PUBLIC ADMINISTRATION IN CANADA

A TEXT

. . . .

SECOND EDITION

KENNETH KERNAGHAN
DAVID SIEGEL

BROCK UNIVERSITY

Nelson Canada

© Nelson Canada
A Division of Thomson Canada Limited, 1991
1120 Birchmount Road
Scarborough, Ontario
M1K 5G4

Every effort has been made to trace ownership of all copyrighted material and to secure permission from copyright holders. In the event of any question arising as to the use of any material, we will be pleased to make the necessary corrections in future printings.

Canadian Cataloguing in Publication Data
Kernaghan, Kenneth, 1940-
Public administration in Canada: a text

2nd ed.
Includes bibliographical references and index.
ISBN 0-17-603496-X

1. Public administration - Canada. 2. Canada -
Politics and government. I. Siegel, David. II. Title.
108.K45   1991   354.71   C91-093044-9

Publisher   Ric Kitowski
Acquisitions Editor   Dave Ward
Manager, Editorial Services   Jean Lancee
Editor   Sarah Robertson
Art Director   Lorraine Tuson
Cover Design   Tracy Walker

Printed and bound in Canada
   2 3 4   BP   94 93 92

To Helgi, Kevin, Scott, and Kris
and
To Nancy and Sarah

ABOUT THE AUTHORS

Kenneth Kernaghan is Professor of Politics and Management at Brock University. He received his Honours B.A. in Economics and Political Science from McMaster University and his M.A. and Ph.D. in Political Science from Duke University. He is the author or editor of many books, monographs, and articles on Canadian public administration and public policy. He has served as President of the Institute of Public Administration of Canada, Editor of *Canadian Public Administration,* founding Director of the Case Program in Canadian Public Administration, Vice-President of the International Association of Schools and Institutes of Administration, and Chairperson of the Academic Advisory Committee of the Ontario Council on University Affairs. He is currently Editor of the *International Review of Administrative Sciences.*

David Siegel is Associate Professor of Politics at Brock University. He received his undergraduate degree in accounting from the University of Louisville and is a Certified General Accountant. He has also received an M.A. in Public Administration from Carleton University and a Ph.D. in Political Science from the University of Toronto. He has written articles for *Canadian Public Administration, Municipal World, Optimum,* and *CGA Magazine.* He has served as Director of the Case Program in Canadian Public Administration and is currently President of the Canadian Association of Programs in Public Administration.

CONTENTS

PREFACE

The warm response that the first edition of this book received is very gratifying. Nevertheless, in this second edition, we have taken account of suggestions for improvement. We recognize that our text is already more comprehensive than most public administration texts, including the many texts published in the United States. We have, therefore, resisted the temptation to extend the length of the text. We have aimed for comprehensiveness in the dictionary sense of "covering much" rather than in the Thesaurus sense of "all-inclusive"; a single volume cannot cover every relevant topic in depth. We have retained the popular features of the glossary, the advice on how to write a research paper, the lengthy bibliographies, and the case references.

In general, the organization of the book is similar to the first edition. However, there are now separate Parts covering the policy dimension of public administration and the role of the bureaucracy in the political system.

Each chapter has been revised or updated, or both, and there are several new chapters. Part I now consists of two introductory chapters; the first chapter is an introduction to public administration and the second chapter is an introduction to public bureaucracy, including an examination of theories of bureaucracy and the state. Part III, which is a new Part on the policy dimension of public administration, contains a new chapter on the implementation and evaluation of public policy. Part IV now contains a chapter on responsibility, accountability, and ethics that incorporates much of what was included in the first edition's chapter on administrative values and ethics. Part VI contains a new chapter on representative bureaucracy and employment equity, and a new chapter on the management of government programs. This latter chapter includes an examination of such current management issues as management information systems, strategic planning, downsizing, and contracting out.

The purpose of this book is to promote better understanding of the study and practice of public administration in Canada. We hope to enhance our readers' knowledge of the unique nature of administration in the public sector, and their appreciation of the challenges and opportunities of a career in the public service. The readership for the first edition of the book has included university and college students in public administration courses, public servants at all levels of government engaged in training and development courses, and knowledgeable lay readers.

We have tried to provide a balanced treatment of the diverse features of public administration by relating theoretical considerations to practical experience, by examining both the political and managerial dimensions of the field, and by covering both enduring and current issues. The book reflects the fact that writings on public administration in Canada have focussed primarily on the federal government. We have, however, made a special effort to provide coverage of the provincial and municipal spheres by supplementing secondary research materials with our own research.

Some of the material in this book appeared originally either in scholarly journals, in *Public Administration in Canada: Selected Readings,* or in monographs published by the Institute of Public Administration of Canada. For permission to reprint previous work, we are grateful to the Institute and to the journals *Canadian Public Administration, Canadian Public Policy, Public Administration* (Britain), and *Public Administration* (Australia).

For the scholarly foundation on which this book is based, we are indebted to the many academics and practitioners who have contributed to our understanding of the discipline and practice of public administration in Canada and elsewhere. The written contributions of most of these people are acknowledged in the book's endnotes and bibliography. However, we also wish to recognize the wealth of information and insights we have gained from formal and informal discussions with our academic colleagues and with public servants from all spheres of Canadian government. We express appreciation to students past and present who have shared—or endured—our fascination with the field of public administration.

In addition to the public servants and academic colleagues whose assistance we acknowledged in the preface to the first edition, we wish to express warm appreciation to the following people who have been especially helpful with this second edition: Peter Aucoin, Nicolas Baxter-Moore, Stephen Brooks, Ian Clark, William Gibson, Kim Graybeil, James Harlick, George Hoberg, Evert Lindquist, Rick Loreto, J. A. Macdonald, Graham Parsons, Lise Pigeon, Moira Russell, and Carol Sales. As with the first edition, we are responsible for any errors that remain.

Kenneth Kernaghan
David Siegel
December 1990

INTRODUCTION

This book is organized to cover the field of public administration in a logical, coherent fashion. The organization of the book comes from our conviction that the study of public administration requires the use of concepts and insights from several disciplines, especially political science and organization theory. Wamsley and Zald argue persuasively that

> organization analysis can provide a rigour and conceptual sophistication currently lacking in public administration; political science brings an awareness of political influences and environmental pressures upon public agencies... that often seems slighted in organization theory and analysis; and public administration reminds us of the range of tasks and organizational problems of public agencies.[1]

Thus, Part I of this book deals with the importance of theories of bureaucracy, organization, and management for the study and practice of public administration. Chapter 1 examines the meaning of public administration, differences between public and private administration, the study of public administration, and the growth and environment of the public service. Chapter 2 reviews the evolution and major theories of public bureaucracy, with special emphasis on the relationship between bureaucracy and the state. Chapters 3 and 4 study the relationship between public administration and organization theory. While Chapter 3 focusses on the early structural and mechanistic theories of organization, Chapter 4 traces the evolution of humanistic theories from their beginnings to contemporary theories of employee participation and development. Chapter 5 draws on some of these theories to discuss the closely related management issues of motivation, leadership, and communication.

Part II deals with the policy dimension of public administration. Chapter 6 examines the primary models that have been developed to explain the making of public policy. Chapter 7 focusses on the two important phases of the policy cycle that follow policy-making, namely policy implementation and policy evaluation.

Using the organization theories and principles discussed in Parts I and II as a base, Part III covers the structure and standard methods of operation of the main organizational forms employed in parliamentary governments. The theme tying these chapters together is what we call *the choice of organizational form*. We explain how the various organizational forms differ and why governments choose a particular organizational form for a particular responsibility. Therefore, each chapter deals with the characteristics of a different organizational form and details the advantages and disadvantages of using each. Chapter 8 focusses on the central agencies and the most commonly used organizational form—the operating department. Chapter 9 discusses public enterprises, and

Chapter 10 deals with regulatory agencies. Chapter 11 examines a number of important, but less widely used, organizations and instruments—Royal commissions, task forces, and advisory councils.

Many of the insights provided in the first three Parts of this book are used in Part IV to develop a frame of reference for examining interactions between bureaucrats and other political actors, which are the focus of Part V. Chapter 12 explains the institutional and value frameworks that provide the conceptual and organizational basis for the chapters in Part V. Chapters 13 and 14 examine in turn the enduring and interrelated themes of bureaucratic power and responsibility. Chapter 14 includes an examination of public service ethics.

The themes of values, power, and responsibility are pervasive in Part V, which deals with the role of the bureaucracy in the political system. The seven chapters in this Part examine relationships between bureaucrats, on the one hand, and political executives, legislators, courts, officials in other governments, pressure groups, political parties, the public, and the media on the other. This Part contains broad coverage of the bureaucrats' interaction with political actors found both within and outside government.

Part V provides an essential base of knowledge for the examination in Part VI of the management of organizational resources. Many of the administrative organizations and administrative values discussed in Parts III to V appear again in Part VI. Chapter 22 examines the management of government programs. Human resource management, representative bureaucracy, and collective bargaining are studied in Chapters 23 to 25, and the book concludes with a discussion of the budgetary process and financial management in Chapters 26 and 27.

Bibliographies at the end of each chapter contain valuable references for further reading. For a comprehensive bibliography on Canadian public administration, readers should consult W.E. Grasham and Germain Julien, *Canadian Public Administration Bibliography*,[2] including supplements 1-4.

At the end of most chapters is a list of case studies that can be used to relate the theoretical and descriptive material in the text to actual administrative situations. Most cases are taken from the *Case Program in Canadian Public Administration*, which is published by the Institute of Public Administration of Canada. Other cases have been developed by the Canadian Centre for Management Development and are available through the *Case Program in Canadian Public Administration*.

Some readers may wish to use the chapters of this book in an order that suits their own purposes. We have, therefore, tried to make each chapter as self-contained as possible and to give cross-references to other chapters that elaborate on certain subjects. We have provided a definition and/or detailed explanation of new terms the first time they appear in the text. If the chapters are used in some other order, readers may wish to consult the Glossary at the end of the book for both a definition and a page reference to where key terms are discussed in more detail.

NOTES

1. Gary L. Wamsley and Mayer N. Zald, *The Political Economy of Public Organizations* (Bloomington, Ind.: Indiana University Press, 1976), p. 83.
2. (Toronto: Institute of Public Administration of Canada, 1972) and supplements 1-4 dated 1974, 1977, 1980, and 1985 respectively.

I

INTRODUCTION TO PUBLIC ADMINISTRATION

1

What Is Public Administration?

THE IMPORTANCE OF PUBLIC ADMINISTRATION

During this century, and especially since the beginning of the Second World War, there has been an enormous expansion in the activities of Canadian governments. The continuing growth of responsibilities in all spheres of Canadian government—federal, provincial, and municipal—has a great impact on the daily lives and future prospects of Canadian citizens. The degree of happiness and prosperity or misery and poverty experienced by Canadians is affected by the countless decisions made each day by our governments. The range of governmental activities includes the traditional functions of administration of justice, the conduct of external relations, and the defence of the country, as well as such newer responsibilities as medicare, environmental protection, and atomic energy research.

The two major areas of government activities are the provision of services and the enforcement of regulations. The service functions include mail delivery, the maintenance of roads and highways, and grants and loans for new housing. Among the regulatory functions are the setting of standards for food and drugs, the prevention and restraint of restrictive trade practices, and the enforcement of fair housing and employment regulations. In order to carry out these and other responsibilities as effectively as possible, governments are actively engaged in research on matters ranging from the inspection of food and drugs to scientific and medical concerns. Virtually every government department and agency is involved in research related to its service or regulatory functions. Research activities are a costly but essential component of the total responsibilities of government.

Few Canadians are aware of the importance and the magnitude of their governments' operations. Canadians, like citizens of other countries, tend to be conscious of only those government activities that affect them directly and significantly—for example, the collection of taxes, the provision of family allowances, or the payment of unemployment insurance benefits. Many important functions of government, such as the preservation of internal law and order or the administration of justice, are taken for granted unless the services are discontinued or disrupted for some reason. An excellent example is the sudden public concern about postal operations when normal service is disrupted by labour disputes.

The impact of government activities on the lives of Canadians during a typical working day is vividly demonstrated by the following example of government regulation:

> In the morning the clock radio awakens us with the sound of music subject to Canadian content regulations. The price, at the farm gate, of the eggs we eat for breakfast has been set by a government marketing board. We drive to work on tires that must meet federal minimum safety standards and in a car whose exhaust is subject to pollution emission regulations. At lunch, the restaurant in which we eat has been subject to the scrutiny of public health inspectors. The monthly rate for the telephone we use at the office is set by a federal or provincial regulatory agency. Shopping in the supermarket on the way home, we note the unpronounceable names of certain chemical preservatives that, by government regulation, are disclosed to us on a finely printed label. As we turn down the thermostat before retiring, we are confident that a government agency has protected our purse by setting the price we will be charged by the monopoly supplier of natural gas. Putting on our sleepwear, we are secure in our knowledge that it is not impregnated with a hazardous substance.... If we live in certain cities, we approach our rest reassured that the smoke detector we were required to install will stand on guard throughout the night.[1]

What do these extensive and pervasive activities of Canadian governments have to do with public administration? A great deal! Public administrators play a very large role in formulating and implementing policies to fulfill their government's service and regulatory responsibilities. These responsibilities are performed through what is known as the public bureaucracy, which is a system for achieving government objectives. Elected representatives, especially political executives (e.g., Cabinet ministers, city mayors), are centrally involved in the making of public policies. However, we shall see in later chapters that bureaucrats (also called public servants, civil servants, or government employees) have considerable influence on the content of these policies and make most of the decisions required to implement them. Thus, while a recurring theme in this book is the importance of relations between the political and bureaucratic realms of government, the role of the bureaucracy is the major focus of attention.

The rest of this chapter examines the meaning and the study of public administration and the environment in which public administration is set. The next chapter focusses on public bureaucracy.

Definition and Scope of Public Administration

Public administration is a term more easily explained than defined. This fact has not discouraged several scholars from trying to capture the meaning of the term in a single sentence. Some typical one-sentence definitions of public administration are:

> The study and practice of the tasks associated with the conduct of the administrative state.[2]

All processes, organizations and individuals (the latter acting in official positions and roles) associated with carrying out laws and other rules adopted or issued by legislators, executives, and courts.[3]

The coordination of individual and group efforts to carry out public policy.[4]

The application of organizational decision-making, and staffing theory and procedures to public problems.[5]

These brief definitions indicate the scope and purpose of public administration, but they are incomplete in their coverage and very general in their wording. The emphasis in these and most other definitions of public administration is on the implementation of policy; there is insufficient recognition of the role of bureaucrats in policy development. Moreover, these definitions contain abstract words and terms that tend to leave the reader with more questions than answers. For example, what *are* the tasks associated with the conduct of the administrative state? What *are* the relationships between bureaucrats and such institutions as legislatures, executives, and courts? Is public administration confined to the *carrying out* of public policy? What is distinctive about organization and management in public administration as opposed to private administration? This book provides answers to these and many other questions about public administration.

The terms public administration and public bureaucracy are often used interchangeably, but they do not mean the same thing. Public administration refers to a field of practice (or an occupation) *and* to a field of study (often referred to as a discipline). **Public bureaucracy** is the system of authority, people, offices, and methods that government uses to achieve its objectives. It is the means whereby the practice of public administration is carried on; it is also the main focus of the study of public administration. In this book, the term public administration refers to its practice unless we indicate otherwise by specific reference to its study. The book is devoted to studying the practice of public administration, as that practice is conducted through the system known as public bureaucracy.

The scope of the practice and study of public administration is so broad that it is difficult to achieve agreement on where the boundaries of the field should be drawn. The size of the field could be demonstrated simply by listing the hundreds of departments and agencies at all levels of Canadian government that collectively carry out an enormous range of activities. It could also be demonstrated by showing the range of concerns shared by teachers and practitioners of public administration. For example, the themes discussed in recent years at the national seminars of the Institute of Public Administration of Canada[6] have included the administration of such public policy fields as transportation, energy, and criminal justice. Other themes have included the implications for public administration of such matters as intergovernmental relations, public sector collective bargaining, pressure group activity, program evaluation, and information management. Moreover, among the issues covered during a recent two-year period in *Canadian Public Administration,* the learned journal of the **Institute of Public Administration of Canada**, are cutback management, privatization, provincial budgetary policy, service efficiency in municipalities, human resources management, employment equity, automation in government offices, public service ethics, administrative tribunals, the management of regional economic development policy, and aging policy and process.

Public Administration versus Private Administration

The meaning of public administration can be clarified by comparing it to private (or business) administration. Wallace Sayre's assertion that "business and government administration are alike in all unimportant respects"[7] has been widely quoted. There is, in fact, much that is similar in public and private administration. Administration in all organizations involves cooperative group action. Moreover, all large organizations, whether they are government departments, hospitals, universities, labour unions, factories or commercial enterprises, must provide for the performance of such functions of general management as planning, organizing, staffing, and budgeting. There are, however, many differences in the administration of public sector organizations and these differences have important implications for the study and practice of public administration. At the very least, these differences suggest the need for caution in transferring practices and technologies from private sector organizations to public sector organizations.

In contemporary Canadian society the line between public and private administration is somewhat blurred. Public and private sector organizations can be shown on a continuum running from typical operating departments of government, to private sector corporations largely free from governmental control or assistance. In the middle section of this continuum are a variety of organizations characterized by a mix of public and private elements. These organizations can be divided into three categories. The first is public corporations (e.g., Via Rail and Petro-Canada) which compete with, and operate much like, private corporations. The second category consists of mixed enterprise corporations that are owned or controlled by different governments (e.g., the St. John Harbour Bridge Authority) or by governments and private organizations (e.g., Canarctic Shipping). The final category is private sector organizations that are subject to close government regulation (e.g., pharmaceutical companies), or companies that depend heavily on government financial assistance (e.g., textile firms), or those companies that do 100 percent of their business with government (e.g., defence contractors). Despite this public-private "grey area," for analytical purposes a broad distinction can be made between the public and private spheres of administration.

The first and most frequently cited difference is that the overall mission of public administration is service to the public, whereas the primary *raison d'être* of private administration is profits or what is often described as "the bottom line." The service orientation of public administration results from the need for bureaucrats to assist elected politicians to respond to public demands and requirements for government services. Private administration is profit-oriented because the survival of private sector organizations ultimately depends on making a profit.

A federal deputy minister has explained that the challenge to governments is to manage "beyond the bottom line." She contends that

> in government, we face a tremendous onus to be fair and equal both in the way we treat our customers and the way we run our operations. Our management decisions must be seen to give all Canadians, regardless of province, region, gender or language, an equal shot at the benefits Canada offers. . . .
>
> It means, for example, that many government departments keep offices in every province whether they need them or not.
>
> It means that departments have to provide service of comparable quality to citizens of Kingston and Baker Lake, regardless of the differential in cost. . . .
>
> It has meant employment equity, affirmative action, and equal pay for work of equal value—long before the private sector.
>
> It's what comes from having to be government for all of the people in a country as large and diverse as Canada. And it affects not only the speed and quality of our operations.
>
> It also affects the cost.[8]

It is commonly argued that a second difference, following directly from the service versus profit distinction, is that public administration operates less efficiently than private administration. It is suggested that since government departments receive their funds largely through annual appropriations from the public treasury, they do not have to worry about profits; thus, they have less incentive to cut costs and operate efficiently. Business organizations are motivated to operate efficiently because they must compete in the marketplace; most government operations, however, are monopolistic (e.g., the police) so that the public does not have a choice among competing organizations for the delivery of services. It is argued that public organizations are less inclined to be efficient because they do not have to be as sensitive as private organizations to the preferences and grievances of their "consumers." Finally, many services are provided by government because they would not produce sufficient profits to interest private sector organizations. Many people argue that when government activities produce a profit, they should be turned over to private enterprise.

Governments also provide what are called "public" goods; these are goods which, when provided at all, benefit all members of society. People cannot be charged for the services in the marketplace, because no one can be excluded from benefiting from them. Examples of public goods include national defence and pollution controls, which are funded through the general tax system rather than on the "user-pay" principle that is characteristic of "private" goods (e.g., a bottle of milk). The benefits of public goods are available to many people, and the benefits are not easily measured. Indeed, it is very difficult to measure the efficiency of many government expenditures (e.g., on health services).

Public administration does not have the measuring rods of prices and profits that are so central to efficiency considerations in the private sector. Nevertheless, government departments and agencies do have incentives to operate efficiently. For example, the many administrative units within government compete with one another for public funds; this competition is especially vigorous during a period of financial restraint in government. Recently, treasury officials have paid much more attention to the economy, efficiency, and effectiveness of departmental operations, and an increasing number of government programs are operated on a cost-recovery basis. Another spur to efficiency in government is the threat of public criticism that may embarrass elected politicians and, in turn, damage the career prospects of the government employees involved.

The achievement of business-like efficiency in government is greatly affected—and often hampered—by the demands of the political environment. In a study of productivity in the public sector, Canada's Auditor General noted that departmental recommendations to cut operating costs are sometimes incompatible with political priorities. He observed that "private sector firms are not required, to the same extent as the public sector, to reconcile questions of productive management with concerns such as national unity, regional development and national well-being."[9]

A third difference between public and private administration hindering efficiency in government is the greater emphasis in the public sector on accountability. The Auditor General concluded that a major constraint on productive management "is the body of administrative regulations and the conflicting accountability requirements that limit managerial authority and autonomy."[10] The lines of authority and responsibility tend to be much clearer in private sector organizations. In government, such factors as the scale and complexity of operations, the desire for political control of the bureaucracy, and the search for consistency and coordination have resulted in a proliferation of accountability mechanisms that lengthen and complicate the decision-making process. For example, deputy ministers in the federal government are directly accountable to their minister, the Prime Minister, and several central agencies. Moreover, they are indirectly accountable through their minister to Parliament and the public. While excessive and conflicting accountability requirements are most evident at the senior levels of the bureaucracy, the middle levels are also affected. The negative impact these requirements have on government efficiency is demonstrated by the Auditor General's concern that "when constraints become a spider's web of rules, regulations, directives, prohibitions, and controls, managers lose sight of value-for-money concerns."[11] To illustrate, the pursuit of efficiency through speedy program implementation may be hampered by numerous financial and personnel constraints.

A fourth difference between public and private administration is that the personnel management system is much more complicated and rigid in government than in private sector organizations. In general, it is harder both to hire and to fire government employees. In the public sector, the merit system of hiring and promoting employees includes several criteria that go well beyond the idea of technical proficiency. To promote sensitivity and responsiveness to the needs of a certain minority group, for example, the government may hire a person from that group who is not as well qualified as other candidates in terms of education and experience. The complexity and inflexibility of public personnel management systems also result from the general emphasis on accountability. Of the top ten constraints on management productivity identified by federal public service managers, three lie squarely in the personnel field, in the areas of job classification, personnel rules, and staffing.[12]

Fifth, and finally, the "public" nature of public administration requires that much of it be conducted in a "goldfish bowl" of publicity. Many government deliberations are conducted behind closed doors but, compared to the private sector, many more government decisions are subjected to public scrutiny. Taxpayers insist on the right to know how much public money is being spent and for what purposes. Thus, a government decision to construct a new airport in a particular area will probably receive much more public and media examination than a decision by a major manufacturer to construct or close a plant in the same area, even if the latter decision has a greater economic or social impact. The media will report on the effects of such private sector decisions, but they do not expect these decisions to be made in public. An important consequence of public scrutiny of government activities is greater emphasis in the public sector on such considerations as responsiveness and accountability. This emphasis explains in part the presence of what is popularly described as bureaucratic "red tape" and the consequent slowness in decision-making.

It is clear that two major characteristics of government account in large part for the differences between public administration and private administration. These are (1) the vast scope and complexity of government activities, and (2) the political environment within which these activities are conducted. Given these considerations, the issue of whether public or private administration is more efficient is not the most relevant concern. The critical question is whether public administration is conducted as efficiently as can reasonably be expected.

The Study of Public Administration

The systematic study of public administration in North America is a relatively recent development. In the United States, the study of the field is generally acknowledged to date from 1887 with the publication of Woodrow Wilson's celebrated essay on "The Study of Administration."[13] In Canada, although no single date or publication marks the formal beginning of the study of public administration, there are several noteworthy developments in the evolution of the formal study of Canadian public administration.[14]

Several of the twenty-three volumes on *Canada And Its Provinces*, written by A. Shortt and A.G. Doherty and published in 1914, covered aspects of public administration and public bureaucracy in Canada. Then, in 1918, the first work focussing on a particular problem in Canadian public administration was written by two scholars from the United States. [15] The earliest general work in the field was R. MacGregor Dawson's *The Civil Service of Canada*, published in 1929.[16] It was not until 1936 that Luther Richter and R.A. Mackay established the first degree program in Canadian public administration at Dalhousie University. Carleton College (now Carleton University) graduated students with a Bachelor of Public Administration degree in 1946, and the university's School of Public Administration was established in 1952. However, it was not until the early 1950s that a handful of academic scholars [17] made the first of their many contributions to the literature on public administration in Canada. *Canadian Public Administration*, the scholarly journal devoted to the study of public administration, commenced publication in 1958.

The academic study of public administration really began to flourish in the late 1960s. Indeed, progress in the study of Canadian public administration since 1970, as measured by research, publications, teachers, and programs, has been greater than all the preceding years combined. This increased attention to research and teaching of public administration is largely due to the growth of the operations, expenditures, and size of the federal, provincial, and municipal bureaucracies. It also coincided with the expansion of Canadian universities and colleges, which were thereby able to devote more resources to teaching and research in public administration.

The study of public administration is commonly described as a discipline, but it is not a discipline in the restrictive sense of an intellectual endeavour with a body of coherent and accepted theory. Even if the term discipline is defined less rigorously as a field of study with a nucleus of unifying beliefs, public administration has not yet achieved agreement on what those beliefs are. The matter is complicated by what has often been called the field's "crisis of identity," which arises from two distinct and largely countervailing developments. The first is the evolution of public administration under the parentage of political science. The second is the continually expanding dimensions of the study and practice of public administration, and the increasingly interdisciplinary approach to its study and teaching. Should public administration be considered a subdiscipline (or subfield) of political science or of administrative science (i.e., organization theory and management science)? The administrative science approach involves considerable borrowing from such disciplines as economics, sociology, and psychology.

Political Science or Administrative Science?

The two opposing positions on the appropriate theoretical base for the organization of studies in public administration have been succinctly expressed as follows:

> Any tendency for public administration to break away from the parent discipline must ultimately weaken both political science as a whole and the study of public administration. It will weaken political science by removing the part of it which brings the teacher into closest relationship with the practical business of government. It will weaken the study of public administration by divorcing it from political theory and the principles of government which underlie political and administrative institutions.[18]

> The greatest promise for study of public administration in the universities will be in association with the growth of an integrative, organizing, generic concept of administration. From the nucleus of general administrative studies, it may be possible to interrelate more meaningfully the study of administration to the various disciplines and professions. In the modern world, no clear line separates administration in government from the administrative processes of the total society. The organization of administrative studies in the university must ultimately correspond to this reality.[19]

There are sound theoretical grounds for teaching public administration as part of political science. Knowledge of the administrative structures of government and the political and legal environment in which the public administrator works is essential to an adequate understanding of the political system. In addition, the bureaucracy plays a central role in the political system through its active involvement in the development, enforcement, and adjudication of laws and regulations. Significant intellectual bonds lie between public administration and political science in their shared concern for inquiry into such key theoretical concepts as responsibility, authority, and the public interest. Political theorists who fail to explore the meaning of these themes in the particular milieu of public administration omit a perspective essential to adequate analysis. All these factors attest to the status of public administration as an integral part of the study of political science.

The most productive approach for political scientists may be to treat public administration as a *subdiscipline* on the basis of existing organizational patterns and theoretical links between public administration and political science. Political scientists may resolve the identity crisis, at least to their own satisfaction, by ceasing to agonize over the vast scope of public administration and by seeking a general theory of public administration.

Those who view public administration as a part of administrative science contend that the study of administration may be most fruitfully pursued by dividing the general field of administration into public, business, hospital, educational, police, and other types of administration. To proponents of this view, the similarities between these forms of administration are greater than their differences. This belief has led to the establishment of "professional" schools or faculties of administrative studies.

Moreover, some scholars are convinced that intellectual developments are moving inexorably in the direction of a rigorous *discipline* of administrative studies. This form of study will be interdisciplinary and integrative in its subject content and teaching approach. Its program will be characterized by a combining of the present "academic" and "professional" streams in administrative studies for mutual enrichment. Discussion of the distinctive nature of "public" administration will be founded on a solid base of knowledge about the concepts and techniques of administration generally. All students will be required to take a group of "core subjects" in administration, regardless of the type of administration in which they are primarily interested, (e.g., public, business, educational). The "core subjects" will normally include organizational behaviour, accounting, economics, administrative law, and quantitative methods. Later specialization in a particular type or problem of administration will be founded on this base of common knowledge.

Public Administration as Public Administration

A variety of structural arrangements exists for the Master's level education of current and aspiring public servants. Programs leading to a Master of Public Administration (MPA) degree, or to a degree in political science or public sector management, are available in departments of political science or in schools or faculties of administrative studies. However, the most common route to an MPA degree is through one of the several specialized schools of public administration that have grown rapidly during the last twenty years. These schools offer an interdisciplinary approach with a professional emphasis. Programs are designed to accommodate students proceeding directly from their Bachelor's degree as well as mid-career public servants. The schools require a similar group of core courses (e.g., government structure and organization, policy formulation, quantitative methods, applied economics, the management process in government, and public sector financial management and accounting) and a range of elective courses in specialized areas such as local government administration and intergovernmental relations.

Most of the schools have adopted a policy-management approach to program content that combines political science and administrative science with an examination of public policy. This approach focusses on public administration as a distinct field of study rather than as a subdiscipline or subfield of political science or administrative science.

THE ENVIRONMENT AND EXPANSION OF PUBLIC ADMINISTRATION

Public administration is greatly influenced by the broad environment within which it is conducted. Aside from the political and legal environment of public administration, discussed in detail elsewhere in this book, the most important environmental influences are geography, technological change, culture, demography, and the economy.[20] The influence of *geography*, manifested in large part by the need to disperse government operations and personnel across the country, or throughout a province, is discussed in Chapters 4 and 8. Canada's vast expanse also helps to explain the existence and nature of our federal system of government and the enduring impact of regionalism on politics and public administration—a subject to which we return later, notably in Chapter 19 on the management of intergovernmental relations.

The environment within which contemporary governments work has also been greatly affected by *technological* developments. The problems for government arising from the widespread use of such inventions as the automobile, the airplane, and television have become more critical as transportation routes have become snarled, airports have become too small for huge jetliners, and intercontinental television transmission has become possible. The opportunities brought about by more recent technological developments involving automation, computers, and atomic energy have created such problems as technological unemployment, invasion of privacy, and possible misuse of atomic energy. Scientific and technical advances, such as increasing numbers of human tissue transplants, test-tube babies, and instruments of instant communication, also present challenging issues for government. The internal management and operations of the public service have, of course, been transformed by technological developments in areas such as word processing and communications systems. Indeed, this development is so important that the impact of management information systems (MIS) resulting from advances in computer technology is examined separately in Chapter 22.

Cultural factors have also been influential in moulding the public service. For example, the powerful influence of the United States on Canadian culture has led to such measures as "Canadian content" regulations in radio and television broadcasting. Both the United States and Britain have exercised significant influence on the organization and administrative arrangements of the public service in Canada. Finally, the public service has been required to adapt to two extremely important cultural factors within Canada itself—the constitutional guarantees to the use of the English and French languages and the increasingly multicultural character of Canadian society. [21]

The impact of *demographic* factors on the public service is becoming increasingly important. Rapid population growth in Canada (from 5.4 million in 1901 to well over 25 million in 1990) was, until recently, accompanied by a movement of Canadians from rural-agricultural areas to urban-industrial centres. The urban population in Canada rose from 19.6 percent in 1871 to 76.1 percent in 1971, but has declined slightly since then. Over 70 percent of Canadians now live in cities, towns, and villages with a population of 1,000 or more, and over 50 percent of the population is found in urbanized areas of more than 100,000 inhabitants (called census metropolitan areas). This urbanization of the Canadian population has brought enormous problems for governments in the form of inadequate housing and air and water pollution. The resolution of these problems continues to require large government expenditures and close cooperation between governments. It is notable that a counter-urbanization movement began in the early 1970s. More people have been moving to rural and fringe areas from urban areas than the reverse. Medium-sized urban areas are growing faster than large and small ones. The total population of the metropolitan areas is the same now as in 1971, and within these areas, people are selecting the semi-urban and rural fringes rather than the core districts. If it continues, this population redistribution will require reconsideration of land development and environmental protection policies because the trend to increasing encroachments on rural areas will increase demand for the limited supply of arable land.[22] Moreover, these people tend to bring with them "urban tastes" in the form of demands for improved services in such fields as transportation, recreation, and education.

Another demographic factor with enormous implications for public administration is the changing age composition of the Canadian population.[23] The percentage of Canadians over sixty-five years of age rose from 5.0 percent in 1901 to 8.6 in 1976 and is projected to rise to 13.3 percent by 2011 and to 22.2 percent by 2031.[24] As the number of elderly people increases, their needs for health, housing, and community services will also increase. There will be an increasing need for different orders of government and different administrative units within each order of government to find the financial and human resources to meet these needs.

Among the most important *economic* factors affecting the public service has been the reliance of the Canadian economy on exploiting and marketing such staple products as fish, fur, wheat, timber, minerals, and pulpwood. Several of the original departments of the federal government (e.g., Agriculture, Marine and Fisheries) were created specifically to deal with problems connected with the production, transportation, and trade of staple products and several departments are still concerned with these problems.

Another important economic influence has been the growth during this century of large industrial and commercial organizations (e.g., multinational corporations, such as General Motors and IBM, which are not totally Canadian-controlled) and of large and powerful labour organizations (e.g., the Canadian Automobile Workers and the Canadian Labour Congress). Employer-employee disputes over such matters as wage levels and the effects of technological change on existing jobs can result in lengthy strikes. Such strikes may not only bring much personal strife and misfortune to those directly involved in the dispute, but may also have an injurious impact on innocent third parties and on the economy as a whole. To protect the public interest, governments have been increasingly obliged to regulate the activities of business and labour organizations and to arbitrate disputes between them.

This brief discussion of environmental factors shows that the operations of governments are extremely complex and the demands on government are constantly changing. Governments must provide rapid solutions to urgent current problems while planning for the solution or avoidance of future problems. They must be conscious of the widespread ramifications of major governmental decisions on various sectors of Canadian society. For example, the federal government must assess the probable impact that changes in the economic policies of other nations will have on Canada. They must then decide how to counteract the adverse effects these changes might have on the prosperity of businesses, on provincial and municipal governments, and on the level of employment. After an evaluation of the likely consequences, the government may have to alter its existing plans and programs to take account of these changes. Clearly, governments operate in a constant state of flux and must have the capacity and the inclination to adapt quickly to change.

The Growth of the Public Service

In Canada, as elsewhere, expansion in the scope and complexity of government activities since the end of the Second World War has been accompanied by a striking growth in expenditures and in the number of government employees.

Expressed as a percentage of the Gross National Product (i.e., the total output of final goods and services without allowance for depreciation), government expenditures rose from about 30 percent in 1960 to about 40 percent in the mid-1970s and have remained relatively stable since then. During the Second World War, the federal government took control of the economy to promote the war effort with the result that, by the end of the war, federal expenditures had risen to 82 percent of total government expenditures. During the post-war period, the total amount of money spent by governments has greatly increased. The federal percentage of total expenditures, however, has declined steadily, while provincial and municipal expenditures have increased. The substantial increase in expenditures by the ten provincial governments combined is a result of the increasing revenue available to the resource-rich provinces, and the increased demand for provincially provided services, particularly in the areas of education, health and social welfare. Over the past 60 years, there has been a steady rise in the proportion of government spending devoted to these areas. However, expenditures on transportation and communications, natural resources, and international aid have risen much more slowly, and expenditures on defence have declined substantially since 1960.[25]

The increase in total expenditures at all levels of Canadian government has been accompanied by a related growth in the number of public employees required to carry out these increasing governmental responsibilities. Much public criticism has centred on the size and growth of public sector employment in Canada, especially at the federal level of government. Certainly the absolute size of public sector employment has increased greatly since the Second World War. But, as a percentage of the total labour force, public sector employment was the same in 1982 as in 1960. It rose from 17.9 percent in 1960 to 20.3 percent in 1975 and fell back to 17.9 percent by 1982.[26]

The hiring of public sector employees has been especially slow since the mid-1970s as a result of fiscal restraint and hiring freezes imposed on government departments and agencies. It is particularly notable that the federal public service constitutes a comparatively small proportion of total public sector employment, and that since the mid-1960s growth has been slower in the federal than in the provincial and municipal governments. In general "it is clear that Canada does not have a large public sector presence. Total employment by all levels of government in Canada is far below that of most modern western democracies and very close to that of the United States."[27]

The variety and change in the occupational composition of the public service is related to the growth in the number of government employees. Virtually every occupation, trade, and skill can be found in the public service. The Royal Commission on Government Organization in Canada (the Glassco Commission) noted that occupations in the federal public service range "from actuaries and anthropologists through bee keepers, dry dock riggers, map compilers and pharmacists, to veterinarians and X-ray operators. An element of mystery is created by the listing of such intriguing operations as insect sampling, . . . receivers of wreck, . . . strippers and layouters."[28] Clearly, a wide variety of job opportunities is available to those who aspire to become Canadian public servants.

The increasingly complex and technical nature of government operations has brought about a significant qualitative change in the public service. Especially over the past few decades, the rate of growth in the administrative, professional, scientific, and technical occupational categories has been more rapid than that in the traditional clerical and operational categories. This change in the occupational makeup of the public service is often referred to as the "professionalization" of the service. One result of this development is that students must not only spend a longer time in school to obtain the education necessary for appointment to the public service, but also must return to school in later years to keep informed about new developments affecting their jobs.

To fulfill the growing responsibilities of government, additional administrative units have been created in the form of new departments, new sections of existing departments, and new agencies, boards, and commissions. These units enjoy varying degrees of independence from political (i.e. Cabinet and parliamentary) control. There are now twenty-seven federal government departments, including, for example, the Departments of Agriculture, Justice, and National Revenue. Among the government agencies, boards and commissions, of which there are more than four hundred, are such Crown corporations as the Canadian Broadcasting Corporation and the Canadian National Railways, and such regulatory agencies as the Canadian Radio-television and Telecommunications Commission and the National Energy Board.

A variety of explanations has been offered for the growth of the public sector. The three main types of explanatory models suggested by Butler and Macnaughton are the socio-economic, organizational, and political models.[29] *Socio-economic* explanations for public sector growth focus on external social and economic influences such as inflation, population growth rates, demographic change, and the level of real personal disposable income. *Organizational* explanations emphasize pressures that emerge within the bureaucracy itself, including responsiveness to clientele demands, bureaucratic empire-building, and incremental decision-making. *Political* explanations stress the pressures to expand government expenditures, therefore increasing employment, that result from such factors as electoral competition, party ideology, and pressure group demands. It is difficult to determine with precision which of these explanatory models best accounts for growth in any particular government; usually, reference to factors from all three models is necessary for a full explanation.

The discussion in this chapter of the meaning, the study, the environment, and the expansion of public administration provides a basis for an examination in the next chapter of the integrally related concept of public bureaucracy.

NOTES

1. Economic Council of Canada, *Responsible Regulation* (Ottawa: Supply and Services, 1979), p. xi.

2. Ivan L. Richardson and Sidney Baldwin, *Public Administration: Government in Action* (Columbus, Ohio: Charles E. Merrill, 1976), p. 3.

3. George J. Gordon, *Public Administration in America* (New York: St. Martin's Press, 1978), p. 8.

4. John M. Pfiffner and Robert Presthus, *Public Administration*, 5th ed. (New York, Ronald Press, 1967), p. 7.

5. Thomas Vocino and Jack Rabin, *Contemporary Public Administration* (New York: Harcourt Brace Jovanovich, 1981), p. 4.

6. The Institute of Public Administration of Canada is an association of public servants—from all levels of government—and academics. It is devoted to improving the study and practice of public administration in Canada.

7. Quoted in Joseph L. Bowen, "Effective Public Management," *Harvard Business Review* 55 (March-April 1977): 132.

8. Jennifer McQueen, Deputy Minister of Labour, *The Globe and Mail*, April 26, 1990.

9. Auditor General, *Annual Report—1983* (Ottawa: Supply and Services, 1983), p. 57.

10. Ibid., p. 60.

11. Ibid.

12. Ibid., p. 62. See also Chapter 23 in this book.

13. Reprinted in Peter Woll, ed., *Public Administration and Policy* (New York: Harper and Row, 1966), pp. 15-41.

14. For an account of the development of the study of public administration in Canada, see A. Paul Pross and V. Seymour Wilson, "Graduate Education in Canadian Public Administration: Antecedents, Present Trends and Portents," *Canadian Public Administration* 19 (Winter 1976): 515-41.

15. H.S. Villard and W.W. Willoughby, *The Canadian Budgetary System* (New York: Appleton, 1918).

16. R. McGregor Dawson, *The Civil Service of Canada* (Oxford: Oxford University Press, 1929). For a discussion of Dawson's views on the role of the public service, see Ken Rasmussen, "The Administrative Liberalism of R. McGregor Dawson," *Canadian Public Administration* 33 (Spring 1990): 37-51.

17. Prominent among these scholars were Albert Abel, Roch Bolduc, J. E. Hodgetts, J. R. Mallory, D. C. Rowat, and Malcolm Taylor.

18. William Robson, *The University Teaching of Social Sciences: Political Science* (UNESCO, 1954), p. 47.

19. Lynton Caldwell, "Public Administration and the Universities: A Half Century of Development," *Public Administration Review* 25 (March 1965): 60.

20. J. E. Hodgetts, *The Canadian Public Service: A Physiology of Government* (Toronto: University of Toronto Press, 1973), p. 17. See also, by the same author, "Challenge and Response: A Retrospective View of the Public Service of Canada," *Canadian Public Administration* 7 (December 1964): 409-21.

21. See the discussion in Chapter 24 of representative bureaucracy and employment equity.

22. For an examination of urbanization in Canada, see Statistics Canada, *Urban Growth in Canada* (Ottawa: Supply and Services, 1984).

23. See Kenneth Kernaghan, "Politics, Public Administration and Canada's Aging Population," *Canadian Public Policy* 8 (Winter 1982): 69-79.

24. Ibid., 70.
25. See Douglas J. McCready, *The Canadian Public Sector* (Toronto: Butterworths, 1984), p. 18, Table 2.3.
26. See Sharon L. Sutherland, "Federal Bureaucracy: The Pinch Test," in Michael J. Prince, ed., *How Ottawa Spends, 1987-88: Restraining the State* (Ottawa: School of Public Administration, Carleton University, 1987), pp. 84-85. See also David Siegel, "The Changing Shape and Nature of Public Service Employment," *Canadian Public Administration* 31 (Summer 1988): 159-93.
27. Sutherland, "Federal Bureaucracy," 73.
28. Canada, *Report of the Royal Commission on Government Organization* 1 (Ottawa: Queen's Printer, 1962-1963): 21.
29. Dan Butler and Bruce Macnaughton, "More of Less for Whom?: Debating Directions for the Public Sector," in Michael S. Whittington and Glen Williams, eds., *Canadian Politics in the 1980s,* 2nd ed. (Toronto: Methuen, 1984), pp. 17-22. See also Richard Bird, *The Growth of Public Employment in Canada* (Montreal: Institute for Research on Public Policy, 1979), ch. 8.

BIBLIOGRAPHY

Public Administration - General

Baker, R. S. *Administrative Theory and Public Administration.* London: Hutchinson, 1972.

Barton, Rayburn, and William L. Chappell Jr. *Public Administration: The Work of Government.* Glenview, Ill.: Scott, Foresman, 1985.

Bernstein, Samuel J., and Patrick O'Hara. *Public Administration.* New York: Harper and Row, 1979.

Bozeman, Barry. *Public Management and Policy Analysis.* New York: St. Martin's Press, 1979.

Chapman, Brian. *The Profession of Government.* New York: Macmillan, 1959.

Dunsire, A. *Administration: The Word and the Science.* New York: John Wiley & Sons, 1973.

Gordon, George J. *Public Administration in America.* New York: St. Martin's Press, 1978.

Heady, Ferrel. *Public Administration: A Comparative Perspective.* 3rd ed. New York: Marcel Decker, 1984.

Henry, Nicholas. *Public Administration and Public Affairs.* 2nd ed. Englewood Cliffs, N.J.: Prentice-Hall, 1980.

Hodgson, J. S. *Public Administration.* Toronto: McGraw-Hill, 1969.

Kramer, Fred A. *Dynamics of Public Bureaucracy.* 2nd ed. Cambridge, Mass.: Winthrop Publishers, 1981.

Marini, Frank, ed. *Toward a New Public Administration: The Minnowbrook Perspective.* Scranton, Pa.: Chandler, 1971.

McCurdy, Howard E. *Public Administration: A Synthesis.* Menlo Park, Calif.: Cummings, 1977.

Miewald, Howard E. *Public Administration.* New York: McGraw-Hill, 1978.

Mosher, Frederick C. *Democracy and the Public Service.* New York: Oxford University Press, 1968.

Nigro, Felix A., and Lloyd A. Nigro. *Modern Public Administration.* 6th ed. New York: Harper and Row, 1984.

Ostrom, Vincent. *The Intellectual Crisis in American Public Administration.* University, Ala.: University of Alabama, 1973.

Presthus, R. V. *Public Administration.* 6th ed. New York: Ronald Press, 1975.

Pursley, Robert D., and Neil Snortland. *Managing Government Organizations.* Belmont,

Calif.: Wadsworth, 1980.

Rehfuss, John. *Public Administration as Political Process*. New York: Charles Scribner's Sons, 1973.

Richardson, Ivan L., and Sydney Baldwin. *Public Administration*. Columbus, Ohio: Charles E. Merrill, 1976.

Rosenbloom, David. *Public Administration: Understanding Management, Politics and Law in the Public Sector*. New York: Random House, 1986.

Self, Peter. *Administrative Theories and Politics*. 2nd ed. London: George Allen and Unwin, 1977.

Sharkansky, Ira. *Public Administration: Agencies, Politics and Policies*. San Francisco: W. H. Freeman, 1982.

Simmons, Robert H., and Eugene P. Dvorins. *Public Administration*. Port Washington, N.Y.: Alfred Publishing, 1977.

Simon, Herbert A., D. W. Smithburg, and V. A. Thompson. *Public Administration*. New York: Knopf, 1950.

Starling, Grover. *Managing the Public Sector*. Homewood, Ill.: Dorsey Press, 1977.

Stein, Harold. *Public Administration and Policy Development: A Casebook*. New York: Harcourt Brace, 1952.

Straussman, Jeffrey D. *Public Administration*. New York: Holt, Rinehart and Winston, 1985.

Vocino, Thomas, and Jack Rabin, eds. *Contemporary Public Administration*. New York: Harcourt Brace Jovanovich, 1981.

Waldo, Dwight. *The Administrative State: A Study of the Political Theory of American Public Administration*. New York: Ronald Press, 1948.

Waldo, Dwight, ed. *Public Administration in a Time of Turbulence*. Scranton, Pa.: Chandler, 1971.

Williams, J. D. *Public Administration: The People's Business*. Boston: Little Brown, 1980.

Public Administration - Canada

Adie, Robert F., and Paul G. Thomas. *Canadian Public Administration: Problematical Perspectives*. 2nd ed. Scarborough, Ont.: Prentice-Hall, 1987.

Borgeat, Louis, René Dussault, and Lionel Ouellet. *L'administration Québecoise: organisation et fonctionnnement*. Québec: Presses de l'Université du Québec, 1984.

Cole, Taylor. *The Canadian Bureaucracy, 1939-1947*. Durham, N.C.: Duke University Press, 1949.

Dawson, R. McGregor. *The Civil Service of Canada*. Oxford: Oxford University Press, 1929.

Doerr, Audrey. *The Machinery of Government in Canada*. Toronto: Methuen, 1980.

Garant, Patrice. *La fonction publique: Canadienne et Québecoise*. Québec: Les Presses de l'Université Laval, 1973.

Gow, Iain, ed. *Administration publique québecoise*. Montreal: Librairie Beauchemin Limitée, 1970.

Hodgetts, J. E. "Challenge and Response: A Retrospective View of the Public Service of Canada." *Canadian Public Administration* 7 (December 1964): 409-21.

Hodgetts, J. E., *The Canadian Public Service: A Physiology of Government, 1867-1970*. Toronto: University of Toronto Press, 1973.

Hodgetts, J. E. "The Public Service: Its Past and the Challenge of its Future." *Canadian Public Administration* 17 (Spring 1974): 17-25.

Hodgetts, J. E., and D. C. Corbett, eds. *Canadian Public Administration*. Toronto: Macmillan, 1960.

Kernaghan, Kenneth, ed. *Bureaucracy in Canadian Government*. 2nd ed. Toronto:

Methuen, 1973.

Kernaghan, Kenneth. "Canadian Public Administration: Progress and Prospects." *Canadian Public Administration* 25 (Winter 1982): 444-56.

Kernaghan, Kenneth, ed. *Canadian Public Administration: Discipline and Profession.* Toronto: Butterworths, 1983.

Kernaghan, Kenneth, ed. *Public Administration in Canada: Selected Readings.* 5th ed. Toronto: Methuen, 1985. (1st ed., 1968; 2nd ed., 1971; 3rd ed., 1977; 4th ed., 1982).

Laframboise, H. L. "The Future of Public Administration in Canada." *Canadian Public Administration* 25 (Winter 1982): 507-19.

McReady, Douglas J., *The Canadian Public Sector.* Toronto: Butterworths, 1984.

Sutherland, Sharon L., and G. Bruce Doern. *Bureaucracy in Canada: Control and Reform.* Research Study no. 43 for the Royal Commission on the Economic Union and Development Prospects for Canada (Toronto: University of Toronto Press, 1985).

Wilson, V. Seymour. *Canadian Public Policy and Administration.* Toronto: McGraw-Hill Ryerson, 1981.

2

What Is Public Bureaucracy?

In the previous chapter, public bureaucracy was distinguished from public administration and was defined as "the system of authority, people, offices, and methods that government uses to achieve its objectives." Large business and other non-governmental organizations are often described as bureaucracies, but the concept of bureaucracy is so closely associated with government that the terms "bureaucracy" and "public bureaucracy" are commonly used interchangeably. This chapter will illustrate that the neutral definition provided above for the term public bureaucracy is not shared by everyone. The chapter begins with a review of the evolution and criticisms of public bureaucracy. This review is followed by an explanation of theories concerning the relationship between bureaucracy and the state.

ORIGINS AND CRITICISMS OF PUBLIC BUREAUCRACY

Evolution of Public Bureaucracy

Many of the central features of contemporary public bureaucracy (e.g., chain of command, specialization, delegation of authority) were evident in the ancient civilizations of Egypt and China. In the West, many characteristics of present-day public bureaucracy existed during the period of the Roman Empire. After the fall of the Empire and the onset of the Dark Ages, some of the Roman achievements in administration were kept alive by the Roman Catholic Church. It is generally acknowledged, however, that the modern type of administrative system began in the seventeenth century after the emergence of nation-states from the feudal societies of Europe. It was not until the 1800s that Europe, Great Britain, the United States, and Canada developed their distinctive systems of public bureaucracy that have endured to the present.

Despite the long history of bureaucratic forms of administration, use of the word bureaucracy is comparatively recent. It appears to have been first used in eighteenth century France by Vincent de Gournay to signify a form of government in which appointed officials play a central role. In France at this time the word "bureau" referred not only to a writing-table (or, according to some scholars, a cloth covering the desks of government officials); it also referred to a place where officials worked. A Greek word meaning "rule" was added as a suffix to "bureau" and by 1798 the Dictionary of the French Academy defined bureaucracy as: "power, influence of the heads and staff of governmental bureaux."[1] An indication of the subsequent pejorative interpretations of the term was provided by the Academy's approval of the term bureaucratic to signify "the influence of governmental bureaux, and also a regime where bureaux multiply without need."[2] Use of the term spread quickly to other European countries and eventually throughout the world.

During the past two centuries, the term bureaucracy has been interpreted in a wide variety of ways. On the basis of an exhaustive study of interpretations and theories of bureaucracy, Martin Albrow has identified seven "modern concepts of bureaucracy."[3] These are bureaucracy as rational organization, as organizational inefficiency, as rule by officials, as public administration, as administration by officials, as the organization, and as modern society.

Criticisms of Public Bureaucracy

Regardless of the neutral meaning assigned to bureaucracy at the beginning of this chapter, the most frequent usage of the term throughout history and in current conversation is a pejorative one. The word bureaucracy normally conjures up images of government employees and organizations characterized by unresponsiveness, inaccessibility, inflexibility, inefficiency, arbitrariness, and empire-building.

Among those groups whose negative views on the bureaucracy have been most widely disseminated are novelists, journalists, politicians, business people, and academics. As early as 1836, in his novel *Les Employés*, Honoré de Balzac described bureaucracy as "the great power wielded by pygmies" and noted that bureaucracy was organized "under a constitutional government with a natural kindness for mediocrity, a predilection for categorical statements and reports, a government as fussy and meddlesome, in short, as a small shopkeeper's wife."[4] And in 1885, the English novelist Charles Dickens wrote in *Little Dorrit* about the Circumlocution Office where "numbers of people were lost." In this office, "unfortunates with wrongs, or with projects for the general welfare.... who in slow lapse of time and agony had passed safely through other public departments; who, according to rule, had been bullied in this, over-reached by that, and evaded by the other; got referred to the Circumlocution Office, and never reappeared in the light of day."[5]

Similar anti-bureaucratic sentiments have pervaded a great deal of fictional literature during the past century. Novelists have been joined by satirists whose works on bureaucracy include *Parkinson's Law, When in Doubt: Mumble,* and *Cover Your Ass.* In *The Completely Civil Servant*, a Canadian writing under the pseudonym of G. Arthur Sage describes his book as "the bible for survival, therapy and reform" for public servants and as a means by which "the taxpayer will get an insider's view of the practices that have mushroomed under the justification of improved service to a demanding citizenry."[6] Movies, popular magazines, professional journals, and public affairs shows on both television and radio all engage in the national sport of bashing bureaucrats.

Journalists make a major contribution to the bureaucracy's negative image through provocative headlines and reports that trumpet the bureaucracy's deficiencies and failures. Many of these headlines and stories reflect attacks on bureaucrats by politicians. An enduring theme of election campaigns at all levels of Canadian government is the need to control the bureaucracy, to make it more efficient, and to reduce its size. Journalists and politicians find a very receptive audience for anti-bureaucratic assertions among the general public and especially among business people. The kind of distorted picture of bureaucracy painted by some business publications is illustrated in an issue of *Canadian Business* where a writer is discussing the problems of running a restaurant:

> A restaurant... is the natural prey of petty bureaucrats who will obstruct and complicate everything you do. All of them will hunt you down, and any of them, on a whim, can shut you down. A mouse in the house, you get a cat. A mouse in a restaurant, you get a visit, an hour's lecture and a warning notice (this time about the cat); and a series of visits and letters from the building inspector who wants to see the drawings for the cat box.[7]

In addition to these journalistic and popular accounts, there have been serious scholarly analyses of bureaucracy where the bureaucracy has received mixed reviews from the academic community. Victor Thompson refers to "bureau-pathic" behaviour in large-scale organizations that takes the form of "excessive aloofness, ritualistic attachment to routines and procedures, and resistance to change; and associated with these behavior patterns is a petty insistence upon rights of authority and status."[8]

Other scholars sing the bureaucracy's praises. Charles Perrow contends that "the sins generally attributed to bureaucracy are either not sins at all or are consequences of the failure to bureaucratize sufficiently."[9] For example, the impersonality and rigid adherence to rules found in bureaucracies are frequently criticized. However, the fact that a bureaucrat responds to people according to the objective merits of their case rather than to factors such as their skin colour or religion is a very positive aspect of bureaucracy. A bureaucratic response based on prejudice or other inappropriate considerations would, in Perrow's view, be evidence of "failure to bureaucratize sufficiently."

One of the strongest proponents of the positive elements of bureaucracy is Charles T. Goodsell. In his book, *The Case for Bureaucracy*,[10] he argues that bureaucracy in the United States has been the victim of unfortunate stereotyping and myth. He notes that while people rail against the evils of bureaucracy in the abstract, when they are asked how *they* have been treated by bureaucrats in specific situations, they tend to see the bureaucrats as being fair and helpful. After reviewing a great deal of evidence, he concludes that while bureaucracy is not perfect by any means, it does have an enviable record of providing services.

Goodsell's point about the contradictory nature of the public's perception of the bureaucracy is supported by two major studies of Canadian attitudes toward the federal public service.[11] The two studies demonstrate that despite favourable personal interactions with bureaucrats, many Canadians have a negative image of the bureaucracy as a whole. For example, when asked about their personal experience, more than 80 percent of those Canadians surveyed in 1978 indicated that public servants had been helpful and courteous and 75 percent indicated that their problems had been handled promptly; however, when asked about their view of public servants in general, only 65 percent of the respondents expected courteous treatment, only 50 percent expected public servants to be helpful, and only 40 percent expected prompt handling of their problems.[12] "In the final assessment, it appears that the public weighs more heavily media and other reports of government inefficiencies than their own experiences with government services and public servants."[13]

BUREAUCRACY AND THE STATE

This section reviews classical and modern theories of bureaucracy within the broad framework of theories of the role of the state.[14] These theories are especially concerned with the effects of bureaucracy on the power structure of society. The next two chapters cover, among other topics, theories of organization; these theories are more narrowly focussed on the internal management of organizations.

Classical Theories of Bureaucracy

Karl Marx (1818-1883)

Marx's ideas on bureaucracy must be examined in the context of his theory of class conflict in capitalist societies and the advent of communism. According to Marx, the state in capitalist societies does not represent the general interest, but rather the interests of the dominant or ruling class. He regards the state as "nothing more than the form of organization which the bourgeois necessarily adopt...for the mutual guarantee of their property and interests."[15] The bureaucracy of the state is viewed as an instrument that the dominant class uses to exercise its power over other social classes. Bureaucracy is, in fact, one of the primary means for perpetuating class division and consolidating the power of the dominant class. The state becomes more oppressive as class conflict intensifies. For Marx, the increasing bureaucratization of the state under capitalism accompanies the intensification of the class struggle.

This class struggle eventually leads to a proleterian revolution and the gradual development of a classless society. With the advent of communism, the state and the exploitative elements of the bureaucracy will ultimately wither away. Administrative tasks will be everyone's concern and will involve the administration of things rather than of people.

In his early writings, Marx argued that bureaucracy contributes to the general process of alienation in society; it becomes an autonomous and oppressive force beyond the control of the people. He also asserted that bureaucracy is characterized by secrecy, incompetence, empire-building, and self-interest. In his later writings, Marx downplayed the idea of bureaucracy as an autonomous social force by referring to bureaucracy simply as part of the state that would wither away with the state itself. Allowing for the possibility of bureaucracy exercising autonomous power would have been inconsistent with his later view that "nothing could prevent economic forces producing the polarization of society into bourgeoisie and proletariat."[16]

Classical Elite Theory

Gaetano Mosca (1885-1941) and Robert Michels (1876-1936). Mosca and Michels belong to the *elite* school of classical theorists. Mosca, in his book *The Ruling Class*, contends that all societies are composed of two classes—a class that rules and a class that is ruled. The ruling class is a minority that rules the majority, not simply by coercion, but through ability to organize and by reference to such abstract principles as the sovereignty of the people or divine right.

Mosca divides states into two types, which he calls the feudal and the bureaucratic. In the feudal state, any member of the ruling class can carry out all the functions of government, whether economic, judicial, administrative, or military. In the bureaucratic state, however, these functions are separated and become the exclusive territory of particular sections of the ruling class, including the bureaucracy and the military establishment. The government taxes a portion of the national wealth to support a large number of salaried administrative and military officials.

Mosca does not accept the Marxian notion of an identity of interests among persons in a similar class position. He looks to the election of members of the ruling class to legislative bodies as a means of constraining bureaucratic power. He is, however, uncertain as to whether elected bodies would in practice be able to exercise adequate control over the bureaucracy.

Michel's major focus is not on the state bureaucracy; rather, it is on the internal political structures of large-scale organizations. On the basis of his study of political parties and trade unions, he formulated his famous "iron law of oligarchy." According to this law, large-scale organizations are necessarily oligarchic because they tend to develop a bureaucratic structure that precludes internal democracy. In Michel's words, "who says organization, says oligarchy." Power becomes concentrated at the top of the organization and is wielded in a dictatorial manner by an organizational elite.

For Michels, the iron law of oligarchy has broad implications in that oligarchic bureaucratic structures undermine the democratic institutions of society. The eventual result is an oligarchic political regime that resists demands for change made by the general populace.

Michels views bureaucracy as inevitable in the modern state. Through bureaucracy, the politically dominant classes secure and preserve their power. They use, indeed they expand, positions in the bureaucracy to provide security for middle-class intellectuals who, in turn, support the state. The bureaucracy tends to oppress the rest of society. Lower-level bureaucrats, in particular, suppress individual liberty and initiative.

Max Weber (1864-1920)

Max Weber, a German scholar, has had more influence on the study of bureaucracy than any other theorist. Weber does not agree with Marx that bureaucracy will eventually wither away. Indeed, he predicts that bureaucratic administration will pervade all forms of organization, whether in the religious, educational, or economic spheres of life. He asserts that "the needs of mass administration make (bureaucratic administration) completely indispensable. The choice is only that between bureaucracy and dilletantism in the field of administration."[17] Weber also disagrees with Michels's view that bureaucratic domination of elected politicians is inevitable. But Weber is ambivalent about the power of the bureaucracy. Support can be found in his writings both for the view that in a democracy the bureaucracy must be subordinate to elected politicians and for the view that, in certain circumstances, bureaucrats could dominate their political superiors.

Like Marx and Michels, Weber sets his ideas on bureaucracy within the context of a study of the power structure of society. He examines the concept of bureaucracy within a broad and complex framework of political sociology. Unlike Marx and Michels, he treats bureaucracy as the central concept in his analysis and as a general phenomenon in modern society.

Weber relates bureaucracy to his analysis of three sources of authority which he distinguishes on the basis of their claim to legitimacy. Under *traditional* authority, the right to rule is legitimated by such factors as heredity, religious beliefs, or divine right. *Charismatic* authority is based on the outstanding personal characteristics of an individual (e.g., Jesus, John Kennedy, Adolph Hitler). Finally, *legal* authority is legitimated by laws and regulations obeyed by both the rulers and the ruled. In this system, "obedience is owed not to a person— whether a traditional chief or charismatic leader—but to a set of impersonal principles."[18] Each of the types of authority is associated with different administrative arrangements; the usual administrative system under legal authority is bureaucracy.

From his knowledge of Western European bureaucracies, notably the German and the British, Weber developed his celebrated ideal-type of bureaucracy, which is discussed in the next chapter.

Modern Theories of Bureaucracy

Pluralism

According to pluralist theory, political power in contemporary Western democracies is fragmented and diffused among many groups that check and balance one another. While certain groups have more influence on government than others, all have some influence. There is no power elite that dominates the decision-making process; rather there is a plurality of elites. Success in influencing government decision-making depends not only on access to such resources as money and expertise, but also on a determination to have one's voice heard.

The structure of modern governments and, in particular, modern bureaucracies, reflects and facilitates this pluralism because their complexity provides numerous points of access for groups wishing to influence government decision-makers. In a pluralist political system, bureaucrats are influenced and constrained by a wide variety of political actors who pursue their interests by forming alliances with administrative agencies. Bureaucrats, in turn, influence and constrain these actors and welcome alliances that enable their agencies to achieve their objectives. This practice is especially characteristic of the United States, where administrative agencies act like pressure groups, mobilizing support from various groups to influence legislators and the public. In Canada, departments that operate in a similar fashion are often referred to as clientele departments; they include such departments as Agriculture (in alliance with farmers) and Veterans Affairs (in alliance with veterans).

In addition, the bureaucracy itself, like the state, is a pluralist structure. It is composed of a large number of administrative agencies that are interdependent, yet are also rivals for scarce government resources. Again, this is most easily demonstrated in the United States where administrative agencies use alliances within or outside the bureaucracy in competition with other agencies for resources and, in some instances, for survival.

Elitism and Technocracy

Modern elite theory draws on the contributions of such classical elite theorists as Mosca and Michels who contend that societies consist of a class that rules and a class that is ruled. In contrast to the pluralists, modern elite theorists contend that public policy is decided by a small number of ruling elites who are drawn largely from the upper socio-economic level of society, who agree on the basic values of the social system, and whose decisions are little influenced by the masses.[19] C. Wright Mills,[20] a leading representative of this school of thought, argues that American society is dominated by a power elite that occupies key posts in government, business corporations, and the military.

Elite theorists view the bureaucratic-technocratic elites as only one element of the ruling elites. However, *technocratic* theory holds that the technocratic elite, or experts, in both public and private sector organizations, exercise the greatest influence on public policy. James Burnham[21] argued as early as 1942 that these experts would become the rulers of society. While contemporary proponents of the technocratic school of thought do not share this view, they are concerned that the power of technocrats, notably government bureaucrats, is a threat to democracy.

Several reasons for the increasing power of senior bureaucrats are offered:[22] the scope and complexity of government activities require a greater number of bureaucrats with expert technical knowledge; political leaders are obliged to rely on bureaucrats for information and advice; since elected officials have limited time and little interest or expertise in certain areas, much is left for bureaucratic decision; and finally, politicians come and go, but bureaucrats are permanent.

It must be acknowledged that bureaucrats exercise substantial power in the political system and that much of this power is based on expertise. However, it can be argued that this expertise does not put the bureaucracy in a dominant position. Moreover, generalists, rather than experts, occupy the top posts in contemporary bureaucracies. It is notable that, while a powerful bureaucracy poses some danger to democracy, it can also constrain abuses of the democratic process by elected officials.

Corporatism

Corporatism can be defined as

> an institutional arrangement whereby public policy is worked out through an interaction between top state elites and the leadership of a limited number of corporate organizations (mainly business and industrial corporations on the one hand and labour unions on the other). Under this arrangement, the corporate organizations are granted a deliberate representational monopoly within their respective areas of interest in exchange for submitting themselves to certain constraints imposed by the state.[23]

There is, however, much debate among writers on corporatism as to the exact meaning of the term, the countries where it exists, whether present trends are in the direction of its expansion, and its implications for relations between bureaucracy and the state.

While pluralist theory holds that government decisions are influenced by a considerable number of groups acting in a voluntary and competitive fashion, corporatist theory holds that these decisions are influenced by a small number of non-competitive and functionally differentiated groups that are recognized or licenced by the state. Corporatist arrangements and tendencies are much less common in Canada[24] and the United States than in Western Europe (notably Austria, Denmark, West Germany, and the United Kingdom) where business organizations and trade unions are more integrated into economic policy-making through various consultative bodies and processes.

Some scholars contend that a corporatist state is less bureaucratic than other forms because the state can work through indirect and informal mechanisms to negotiate agreements with a small number of dominant groups. Other scholars argue, however, that in a corporatist state the government would require "an autonomous bureaucratic arm with independent access to information and capable of supervising the operations of capital."[25] Moreover, bureaucratic power is likely to be greater because of the close interaction between senior bureaucrats and the dominant groups.[26] It is notable that in a corporatist state, weaker groups and unorganized people would tend to be frozen out of the decision-making process.

Modern Marxist Theory

Contemporary Marxist scholars are not agreed on a generally acceptable theory of the state. They do agree, however, that the state serves three major functions, namely, accumulating wealth and power for the capitalist class, legitimizing to workers the value of the capitalist state, and, if necessary, repressing or coercing workers to ensure social order. In Chapter 6 these functions will be elaborated in the examination of Marxist analysis as a model of public policy-making. The focus here is on the modern Marxist view of the role of bureaucracy in the power structure of society.

Like Marx, modern Marxists contend that state institutions, notably the bureaucracy, serve the interests of the capitalist ruling class. Ralph Miliband, a leading theorist on Marxism, offers several reasons for this.[27] First, members of the ruling class and senior officials in state institutions have personal ties of friendship, kinship, and experience because of their similar social origins. Indeed, members of the ruling class are direct participants in the bureaucracy and other state institutions. Second, the ruling class, because of its economic power, is the most influential pressure group in capitalist society. Third, the state operates in a capitalist system of production and is, therefore, constrained by structure to promote the capitalist economy. By doing so, it serves both its own interests and those of the capitalist class. According to Miliband, "a capitalist economy has its own 'rationality' to which any government and state must sooner or later submit, and usually sooner."[28] Nicos Poulantzas, another leading theorist, contends that the bureaucracy serves the capitalist class, not because of similar social origins, but because of Miliband's third point, namely that structural constraints mean that the interests of the bureaucracy and the ruling class coincide.[29]

Miliband and Poulantzas agree, however, that bureaucracy has become the dominant state institution. The power of the legislatures and, therefore, of those who elect them, has declined; legislators have little direct contact with bureaucrats. Similarly, the accompanying decline in the power of political parties means that they no longer serve as mechanisms for channeling class interests to bureaucratic decision-makers. The threat to democracy is aggravated further in some countries by the politicization of the bureaucracy, which enables the government party to appoint its supporters to senior public service posts. The increased power of the bureaucracy is dangerous also because it tends to promote and sustain conservative forces.

Eva Etzioni-Halevy criticizes Marxists for turning into a dogma the idea that the state, and therefore the bureaucracy, promotes the interest of the capitalist ruling class.[30] She notes the Marxist argument that "if the state elite is conservative in its policies, then, obviously, it works in the interests of the ruling class." If, however, "it introduces reforms that benefit the lower classes . . ., this too is interpreted . . . as serving merely to co-opt those classes and make them more willing to accept the capitalist system." She contends that a more realistic approach than treating the state elites as servants of the ruling class would be to treat them "as two groups, each of which is intent on using the other to serve its own interests." She also criticizes the Marxists for arguing on the one hand that bureaucracy is simply a servant of the ruling class and on the other that bureaucracy is becoming too powerful in its own right.

Libertarian Theory

The school of thought represented by such thinkers as Frederich Hayek and Milton Friedman is called Libertarianism. In the tradition of Adam Smith and John Stuart Mill, Hayek and Friedman are concerned about the threat that the expansion of both government activities and bureaucracy poses for economic liberty. Indeed, they argue that this expansion threatens political as well as economic liberty.

Frederich A. Hayek (1899-   ). Hayek's best-known book, *The Road to Serfdom,*[31] is based on principles of nineteenth-century economic liberalism. He argues that economic liberty is possible only in a capitalist system and that all forms of collectivism (e.g., socialism) are incompatible with democracy because the social planning involved in collectivism tends to destroy both political and economic freedom. Hayek is not opposed to the idea of a welfare state, but he is concerned that even the moderate planning involved in creating a welfare state will have consequences, neither foreseen nor desired by the planners, that will put the state on the road to serfdom, that is, totalitarianism. Moreover, the bureaucracy will play a critical role in putting the state on this path.

Hayek notes that economic planning and regulation in the welfare state lead to very substantial growth in the size and power of the bureaucracy, some of whose members exercise extensive discretionary powers over individual citizens. In addition, the bureaucracy is composed of people whose careers depend significantly on the expansion of government services. According to Hayek, in the welfare state the rule of law is breached in that bureaucrats are delegated powers to make decisions that discriminate between individuals and against which appeal is very difficult. Efficiency is also reduced in that the welfare system doesn't really help those for whom it was designed; for example, a progressive income tax benefits middle-income persons rather than the poor.

Milton Friedman (1912-   ). Friedman's best-known books include *Capitalism and Freedom*[32] and *Free to Choose.*[33] Like Hayek, Friedman worries about the threat to economic and political liberty from the expansion of both government activities and bureaucracy. This expansion is the unavoidable result of the growth of the welfare state which, in his view, diverts important economic resources away from the private sector of the economy and creates a kind of government paternalism that undermines the very foundations of the capitalist system. Among government activities to which he objects are rent control, minimum wage rates, legal maximum prices, detailed regulation of industries, and public housing.[34]

Friedman warns that the United States is moving in the same direction as other countries that have lost their economic and political liberty as a consequence of the expansion of the welfare state. He cites the examples of Chile, Britain, and New York City to support his view that the expanded role of the state, the increased volume of government regulations, and the growth of government spending, no matter how well-intended, threaten individual liberty. He contends that "the Welfare State's fundamental fallacy, which leads to both financial crisis and the destruction of freedom, is the attempt to do good at someone else's expense."[35] This happens because people do not spend someone else's money with as much care as they do their own. Moreover, to do good at someone else's expense, you have to take the money away from that person. Thus, the use of force and coercion, which destroy freedom, is necessary to do good at somebody else's expense.

Friedman distinguishes between the economic market where you get what you vote for (by paying) and the political market where there is very little relation between what you vote for and what you get. In the economic market, "each man can vote, as it were, for the color of the tie he wants and get it; he does not have to see what color the majority wants and then, if he is in the minority, to submit."[36] One of the myths about the political market is that a government bureaucrat can be distinguished from someone in private enterprise on the grounds that the bureaucrat serves a *public* interest rather than a *private* interest. Friedman contends that "a government bureaucrat is seeking to serve his private interest just as much as you or I or the ordinary businessman."[37] In the economic market, our self-interest motivates us to serve our customers' interests, but in a government bureaucracy the customers have nowhere else to go. Thus, the bureaucrats can serve their self-interest at their customers' expense by expanding their empire and reducing their workload.

The Libertarian school of thought has had a great deal of influence on the views of those people associated with the contemporary neo-conservative movement. The term neo-conservatism[38] emerged in the mid-1970s to describe the views of a group of American intellectuals (e.g., Irving Kristol, Nathan Glazer, and Norman Podhoretz) who believe that big government is a threat to freedom and economic prosperity and who tend to ally themselves with business interests on many political and economic issues. Neo-conservatism has had very significant influence on the Reagan and Bush administrations in the United States and on the Thatcher government in Britain. It also has followers in Canada (e.g., Michael Walker of the Fraser Institute in Vancouver, writer Barbara Amiel, and John Bullock of the Canadian Federation of Independent Business).

A practical application of neo-conservative thinking can be seen in efforts over the past fifteen years, in Canada and elsewhere, to reduce both government spending and the size and influence of the bureaucracy. In Canada, the Progressive Conservative government of Prime Minister Brian Mulroney has pursued these objectives by such means as abolishing or cutting back government programs; privatizing government activities and ownership; deregulating industry; emulating the management model provided by private enterprise; downsizing the public service; and increasing political control over the bureaucracy.

Bureaucracy and Democracy

The foregoing theories are concerned, in varying degrees, with one of the most central and enduring issues in public administration, namely the relationship between bureaucracy and democracy. Indeed, a pervasive theme in this book— and the primary concern of Chapters 12 to 14—is the nature of bureaucratic power and bureaucratic responsibility in Canadian democracy. Etzioni-Halevy captures the essence of the problematic relationship between bureaucracy and democracy in three theses.[39] Her first thesis is that "bureaucracy generates a dilemma for democracy." She contends that bureaucracy threatens democratic political institutions because it is becoming increasingly powerful and independent, and because the rules affecting the exercise of its power are ill-defined. At the same time, however, a powerful, independent bureaucracy is required to prevent political corruption and to safeguard democratic procedures. "Bureaucracy is thus a threat to, but also indispensable for, democracy."

The second thesis is that "democracy generates a dilemma for bureaucracy." Because democracy's rules are self-contradictory, bureaucracy finds itself in a double-bind. It "is expected to be both independent and subservient, both responsible for its own actions and subject to ministerial responsibility, both politicized and non-politicized at the same time." Public servants are centrally involved in policy development, but are expected to be neutral in regard to party politics.

The third thesis is that "these dilemmas exacerbate strains and power struggles on the political scene," notably between senior bureaucrats and senior politicians. It is often unclear as to whether certain responsibilities belong to public servants or politicians. Thus, public servants and politicians, especially Cabinet ministers, can become involved in serious disagreements over jurisdiction.

We shall see in subsequent chapters that the tensions resulting from these dilemmas explain a great deal about the organization and management of Canadian government in general and public bureaucracy in particular.

NOTES

1. Martin Albrow, *Bureaucracy* (London: Macmillan, 1970), p. 17.
2. Ibid., pp. 17-18.
3. Ibid.
4. Translated by E. Marriage as *Bureaucracy* (1898), p. 84. Cited in ibid., p. 18.
5. Cited in E.N. Gladden, *The Essentials of Public Administration* (London: Staples Press, 1964), p. 66.
6. G. Arthur Sage, *The Completely Civil Servant* (n.p.: Eden Press, 1985).
7. James Barber, "Cordon Blues," *Canadian Business* (June 1981), p. 116.
8. Victor Thompson, *Modern Organization* (New York: Knopf, 1961), pp. 152-53.
9. Charles Perrow, *Complex Organizations: A Critical Essay*, 2nd ed. (Glenview, Ill.: Scott Foresman, 1979), p. 5.
10. Charles T. Goodsell, *The Case for Bureaucracy*, 2nd ed. (Chatham, N.J.: Chatham House, 1985).
11. Task Force on Government Information, *To Know and Be Known* (Ottawa: Queen's Printer, 1969) and *Task Force on Service to the Public, Surveys Among the Public on the Quality of Service to the Public from the Federal Government* (unpublished report, 1978).
12. David Zussman, "The Image of the Public Service in Canada," *Canadian Public Administration* 25 (Spring 1982): 77.
13. Ibid., 78.
14. For elaboration on these theories, see Eva Etzioni-Halevy, *Bureaucracy and Democracy* (London: Routledge and Kegan Paul, 1983), Nicos P. Mouzelis, *Organization and Bureaucracy* (Chicago: Aldine, 1967), and B.C. Smith, *Bureaucracy and Political Power* (Sussex: Wheatsheaf Books, 1988).
15. Karl Marx and Friedrich Engels, *The German Ideology* (1846), p. 78. Cited by Martin Albrow, *Bureaucracy*, p. 70.
16. Albrow, ibid.
17. Max Weber, *Economy and Society* (New York: Bedminster Press, 1968), p. 223.
18. Peter Blau and Richard W. Scott, *Formal Organizations* (San Francisco: Chandler, 1962), p. 32.

19. See Thomas R. Dye and Harmon Ziegler, *The Irony of Democracy*, 6th ed. (Monterey, Calif.: Brooks/Cole, 1984), p. 6.
20. C. Wright Mills, *The Power Elite* (New York: Oxford University Press, 1956).
21. James Burnham, *The Managerial Revolution* (London: Putnam, 1942).
22. Etzioni-Halevy, *Bureaucracy and Democracy*, pp. 57-59.
23. Ibid., p. 63.
24. For a discussion of the possible adoption of corporatist arrangements in Canada, see William D. Coleman, *Business and Politics* (Kingston and Montreal: McGill-Queen's University Press, 1988).
25. Leo Panitch, "Recent Theorizations of Corporatism: Reflections on a Growth Industry," *British Journal of Sociology* 31 (1980): 165.
26. Diamant, "Bureaucracy and Public Policy in Neo-Corporatist Settings," *Comparative Politics* 14 (1981): 110.
27. Ralph Miliband, *The State in Capitalist Society* (London: Weidenfeld and Nicolson, 1969), pp. 48-68.
28. Ralph Miliband, *Marxism and Politics* (Oxford: Oxford University Press, 1977), p. 72.
29. Nicos Poulantzas, *Political Power and Social Classes* (London: NLB and Sheed and Ward, 1975), pp. 331-40.
30. Etzioni-Halevy, *Bureaucracy and Democracy*, pp. 82-84.
31. (Chicago: University of Chicago Press, 1944).
32. (Chicago: University of Chicago Press, 1962).
33. (New York: Harcourt Brace Jovanovich, 1980).
34. *Capitalism and Freedom*, pp. 35-36.
35. Milton Friedman, "The Threat to Freedom in the Welfare State," *Business and Society Review* (Spring 1977): 8-16.
36. Ibid., 15.
37. Ibid., 12.
38. See Peter Steinfels, *The Neoconservatives* (New York: Simon and Schuster, 1979).
39. Etzioni-Halevy, *Bureaucracy and Democracy*, p. 87.

BIBLIOGRAPHY

Albrow, Martin. *Bureaucracy*. London: Macmillan, 1970.

Blau, Peter M., and Marshall W. Meyer. *Bureaucracy in Modern Society*. 2nd ed. New York: Random House, 1971.

Blau, Peter M., and Richard W. Scott. *Formal Organizations*. San Francisco: Chandler, 1962.

Burnham, James. *The Managerial Revolution*. Middlesex: Penguin Books, 1962.

Crozier, Michael. *The Bureaucratic Phenomenon*. Chicago: University of Chicago Press, 1964.

Downs, Anthony. *Inside Bureaucracy*. Boston: Little, Brown, 1967.

Etzioni-Halevy, Eva. *Bureaucracy and Democracy*. London: Routledge & Kegan Paul, 1983.

Friedman, Milton. *Capitalism and Freedom*. Chicago: University of Chicago Press, 1962.

Friedman, Milton. *Free to Choose*. New York: Harcourt Brace Jovanovich, 1980.

Goodsell, Charles T. *The Case for Bureaucracy*. 2nd ed. Chatham, N.J: Chatham House, 1985.

Hayek, Frederich A. *The Road to Serfdom*. Chicago: University of Chicago Press, 1944.

Hummel, Ralph P. *The Bureaucratic Experience*. New York: St. Martin's Press, 1977.

Merton, Robert K. et al., eds. *Reader in Bureaucracy*. Glencoe, Ill.: Free Press, 1953.

Michels, Robert. *Political Parties*. Translated by E. and C. Paul. London: Jarrold, 1915.

Miliband, R. *The State in Capitalist Society*. London: Weidenfeld and Nicolson, 1969.

Miliband, R. *Marxism and Politics*. Oxford: Oxford University Press, 1977.

Morstein Marx, F. *The Administrative State*. Chicago: University of Chicago Press, 1957.

Mouzelis, Nicos P. *Organization and Bureaucracy: An Analysis of Modern Theories*. Chicago: Aldine, 1968.

Pal, Leslie A. *State, Class and Bureaucracy*. Kingston and Montreal: McGill-Queen's University Press, 1988.

Perrow, Charles. *Complex Organizations: A Critical Essay*. 2nd ed. Glenview, Ill.: Foresman, 1979.

Poulantzas, N. *Political Power and Social Classes*. London: New Left Books and Sheed and Ward, 1975.

Smith, B. C. *Bureaucracy and Political Power*. Sussex: Wheatsheaf, 1988.

Thompson, Victor A. *Bureaucracy and the Modern World*. Morristown, N.J.: General Learning Press, 1976.

Thompson, Victor A. *Modern Organization*. New York: Knopf, 1961.

Weber, Max. *Economy and Society*. New York: Bedminster Press, 1968.

Weber, Max. From *Max Weber: Essays in Sociology*. Edited and translated by H. H. Gerth and C. Wright Mills. New York: Oxford University Press, 1946.

Weber, Max. *The Theory of Social and Economic Organization*. Translated by A.M. Henderson and Talcott Parsons. Fair Lawn, N.J.: Oxford University Press, 1947.

3

Public Administration and Organization Theory: The Structural Foundation

Early cave-dwellers who decided to join forces and divide responsibilities to improve their chances in hunting probably created the first organization. Given this lengthy history of organization, it is surprising that bureaucracy, as we know it today, has had a relatively short history. As noted in Chapter 2, bureaucratic forms existed in ancient China and in the medieval Roman Catholic Church. While these organizations had characteristics in common with modern forms of bureaucracy, they all lacked one or more of the essential features found in modern bureaucracies. The remaining chapters in this Part of the book will discuss theories that have been used to explain bureaucracy or to attempt to improve its operation. The approach will be roughly chronological, beginning with the earliest theorists and moving, in the next chapter, to some contemporary writers.

It is useful to begin by explaining why something that sounds as dry and other-worldly as organization theory should be studied. Frequently, theory is contrasted with action and, not surprisingly, most managers seem to prefer the latter and disdain the former. This is unfortunate because it ignores the fact that every member of society approaches organizations, other members of society, and tasks to be accomplished with a particular group of attitudes. Most people would not consider those attitudes as constituting a theory of organization, but they do. Whether we realize it or not, commonly held attitudes such as, "If I didn't watch my employees all the time, they'd just goof off" or "My boss treats me like a child—if she just let me decide how I wanted to do the work, I could do it much better" are really important parts of highly developed organizational theories. The problem with disparaging any systematic study of good theory is that members of organizations have attitudes which are theories, and which they use in the operation of their organizations.

MAX WEBER AND CLASSICAL BUREAUCRATIC THEORY

It would be difficult to locate the first bureaucratic organization, but the most noted person who systematically studied the emerging phenomenon of bureaucracy was Max Weber (1864-1920). As explained in the previous chapter, Weber was a brilliant scholar whose interests spanned many fields. Chapter 2 explained his views on the role of bureaucracy in society; this chapter will focus mainly on his discussion of the internal organization of bureaucracies.

The Characteristics of Weberian Bureaucracy

Weber's empirical study of the German bureaucracy suggested to him that the modern bureaucratic form consisted of a number of related characteristics. When these characteristics were combined in the same organization, the result was what he called the "ideal-type" bureaucracy.[1] The main components of this "ideal-type" bureaucracy were:[2]

- hierarchical structure;
- unity of command;
- specialization of labour;
- employment and promotion based on merit;
- full-time employment;
- decisions based on impersonal rules;
- importance of written files; and
- bureaucratic employment totally separate from the bureaucrat's private life.

Hierarchical structure. A bureaucratic organization is arranged in a series of superior-subordinate relationships, at the pinnacle of which is one, and only one, superior. This can also be described as **unity of command**, which means that for each position in the hierarchy, there is one, and only one, supervisor. Thus, Weber identified what is now a commonplace characteristic of an organizational chart. The clear line of authority produced by unity of command was one reason why Weber felt that bureaucracy was more efficient than previous forms of organization, but there were also other reasons for his belief.

Specialization of labour. The purpose of the hierarchical structure was to allocate responsibilities to subordinates in a clear and unambiguous fashion. This division of responsibilities was significant because a person may become very efficient when able to concentrate on a specific job. Specialization of labour, however, is not enough if the employees are not qualified to learn to perform the work.

Employment and promotion based on merit. In earlier times, people often obtained organizational positions through either heredity or outright purchase. Obviously, this method of staffing provided no guarantee that the person in a particular position was the best person for the job or even a competent one. Without some assurance of competence, no organization could operate in an efficient manner. In the German bureaucracy that Weber studied, employment and promotion based on an objective test of merit provided this assurance and, therefore, increased the efficiency of operation.

Full-time employment. An important principle related to employment based on merit was that employment in the bureaucracy was the full-time activity and major source of income of the official. This ensured that the official would develop allegiance to the bureaucracy and that the bureaucrat's hierarchical superior could exercise real *control* over the day-to-day activities of the official. The superior needed effective control to force the subordinate to abide by organizational regulations in carrying out duties. This led to another important characteristic of modern bureaucracy.

Decisions based on impersonal rules. Bureaucrats are bound by certain rules in dealing with the public. These rules are "impersonal" in the sense that they apply equally to all clients in a similar situation. Thus, bureaucrats cannot substitute their own set of rules for those legitimately proclaimed by superiors. If a particular benefit is to be provided without regard to race or religion, then a member of a bureaucracy would risk severe penalties if he or she allowed personal prejudice to affect the decision made. Reliance on impersonal rules in dealings between the bureaucracy and the general public increases confidence in the bureaucracy by establishing a regime of certainty in dealings.

Importance of written files. The importance of these rules leads to the importance of written files. If the bureaucrat must prove that he or she has abided by the rules in making decisions, then it is important to maintain written records, first, of the rules themselves, and then of all decisions made, and the rationale for those decisions. It is worth noting here that the bureaucrat's allegiance to the rules takes precedence over allegiance to his or her superior. A superior can exercise judgment in an area that is unclear under the rules, but cannot order a subordinate to violate those rules.

Bureaucratic employment is totally separate from the individual bureaucrat's private life. This is a recognition both of the autonomous nature of the bureaucracy as an organization and of the fact that the bureaucrat does not "own" his or her position and the rights that go with it. Bureaucrats possess very powerful authority. In the case of members of a government bureaucracy, this could be highly coercive authority. However, it is always clear that the power is attached to the position rather than to the individual. This was a distinction that was not always clear among members of the monarch's retinue in pre-bureaucratic times. An obvious result of this division is that the bureaucrat is not permitted to obtain any personal gain, other than a fixed salary, from his or her position.

Weber seems to have had a rather difficult love-hate relationship with this new organizational form called bureaucracy. As a serious, objective scholar, he documented the characteristics of the German bureaucracy as he saw them without favourable or critical comment.

Beyond that, though, he seems to have been of two minds about bureaucracy. On one hand, he argued that bureaucracy was the most efficient method of organization—a position that has been attacked by some contemporary critics. In fairness to Weber, he was likely suggesting that bureaucracy was more efficient than any *previous* system—an argument that would be difficult to refute. However, Weber did foresee many of the problems that contemporary critics find in bureaucracy.

This passion for bureaucratization ... is enough to drive one to despair. It is ... as though we knowingly and willingly were *supposed* to become men who need "order" and nothing but order, who become nervous and cowardly if this order shakes for a moment and helpless when they are torn from their exclusive adaptation to this order. That the world knows nothing more than such men of order—we are in any case caught up in this development, and the central question is not how we further and accelerate it but what we have to *set against* this machinery, in order to preserve a remnant of humanity from this parcelling-out of the soul, from this exclusive rule of bureaucratic life ideals.[3]

In this quotation, Weber touched upon the crucial aspects of bureaucracy that still confound us today. On the one hand, it seems to be the most efficient way of arranging a large number of offices and accomplishing complex, repetitive tasks. But, on the other hand, we condemn the impersonal, mind-numbing aspects of its operation.

Criticisms of Weber

The general criticism of Weber's work is that he dwelt too much on the structural aspects of bureaucracy and not enough on the human side of organization. It is suggested that because Weber viewed bureaucrats as mere cogs in the mechanism, he overstated the efficiency of bureaucracy and overlooked the effect that it would have on its members.

Robert Merton was concerned about the effect that the Weberian "ideal-type" of bureaucracy would ultimately have on the personality of the bureaucrat. He noted that situations occurred in which the application of general rules produced either inefficient results or results that seemed unfair to the client. In this situation, the Weberian bureaucrat must either abide by the general rule and produce an undesirable result or violate the rule and produce a desirable result. The bureaucrat who really values his or her career has little choice but to follow the rules. Thus, there is an inevitable tendency toward "an over-concern with strict adherence to regulations which induce timidity, conservatism, and technicism."[4]

Philip Selznick questioned the presumed efficiency of Weberian bureaucracy. He argued that the informal system of worker relationships could be just as important and influential as the formal system established in the rules of the organization.[5] To illustrate this point, he first distinguished between professed and operational goals. The professed goals are the original, overarching goals of the organization as a whole. The operational goals relate to the day-to-day functions and needs of the workers within the organization. He gave the example of a boys' reformatory that had adopted progressive ideals of rehabilitation as its professed goal, but continually slipped into the use of such techniques as discipline, regimentation, and spying to solve its practical, day-to-day problems. Thus, operational goals can easily diverge from professed goals and so weaken the efficiency of the organization.

He suggested that these two kinds of goals can come into play in any case where there is delegation of function—an important part of bureaucratic operation. This delegation has a tendency to create a "*bifurcation of interest between the initiator of the action and the agent employed.*"[6] The initiator wants a particular thing done in a particular manner (the professed goal), but the agent who must deal with practical problems frequently is unable to do exactly what is desired and so must do something else instead (the operational goal). This raises the question of *control*, which Weber implies is automatically attained. The initiator will not always be able to control the agent absolutely. The struggle for control leads to the creation of an informal system in which rank-and-file workers interact to attempt to control their work environment and fend off any capricious demands of senior officials.

Warren G. Bennis and Philip E. Slater take a radical stance in arguing that bureaucracy is currently outmoded as a form of organization.[7] They suggest that modern trends such as rapid change and the increasing professionalization of the workforce make bureaucracy, with its emphasis on rigid rules and hierarchy of control, obsolete.

The next chapter examines contemporary theories of organization that purport to maintain the positive aspects of bureaucracy and circumvent its less desirable aspects. However, it is useful first to examine an American contemporary of Weber who was also very influential in the study of organizations.

FREDERICK W. TAYLOR AND SCIENTIFIC MANAGEMENT

Max Weber was a philosopher who could stand at arm's length from organizations and describe in broad terms their general characteristics. By contrast, Frederick Winslow Taylor (1856-1915) was a mechanical engineer who began his career working as a technician on the factory floor and spent much of his later life in either a supervisory or advisory capacity dealing with problems of production management. His major concern was the proper arrangement of the human and mechanical resources of the factory so as to minimize waste, particularly waste of workers' time.

Taylor's experience in the factory showed him that a great deal of "soldiering," i.e., slacking off, was taking place, and that there were two reasons for this. One was what he regarded as the natural tendency of employees to do as little work as possible. The second was that work was sometimes arranged in such an awkward manner that no reasonable human being, regardless of how ambitious or honest he or she was, could physically perform what was expected by superiors. Since "soldiering" constituted the squandering of a resource, it was important for management to end it. Taylor argued that the resulting increased productivity would benefit both employers and employees.

The employee's natural tendency toward "soldiering" could be eliminated if the employer used scientific methods rather than "rule-of-thumb" methods to determine an employee's appropriate workload. Some "soldiering" was caused by the employee's rational reaction to the method of piece-work payment that was prevalent in Taylor's time. Employees knew that in the short run they could earn more by working hard and producing above standard, but they realized that in the long run this was counter-productive because employers simply raised the standard. Therefore, it was better to work at a steady pace and receive adequate pay than to be a "rate-buster." The problem was that employers had no idea what an employee *could* do in an average shift. Therefore, most employers used rules-of-thumb to establish standards and so did not have the confidence of their employees. The obvious solution to the problem was to establish *scientific standards* based on the proven physical capacities of workers and then refrain from adjusting those standards arbitrarily.

Taylor's usual approach in establishing these scientific standards was to select employees who performed a particular task exceptionally well, (e.g., moving the most pig iron, shoveling the most coal). Then, a trained management employee would carefully scrutinize the actions of these employees, watching and *timing* their every movement. This was the beginning of the time-and-motion study that has stirred so much controversy on factory floors. The purpose of these studies was to learn the ideal method of performing a particular task from the most efficient employees. This is the "one best way" employed by Frank and Lillian Gilbreth and popularized with humourous effect by their children in the book and movie *Cheaper by the Dozen*.[8] When the best set of physical motions was determined, then it was the responsibility of managers to teach this technique to all employees.

The second cause of "soldiering" was the simple inability of workers to maintain the pace that was expected of them because of the manner in which the work was organized. Taylor pointed out that workers could be more productive if management took greater care in organizing the work. He put particular emphasis on things such as determining the optimal working rhythm necessary to maximize output. The next time you are working in the garden or shoveling snow it might be useful to know that, according to Taylor, the greatest tonnage per day can be shoveled when the worker moves twenty-one pounds on each shovel-load.[9]

Taylor felt that it was important to have a clear division of duties between management and labour. It was the job of management to select employees for specific jobs in a scientific manner so that the physical and mental characteristics of the individual fit the job. It was then the role of management to teach labourers the optimum way to perform their duties. It was the job of labourers to supply strong backs, but since in Taylor's mind a strong back connoted a weak mind, it would be impossible for labourers to arrange their own duties.

Taylor also emphasized the importance of financial factors as a motivating force. However, he eschewed the crude principle of piece-work, because he knew that workers could easily manipulate the standard. Instead, he singled out the best workers for the privilege of working in a higher-paid group. By examining their actions as described above, he was able to determine in a scientific manner how much work should be accomplished. In one experiment, workers who had met the standard in their previous day's work were given white slips at the beginning of their next shift, while those who had not were given yellow slips. Those receiving yellow slips obviously did not understand fully how their job should be done, so it was the responsibility of management to provide additional training. The consistent receipt of yellow slips would cause one's return to the lower-paid gang.[10] This was Taylor's method of using financial incentives without the drawbacks identified with piece-work.

   Some writers suggest that Taylor showed a lack of concern for the workers. It is clear that he saw management as very enlightened and he viewed workers in a rather condescending manner. This attitude is exemplified in the unintended humour in this quotation:

> Now one of the very first requirements for a man who is fit to handle pig iron as a regular occupation is that he shall be so stupid and so phlegmatic that he more nearly resembles in his mental make-up the ox than any other type . . . Therefore the workman who is best suited to handling pig iron is unable to understand the real science of doing this class of work. He is so stupid that the word "percentage" has no meaning to him, and he must consequently be trained by a man more intelligent than himself into the habit of working in accordance with the laws of this science before he can be successful.[11]

Given this attitude, it is not surprising that Mr. Taylor was once advised by some of his employees that it might be unsafe for him to take a particular route home in the evening.[12]

   However, Taylor did strive for harmony between management and workers and was sensitive to the need of not alienating unions. He always argued that cooperation was the best way to maximize productivity—but one gets the impression that it would be cooperation on management's terms. Furthermore, he was strongly opposed to over-working employees in sweat-shop conditions. Although this might well have been more for reasons of productivity than humanity, it apparently was still a fairly radical idea for his time.

   Taylor did not confine his emphasis on improvement and innovation to the factory floor. An avid tennis player, he and Clarence M. Clark won the first United States Lawn Tennis Association doubles championship in 1881. Not content to just play the game, he also invented an improved tennis net and the sprocket device that is still used to tighten the net. These changes were quickly accepted, but his spoon-shaped racket was just as quickly made the subject of ridicule.[13]

   Taylor's main contribution to organization theory was his emphasis on the scientific approach to work management—the "one best way"—and his emphasis on the important role of management in organizing the work. However, there were certain problems with the manner in which Taylor's ideas were implemented. Management, in some cases, used time-and-motion studies to attempt to extract the maximum possible production from workers. This led to worker resistance to the entire concept. The idea of the narrow subdivision of work into its smallest components created monotony, which led to further unrest on the part of workers. All of these problems in the application—some might say misapplication—of Taylor's ideas became evident eventually, but not before his ideas were tried in a number of places including the Canadian federal government.

THE CANADIAN EXPERIENCE—FROM PATRONAGE TO MERIT

The Canadian federal government gradually began adopting some of Taylor's ideas to speed the move from a patronage-based public service to a merit-based one, thus simultaneously moving toward the Weberian concept of bureaucracy.

The Civil Service Commission (CSC) was established in 1908 to act as guardian of the merit principle. The CSC was the outgrowth of a number of reports indicating that the prevalence of patronage appointments in the Canadian civil service was having a detrimental impact on its efficiency. The CSC began the process of entrenching the merit principle by administering competitive examinations to applicants for government positions. However, the CSC soon discovered that a serious problem existed because the duties of specific positions were not usually well-defined. Without a clear description of duties, a meaningful competitive examination was somewhat problematic.

Gradually the powers and responsibilities of the CSC evolved, until in 1918 it was given the power to actually make appointments and to reorganize departments, whether this was sought by the department or not. This legislation seemed to be influenced by officials of the CSC, who were in turn influenced by the principles of scientific management that were so prevalent at the time.[14]

The commissioners and the executive secretary of the CSC hired the American consulting firm of Arthur Young & Co. to introduce the principles of scientific management into the Canadian federal government. The exercise began with the systematic description and classification of 50,000 positions. The positions had to be described in great detail because this was the starting point for the mechanistic process of matching the person possessing the proper qualifications with the appropriate position. The next step was to be a sweeping reorganization of the entire governmental bureaucratic apparatus, streamlining and reducing the number of departments and agencies. Obviously, the idea of government reform is not as new and radical as some think.

Arthur Young & Co.'s involvement became bogged down in a series of problems and as a result the reorganization did not occur. The sole, but significant, result of the exercise was an extensive and systematic classification of all government positions. Not everyone was pleased with the result. The basis of the scientific management approach to job classification made it possible to match, in a mechanical fashion, the skills required in a particular job with the skills possessed by a particular person. When the match was complete, presumably the process would be like pushing a plug into a wall socket—an automatic perfect connection that would last until it was unplugged. Not everyone was impressed by the neatness of this arrangement. For example, R. MacGregor Dawson observed

> [A]ll positions are deemed to call for special talents, and each is filled through an examination of its own designed to test those special qualifications. But therein lies its basic weakness. Some civil servants—a plumber, a chemist, a stenographer, an entomologist, an accountant, an engineer—should unquestionably be chosen because of the special knowledge or skill which they happen to possess at the

moment of their candidature; but for others, such as a clerical or administrative official, the knowledge of their duties which they might have at entrance is comparatively unimportant. The really vital question is their inherent ability and what they will be capable of doing after they have been trained by years of experience in the department.[15]

These words could have been written as easily in 1991 as they were in 1936. The classification system has undergone a number of revisions since the original exercise. The most recent was in the late 1960s, in preparation for the beginning of collective bargaining. However, each revision has brought forth complaints about the complexity and inflexibility of the system. As discussed in Chapter 23, some flexibility has been introduced into the most senior positions, but for the vast majority of positions the job description and classification process is still the spiritual successor of the original Arthur Young work.

At roughly the same time that Taylor and consultants such as Arthur Young were concerned with the classification and arrangement of individual jobs, there was a movement afoot to consider broader questions of the appropriate overall structure of organizations.

GULICK AND URWICK AND THE SCIENTIFIC THEORY OF ORGANIZATION

In the United States in the 1930s, the work of the President's Committee on Administrative Management spurred a great deal of interest by trying to develop a scientific theory of organization. Taylor's work dealt with how to organize work on the factory floor, but Luther Gulick and Lyndall Urwick were concerned with developing broader theories about the ideal structure for any organization. Their concerns were span of control and the proper alignment of related functions.

The Scientific Theory of Organization

Span of control refers to the number of subordinates who report to one supervisor. There has long been controversy about what that ideal number should be. For adequacy of supervision, the smaller the span of control the better, but too narrow a span of control leads to too many supervisors and too much overhead.

This point is illustrated in Figure 3.1, which compares two different organizations, both of which have sixty-four production workers. In Figure 3.1a, the span of control in every case is four. This narrow span of control results in a total organization of eighty-five employees with two levels of management between the chief executive and the workers. In Figure 3.1b, the span of control is eight. This results in a total of seventy-three employees and only one level of management between the chief executive and the workers. In the latter case, not only are there fewer total employees and therefore less cost, but the presence of only one intermediate level of management makes communication considerably easier.

Figure 3.1
EXAMPLES OF DIFFERENT SPANS OF CONTROL

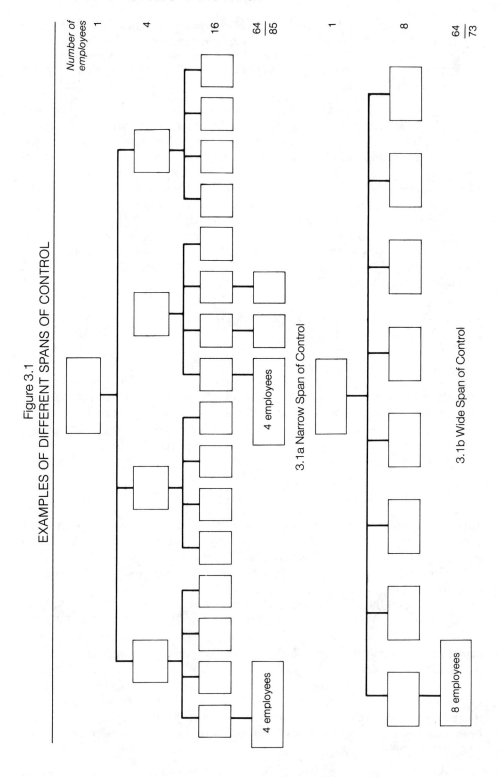

3.1a Narrow Span of Control

3.1b Wide Span of Control

However, the intangible cost of using this system is that supervisors cannot supervise eight people as closely as they can four. This could lead to production problems. McLaren points out the nature of this dilemma quite well;

> Small spans of control may appear to tighten control for the superior-subordinate relationship, but they loosen the overall control of the organization by extending the number of levels and thereby making the top that much more removed from the bottom. To cut down on the number of levels will reduce the distance between top and bottom, but the resulting increase in the span of control at each level will lessen the control that each level can maintain.[16]

The question of the appropriate span of control is still answered much as it was in Gulick and Urwick's time: it depends on the interaction of several things:

- the nature of the work supervised (routine procedures allow for a broader span of control, but supervision of several heterogeneous activities requires a narrower span of control);
- the level of training of the subordinates;
- the extent of geographical decentralization of the work; and
- the overall stability of the organization.[17]

Aside from span of control, Gulick and Urwick were concerned with the problem of the ideal arrangement of duties within the organization. They argued that the process of organizational design should work simultaneously from the top-down and from the bottom-up.[18] When working from the top-down, the primary criterion was to limit the span of control. Gulick reflected the conventional wisdom of the time that the senior executive should not have more than three direct subordinates. Working from the bottom-up, the important factor was to combine homogeneous activities to facilitate coordination and supervision. The analyst then simply built in both directions until the two were joined.

When working from the bottom-up it was important to have an appropriate definition of homogeneity. The definition suggests that people doing similar work ought to be grouped together, but on further analysis this idea is difficult to apply. Gulick suggested that each worker could be characterized in four different ways:

1. The major *purpose* he is serving, such as furnishing water, controlling crime, or conducting education;
2. The *process* he is using, such as engineering, medicine, carpentry, stenography, statistics, accounting;
3. The *persons or things* dealt with or served, such as immigrants, veterans, Indians, forests, mines, parks, orphans, farmers, automobiles, or the poor;
4. The *place* where he renders his service, such as Hawaii, Boston, Washington, the Dust Bowl, Alabama, or Central High School.[19]

In designing an organization, employees who had all four things in common would be grouped together in the same organizational unit. If an employee was different in one category, for example, if he or she worked in a slightly different location, then that would suggest that he or she ought to be in another unit, but Gulick emphasized the importance of pragmatism and judgment applied to individual cases. Where employees had only one or two things in common, they would likely be in separate units.

The question remains as to which of the four should be the dominant organizing principle.

> Each of the four basic systems of organization is intimately related with the other three, because in any enterprise all four elements are present in the doing of the work and are embodied in every individual workman. Each member of the enterprise is working for some major purpose, uses some process, deals with some person, and serves or works at some place.

> If an organization is erected about any one of these four characteristics of work, it becomes necessary to recognize the other characteristics in constructing the secondary and tertiary divisions of the work. For example, a government which is first divided on the basis of place will, in each geographical department, find it necessary to divide by purpose, by process, by clientele, or even again by place; and one divided in the first instance by purpose, may well be divided next by process and then by place. While the first or primary division of any enterprise is of very great significance, it must none the less be said that there is no one most effective pattern for determining the priority and order for the introduction of these interdependent principles. It will depend in any case upon the results which are desired at a given time and place.[20]

This problem occurs in a very practical way when deciding how to arrange the legal services function in a large, multi-function organization. One legal department containing all lawyers illustrates a process form of organization. If instead, the lawyers are divided and assigned to the units that handle the programs, organization by purpose is being used. At first glance, one arrangement seems to have as many advantages and disadvantages as the other. Gulick admitted that the lack of empirical evidence made serious discussion difficult, but he did suggest some of the pros and cons of each method.[21]

It is difficult to resolve this question of the best method of organization. In general it can be said that provincial governments are organized by purpose, e.g., departments of health, education, social assistance, and so forth. However, recently there has been a trend in some provinces to establish departments having a special mandate to look after the unique problems of the northern areas of those provinces. In some cases these new departments actually deliver services provided by the "purpose" departments in the south, and in others they act as coordinating bodies. There is usually some tension between this new "place" department and the traditional "purpose" departments over the appropriate role of each.

Gulick also dealt with the activities of the executive. He argued that words like "administration" and "management" had lost their specific content. He felt that the job of the executive could be summed up by the acronym POSDCORB,[22] which stood for the following activities:

- planning;
- organizing;
- staffing;
- directing;
- coordinating;
- reporting;
- budgeting.

Carrying out all of these functions as part of managing a complex organization posed a very difficult problem, particularly as each of these functions was becoming more complex in itself. Urwick noted that one way in which many organizations were dealing with this problem was by the use of separate line and staff functions.[23] A **line function** is usually considered to be directly involved in producing and distributing the goods or services provided by the organization. A classic example would be the manufacturing section of an industrial organization. Some typical examples in government would be public health nurses, social workers, or officers dealing directly with social assistance claimants.

A **staff function** is a function that aids, advises, and supports the employees providing the line function, usually without dealing directly with the clients or output of the organization. The obvious examples are accounting, legal, and personnel services.

Some writers distinguish between three categories—line, staff, and auxiliary.[24] Auxiliary is used to refer to such repetitive "housekeeping" kinds of activities as personnel and accounting, while staff refers to such non-repetitive functions as policy advice and coordination. This distinction has some value, but it can be difficult to make these kinds of distinctions in practice, which is probably why one is more likely to see the twofold distinction used in organizations.

When organizations are structured in this typical line-staff manner, the organization chart resembles Figure 3.2. Ideally, the two functions work together closely to further the objectives of the organization. The staff units can provide specialized advice to the line units about handling unusual situations. This means that line officers can concentrate on their standard repetitive tasks and do not have to be trained to cope with every eventuality. Another function frequently provided by staff employees is specialized record-keeping. Again, this relieves the line officers of the responsibility for a routine, repetitive task and allows them to concentrate on their major function. Thus, one would expect a smooth, complementary relationship between these two functions, and this is the case in many organizations.

When problems do crop up in the line-staff relationship, they usually concern the question: is the staff function a *service* or a *control* function? If the answer to the question is ambiguous, there can be serious problems. The organization chart in Figure 3.2 illustrates how the presence of the staff function could lead to a violation of the principle of unity of command. The Regional Director in Halifax is responsible to the Assistant Deputy Minister, Field Opera-

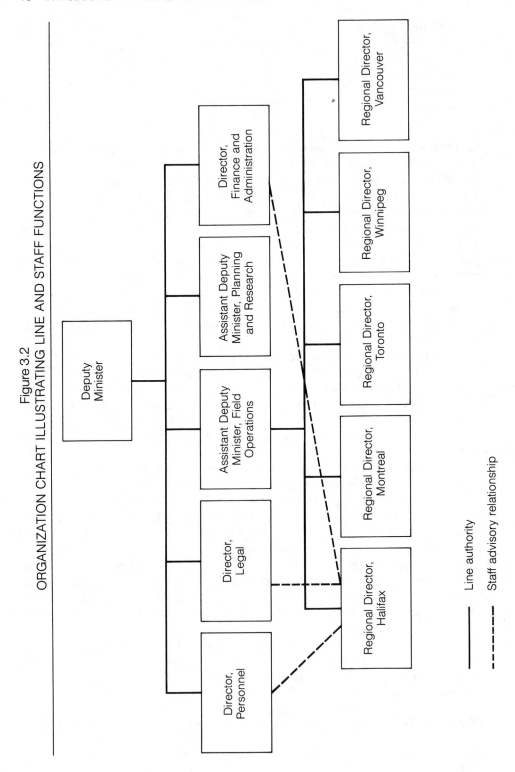

Figure 3.2
ORGANIZATION CHART ILLUSTRATING LINE AND STAFF FUNCTIONS

tions for most things, but may also be responsible to the various staff officers. In some cases the staff department will render advice that the line department would rather not hear or act upon. Line officials argue that to carry out their duties appropriately, they cannot be constrained by the whims of some group that does not fully understand the operation of the organization. The line manager may point out the amount of profit or units of production that his or her unit has contributed to the organization and ask rhetorically how much the staff units have contributed.

The real problem for senior management arises from the fact that the staff unit usually has good arguments grounded in the long-term good of the organization. For example, it might seem expedient to ignore the advice of the legal department at the moment, but this may prove short-sighted if the organization starts facing legal action in a few years. Organizations usually try to resolve this difficulty by establishing clear lines of authority and procedures to be followed in particular cases. These procedures seldom anticipate every circumstance. Obviously, both line and staff functions are important in an organization. How well they work together is frequently what separates good organizations from those that simply limp along from one crisis to the next.

Gulick and Urwick contributed to organizational behaviour by synthesizing and disseminating other people's ideas. Nevertheless, these two men made a valuable contribution both by forcing people to think about management in a systematic manner, and in beginning to set out certain principles—many of which are still seen as beneficial guides to action today. However, not everyone treated these scientific principles with reverence.

Herbert Simon and the Proverbs of Administration

Herbert Simon is a prolific writer on many topics of administration. One of his most widely quoted passages deals with the scientific principles of administration:

> It is a fatal defect of the current principles of administration that, like proverbs, they occur in pairs. For almost every principle one can find an equally plausible and acceptable contradictory principle. Although the two principles of the pair will lead to exactly opposite organizational recommendations, there is nothing in the theory to indicate which is the proper one to apply.[25]

One example of this kind of problematic pair of proverbs is: "Look before you leap," and "He who hesitates is lost." If the so-called scientific principles of management could be seen to have similar flaws, then their validity was in doubt.

Simon gives the example of the juxtaposition of two principles:

> Administrative efficiency is supposed to be enhanced by limiting the number of subordinates who report directly to any one administrator to a small number—say six . . .

Administrative efficiency is enhanced by keeping at a minimum the number of organizational levels through which a matter must pass before it is acted upon.[26]

Obviously, it cannot be both ways. Earlier in this chapter, Figure 3.1 showed that a narrow span of control always results in a large number of layers in the organization. A truly scientific principle of management would not leave this dilemma. If one must exercise judgment and discretion in achieving a blend of the two rules, the rules are not very scientific.

Simon saves most of his attack for the idea of organizing by purpose, process, people, or place. He points out that not only is the overall idea contradictory in that one of the four must take precedence, but that the concepts themselves are somewhat fuzzier than Gulick had suggested, so that some of them shade into one another.

Presumably, the rebuttal could be made here that Simon is being too fussy. The principles are simply guides to action; they are considerations to be taken into account before acting, to be used to shape our judgment and guide our discretion. The rebuttal might well be valid, but the crucial point is: if judgment and discretion are so important in applying these principles, then can they really be called "scientific"?

Simon's solution recognizes this point. He argues that these ideas should not be discarded because all have real value in certain cases. The trick is to find the proper combination of them to work in different cases. To accomplish this, Simon argues that good empirical work on the efficiency of existing organizations is needed more than additional theories.

CENTRALIZATION/DECENTRALIZATION

Gulick and Urwick's discussion of methods of organization opened the way for a serious discussion of decentralization of government services, which is a very important issue in a country as large and heterogeneous as Canada. The size and diversity of most provinces and even some of our larger cities make it an issue for provincial and municipal governments as well.

An important distinction must be made between decentralization and deconcentration. The difference between the two lies in the amount of *real decision-making authority* vested in the outlying unit. **Decentralization** suggests a vesting of real discretionary authority in the outlying unit. In some cases this might mean that the unit will also be physically removed from the centre to facilitate an understanding of local conditions, but physical dispersal is not a prerequisite for decentralization. **Deconcentration**, on the other hand, suggests a physical dispersal of members of the organization with only very limited delegation of decision-making authority.

Obviously, the line between the two is sometimes unclear. Even in deconcentration, there is virtually always some limited amount of discretion vested in field officials just as in decentralization there are always some kinds of decisions that can only be made after consultation with head office. Sometimes authority to deal with matters of an operational nature will be decentralized, while matters of a policy or program nature will be retained within the control of head office.

It is probably the large size and diversity of Canada that usually causes Canadians to think of decentralization in terms of the physical dispersal of operating units. This is an appropriate use of the term, but it has a more general meaning as well. Geographic decentralization is decentralization by place, but decentralization can also be based on any of Gulick and Urwick's other classical methods of organization—process, purpose, or people.[27] Even an organization with all of its divisions located in the same building can be decentralized, if real decision-making authority is vested in each of the separate units.

More than two-thirds of federal employees in regular government departments work outside the National Capital Region (i.e., the Ottawa-Hull area). These employees are located across the vast expanse of Canada in field units that vary greatly in purpose, size, and organization. This deconcentration of the federal government's operations is essential to the successful development and implementation of its policies and programs.

The present balance in each department or agency between the number and level of employees at headquarters and in the field is a culmination of more than a century of political, administrative, economic, and geographical factors. In the earliest days of the Canadian federation, it was necessary to establish outposts for such government services as the post office and customs. The subsequent geographical dispersal of the public service is a government response to the challenge of providing a broad range of services to a population that is spread across a continent. Virtually all government departments now have field units, although the size of these units varies enormously. In 1989, the percentage of employees located outside the National Capital Region ranged from 0.7 percent in the Department of Finance and 21.1 in Energy, Mines and Resources to 87.9 percent in Fisheries and Oceans and 88.1 percent in Employment and Immigration.[28]

Whether this represents decentralization or deconcentration, the problem remains the same. There must be a balance between accountability to rules specified in head office and responsiveness to regional needs. Officials in the field always feel pulled between the two. On the one hand, the rules and procedures set out by head office must be followed. On the other hand, field workers are sufficiently close to clientele in their everyday work to perceive an injustice in the manner in which the general rule must be applied to the specific case. The pressures to bend the rule are sometimes irresistible.

From the standpoint of head office, the problem is to maintain mechanisms to ensure that officials in the field are complying with head office rules and procedures without unnecessarily restricting the freedom of field officials to be responsive to local conditions. After all, it is these officials who are closest to the situation and are most knowledgeable about what should be done. However, they cannot be given carte blanche to do whatever they like without regard to the overall objectives of the department.

Specific approaches to departmental decentralization in Canada will be discussed in Chapter 8, but at this point it is important to consider the general form that decentralization or deconcentration can take. In any organization serving a large geographic area, there must be some form of decentralization. Oversimplifying somewhat, this decentralization can take one of two forms. Figure 3.3 illustrates the two possibilities for an organization carrying out three different functions across the country.[29]

Figure 3.3a illustrates decentralization by place. This style of decentralization is more likely to be true decentralization rather than deconcentration. In this case there is one main office in each region and that office is subdivided based on the three functions. This kind of structure will tend to improve coordination between the three functions within each region. Because of this ease of coordination and because of the orientation toward place, the regional office of an organization of this kind is likely to be highly responsive to the needs of its geographic area. In fact, with this kind of structure there is usually some concern that officials will become too sensitive to their geographic area and possibly deviate from the national objectives of their programs. For this reason, there is usually a group of staff advisors in head office who have some sort of functional authority over the people delivering the programs in the regional offices. This is illustrated by the dotted lines in Figure 3.3a. This group is necessary to ensure uniformity of the programs across the country. However, it can create the sort of line-staff problems discussed earlier in this chapter.

The advantages of this form of organization include good coordination within each region and responsiveness to regional needs. The disadvantages include possible departures from national objectives and a complex form of organization.

Figure 3.3b illustrates decentralization based on purpose, although this same form would also be applicable to decentralization based on process or people. This form is more likely to result in deconcentration than decentralization. In this case, the primary division is by purpose with the senior managers responsible for each function remaining in head office. Within each branch there is a subdivision by region, although the geographic areas covered by the regions are not necessarily the same for each branch. This reflects the fact that some programs might be more important in certain areas of the country than in others. Because each branch and each regional office specialize in providing only one function, it is relatively easy to ensure uniformity of administration across the entire country without the awkward organizational structure required in the case of decentralization by place.

The advantages of this style of organization are the simpler form of organization and the uniformity of administration of the program across the country. Its disadvantages are a lack of coordination of the programs at the regional level, and a weaker responsiveness to regional needs.

The style of organization depends upon the nature of the programs to be delivered and the need for regional responsiveness. If good coordination between programs at the regional level and a sensitivity to regional needs is important, then the preferable style is decentralization by place as illustrated in

Figure 3.3
TWO TYPES OF ORGANIZATIONAL STRUCTURES

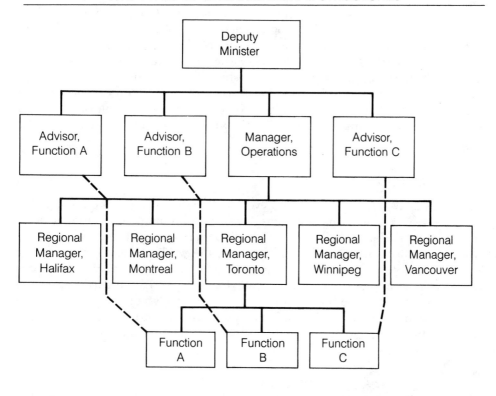

3.3a Organization by Place

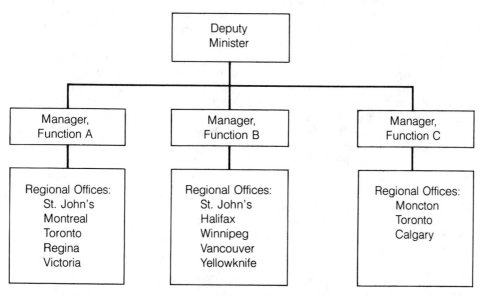

3.3b Organization by Purpose

Figure 3.3a. An example of this kind of program would be one aimed at regional economic development. Uniform administration across the country is less important than responsiveness to local conditions. On the other hand, if uniform administration of the program across the country is more important than regional sensitivity, then deconcentration by program as illustrated in Figure 3.3b would be preferable. The word deconcentration is used here because if there is uniformity of administration across the country, then, by definition, there will be little scope for decision-making within each region. An example of this kind of organization would be a tax collection organization where fairness and equity demand that the same rules apply to everyone in the country.

CONCLUSION

The ideas of Weber and Taylor, and even the later contributions of Gulick and Urwick, viewed good management as devising an optimal organizational structure to maximize output. They took little account of the needs and desires of the workers themselves. In these early theories, the worker is just like any other interchangeable machine part to be moved at the whim of management in order to create a better organizational chart. Taylor, in particular, seemed to view the worker as simply an extension of the machine. Gradually a different approach to management emerged—one that took a more human and humane view of the worker. This later approach will be the subject of the next chapter.

NOTES

1. The phrase "ideal-type" has a particular meaning in this context. It is not "ideal" in the sense of "perfect" or "cannot be improved upon"; rather it suggests that Weber's characterization is a polar or extreme description that probably does not exist exactly in the real world. For a good explanation of this, see Michael M. Harmon and Richard T. Mayer, *Organization Theory for Public Administration* (Boston: Little, Brown, 1986), pp. 71-74, 83.
2. Weber's famous discourse on bureaucracy, originally published in his *Wirtschaft und Gesellschaft*, has been translated and published in many places, but one of the most commonly cited references is *From Max Weber: Essays in Sociology*, eds. and trans. H. H. Gerth and C. Wright Mills (New York: Oxford University Press, 1946), pp. 196-244.
3. *Gesammelte Aufsatze zur Sozial und Wissenschaftslehre*, as quoted in Arthur Mitzman, *The Iron Cage: A Historical Interpretation of Max Weber* (New York: Knopf, 1970), p. 178. (Emphasis in Mitzman.)
4. "Bureaucratic Structure and Personality," *Social Forces* 18 (May 1940): 564.
5. "An Approach to the Theory of Bureaucracy," *American Sociological Review* 8 (February 1943): 47-54.
6. Ibid., 51. (Emphasis in original.)
7. *The Temporary Society* (New York: Harper & Row, 1968), ch. 3.
8. Frank B. Gilbreth, Jr., and Ernestine Gilbreth Carey, *Cheaper by the Dozen* (New York: Thomas Y. Crowell, 1948).

9. Frederick Winslow Taylor, *The Principles of Scientific Management* (New York: W. W. Norton, 1967), p. 65.
10. Ibid., pp. 67-68.
11. Ibid., p. 59.
12. Ibid., pp. 51-52. *See also* Frank Barkely Copley, *Frederick W. Taylor: Father of Scientific Management*, vol. 1 (New York: Augustus M. Kelley, 1969), pp. 166-67.
13. Copley, *Frederick W. Taylor*, p. 143.
14. J. E. Hodgetts et al., *The Biography of an Institution* (Montreal: McGill-Queen's University Press, 1972), ch. 4.
15. "The Canadian Civil Service," *Canadian Journal of Economics and Political Science* 2 (August 1936): 293.
16. Robert I. McLaren, *Organizational Dilemmas* (Chichester, U. K.: John Wiley & Sons, 1982), pp. 45-46. Reproduced by permission of John Wiley & Sons, Ltd.
17. Luther Gulick, "Notes on the Theory of Organization," in Luther Gulick and L. Urwick, eds., *Papers on the Science of Administration* (New York: Augustus M. Kelley, 1969), pp. 7-9.
18. Ibid., pp. 11-12.
19. Ibid., p. 15. (Emphasis in original.)
20. Ibid., pp. 31-32.
21. Ibid., pp. 21-30.
22. Ibid., p. 13.
23. Urwick, "Organization as a Technical Problem," in ibid., pp. 47-88.
24. J. E. Hodgetts, *The Canadian Public Service: A Physiology of Government, 1867-1970* (Toronto: University of Toronto Press, 1973), ch. 9.
25. *Administrative Behavior* (New York: The Free Press, 1957), p. 20.
26. Ibid., p. 26.
27. McLaren points out that decentralization can occur in several dimensions. *Organizational Dilemmas*, ch. 2.
28. Public Service Commission of Canada, *Annual Report 89* (Minister of Supply and Services, 1990), pp. 78-79.
29. McLaren's enlightening treatment takes a slightly different approach, but deals with the same issues. *Organizational Dilemmas*, pp. 12-17.

BIBLIOGRAPHY

Bennis, Warren G., and Philip E. Slater. *The Temporary Society*. New York: Harper & Row, 1968.

Copley, Frank Barkely. *Frederick W. Taylor: Father of Scientific Management*. 2 vols. New York: Augustus M. Kelley, 1969.

Dawson, R. MacGregor. "The Canadian Civil Service." *Canadian Journal of Economics and Political Science* 2 (August 1936): 288-300.

Gilbreth, Frank B., Jr., and Ernestine Gilbreth Carey. *Cheaper by the Dozen*. New York: Thomas Y. Crowell Company, 1948.

Gulick, Luther, and L. Urwick, eds. *Papers on the Science of Administration*. New York: Augustus M. Kelley, 1969.

Harmon, Michael M., and Richard T. Mayer. *Organization Theory for Public Administration*. Boston: Little, Brown and Company, 1986.

Heffron, Florence. *Organization Theory and Public Organizations: The Political Connection.* Englewood Cliffs, N.J.: Prentice-Hall, 1989.

Hodgetts, J. E. *The Canadian Public Service: A Physiology of Government, 1867-1970.* Toronto: University of Toronto Press, 1973.

Hodgetts, J. E., William McCloskey, Reginald Whitaker, and V. Seymour Wilson. *The Biography of an Institution.* Montreal: McGill-Queen's University Press, 1972.

McLaren, Robert I. *Organizational Dilemmas.* Chichester, U. K.: John Wiley & Sons, 1982.

Merton, Robert K. "Bureaucratic Structure and Personality." *Social Forces* 18 (May 1940): 560-68.

Mitzman, Arthur. *The Iron Cage: A Historical Interpretation of Max Weber.* New York: Knopf, 1970.

Selznick, Philip. "An Approach to the Theory of Bureaucracy." *American Sociological Review* 8 (February 1943): 47-54.

———. *TVA and the Grass Roots.* New York: Harper & Row, 1966.

Simon, Herbert. *Administrative Behavior.* 2nd ed. New York: The Free Press, 1957.

Taylor, Frederick Winslow. *The Principles of Scientific Management.* New York: W. W. Norton, 1967.

Weber, Max. *From Max Weber: Essays in Sociology.* Edited and translated by H. H. Gerth and C. Wright Mills. New York: Oxford University Press, 1946.

4

Public Administration and Organization Theory: The Humanistic Response

Gradually, organization theory began to emphasize the human, rather than the mechanical, nature of the worker. This chapter will trace the history of organization theory from the original humanistic, but still highly paternalistic, approach to some present-day theories that emphasize genuine worker participation in organizational decision-making.

ORGANIZATIONAL HUMANISM

Just as scientific management bore the imprint of production engineers, such as Frederick Taylor, organizational humanism, or the **human relations school**, bore the imprint of the social psychologists who were its prime movers. Taylor focussed on what *should* happen in the factory to maximize production. The organizational humanists focussed instead on what *actually* happened on the factory floor. Their findings seem rather unspectacular now, but they totally upset scientific management. They found that in addition to the formal system of authority through which management controlled workers, there was an informal system of worker control that was in some cases more powerful than the formal system. The informal system was characterized by the network of friendships, friendly banter, and informal sanctions that occur in every work setting. The devastating impact that this had on the scientific management theory was obvious. Of course, Taylor and his disciples could continue to set their standards, but workers would simply not comply with them if it meant the ostracism that is frequently accorded the "rate-buster." This meant that Taylor's emphasis on scientific principles to set the work pace and on financial incentives to improve productivity was somewhat misplaced. While these factors had some value, it was becoming clear that another route to increased productivity lay with the informal system.

Mary Parker Follett

One of the first people to understand the importance of the informal system was not a conventional researcher, but rather a very perceptive student of human nature. Mary Parker Follett (1868-1933) did not study organizations systematically in the ordinary sense, but she did use every opportunity to discuss organizational questions with everyone from senior executives to factory workers. From these discussions, she developed a number of important ideas.

Her basic philosophy stemmed from the fact that she rejected the conventional use of raw power in organizations. She felt that its use was either futile or, in some cases, totally counter-productive. Instead, she focussed on two related points—circular response and integration.

She rejected the biological concept of unidirectional stimulus-response relationships as inapplicable in the human setting. Instead, she emphasized shared interaction.[1] *Circular response* means no one unilaterally acts on someone else; rather people interact with one another in ways that influence both parties. It was this view that caused her to reject the idea of power as a one-way street.

Integration referred to the need to combine diverse elements into a useful whole. In some ways, this could be seen as simply a restatement of the old idea of division of labour, but Follett realized that integration was a dynamic concept and not simply the static arrangement of slots on an organizational chart. She understood that conflict would inevitably develop in any organization because of the existence of circular response and the informal organization.

> It was, however, the particular genius of Mary Follett's contribution that she recognized and held fast to the notion that the process of change that generates conflict also provides the opportunity for the further changes necessary to resolve that conflict. Each solution contains the seeds of new differences, but these differences also contain the seeds of new solutions. What they need is freedom to grow within a milieu of intelligent and sympathetic cultivation.[2]

This latter point was a very important one for Follett. She frequently emphasized the importance of executives exercising leadership rather than wielding power. She felt that the way to motivate employees was through a rational appeal to a person's higher instincts rather than a reliance on fear or threats.

Follett was an important influence because she lectured widely and knew many of the senior business people of her time, but it is questionable whether her rather unscientific views had any influence on some of the more scientific researchers of her time. For this reason, her role in the development of the human relations school is sometimes overlooked.

Roethlisberger and Dickson and the Hawthorne Experiments

The beginnings of the human relations school are usually traced to an experiment conducted with workers at the Hawthorne Works (near Chicago) of Western Electric in 1924. The idea was to test the impact of different levels of lighting on employee productivity. The experiments were organized and conducted by an industrial psychologist from Harvard, F. J. Roethlisberger, and a Western Electric management employee, William J. Dickson. They were later joined by another Harvard professor, Elton Mayo.[3] The experimenters assumed that improving physical working conditions by increasing levels of lighting would increase productivity. The research was poorly designed and the results inconclusive because production tended to move erratically up or down without much regard to changes in the level of lighting. The experimenters had to discard their original hypothesis because the ambiguity of the results indicated that the physical conditions surrounding work did not have the paramount influence assumed.

The Hawthorne experiment was followed by a series of experiments that tested many other changes in physical conditions in the workplace, to see which would produce changes in the level of output. Again, the results were ambiguous. This caused experimenters to think about a characteristic of the experiments that they had not considered previously. In every case, the tests were conducted using a group of people who were selected from the workroom, moved to a special place, and singled out for significant amounts of attention from researchers. This led experimenters to focus on the *Hawthorne* or *sympathetic observer effect*—the idea that workers singled out for special attention will experience an increase in morale, which will lead to greater productivity. This finding has been criticized widely over the years.[4] Some critics have pointed to the poor design of the research, while others have argued that the findings of the research do not support the conclusions usually drawn from them. However, this did not seem to matter at the time. The human relations school grew and thrived over these years in both academic and business circles.

Chester Barnard and the Importance of Cooperation

Chester Barnard (1886-1961) was a career business executive who rose to become President of the New Jersey Bell Telephone Company. In 1938, after his retirement, he wrote his landmark work *The Functions of the Executive*.[5] His crucial idea was that an organization is a cooperative system held together by a good communication system and by the continuing desire of individual members to see the organization thrive. Members of the organization make *contributions* to it, but only when they receive adequate *inducements* to encourage them to continue to do so. It is important to balance contributions and inducements. If inducements exceeded contributions, business failure will result. On the other hand, if inducements were inadequate, then workers would cease making contributions and business failure will result. The inducements offered to workers could be in the form of monetary rewards, but Barnard felt that other forms of inducement such as loyalty, good working conditions, and pride in both work and the organization were probably more effective.

Barnard tried to be sensitive to the needs of workers, but it must be said that his basic attitude to workers was somewhat patronizing. The title of his book, *The Functions of the Executive*, did not come about by accident. He felt that workers were rather docile, uninspired creatures who depended upon leadership to accomplish anything. It was the responsibility of the executive to establish good communications systems that would, in turn, instill the appropriate company spirit in employees.

He recognized that there was an informal organization that could thwart the desires of management, but he argued that it was the responsibility of management to use the idea of cooperation to harness that informal system for the benefit of the organization.

Abraham Maslow's Hierarchy of Needs

Scientific management focussed on the idea of monetary rewards as an incentive for good work performance. Maslow argued that this was too simplistic. He said that people are motivated by a hierarchy of five categories of needs ranging from the physiological to self-actualization. He believed that a person will first be motivated by a desire to satisfy the most basic physiological needs, but as these are satisfied, the person will strive to meet the next level of needs and so on up the hierarchy. As an employee attains each succeeding level in the hierarchy, he or she will no longer be motivated by rewards directed at the more basic needs. The five levels in the **hierarchy of needs** are:

1. *Physiological*–food, shelter, clothing, sex, and sleep;
2. *Safety*–security, stability, freedom from fear;
3. *Belongingness and Love*–friendship, love, membership in some community;
4. *Esteem*–achievement, competence, independence, prestige, status;
5. *Self-Actualization*–self-fulfillment, attaining ultimate goals in life.[6]

Maslow's contention was that there is no "one best way" to motivate employees. Instead, management must be sensitive to the fact that people have a variety of needs beyond the simple need for money. Thinking about employee needs such as self-esteem and self-actualization posed serious problems for managers who were accustomed to thinking in simple piece-work terms.

A discussion of Maslow's complex theory of motivation appears in almost every management textbook, and it is the basis for most participative management philosophy. It also seems to strike a more responsive note than the simpler, one-dimensional approach of the scientific management school. It agrees with the usual observation that different people are motivated by different kinds of things and even the same person is motivated by different things at different times.

However, the model is very difficult to test in the workplace. Salancik and Pfeffer have argued that "the need-satisfaction model must be seriously re-examined and does not warrant the unquestioning acceptance it has attained in organizational psychology literature."[7]

Douglas McGregor's Theory X and Theory Y

In spite of Maslow's caveats, McGregor built on his ideas and related them to the attitudes of individual managers. He noted that some managers simply do not trust or respect their employees. These Theory X managers make the following assumptions about their employees:

1. *The average human being has an inherent dislike of work and will avoid it if he can;*
2. *Because of this human characteristic of dislike of work, most people must be coerced, controlled, directed, threatened with punishment to get them to put forth adequate effort toward the achievement of organizational objectives;*
3. *The average human being prefers to be directed, wishes to avoid responsibility, has relatively little ambition, wants security above all.*[8]

On the other hand, Theory Y managers are more positive and more respectful of their employees' needs. These managers operate under the assumptions that:

1. *The expenditure of physical and mental effort in work is as natural as play or rest.* The average human being does not inherently dislike work. Depending upon controllable conditions, work may be a source of satisfaction (and will be voluntarily performed) or a source of punishment (and will be avoided if possible);
2. *External control and the threat of punishment are not the only means for bringing about effort toward organizational objectives. Man will exercise self-direction and self-control in the service of objectives to which he is committed;*
3. *Commitment to objectives is a function of the rewards associated with their achievement.* The most significant of such rewards, e.g., the satisfaction of ego and self-actualization needs, can be direct products of effort directed toward organizational objectives;
4. *The average human being learns, under proper conditions, not only to accept but to seek responsibility.* Avoidance of responsibility, lack of ambition, and emphasis on security are generally consequences of experience, not inherent human characteristics;
5. *The capacity to exercise a relatively high degree of imagination, ingenuity, and creativity in the solution of organizational problems is widely, not narrowly, distributed in the populations;*
6. *Under the conditions of modern industrial life, the intellectual potentialities of the average human being are only partially utilized.*[9]

McGregor's basic message was that employees react differently depending upon how they are treated. If managers convey the impression that they believe that their employees are Theory X types of workers, then the workers will likely meet those expectations. On the other hand, managers who treat employees in a Theory Y manner will likely be more successful.

Summary of the Principles of Organizational Humanism

The important, key beliefs that characterize the organizational humanists are:

- Respect for workers as complex human beings with diverse sets of needs;
- Distrust of simple, one-dimensional theories of motivation;
- Recognition that the informal organization can be as influential as the formal one in setting work rules.

CRITICISMS OF ORGANIZATIONAL HUMANISM

There have been many criticisms of the philosophy of the human relations school. The most significant are based on the idea that the presumed community of interest between workers and management does not exist and therefore the entire human relations concept is simply a method to manipulate employees to behave in the interests of management.

It is obviously in management's interest to extract as much work as possible from employees. This is the profit motive. However, it is in the employees' interest to restrict their output to what they can do in physical comfort. Employees are also aware that the amount of work to be done is usually finite and that their reward for working hard might be a lay-off slip when the work is completed. When one views the workplace in this way, the cooperation treasured by the organizational humanists is somewhat illusory.

Critics charge that this is precisely the point where the theories developed by the organizational humanists become important. How does management convince workers to behave in the best interests of management rather than in their own best interests? The human relations response is to establish a feeling of caring and unity in the workplace that can then be used to manipulate employees. Critics like to point to one aspect of the work done at Hawthorne that involved hiring 300 employees to wander the factory floor and listen to complaints of other employees. Management never did anything about the complaints and never intended to do anything; the sole purpose of this action was to create the impression that management actually cared about workers.[10]

> In the end, therefore, the human relations approach to management proves to be simply another technique for managerial control. Although the human relations approach provides a recognition of the human factors in organizational life, it ultimately treats these as just another set of inducements to be manipulated in the pursuit of managerial control. Where conflicts arise between the individual and the organization, managers are admonished to resort to their hierarchical authority. Ultimately, this approach remains simplistic and unfulfilling and, in any case, hardly leads toward a true alternative to the rational model of administration. Though appearing humanistic, the human relations approach may simply be more subtle.[11]

There was also a management-oriented critique of the human relations approach. Some managers were concerned that this school was *too* employee-centred. Their criticism was that in its revulsion from scientific management, it tipped the balance too far in the other direction. Some derisively referred to human relations as "country club" management meaning that the ideal workplace ought to resemble a country club. Others suggested that for human relations the "one best way" was employee satisfaction rather than concern for production.

In the face of this criticism from both sides, organizational humanism had to evolve. The next step was a cluster of ideas that attempted to meet both kinds of criticisms. These varying concepts can be loosely grouped under the heading of participatory management.

PARTICIPATORY MANAGEMENT

Gradually it became accepted that there was an innate tension and conflict in the workplace. This could centre around universal issues such as rates of pay and speed of the production process, or specific issues such as the attitude of a particular supervisor or the quality of food served in the lunchroom. Organizational humanism tried to cover over this tension by "bribing" employees to accept management views. The participatory theories held that the tension could be controlled and directed, but probably not totally eliminated, by allowing workers a real decision-making role in the workplace.

There are many approaches to **participatory management**. Two recent and important approaches are discussed here.

Management by Objectives

Peter Drucker is usually considered the founder of **Management by Objectives (MBO)**.[12] Drucker's basic argument absolutely opposed Weber's views of bureaucracy. Drucker argued that the very things that Weber saw as such powerful engines of *efficiency*—bureaucracy, hierarchical structures, and specialization— were, in fact, powerful forces for *misdirection*.

Drucker felt that in large organizations managers and employees became too involved in their specialty and had a tendency to emphasize this at the expense of the overall good of the organization. For example, if the purchasing department emphasizes buying at low prices rather than the high quality of the product or security of supply, then the production department can suffer precisely because the purchasing department is doing its job well—at least, in the view of people in that department. Thus, it frequently happens that inefficiency and misdirection occur *because* of hierarchy and specialization of labour. The problem is the inability to focus on the overall organizational goal; the solution is management by objectives.

George S. Odiorne was another of the early gurus of management by objectives.

> In brief, the system of management by objectives can be described as a process whereby the superior and subordinate managers of an organization jointly identify its common goals, define each individual's major areas of responsibility in terms of the results expected of him, and use these measures as guides for operating the unit and assessing the contribution of each of its members.[13]

There is no one standard way in which MBO is implemented. On the contrary, the literature is filled with debate about the ideal, precise steps to be followed. However, there is general agreement that the framework consists of six steps:

1. *Consultation between top managers and their immediate subordinates to determine the broad goals of the organization.* This should be a truly participative exercise during which subordinates can state their views and have them considered

seriously by top management. It should not be an exercise in which top management sells its ideas to subordinates.

2. *Statement by top management of the overall results expected in the upcoming year.* This makes it clear that, while there is meaningful participation, in the final analysis the responsibility for setting objectives rests with senior management.

3. *Top managers and their subordinates then meet again to parcel out the responsibility for these results to individual organizational units.* These responsibilities are not simply imposed upon subordinate managers, but rather they agree that they will be able to fulfill the goals set. As a part of this exercise, three types of objectives are set for each unit. *Routine objectives* are the results expected from the normal operating activities of each unit—number of files processed, number of widgets manufactured. The *problem-solving* objective deals with clearing up some past problem. This might be the difficulty experienced between the purchasing and production departments mentioned above. The *innovative objective* should lead to some results beyond the anticipated goals. For example, this could be a new production process. The purpose of having three different kinds of objectives is to force managers to look beyond immediate problems. There is a tendency for a manager to concentrate on one kind of objective, usually the routine, until some crisis develops, which then forces him or her to devote full time to the crisis and neglect the routine, production function. The MBO approach encourages managers to deal with problems before they become crises.

4. *Repeat the process of parcelling out the responsibilities outlined in step 3 throughout the organization.* As a result of this iterative process, a plan showing the assigned role of each organizational unit is developed.

5. *Management reviews this plan for consistency and to ensure that the desired goals are met.*

6. *Year-end comprehensive performance review.* The significance of this review is that managers are evaluated according to goals that they helped set and to which they agreed at the beginning of the year. Thus, no manager is able to duck substandard results by saying that the goals were unrealistic or were unfairly imposed by top management.

MBO has been used extensively in both business and government organizations. It is particularly well-suited for use by government because the objectives do not have to be stated in financial terms. However, it has not been without its critics. One stream of criticism suggests that MBO is simply organizational humanism with a few bells and whistles attached. This view holds that the participation that occurs is not really meaningful because top management always makes the final decisions.

Clearly, some attempts to implement MBO have foundered on this problem, but there is some question about whether this is a criticism of MBO as a concept or simply a criticism of errors some organizations have made attempting to implement it.

Another criticism raises the difficulty of establishing meaningful, easily measurable objectives. Clearly, this can be a problem in some organizations, but not an insurmountable one. Still another criticism is that the implementation and operation of MBO consumes significant amounts of time and other organizational resources. Proponents of MBO point out that this is more of a problem in the first year of operation than in subsequent years when people are more familiar with the functioning of the system.

The consensus about MBO is that it is a useful tool, but only when implemented in a sensitive manner. There is general agreement that all of the criticisms discussed above can be justified if implementation is not properly handled.

Organization Development

Organization development is another participative approach to management, but it is considerably more all-encompassing than MBO. It is so amorphous that there are many different definitions.[14] However, the following definition incorporates many of the ideas that have been associated with OD over the years.

> Organization development is a process which uses behavioural science knowledge to examine the entire organizational unit as a system and to institute planned change in those aspects of the unit which are impediments to its health and efficiency. The exercise usually uses an outside change agent employing action research techniques and involves all members of the organizational unit.

A better understanding of OD can be obtained by elaborating on each aspect of the definition.

OD is a multi-disciplinary approach to organizational change "in which theories, concepts, and practices from sociology, psychology, social psychology, education, economics, psychiatry, and management are brought to bear on real organizational problems."[15] This separates it from earlier approaches to organizational change that were based on only one discipline, frequently engineering or, later, psychology.

OD deals with the entire organizational unit, which is defined as all segments of the organization that interact closely on a regular basis. This could be the total organization or it could be a group of work units smaller than the full organization. The decision about the appropriate units to be covered is somewhat subjective, but it is important to understand that OD cannot be effective if it is confined to only one small unit.

OD views the entire organization as a system—a set of interacting parts. Any change in one aspect of the system will have repercussions for the entire system. Therefore, attempts to remedy only one aspect of a systemic problem will be futile, or even counter-productive.

One of the main tasks of OD is to identify the impediments to the development of an efficient and healthy organization—an organization that is concerned with both efficiency in production and ensuring that individuals in the organization have the maximum opportunity to realize their full potential.[16]

After the organization's problems are identified, the participants are then required to plan the changes necessary to make the organization more efficient.

Changes specified could deal with improved teamwork, the physical layout of the operation, the attitudes of workers or managers, the organizational structure, or any other aspect of the organization. Unlike earlier approaches, OD does not focus solely on one factor in the workplace and assume that all problems can be corrected by altering that one factor.

It is usually desirable to employ an outside change agent for three reasons. First, the size and complexity of an exercise of this sort normally require someone who is very knowledgeable about a range of behavioural science techniques. Second, the OD intervener might be the only person who can see, and is really concerned about, the whole organizational system. Members of the organization tend to be more concerned about their part of the organization than the organization as a whole.[17] Third, since OD can potentially involve major realignments of the power structure of an organization, it is better that the project leader have no vested interest in the changes recommended.

The general approach of action research is to gather data about a client group, assist the client group in analysing the data, and establish some action plan based on the findings of the data. Thus, action research combines research and action. It involves research not just to shed light on some academic hypothesis, but research undertaken for the purpose of stimulating action.

It is important that the exercise involve all employees in the unit because

> wider participation in goal setting leads to a greater utilization of an organization's resources, human and technical, and results in significantly better plans. In addition, the plans that have been the contribution of many people at all levels of the organization probably have more chance of being realistic and attainable and also have some built-in support for carrying them out.[18]

To further clarify the definition, Huse discusses a few things that OD is *not*:

> OD is *not* management development. Management development is focused on a particular manager or group of managers to change individual managerial behavior. OD is focused on the broader system of which the manager is a subsystem.

> OD is *not* a specific technique, such as sensitivity training, job enrichment, group team building, or management by objectives. OD may *use* specific techniques, but only after the relevance and utility of a specific technique has been clearly demonstrated by careful diagnosis.

> OD is concerned *not* only with "making people happy." Rather, OD is concerned with organizational competence, including both effectiveness and efficiency.[19]

The basic concern addressed by organization development is that all organizations tend to become rigid or "frozen." As the environment of the organization changes while the organization remains rigid, this has serious consequences. Usually conditions gradually deteriorate until a serious crisis occurs, which causes either radical restructuring, or even the collapse of the organization. The purpose of OD is to locate the barriers to change and to show the organization how to engage in planned, goal-directed change, not directionless evolution or radical revolution.

Organization development recognizes that all organizations have a history that creates an organizational culture.[20] In some cases this can be a good thing, but in many cases it is not. This history, or culture, develops as a result of the organization's past successes and failures. For example, when someone responds to a new proposal by saying: "We can't do that because we tried something like it ten years ago and it didn't work," an example of history is at work. Of course, the fact that something similar was unsuccessful ten years earlier might or might not be relevant now, but in many cases this kind of argument will win. When the culture or history of an organization has this kind of negative influence, it is referred to as "drag."

Practitioners of OD warn that the patterns and procedures that create drag are merely symptoms of a more serious underlying problem in the culture. It is pointless to change these patterns and procedures—merely the manifestations of the basic problems—without also changing the underlying culture. Such changes would meet strong resistance, and inappropriate new patterns could possibly be imposed on an unfriendly environment.

There are many practitioners of OD, and each has a slightly different approach.[21] However, they all share a belief in a general three-phase approach— "unfreezing, moving, and freezing of group standards."[22] The unfreezing stage involves identifying current dysfunctional behaviour and helping the organization to "un-learn" that behaviour. In the second phase, the improvements needed are identified and implemented. The third stage involves re-freezing the organization with its new behaviour in place so that the organization does not unconsciously revert to the old behaviour.

CRITICISMS OF THE PARTICIPATIVE APPROACH

One of the criticisms frequently leveled at the participative approaches is that they require a huge commitment of resources on the part of the organization, and that they are so disruptive that they can lead to rather lengthy periods of turmoil. The entire idea of the approach is that virtually all employees of the organization must become involved and, in some cases, for fairly lengthy periods. This imposes a heavy cost on the organization, in addition to the usual consulting fees charged by the outside consultants.

Moreover, there is usually a psychological cost to the organization from undergoing this kind of radical surgery. Even though the actual organizational changes themselves can be planned in an incremental and minimally disruptive manner, the rumour mill that always works full-time in these situations can wreak havoc on morale. The obvious response to this criticism is that the end result is worth the short-term trauma, and, in many cases, this has proven correct. However, given the cost and turmoil engendered in the short run, management's frequent reluctance to become fully involved in a participative management exercise is understandable.

Many of the criticisms of the idea of participative management echo those directed against the organizational humanists. There seems to be a lingering concern that the process is not really and truly participative, but rather is guided—not to say manipulated—by management. "Frederick Taylor was satis-fied if he could control the physical movements of the workers; OD wants their hearts, souls, and minds."[23]

While organizational humanism and participative management stress con-cern for the whole person, they both focus on "the person as a worker" with less concern for the non-work-related aspects of the person's life. For example, it is not hard to determine how they would view an employee who refused to work more than forty hours a week, even though it meant passing up a promotion, because the person wanted more time to spend with his or her family, or to take part in other activities.

As mentioned above, this stands more as a criticism of the manner in which the process has been applied in certain cases than a basic criticism of the process itself. However, it does raise a difficult conundrum. In a true hierarchical setting, those at the pinnacle of the hierarchy have authority over those at lower levels. Some things have not changed since Weber. Given this fact, is real participation possible?

This leads to a particular concern with the use of participative management in the public sector. The most serious concern is whether a bottom-up participa-tive approach to decision-making fits with concepts of accountability of the minister for the activities of his or her department. Sometimes it is suggested that not only should employees of the organization "participate," but also clients who are affected by agency decisions. However, this has problems as well. It is usually the case that the clients of any program represent a special interest group rather than the broader public interest.

In practice, the concern for top-down accountability has won out over bottom-up participation. At the risk of generalizing, it seems that few govern-ment agencies give more than lip-service to participatory management.

However, this does not preclude certain kinds of OD interventions that are geared more to operation of the agency than basic public policy decision-making. Robert T. Golembiewski, a recognized expert on OD in the public sector, has argued that there are particular problems with the use of OD in the public sector, and even agrees that these problems result in a "lower batting average" in the success of OD in the public sector. After an extensive review of the literature on OD attempts, he arrives at the conclusion that "the 'lower batting average' is still 'pretty high.'"[24]

Both MBO and OD have been used in various government organizations. We will now examine some of these practical experiences.

THE CANADIAN EXPERIENCE—FROM TAYLOR TO MBO

In the previous chapter, the status of scientific management in the federal government was considered. In this chapter, many other styles of management have been discussed, but there has been no comment on their impact on Canadian governments. The reason is quite simple—they seem to have had little impact. V. S. Wilson describes the impact that the organizational humanists had in the United States, and then addresses the Canadian situation in this manner:

In Canada no developments of this sort surfaced in the public sector. The federal government, for example, continued in its well-established role as omnipotent employer. Institutions of employer-employee relationships created during this time . . . had as their central focus "the problems of the government as employer and not those of the employees."[25]

It might be unfair to say that nothing of the organizational humanist school filtered into the Canadian public sector. Since the human relations school is, in large part, a prescription for changes in the actions of individual managers, it is possible that certain managers did follow the advice of the organizational humanists without any system-wide documentation of the practice. But Wilson is surely correct in his overall assessment of the situation. Throughout the time of the organizational humanists, Canadian governments continued to exhibit rigid hierarchies, inflexible job classification structures, and the other trappings of scientific management.

However, when the participatory style of management came into full flower, it found easier acceptance. After the Second World War, the way was made ready by the gradual emergence of the personnel function as a legitimate and important staff activity providing advice to management. Referring to this time, a later Chairman of the Public Service Commission stated that "the use of the title personnel officer or training officer would have been sufficient to have one tried for witchcraft."[26] Gradual change occurred between the end of the war and the early 1960s, but in the face of many negative comments on the quality of management, including a ringing indictment by the Royal Commission on Government Organization in 1962, changes occurred rapidly in the 1960s.

The name of the Civil Service Commission was changed to the Public Service Commission (PSC) in 1967, but there was much more than just a change of name occurring. Without abandoning its former role as guardian of the merit principle, the PSC moved into more active areas of personnel management, such as human resource planning and training. Similar changes were occurring within operating departments as personnel officials became both more numerous and more influential. There was, therefore, more emphasis on training managers in management skills. Courses with titles such as "supervisory skills" and "effective motivation" became very popular when offered by both the PSC and educational institutions. Governments were belatedly discovering the marvels of the organizational humanists at the same time that they were experimenting with participatory management.

Changes started coming so quickly that there were real fears that managers would not be able to cope with them all. H. L. Laframboise's insightful article on the "saturation psychosis" became required reading for every manager. Laframboise argued that the implementation of major management reforms, the introduction of collective bargaining, and the movement to a truly bilingual public service—all at the same time—were making it very difficult for managers to cope with their rapidly changing environment.[27]

The major management reforms discussed by Laframboise involved a more systematic approach to managing both financial and human resources. This led to a more sophisticated approach to planning in both operating departments and central agencies, which will be discussed in more detail in later chapters. One of the most commonly used reforms was Management by Objectives or a similar technique with a different name.[28] Many departments experimented with MBO with some degree of success. Most managers treaded a bit more warily around Organizational Development,[29] but some became involved enthusiastically.

These various reforms have probably produced a higher quality of management, but they have also created problems. While new innovations have been implemented, few of the trappings of the older systems have been discarded. The entire arrangement is reminiscent of an old European building with a basic structure from one era and many additions, each bearing the architectural style of the era in which it was added. There is nothing wrong with each separate part, but it creates a very unusual overall impression. For example, team-building exercises that emphasize flexibility and cooperation have been combined with lengthy, complex job descriptions that emphasize rigidity and differentiation of duties.

On balance, though, the system has improved over the last few years. The fact that there is a greater attempt to keep in step with modern management development sets the current period apart from earlier times. Large governmental organizations will probably always suffer from rigidities that will hamper their rapid employment of new techniques, but at least there is now an awareness of the need for improvement.

While such practical changes as MBO and OD were being imported into the Canadian scene, progress continued in the theoretical study of organizations. Many of these new approaches were significant improvements in organizational theory, but were still basically embellishments of ideas coming from the participatory approach.

KATZ AND KAHN'S OPEN SYSTEMS APPROACH

One such theory is the **open systems theory**. Some social psychologists such as Robert Merton, Talcott Parsons, Daniel Katz, and Robert L. Kahn became disenchanted with the earlier organizational theories because they placed too much emphasis on activities of individuals within organizations and on the activities of the organization as a monolithic body without consideration of the environment within which the organization operated. They criticized this kind of thinking as the "closed system" approach, because, in their eyes, it considered the organization only as a closed system and not as a part of its environment:

> The closed system metaphor depicts a self-contained entity in which the functioning of the component parts and their inter-relations are the primary objects of inquiry. Any simple machine operating as a self-contained mechanism, such as a lawn mower or an automobile, is a prototypical closed system. Similarly, bureaucracy is often seen as an organizational equivalent of a closed system. Its relationship to its environment is regulated and stabilized in such a way that one can, analytically, ignore that environment when describing, dissecting, and manipulating the system. This is what

Max Weber does, for instance, when describing the characteristics of ideal-typical bureaucracy. In the same way, Frederick Taylor's discussion of the functions of the planning department essentially assumes that the firm's environment is stable, calculable, and likely to have little impact, in the sense of changing the work of the department.[30]

Followers of the open systems approach were influenced by biological models that dealt with both the internal organization of organisms and the manner in which they interacted with their environment. Natural scientists did this by thinking in terms of inputs-throughputs-outputs-feedback. To continue in existence, any organism must receive certain inputs from its environment. It then converts these to outputs which, through feedback, help it to attain more inputs. In the case of simple one-cell organisms, this means capturing some nourishment and converting it to energy, which it uses to move about to capture more nourishment. Human beings operate on the same principle, only with a more complex interaction system. Human beings need nourishment, shelter, and psychic encouragement, which they convert to work effort that can be sold for cash or traded to satisfy such needs as food, shelter, and psychic encouragement.

The open systems theorists felt that organizations could be approached in the same manner. Organizations need inputs in the form of labour power, raw material, and so forth. These are then converted to finished products, which are sold for cash so that more inputs can be purchased. Not-for-profit organizations do not follow exactly the same cycle, in that their products are usually not sold, but they still must produce an acceptable level of output so that some organization such as a government will provide inputs to them.

Katz and Kahn argued that successful organizations arrange the input-throughput-output process so as to reverse the normal entropy to which living organisms are subject. Entropy is the process through which organisms are subject to deterioration. In complex physical systems, as the size of the system becomes larger, the individual parts of the system become more disorganized until they are no longer able to sustain the organization as a whole. At this point, the system perishes.

A successful organization overcomes this process by developing *negative entropy*, which is the process of importing and storing more energy than it expends. This allows the organization to expand and to survive in difficult times by drawing on the stored reserve.[31] This stored reserve could take several forms. An obvious one is cash and other hard assets, but some other forms of stored energy could be the trust and goodwill of important people or a high quality management team.

The crucial lesson for managers in open systems theory is that all organizations are a part of their environments. Previous thinkers such as Frederick Taylor and, to a lesser extent, the organizational humanists, attempted to see the organization as a closed system unaffected by its environment. The open system concept reminds managers that, in addition to managing the internal aspects of their organization, they must also be sensitive to the rapidly changing environment that affects such things as the acceptance of their product, their relationship with their clientele, and the attitudes of their employees.

This next theory continued this open system approach and focussed on the way in which an organization must fit in with its environment.

CONTINGENCY THEORY

Contingency theory was first developed in a systematic fashion in the 1960s.[32] It argues that there is no "one best way" of structuring an organization. Instead, contingency theory suggests that the best way to structure an organization is contingent on a number of factors affecting the organization.[33] The most commonly cited factors are "the task environment of the organization, the technology used within the organization, and the organization's size."[34]

> Enterprises with highly predictable tasks perform better with organizations characterized by the highly formalized procedures and management hierarchies of the classical approach. With highly uncertain tasks that require more extensive problem solving, on the other hand, organizations that are less formalized and emphasize self-control and member participation in decision making are more effective. In essence, according to these newer studies, managers must design and develop organizations so that the organizational characteristics *fit* the nature of the task to be done.[35]

The "task environment" of an organization consists of its clients or customers, competitors, suppliers, regulatory agencies, and, in the case of public organizations, the legislature that established it and provides its funding.

Some organizations face a task environment that is uncertain and rapidly changing. These organizations must be very flexible and able to change as rapidly as their environment. Other task environments are considerably more stable and organizations operating in them can become a little complacent.

Technology refers to "*the process by which an organization converts inputs into outputs.*"[36] In a manufacturing environment, this is the assembly line or other mechanism used to produce the finished product. However, service organizations and even organizations producing such ephemeral products as "policy advice" also have production processes.

Where a technology is very routine and repetitive, such as an assembly line, the organization can have a very broad span of control, because problems are not likely to occur and when they do, there is usually a prearranged solution. Where the production process is less highly specified, such as in a policy advice unit, the span of control must be considerably smaller, because each new task is different from previous tasks and superiors and subordinates must work closely together.

The size of the organization also has an impact on its organizational structure. In very small organizations, the chief executive is in daily contact with all of his or her subordinates and everyone understands almost by tradition what is to be done. As organizations become larger, layers of hierarchy are established, and written job descriptions and standard operating procedures are required to delineate responsibilities.

The usual procedure to conduct empirical inquiries into the validity of contingency theory is to use survey research to compare a large number of organizations. Sometimes the investigator will select organizations engaging in the same activity, but with varying degrees of success. In this case, the hypothesis is that successful organizations will possess congruence of the various factors and unsuccessful ones will not. Another approach is for an investigator to choose organizations engaged in very different kinds of activity. In this case, the hypothesis is that organizations engaged in different kinds of activities will be structured differently and have different approaches to management.

In general, the results of these inquiries have been mixed. An early study conducted by Morse and Lorsch consisted of a study of four firms—two engaged in predictable manufacturing tasks and two in unpredictable research and development tasks.[37] Their results strongly supported contingency theory in that for each pair, the one with congruence between the nature of its task and its organizational structure was the more effective performer. More recent studies employing larger samples have usually not produced such unambiguous results. Many have found, at most, moderate support for the linkages posited in contingency theory.[38]

Probably the safest thing to be said about contingency theory is that the jury is still considering the final verdict. Almost all the studies do find some kinds of linkages, although they seldom find all of those expected and those found are sometimes weaker than expected. The authors of the studies usually conclude with a plea for more research in this area to search out other variables or refine measurement techniques. It is likely that contingency theory has some value, although it probably does not hold out the promise suspected initially.

One of the strengths of contingency theory is that, unlike many of the other theories that have been discussed, it is a dynamic approach to organizations. Managers must be aware constantly that there is no "one best way" to organize their operation. The structure that was highly successful last year might be a dismal failure with the changed conditions of the new year. The need to adjust to the rapidly changing environment is a challenge to all modern organizations.

THE EMERGENT PROCESS VIEW

The organization theories discussed to this point have been based on the idea that managers have a great deal of control in making decisions about organizational structure and that they always exercise that control in a rational manner and after extensive evaluation of alternatives.

A newly developing view suggests that organization design should be seen "as an emergent process, partially under the manager's control and partially beyond control ... [Managers are] partly proactive and partly reactive, capable of influencing organization design but not being the dominant influence."[39] This idea recognizes that external constraints play an important role in influencing organizational design, but that there is a significant element of chance or luck involved in organizational design as well.

One of the first discussions of this idea was an article colourfully titled "A Garbage Can Model of Organizational Choice."[40] This article described organizations as "organized anarchies."

> The organization operates on the basis of inconsistent and ill-defined preferences. It can be described better as a loose collection of ideas than as a coherent structure; it discovers preferences through action more than it acts on the basis of preferences.[41]

The decision-making process can be viewed as a garbage can into which four items are thrown:

- problems looking for solutions;
- solutions looking for problems;
- participants, each having different interests and different amounts of time to devote to a situation; and
- choice opportunities, or occasions when organizations are forced to undertake some action.

These items are thrown into the garbage can on a random basis and stirred about. Thus, problems do not always precede solutions. In some cases, solutions that have not yet discovered a problem are available. The decision made is a function, not of cold, rational logic, but rather of the chance factor of how these four elements are thrown into and stirred about in the garbage can. It is well understood in organizations that decisions are frequently influenced by the particular people who attend a key meeting. Thus, a bout of the flu or a flat tire that prevents a particular person from attending a meeting can determine which decision is made.

However, one should not go too far in emphasizing the randomness of decision-making. Clearly, managers have the legal and effective authority to make decisions and they do utilize rational processes in making those decisions. The significance of the **emergent process view** is that it recognizes that managers do face certain uncontrollable factors in making decisions and that managers do sometimes temper their rationality with impulse and irrational bias in making decisions.

CONCLUSION

The history of organizational theory begins with the mechanistic views of Weber and Taylor and progresses to the considerably more humanistic views of the social psychologists and organizational development specialists.

> Organization theory has indeed come full circle, and the enduring conflicts that characterize the field remain unresolved: formal versus informal structure as the proper focus of analysis, rationality versus humanism as the proper approach, equity versus efficiency as the goal of organizations, and the responsibility or lack thereof of the organization for the development and satisfaction of its employees—ultimately, conflicting theories of human nature and personality. What becomes apparent is

that organizations are far more complex and complicated than was initially believed; as important as it is to understand them, we are a long way from that understanding.[42]

The thread that runs through all of these theories is an emphasis on motivating employees to perform better. No organizational "quick fix" or even long-term structural reform can ever be effective if the most basic components of any organization—the people who make it work—do not carry out their duties in an efficient and effective manner. The next chapter will continue to focus on the behaviour of people in organizations by examining the related issues of motivation, leadership, and communication in organizations.

NOTES

1. Mary Parker Follett, *Creative Experience* (New York: Peter Smith, 1951), ch. 3; Mary Parker Follett, *The New State* (Gloucester, Mass.: Peter Smith, 1965), pp. 25-26.

2. Mary Parker Follett, *Dynamic Administration: The Collected Papers of Mary Parker Follett,* Elliot M. Fox and L. Urwick, eds. (London: Pitman, 1973), p. xxv.

3. Their work is described in great detail in Roethlisberger and Dickson's book *Management and the Worker* (Cambridge, Mass.: Harvard University Press, 1964).

4. Two of the more trenchant critics are Charles Perrow, *Complex Organizations: A Critical Essay* (Glenview, Ill.: Scott, Foresman, 1972), pp. 97-106; and Amitai Etzioni, *Modern Organizations* (Englewood Cliffs, N.J.: Prentice-Hall, 1964), pp. 39-49. A good overview of many of the critical articles can be found in Michael M. Harmon and Richard T. Mayer, *Organization Theory for Public Administration* (Boston: Little, Brown, 1986), p. 97.

5. (Cambridge, Mass.: Harvard University Press, 1962).

6. Abraham H. Maslow, *Motivation and Personality* (New York: Harper & Row, 1970), ch. 4.

7. Gerard R. Salancik and Jeffrey Pfeffer, "An Examination of Need-Satisfaction Models of Job Attitudes," *Administrative Science Quarterly* 22 (September 1977): 453.

8. Douglas McGregor, *The Human Side of Enterprise* (New York: McGraw-Hill, 1960), pp. 33-34. (Emphasis in original.)

9. Ibid., pp. 47-48. (Emphasis in original.)

10. Perrow, *Complex Organizations*, p. 100.

11. Robert B. Denhardt, *Theories of Public Organization* (Pacific Grove, Calif.: Brooks/Cole, 1984), p. 97.

12. Peter F. Drucker, *The Practice of Management* (New York: Harper & Row, 1954).

13. *Management By Objectives* (New York: Pitman, 1965), pp. 55-56

14. A good summary of some of these definitions is contained in Edgar F. Huse, *Organization Development and Change* (St. Paul, Minn.: West Publishing Company, 1980), pp. 22-25; Wendell L. French, Cecil H. Bell, Jr., and Robert A. Zawacki, "Mapping the Territory"; and Richard Beckhard, "What Is Organization Development?" in Wendell L. French, Cecil H. Bell, Jr., and Robert A. Zawacki, eds., *Organization Development: Theory, Practice, and Research* (Dallas: Business Publications, 1978).

15. French, Bell, and Zawacki, "Mapping the Territory," in French, Bell, and Zawacki, eds., *Organization Development*, p. 11.

16. Richard Beckhard, *Organization Development: Strategies and Models* (Reading, Mass.: Addison-Wesley, 1969), pp. 10-11.

17. Robert T. Golembiewski, *Humanizing Public Organizations* (Mt. Airy, Md.: Lomond Press, 1985), pp. 303, 338, and ch. 8 passim.

18. Wendell L. French and Cecil H. Bell, Jr., *Organization Development: Behavioral Science Interventions for Organization Improvement* (Englewood Cliffs, N.J.: Prentice-Hall, 1978), p. 81.

19. *Organization Development and Change*, pp. 23-24. (Emphasis in original.)

20. A good, complete discussion of the concept of organizational culture is found in Florence Heffron, *Organization Theory and Public Organization: The Political Connection* (Englewood Cliffs, N.J.: Prentice-Hall, 1989), ch. 7.

21. Some interesting examples are Robert R. Blake and Jane S. Mouton, *The Managerial Grid III* (Houston: Gulf Publishing Company, 1985); Matthew B. Miles and Richard A. Shmuck, "The Nature of Organization Development," in French, Bell, and Zawacki, eds., *Organization Development: Theory, Practice, and Research*, p. 24 and passim; Samuel A. Culbert and Jerome Reisel, "Organization Development: An Applied Philosophy For Managers of Public Enterprise," in Robert T. Golembiewski and William B. Eddy, eds., *Organization Development in Public Administration* 1 (New York: Marcel Dekker, 1978).

22. These words were first used by one of the founders of organization development, Kurt Lewin, "Frontiers in Group Dynamics," *Human Relations* 1, no. 1, (1947): 34.

23. Heffron, *Organization Theory and Public Organizations*, p. 161.

24. *Humanizing Public Organizations*, p. 61.

25. "The Influence of Organization Theory in Canadian Public Administration, *Canadian Public Administration* 25 (Winter 1982): 553-54. The quotation within the quotation is from J. E. Hodgetts et al., *The Biography of an Institution* (Montreal: McGill-Queen's University Press, 1972), p. 194.

26. Sylvain Cloutier, as quoted in Wilson, "The Influence of Organization Theory in Canadian Public Administration," 554.

27. "Administrative Reform in the Federal Public Service: Signs of a Saturation Psychosis," *Canadian Public Administration* 14 (Fall 1971): 303-25.

28. For one example, see J. S. Hodgson, "Management by Objectives—The Experience of a Federal Government Department," *Canadian Public Administration* 16 (Fall 1973): 422-31. There have been other programs that are similar to MBO such as Ontario, The Management Board of Cabinet, *Manager's Guidelines to Managing by Results* (Toronto: The Management Board of Cabinet, 1982).

29. For the history of a largely unsuccessful attempt in some Ontario municipalities, see the various documents prepared as a part of the Local Government Management project, such as *The LGMP Experience: Guidelines for Organizational Change in Local Government* (Toronto: Ministry of Treasury, Economics and Intergovernmental Affairs, 1977).

30. Harmon and Mayer, *Organization Theory for Public Administration* , p. 162.

31. Daniel Katz and Robert L. Kahn, *The Social Psychology of Organizations* (New York: John Wiley & Sons, 1966), ch. 2.

32. A good history of contingency theory is found in James L. Gibson, John M. Ivancevich, and James H. Donnelly, Jr., *Organizations: Behavior, Structure, Processes*, 5th ed. (Plano, Tex.: Business Publications, 1985), ch. 14; and John B., Miner, *Theories of Organizational Structure and Process* (Chicago: The Dryden Press, 1982), ch. 9.

33. A very thorough discussion of contingency theory is contained in Henry Mintzberg, *The Structuring of Organizations* (Englewood Cliffs, N.J.: Prentice-Hall, 1979), Part III and passim.
34. Daniel Robey, *Designing Organizations*, 3rd ed. (Homewood, Ill.: Richard D. Irwin, 1990), p. 26.
35. John J. Morse and Jay W. Lorsch, "Beyond Theory Y," *Harvard Business Review* (May-June, 1970): 62. (Emphasis in original.)
36. Robey, *Designing Organizations*, p. 28. (Emphasis in original.)
37. "Beyond Theory Y," *Harvard Business Review*, 61-68.
38. A good review of many of the studies that have been conducted can be found in: Claudia Bird Schoonhoven, "Problems with Contingency Theory: Testing Assumptions Hidden within the Language of Contingency 'Theory,'" *Administrative Science Quarterly* 26 (September 1981): 349-77.
39. Robey, *Designing Organizations*, p. 38.
40. Michael D. Cohen, James G. March, and John P. Olsen, *Administrative Science Quarterly* 17, no. 1 (March 1972): 1-25.
41. Ibid., 1.
42. Heffron, *Organization Theory and Public Organizations*, p. 8.

BIBLIOGRAPHY

Barnard, Chester. *The Functions of the Executive*. Cambridge, Mass.: Harvard University Press, 1962.

Beckhard, Richard. *Organization Development: Strategies and Models*. Reading, Mass.: Addison-Wesley, 1969.

Bennis, Warren G. *Organization Development: Its Nature, Origins, and Prospects*. Reading, Mass.: Addison-Wesley, 1969.

Blake, Robert R., and Jane S. Mouton. *The Managerial Grid III*. Houston: Gulf, 1985.

Denhardt, Robert B. *Theories of Public Organization*. Pacific Grove, Calif.: Brooks/Cole, 1984.

Drucker, Peter F. *The Practice of Management*. New York: Harper & Row, 1954.

Etzioni, Amitai. *Modern Organizations*. Englewood Cliffs, N.J.: Prentice-Hall,1964.

Follett, Mary Parker. *Creative Experience*. New York: Peter Smith, 1951.

———. *The New State*. Gloucester, Mass.: Peter Smith, 1965.

———. *Dynamic Administration: The Collected Papers of Mary Parker Follett*. Edited by Elliot M. Fox and L. Urwick. London: Pitman, 1973.

French, Wendell L., and Cecil H. Bell, Jr. *Organization Development: Behavioral Science Interventions for Organization Improvement* 2nd ed. Englewood Cliffs, N.J.: Prentice-Hall, 1978.

French, Wendell L., Cecil H. Bell, Jr., and Robert A. Zawacki, eds. *Organization Development: Theory, Practice, and Research*. Dallas: Business Publications, Inc., 1978.

Golembiewski, Robert T. *Humanizing Public Organizations*. Mt. Airy, Md.: Lomond Press, 1985.

Golembiewski, Robert T., and William B. Eddy, eds. *Organization Development in Public Administration*. 2 vols. New York: Marcel Dekker, Inc., 1978.

Harmon, Michael M., and Richard T. Mayer. *Organization Theory for Public Administration*. Boston: Little, Brown, 1986.

Harvey, Donald F., and Donald R. Brown. *An Experiential Approach to Organization Development*. Englewood Cliffs, N.J.: Prentice-Hall, 1976.

Heffron, Florence. *Organization Theory and Public Organizations: The Political Connection.* Englewood Cliffs, N.J.: Prentice-Hall, 1989.

Hodgetts, J. E., William McCloskey, Reginald Whitaker, and V. Seymour Wilson. *The Biography of an Institution.* Montreal: McGill-Queen's University Press, 1972.

Hodgson, J. S. "Management by Objectives—The Experience of a Federal Government Department." *Canadian Public Administration* 16 (Fall 1973): 422-31.

Huse, Edgar F. *Organization Development and Change.* 2nd ed. St. Paul, Minn.: West Publishing Company, 1980.

Katz, Daniel, and Robert L. Kahn. *The Social Psychology of Organizations.* New York: John Wiley & Sons, 1966.

Laframboise, H. L. "Administrative Reform in the Federal Public Service: Signs of a Saturation Psychosis." *Canadian Public Administration* 14 (Fall 1971): 303-25.

LGMP Team, The. *The LGMP Experience: Guidelines for Organizational Change in Local Government.* Toronto: Ministry of Treasury, Economics and Intergovernmental Affairs, 1977.

McGregor, Douglas. *The Human Side of Enterprise.* New York: McGraw-Hill, 1960.

McLaren, Robert I. *Organizational Dilemmas.* Chichester, U.K.: John Wiley & Sons, 1982.

Maslow, Abraham H. *Motivation and Personality.* New York: Harper & Row, 1970.

Mintzberg, Henry. *Structure in Fives: Designing Effective Organizations.* Englewood Cliffs, N.J.: Prentice-Hall, 1983.

———. *The Structuring of Organizations.* Englewood Cliffs, N. J.: Prentice-Hall, 1979.

Morse, John J., and Jay W. Lorsch. "Beyond Theory Y." *Harvard Business Review* 48 (May-June, 1970): 61-68.

Odiorne, George S. *Management By Objectives.* New York: Pitman, 1965.

Ontario. The Management Board of Cabinet. *Manager's Guidelines to Managing by Results.* Toronto: The Management Board of Cabinet, 1982.

Perrow, Charles. *Complex Organizations: A Critical Essay.* Glenview, Ill.: Scott, Foresman, 1972.

Roethlisberger, F. J., and William J. Dickson. *Management and the Worker.* Cambridge, Mass.: Harvard University Press, 1964.

Salancik, Gerard R., and Jeffrey Pfeffer. "An Examination of Need-Satisfaction Models of Job Attitudes." *Administrative Science Quarterly* 22 (September 1977).

Schoonhoven, Claudia Bird. "Problems with Contingency Theory: Testing Assumptions Hidden within the Language of Contingency Theory." *Administrative Science Quarterly* 26 (September 1981): 349-77.

Wilson, V. Seymour. "The Influence of Organization Theory in Canadian Public Administration." *Canadian Public Administration* 25 (Winter 1982): 545-63

CASES

In *Case Program in Canadian Public Administration* (Toronto: Institute of Public Administration of Canada):

Bureaucratie. By Guy Demers

Case Studies in Government Operations and Procedures. By R. H. McLaren

A Taxing Problem. By Roy S. Gunn

Cases developed by the Canadian Centre for Management Development and distributed by the Case Program in Canadian Public Administration:

Impasse: Team Building. By John Hunter

Reorganizing Human Resources at Statistics Canada. By Philippe Clément

5

Communications, Leadership, and Motivation

The previous two chapters focussed on organizations as organizations much more than on the actions and motivations of the people within them. This chapter will focus on the individual members of the organization.

It is frequently said that the most important resource that any organization possesses is its human resources—its employees. Yet it is shocking to see how carefully some organizations preserve and protect their other resources, but neglect their human resources. This chapter will first consider two important aspects of motivation—communications and leadership—and then tie these together with a discussion of some general theories concerning the motivation of employees.

Communications, leadership, and motivation are very closely related concepts. Good communications and sound leadership are important in producing highly motivated employees; and highly motivated employees can make the organization operate more efficiently.

COMMUNICATIONS

Communications are the lifeblood of any organization and one of the main purposes of communication is to effect coordination between the various elements in an organization. If an organization is to function properly, people in the organization must understand what is taking place in other parts of it. Communication takes place in several ways. At one extreme are the formal, written instructions found in an organization manual or on a list of standard operating procedures. At the other extreme, communication can be by example. When senior managers all dress very conservatively, work long hours, and take short breaks, they are communicating something very significant to those below them in the hierarchy—without saying a word.

Pursley and Snortland capture the full subtlety of the situation when they define communication as "the transfer and reception of information, emotions, ideas, and orders."[1] Notice that this definition considers communication as a two-step process; communication is not just the sending of a message, but the reception of that message as well. We are all aware of situations where the message that was sent was not the same message received—either accidentally or intentionally.

Different Kinds of Communications

Formal and informal communications. In many ways, formal and informal communications parallel the formal and informal organizations discussed in Chapter 4. All organizations provide certain formal communications to members. These take such forms as the orientation package for new employees, training materials, and operating manuals. These set out the formal rules of the organization and tell employees what is expected of them. However, as new employees become socialized in an organization, they also receive many informal communications that modify communications they have received through the formal channel. For example, the operating manual might say that employees are entitled to be paid at a premium rate for all overtime worked. However, the informal channel of communications might suggest that if you value your future in the organization and want to be seen as a "team player," you will simply work the overtime and not bother to ask for the extra pay. In many cases, the information conveyed through the informal communication system can be as important as that conveyed through the formal system.

Management should attempt to keep track of communication flowing through the informal system. It will frequently provide advance notice of employee dissatisfaction or other problems in lower levels of the organization. There is also much misinformation which is passed through the "grapevine." This can be a sign that the more formal methods of communication are not adequate. An "organization's informal communications network begins to hum whenever the formal channels are silent or ambiguous on subjects of importance to its members."[2] Management must be conscious of this tendency and head it off by providing a steady flow of accurate formal communications. Thus, if the formal system communicated that there was soon to be a major reorganization and then was silent, the informal system might begin to buzz with information about imminent huge layoffs. However, if senior management used the formal system to keep employees informed about the reorganization, there would be less misinformation in the informal system.

Downward communications involve the communication of official organizational pronouncements from the top levels of the hierarchy down to operating employees. Downward communication is used by senior management to coordinate the activities of lower-level employees. This is usually done through formal communications such as policy directives, operating manuals, or notices on bulletin boards, but, as mentioned earlier, downward communication can also be informal.

Great care must be taken to ensure that the message sent by senior managers is the same received by operating employees. This problem increases with the number of levels in the hierarchy and with functional specialization. One of the barriers to communication discussed below is caused because the language spoken varies at different levels in the organization, and in its different functional areas. A communication that begins at the top level of the organization as a one-page statement about the need for better safety in the factory will be "translated" as it passes down the chain of command. It will develop into lengthy statements about who must wear safety shoes, hard hats, and protective glasses, when they must be worn, and how they will be paid for. In this translation process, the policy as implemented on the factory floor might or might not be the same one articulated by senior management.

Upward communications, sometimes called *feedback*, are messages from lower levels of the organization to higher levels. This is the most unnatural form of communication in the organization because it runs counter to the normal chain of command, but it can also be the most important. Operating-level employees are in a much better position to know about problems as they are developing than are senior managers. Operating-level employees deal with clients on a daily basis and so have immediate feedback about dissatisfaction among clients; factory employees see how a product is being assembled and so can frequently point to quality control problems and bottlenecks in operations.

Senior managers should always encourage upward communication, but this is easier said than done. Lower-level employees are sometimes reluctant to discuss problems with senior employees either because of the social distance involved, or the unnaturalness of upward communications, or for fear that managers will "kill the messenger bearing the bad news." The major inhibition on the upward flow of information is simply that lower-level employees do not want to pass upward information that can be used against them.

Thus, there is a natural tendency to pass upward positive information, but not negative information. The cumulative impact of this tendency can be so severe that senior managers are totally out of touch with what is actually happening at the operating level. David Halberstam suggests that the American involvement in Vietnam in the 1960s was characterized by this attitude of telling superiors what they wanted to hear. He states that one journalist felt that senior officers in the military "had created an elaborate machine to lie to them, only to become prisoners of their own lies."[3] Wartime situations bring about extreme cases, but it is not unusual for senior managers to be forced to deal quickly with a crisis that could have been headed off easily if they had had some advance warning. Junior officials did not provide that advance warning because they tried to hide the problem.

Some companies have formal programs such as suggestion boxes or plans that reward employees for ideas to improve productivity, but these plans frequently meet with mixed success. One interesting method of stimulating upward communication is "management by wandering around" (MBWA).[4] MBWA, also called "the technology of the obvious," urges managers to put aside computer printouts and marketing surveys periodically and escape from their offices to wander about and see their product or service as customers see it and experience their work environment as their employees do. Some managers' findings when they attempted this were obvious, basic, and brilliant at the same time. One manager insisted on cleaner washrooms in the factory because he did not see how employees could have a sense of pride in their work when they had to put up with the stench from stinking washrooms on the assembly line.[5] Some of the things that have the greatest effect on working conditions never find their way into computer printouts.

Lateral communication "takes place among workers of the same level in the hierarchy, or among individuals of different levels who are not in a superior-subordinate relationship."[6] *Most* communication in organizations could well be of the lateral variety, although it is impossible to measure this precisely. Some kinds of lateral communication are encouraged by the formal organization, but some kinds are discouraged or even prohibited.

Lateral communication between employees within the same work team is usually encouraged because it promotes coordination. It is impossible for standard operating procedures to foresee every future working condition; lateral communication between employees fills this void by facilitating informal solutions to work problems.

However, lateral communication between employees in different organizational units is more problematic. Strictly speaking, all communication within an organization should flow "through channels." This means that people at the same level, but reporting to different supervisors, do not consult directly with one another. Figure 5.1 shows the proper formal communication route in a bureaucracy. If X desires to communicate with Y, X passes the communication up the hierarchy until it reaches someone who has line authority over both X and Y. This person then makes some decision and passes that decision down.

However, people working in organizations quickly discover the difficulties with this communication "through channels." Not only is it time-consuming, but there is also a risk that relatively small issues will be caught up in larger concerns of "office politics" or territoriality. Subordinates learn quickly that it is much faster and easier to resolve minor problems through informal lateral communication than through the hierarchy. Thus, the rigid standard operating procedures found in formal communications are frequently modified in practice because people at lower levels in the organization have found better ways to coordinate their activities.

There is some risk to subordinates in ignoring the chain of command. If it is really a small matter that does not affect others, then it will be acceptable to ignore the channels, but if something larger goes awry as a result of these informal agreements, subordinates can be in a great deal of trouble for not keeping their bosses informed.

Some organizations see real value in encouraging lateral communication. It can smooth out many problems quickly and be a source of innovation. Henri Fayol developed the idea of the "gang plank," which allows lateral communications to occur while still preserving the concept of the chain of command. He strongly argued that lateral communications were highly preferable to the roundabout method of following channels as long as the communicators' immediate supervisors were kept informed of what was happening.[7]

Lateral communication can also occur between different organizations. This can be routine, such as when someone in a regional office communicates directly with a head office counterpart, or it can involve the transfer of major

Figure 5.1
BUREAUCRATIC FLOW OF COMMUNICATION

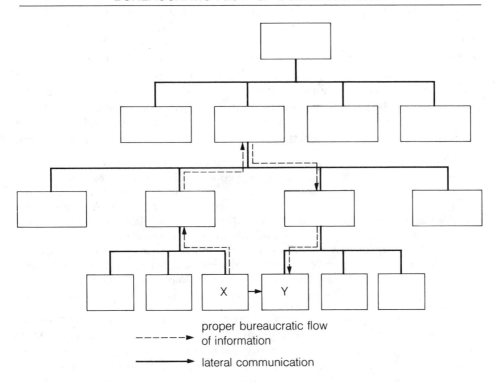

proper bureaucratic flow
- - - - - - ▶ of information

—————————▶ lateral communication

innovations from one organization to another. People performing the same function in different organizations frequently belong to associations that allow them to meet and discuss changes in their field. These can be as formal as the provincial engineers' or accountants' associations, or as informal as a periodic breakfast meeting of personnel officers employed in municipal governments in a certain area. These people engage in lateral communication about new activities in their organizations. This allows for sharing of new ideas.

Lateral communications can have substantial value in certain cases. They aid problem solving and can foster innovation and the dissemination of new ideas. However, some organizations are fearful of this form of communication because it can appear to subvert the formal chain of command.

Obstacles to Communication

Good, clear lines of communication are important in coordinating activities and ensuring organizational effectiveness, but there are a number of factors that inhibit effective communications.

Territoriality and other organizational tensions occur in organizations where there is a climate that encourages managers to think solely about the further-ance of their own goals. In this environment, communication is discouraged because managers do not want to "tip their hands" too early and allow other departments to know what they are doing. This attitude is clearly dysfunctional to organizational health, but it is found all too often in organizations.

Language differences exacerbate problems that might already exist between various occupational specialties and organizational units. Andrew Dunsire com-pares a typical organization to a high-rise building that he calls the "Babel house." Each ascending floor is a higher level in the hierarchy, and the horizontal separation on each floor represents different functional specialties:

> The building is a Tower of Babel because a different tongue (concepts, vocabulary) is talked on each floor—amounting to a considerable linguistic disparity between top-floor speech and ground-floor speech—and different jargons and dialects are spoken on any one floor, in each of the corners and other areas. As between one floor and the next, or as between one office and its neighbour on the same floor, differences in language and habitual style of doing business can usually be noted, though it is quite easy for adjacent ranks, and denizens of adjacent offices, to understand one another. Messages from distant locations in any direction—from a far-away corner, or from a much higher or much lower floor—do not by contrast, make much sense on first hearing or reading: the more distant, the less intelligible.[8]

These different languages and dialects come about as a result of professional and functional specialization. For example, both economists and accountants talk about "depreciation" and "rents," but the two groups have different meanings for those same terms which are, in turn, different from their more common usage by members of the public. In a factory, a document which is clearly identified on its face as "Form No. C31-a" might be called a "requisition form" or "green sheet" in different parts of the plant.

Communications overload occurs when there are so many communications taking place that they overload the channels for processing them, causing organizational dysfunctions. In the popular novel and film *The Day of the Jackal* the French authorities know that the Jackal has entered the country to assassi-nate President DeGaulle. And someplace in the elaborate French bureaucracy they have the information they need to find him. The problem is that they also have so much other information that they are unable to locate the relevant bits. This sort of thing is a relatively frequent occurrence in large organizations. Senior executives are inundated with communications so that it is difficult for them to decide which are the most relevant ones.

Noise or *distortion* occurs when messages are altered as they pass through the various steps in the hierarchy. Almost everyone has played the game that involves saying something to one person who, in turn, passes the information to someone else and so forth until it has passed through many people. The message in its final form usually bears little resemblance to its original statement. This problem can be even more severe in large organizations when there is the possibility that territoriality or language differences can add to the distortion.

Organizations can attempt to minimize these distortions by relying on formal, written communications, and hoping that there is less likelihood of misinterpretation of written documents than of word-of-mouth communication. However, even written documents can suffer from poor translation as information is passed from senior managers down the hierarchy.

One of the other factors that can be used to coordinate activities within any organization is good leadership. It can be used to supplement communications by putting unclear or distorted communications back into perspective.

LEADERSHIP

Leadership is usually considered to be an important factor in the motivation of employees. It is necessary to be a good leader in order to be a good manager, but the words are not synonymous. Managers possess power as a result of their organizational position; leaders possess power as a result of the concurrence of their followers. Some managers are leaders in the sense that their relationship with subordinates is such that subordinates comply with their requests not just out of fear for the consequences, but because they are willing followers. Katz and Kahn "consider the essence of organizational leadership to be the influential increment over and above the mechanical compliance with the routine directives of the organization."[9] Pursley and Snortland provide a more detailed distinction between a leader and a manager:

> Managers are appointed and have formal authority within an organization; leaders may be elected, appointed, or merely emerge from within a group. A manager has a formal position; a leader may or may not have a formal position. A manager usually can expect people to follow proper, official orders; leaders may be able to move people to do things far beyond the call of duty. Although every manager should be a leader, not all leaders are managers. A manager is expected to be able to organize, plan, and evaluate; some leaders may not be able to perform these management tasks. A manager's formal authority provides the resources that the manager may be able to use to influence the behavior of people—in short, to lead. However, not every manager is a leader or even understands the importance of leadership.[10]

This raises the question of why a leader is even needed in a bureaucratic organization. After all, the rules are the rules and even totally uninspired managers can stand over workers and be certain that they follow the rules. Who needs a leader?

There is something to be said for this line of reasoning. Most people are familiar with organizations that stagger along without effective leadership— forms are processed, decisions are made, and so forth. However, such an organization is really only "staggering along." Good leaders do a number of things that allow organizations to develop and thrive rather than just stumble from one crisis to the next.

Leaders instill the desire to excel in subordinates. When you visit a store or office, it is very easy to distinguish organizations in which the employees are striving to do their job as well as possible, from organizations where employees are simply going through the motions to get a paycheque. Usually, the difference will be the presence of a true leader rather than a "by the book" manager.

Leaders also help organizations survive crises. It is relatively easy to manage an organization in a stable situation, but a good leader is necessary when the organization is facing a threat to its continued existence, or must make a major change in its operations.

The difficulty of defining leadership in an unequivocal manner is evidenced by the fact that Stogdill, in his compendium review of the literature on leadership, devotes an entire chapter to definitions in which he lists eleven different categories of definitions.[11] However, this lack of a precise definition has not restricted the amount of research undertaken in the area of leadership.

This voluminous research has yielded a number of different perspectives on the issue of leadership. One of the earliest approaches was to attempt to locate those *traits* that always seemed to be present in a successful leader. This was followed by a trend toward research to determine which *skills* were most likely to be of use to leaders.

Traits are genetically a part of the individual, whereas skills can be learned and developed. The switch to an emphasis on skills led to a concern for the development of an ideal leadership *style*—democratic, authoritarian, or laissez-faire. In recent years there has been a trend to a belief that there is no one ideal style, but that the most appropriate style is a function of the relationship between, on the one hand, both traits and skills of leaders and, on the other hand, the characteristics of followers and the environment of the organization. This is called the situational or *contingency* theory of leadership. Each of these approaches to the study of leadership will be discussed in this chapter.

Leadership Traits or Skills

One of the earliest approaches to the study of leadership was an analysis of a group of people who were commonly regarded as successful, or "natural leaders," to determine what traits these individuals had in common. The basis of this research was that there were certain inherited traits that would always mark a leader. Some studies suggested that leaders tended to be older, taller, weigh more, and have greater athletic and speaking ability than non-leaders.[12] However, this line of research fell out of favour when other studies did not produce consistent results.[13]

A second wave of research applied some of the same techniques used in the studies of "natural leaders" to locate the traits and skills common to successful leaders in the workplace—managers and supervisors. This focus was considerably more productive. Stogdill has summarized the findings of these studies:

> The leader is characterized by a strong drive for responsibility and task completion, vigor and persistence in pursuit of goals, venturesomeness and originality in problem solving, drive to exercise initiative in social situations, self-confidence and sense of personal identity, willingness to accept consequences of decision and action, readiness to absorb interpersonal stress, willingness to tolerate frustration and delay,

ability to influence other persons' behavior, and capacity to structure social interaction systems to the purpose at hand.[14]

A more recent study of two thousand managers in twelve organizations identified several characteristics usually found in successful managers: efficiency orientation; proactivity; diagnostic use of concepts; concern with impact; self-confidence; use of oral presentations; conceptualization (middle-level managers and executives only); use of socialized power; managing group process (middle-level managers and executives only); perceptual objectivity; self-control; stamina and adaptability.[15]

Some commentators see the situation more simply and suggest that management abilities can be identified in two or three clusters of skills. Katz's three-skills typology was first developed in 1955, but is still considered relevant:

Technical Skills: "An understanding of, and proficiency in, a specific kind of activity, particularly one involving methods, processes, procedures, or techniques. . . Technical skill involves specialized knowledge, analytical ability within that specialty, and facility in the use of the tools and techniques of the specific discipline."[16]

Human Skills: "The executive's ability to work effectively as a group member and to build cooperative effort within the team he leads. As *technical* skill is primarily concerned with working with 'things' (processes or physical objects), so *human* skill is primarily concerned with working with people."[17]

Conceptual Skills: "The ability to see the enterprise as a whole; it includes recognizing how the various functions of the organization depend on one another, and how changes in any one part affect all the others; and it extends to visualizing the relationship of the individual business to the industry, the community, and the political, social, and economic forces of the nation as a whole. Recognizing these relationships and perceiving the significant elements in any situation, the administrator should then be able to act in a way which advances the over-all welfare of the total organization."[18]

All managers must possess these skills to some degree, but managers at different levels in the organization need different quantities of each. The first-line supervisor must have high levels of technical skills because he or she must be able to advise workers on production problems. First-line supervisors must also possess human relations skills to maintain satisfaction and motivation among group members and direct them toward organizational goals. Conceptual skills are less necessary for first-line supervisors because the problems facing them are fairly well-defined and recurring, and usually involve problems within the organization, rather than in its environment.

The skill needs of senior managers are reversed. Technical skills are not very important because there are large numbers of skilled operatives at lower levels to solve those kinds of problems. Conceptual skills are much more important for senior managers because they are constantly facing new and unstructured problems involving relationships between different units of the organization, or the organization and its environment.

One of the outcomes of this type of research was a debunking of the myth that "leaders are born, not made." If the traits and skills commonly found in good leaders could be identified, then these same characteristics could be nurtured in other promising people, so that possibly good leaders—or at least passable managers—could be developed.

This idea led many organizations to establish what are called *assessment centres*. These centres administer a battery of various kinds of tests to current and potential managers to locate the most promising managers and point out the skills they need to develop. This battery of tests usually lasts for several days and ranges from objective intelligence tests to role-playing exercises to determine human relations skills. Intended or accidental bias is reduced by the use of multiple testing instruments and multiple human evaluators.

These assessment centres are used quite widely in the private sector, and there is some evidence that they are effective in identifying managers.[19] However, government organizations have been somewhat slower to adopt this concept because of the rigidities imposed by the mechanistic application of the merit system (discussed in Chapters 3 and 4.) The assessment centre technique can be construed as identifying "high flyers" and providing them with preferential training and development. This runs counter to the mechanistic application of the merit principle that requires that individuals be matched to jobs for which they possess the necessary skills right now.

The study of leadership traits and skills led to a realization that leadership was not something contained only in the leader, but rather that leadership described a reciprocal relationship between the leader and followers. The next approach to leadership studied the exchange relationship between these two.

Styles of Leadership: Authoritarian, Democratic, Laissez-Faire

There are probably as many different leadership styles as there are leaders. Recently developed situational theories of leadership stress this fact, but many earlier studies have focussed on three broad categories of leadership styles— authoritarian, democratic, and laissez-faire. The *authoritarian* style involves the leader making all decisions and communicating work tasks to followers in a highly detailed manner so that followers have no role in making decisions or organizing their work. The *democratic* or participative style of leadership involves a more open relationship in which leaders encourage followers to work together in seeking and implementing solutions. Leaders guide the group by advising on alternative possibilities. The *laissez-faire* style allows followers to "do their own thing" with no direction or involvement on the part of the leader. This usually comes about as a corruption or a misapplication of the democratic style.[20]

The relative effectiveness of these different styles has been tested many times and the results have always been very similar. The laissez-faire style is universally rejected as having no redeeming value. It results in groups deteriorating into chaos, and produces neither organizational effectiveness nor member satisfaction. The democratic leadership style seems to further member satisfaction and group cohesion more than the other two. The evidence is less clear concerning the effect of leadership style on group productivity. Stogdill's comprehensive review of studies suggests that leadership style (authoritarian or democratic) had little impact on productivity.[21]

However, some researchers began to delve a little more deeply into this issue.[22] They found that authoritarian styles seemed to be more functional in cases where the task to be accomplished was clearly defined and could be well-structured, e.g., factory assembly line. Democratic styles were more productive where tasks were ill-defined and non-repetitive, e.g., research laboratory. This was one of the findings that led to the idea that there was no "one best way" of establishing leadership, but that different leadership styles were more effective in different situations.

Situational or Contingency Theories

The contingency theory of organization discussed in Chapter 4 holds that the ideal structure for an organization is a combination of a number of factors such as the backgrounds of employees in the organization and the task to be accomplished. The situational theory of leadership borrows this concept in arguing that the best style of leadership is a product of a number of factors relating to:

- characteristics of the leader;
- characteristics of the members of the group;
- nature of the decision to be made; and
- the situation or environment.

A number of researchers have developed different forms of situational theories.[23] The Vroom-Yetton normative model will be discussed here as representative of this general approach.

Vroom and Yetton focus on how leaders ought to make decisions if they are to be perceived as good leaders.[24] This is a normative model, meaning that it is Vroom and Yetton's idea of how decisions *ought* to be made. They are not saying that decisions are made this way, only that managers would be better leaders if they did. It is clear that their work is influenced by participative approaches to management, but they recognize that participation is not necessary, or even productive, in every decision.

First, they identify five different decision-making styles. Two are autocratic:

A1. You solve the problem or make the decision yourself, using information available to you at the time.

A2. You obtain the necessary information from your subordinates, then decide the solution to the problem yourself. You may or may not tell your subordinates what the problem is in getting the information from them. The role played by your subordinates in making the decision is clearly one of providing the necessary information to you, rather than generating or evaluating alternative solutions.[25]

Two are consultative:

C1. You share the problem with the relevant subordinates individually, getting their ideas and suggestions without bringing them together as a group. Then *you* make the decision, which may or may not reflect your subordinates' influence.

C2. You share the problem with your subordinates as a group, obtaining their collective ideas and suggestions. Then you make the decision, which may or may not reflect your subordinates' influence.[26]

One is group:

G1. You share the problem with your subordinates as a group. Together you generate and evaluate alternatives and attempt to reach agreement (consensus) on a solution. Your role is much like that of chairman. You do not try to influence the group to adopt "your" solution, and you are willing to accept and implement any solution which has the support of the entire group.[27]

Each of these methods of decision-making is beneficial in certain circumstances. Vroom and Yetton's next step is to provide the decision rule that determines which method should be used in a particular set of circumstances. They identify eight factors to be considered in choosing a method. Among the most significant factors are:[28]

- the importance of the decision for the health of the organization;
- the adequacy of knowledge possessed by the decision-maker;
- the importance of subordinates' acceptance of the decision; and
- the likelihood that subordinates would make a decision based on the best interests of the organization.

Vroom and Yetton present the relationships between the types of decisions and these situational factors in a fairly complex decision-tree. However, it is possible to capture their general idea by an illustration. If subordinates' acceptance of the decision is important, then you would be more likely to use the group or consultative mode of decision-making, unless the group could not be trusted to act in the best interest of the organization, in which case you would have to use the autocratic style.

However, leadership is not something to be valued in itself. Leadership must have some purpose; one of the main purposes of leadership is to improve organizational effectiveness by motivating employees. The next section of this chapter reviews some theories of motivation.

MOTIVATION

Earlier ideas of motivation were rather simple. Bosses simply told workers what to do and they did it—or were fired. Henry Ford is purported to have said that the best incentive to an employee is the presence of unemployed workers outside the factory gate. Chapters 3 and 4 described how ideas of external motivation based on reward or fear of punishment have recently been replaced with ideas of the importance of internal motivators such as self-actualization or pride in accomplishment.

Table 5.1
SUMMARY OF MOTIVATING MECHANISMS

Management School	Communication Style	Leadership Style	Motivating Mechanism
Weberian	Formal Downward	Authoritarian	Commands Authority
Scientific Management (Taylor)	Formal Downward	Authoritarian	Authority Financial Rewards
Human Relations (Theory X-Theory Y) (Hierarchy of Needs)	Upward Downward	Democratic Potentially Laissez-faire	Self-actualization
Participative (Organization Development)	Upward Downward Lateral	Democratic	Self-actualization Participation

Traditional forms of motivation based on punishment have fallen into disuse for a number of reasons. The strength of unions and recent changes in labour laws to protect workers have reduced the unilateral power that employers once had to discipline employees. However, research indicates that motivation by fear of punishment is not very efficient, anyway.[29] Negative forms of motivation might well encourage employees to do just enough to avoid being disciplined. The result could be a continual game of employees trying to find out how much they can "get away with" before they are disciplined. This could then lead to management continually imposing new controls and restrictions as employees find ways of circumventing them. Positive methods of motivating people are probably much more effective.

Chapters 3 and 4 discussed some of the motivating mechanisms employed in various schools of management. Table 5.1 summarizes the main points made in those chapters. This chapter will build on the general findings presented earlier and provide additional details on motivating mechanisms.

Chris Argyris's Maturity-Immaturity Theory

Chris Argyris points out that all social organizations are composed of individuals and a formal structure, but that tensions inevitably develop because there is a basic incongruence between the behaviour pattern of mature individuals and the needs of the formal organization. He suggests that the characteristics of a maturing individual are:

- increasing activity or self-determination;
- independence rather than dependence;
- multi-faceted behaviour;
- deepening interest in stimulating challenges;
- longer time perspective;
- feelings of equality with peers; and
- self-awareness.[30]

He goes on to point out that formal organizations are based on such principles as: task or work specialization, chain of command, unity of direction, and span of control.[31] Most of these principles require not mature, but *immature*, behaviour on the part of the individual. For example, mature individuals capable of complex behaviour and interested in challenges are placed in jobs that require boring, repetitive actions. "[O]rganizations are willing to pay high wages and provide adequate seniority if mature adults will, for eight hours a day, behave in a less than mature manner!"[32]

It is quite normal for individual employees to react negatively when confronted with this situation. They could simply leave the organization. Or they could stay in the organization and become apathetic and/or establish an informal work group that could have a detrimental effect on production. Or they could resolve to work their way up the organizational ladder, because the incongruity between personality and organizational demands is less pronounced at the higher levels.[33]

In a later work, Argyris presents some tentative suggestions for resolving this basic incongruity.[34] He suggests that organizations of the future will emphasize the pyramidal organizational structure less, and recognize that there are other, less formal structures in place that are also important. He strongly supports a form of job enlargement (discussed in more detail below) that would ensure that employees develop a greater understanding of, and concern for, the activities of the *entire* organization, rather than only their narrow portion of it. This should be supplemented by employees meeting in small groups to discuss problems of the organization and possibilities for improvement. He argued that autocratic leadership styles should be replaced by situational approaches to leadership—different types of employees and situations call forth different leadership styles. Control mechanisms should be less negatively oriented toward detecting transgressions and more oriented toward helping individuals achieve greater "self-responsibility and psychological success."[35]

A standard criticism of Argyris's approach is that he views human nature as too homogeneous. His view that *everyone* is mature and wants interesting, challenging work is too simplistic. Robert Presthus argues that different personalities react differently to bureaucratic structures. He labels the three different bureaucratic personality types as "upward-mobiles," "indifferents," and "ambivalents."[36]

One might disagree with the specifics of Presthus's categories, but it does seem to be the case that different individuals behave differently in bureaucratic settings; most seem to hate the boredom, but some people can enjoy aspects of even the most boring job.[37]

Possibly it is the characterization of "bureaucracy" as homogeneous that misses the mark. The characteristics of particular jobs can vary quite widely; an employee's positive or negative feelings might have more to do with how the employee views his or her job than with how he or she relates to the overall bureaucracy.

Table 5.2
HERZBERG'S MOTIVATION AND HYGIENE FACTORS

Motivators	Hygiene
Achievement	Company Policy & Administration
Recognition	Supervision—Technical
Work itself	Salary
Responsibility	Interpersonal Relations—Supervision
Advancement	Working Conditions

Frederick Herzberg's Motivation-Hygiene Theory

People frequently assume that the factors that cause *satisfaction* in the work environment are simply the reverse of those factors that cause *dissatisfaction*. Frederick Herzberg tested this conventional wisdom by asking a number of employees to describe work occurrences that led to satisfaction and dissatisfaction. In many cases, the factors causing satisfaction were very different from those causing dissatisfaction.[38] For example, Table 5.2 indicates that a feeling of achievement tended to satisfy workers, but its absence did not make them dissatisfied; it simply reduced their satisfaction. Conversely, company policy and administration were a frequent source of dissatisfaction, but correcting problems in this area merely lessened dissatisfaction; it did not increase satisfaction.

Herzberg referred to the factors that led to dissatisfaction as *hygiene factors* because "they act in a manner analogous to the principles of medical hygiene. Hygiene operates to remove health hazards from the environment of man. It is not curative; it is, rather, a preventive."[39] The factors that led to satisfaction, Herzberg labeled *motivators* because they had a highly positive effect on people's feelings about their job.

Herzberg noted a very interesting difference between the hygiene and motivating factors. The hygiene factors all relate to the general work environment, while the motivating factors are all intrinsic to the nature of the job itself. The implications of Herzberg's theory for management are clear: the general work environment should be pleasant enough to avoid dissatisfaction, but any major improvements in motivation can be made only through changes in the nature of the job itself.

The specific remedy suggested by Herzberg was job redesign or job enrichment.

Job Redesign

The theories of both Argyris and Herzberg focussed on the ability to improve motivation through careful job design. However, two experts on job design remind us that sometimes the problem is not with the nature of the job itself. They emphasize the need for proper selection and training techniques to ensure that there is a good fit between the person and the job.[40]

> When people are well matched with their jobs, it rarely is necessary to force, coerce, bribe, or trick them into working hard and trying to perform the job well. Instead, they try to do well because it is rewarding and satisfying to do so.[41]

However, the job itself must be reasonably attractive. A number of different approaches to improving job designs have been tried.

Job rotation involves keeping the job descriptions for all positions the same, but shifting the people who fill the position. This could be done for only a half-day at a time or for a few weeks. It adds some variety to an employee's workday and could increase his or her sense of accomplishment and responsibility if he or she knows how to do several jobs instead of just one.

The rigidities introduced into the workplace by collective agreements and the merit system can limit the possibility of job rotation. Moving a person into a job temporarily could be seen as giving that person an advantage in any future competition for the job. When people try to perform too many tasks, they might not be properly trained, which could lead to mistakes or even serious accidents. Employees sometimes resist job rotation on the basis that it is no more interesting to do two boring jobs than to do one boring job.

Job enlargement tries to relieve the boredom in a job by expanding the size of the job. Instead of spending all day simply examining and filing forms, an employee might also be responsible for working at a counter and helping members of the public fill out forms. Having broader responsibilities and being able to see more of the total process should increase an employee's sense of belonging and accomplishment.

Job enlargement has been tried in many places, and has been quite successful,[42] but, again, bureaucratic rigidities can cause problems. A job description with more duties probably means that the job will receive a higher rate of pay. If this is the case, management will likely want to stay away from job enlargement.

Job enrichment or *vertical job loading* is a variant of job enlargement proposed by Hackman and Oldham, Argyris, and Herzberg, among many others. Herzberg, in particular, emphasized the importance of expanding jobs not just by arbitrarily adding more duties, but by considering the needs of the mature employee. He pointed out the difference between horizontal job loading, which meant simply loading a person with more work, and vertical job loading, which meant expanding the job through such means as:[43]

- removing some detailed controls and making the employee more responsible for his or her own work;
- carving out a "natural unit of work" for the person and granting him or her additional responsibility for dealing with all problems in that area; and
- introducing more specialized and difficult tasks.

Herzberg felt that these improvements in the job itself would increase an employee's satisfaction, but other theories argue that more extensive changes in the overall work environment are beneficial.

Expectancy Theory

Expectancy theory was originally developed by Victor Vroom in his 1964 book *Work and Motivation*,[44] and has been developed further by a number of other writers, most notably Edward Lawler and Lyman Porter. It is a fairly complex theory, but it has gained many followers in the last few years, and is certainly a very influential theory now.

It is based on four assumptions:[45]

- An individual's behaviour is determined by the interaction of forces in the individual and in the environment;
- While there are some constraints on the behaviour of individuals within organizations, people still have significant scope to make their own decisions. In particular, they make decisions about joining and remaining within an organization, and about the amount of effort they will expend on particular activities;
- Different people have different needs, desires, and goals;
- People choose among alternative behaviours based on their *expectations* about the impact that the behaviour will have on their ability to satisfy their needs, desires, and goals.

Expectancy theory has its own specialized vocabulary. *First-level outcomes* relate to the performance of the job itself (e.g., completing a report by a deadline). *Second-level outcomes* "are those events (rewards or punishments) that the first-level outcomes are likely to produce, such as merit pay increase, group acceptance or rejection, and promotion."[46] *Instrumentality* is the person's perceived connection between the first-order and second-order outcomes. For example, most people like to believe that there is a connection between satisfactory work performance and a positive performance appraisal. A *valence* is the importance that a person attaches to specific first- and second-level outcomes. If an outcome is desired, it is positively valent; if it is not desired, it is negatively valent. Valences also have strengths associated with them to indicate the intensity of the person's feelings.

Figure 5.2 provides an illustration of the relationship between these various elements. An individual's performance will be determined by his or her level of motivation and ability. If a person has a great deal of ability to perform a particular task, then he or she would need little motivation; but a person must have a great deal of motivation to perform a task he or she finds difficult. The amount of motivation that a person will be able to muster will depend on the level of importance that a person attaches to the first- and second-level outcomes (valences), and the person's perception of the strength of the linkages at points A and B (instrumentality).

This can be illustrated by the case depicted in Figure 5.3. The first-order outcome is the need to complete a report on time even though that will require extra effort. This worker envisions several second-level outcomes flowing from that. They are arrayed here from the "highly positive" to the "highly negative."

Figure 5.2
CONCEPTUAL DEPICTION OF EXPECTANCY THEORY

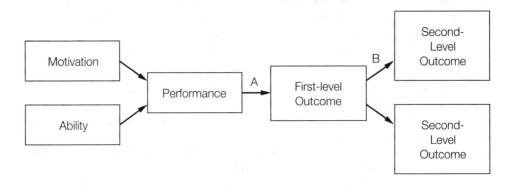

Not everyone would have the same list of second-order outcomes and not everyone would order them in the same manner.

There are a number of lessons that managers should obtain from expectancy theory. The first is that not all people are motivated by the same factors and not all motivating factors have the same level of influence. Thus, one person will be strongly motivated by a sense of personal accomplishment, whereas someone else might be more interested in the praise of his or her supervisor.

The second lesson for managers is that linkages between performance and first-level outcomes must be clear and attainable. It is very difficult to motivate someone to attain a high level of performance when the first-order outcome is virtually unattainable. Some people attribute the high rate of burnout of social service workers to the fact that they realize very quickly that whatever their level of performance, they will never be able to eliminate various social problems. Maybe people in this line of work need to focus on some more easily attainable first-order outcome.

The third lesson is that it is important to establish clear linkages between first- and second-level outcomes, or, put more simply, rewards are important. A person will be highly motivated to produce a first-level outcome (completing a report on time) if it is clearly tied to a desirable second-level outcome (improving the possibility of obtaining a promotion). However, if an organization makes it clear that promotions will be based on seniority, then it is very difficult to use promotion as a way to motivate someone to perform well. "Organizations usually get what they reward, not what they want."[47]

Expectancy theory is gaining a great deal of prominence in the literature on organizational behaviour. However, it also has its critics. It is admittedly a very complex theory to understand and apply. Managers feel more comfortable with the more straightforward theories of Maslow and Herzberg. Some people have suggested that workers are not as coldly rational or as conscious about their motivation as this theory suggests. Most of us have only vague ideas of what really

Figure 5.3
REAL-LIFE APPLICATION OF EXPECTANCY THEORY

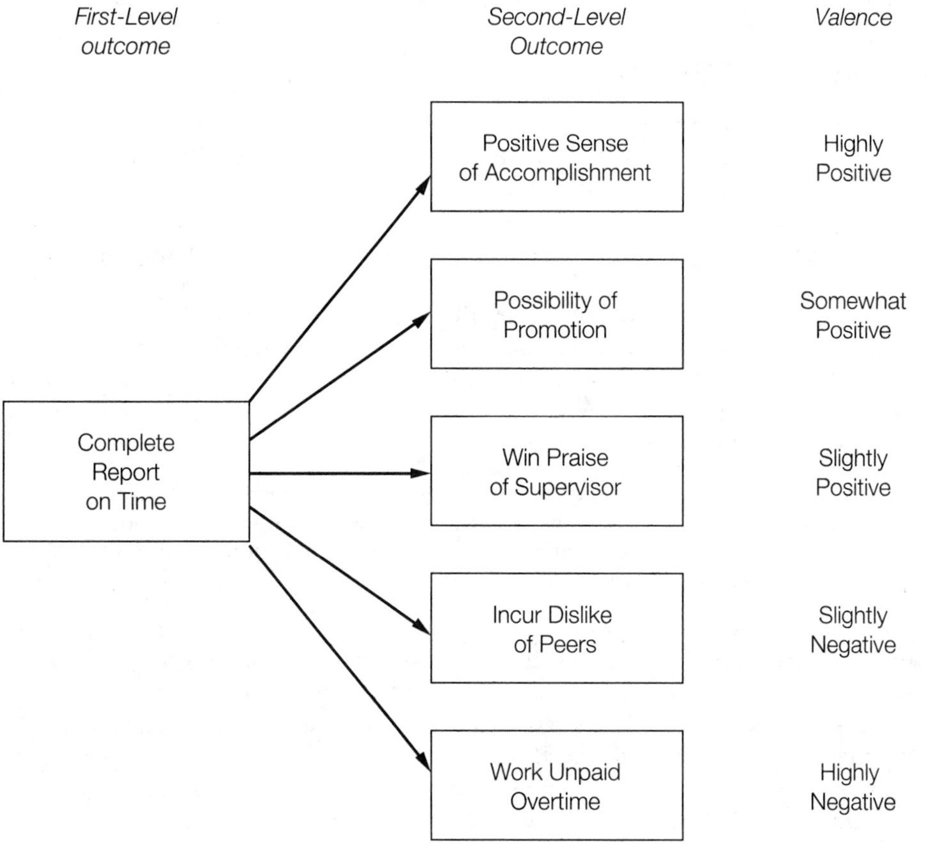

First-Level outcome	Second-Level Outcome	Valence
	Positive Sense of Accomplishment	Highly Positive
	Possibility of Promotion	Somewhat Positive
Complete Report on Time	Win Praise of Supervisor	Slightly Positive
	Incur Dislike of Peers	Slightly Negative
	Work Unpaid Overtime	Highly Negative

motivates us and some highly motivated people seem motivated to do things that are clearly detrimental to their own welfare (e.g., abuse drugs, go over Niagara Falls in a barrel.)

Expectancy theory also seems to pose an impossible task for managers. Is it really possible for a busy manager to understand the desired second-level outcomes of all employees and the valences that they attach to them? In many job situations, responding appropriately would be impossible anyway. The union would certainly frown on reducing someone's pay in exchange for greater praise from superiors, even if that is what the employee wanted.

However, expectancy theory principles cannot, and should not, be applied mechanistically. Maybe it is enough if expectancy theory reminds managers that people respond to different stimuli and that reward systems matter.

One important caveat about all of the theories discussed is that they have focussed predominantly on employee motivation. Their only concern with productivity is their implicit assumption that a well-motivated worker will be a more productive worker. While this line of reasoning seems attractive, it is important to remember that this can be a contentious point.

Quality of Working Life

In recent years, workers have become more vocal and more sophisticated in their complaints about their work environment. This has been reflected in such problems as more militant union actions, demands for higher pay and improved working conditions, and greater employee dissatisfaction evidenced through high absenteeism. Quality of working life (QWL) has come to signify a number of different specific programs all directed at "renovat[ing] working patterns and environments in order that there might be a better fit between what people *expected* from their jobs and what they actually *found* in their jobs."[48]

The purpose of QWL is to analyze the reasons for the discrepancy between employee expectations and actual conditions and prescribe what ought to be done to correct that discrepancy.

> QWL techniques or approaches cannot be purchased as one buys candy from a store, with thought given only to the sweetness of the commodity. The choice of the "candy" must be integrated with the needs of the organization's social and technical system. A "best fit" between the two must be sought.[49]

The innovations adopted as a result of a QWL undertaking could consist of anything from minor changes in job descriptions to major organizational development projects. Barry A. Stein provides a list of some of the possible changes: employee opinion surveys, all-employee meetings, management by objectives, open-door policies, flexible schedules, team-building, job enrichment, and self-managed work teams.[50]

However, the purpose of a good QWL exercise is not to "mollycoddle" employees and make their work easier. The intent of QWL is to improve both worker satisfaction and organizational productivity. As has been mentioned before, these two do not always occur together.

QWL is a way of effecting change so that employees will be better motivated. There are other management systems that also promise better motivation and organizational performance. This chapter will look at two of these.

Theory Z—Japanese Management

One of the great success stories of recent years has been the performance of the Japanese economy. Japanese companies are both envied and feared by their North American competitors. Japan is a country with virtually no natural resources, but its companies have shown an ability to enter almost any market and produce a very high quality product at a competitive price. This success is usually linked to the high productivity of the Japanese worker. This has produced an interest in Japanese management techniques to determine if any can be exported.[51] This section will discuss some of those techniques and some of the impediments to their use in Canada.

Lifetime employment. The large firms that employ approximately one-third of the labour force in Japan virtually guarantee lifetime employment to their management workforce. New employees are recruited once each year from that year's crop of university graduates. These people are not recruited to fill specific positions, but rather employers seek to hire a group of employees whose interests and temperament are compatible with the milieu of the firm. In some cases, there might not be a position available immediately for a new recruit, but this is not a concern because it is more important to hire good people for the long run than to fill specific positions in the short run.

After someone is hired, he (even today, Japanese firms tend not to hire women managers[52]) has a virtual guarantee that he will not be laid off or fired for anything short of a criminal offence. This is one of the things that creates the system of trust on which much of Japanese management is based. Ouchi points out a number of situations in which managers agree to do things that benefit the firm, but leave them very vulnerable personally.[53] Canadian managers would be loathe to put themselves in this position, but in the Japanese system managers trust that their sacrifices for the firm will be remembered and rewarded in the long run. After all, if you know that you will be spending the rest of your working life with a person, it would not do to take advantage in the short term.

The fact that a person has lifetime tenure with an organization does not eliminate any sort of incentive to perform. On the contrary, good performance is very important to attain promotions and to maintain credibility with your life-long peer group.

Non-specialized career paths. The new recruit embarks on an orientation program that involves rotation through a number of different units in the company. In a Japanese firm, no one spends an entire career specializing in one function; people are systematically rotated through a number of different functions. There is a cost to doing this; Japanese firms do not have people with a high degree of specialization in particular functions. What they have instead is an entire workforce that understands the total operation of the organization, the problems encountered in other organizational units, and is familiar with a great many of the people working in those units. This is another method to engender the trust mentioned above, as well as a concern for the total company rather than only one portion of it.

Slow evaluation and promotion. After the new employee is hired, he moves through a number of different assignments, usually with progressively more responsibility, but he will not receive a formal evaluation or a promotion until he has been with the firm approximately ten years. This focus on the long term has a number of consequences.

Everyone has heard stories of the dysfunctional corporate "game-playing" in Canadian companies—managers play tricks to make themselves look good in the short term and win a promotion. If evaluation is done only after ten years, there is simply no point to this kind of behaviour. Also, managers being evaluated over such a long term can take the risk of being innovative and experimenting with new ideas; they know that one project gone sour will not destroy a career.

The fact that a person does not receive a formal promotion does not mean that he is not given additional responsibilities. Canadians are sometimes confused in dealing with Japanese firms because titles—which are so important to Canadians—are frequently not commensurate with responsibility in Japanese firms. Promotions, once given, are seldom reversed. Therefore, aspiring senior managers are given great scope for decision-making while still at apparently junior levels, in order to test their abilities before they are given the title to go with the responsibility.

Large bonuses based on total company performance. As much as one-third of a Japanese manager's annual pay can come in the form of a bonus. The most significant aspect of the bonus is that all employees receive the same percentage, which is based on *total company performance* and not personal, or even divisional, performance. This is another example of an incentive system that encourages managers to place the performance of the overall company ahead of their own personal good.

Slow, collective decision-making. In Canadian companies, there is frequently a sense of individual responsibility for decisions. Managers take pride in saying: "The buck stops here." The Japanese system requires collective decision-making, but a form of collective decision making that goes far beyond the standard prescriptions of participative management discussed in the previous chapter. A small team is assigned to prepare a report; its members must consult widely in the organization. The decision finally made reflects the needs and interests of a broad cross-section of employees. The system works well in Japanese firms because all employees are socialized to have a greater concern for the overall good of the company than for their own unit.

Canadians dealing with Japanese companies are frequently frustrated at the slow pace at which this kind of decision-making proceeds. However, the slowness in decision-making can be more than offset in the speed of implementation because everyone understands the aims of the decision and is in agreement with it.

A *quality circle* consists of a small group of employees who meet on a *voluntary* basis to discuss work-related concerns. Because of the title, there is usually an incorrect assumption that quality circles are concerned with quality control. The group might discuss work factors that would improve quality control, but this is only one aspect of their concerns. Group discussions could involve "increasing output, improving work procedures, utilizing equipment better, and even improving product design. Quality circles also discuss ways to improve job satisfaction or morale."[54]

Can Theory Z Work In Canada?

Most of the reservations about the adoption of the Japanese management system in Canada revolve around the belief that it is culture-bound, i.e., it works in

Japan because of certain aspects of its culture that are not present elsewhere.[55] For a variety of reasons, Japanese society is considered to be characterized by a degree of trust between individuals and a concern for the collective good that does not seem to exist in other societies.[56] This is reflected in management techniques. The Japanese management system built on trust contrasts rather sharply with the Canadian one built on elaborate labour laws and collective agreements. Ouchi suggests that these obstacles can be overcome, but the distance to be traversed by labour and management is significant.

Certain aspects of the Japanese system might not sit well with other aspects of the Canadian value system. By Canadian standards, the Japanese system could be considered frankly exploitative. It works well for shareholders and, to a lesser extent, for—predominantly male—managers. It does not work so well for others. The fact that managers receive such a large portion of their incomes in the form of a bonus gives the company a nice cushion in difficult times. Bonuses are reduced so that managers, not shareholders, bear the risks. However, the male managers fare better than the female operating employees. The lifetime guarantee of security of employment applies only to managers; operating employees are laid-off and recalled very quickly in response to market demands.

The utility of quality circles in the North American context has also been questioned. The fact that they are based on Japanese systems of management means that they have the same cultural obstacles discussed above.[57] A review of the literature evaluating quality circles indicates that in many cases they have not improved the work environment.[58]

The Japanese system has worked very well—in Japan. There is also evidence that some of the best-managed American companies have adopted some of its ideas.[59] Canadians would be foolish not to examine it and consider the lessons it holds. However, it can be very difficult to adapt motivational techniques from other societies. It could well be that there are lessons to be learned from experiences closer to home.

In Search of Excellence

One of the most widely read books of the 1980s on management has been Thomas J. Peters and Robert H. Waterman, Jr.'s *In Search of Excellence*.[60] These two management consultants set out to determine the factors that created maximum organizational effectiveness. Their work considered far more than just motivation, but since many of their findings dealt with the relationship between the organization and its people, it is logical to discuss these findings in conjunction with employee motivation.

They conducted extensive research on forty-three excellent American companies in various industries. The companies were selected on the basis of their financial performance, their financial position in comparison to other companies in the same industry, and a subjective assessment of their innovativeness. The research indicated that these companies possessed eight factors that contributed to their excellence.

- *a bias for action*—continual small-scale experimentation is better than studying a problem to death;
- *close to the customer*—listen carefully to what customers are saying all the time, not just immediately before you are selling them something;
- *autonomy and entrepreneurship*—insulate creative people from the deadening effect of bureaucracy so that they can remain creative;
- *productivity through people*—trust your employees and treat them like they are competent human beings;
- *hands-on, value driven*—develop a company philosophy to help mould employees into a cohesive group;
- *stick to your knitting*—"Never buy a business you don't know how to run."[61]
- *simple form, lean staff*—complex management structures confuse people and divide their efforts;
- *simultaneous loose-tight properties*—give employees a great deal of operating autonomy as long as they do not violate certain strongly held central tenets of the organization.

Even though this research was done exclusively in the private sector, there are some lessons for public sector organizations. Admittedly, there are limits on the appropriate entrepreneurship of public administrators; initiating new programs is clearly the job of politicians. However, if administrators stayed closer to their clients [customers] they would probably have a much better understanding of problems in service delivery, and they would also be able to provide better policy advice to their political masters. The high concern for employees is fairly adaptable to public organizations, although the scope in public sector organizations for decentralization and "messiness" can be somewhat limited. Some of the lessons contained in *In Search of Excellence* are not relevant to the public sector, but many are.

THE CURRENT STATE OF COMMUNICATIONS, LEADERSHIP, AND MOTIVATION IN THE CANADIAN PUBLIC SERVICE

The general thrust of the theories of motivation discussed in this chapter is the need for better communications strategies and greater flexibility in leadership styles, organizational structures, and job design. There is substantial evidence that suggests that improved communications and more flexibility are highly conducive to achieving worker satisfaction, and there is weaker evidence that worker satisfaction is related to organizational effectiveness.

How do Canadian governments rate in terms of their use of the techniques mentioned in this chapter? The answer is mixed. Many governments are trying to improve communications and introduce the flexibility prescribed by most of the theories discussed in this chapter, but the obstacles facing them are great. This does not bode well for attempts at job redesign, situational approaches to leadership, or quality of working life projects.

There is little hard evidence on this point, but there is a general feeling that morale has declined in most public service organizations in the last few years.

One reason for this is the resource constraints that most of these organizations are facing, but the major reason is probably that public servants see the general public (including, in some cases, their political masters) engaging in an orgy of bureaucrat-bashing. At a time when public servants are being asked to do more with less, they are criticized for being excessively wasteful. At a time when public servants are being forced to cope with rapid changes, both within the public service and in the broader environment, they are criticized for being rigid and inflexible. At a time when public servants are being fired or laid-off, they are criticized for having cushy, permanent sinecures. These events have an obvious impact on morale.

John L. Manion, a long-time public servant and astute observer of the Ottawa scene, summed up the situation this way:

> [I]f our public services are *perceived* to be second-rate at home, unfortunately they will become second-rate. We cannot continue to maintain the quality of the public service if we cannot continue to attract the best young Canadians to our ranks. *They will not devote their lives to serving people who demean them.*[62]

Two academics from the University of Ottawa have done extensive surveys of senior managers in the federal government and compared their attitudes to senior managers in the private sector. At this time only the results of the 1986 study are available,[63] but they do not paint a very positive picture of communications, leadership, or employee satisfaction [64] in the federal public service. This book caused quite a stir in Ottawa when it was published because it clearly documented a malaise of which most people had been only dimly aware.

Their most significant finding is embodied in the title of their book—*The Vertical Solitude.* They found that there was no uniform organizational culture or organizational perspective that was widely held even among the senior managers within the service. By extension, if even the small cadre of senior managers do not possess a similar organizational view, then what hope is there for the large number of lower-level employees who receive their organizational culture through their senior managers?

It is impossible to do justice to Zussman and Jabes's excellent work in a short summary, but a few quotations capture some of their findings.
About communications:

> There appears to be a serious breakdown in the communication flow between the executive ranks and the managerial cadre in the federal public service. This breakdown suggests that it is unlikely that public servants working below the managerial level, and who are in constant contact with the public and client groups, will develop a valid understanding of the expectations of their ministers and the other people who set the tone and direction of their departments.[65]

About leadership:

> Comparing perceived leadership behaviour in the private and public sectors, we were struck by differences in perceived instances of leadership in the two sectors. . . With regard to DM/CEO leadership, more than 80 per cent of private sector respondents reported that their most senior officer demonstrated leadership to a great or

very great extent. The comparable figure for public sector managers was 51 per cent.[66]

About worker attitudes:

> We found, within the public service management cadre, divergent views among the five managerial levels with regard to almost all managerial practices. The differences were almost always dependent on where one worked in the management structure. This effect, which we have called "the vertical solitude", (sic) suggests that, as one moves down the bureaucratic hierarchy, managers are less satisfied and less positive about managerial practices in their organization. As a counterpoint, we did not find this effect to any significant degree in the private sector.

> The data also revealed that levels of work satisfaction among the [lower levels of senior management] . . . were substantially lower than those of their private sector counterparts and, in our opinion, were too low for managers occupying such pivotal positions in the organization.[67]

Given these negative findings, this comment that reflects on the morale of senior managers should not be surprising:

> Few managers in the private sector are contemplating career moves out of the private sector, whereas close to one-half of the most senior managers in the public service of Canada show a keen interest in working for the private sector.[68]

In fairness to governments, they face certain environmental constraints not present in the private sector. The most significant of these is the comparative openness of government. This openness makes governments hypersensitive about failure and gaps in their systems of control, since government failures are so public and are handled so brutally by the media. This sensitivity to failure influences many characteristics of government organization. It creates a bias for *inaction* and constant study; it gravitates against autonomy; it gravitates in favour of strong central control agencies. Because of government's basic concern about failure, there would be a great deal of difficulty in establishing in government organizations the characteristics that Peters and Waterman see as essential for excellence.

One should not conclude on a totally negative note. Whatever problems our public service might be experiencing now, it is widely recognized on the international scene that Canada has a very high-quality and professional public service. This is clear from the requests that come from other countries for Canada's advice on issues in public administration. It is also clear to any Canadian who participates in international public administration associations. There are some initiatives, such as Public Service 2000 (discussed later), which are system-wide attempts to show greater concern for motivation of employees. There are also many bright spots in government departments where individual managers have realized the importance of improving the system. It will be interesting to see how these initiatives fare in the face of a very long history of inflexibility.

NOTES

1. Robert D. Pursley and Neil Snortland, *Managing Government Organizations: An Introduction to Public Administration* (North Scituate, Mass.: Duxbury Press, 1980), p. 218.
2. Eugene Walton, "How Efficient Is the Grapevine?" *Personnel* 38 (March-April 1961): 45.
3. *The Best and the Brightest* (Greenwich, Conn.: Fawcett, 1973), p. 771.
4. Tom Peters and Nancy Austin, *A Passion for Excellence: The Leadership Difference* (New York: Random House, 1985), ch. 2 and passim.
5. Ibid, pp. 228-29.
6. Felix A. Nigro, *Modern Public Administration* (New York: Harper & Row, 1965), p. 197.
7. *General and Industrial Management,* Constance Storrs, trans., (London: Pitman, 1971), pp. 35-36.
8. *Implementation in a Bureaucracy* (Oxford: Martin Robertson, 1978), p. 176.
9. Daniel Katz and Robert L. Kahn, *The Social Psychology of Organizations,* 2nd. ed. (New York: John Wiley & Sons, 1978), p. 528.
10. *Managing Government Organizations*, p. 186.
11. Ralph M. Stogdill, *Handbook of Leadership: A Survey of Theory and Research* (New York: The Free Press, 1974), ch. 2.
12. Ibid., ch. 5.
13. Dorwin Cartwright and Alvin Zander, "Leadership and Performance of Group Functions: Introduction," in Dorwin Cartwright and Alvin Zander, eds., *Group Dynamics: Research and Theory,* 3rd ed. (New York: Harper & Row, 1968), p. 303; Gary A. Yukl, *Leadership In Organizations,* 2nd. ed. (Englewood Cliffs, N.J.: Prentice-Hall, 1989), p. 202.
14. Stogdill, *Handbook of Leadership,* p. 81.
15. Richard A. Boyatzis, *The Competent Manager: A Model for Effective Performance* (New York: John Wiley & Sons, 1982), p. 229.
16. Robert L. Katz, "Skills of an Effective Administrator," *Harvard Business Review* 33 (January-February 1955): 34.
17. Ibid. (Emphasis in original.)
18. Ibid., 35-36.
19. James R. Huck, "Assessment Centres: A Review of the External and Internal Validities," *Personnel Psychology* 26 (Summer 1973): 191-212.
20. These depictions of the styles come from one of the earliest studies: Ronald Lippitt and Ralph K. White, "The 'Social Climate' of Children's Groups," in Robert G. Barker, Jacob S. Kounin, and Herbert F. Wright, eds., *Child Behavior and Development: A Course of Representative Study* (New York: McGraw-Hill, 1943), pp. 485-508. See also the more widely cited Ralph K. White and Ronald Lippitt, *Autocracy and Democracy* (Westport, Conn.: Greenwood Press, 1972), pp. 26-27.
21. *Handbook of Leadership,* ch. 32.
22. A good review of these different approaches is contained in J. D. Williams, *Public Administration: The People's Business* (Boston: Little, Brown and Company, 1980), pp. 147-48; Richard H. Hall, *Organizations: Structure and Process,* 3rd ed. (Englewood Cliffs, N. J.: Prentice-Hall, 1982), pp. 163-66; Alan C. Filley and Robert J. House, *Managerial Process and Organizational Behavior* (Glenview, Ill.: Scott, Foresman and Company, 1969), pp. 401-405. Some of the specific studies that support this view are Fred E. Fiedler, "Personality and Situational Determinants of Leadership Effectiveness," in Cartwright and Zander, eds., *Group Dynamics,* 3rd ed. (New York: Harper &

Row, 1968): 362-80; and Kurt Lewin, Ronald Lippitt, and Ralph K. White, "Patterns of Aggressive Behaviour in Experimentally Created 'Social Climates,'" *Journal of Social Psychology* 10 (1939): 273.

23. A good review of the best-known theories is found in Yukl, *Leadership in Organizations*, ch. 6.

24. The Vroom-Yetton model has been criticized and extended by Vroom and Arthur G. Jago. This model will not be discussed here because it is even more complex than Vroom and Yetton's original work and the recent publication of the Vroom-Jago work means that it has not yet been subjected to serious review. *The New Leadership: Managing Participation in Organizations* (Englewood Cliffs, N.J.: Prentice-Hall, 1988).

25. Victor H. Vroom and Philip W. Yetton, *Leadership and Decision-Making* (University of Pittsburgh Press, 1973), p. 13.

26. Ibid. (Emphasis in original.)

27. Ibid.

28. Ibid., pp. 21-31.

29. Leonard R. Sayles and George Strauss, *Managing Human Resources* (Englewood Cliffs, N.J.: Prentice-Hall, 1977), p. 132.

30. *Personality and Organization: The Conflict Between System and the Individual* (New York: Harper & Row, 1957), pp. 50-51.

31. Ibid., ch. 3.

32. Ibid., p. 66.

33. Ibid., ch. 4.

34. *Integrating the Individual and the Organization* (New York: John Wiley & Sons, 1964).

35. Ibid., p. 275.

36. *The Organizational Society*, rev. ed. (New York: St. Martin's Press, 1978).

37. Henry Mintzberg, *Structure in Fives: Designing Effective Organizations* (Englewood Cliffs, N.J.: Prentice-Hall, 1983), pp. 178-79.

38. The results of this research were reported in detail in Frederick Herzberg, Bernard Mausner, and Barbara Bloch Snyderman, *The Motivation to Work* (New York: John Wiley & Sons, 1959). A more elaborate discussion and further verification of the theory is contained in Frederick Herzberg, *Work and the Nature of Man* (Cleveland: The World Publishing Company, 1966).

39. Herzberg et al., *The Motivation to Work*, p. 113.

40. J. Richard Hackman and Greg R. Oldham, *Work Redesign* (Reading, Mass.: Addison-Wesley, 1980), ch. 2.

41. Ibid., p. 71.

42. Roy W. Walters, "Job Enrichment Isn't Easy," *Personnel Administration Review* (September-October 1972).

43. Frederick Herzberg, "One More Time: How Do You Motivate Employees?" *Harvard Business Review* 46 (January-February 1968): 59-62.

44. (New York: John Wiley & Sons, 1964).

45. David A. Nadler and Edward E. Lawler, III, "Motivation: A Diagnostic Approach," in Patrick E. Connor, ed., *Organizations: Theory and Design* (Chicago: Science Research Associates, 1980), pp. 212-13.

46. James L. Gibson, John M. Ivancevich, and James H. Donnelly, Jr., *Organizations: Behavior, Structure, Processes* (Plano, Tex.: Business Publications, 1985), p. 155.

47. Nadler and Lawler, "Motivation: A Diagnostic Approach," p. 216.

48. "Introduction," in J.B. Cunningham and T.H. White, eds., *Quality of Working Life: Contemporary Cases* (Ottawa: Minister of Supply and Services Canada, 1984), p. 2. (Emphasis in original.)

49. Eric Trist, "Preface," in ibid., p. x.
50. *Quality of Work Life In Action: Managing for Effectiveness* (New York: American Management Associations, 1983), pp. 32-34.
51. Most of the following commentary is derived from one of the most prolific writers on Theory Z: William G. Ouchi, *Theory Z: How American Business Can Meet the Japanese Challenge* (New York: Avon Books, 1981).
52. Ibid., p. 21.
53. Ibid., pp. 5, 16-17, 40.
54. Jan P. Muczyk, Eleanor Brantley Schwartz, and Ephraim Smith, *Principles of Supervision: First- and Second-Line Management* (Columbus, Ohio: Charles E. Merrill, 1984), p. 206. See also Richard J. Schonberger, *Japanese Manufacturing Techniques* (New York: The Free Press, 1982), ch. 8; Edward E. Lawler, III, *High-Involvement Management* (San Francisco: Jossey-Bass, 1986).
55. Sandford F. Borins, "Management of the Public Sector in Japan," *Canadian Public Administration* 29, no. 2 (Summer 1986): 175-96; Ouchi, *Theory Z*, pp. 54-57.
56. S. Prakash Sethi, Nobuaki Namiki, and Carl L. Swanson, *The False Promise of the Japanese Miracle* (Boston: Pitman, 1984).
57. Gerald R. Ferris and John A. Wagner, III, "Quality Circles in the United States: A Conceptual Reevaluation," *The Journal of Applied Behavioral Science* 21, no. 2 (1985): 155-67.
58. Robert P. Steel and Gary S. Shane, "Evaluation Research on Quality Circles: Technical and Analytical Implications," *Human Relations* 39, no. 5 (1986): 449-68.
59. Ouchi, *Theory Z*, pp. 57-59.
60. (New York: Warner Books, 1982).
61. Ibid., p. 15.
62. "New Challenges in Public Administration," *Canadian Public Administration* 31, no. 2 (Summer 1988): 237. (Emphasis in last sentence added.)
63. David Zussman and Jak Jabes, *The Vertical Solitude: Managing in the Public Sector* (Halifax: The Institute for Research on Public Policy, 1989).
64. Zussman and Jabes were measuring "employee satisfaction" rather than motivation. The concepts are not identical, although they are closely related.
65. Ibid., p. 3.
66. Ibid., pp. 62-63.
67. Ibid., p. 196.
68. Ibid., p. 128.

BIBLIOGRAPHY

Argyris, Chris. *Integrating the Individual and the Organization.* New York: John Wiley & Sons, 1964.

――. *Personality and Organization: The Conflict Between System and the Individual.* New York: Harper & Row, 1957.

Argyris, Chris, with Roger Harrison. *Interpersonal Competence and Organizational Effectiveness.* Homewood, Ill.: Richard D. Irwin, 1962.

Blau, Peter M., and W. Richard Scott. *Formal Organizations: A Comparative Approach.* San Francisco: Chandler, 1962.

Borins, Sandford F. "Management of the Public Sector in Japan." *Canadian Public Administration* 29, no. 2 (Summer 1986): 175-96.

Boyatzis, Richard A. *The Competent Manager: A Model for Effective Performance.* New York: John Wiley & Sons, 1982.

Cartwright, Dorwin, and Alvin Zander, eds. *Group Dynamics: Research and Theory.* 3rd ed. New York: Harper & Row, 1968.

Cunningham, J. B., and T. H. White, eds. *Quality of Working Life: Contemporary Cases.* Ottawa: Minister of Supply and Services Canada, 1984.

Dubin, Robert, George C. Homans, Floyd C. Mann, and Delbert C. Miller. *Leadership and Productivity.* San Francisco: Chandler, 1965.

Dunsire, Andrew. *Implementation in a Bureaucracy.* Oxford: Martin Robertson, 1978.

Fayol, Henri. *General and Industrial Management.* Translated from the French by Constance Storrs. London: Pitman, 1971.

Ferris, Gerald R., and John A. Wagner, III. "Quality Circles in the United States: A Conceptual Reevaluation." *The Journal of Applied Behavioral Science* 21, no. 2 (1985): 155-167.

Fiedler, Fred A. *A Theory of Leadership Effectiveness.* New York: McGraw-Hill, 1967.

Fiedler, Fred A., Martin M. Chemers, with Linda Mahar. *Improving Leadership Effectiveness: The Leader Match Concept.* Rev. ed. New York: John Wiley & Sons, 1977.

Filley, Alan C., and Robert J. House. *Managerial Process and Organizational Behavior.* Glenview, Ill.: Scott, Foresman, 1969.

Gibson, James L., John M. Ivancevich, and James H. Donnelly, Jr. *Organizations: Behavior, Structure, Processes.* Plano, Tex.: Business Publications, 1985.

Hackman, J. Richard, and Greg R. Oldham. *Work Redesign.* Reading, Mass.: Addison-Wesley, 1980.

Hall, Richard H. *Organizations: Structure and Process.* 3rd ed. Englewood Cliffs, N. J.: Prentice-Hall, 1982.

Heffron, Florence. *Organization Theory and Public Organizations: The Political Connection.* Englewood Cliffs, N.J.: Prentice-Hall, 1989.

Hersey, Paul, and Kenneth H. Blanchard. *Management of Organizational Behavior: Utilizing Human Resources.* 3rd ed. Englewood Cliffs, N. J.: Prentice-Hall, 1977.

Herzberg, Frederick. "One More Time: How Do You Motivate Employees?" *Harvard Business Review* 46 (January-February 1968): 53-62.

——. *Work and the Nature of Man.* Cleveland: The World Publishing Company, 1966.

Herzberg, Frederick, Bernard Mausner, and Barbara Bloch Snyderman. *The Motivation to Work.* New York: John Wiley & Sons, 1959.

Huck, James R. "Assessment Centres: A Review of the External and Internal Validities." *Personnel Psychology* 26 (Summer 1973): 191-212.

Johnston, Carl P., Mark Alexander, and Jacquelin Robin. *Quality of Working Life: The Idea and its Application.* Ottawa: Minister of Supply and Services Canada, 1980.

Katz, Robert L. "Skills of an Effective Administrator." *Harvard Business Review* 33 (January-February 1955): 33-42.

Katz, Daniel, and Robert L. Kahn. *The Social Psychology of Organizations.* 2nd ed. New York: John Wiley & Sons, 1978.

Lewin, Kurt, Ronald Lippitt, and Ralph K. White. "Patterns of Aggressive Behavior in Experimentally Created Social Climates." *Journal of Social Psychology* 10 (1939): 271-99.

Likert, Rensis. *The Human Organization.* New York: McGraw-Hill, 1967.

——. *New Patterns of Management.* New York: McGraw-Hill, 1961.

Lippitt, Ronald, and Ralph K. White. "The 'Social Climate' of Children's Groups." In Robert G. Barker, Jacob S. Kounin, and Herbert F. Wright, eds., *Child Behavior and Development: A Course of Representative Study.* New York: McGraw Hill, 1943, pp. 485-508.

Manion, John L. "New Challenges in Public Administration," *Canadian Public Administration* 31, no. 2 (Summer 1988): 234-46.

Mintzberg, Henry. *Structure in Fives: Designing Effective Organizations.* Englewood Cliffs, N.J.: Prentice-Hall, 1983.

Muczyk, Jan P., Eleanor Brantley Schwartz, and Ephraim Smith. *Principles of Supervision: First- and Second-Line Management.* Columbus, Ohio: Charles E. Merrill, 1984.

Nadler, David A., and Edward E. Lawler, III. "Motivation: A Diagnostic Approach." In Patrick E. Connor, ed., *Organizations: Theory and Design.* Chicago: Science Research Associates, Inc., 1980, pp. 212-18.

Nigro, Felix A. *Modern Public Administration.* New York: Harper & Row, 1965.

Ondrak, D. A., and M. G. Evans. *Quality of Working Life: Evaluation and Measurement.* Ottawa: Minister of Supply and Services Canada, 1981.

Ouchi, William G. *Theory Z: How American Business Can Meet the Japanese Challenge.* New York: Avon Books, 1981.

Peters, Thomas, and Robert H. Waverman, Jr. *In Search of Excellence.* New York: Warner Books, 1982.

Peters, Tom, and Nancy Austin. *A Passion for Excellence: The Leadership Difference.* New York: Random House, 1985.

Presthus, Robert. *The Organizational Society.* Rev. ed. New York: St. Martin's Press, 1978.

Pursley, Robert D., and Neil Snortland. *Managing Government Organizations: An Introduction to Public Administration.* North Scituate, Mass.: Duxbury Press, 1980.

Quality of Working Life: The Canadian Scene. (A periodical published by the federal Department of Labour from 1978 to 1986.)

Sayles, Leonard R., and George Strauss. *Managing Human Resources.* Englewood Cliffs, N.J.: Prentice-Hall, 1977.

Schonberger, Richard J. *Japanese Manufacturing Techniques.* New York: The Free Press, 1982.

Scott, William G., Terence R. Mitchell, and Philip H. Birnbarum. *Organization Theory: A Structural and Behavioral Analysis.* 4th ed. Homewood, Ill.: Richard D. Irwin, 1981.

Sethi, S. Prakash, Nobuaki Namiki, and Carl L. Swanson. *The False Promise of the Japanese Miracle.* Boston: Pitman, 1984.

Steel, Robert P., and Gary S. Shane. "Evaluation Research on Quality Circles: Technical and Analytical Implications." *Human Relations* 39, no. 5 (1986): 449-68.

Stein, Barry A. *Quality of Work Life In Action: Managing for Effectiveness.* New York: American Management Association, 1983.

Stogdill, Ralph M. *Handbook of Leadership: A Survey of Theory and Research.* New York: The Free Press, 1974.

Tannenbaum, Robert T., and Warren H. Schmidt. "How to Choose A Leadership Style." *Harvard Business Review* 36 (March-April, 1958): 95-101.

Vroom, Victor H., and Arthur G. Jago. *The New Leadership: Managing Participation in Organizations.* Englewood Cliffs, N.J.: Prentice-Hall, 1988.

Vroom, Victor H., and Philip W. Yetton. *Leadership and Decision-Making.* Pittsburgh: University of Pittsburgh Press, 1973.

Walters, Roy W. "Job Enrichment Isn't Easy." *Personnel Administration Review* (September-October 1972): 61-66.

Walton, Eugene. "How Efficient Is the Grapevine?" *Personnel* 38 (March-April 1961): 45-49.

White, Ralph K., and Ronald Lippitt. *Autocracy and Democracy.* Westport, Conn.: Greenwood Press, 1972.

Williams, J.D. *Public Administration: The People's Business.* Boston: Little, Brown and Company, 1980.

Yukl, Gary A. *Leadership In Organizations.* 2nd ed. (Englewood Cliffs, N. J.: Prentice-Hall, 1989.

Zussman, David, and Jak Jabes. *The Vertical Solitude: Managing in the Public Sector.* Halifax: The Institute for Research on Public Policy, 1989.

CASES

In *Case Program in Canadian Public Administration* (Toronto: Institute of Public Administration of Canada):

  The Administrative In-Basket Case. By C. Lloyd Brown-John
  The Police Chief's In-Basket. By R. H. McLaren
  Trying to Fire the Medical Officer of Health: A Case Study. By Alison McGear, Ted Darby, and Raisa B. Deber

Cases developed by the Canadian Centre for Management Development and distributed by the Case Program in Canadian Public Administration:

  Pressures on the President. By John William Pullen
  The Chairman's Challenge. By John William Pullen

II

THE POLICY DIMENSION OF PUBLIC ADMINISTRATION

6

Making Public Policy

Part I of this book discussed some of the theories of organizing and motivating employees. These theories are not ends in themselves; rather they assist in the making and implementing of public policy, which is the real core of government activity.

This Part of the book will examine the entire policy cycle. This chapter will examine a number of theories about how government policies are made, and will also discuss an important instrument of policy-making—coloured papers. Chapter 7 will discuss two relatively new areas of study in public administration— policy implementation and policy evaluation.

In the past, the area of policy implementation was given very little attention because there seemed to be an assumption that once policy was articulated, implementation was automatic, with little friction or tension. In the last decade, there has been a growing awareness that the relationship between making and implementing policy is not always so smooth. There has also been greater concern in recent years about the systematic evaluation of public policy. Has the policy had the desired effect? Has it been worth the resources that have been spent to implement it? Policy evaluation attempts to answer these questions.

Figure 6.1 illustrates one view of the total policy cycle. The first step is policy formulation. The Cabinet and the legislature are dominant in this part of the process, but the public service also has an important advisory role. The next step is implementation. In this part of the process, the public service has the dominant role, but Cabinet and the legislature have an important oversight role. The final step is evaluating the ultimate worth of the policy. This evaluation can be formal, employing sophisticated social science techniques, or it can be as informal as legislators responding to complaints of citizens.

Figure 6.1 conveys the impression that these three steps are totally separate and discrete processes. Figure 6.2 conveys a more realistic impression of the policy cycle as a dynamic process with a considerable degree of overlap between the three stages in the process. As will be discussed in this and the following chapter, implementation frequently begins before policies are firmly established, and evaluation frequently leads to changes in policies. In practice, policies are seldom finally set or carved in stone. Policies are always being revised. Most policies are subject to extensive revisions every few years as a result of major studies or initiatives, and to minor fine-tuning more frequently.

Figure 6.1
SIMPLIFIED VERSION OF THE POLICY PROCESS

Figure 6.2
THE POLICY PROCESS IN ACTION

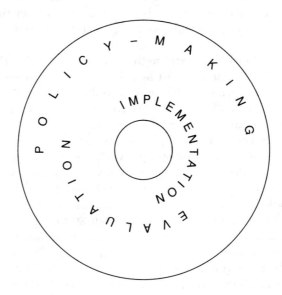

WHAT IS PUBLIC POLICY?

There are a number of definitions of the phrase **public policy**. This book will use Thomas R. Dye's simple, yet effective, definition that "[p]ublic policy is whatever governments choose to do or not do."[1] He explains that

> [g]overnments do many things. They regulate conflict within society; they organize society to carry on conflict with other societies; they distribute a great variety of symbolic rewards and material services to members of the society; and they extract money from society, most often in the form of taxes. Thus, public policies may regulate behavior, organize bureaucracies, distribute benefits, or extract taxes—or all of these things at once. . .
>
> Public policies may deal with a wide variety of substantive areas—defense, energy, environment, foreign affairs, education, welfare, police, highways, taxation, housing, social security, health, economic opportunity, urban development, inflation and

recession, and so on. They may range from the vital to the trivial—from the allocation of tens of billions of dollars for a mobile missile system to the designation of an official national bird.[2]

Several aspects of this definition are important. First, unlike other definitions of public policy, there is no discussion of "goals" or "objectives." Policies are specific courses of action; the adoption of a policy does not imply that all those who agree on a specific policy share the same goals. In fact, some policies come about not because of an agreement on goals, but because several groups all favour a particular policy, although for totally different reasons. This phenomenon will be discussed in more detail later.

Second, Dye's definition recognizes that policies are reflected in choosing *not* to act, as well as in choosing to act. These "non-decisions" can be as important as decisions, especially for groups attempting to effect change.

This definition also suggests that a policy can be either *a specific action* by a government (e.g., the decision by a municipality to allow development in a particular area), or *the result of a series of diverse decisions* (e.g., health care policy, which is really the combination of a large number of decisions—and non-decisions—by many governments).

The other point about public policy that will be emphasized in this book is that policy is not merely a *statement* by a government about some problem; rather policy is what is actually *implemented*. Thus, Dye's definition refers to what governments "do," not what they say they want to do or plan to do. Peter Aucoin takes this into account in his definition of public policy. "Public policy must be considered to encompass the actual activities undertaken by a government, whether or not a government's objectives and strategies are explicit, or are congruent with its activities."[3] As will be explained in Chapter 7, there can be significant slippage between policy statements and actual policy, and then further slippage between policy as adopted and policy as implemented.

Political scientists and other students of public policy have developed several models of how public policies are made. These models are ways of describing how policy-makers, such as Cabinet ministers and legislators, think about public policy and interact in the policy-making process. However, policy-makers usually do not consciously think about these models when they are making policy; the models have been developed by academics and others who analyze policy decisions after they have been made.

Models of public policy can be divided into normative and descriptive models. *Normative* models prescribe how decisions *should* be made. Thus, a normative model is an ideal model of how a particular theorist feels that the policy process *ought* to work. *Descriptive* models attempt to explain how decisions *are* made in practice. The formulation of a descriptive model involves the study of how a number of policies have been made and some generalization about how the system works. As discussed below, some models purport to be both normative and descriptive.

This section will consider different models of the policy-making process; most of the major models will be reviewed, but this is not meant to be comprehensive.

COMPREHENSIVE RATIONALITY

The **comprehensive rationality** model suggests that policies are subjected to a multi-step analysis before a decision is made. Different writers list slightly different steps, but Anderson's list is typical:

1. The decision-maker is confronted with a given problem that can be separated from other problems or at least considered meaningfully in comparison with them.
2. The goals, values, or objectives that guide the decision-maker are clarified and ranked according to their importance.
3. The various alternatives for dealing with the problem are examined.
4. The consequences (costs and benefits, advantages and disadvantages) that would follow from the selection of each alternative are investigated.
5. Each alternative, and its attendant consequences, can be compared with the other alternatives.
6. The decision-maker will choose that alternative, and its consequences, that maximizes the attainment of his or her goals, values, or objectives.[4]

The attractions of this style of decision-making are obvious. It has an aura of careful forethought and scientific precision that contrasts with some of the more rudderless models of policy-making that will be discussed below. Some of the techniques used in rational decision-making are operations research, cost-effectiveness analysis, and cost-benefit analysis. Because comprehensive rationality involves careful analysis, it ought to provide a solution that produces the desired result with the most efficient use of resources.

However, there are many criticisms of this model. Most of them flow from the second step identified above—clarification and ranking of goals. In democratic, pluralistic societies, it is very difficult to rank "goals, values, or objectives" in order of priority. The question becomes whose goals and whose values will be reflected in the final decision. The best technical analysis available is useless if there is no agreement on this point, and there seldom is. Dunn points out this problem by suggesting that there are at least five different types of "rationality," which are frequently in conflict with one another.[5]

Even if there were agreement on goals, the requirement for *comprehensive* analysis would introduce severe complications. The model requires that the decision-maker find and compare *all* potential solutions. At what point can the decision-maker be confident that he or she has actually identified *all* possible solutions? And how far must one go in identifying all consequences (desirable and undesirable) of a decision? Because of these problems, comprehensive rationality is sometimes dismissed as "paralysis by analysis."

Given these difficulties, it is not surprising that the concept of comprehensive rationality is not applied very often in practice.

With the possible exception of those few instances when there is the appearance of a full-scale review and analysis of policy alternatives, the empirical investigation of the making of a public policy usually tends to illustrate how logical procedures were overrun by a dominant political leader, a pressure group of some sort, or perhaps an influential section of the bureaucracy.[6]

It is difficult to think of examples of public policy decisions made in a purely rational manner, although most decisions are subjected to some limited form of rational analysis at some stage in the decision-making process. For example, in government purchasing decisions, the many alternatives available are frequently reduced to a smaller number on a fairly rational basis, e.g., minimum cost, security of supply, but "non-rational" elements such as the number of jobs provided in particular areas of the country, frequently intrude on the final decision.

INCREMENTALISM

Charles E. Lindblom argued not only that comprehensive rationality is impossible, but also that policies are seldom changed radically as a result of extensive reviews.[7] In effect, he suggested that comprehensive rationality failed as both a normative and a descriptive model. Instead, he argued that policies are changed incrementally as a result of "successive limited comparisons" between the status quo and some very close alternatives. If some improvement on the status quo is desired, policy-makers do not really search far and wide for the best possible alternative. Instead, they usually find some marginal improvement that makes the policy more acceptable to those affected by it.

Lindblom further argued that this "successive limited comparisons" approach, or **incrementalism**, was not only an accurate descriptive model, but also a normatively desirable one. He pointed out that comprehensive rationality tends to ignore the fact that new policies must be accepted by existing organizations and clientele groups. It might well be true that some radically different policy would be ideal if there were no ingrained ideological or institutional biases. However, these biases invariably exist. If a new policy recommendation is not acceptable to established players, then it will be very difficult to implement.

This is one of the reasons why Lindblom argues that the best test of the worth of a policy is its acceptance by most relevant actors, and not its rigid conformity to some preset objectives. It is difficult enough to implement policies when all are in agreement; if there is no consensus, then the problems are magnified greatly.

Incrementalism also recognizes that policy-making is an ongoing process.[8] When a particular decision is made it will not be carved in stone to remain unchanged for the next hundred years. On the contrary, the policy-making process proceeds slowly by successive small iterations. If a particular marginal adjustment does not seem to move the policy in the desired direction, then a different change is made.

The incremental model also has its critics. Etzioni has expressed the fear that incrementalism goes too far in buttressing the established order.[9] If the status quo is satisfactory, then there is no point in searching widely for improvements. However, if the status quo is not acceptable to major groups in society, then incrementalism is a less suitable guide to action. It assigns too great a role to established and powerful interest groups and does not recognize the need to protect those who are unorganized.

Incrementalism does not lend itself very well to some kinds of "all or nothing" decisions. If a society favours a system of state-run unemployment insurance, then incrementalism provides a mechanism to determine such details of the plan as conditions for eligibility, amounts of payment, and so forth. Incrementalism does not work very well on such "all or nothing" decisions as going to war, capital punishment, or abortion. Moreover, incrementalism does not work very well in dealing with new problems. For example, it does not help very much in dealing with new scientific breakthroughs such as genetic engineering or *in vitro* fertilization.

In practice, incrementalism explains some kinds of decisions better than others. Lindblom is right that *most* decisions are simply minor variations from previous decisions, but some *very important* decisions are not. It would be rather difficult to argue that the establishment of the Canada and Quebec Pension Plans or the founding of the Canadian Radio Broadcasting Commission and Trans-Canada Airlines were incremental decisions. It is true that only a *small* number of decisions fit in this category, but they are almost all very important decisions.

Yehezkel Dror is concerned about incrementalism because it provides a rationale for the inertia and lack of innovation that are too frequently found in large organizations. He argues that incrementalism acts

> as an ideological reinforcement of the pro-inertia and anti-innovation forces preva-
> lent in all human organizations, administrative and policy making. The actual
> tendency of most organizations is to limit the search for alternatives to the mini-
> mum; there is little danger in real life, then, that administration will become bogged
> down in exhaustive search for all alternatives and full enumeration of consequences,
> in order to achieve "rational-comprehensive" policy making. The "rational-com-
> prehensive" model has at least the advantage of stimulating administrators to get a
> little outside their regular routine, while Lindblom's model justifies a policy of "no
> effort."[10]

Given the various shortcomings identified in both the rational comprehensive and incremental approaches, it is not surprising that a number of attempts have been made to synthesize certain elements of the two into a better model.

BOUNDED RATIONALITY AND SATISFICING

Herbert Simon argued that, in practice, people do not really spend huge amounts of time searching for the *ideal* solution to a problem, and, that even if they did, their attempts at rationality would fail because of the complexity of the problem.

> It is impossible for the behavior of a single, isolated individual to reach any high degree of rationality. The number of alternatives he must explore is so great, the information he would need to evaluate them so vast that even an approximation to objective rationality is hard to conceive. Individual choice takes place in an environment of "givens"—premises that are accepted by the subject as bases for his choice; and behavior is adaptive only within the limits set by these "givens."[11]

The presence of these "givens" and the innate limitations on human abilities provide boundaries that define the search for alternatives. In the real world, when people determine that the status quo is no longer working, they begin their search for alternatives by starting with solutions that are very similar to the *status quo* and gradually move further and further away, searching only until they find a *satisfactory*, not an ideal, solution. Simon coined the term "satisficing" to describe this type of behaviour.

> *Most human decision-making, whether individual or organizational, is concerned with the discovery and selection of satisfactory alternatives; only in exceptional cases is it concerned with the discovery and selection of optimal alternatives. . .* To optimize requires processes several orders of magnitude more complex than those required to satisfice. An example is the difference between searching a haystack to find the sharpest needle in it and searching the haystack to find a needle sharp enough to sew with.[12]

Bounded rationality or optimal policy-making uses the *process* identified with comprehensive rationality, but instead of searching for *all* possible alternatives, it searches for alternatives only within some limited range.[13] Also, it does not seek the *best* possible policy, but rather searches for an *optimal* policy. For example, when a politician says: "We must find a better solution to this problem, but we can't afford to increase our expenditure on it," that is a request for bounded rationality. Alternatively, the boundary could be a structural one in that a desire to improve the delivery of a service would be "bounded" by a need to retain the basic structure of the organization currently delivering the service.

Bounded rationality is obviously considerably easier to accomplish than comprehensive rationality, and it does not simply give up any hope of furthering rationality as do some of the models to be discussed below. However, it does require the difficult and stressful agreement on goals and objectives mentioned as a problem with comprehensive rationality.

MIXED SCANNING

Amitai Etzioni has developed a different way of combining rationality and incrementalism. He argues that governments really make two different kinds of decisions—fundamental and incremental. Fundamental (or "contextuating") decisions are radical changes in policy, while incremental decisions are used either to pave the way for fundamental decisions or to fine-tune fundamental decisions after some of their consequences have been identified.

> Fundamental decisions are made by exploring the main alternatives the actor sees in view of his conception of his goals, but—unlike what rationalism would indicate—details and specifications are omitted so that an overview is feasible. Incremental decisions are made but within the contexts set by fundamental decisions (and fundamental reviews). Thus, each of the two elements in mixed-scanning helps to reduce the effects of the particular shortcomings of the other; incrementalism reduces the unrealistic aspects of rationalism by limiting the details required in fundamental decisions, and contextuating rationalism helps to overcome the conservative slant of incrementalism by exploring longer-run alternatives.[14]

Etzioni cites the history of the U.S. space program as an example of how this system operates.[15] First, the Congress made a *fundamental* decision to embark on a space program. Over the years, it has made a number of related *incremental* decisions to provide more or less funding, to proceed rapidly with some parts of the program, and to scrap other parts. This illustrates the interaction between fundamental and incremental decisions.

The framework of incremental and rational decisions and the many models in between are still used quite extensively, but there are some newer models of policy-making that do not rely so heavily on these concepts.

PUBLIC CHOICE

Public choice is one of the newest models of public policy-making and for this reason it seems to mean different things to different writers. The basic element of public choice is the application of economic styles of thinking to the analysis of political behaviour. "Public choice can be defined as the economic study of nonmarket decision-making, or simply the application of economics to political science."[16] Public choice uses the concept of the market except that, instead of seeing a market for tangible goods and services, public choice theorists think in terms of a market for votes and for specific public policies.[17]

In the public choice model, the basic building-block of political action is the self-interested, utility-maximizing individual. The aim of the public choice model is "to explain collective decisions (about what are often thought to be political matters) in terms of the self-seeking behaviour of rational individuals."[18] The desire to maximize income, security, or, more generally, utility is the motivating force behind all actions—including voting. "Each citizen . . . votes for the party he believes will provide him with a higher utility income than any other party during the coming election period."[19]

Of course, citizens can participate in the political process in ways other than voting. Breton suggests that individuals will begin to participate more actively in the political process when their perceived costs as a result of government policies exceed their benefits from them. The nature and intensity of their organizing efforts are a function of the distance between costs and benefits.[20]

This "market" for votes and other political activity leads politicians who want to be elected to espouse policies that will please voters—but not just any voters. Politicians would be advised to ignore committed voters—regardless of whether they are committed for or against the politician or party in question. It would be a better use of resources to try to sway undecided voters, since this is the group that normally determines electoral outcomes.[21]

This might explain the continuing allegation that both the Liberal and Progressive Conservative Parties are more concerned about voters in Eastern Canada than in Western Canada. The Liberals do not bother to curry the favour of westerners because it is clear that westerners always vote Conservative; the Conservatives can ignore westerners for the same reason.

Public choice can also explain the actions of public servants. Public servants will ordinarily attempt to increase their department's mandate and the sizes of its staff and budget because this will increase the individual public servant's income and status.[22] This desire for increased status will also cause public servants to favour particular kinds of policies. For example, Breton and Wintrobe have argued that income and price controls are imposed by governments, not because they are successful, and not because politicians or citizens want them, but because they make it easier for bureaucrats to obscure accountability and so take credit for successes and shift blame for failures.[23]

Public choice explains the behaviour of individual voters, politicians, and bureaucrats, but it can also be used to explain the interactions of these groups. Hartle discusses public policy-making as a series of interacting games:

> Individuals involved in public policy decision making are self-seeking players . . . engaged in sets of interrelated "games." Each of the several "games" (political, bureaucratic, lobbying, media) has its own set of unique rules including rules of entry and exit, rules of play, and rules of reward and punishment. In each "game" also, any one player makes decisions in the face of ubiquitous uncertainty concerning the actions and reactions of other players.[24]

He goes on to summarize a part of the game in the following manner:

> The bureaucracy extracts rents from the governing party as the price for its active cooperation in assisting the party to stay in power by pacifying the special interest groups with rents transferred from the uninformed, from the unorganized, and from their committed opponents in never-to-be-won constituencies. The more successful the bureaucrats in their rent seeking, the greater the administrative budget . . .[25]

The overall policy game consists of the interaction of these four games, because everyone in the system needs everyone else. Media people need politicians to give them "scoops," but politicians also need media people to help establish their image. However, not all players in the game are equal; depending on the issue at stake and the resources (financial or other) of the various players, different outcomes can be expected. Thus, public policy is the result of the interaction of these games.

One of the problems with the public choice model is that it presents few testable hypotheses. People are presumed to act based on certain motivations, but since these are subjective motivations, they cannot be measured or tested.

> What is developed is a logical progression based on untested and indeed unlikely hypotheses about how human beings actually behave. Norton Long makes this point sharply by concluding that public choice theorists "argue with elegant and impeccable logic about unicorns."[26]

For example, it is sometimes pointed out that many people do not act in the self-interested, rational manner posited by the model. Public choice theorists would suggest that such a person is, in fact, acting in some longer-term self-interest or taking additional things into account. This sounds suspiciously like "saving the hypothesis," but it is impossible to counter.

GOVERNMENTAL OR BUREAUCRATIC POLITICS

Public choice theory attempts to explain virtually all political actions in society as a result of the actions of various groups and their involvement in the making of major policy decisions. The governmental or bureaucratic politics model has some factors in common with public choice, but the bureaucratic politics model is generally confined more narrowly to a discussion of public policy-making.

Elements of this model have been the subject of much discussion, but these elements were drawn together and the model was given greater recognition as a full-blown theory of policy-making by Graham Allison in his book *Essence of Decision*.[27]

In many ways, this model is the exact opposite of the rational model. The rational model sees "the government" as a monolithic actor guided by a dedication to efficiency, effectiveness, and rationality, however those concepts might be defined. The governmental or bureaucratic politics model sees government as composed of a number of different departments and agencies, each with its own goals and each trying to mould policy to further its own interests. Thus, government is a coalition of various interests, and government policies are the outcome of the interactions of these various entities. For that reason, this model is sometimes referred to as the *bargaining* model.

When a decision needs to be made, each department or agency within a government could well have a different perspective on it. For example, if Canada were called upon to act because one country had invaded another, there could be a number of different responses. The military might propose some sort of retaliation or other military solution. External Affairs might propose such diplomatic initiatives as international negotiations or actions through the United Nations, including possibly a trade embargo. Industrial development officials might propose that there be an embargo on food products, since Canadian manufacturers should not suffer. The Department of Agriculture might favour an embargo on manufactured goods so that Canadian farmers would not suffer. Each organization sees the problem and the solution in a different way depending on how its interests are affected. This gives rise to the statement: "Where you stand depends on where you sit."[28]

There is no question of disloyalty to the public interest or the common good when different entities adopt different positions. All of these organizations are firmly committed to the public interest, but they all see that interest being served in a different manner.

The decision ultimately taken is the outcome of compromise and negotiation between the various interested parties and thus is heavily influenced by the relative power of the various organizations. In almost every policy area, there is a "lead ministry" that is most directly involved in the area, and whose opinions carry the greatest weight, but there are a number of other interested departments that also have some influence on the final policy.

> Government decisions are made, and government actions are taken, neither as the simple choice of a unified group, nor as a formal summary of leaders' preferences. Rather, the context of shared power but separate judgments about important choices means that politics is the mechanism of choice. Each player pulls and hauls with the power at his discretion for outcomes that will advance his conception of national, organizational, group, and personal interests.[29]

This theory is easier to see at work in the open presidential system of the United States than in the Canadian parliamentary system, where decisions tend to be made in Cabinet behind closed doors and Cabinet solidarity prevails after the decision has been made. However, this model has been used to describe the federal budgetary process[30] and intergovernmental policy-making in a number of areas.[31] Nossal has suggested that it could also be used to analyze the making of Canadian foreign policy.[32]

SOCIO-ECONOMIC DETERMINANTS

The socio-economic determinants model of public policy suggests that policies evolve in response to certain changes in the socio-economic environment of a society. It does not suggest that individuals and groups are powerless in the policy process, but it says that their scope for autonomous action is severely limited by the environmental constraints that they face.

Ronald Manzer has developed one of the most interesting and innovative approaches to relating socio-economic development to changes in public policy. He has divided the economic history of Canada into three broad phases, and he argues that each phase has been characterized by different kinds of policy.

The first phase (sixteenth century to early twentieth century) was identified by what Manzer calls "economic growth by resource appropriation,"[33] which is economic growth as a result of "private individual enterprise in settling and developing the land and exploiting its resources."[34] This is characterized by individualistic units of production in such areas as fishing, fur trading, and lumbering. The individualistic culture of the time meant that government income security policy was rudimentary at best.[35] Short-term unemployment, if it existed at all, was mitigated by family, and charitable or religious organizations. Government programs were limited to institutional care for "children and old people with no family or friends to support them" and "insane or physically disabled persons whose requirements for care exceeded the simple facilities of family homes."[36]

The next stage identified by Manzer is "economic growth by capital accumulation"[37] (late nineteenth century to 1930s or 1940s), which is characterized by the growth of large industrial enterprise and the mass market needed by this form of industrial organization. This period was also characterized by mass migration from rural to urban areas, with the attendant weakening of family ties. The dependence of labour on large enterprises increased unemployment, and the weakening of family support mechanisms made this unemployment a societal, and not just a family or community, problem. Government was forced to become more involved in providing real income security programs. These programs changed from institutional care to such income transfers as mothers' allowance, workers' compensation, and old age pensions.[38]

Manzer's third stage is "economic growth by economic stabilization."[39] This stage is the maturing of the second stage with the economy being almost totally driven by large enterprise, which needs economic stability to function smoothly. Government must respond to this need for stability by employing economic tools "to minimize fluctuations in the level of economic activity"[40] and so keep the economy running smoothly. Government income security policy in this period is characterized by what are commonly called welfare state programs—de facto guaranteed income levels through programs such as unemployment insurance. These programs have a counter-cyclical impact in that they automatically increase in times of high unemployment and so stimulate the economy.

The important point of Manzer's argument is that there have been distinct stages in Canada's economic development that have produced distinctive public policies as a product of those times. This flies in the face of the analysis that focusses on the importance of partisan and ideological factors in policy-making.

The conventional wisdom one reads in some political science textbooks and most popular journalism says that public policies are a product of the ideology of the political party in power or possibly of the configuration of the present legislature, e.g., a weak minority government. Anyone who spends a great deal of time and energy studying the political system (such as political scientists and journalists) would like to believe that these political factors are highly influential. However, in the last twenty years the evidence has begun to mount in a number of jurisdictions that socio-economic variables are more important determinants of public policy than political ones.

Figure 6.3a illustrates the conventional wisdom about the central role of political factors in policy-making. It suggests that there are certain socio-economic factors that influence the decision of voters to support a particular political party. For example, union members vote for the NDP; wealthy business people vote for the Conservatives. The political party elected would then make policies that supported the political predispositions of those who voted for it. Over time, these socio-economic factors change, e.g., increase in union mem-

Figure 6.3
ALTERNATE MODELS OF THE POLICY PROCESS

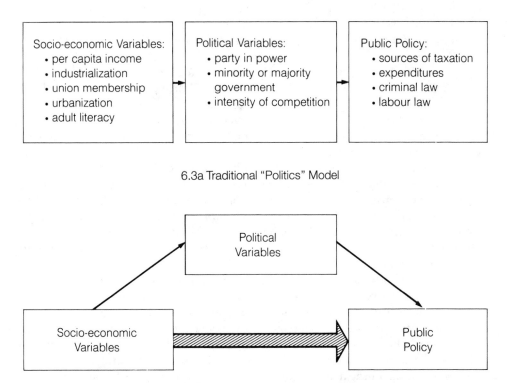

6.3a Traditional "Politics" Model

6.3b Socio-economic Variables Model

bership, a fact that could put a different political party in power and so bring about changes in public policy. Not only does this sound like the way a democratic system "ought" to work, but it coincides nicely with the legal arrangements of the situation.

Quantitative studies, first in the United States, then in a number of other countries, including Canada, indicate that, in fact, political variables may be less influential than had been thought. The general argument is that the model shown in Figure 6.3b is a more accurate depiction of the process than that in Figure 6.3a. Note that this refinement does not suggest that "politics doesn't matter," but it does suggest that political variables matter somewhat less than certain socio-economic variables.

The evolution of this style of thought can be illustrated by a brief discussion of how the idea developed in the United States. At one time, there was a widely held view that the level of inter-party competition in state politics had a major impact on the level of public expenditure, particularly in such functions as education and social welfare.[41] This was supported by comparing southern states with little party competition and low expenditures with New England states with high competition and high expenditure. The rationale for this was that where there was a high level of competition for office, the party in power was forced to provide "goodies" to the public to increase its chance of re-election.

However, one could also note that these two groups of states differed not just in level of inter-party competition, but also in such socio-economic factors as per capita income, levels of adult literacy, education, urbanization, and industrialization. This finding led to the use of such quantitative techniques as partial correlation and multiple regression to test the relative power of political versus socio-economic variables as explanatory agents. In the various tests, the strength of the relationship has varied, but the overall conclusion of these studies has almost invariably been that socio-economic factors have a greater influence on public policy than political factors.

Falcone and Whittington have conducted a comprehensive study of this question in Canada.[42] They tested the strength of such political variables as party in power, minority versus majority government, and social background of legislators. Their Canadian findings were substantially in agreement with the American results reported above. They found that such socio-economic variables as income and urbanization had a greater influence on levels of public expenditure than the political variables.

However, it is important to note that none of these studies has found that all changes in public policy can be explained by socio-economic factors. As Richard Simeon has pointed out, the environment determines what issues will move to the forefront of the agenda, what constraints decision-makers will face, and what resources will be available to them, but environment does not determine exactly what response they will make to an issue. "Urbanization generates the need to move people around, it does not tell us how the costs will be distributed."[43] *Politics does matter*, but probably not as much as some have believed in the past.

On further analysis, this should not be so surprising. In Canada, political parties seldom disagree on basic societal values. For example, all major parties believe in economic prosperity shared by all, lower inflation, lower unemployment, more equitable distribution of wealth, sunny weather in summer, and good snow on the ski slopes in winter. The strongest arguments at election times usually revolve around which party is more adept at furthering the basic societal values on which all agree. Richard Rose described this phenomenon in British politics:

> Parties can compete with each other by claiming to be more proficient in achieving goals generally valued by the electorate. For example, the Conservative and Labour parties do not compete by one party favouring full employment, and the other unemployment, or one favouring inflation and the other price stability. The parties compete by each claiming to be *better* qualified to achieve both full employment and stable prices. Instead of taking different positions, the parties take the same position, but differ in boasting of their competence in handling . . . conditions commonly valued by the majority of the electorate.[44]

Therefore, it should not be surprising that *all* parties are more likely to be influenced by general societal trends than by rigid, historical ideological positions. For example, in recent years all parties have seen the value of privatizing Crown corporations—the Social Credit in British Columbia, the Conservatives in the Alberta, Saskatchewan, and federal governments, even the provincial Liberal governments in Ontario and Quebec, in spite of the presumed Liberal ideological support for big government.

One reason for the similarity of policies is that parties, once in power, face a similarity of external constraints. In commenting on the British situation, Richard Rose points out that whichever party is in power is so constrained in the making of economic policy by the power of big business and big labour, export policies of foreign governments, and the price of North Sea oil, that it has great difficulty engaging in a policy significantly different from its predecessor, which faced the same constraints. Thus, parties tend to arrive at the same policies regardless of their ideological differences.

> To emphasize the force of a relatively consensual electorate and powerful secular trends is *not* to assert that the beliefs and interests of Conservative and Labour politicians are identical. Similarity in behaviour need not imply an identity of values. It can occur in spite of underlying differences if the specifics of a given circumstance are sufficiently powerful to lead people with different perspectives to arrive at the same conclusion about what must be done. *Necessity more than ideological consensus is the explanation for similarities in behaviour.*[45]

In sum, the thrust of the socio-economic determinants model of policy-making is that variables relating to the stage of a society's socio-economic development are more important in determining the types of policies formulated than are some of the political variables that are discussed so frequently. The Marxist theory of the state also emphasizes the significance of socio-economic factors.

MARXIST ANALYSIS

Chapter 2 discussed the Marxist approach to the role of the state in society. Marxists feel that the ultimate aim of the capitalist state is to organize society in such a manner as to ensure that the economic elite will be able to exploit the working class. Neo-Marxists argue that the state has three roles—fostering accumulation, providing legitimation, and imposing social order.[46]

In the Marxist view, the overriding concern of the state is assisting capitalists in *accumulating* large amounts of wealth and power. The state can aid in accumulation directly through such means as the provision of industrial development grants to wealthy corporations; or it can act indirectly through labour laws that inhibit unionization; or it can act through "non-decisions" such as refusal to enforce aggressively pollution or occupational health and safety laws. All of these policies result in what has been described as the privatization of profit and the socialization of costs, or public costs and private benefits.[47]

However, neo-Marxists argue that accumulation must be restrained somewhat, and capitalists must be saved from themselves, i.e., too much heavy-handed pure exploitation would incite armed rebellion or at least concerted actions on the part of workers. The state could use its coercive force to prevent such action, but that would be dysfunctional.

> [T]he state must try to maintain or create the conditions in which profitable capital accumulation is possible. However, the state also must try to maintain or create the conditions for social harmony. A capitalist state that openly uses its coercive forces to help one class accumulate capital at the expense of other classes loses its legitimacy and hence undermines the basis of its loyalty and support.[48]

Therefore, the state also attempts to illustrate to workers the value of the present system by providing *legitimation*, which is, in a sense, the benevolent face of capitalism.

> Legitimation policies are those that reduce inter-class conflict by providing subordinate classes with benefits that reduce their dissatisfaction with the inequalities generated by the capitalist economy. Social welfare policies and labour legislation are examples of state actions that promote social harmony by legitimizing the existing capitalist system in the eyes of those classes who, it is argued, benefit least from its operation.[49]

However, if workers cannot be kept in line through the persuasion inherent in legitimation, then the state stands ready to use *coercion to impose the appropriate social order*, such as legislation making union organization more difficult (the so-called "Michelin law" in Nova Scotia) and limitations on the right to picket during strikes.

The role of the state, and by extension of public policy, in the Marxist view is to mediate between the various conflicting interests present in society. However, this is not a neutral style of mediation. In the Marxist view, the state always acts in the long-term interests of the capitalist class. This might involve taking actions that have a short-term detrimental effect on accumulation and so are opposed by the capitalist class, e.g., extension of workers' compensation or unemployment insurance plans. However, these are necessary for legitimation and so benefit the capitalist class in the long run. In this sense, the role of the state is to maintain a relative autonomy[50] from *all* classes so that it can save the capitalist class from its own greed.

Evidence to support the Marxist model of the state can be seen in tax laws that provide generous benefits to people able to invest large sums while taxing wage-earners on the basis of each dollar earned. Another example is the case of the legislators who have great difficulty passing legislation preventing business combinations that limit competition, but have no such difficulty passing legislation ordering the end of legal strikes and the jailing of union leaders. Not many Canadians accept this Marxist view of the state, but it seems to be a valid explanation of certain actions of the state.

COLOURED PAPERS

Coloured papers are an important part of the policy-making process. They are documents prepared by government departments to communicate current government thinking on a particular issue to interested individuals or groups and to stimulate public discussion on the issue. One of Canada's foremost students of the use of coloured papers argues that they have three basic purposes:

- to provide information to interested parties;
- to involve Parliament and the public in decision-making;
- to stimulate federal-provincial consultation.[51]

Coloured papers are not always a part of the policy-making process, although they have become more common since the Trudeau era.[52] When both kinds of coloured papers are used, a green paper would be followed by a white paper, although there is no set pattern, and sometimes one is used without the other.

A **green paper** is prepared fairly early in the policy-making process to stimulate discussion about the possibility of changing policy in a particular area. It is *not* a statement of government policy, but, rather, usually attempts to set out a list of the options that the government is considering and the advantages and disadvantages of each. This is a signal to those interested in a particular policy area that the government is contemplating modifying a policy, and that they should make their views known to the government at this time.

The phrase "green paper" is used generically to describe all government communications of this sort. The actual colour of the covers of the papers varies widely; it is becoming more common to refer to specific documents by their actual colours such as the "blue paper" on Crown corporations[53] or the "orange paper" on social security[54] (sometimes irreverently called the "Halloween paper" after its rather garishly coloured cover).

A **white paper** is a statement of government policy. It usually provides a statement of policy in everyday, non-legislative language, accompanied by an explanation and defence of the particular course of action chosen. It is the government's way of saying that it has reviewed the thinking in a particular area, possibly through the use of a green paper, and this is its decision about how to proceed. This is the government's opportunity for the "hard sell."

A white paper is less specific than draft legislation, and so groups still have an opportunity to effect some modifications in the government's approach to an issue. However, a white paper is meant to be government policy, and if the government is forced to make a major change after the white paper stage, the Opposition will use this opportunity to embarrass it.

Coloured papers have been prepared on such wide-ranging topics as energy, immigration, social security, and the constitution.[55] It is difficult to think of a major policy field that has not been the subject of a coloured paper.

Coloured papers are handled in a variety of ways after their release. They are frequently sent to parliamentary committees for formal discussion and review. This can sometimes lead to very wide-ranging participation in the policy-making process:

For example, the 1969 paper on tax reform was examined by two parliamentary committees. The Commons committee held a total of 146 meetings and heard 211 briefs presented by 820 individuals. Two sub-committees traveled across Canada and held 31 meetings to hear 68 briefs. In total, 524 briefs and 1,093 letters and other submissions were received by the Commons committee. The Senate committee received a total of 345 briefs from organized groups and individuals, of which it heard 118.[56]

This is an extreme case in terms of numbers of participants, but there is always great interest on the part of certain parties in the discussions on coloured papers.

Coloured papers play an important role in the policy development process because they encourage debate about a policy at a time when the government has that policy under review. Green papers provide a way for the government to gauge the depth and breadth of feelings about an issue without having to commit itself. White papers provide the government with the opportunity to state its case for a particular decision. Both devices encourage citizen participation in the policy-making process and help inform the public.

CONCLUSION

This chapter has discussed some of the theories of policy-making. The obvious question now is: which one best describes reality? There is no easy answer to that question. The discussion of each theory included examples of policies that seemed to fit that theory, so it seems clear that all of the theories discussed can be used to explain something. So the answer to the question might be the admittedly vague idea that each theory has some value depending on the policy, the environment, the predispositions of the observer, and a whole series of other factors.

Is there any way of making these theories fit together? Richard Simeon suggests that different aspects of the policy process and different theories will be relevant at different points in the policy process. He describes what he calls a "funnel of causality."

> At the most general level, and most remote from the particular choice of alternative A or B, is the socioeconomic environment; next come the fundamental political variables, power, culture and ideology, and institutions; finally the most proximate source of decision is the operation of the decision-making process itself. To some extent, the more concerned one is with broad patterns of policy, and with international comparisons, the more one will concentrate on environmental, ideological, and structural variables; the more concerned with day-to-day shifts in policy, the more one will assume those prior factors as given and focus on the decision-makers themselves, though some environmental constraints may enter here too. Much of the literature has tended to focus on one end of the funnel without taking account of the other.[57]

This is a partial but reasonably representative explanation of the various theories. However, it is not enough for a government simply to make a policy; policies are only truly relevant when they are implemented. The next chapter discusses what happens during the implementation phase.

NOTES

1. *Understanding Public Policy*, 5th ed. (Englewood Cliffs, N.J.: Prentice-Hall, 1984), p. 1.
2. Ibid., pp. 1-3.
3. "Public-Policy Theory and Analysis," in G. Bruce Doern and Peter Aucoin, eds., *Public Policy in Canada* (Toronto: Macmillan, 1979), p. 2.
4. James R. Anderson, *Public Policy-Making*, 3rd ed. (New York: Holt, Rinehart and Winston, 1984), p. 8.
5. William N. Dunn, *Public Policy Analysis* (Englewood Cliffs, N.J.: Prentice-Hall, 1981), pp. 225-26.
6. Peter Aucoin, "Theory and Research in the Study of Policy-Making," in G. Bruce Doern and Peter Aucoin, eds., *The Structures of Policy-Making in Canada* (Toronto: Macmillan of Canada, 1971), p. 24.
7. Lindblom's ideas on incrementalism have been elaborated in several places. The shortest and most succinct treatment is in "The Science of 'Muddling Through,'" *Public Administration Review* 19 (Spring 1959): 79-88. Some of the other more thorough treatments are David Braybrooke and Charles Lindblom, *A Strategy of Decision* (New York: The Free Press, 1970); Charles Lindblom, *The Policy-Making Process* (Englewood Cliffs, N.J.: Prentice-Hall, 1968); and Robert A. Dahl and Charles E. Lindblom, *Politics, Economics, and Welfare* (New York: Harper & Row, 1953).
8. Braybrooke and Lindblom, *A Strategy of Decision*, pp. 99-102.
9. "Mixed-Scanning: A 'Third' Approach To Decision-Making," *Public Administration Review* 27 (1967): 387.
10. "Muddling Through–'Science' or Inertia?" *Public Administration Review* 24 (1964): 155.
11. *Administrative Behaviour*, 2nd ed. (New York: The Free Press, 1957), p. 79.
12. James G. March and Herbert A. Simon, *Organizations* (New York: John Wiley & Sons, 1958), pp. 140-41. (Emphasis in original.)
13. Yehezel Dror, *Public Policymaking Reexamined* (Scranton, Pa.: Chandler Publishing Company, 1968), chs. 13-15 and passim.
14. Etzioni, "Mixed Scanning," pp. 389-90.
15. Ibid., p. 388.
16. Dennis C. Mueller, *Public Choice* (Cambridge: Cambridge University Press, 1979), p. 1.
17. One of the clearest statements of the public choice approach is in M. H. Sproule-Jones, *Public Choice and Federalism in Australia and Canada* (Canberra: Centre for Research on Federal Financial Relations, The Australian National University, 1975), ch. 2; see also Mark Sproule-Jones, "Institutions, Constitutions, and Public Policies: A Public-Choice Overview," in Michael M. Atkinson and Marsha A. Chandler, eds., *The Politics of Canadian Public Policy* (Toronto: University of Toronto Press), pp. 127-50.
18. D. G. Hartle, *A Theory of the Expenditure Budgetary Process* (Toronto: University of Toronto Press, 1976), p. 12.
19. Anthony Downs, *An Economic Theory of Democracy* (New York: Harper & Row, 1957), pp. 38-39.
20. Albert Breton, *The Economic Theory of Representative Government* (Chicago: Aldine, 1974), ch. 5 and passim. One of the most complete formulations of public choice theories of collective action is contained in Mancur Olson, *The Logic of Collective Action* (Cambridge: Harvard University Press, 1965).
21. Hartle, *A Theory of the Expenditure Budgetary Process*, p. 65.

22. William A. Niskanen, Jr., *Bureaucracy and Representative Government* (Chicago: Aldine-Atherton, 1971), ch. 4.
23. Albert Breton and Ronald Wintrobe, *The Logic of Bureaucratic Conduct* (Cambridge: Cambridge University Press, 1982), pp. 146-54. For a similar point, see also Breton, *The Economic Theory of Representative Government*, p. 163.
24. Douglas G. Hartle, *The Expenditure Budget Process of the Government of Canada: A Public Choice—Rent-Seeking Perspective*, Canadian Tax Paper no. 81 (Toronto: Canadian Tax Foundation, 1988), p. 35. (Footnote omitted.)
25. Ibid., p. 60.
26. Richard B. Denhardt, *Theories of Public Organization* (Pacific Grove, Calif.: Brooks/Cole, 1984), p. 146. (Footnote omitted.)
27. (Boston: Little, Brown, 1971), ch. 5.
28. Ibid., p. 176.
29. Ibid., p. 171.
30. Richard D. French, *How Ottawa Decides* (Toronto: James Lorimer, 1980), ch. 2 and passim.
31. Richard J. Schultz, *Federalism, Bureaucracy, and Public Policy* (Montreal: McGill-Queen's University Press, 1980); Simon McInnes, "Federal-Provincial Negotiation: Family Allowances 1970-1976" (Ph.D. diss., Carleton University, 1978); David Siegel, "Provincial-Municipal Relations in Ontario: A Case Study of Roads" (Ph.D. diss., University of Toronto, 1984).
32. Kim Richard Nossal, "Allison through the (Ottawa) Looking Glass: Bureaucratic Politics and Foreign Policy in a Parliamentary System," *Canadian Public Administration* 22 (Winter 1979): 610-26.
33. *Public Policies and Political Development in Canada* (Toronto: University of Toronto Press, 1985), p. 22.
34. Ibid.
35. Manzer illustrates his argument with references to a number of different policy areas; the examples here will be drawn strictly from the one field of income security.
36. Manzer, *Public Policies and Political Development in Canada* (Toronto: University of Toronto Press, 1985), p. 52.
37. Ibid., p. 29.
38. Ibid., pp. 54-59.
39. Ibid., p. 39.
40. Ibid., p. 40.
41. A good general history of this approach is contained in Dye, *Understanding Public Policy*, ch. 12.
42. David J. Falcone and Michael S. Whittington, "Output Change in Canada: A Preliminary Attempt to Open the 'Black Box'" (Paper presented to the Annual Meeting of the Canadian Political Science Association, Montreal, Quebec, June 4, 1972.)
43. "Studying Public Policy," *Canadian Journal of Political Science* 9 (December 1976): 567.
44. *Do Parties Make A Difference?* (London: Macmillan, 1980), p. 12. (Emphasis in original; footnote omitted.)
45. Ibid., p. 145. (Emphasis in original.)
46. Leo Panitch, "The Role and Nature of the Canadian State," in Leo Panitch, ed. *The Canadian State: Political Economy and Political Power* (Toronto: University of Toronto Press, 1977), p. 8 and passim.

47. Rick Deaton, "The Fiscal Crisis of the State and the Revolt of the Public Employees," *Our Generation* 8 (October 1972): 11-51.
48. James O'Connor, *The Fiscal Crisis of the State* (New York: St. Martin's Press, 1973), p. 6.
49. Stephen Brooks, *Public Policy in Canada* (Toronto: McClelland & Stewart, 1989), p. 56.
50. Nicos Poulantzas, *Political Power and Social Classes* (London: Verso Editions, 1978), 255ff. and Part IV passim.
51. Audrey D. Doerr, "The Role of Coloured Papers," *Canadian Public Administration* 25 (Fall 1982): 370-76.
52. For a good history of the process, see A. D. Doerr, "The Role of White Papers," in Doern and Aucoin, eds., *The Structures of Policy-Making in Canada*, pp. 180-87.
53. Canada, Privy Council Office, *Crown Corporations: Direction-Accountability-Control* (Minister of Supply and Services Canada, 1977).
54. Marc Lalonde, Minister of National Health and Welfare, *Working Paper on Social Security in Canada*, 2nd ed. (1973).
55. A more complete list of recent coloured papers is contained in Doerr, "The Role of Coloured Papers," pp. 378-79.
56. Ibid., p. 372.
57. "Studying Public Policy," p. 556.

BIBLIOGRAPHY

Allison, Graham. *Essence of Decision: Explaining the Cuban Missile Crisis*. Boston: Little, Brown , 1971.

Anderson, James R. *Public Policy-Making*. 3rd ed. New York: Holt, Rinehart and Winston, 1984.

Atkinson, Michael M., and Marsha A. Chandler, eds. *The Politics of Canadian Public Policy*. Toronto: University of Toronto Press, 1983.

Beer, Samuel H. "Federalism, Nationalism and Democracy in America." *American Political Science Review* 72 (March 1978).

Braybrooke, David, and Charles Lindblom. *A Strategy of Decision*. New York: The Free Press, 1970.

Breton, Albert. *The Economic Theory of Representative Government*. Chicago: Aldine, 1974.

Breton, Albert, and Ronald Wintrobe. *The Logic of Bureaucratic Conduct*. Cambridge: Cambridge University Press, 1982.

Brooks, Stephen. *Public Policy in Canada*. Toronto: McClelland & Stewart, 1989.

Cohen, Michael D., James G. March, and Johan P. Olson. "A Garbage Can Model of Organizational Choice," *Administrative Science Quarterly* 17, no. 1 (March 1972): 1-25.

Dahl, Robert A., and Charles E. Lindblom. *Politics, Economics, and Welfare*. New York: Harper & Row, 1953.

Deaton, Rick. "The Fiscal Crisis of the State and the Revolt of the Public Employees." *Our Generation* 8 (October 1972): 11- 51.

Denhardt, Robert B. *Theories of Public Organization*. Pacific Grove, Calif.: Brooks/Cole, 1984.

Doern, G. Bruce, and Peter Aucoin, eds. *Public Policy in Canada*. Toronto: Macmillan, 1979.

——. *The Structures of Policy-Making in Canada*. Toronto: Macmillan, 1971.

Doern, G. Bruce, and Richard W. Phidd. *Canadian Public Policy: Ideas, Structure, Process*. Toronto: Methuen, 1983.

Doern, G. Bruce, and V. Seymour Wilson, eds. *Issues in Canadian Public Policy*. Macmillan, 1974.

Doerr, Audrey D. *The Machinery of Government in Canada*. Toronto: Methuen, 1981.

———. "The Role of Coloured Papers." *Canadian Public Administration* 25 (Fall 1982): 366-79.

Downs, Anthony. *An Economic Theory of Democracy*. New York: Harper & Row, 1957.

Dror, Yehezkel. "Muddling Through—"Science" or Inertia?" *Public Administration Review* 24 (1964): 153-58.

———. *Public Policymaking Reexamined*. Scranton, Pa.: Chandler, 1968.

Dunn, William N. *Public Policy Analysis*. Englewood Cliffs, N.J.: Prentice-Hall, 1981.

Dye, Thomas R. *Policy Analysis: What Governments Do, Why They Do It, and What Difference It Makes*. University, Ala.: The University of Alabama Press, 1976).

———. *Understanding Public Policy*. 5th ed. Englewood Cliffs, N.J.: Prentice-Hall, 1984.

Etzioni, Amitai. "Mixed-Scanning: A 'Third' Approach To Decision-Making." *Public Administration Review* 27 (1967): 385-92.

Falcone, David J., and Michael S. Whittington. "Output Change in Canada: A Preliminary Attempt to Open the 'Black Box.'" Paper presented to the Annual Meeting of the Canadian Political Science Association, Montreal, Quebec, June 4, 1972.

French, Richard D. *How Ottawa Decides*. Toronto: James Lorimer, 1980.

Granatstein, J. L. *The Ottawa Men*. Toronto: Oxford University Press, 1982.

Hartle, D. G. *The Expenditure Budget Process of the Government of Canada: A Public Choice—Rent-Seeking Perspective*. Toronto: Canadian Tax Foundation, 1988.

———. *A Theory of the Expenditure Budgetary Process*. Toronto: University of Toronto Press, 1976.

Kernaghan, Kenneth, and T. H. McLeod. "Mandarins and Ministers in the Canadian Administrative State." In O. P. Dwivedi, ed., *The Administrative State in Canada*, pp. 17-30. Toronto: University of Toronto Press, 1982.

Laframboise, H. L. "Moving a Proposal to a Positive Decision: A Case Study of the Invisible Process." *Optimum* 4, no. 3 (1973): 31-41.

Lindblom, Charles E. *The Policy-Making Process*. Englewood Cliffs, N.J.: Prentice-Hall, 1968.

———. "The Science of 'Muddling Through.'" *Public Administration Review* 19 (Spring 1959): 79-88.

Manzer, Ronald. *Public Policies and Political Development in Canada*. Toronto: University of Toronto Press, 1985.

March, James G., and Herbert A. Simon. *Organizations*. New York: John Wiley & Sons, 1958.

McInnes, Simon. "Federal-Provincial Negotiation: Family Allowances 1970-1976." Ph.D. diss., Carleton University, 1978.

Mueller, Dennis C. *Public Choice*. Cambridge: Cambridge University Press, 1979.

Niskanen, William A., Jr. *Bureaucracy and Representative Government*. Chicago: Aldine-Atherton, 1971.

Nossal, Kim Richard. "Allison through the (Ottawa) Looking Glass: Bureaucratic Politics and Foreign Policy in a Parliamentary System." *Canadian Public Administration* 22 (Winter 1979): 610-26.

O'Connor, James. *The Fiscal Crisis of the State*. New York: St. Martin's Press, 1973.

Olson, Mancur. *The Logic of Collective Action*. Cambridge: Harvard University Press, 1965.

Panitch, Leo. "The Role and Nature of the Canadian State." In Leo Panitch, ed., *The Canadian State: Political Economy and Political Power*. Toronto: University of Toronto Press, 1977.

Poulantzas, Nicos. *Political Power and Social Classes.* London: Verso Editions, 1978.

Rose, Richard. *Do Parties Make A Difference?* London: The Macmillan Press, 1980.

Schultz, Richard J. *Federalism, Bureaucracy, and Public Policy.* Montreal: McGill-Queen's University Press, 1980.

Siegel, David. "Provincial-Municipal Relations in Ontario: A Case Study of Roads." Ph.D. diss., University of Toronto, 1984.

Simeon, Richard. "Studying Public Policy." *Canadian Journal of Political Science* 9 (December 1976): 548-80.

Simon, Herbert. *Administrative Behavior.* 2nd ed. New York: The Free Press, 1957.

Sproule-Jones, M. H. *Public Choice and Federalism in Australia and Canada.* Canberra: Centre for Research on Federal Financial Relations, The Australian National University, 1975.

Trebilcock, M. J., R. S. Prichard, D. G. Hartle, and D. N. Dewees. *The Choice of Governing Instrument.* Ottawa: Minister of Supply and Services Canada, 1982.

Wilson, V. Seymour, "What Legacy? The Nielsen Task Force Program Review," in Katherine A. Graham, ed., *How Ottawa Spends–1988/89.* Don Mills, Ont.: Oxford University Press Canada, 1988, pp. 23-47.

CASES

In *Case Program in Canadian Public Administration* (Toronto: Institute of Public Administration of Canada):

L'Affaire Caloil. By Michel Paquin

The Draft Memorandum to Cabinet. By Douglas G. Hartle

The Toronto Airport(s). By Sandford F. Borins

Assessing Housing Needs in Manitoba's Remote Communities. By Nelson Wiseman

Policy Analysis: A Case Study. By David Zussman

Screening the Boat People? Case Studies in Health Policies. By Peter Owen, Peggy Purvis, and Raisa B. Deber

All Things to All People: Government and Its Client Groups. By Sharon Bider and Peter McNaughton

We'll Take You On, Mr. Toyota: A Case Study on Japanese Imports and the Future of the Canadian Automobile Industry. By Sandford F. Borins, John M. Curtis, R. Moroz, and Tony R. Washington

The Allocation of a National Housing Budget. By Barbara Carroll

The Commissioner's Dilemma: Body Cavity Searches in the Canadian Penitentiary Service. By Edd LeSage

Cases developed by the Canadian Centre for Management Development and distributed by the Case Program in Canadian Public Administration:

Competition Act: Stages 1 to 6. By Lynne Tyler and Glen G. D. Milne

7

Implementing and Evaluating Public Policy

As discussed at the beginning of Chapter 6, the formulation of public policy is only one part of the overall policy process. This chapter will examine what happens after the initial decision about the adoption of a policy is made. It will examine how the policy is implemented and then how it is evaluated to determine its ultimate worth.

IMPLEMENTATION

Traditionally, political scientists have been predominantly concerned with the study of political institutions, e.g., cabinets or legislatures, and their impact on policy-making. The general implication was that after policy decisions were made, they were simply automatically carried out, so that there was nothing of interest to political scientists in the implementation process. At best, there were a few questions of organization and motivation, which were considered to be more properly in the realm of those who study administration than of those who study important things like political science.

This attitude began to change in the 1970s, at least partly as a result of an increasing interest in policy-impact studies. These studies found that public policies frequently did not have the impacts that were envisaged when they were first formulated by the executive or legislature. For example, it was discovered that children were not learning as much in school as some thought they should be, that poverty was no closer to elimination in spite of the expenditure of significant amounts of money, and that courts were experiencing such a backlog that justice was seriously delayed. This led to a clear understanding that there was some slippage between policy-making and policy impact; this, in turn, led to the realization that implementation is an integral part of the political process.

> [T]he bargaining and maneuvering, the pulling and hauling, of the policy-adoption process carries over into the policy-implementation process. Die-hard opponents of the policy who lost out in the adoption stage seek, and find, means to continue their opposition when, say, administrative regulations and guidelines are being written. Many who supported the original policy proposal did so only because they expected to be able to twist it in the implementation phase to suit purposes never contemplated or desired by others who formed part of the original coalition.[1]

136

Clausewitz wrote that war was simply the conduct of foreign relations by other means; on the domestic scene, implementation can be seen as the conduct of politics by other means.

The Implementation Process

Successful implementation is very difficult. Ripley and Franklin explain why:

> Implementation processes involve *many important actors* holding *diffuse and competing goals and expectations* who work within a *context of an increasingly large and complex mix of government programs* that require *participation from numerous layers and units of government* and who are affected by *powerful factors beyond their control.*[2]

They go on to describe implementation as a game. However:

> [t]he game does not resemble some nicely ordered sport with small team size and well-defined rules like basketball. Rather it resembles lacrosse in its original form— played between two tribes with the number of players, the boundaries, the duration, and other important aspects of the game all somewhat nebulous.[3]

One of the keys to understanding the implementation process is a better grasp of the complex relationship between those who make policy and those who implement it. Nakamura and Smallwood suggested that there could be five different styles of linkage between them.[4]

The *"classical" technocratic* linkage closely approximates the Weberian ideal-type. It assumes that formulators state goals clearly and unequivocally and delegate the technical responsibility for carrying out those goals to implementers, and that implementers automatically carry out those duties in the desired manner.

The *instructed delegate* approach is similar to the classical technocratic approach in that formulators specify goals and implementers agree with those goals, but it differs in that formulators delegate a somewhat broader area of discretion to the implementers. Implementers are not simply automatons; they have limited authority to make decisions about programs during the implementation process.

In the *bargaining approach*, the formulators and implementers do not agree on policy goals. However, since each needs the cooperation of the other in order to carry out any program, bargaining occurs. "The final outcome of bargaining between policy makers and implementers is determined by the distribution of relative power resources (actual or perceived) among the two groups."[5] This plays havoc with the traditional Weberian notion of bureaucracy in that it suggests that implementers could have some influence over formulators.[6]

The *discretionary experimenter* approach occurs when formulators can decide on broad general goals, but do not have enough knowledge to specify precise goals or directions. In this case, formulators have little choice but to convey general goals to implementers and to provide them with wide discretionary powers to carry out these general abstract goals.

The *bureaucratic entrepreneur* approach turns the traditional relationship between formulators and implementers on its head. In this style of interaction, implementers begin by formulating their goals and then marshalling support for those goals among various significant groups. After this is done, the implementers approach the formulators to obtain the necessary resources, including legitimation, to undertake the program. This is the most radical approach, but it is also a very common one. Samuel H. Beer had this sort of relationship in mind when he made this comment on the political process in the United States.

> I would remark how rarely additions to the public sector have been *initiated* by the demands of voters or the advocacy of pressure groups or the platforms of political parties. On the contrary, in the fields of health, housing, urban renewal, transportation, welfare, education, poverty, and energy it has been, in very great measure, people in government service, or very closely associated with it, acting on the basis of their specialized and technical knowledge, who first perceived the problem, conceived the program, initially urged it on the President and Congress, went on to help lobby it through to enactment, and then saw to its administration.[7]

The closed nature of the parliamentary system makes it difficult to see this process at work in Canada, but cases can be cited where implementers have, in fact, had a major role in formulating policies.[8]

The "classic technocratic" approach is the approach that most closely corresponds with traditional democratic theory. The opposite extremes—the discretionary experimenter and bureaucratic entrepreneur approaches—seem to be at odds with the classic idea of "politicians on top, experts on tap." However, there are frequently situations where some slippage between the policy as originally stipulated, and as implemented, is necessary or even beneficial.

Paul Berman has identified what he calls *adaptive implementation*. He defines this as "processes that enable initial plans to be adapted to unfolding events and decisions."[9] He argues that the traditional style of implementation, which he calls *programmed implementation*, is frequently insensitive to the existing bureaucratic culture and so can result in symbolic implementation that amounts to no real change in how things are done.

He recognizes that adaptive implementation is at variance with traditional ideas of political control of implementation. However, he argues that for certain kinds of new programs, it is not only an accurate description of what generally happens, but it is actually preferable.

> Implementation problems arise because of the overspecification and rigidity of goals, the failure to engage relevant actors in decision-making, and the excessive control of deliverers. The ideal of adaptive implementation is the establishment of a process that allows policy to be modified, specified, and revised—in a word, adapted—according to the unfolding interaction of the policy with its institutional setting. Its outcomes would be neither automatic nor assured, and it would look more like a disorderly learning process than a predictable procedure.[10]

In particular, he feels that where policies involve radical changes in the status quo, where the technology to be employed is uncertain, where there is high conflict over the policy, and where there is an unstable environment, adaptive implementation might be the most beneficial approach.[11]

One of the keys to good implementation is understanding what conditions will improve the possibility of implementation, and what problems stand in the way of implementation. The next two sections of this chapter focus on those two points.

Making Implementation Easier

Two long-time students of implementation list five conditions that they feel are necessary for effective implementation.[12]

"Condition 1. The program is based on a sound theory relating changes in target group behavior to the achievement of the desired end-state (objectives.)" It must be clear that acting on the target group will actually cause progress toward the desired goal. For example, imposing stringent environmental standards on one group will not have much overall impact on pollution if that group is not a major contributor to pollution. In fact, such a policy could be very expensive to enforce if it incited resentment on the part of the target group.

"Condition 2. The statute (or other basic policy decision) contains unambiguous policy directives, and structures the implementation process so as to maximize the likelihood that target groups will perform as desired." Clear guidance from legislators allows implementers to stay on track, and helps them resist forces that would try to deflect or change the policy as it is being implemented. It is also important that responsibility for implementation is assigned to an organization that is supportive of the program and that adequate resources are allocated to that agency to carry out its responsibilities.

"Condition 3. The leaders of the implementing agencies possess substantial managerial and political skills and are committed to statutory objectives." Usually, there are a number of agencies that could be assigned the responsibility for implementation. Legislators must exercise care in assigning a policy to an organization whose management is both competent and committed to the policy.

"Condition 4. The program is actively supported by organized constituency groups and by a few key legislators (or the chief executive) throughout the implementation process, with the courts being neutral or supportive." This seems quite straightforward, but it can be more difficult to achieve than it might at first seem. The problem is the very short attention span of individuals and groups that causes them to lose interest in a cause quickly after initial legislation has been passed.

Sabatier and Mazmanian suggest that two factors should be present to achieve this condition. First, they recommend an individual whom they call a "fixer," but who might be called a "champion" by others. This is someone who will make it his or her mission to push for or "champion" a particular policy. This person will not allow others to forget commitments that they made in the heat of the moment. Second, there is a need for a supportive interest group that will monitor the activities of the implementing agency and ensure that it is making progress in the desired direction. Consumers' and women's groups have carried out this function very well in some policy areas.

"Condition 5. The relative priority of statutory objectives is not significantly undermined over time by the emergence of conflicting public policies or by changes in relevant socioeconomic conditions that undermine the statute's 'technical' theory or political support." The importance of specific policies can ebb and flow over time. In recent years, concerns about improving social programs have run head-on into concerns for reducing the deficit. When this happens, it is very difficult to maintain the interests of legislators in the policy that is falling out of fashion.

Difficulties of Implementation

Implementation is frequently much more difficult than it is perceived to be. All sorts of problems develop during implementation that were only dimly seen when the original policies were made.

Communications Problems. Chapter 3 discussed the Weberian idea of bureaucracy, which held that senior officials gave orders and subordinates simply carried them out. Chapters 4 and 5 went on to suggest that it was not quite that simple. Subordinates are not programmed automatons; they have minds of their own and are capable of misunderstanding or misinterpreting (either accidentally or intentionally) the desires of senior officials. The need to communicate between policy formulators and policy implementers presents problems.

> [C]ommunications linkages within any policy system can be replete with potential pitfalls. Mishaps can occur because of (1) garbled messages from the senders; (2) misinterpretation by the receivers; or (3) system failure in terms of transmission breakdowns, overload, "noise," and inadequate follow-though or compliance mechanisms.[13]

These possible problems can be magnified by the presence of organizational and other kinds of systematic bias on the part of implementers.

Organizational Rigidities. These communication difficulties raise the possibility of some sort of selective perception on the part of implementers. There are cases where this is deliberate and malicious, but that need not be the case. Most people have a strong predisposition to handle particular problems in a particular manner. When confronted with new problems, there is a tendency to continue to respond in the old manner. For example, most professions possess what has been described as a "trained incapacity." Professional training teaches people one specific way to deal with a problem and so makes them unable to develop new approaches. In the 1960s and 1970s when there were acrimonious disputes about expressways versus public transit, it was suggested that one of the problems was that engineers had been trained in one way of moving people— private cars on roads; they had developed a "trained incapacity" to see that other ways of moving people could be developed.

Policy-makers frequently ignore the existence of these organizational biases when they are deciding on new policies. This means that policies are produced under the assumption that organizations will change to implement the policies; in fact, it is more likely that policies will be changed to fit the organization.

Insufficient Resources. Even when people are willing and able to implement policies, there can still be difficulties if adequate resources are unavailable. This problem is sometimes compounded when policy-makers who are instrumental in the adoption of a policy deliberately underestimate the resources needed to implement it, to facilitate adoption of the policy. Implementers then suffer from a shortage of funds, but this is not the only resource necessary to implement some policies. In the case of scientific programs in particular, there are sometimes not enough people with appropriate training to carry out a project, regardless of the funds available to pay them.

Implementers also complain that they do not receive enough political support at key points in the implementation phase. Frequently, politicians lose interest in a particular policy after it has been approved; they simply assume it will be implemented properly. However, implementers can have difficulty battling inertia or even hostile forces in the environment. Without continuing political support, implementers can be left like the proverbial explorers up the creek without a paddle. Political support is particularly necessary when there are a number of different organizations involved in implementation.

Interorganizational Complexity. The problem of implementing programs that have intergovernmental or interorganizational implications is given a special place in the literature on implementation because of the great difficulties encountered. These problems arise because of the number of different organizations involved, and because each of these organizations has different goals. At times, the numbers alone can be devastating. Pressman and Wildavsky's analysis of an economic development program found that it was necessary to arrive at seventy different agreements involving fifteen different organizations. They calculate that with this number of agreements needed, if each has an 80 percent probability of success, then the probability that all seventy would be arrived at successfully is .000000125. One would have to assume a 99 percent probability of success for each contract to have close to a 50 percent chance of having all seventy contracts completed successfully.[14] They also point out the importance of speed in arriving at agreements, because agreements once made can still be abrogated if later decisions are not made promptly.

> It could be said that the EDA public works program was characterized by the slow dissolution of agreement. As one delay succeeded another, the major individual participants changed and so did the understandings they had with one another. Agreements were reached, eroded, and remade. The frequent calls for coordination . . . reflected the inability of the machinery for implementation to move fast enough to capture the agreements while they lasted. Allow enough time to elapse in a rapidly changing external world and it is hard to imagine any set of agreements remaining firm.[15]

Fullness of Time. One of the things many people do not understand about implementation can be symbolized by the fact that you cannot produce a child in one month by impregnating nine women. When a large organization with many accumulated organizational structures and biases is asked to accept a new idea, it takes a while for that idea to sink in. This is particularly important because in "the implementation process . . . politics appears primarily *defensive*. Actors seem more concerned with what they in particular might lose than with what all in general might gain."[16]

Many times the best implementation strategy is a very low-key one that involves simply mentioning a new idea that is currently being floated, without activating defence mechanisms by suggesting it be adopted. Then, after there has been some discussion of it, the idea begins to seem more palatable. Finally, it comes to be accepted by most people in the organization and the time is ripe for implementation. A great deal of damage can be done by trying to ram through a new idea without taking time to let people feel comfortable with it. In spite of the old saying, the shortest distance between two points is not necessarily a straight line.

Inadequate Participation. The importance of participation was discussed in Chapters 4 and 5, but it is important to realize that participation is not just therapeutic for the individual; there is some evidence that it can have real benefits for the organization. Some studies have indicated that when people have the opportunity to participate in the early stages of policy design, the implementation process works much more smoothly.[17] There are at least two reasons for this. First, people who have been consulted about a policy will feel that they own a part of the policy and will feel comfortable with it during the implementation phase; the defence mechanisms mentioned above will never be activated. Second, early consultation with administrators will allow them to identify certain problems that can be corrected sooner rather than later.

The discussion in this and the preceding section makes it clear that a great deal of care must be exercised in choosing the means of implementing a policy. A unique Canadian contribution to this discussion has been the development of theories about how governments choose these instruments of implementation.

Choice of Governing Instrument

In recent years, there has been emerging literature in the field of the "choice of governing instrument." This approach to public policy-making recognizes that policy-making is not simply the choice of a policy objective, but rather it also involves a decision about *how* the policy will be implemented. Doern and Phidd define governing instruments as "the major ways in which governments seek to ensure compliance, support and implementation of public policy."[18]

When most people think of government policy, they think of the more visible aspects of government activity, usually government expenditure or regulation. However, in attempting to implement some policies, governments have a number of techniques, or instruments, at their disposal. Doern and Phidd categorize these under a number of headings:

- exhortation and symbolic policy outputs
- expenditure
- taxation
- regulation, and
- public enterprise.[19]

This section will discuss three theories of how governments go about selecting which instrument or mechanism they will employ to implement a policy. All three operate on the somewhat questionable assumption that governments have free rein to make more or less conscious decisions about which instrument to use. Kenneth Woodside has argued that this apparent breadth of choice is frequently limited by such factors as legislation, tradition, or level of experience with particular instruments.[20] For example, Atkinson and Nigol argue that one of the reasons why Ontario has moved to regulate auto insurance rates, rather than establish a government-run insurance corporation, is because the ministry responsible for dealing with this issue has more experience in using regulation than in operating Crown corporations.[21]

Doern and Wilson have developed the *coercion theory*, which holds that in choosing governing instruments, governments will move from the least coercive instruments to more coercive ones. Note that the order in which the instruments were listed above moves from the least to the most coercive. Doern and Wilson have suggested that the choice of governing instrument is made with a keen eye on public acceptability and that the public will more easily accept persuasive than coercive measures:

> This hypothesis would suggest that politicians (especially the collective cabinet) have a strong tendency to respond to policy issues (any issue) by moving successively from the *least coercive* governing instruments to the *most coercive*. Thus they tend to respond first in the least coercive fashion by creating a study, or by creating a new or reorganized unit of government, or merely by uttering a broad statement of intent. The next least coercive governing instrument would be to use a distributive spending approach in which the resources could be handed out to various constituencies in such a way that the least attention is given as to which taxpayers' pockets the resources are being drawn from. At the more coercive end of the continuum of governing instruments would be a larger redistributive programme, in which resources would be more visibly extracted from the more advantaged classes and redistributed to the less advantaged classes. Also at the more coercive end of the governing continuum would be direct regulation in which the sanctions or threat of sanctions would have to be directly applied. It is, of course, obvious that once a policy issue has matured and been on the public agenda for many years, all or most of the basic instruments could be utilized.[22]

Examples of the movement from less coercive policies to more coercive ones can be seen in a number of areas. The issue of equality for women was dealt with first by the use of a Royal commission to highlight the fact that there was a problem. Next, governments took action to improve the ability of women to compete in the labour force by providing innovative kinds of job training and *encouraging* employers not to discriminate against women. These kinds of policies benefited women without imposing an obvious cost on anyone. Next, legislation was passed to force employers to provide equal pay to women. This confers a benefit on women and imposes an obvious cost on only one limited group—employers. To this point, Canadian policy-makers have stopped short of employment quotas that would be the most coercive form of policy, in that they would clearly benefit women and impose a cost on men.

Thus, we see a movement along Doern and Phidd's hierarchy from exhortation to expenditure to regulation. Similar examples could be found in the approach to bilingualism, inflation, and foreign ownership, although the handling of the issue of foreign ownership indicates that one can move both ways on the continuum. Since coming to power in 1984, the Mulroney government seems to be acting in a less coercive manner with regard to foreign ownership.

Nicolas Baxter-Moore has developed a *neo-Marxist approach* to choosing governing instruments. He argues that the state will choose different types of instruments, depending on whether it is attempting to influence dominant or subordinate classes, or whether it is implementing a policy aimed at accumulation or legitimation.[23] He develops two specific hypotheses.

> From the neo-Marxist perspective, we may hypothesize first that the state will generally use less intrusive instruments when seeking the compliance of the dominant capitalist class and deploy more intrusive measures to direct or control the behaviour of subordinate classes.

> But the performance of the (sometimes contradictory) accumulation and legitimation functions often requires the state to disguise its activities on behalf of capital and to emphasize policies orientated towards subordinate groups. Therefore, we may also hypothesize that the state will tend to use less intrusive (or less visible) measures to foster capital accumulation and more intrusive (or more obvious) instruments when pursuing policies aimed primarily at legitimizing its rule.[24]

Woodside also argues that this perspective could explain government actions better than the coercion theory.

> [E]xperience suggests that governments do not always seek to avoid coercive solutions but, indeed, may at times seem to revel in taking a hard line from the start. While there are undoubtedly many reasons for these more heavy-handed responses, surely some of the most important ones include the constituency or group at which the policy is aimed, the circumstances in which the problem has appeared, and the nature of the problem involved.[25]

The example he gives is the much harsher coercive mechanisms available against welfare fraud than tax evasion. He suggests that these offences are treated differently because of the differences in the type of person likely to commit them.

Michael Trebilcock et al. have developed a *public choice theory* about the use of governing instruments. This employs the public choice theory discussed in Chapter 6. They argue that politicians choose governing instruments, not on the basis of policy rationality or efficiency, but rather to improve their electoral position. For example, they point out that there is a tendency for politicians to assign the administration of programs that impose significant costs on voters to "independent" agencies, so that the actions of these agencies are not directly associated with politicians.[26]

Another general rule that they suggest will be followed by politicians, is that benefits will be conferred on a concentrated group of uncommitted voters, while costs will be spread as widely as possible. This strategy could be supplemented by control of information, so that the benefit side could be emphasized and the cost side obscured.[27]

This approach would explain the growing use of tax expenditures as policy instruments. Tax expenditures are benefits in the form of reduced taxes to taxpayers who do (or refrain from doing) something desired by government. Their obvious attraction is that they provide low-visibility benefits, while spreading the cost (in increased taxes to others) so widely that people do not feel coerced.[28]

It is clear that the choice of governing instruments approach has a great deal of value in illuminating certain characteristics of public policy. First, it emphasizes that policy-making is not simply choosing a desired end, but rather it also involves a selection of means to accomplish that end—implementation. Second, it points out that there is a substitutability between the various instruments. Several instruments could potentially be used to accomplish the same ends; if one does not succeed, then policy-makers might try another.

In Part III, we borrow this concept of choice of governing instrument and apply it to the choice that governments make with regard to organizational form. When confronted with a particular task, governments must choose the appropriate organizational form for accomplishing the task. They have available such forms as operating departments, Crown corporations, and regulatory agencies. We will discuss the various characteristics of these organizational forms, with particular reference to why governments would choose one form over the others to deal with a particular problem.

EVALUATION

Evaluation is one of those unfortunate words that has several meanings at different levels. At the most basic level, policies have always been evaluated.

> It could be argued that program evaluations had been conducted virtually from Confederation. Parliamentary committees, central agencies, line departments, and the cabinet had examined and reviewed policies and programs over the years. Royal commissions and, more recently, "colored" papers and task forces were used frequently to examine and evaluate the effectiveness of various government policies and programs... [I]t is... clear that such efforts were sporadic and of uneven quality.[29]

This kind of rough-and-ready evaluation still goes on and its value should not be minimized.

> Assessment takes place constantly, even if it is only carried out on the basis of the intuitive feel of policymakers and even if the criteria are exclusively political in the narrowest sense of "what's in it for me?"[30]

Definitions of Evaluation

However, beginning roughly in the 1960s, the word evaluation began to take on a more rigorous and sophisticated meaning.

> *Program evaluation* is the periodic, independent and objective assessment of a program to determine, in light of present circumstances, the adequacy of its objectives, its design and its results both intended and unintended. Evaluations will call into question the very existence of the program. Matters such as the rationale of the program, its impact on the public, and its cost effectiveness as compared with alternative means of program delivery are also reviewed.[31]

Evaluations run the gamut from rough, seat-of-the-pants judgments, to highly sophisticated, heavily quantitative research documents. Performing evaluations is now a major industry. Most accounting/consulting firms have the capacity to perform evaluations, and there are even consulting firms that specialize in performing evaluations.[32] There is also a professional association of evaluators— the Canadian Evaluation Society—and a journal—the *Canadian Journal of Program Evaluation*.

The more sophisticated, quantitative evaluations can take several forms. Some compare output measures before and after the implementation of some policy, e.g., student test scores before and after introduction of a new program. Others survey participants in a program to determine how they perceive the worth of the program.

Some less quantitative styles of evaluation focus on the process used to implement the policy in order to determine if it is in line with what policy-makers had in mind. The "professional review" approach to evaluation involves a group of established experts reviewing a program and providing their best professional judgment on its value.[33] This is a common way to evaluate university programs or accredit professional programs. This approach is less objective than the previous types, but if the panel is chosen wisely, and its members have professional credibility, its results will be taken seriously.

There can be some confusion between policy analysis and program evaluation because they both tend to use the same kinds of analytical tools. Most writers make the distinction that policy analysis is a prospective, or before the fact, consideration of the likely future impacts of a policy if it is implemented. Program evaluation is a retrospective consideration of how a policy has functioned in the past. While this is a good general distinction, Ray Rist reminds us that the policy process is a bit too dynamic to make these kinds of firm distinctions.

> [W]hat appears at first glance as a clear dichotomy—retrospective and prospective—becomes with closer scrutiny two stages of an interactive process: decisions are made, information is gathered about the effects of those decisions, further decisions are made with data available on the results of previous decisions, etc., etc., etc.[34]

This chapter will not deal with the mechanics of how to conduct an evaluation, because that can become quite complicated and is described well in other books.[35] This chapter will discuss the political issues surrounding evaluation.

An Example: Evaluation of Gun Control Legislation

In 1977, the federal Parliament passed the Criminal Law Amendment Act, which imposed tighter regulations on the purchase and carrying of firearms, provided for search and seizure without a warrant (even when a criminal offence had not occurred), and provided for stiffer penalties for violation of gun control laws.

In the early 1980s, the Solicitor General of Canada entered into a contract with Decision Dynamics Corporation to perform an evaluation of the effects of this legislation. The study lasted for three years and resulted in the publication of a number of preliminary documents and a final report.[36]

There are two types of evaluations, and this study included both. An *outcome evaluation* or *impact evaluation* "is concerned with examining the extent to which a policy causes a change in the intended direction."[37] This kind of evaluation focusses on what the outcome or impact of the policy was supposed to be and compares that to what has, in fact, happened.

A *process evaluation* is

> concerned with the extent to which a particular policy or program is implemented according to its stated guidelines. The content of a particular public policy and its impact on those affected may be substantially modified, elaborated, or even negated during its implementation.[38]

It is important to do both kinds of evaluations, particularly if it appears that the policy is not working well. Some policies do not produce the desired result because they were flawed policies from the outset; other policies do not produce the desired result because they have never been implemented as intended. Performing both kinds of evaluation at the same time helps determine where the problem lies.

In the gun control case, the outcome or impact evaluation consisted of collecting statistics on the incidence of the use of firearms in the commission of various crimes, as well as non-criminal firearms incidents such as accidents and suicides. The evaluator traced the trend of these statistics through a number of years before and after the legislation. By determining if there was any change in the long-term trend at the time of implementation of the legislation, the evaluator was able to arrive at such conclusions as:

- The relative use of firearms in most violent crimes declined in the post-legislation period.
- There has been a moderate displacement of firearms by other weapons in robberies.
- There is a strong relationship between alcohol and drug use and firearms misuse in the two rural jurisdictions.
- Accidents with firearms were declining prior to 1978 but the legislation has contributed to further downward trends.
- Suicides with firearms declined moderately in the post-legislation period.[39]

The process evaluation examined "the implementation and effect of procedures and practices associated with the legislation." Specifically, this involved a review of statistics relating to screening people wanting to purchase firearms, sentencing of people convicted of firearms offences, and prohibiting people from owning firearms. Some of the conclusions of this part of the study were:

- Following 1979, courts imposed more severe sentences on firearms offences.
- Robberies with firearms resulted in longer jail sentences after the implementation of Bill C-51.
- Following 1979, sentences for repeat firearms offenders were more severe.
- The requirement for the mandatory imposition of prohibition orders following specified criminal convictions is seldom met.[40]

The Current State of Evaluation in the Government of Canada

In 1977, the federal Treasury Board instituted a policy requiring that departments evaluate their programs on a regular basis. In 1978, the Office of the Comptroller General (OCG) was established and given the responsibility to oversee all aspects of the federal government's evaluation policy.[41]

> The OCG develops and communicates evaluation policy and assists in the development of government-wide program performance and accountability procedures. The OCG provides guidance on evaluation methods, procedures and standards and; (sic) monitors departmental and agency evaluations, coordinating their plans with the needs of Treasury Board, Cabinet Committees and central agencies.[42]

While the OCG sets standards for evaluations and generally oversees the process, the department—specifically the deputy head of the department—is responsible for conducting evaluations. The OCG has produced a number of documents to assist departments in performing evaluations.[43] It also monitors the activity of departments, to ensure that they are evaluating all programs on a regular basis, and that the evaluations are of an appropriate quality. Currently, approximately 100 evaluations are performed each year. This number will have to approximately double if the OCG's target of evaluating each program on a 3 to 5 year cycle is to be met.[44]

Responsibility for conducting evaluations was situated within the department because the government wanted to emphasize that evaluation is an integral part of the policy-management process, and not a separate process imposed by an outside agency that visits periodically, yet does not really understand the operation of the program. It was hoped that the evaluation process would be more acceptable to managers if it was clear that it was to be used as a management tool.

The deputy head of the department, i.e., the administrative, not the political, head of the department, is viewed as the client for the study. This means that the evaluation will be performed to the deputy head's specifications and will be geared to meeting his or her needs. Of course, the terms of the evaluation must also meet guidelines determined by the OCG. In identifying the client, the government could have cast its net a bit wider and said that the client would be the minister, the full Cabinet, the legislature, the clients of the program, or even society as a whole. The choice of the client will influence the scope of the evaluation.

A *formative evaluation* is targeted at senior management, i.e., the deputy head. It involves "monitoring and feedback activities which enable managers to improve performance by adjusting operations and redesigning programs... "[45] A formative evaluation does not deal with the overall value of the policy, because that is a matter for politicians, not administrators.

A *summative evaluation* is targeted at the minister, full Cabinet, or even the entire community. These evaluations are "comprehensive assessments of the degree of success achieved by programs."[46] This kind of evaluation is directed at the efficacy of the policy itself, and could result in a modification of the underlying policy. This would be of more concern to the minister than the deputy minister.

In sum, a formative evaluation measures how well a program is managed, while a summative evaluation measures whether the policy is attaining its desired end. Both types of evaluation have their uses.

It can be difficult to draw firm lines between formative and summative evaluations, but the federal government's decision to make the deputy head the client for all evaluations has meant that most evaluations have tended to be formative rather than summative.

The public distribution of evaluations has been a contentious issue for the Canadian government. At first, most evaluations were regarded as confidential, and so were available only within the department and OCG. Gradually, this policy has been loosened, so that now all evaluations are available to the public, except those involving sensitive areas such as national security.

Given that a policy evaluation is a very important document in promoting accountability and responsibility in government, it would seem rather extraordinary to keep it confidential. However, this is a more complex issue than it seems at first. The knowledge that an evaluation will be made public can have an impact on which programs will be evaluated, what issues the evaluator will address, and how much cooperation the evaluator will receive from program managers. When a report will be made public, there could be a tendency to focus on the most positive aspects of the program and cover up any problems. This is clearly not in the best long-term interests of the program, the program managers, or the general public. Paradoxically, the desire to make the maximum use of evaluations could result in reducing both the number of evaluations performed and the scope of those that are performed.[47]

Impediments to Good Evaluation[48]

Many of the obstacles to good evaluation are the same *methodological problems* that one encounters in any social science research. These will not be reviewed in detail here, because there are many good, comprehensive reviews of these problems.[49] However, it is worth mentioning just a few to convey the general idea.

Measuring some kinds of intangible outputs of programs is a standard problem. For example, how would one measure the worth of a program designed to improve people's self-confidence and self-esteem?

The establishment of experimental and control groups is always a problem with government programs, because it is politically very difficult to tell some people that, for the good of science, they will not be allowed to benefit from a new program.

Establishing the causal link between a new program and some change is also very difficult in a dynamic world. In the evaluation of gun control legislation discussed earlier, the evaluator drew such conclusions as: the relative use of firearms in most violent crimes declined in the post-legislation period. Notice that she does not say that this decline *was* caused by the legislation. The statistical trend suggests that there could be a causal link between the two, but statistical evidence can never *prove* a linkage of this sort.

The list can go on and on. Walter Williams has used the phrase "the iron law of absolute evaluation flaws" to suggest that no real-life evaluation could ever match the methodological rigour demanded by some social scientists, particularly when they want to attack the program on political grounds, anyway.[50] However, there are a number of other problems more specific to public policy evaluations.

Government programs frequently have *multiple and/or unclear goals*. In order to evaluate a program, there must be a clear understanding of what the program was supposed to accomplish. If a program has several objectives, some of which politicians refuse to acknowledge openly, then it is very difficult to determine how successful the program has been. For example, if the purpose of a regional economic development program is to create permanent jobs in an area, then it might not appear to be successful. However, if the real purpose of the program is to ensure that politicians have the discretion to throw money at selected ridings immediately before an election, it might be highly successful.

There are some things that governments do not want to know. When a government is firmly committed to a particular policy for political, historical, or ideological reasons, it is unlikely to change that policy, regardless of the findings of an evaluation. And if it is unlikely to change the policy, then it does not want to know whether it has been successful; the answer might be negative. Therefore, what purpose would an evaluation serve? "Governments concerned with their popular support are unlikely to take unpopular decisions simply because of the weight of intellectual argument that backs up such proposals."[51]

The best example might be the federal government's policy with regard to a bilingual public service. All three political parties are committed to this policy. If an evaluation were performed that indicated that, in strict economic terms, a unilingual public service would function better, no change in the status quo would occur. The only use of such an evaluation would be to provide a tool for certain groups to attack bilingualism, and in the current environment, the federal government is unlikely to fund such an effort.

Table 7.1
USES OF EVALUATIONS

	%
Improve operations	50
Structural change	17
Confirm program	8
Adjust resources	18
Procedural usage	34
No usage	4

Percentages do not add to 100 because some evaluations had more than one use identified.

A dog will not bring the stick with which he or she will be beaten. Douglas Hartle coined his picturesque phrase when writing about budgetary systems, but it is equally applicable to evaluation. Public servants resist evaluations, in the first place, because they cost too much and take up too much time that could be spent actually administering the program. However, they also fear the results of the evaluation. If the results are negative, it could result in media coverage that could jeopardize the future of the program and therefore their jobs. The fears of the public servant are compounded by a concern that the evaluator (or readers of the evaluation) will misunderstand or overlook some aspect of the program, and provide a negative evaluation based on faulty perceptions. The media, in particular, are notorious for searching for, and magnifying, the one negative comment in an otherwise positive report.

Does Policy Evaluation Matter?

The obvious question that arises from all this discussion of evaluation is: does any of this matter? Are evaluations ever actually used for anything? Keeping in mind the powerful coalitions that frequently grow up in support of programs, do these data have any real impact?

The answer to this question is mixed. Stephen Brooks has argued that there "is an impressive consensus that its impact has been marginal."[52] Many other critics of the process have noted the very low profile of these evaluations in the media, and the fact that there are virtually no well-known cases of programs being terminated as a result of negative evaluations.

Not surprisingly, officials of the OCG have a more positive assessment. They reviewed 150 evaluations undertaken between 1984 and 1988. Table 7.1 lists the uses that have been made of those evaluations.[53] The table indicates that 96 percent of the evaluations were put to some use, even if it was only to reassure managers that the program was working well. The *Government Program Evaluation Plan* describes several of the changes made in detail. Some of these were admittedly quite marginal, but it does list one program that was terminated as a result of an evaluation.

Timothy Plumptre, who has done an extensive review of management in the federal government, provides a rather mixed assessment of the current state of evaluation.

> Is program evaluation in Ottawa "working"? Evaluation is like chastity: people support it in principle, but in practice they prefer if it is mandatory for others and optional for them. Although the OCG's assessment may be coloured somewhat by the fact that evaluation is a mainstay of the Office's mandate, it is clear that some useful work is being done. However, the results are a good deal less than what was originally hoped for: evaluation has not, at time of writing, become a key element in the resource allocation process, and major studies still tend to take place outside the system. In the mid-1980s, five deputy ministers, questioned on the usefulness of the program evaluation system, agreed that there should be more rigorous reviews of program performance, but their assessment of the system in place at that time was broadly consistent: "The jury is out."[54]

It might be that some commentators have expected too much of program evaluation. The OCG suggests that evaluation should not be considered as the definitive final word, but rather should be seen as one element to be used in a very complex decision-making process.

> Program evaluation is one means of providing relevant, timely, and objective findings—information, evidence and conclusions—and recommendations on the performance of government programs, thereby improving the information base on which decisions are taken. In this view, program evaluation, as part of this decision making and management process, should not be seen as an exercise in scientific research aimed at producing definitive "scientific" conclusions about programs and their results. Rather it should be seen as input to the complex, interactive process that is government decision making, with the aim of producing objective but not necessarily conclusive evidence on the results of programs.[55]

CONCLUSION

This chapter has reviewed what happens after a policy has been formulated. The main point of this chapter is to show that the frequently unseen mechanisms that implement and evaluate policies can have as great an impact on the success of those policies as the high-profile legislators who formulated the policy. The next section of this book looks at the organization and operation of those vehicles—operating departments, public enterprises, and regulatory agencies.

NOTES

1. Eugene Bardach, *The Implementation Game: What Happens After a Bill Becomes Law* (Cambridge, Mass.: The MIT Press, 1977), p. 38.
2. Randall B. Ripley and Grace A. Franklin, *Policy Implementation and Bureaucracy*, 3rd ed. (Chicago: The Dorsey Press, 1986), p. 11. (Emphasis in original.)
3. Ibid., p. 13.
4. Robert T. Nakamura and Frank Smallwood, *The Politics of Policy Implementation* (New York: St. Martin's Press, 1980), ch. 7.

5. Ibid., p. 122.
6. This phenomenon of subordinates' power over superiors is also considered in Donald S. Van Meter and Carl E. Van Horn, "The Policy Implementation Process: A Conceptual Framework," *Administration and Society* 6 (February 1975): 454-58.
7. "Federalism, Nationalism and Democracy in America," *American Political Science Review* 72 (March 1978): 17. (Emphasis in original.)
8. H. L. Laframboise, "Moving a Proposal to a Positive Decision: A Case Study of the Invisible Process," *Optimum* 4, no. 3 (1973): 31-41; J. L. Granatstein, *The Ottawa Men* (Toronto: Oxford University Press, 1982); Kenneth Kernaghan and T. H. McLeod, "Mandarins and Ministers in the Canadian Administrative State," in O.P. Dwivedi, ed., *The Administrative State in Canada* (Toronto: University of Toronto Press, 1982), pp. 17-30.
9. "Thinking about Programmed and Adaptive Implementation: Matching Strategies to Situations," in Helen M. Ingram and Dean E. Mann, eds., *Why Policies Succeed or Fail* (Beverly Hills, Calif.: Sage, 1980), pp. 205-206. (Footnote omitted.) A book of case studies influenced by this approach is Dennis J. Palumbo and Marvin A. Harder, eds., *Implementing Public Policy* (Lexington, Mass.: Lexington Books, 1981).
10. Berman, "Thinking about Programmed and Adaptive Implementation," pp. 210-11.
11. Ibid., p. 214.
12. Paul Sabatier and Daniel Mazmanian, "The Conditions of Effective Implementation: A Guide to Accomplishing Policy Objectives," *Policy Analysis* (Fall 1979): pp. 481-504. (Emphasis in original.)
13. Nakamura and Smallwood, *The Politics of Policy Implementation*, p. 24.
14. Jeffrey L. Pressman and Aaron B. Wildavsky, *Implementation* (Berkeley and Los Angeles: University of California Press, 1974), p. 92.
15. Ibid.
16. Bardach, *The Implementation Game*, p. 42.
17. In spite of many pious protestations about the positive value of participation, the hard evidence is not clear on this point. For a good review of this literature, see Neal Gross, Joseph B. Giacquinta, and Marilyn Bernstein, *Implementing Organizational Innovations: A Sociological Analysis of Planned Educational Change* (New York: Basic Books, 1971), pp. 25-29.
18. G. Bruce Doern and Richard W. Phidd, *Canadian Public Policy: Ideas, Structure, Process* (Toronto: Methuen, 1983), p. 110.
19. Ibid.
20. "Policy Instruments and the Study of Public Policy," *Canadian Journal of Political Science* 19, no. 4 (December 1986): 787.
21. Michael M. Atkinson and Robert A. Nigol, "Selecting Policy Instruments: Neo-Institutional and Rational Choice Interpretations of Automobile Insurance in Ontario," *Canadian Journal of Political Science* 22, no. 1 (March 1989): 131-32.
22. G. Bruce Doern and V. Seymour Wilson, "Conclusions and Observations," in G. Bruce Doern and V. Seymour Wilson, eds., *Issues in Canadian Public Policy* (Macmillan, 1974), p. 339.
23. "Policy Implementation and the Role of the State: A Revised Approach to the Study of Policy Instruments," in Robert J. Jackson, Doreen Jackson, and Nicolas Baxter-Moore, eds., *Contemporary Canadian Politics* (Scarborough, Ont.: Prentice-Hall, 1987), pp. 336-55.
24. Ibid., p. 346.
25. "Policy Instruments and the Study of Public Policy," p. 786. (Footnote omitted.)

26. *The Choice of Governing Instrument* (Ottawa: Minister of Supply and Services Canada, 1982), p. 33.

27. Ibid.

28. Kenneth Woodside, "The Political Economy of Policy Instruments: Tax Expenditures and Subsidies in Canada," in Michael M. Atkinson and Marsha A. Chandler, eds., *The Politics of Canadian Public Policy* (Toronto: University of Toronto Press, 1983), pp. 175-76 and passim.

29. R. V. Segsworth, "Policy and Program Evaluation in the Government of Canada," in Ray C. Rist, ed., *Program Evaluation and the Management of Government* (New Brunswick, N.J.: Transaction Publishers, 1990), p. 21. (Footnote omitted.)

30. Ripley and Franklin, *Policy Implementation and Bureaucracy*, p. 9.

31. Office of the Comptroller General, *Guide on the Program Evaluation Function* (Minister of Supply and Services Canada, 1981), p. 19 (Emphasis in original.)

32. The development of the policy analysis industry is described well in Leslie A. Pal, *Public Policy Analysis* (Toronto: Methuen, 1987), ch. 4.

33. Ernest R. House, *Evaluating with Validity* (Beverly Hills: Sage, 1980), p. 34 ff.

34. "Managing of Evaluations or Managing by Evaluations: Choices and Consequences," in Rist, ed., *Program Evaluation and the Management of Government*, p. 4.

35. Office of the Comptroller General, *Principles for the Evaluation of Programs by Federal Departments and Agencies* (Minister of Supply and Services Canada, 1981); David Nachmias, *Public Policy Evaluation: Approaches and Methods* (New York: St. Martin's Press, 1979); Arlene Fink and Jacqueline Kosecoff, *An Evaluation Primer* (Beverly Hills, Calif.: Sage Publications, 1978).

36. The discussion in this section is based on Elisabeth Scarff, Decision Dynamics Corporation, *Evaluation of the Canadian Gun Control Legislation: Final Report* (Ottawa: Minister of Supply and Services Canada, 1983).

37. Nachmias, *Public Policy Evaluation*, p. 5.

38. Ibid.

39. Scarff, *Evaluation of the Canadian Gun Control Legislation*, pp. 71-72.

40. Ibid., pp. 72-73.

41. The Office of the Comptroller General has a number of other responsibilities. It will be discussed in more detail in Chapter 27.

42. *1990-91 Estimates: Part III: Treasury Board of Canada/Comptroller General* (Ottawa: Minister of Supply and Services Canada, 1990), p. 12.

43. Office of the Comptroller General, *Working Standards for the Evaluation of Programs in Federal Departments and Agencies* (Minister of Supply and Services Canada, 1989); *Principles for the Evaluation of Programs by Federal Departments and Agencies* (Minister of Supply and Services Canada, 1981); *Guide on the Program Evaluation Function* (Minister of Supply and Services Canada, 1981).

44. Michael H. Rayner, "Using Evaluation In the Federal Government," *The Canadian Journal of Program Evaluation* 1, no. 1 (April 1986): 3.

45. Rodney Dobell and David Zussman, "An Evaluation System for Government: If Politics Is Theatre, Then Evaluation Is (Mostly) Art," *Canadian Public Administration* 24, no. 3 (Fall 1981): 415-16.

46. Ibid., p. 416.

47. Michael Hicks, "Evaluating Evaluation in Today's Government: Summary of Discussions," *Canadian Public Administration* 24, no. 3 (Fall 1981): 357.

48. One of the best general critiques of evaluation is found in W. Irwin Gillespie, " 'Fools' Gold: The Quest for a Method of Evaluating Government Spending," in G.

Bruce Doern and Allan M. Maslove, eds., *The Public Evaluation of Government Spending* (Toronto: Institute for Research on Public Policy, 1979), pp. 39-59.

49. Felix A. Nigro and Lloyd G. Nigro, *Modern Public Administration*, 4th ed. (New York: Harper & Row, 1977), pp. 279-82.

50. *Social Policy Research and Analysis* (New York: Elsevier, 1971), ch. 7.

51. Stephen Brooks, *Public Policy in Canada* (Toronto: McClelland & Stewart, 1989), p. 83.

52. Ibid.

53. Office of the Comptroller General, *GPEP 89: Government Program Evaluation Plan* (Minister of Supply and Services Canada, 1989), p. 30.

54. *Beyond the Bottom Line: Management in Government* (Halifax: The Institute for Research on Public Policy), p. 267.

55. *Guide on the Program Evaluation Function*, p. 4.

BIBLIOGRAPHY

Adie, Robert F., and Paul Thomas. *Canadian Public Administration: Problematic Perspectives.* 2nd ed. Scarborough, Ont.: Prentice-Hall Canada, 1987.

Atkinson, Michael M., and Marsha A. Chandler, eds. *The Politics of Canadian Public Policy.* Toronto: University of Toronto Press, 1983.

Atkinson, Michael M., and Robert A. Nigol. "Selecting Policy Instruments: Neo-Institutional and Rational Choice Interpretations of Automobile Insurance in Ontario." *Canadian Journal of Political Science* 22, no. 1 (March 1989): 107-35.

Bardach, Eugene. *The Implementation Game: What Happens After a Bill Becomes a Law.* Cambridge, Mass.: The MIT Press, 1977.

Baxter-Moore, Nicolas. "Policy Implementation and the Role of the State." In Robert Jackson, Doreen Jackson, and Nicolas Baxter-Moore, eds., *Contemporary Canadian Politics.* Scarborough, Ont.: Prentice-Hall Canada, 1987, pp. 336-55.

Berman, Paul. "Thinking about Programmed and Adaptive Implementation: Matching Strategies to Situations." In Helen M. Ingram and Dean Mann, eds., *Why Policies Succeed or Fail.* Beverly Hills: Sage Publications, 1980, pp. 205-27.

Dobell, Rodney, and David Zussman. "An Evaluation System for Government: If Politics Is Theatre, Then Evaluation Is (Mostly) Art." *Canadian Public Administration* 24, no. 3 (Fall 1981): 404-27.

Doern, G. Bruce, and Peter Aucoin, eds. *Public Policy in Canada.* Toronto: Macmillan, 1979.

——. *The Structures of Policy-Making in Canada.* Toronto: Macmillan Canada, 1971.

Doern, G. Bruce, and Allan M. Maslove, eds. *The Public Evaluation of Government Spending.* Toronto: Institute for Research on Public Policy, 1979.

Doern, G. Bruce, and Richard W. Phidd. *Canadian Public Policy: Ideas, Structure, Process.* Toronto: Methuen, 1983.

Doern, G. Bruce, and V. Seymour Wilson, eds. *Issues in Canadian Public Policy.* Toronto: Macmillan,1974.

Dunn, William N. *Public Policy Analysis.* Englewood Cliffs, N. J.: Prentice-Hall, 1981.

Dunsire, Andrew. *Implementation in a Bureaucracy.* Oxford: Martin Robertson, 1978.

Dye, Thomas R. *Policy Analysis: What Governments Do, Why They Do It, and What Difference It Makes.* University, Ala.: The University of Alabama Press, 1976.

Fink, Arlene, and Jacqueline Kosecoff. *An Evaluation Primer.* Beverly Hills, Calif.: Sage Publications, 1978.

Gross, Neal, Joseph B. Giacquinta, and Marilyn Bernstein. *Implementing Organizational Innovations: A Sociological Analysis of Planned Educational Change*. New York: Basic Books, 1971.

Hicks, Michael. "Evaluating Evaluation in Today's Government: Summary of Discussions." *Canadian Public Administration* 24, no. 3 (Fall 1981): 350-58.

House, Ernest R. *Evaluating with Validity*. Beverly Hills: Sage Publications, 1980.

Laframboise, H. L. "Moving a Proposal to a Positive Decision: A Case Study of the Invisible Process." *Optimum* 4, no. 3 (1973): 31-41.

March, James G., and Herbert A. Simon. *Organizations*. New York: John Wiley & Sons, 1958.

McInnes, Simon. "Federal-Provincial Negotiation: Family Allowances 1970-1976." Ph.D. diss., Carleton University, 1978.

Nachmias, David. *Public Policy Evaluation: Approaches and Methods*. New York: St. Martin's Press, 1979.

Nakamura, Robert T., and Frank Smallwood. *The Politics of Policy Implementation*. New York: St. Martin's Press, 1980.

Nigro, Felix A., and Lloyd G. Nigro. *Modern Public Administration*. 4th ed. New York: Harper & Row, 1977.

Palumbo, Dennis J., and Marvin A. Harder, eds. *Implementing Public Policy*. Lexington, Mass.: Lexington Books, 1981.

Pressman, Jeffrey L., and Aaron B. Wildavsky. *Implementation*. Berkeley and Los Angeles: University of California Press, 1974.

Rayner, Michael H. "Using Evaluation In the Federal Government," *The Canadian Journal of Program Evaluation* 1, no. 1 (April 1986): 1-10.

Ripley, Randall B., and Grace A. Franklin. *Policy Implementation and Bureaucracy*. 3rd ed. Chicago: The Dorsey Press, 1986.

Rist, Ray C., ed. *Program Evaluation and the Management of Government*. New Brunswick, N.J.: Transaction Publishers, 1990.

Schultz, Richard J. *Federalism, Bureaucracy, and Public Policy*. Montreal: McGill-Queen's University Press, 1980.

Siegel, David. "Provincial-Municipal Relations in Ontario: A Case Study of Roads." Ph.D. diss., University of Toronto, 1984.

Simon, Herbert. *Administrative Behavior*. 2nd ed. New York: The Free Press, 1957.

Trebilcock, M. J., R. S. Prichard, D. G. Hartle, and D. N. Dewees. *The Choice of Governing Instrument*. Ottawa: Minister of Supply and Services Canada, 1982.

Van Meter, Donald S., and Carl E. Van Horn. "The Policy Implementation Process: A Conceptual Framework." *Administration & Society* 6 (February 1975): 445-88.

Woodside, Kenneth, "Policy Instruments and the Study of Public Policy." *Canadian Journal of Political Science* 19, no. 4 (December 1986): 775-93.

CASES

In *Case Program in Canadian Public Administration* (Toronto: Institute of Public Administration of Canada):

L'Affaire Caloil. By Michel Paquin
The Elusive IPB System. By Walter Baker
The Toronto Airport(s). By Sandford F. Borins
Assessing Housing Needs in Manitoba's Remote Communities. By Nelson Wiseman

III

THE CHOICE OF ORGANIZATIONAL FORM

8

Government Departments and Central Agencies

THE CHOICE OF ORGANIZATIONAL FORM

In the first two parts of this book, the emphasis was on the development of certain general principles or theories. The major purpose of this third part is to build on those general ideas and discuss how they apply in the Canadian context. Each chapter in this part covers the structure and standard method of operation of one of the main organizational forms employed in parliamentary governments. Chapters 8, 9, and 10 deal respectively with government departments and central agencies, Crown corporations, and regulatory agencies. Chapter 11 covers a miscellany of other forms of organization, such as Royal commissions and task forces.

The theme that ties these chapters together is the *choice of organizational form*, that is, how do the various organizational forms differ from one another, and why do governments choose a particular organizational form to carry out a particular responsibility.

Chapter 7 pointed out that when a government is confronted with a problem, it has a number of ways of dealing with that problem. The main instruments that government could employ were summarized as:

- exhortation
- expenditure
- taxation
- regulation, and
- public enterprise.[1]

In some cases, the instrument to be employed is fairly obvious. For example, taxation is likely to work better than exhortation in raising revenue. However, in many cases there are a variety of instruments that could be used to accomplish a particular end.

If a government wishes to promote indigenous cultural activity, it can engage in public ownership, as in the case of the Canadian Broadcasting Corporation or the National Film Board; provide direct subsidies to theatre groups; finance granting institutions (e.g. the Canada Council); provide tax incentives, such as capital cost allowance on films or an expense allowance for advertising; and engage in regulation (e.g. through the Canadian Radio-Television (sic) Telecommunications Commission's broadcasting content rules).[2]

Governments have available to them a broad range of organizational forms. When governments organize, or re-organize, they are not simply deciding to carry out a particular function, they are also making a strategic choice about *how* that function ought to be carried out. In most cases, the choice of the appropriate strategy for implementation can be a key determinant of how well the government's objective will be met.

One of the key choices that a government makes is the choice of the organizational structure—operating department, Crown corporation, regulatory agency, or other structure—in which responsibility for the function will be lodged. There are a number of factors that could influence governments in choosing a particular organizational form. This decision is not always made according to the tenets of comprehensive rationality. In many cases, governments simply "follow-the-leader" by adopting the kind of structure that is already employed, for the same or similar purposes, in other jurisdictions.

However, in some cases, governments make conscious decisions about organizational forms. For example, if a particular function is very much like a commercial operation, such as operating an airline or oil company, then the Crown corporation form is likely to be chosen. If a function requires an arm's-length relationship with government, such as regulating broadcasting, then the regulatory agency will likely be the preferred form. Each chapter in this section will consider the unique characteristics of each of the organizational forms.

This chapter starts that process by examining the departmental form of organization. It begins with a discussion of the legal foundations of departments, which requires an examination of interactions between departments, the legislature, and the political executive (that is, the Cabinet).[3] Next, an innovative form of organization employed in the federal government—the ministers and ministries of state—will be described. Then, the role of central agencies such as the Prime Minister's Office and the Privy Council Office will also be discussed. Finally, the organization structure of a typical operating department will be described.

THE LEGISLATURE, THE EXECUTIVE, AND DEPARTMENTS

It is customary to speak of three branches of government—legislative, executive, and judicial. The judicial branch, which consists of the law courts and related institutions, is not discussed in this chapter, but is considered in detail in Chapter 18. In Canada, the legislative branch of the federal government consists of the Queen and two houses or chambers—the House of Commons and the Senate. Each of the provincial legislatures has only one house (e.g., the National Assembly in Quebec, and the Legislative Assembly in several western provinces).

The executive branch is technically headed by the Queen, represented in Canada by the **Governor General** and the Lieutenant Governors of the provinces. In practice, neither the Queen nor any of her vice-regal representatives ever acts except on the advice of the government of the day as embodied in the Prime Minister (or provincial Premier) and the Cabinet. This means that the responsibilities of the executive branch are carried out collectively by Cabinet or what is commonly called "the government." All public servants act under the direction and control of the Cabinet, and are included, therefore, as part of the executive branch. Thus, in this book, the practical, working definition of the executive is the Cabinet and the public service.

One sometimes hears that something is done by the **Governor General in Council** or the **Lieutenant Governor in Council**. This means that the Governor General or Lieutenant Governor has taken some legal action after consultation with the Cabinet. It actually means that the Cabinet has taken some action; the Governor General's or Lieutenant Governor's signature is a formality.

The congressional system of government in the United States is characterized by a balance of powers between the three branches so that no one branch has authority over any other. In parliamentary systems, like Canada's, it is an important principle that the executive branch is accountable to the legislative branch (i.e., the branch most directly responsible to the general public). The two branches are, in fact, joined because Cabinet ministers are almost invariably members of the legislative branch. This institutional arrangement helps the legislature to hold the executive accountable for its actions.

Definition of a Department

It is difficult to establish a precise, working definition of an **operating department**. Legal definitions can be found in both the Financial Administration Act [4] and the Public Service Employment Act.[5] However, not only are these two legislative definitions different, but, since their purpose is to determine which organizations will be subject to a particular regime of financial or personnel administration, they do not capture the essence of a department.

The definition used in this book is that of J. E. Hodgetts, who states that

> [A] department is an administrative unit comprising one or more organizational components over which a minister has direct management and control. This definition restricts our terms of reference to major ministerial portfolios and thereby excludes subordinate units such as Insurance and Public Printing and Stationery that in law actually carry the title 'department.' Since we are also concerned with the ways in which programs are allocated to these units, we can disregard cabinet portfolios to which no duties are assigned: thus the customary minister without portfolio will be excluded from the list.[6]

One characteristic that should be emphasized in distinguishing operating departments from regulatory agencies and Crown corporations is that of direct management and control by the minister. It is a constitutional convention that the minister should very closely and directly control the actions of an operating department. This differs from the minister's relationship with regulatory agencies and Crown corporations in which there are certain understood limits on the direct involvement of the minister in the specifics of their day-to-day management.

Classification Systems for Departments

There are so many departments with so many specialized responsibilities that a number of writers have tried to facilitate understanding of their roles by grouping them in some way. Hodgetts's classification system is based on the *general policy fields* addressed, or functions carried out by the department, such as "public works, communications, and transportation" and "conservation, development, and promotion of physical resources."[7]

Doern focusses on the *relative power* of different departments by developing a classification system that considers size of budget, responsibility for coordination, and knowledge or research capability.[8] He argues that all three of these factors are sources of power, although of different types. Thus, it is very difficult to compare the importance of a department with a large budget, such as National Health and Welfare, and one with a small budget but a broad coordinating role, such as Treasury Board. He identified four types of departments, but one was an experimental structure that is no longer in use. The three remaining types are horizontal policy coordinative, administrative coordinative, and vertical constituency. A contemporary application of Doern's classification scheme results in the grouping of departments shown in Table 8.1.

The *horizontal policy coordinative departments* tend to be the most politically influential:

> They have inherent high policy influence because of the formal authority they possess and because they afford their occupants the highest number of strategic opportunities to intervene in almost any policy issue if the occupant wishes. They each deal respectively with the traditionally most basic horizontal or cross- cutting dimensions of government policy, namely overall political leadership and strategy, foreign policy and the foreign implications of domestic policy fields, aggregate economic and fiscal policy, the basic legal and judicial concepts and values of the state, and the overall management of government spending programmes.[9]

These departments tend to be weak in terms of size of budget, but very strong in the other two dimensions.

The *horizontal administrative coordinative departments* are usually felt to be the least influential, in that they are assumed to be the "nuts and bolts" departments that provide the wherewithal for other departments to operate. However, even these departments have some political and policy-making significance. The Department of National Revenue–Taxation has caused a stir in the past because of its assessment and collection practices, and it is sometimes suggested that the purchasing policy of the Department of Supply and Services could be used as a tool for economic development.

The *vertical constituency departments* are generally involved in providing services directly to the public. These are high-profile departments in that they have the largest budgets and deal with a large constituency. In general, they lack

Table 8.1
DOERN'S CLASSIFICATION OF DEPARTMENTS AND CENTRAL AGENCIES

Horizontal Policy Coordinative Departments
External Affairs
Finance
Justice
Privy Council
Federal-Provincial Relations Office
Treasury Board

Horizontal Administrative Coordinative Departments
National Revenue
Public Works
Supply and Services

Vertical Constituency Departments
Agriculture
Communications
Consumer and Corporate Affairs
Employment and Immigration
Energy, Mines and Resources
Environment
Fisheries and Oceans
Indian Affairs and Northern Development
Industry, Science and Technology
Labour
National Defence
National Health and Welfare
Secretary of State
Solicitor General
Transport
Veterans Affairs

Source: Based on G. Bruce Doern, "Horizontal and Vertical Portfolios in Government," in G. Bruce Doern and V. Seymour Wilson, eds., *Issues in Canadian Public Policy* (Toronto: Macmillan, 1974), pp. 315-16, but updated to reflect changes since the earlier tables were originally prepared.

the power to intervene in the affairs of other departments, which only comes with the responsibility to coordinate, but their large budget and vocal constituency give these departments a significant amount of power. It is difficult for the horizontal coordinative portfolios to intervene too much in the affairs of these departments without raising the ire of the large number of constituents who are dependent on the departments for service.

While it is possible to group departments according to characteristics, it is considerably more difficult to rank these portfolios, or the ministers who hold them, in order of importance. A minister's relative position in Cabinet is determined in part by his or her portfolio, but also in large part by such other factors as regional power base, personal diplomatic and judgmental skills, and relationship with the Prime Minister. In short, no portfolio can be deemed unimportant. All portfolios have significant roles, and they can all lead to substantial embarrassment for the government if the occupant of a portfolio is careless or incompetent.

Departments are the most closely controlled of all government agencies. Other entities such as regulatory agencies and Crown corporations are deliberately insulated, to some extent, from direct control by the legislature and the executive, but departments have no such insulation. It is important to consider some of those avenues of legislative and executive control.

The Legislature and Government Departments

This section will discuss the various methods used by the legislature to control government departments. (A more complete description of the interactions between the legislature and the bureaucracy is contained in Chapter 17.) This control begins at the time of the creation of a new department, because a new department can be created only by an Act of Parliament. This enabling legislation sets out the responsibilities of the department and the limits of its authority. The statute establishing the federal Department of Communications is typical in that it is only two pages long, and its very general wording imposes only rather broad conditions on the department's operation. The statute provides in part that:

> 2. (1) There is hereby established a department of the Government of Canada called the Department of Communications over which the Minister of Communications appointed by commission under the Great Seal shall preside.
>
> (2) The Minister holds office during pleasure and has the management and direction of the Department . . .
>
> 4. The powers, duties and functions of the Minister extend to and include all matters over which Parliament has jurisdiction, not by law assigned to any other department, branch or agency of the Government of Canada, relating to
> (a) telecommunications; and
> (b) the development and utilization generally of communications undertakings, facilities, systems and services for Canada.[10]

In some provinces, this kind of legislation is considerably longer and more detailed and restrictive. In any case, the executive has fairly broad prerogatives to arrange the internal structure of departments. Under the federal Public Service Rearrangement and Transfer of Duties Act,[11] the executive also has the power to transfer responsibilities between departments.

In addition to the initial, enabling legislation, Parliament sometimes passes other legislation affecting departments. This includes both specific legislation, such as setting up a new program and assigning it to a department, and general legislation, such as the Financial Administration Act or the Public Service Employment Act, that binds all departments in certain matters. Thus, Parliament can specify a department's mandate as loosely or as tightly as it wants, although the usual practice is to provide a broad mandate that allows maximum flexibility to the executive.

Another important element of Parliament's relationship to the executive is the annual budget. Each year the executive must seek parliamentary approval to spend funds in the upcoming year. At a minimum, the members of Parliament, particularly Opposition members, use this opportunity to question ministers and public servants about the operation of their departments and programs. In extreme cases, Parliament could decide to reduce, or even entirely eliminate, an appropriation for a department.

While these methods by which the legislature can affect departmental operations are, legally speaking, correct, realism requires some modification in practice. When the government party holds a majority of seats in the legislature, the government has fairly effective control over the legislation passed. Members of the Opposition can introduce amendments to proposed legislation, including reductions of appropriations, but these are unlikely to be passed. In the case of a minority government, the situation is more complex, but the government usually finds some method of exercising a certain amount of control over activities in the legislature.[12] Obviously, if it cannot exert sufficient control, it will not govern long.

However, this should not be taken to mean that the government can totally dominate the legislature. Opposition members have certain tools at their disposal to thwart arbitrary government actions. The legislature is a highly public forum, and the government is very sensitive to the embarrassment that it can suffer when the Opposition rallies public opinion against some unpopular action of the government. The government, particularly in a majority situation, has a strong position, but not an absolutely commanding one. Opposition parties still have means of holding a government accountable for its actions.

This is where the doctrine of *individual ministerial responsibility* becomes important.[13] Conceptually, the principle of ministerial responsibility holds that a minister is responsible for all actions carried out by his or her department. This means that, even if the minister did not approve an action in advance or had no knowledge of it, he or she still must accept responsibility for the action. This principle is an important element in a system of responsible government because the minister is the only link between the legislature and the operating department. If the minister could avoid responsibility for the actions of his or her department, then the legislature would have no effective way of holding the executive accountable for its actions. Since the minister is accountable for the actions of his or her department, it is important that there are adequate methods available for the minister to control the department.

The Executive and Government Departments

In the first place, the minister is the political head of the department and so has line authority over all public servants in the department. Within the provisions of relevant legislation, he or she has full authority to assign duties to departmental employees and supervise their activities. In Chapters 3, 4, and 5, there was some discussion of the difficulties of administrative superiors holding subordinates truly accountable for their actions. The large size and geographical decentralization of most departments, and the incredible demands made on ministers' time in the legislature and in constituency work, make the enforcement of true accountability particularly problematic. However, ministers have a number of tools to assist them in controlling the activities of operating departments.

All ministers have a small personal staff. The members of this staff are selected personally by the minister and are not considered to be public servants; rather they are the minister's political assistants. They are selected partly for their administrative competence, but unlike public servants, they are also selected for their partisan affiliation. Their roles are difficult to define because each minister uses them in somewhat different ways; however, one role they have in common is assisting the minister to exercise political control over the bureaucracy.[14]

Ministers also have more formal, legal means of controlling their departments. The legislation establishing departments and programs seldom specifies in precise detail how all activities are to be carried out, in large part because the legislature is simply unable to foresee every future possibility. There is usually a clause in this kind of legislation that allows either the minister or the Governor in Council (that is, the Cabinet) to make certain regulations as long as they are consistent with the terms of the enabling legislation. In some cases, this is done in strict legal form through an **order in council.** This is a formal regulation approved by the Governor in Council and, in the case of the federal government, published in the **Canada Gazette**, which is a bi-weekly listing of official announcements prepared by the government. Provincial governments have similar official publications.

These orders in council frequently establish the ground rules governing relationships between public servants and members of the public affected by their actions and decisions. For example, there are lengthy orders in council specifying the rules about access to information and privacy. They describe the sorts of information that are not available to the public, but they also restrict public servants by specifying those items that must be released. In this sense, regulations are an important means of controlling the actions of public servants.

In a less formal manner, ministers frequently issue internal departmental regulations. These are also binding on all departmental officials, provided that the regulations are within the terms of the enabling legislation. It is these regulations—covering such matters as which form is to be completed in a particular case and how a particular situation is to be treated—which are the lifeblood of most large organizations. Over the years, these regulations can accumulate to several volumes.

MINISTERS AND MINISTRIES OF STATE IN THE FEDERAL GOVERNMENT

After Prime Minister Trudeau came to power in 1968, he made a number of changes in the way Cabinet and the bureaucracy were organized. One of the major innovations was embodied in the Ministries and Ministers of States Act.[15]

Trudeau wanted more flexibility in the size of Cabinet and in the appointment of Cabinet ministers. In particular, he wanted to be able to bring people into Cabinet to consider problems that did not fit neatly into the existing departmental structure. This was difficult under the legislative arrangements that prevailed at that time. He also wanted to ease the managerial burden that some ministers were feeling in managing the more rapidly growing and diverse departments. And finally, he recognized that to maintain the idea of a representative Cabinet, all this had to be accomplished without creating a hierarchy of senior and junior ministers.

This re-organization resulted in four different kinds of ministers. It is important to remember that, even though these different types of ministers have different levels of responsibility, they are all equal in terms of their formal position in Cabinet.

Departmental Ministers. These are the conventional ministers, who head operating departments. They derive their authority from the statutes that created their departments, and are not really affected by the 1970 legislation.

Ministers of State for Specified Purposes. This was the major innovation in this legislation. The Prime Minister could appoint an unlimited number of new ministers in this category by an order in council approved by a vote of the House of Commons. This was a considerably easier and less formal mechanism than seeking legislation to establish a department. The idea was that this type of minister would head a **Ministry of State**, a small department oriented to the consideration of some specific problem. It would be a "think tank" with some responsibility for coordinating activities of departments, but no responsibility for operating programs. It was understood that this kind of ministry could be a temporary organization that would analyze a problem, propose a solution, and then be put out of business.

The first two ministries created were the Ministry of State for Urban Affairs (MSUA), and the Ministry of State for Science and Technology (MOSST). The Ministry of State for Urban Affairs was created in response to a presumed urban crisis. It conducted a significant amount of research on urban problems, but its abilities to coordinate the activities of operating departments in urban affairs proved to be somewhat limited. It was eliminated in 1979 as a cost-saving move and as a concession to the provinces, which resented any federal involvement in municipal affairs. MOSST was active in coordinating the activities of public and private sector organizations in scientific research until it was folded into the Department of Industry, Science and Technology in 1989.

There were two other short-lived ministries of state. The Ministry of State for Economic and Regional Development (MSERD), and the Ministry of State for Social Development (MSSD) were created in 1979 and 1980, respectively, to be secretariats to the relevant Cabinet committees, and to coordinate the activities of operating departments in their areas. They were abolished by Prime Minister Turner when he took office in 1984, ostensibly as a cost-saving measure.

While there is still provision in the legislation for Ministries of State for Specified Purposes, there are currently none in existence. The consensus on these ministries is that they did not live up to their expectations. The ministry concept was born at a time when the catch phrase was "knowledge is power." It was expected that these ministries would obtain their power from their superior knowledge in particular policy areas. In retrospect, it seems that the ability to control programs and spend money is considerably more powerful than knowledge.[16] The ministries of state had very few successes in using their knowledge and suasion to affect the policies of operating departments. Since these ministries did not have programs, they could never develop a committed clientele. Therefore, when cost-saving or a sop to provincial autonomy was needed, these ministries were the easiest places in which to make cuts.

Minister of State to Assist a Minister. Originally, the reason for this type of portfolio was that some departments were so large, and their duties so diverse, that it seemed that a single minister could not adequately manage the entire department. The solution to this problem was to "hive-off" or divide one portion of a minister's department and make that the responsibility of a Minister of State.

The longest-standing such position is the Minister of State for Fitness and Amateur Sport. Administratively, this organization is a part of the Department of National Health and Welfare, but politically it is the responsibility of a separate Minister of State. The objective of this kind of arrangement is both to relieve some of the work pressure on the minister responsible for the department, and to signal the intentions of the government to give a particular policy area a higher priority. This position has also been used to test the abilities of new ministers and to groom them for more weighty responsibilities.

Recently the roles of some of these ministers have gone beyond the original idea of hiving-off portions of a department, and expanded to include coordinating responsibilities that span several departments. A large number of different organizational arrangements have been employed in using the Minister of State to Assist.[17]

A distinction should be made between a Parliamentary Secretary and a Minister of State to Assist a Minister. The Parliamentary Secretary usually does not have continuing responsibilities in a defined area, but rather does as much or as little as requested by the minister to whom he or she is assigned. The major difference between the two positions is that the Parliamentary Secretary is not a member of Cabinet and so cannot speak for the government in the House or answer questions on behalf of the minister. The Minister of State to Assist a Minister is a member of Cabinet and so speaks for the government in the House, and is conceptually equal to all other ministers.

A recent evaluation of this type of minister has produced a rather mixed judgment. Chenier suggests that there have been some problems in the manner in which it has been employed, but that some valuable lessons were learned which, if applied in the future, could make this a very useful organizational form.[18]

Minister without Portfolio for Designated Purposes. This kind of minister ordinarily has no program responsibilities. Instead, his or her role is to speak in Cabinet for a particular group to ensure that it is appropriately treated by *all* departments and agencies of the government. He or she can be seen as a kind of informal ombudsman for the interests of the group. This is usually a two-way street in that this type of minister is expected to carry the message about the value of government programs to the group. The longest-standing position in this category is in the field of multiculturalism.

This type of minister of state has probably fulfilled expectations better than the others, but comparisons are difficult because much less was expected of this kind of minister.

Ministers have an individual, personal responsibility in managing their departments, but there is also a collective Cabinet responsibility in managing the total affairs of the government. This means that the Cabinet collectively must have some assurance that departments are being managed well, and that coordination between departments is being handled properly. It is to help ensure these objectives that central agencies have developed as mechanisms of *Cabinet control* of government activities.

CENTRAL AGENCIES

Rationale for Central Agencies

The discussion in Chapter 3 of span of control drew attention to the fact that as the number of units reporting to the same person increases, that person has more difficulty maintaining control of the units and coordinating their activities. The organizational chart of the government of Canada in this book demonstrates that the Cabinet's span of control is very broad. The organizational charts of most provinces show only a slightly smaller span of control. This broad organizational structure requires some method of coordinating the activities of the separate departments to prevent overlap and working at cross-purposes. One of the methods employed in Canada is the central agency.

There are other ways of dealing with this problem. In Britain, there are many departments headed by ministers who are not members of Cabinet. Ministers heading related departments are then grouped under a senior minister who is a member of Cabinet. This creates a situation where the span of control is reasonable for both Cabinet, with a relatively small number of senior ministers, and for the senior ministers, each of whom has a reasonable number of non-Cabinet ministers reporting to him or her. It provides for both reasonable spans of control and a relatively small Cabinet.

It is this latter characteristic that precludes the use of this system in Canada. In Canada, the concept of the *representative Cabinet* is very important. This principle means that many diverse interests must be represented in the federal Cabinet. It requires the selection of Cabinet members to provide an appropriate balance of geographic, religious, ethnic, linguistic, gender, and other criteria. As a result, the Cabinet must be fairly large to ensure that all groups are represented adequately.

The principle of a representative Cabinet also requires adherence to the concept that all Cabinet ministers are equal. If there were a distinction between Cabinet and non-Cabinet ministers, it would be impossible to achieve the appropriate representative balance with a limited number of senior ministers. The Clark government of 1979-80 had a small, powerful "inner Cabinet," but Opposition members delighted in pointing out to residents of certain provinces that they had no representative within the important "inner Cabinet." The practice has not been resurrected by subsequent governments.

Definition of a Central Agency

These conventions of representative Cabinet and equality of Cabinet ministers require the wide span of control illustrated in the organization chart. The wide span of control requires the presence of some mechanism to coordinate and control the activities of the operating departments. This is the role of the central agencies. A **central agency** is any agency that has a substantial amount of continuing, legitimate authority to direct and intervene in the activities of departments.

The application of any definition, particularly one that contains words such as "substantial" and "continuing," is somewhat arbitrary, but it is widely acknowledged in the 1990s that there are six full-fledged central agencies in the government of Canada—the Prime Minister's Office, the Privy Council Office, the Federal-Provincial Relations Office, the Treasury Board Secretariat, the Office of the Comptroller General, and the Department of Finance.[19]

Central agencies obtain their power from either legislative authority to operate in a particular area, or proximity to someone with legitimate authority, such as the Prime Minister. They usually do not have a large number of employees, although most of the staff employed are relatively high-level, professional people. Table 8.2 shows the number of people employed in these six agencies, and some of the largest and smallest departments in the fiscal year ending March 31, 1989. Even the smallest departments have more employees than the central agencies, and the largest departments completely dwarf them.

All six agencies discussed in this section have either been created, or experienced significant change, as a result of the style of government brought to office by Prime Minister Trudeau in 1968.[20] Trudeau's predecessor, Prime Minister Pearson, never had a majority government, and so had to be concerned with conciliation and fire-fighting. Trudeau, with a majority government in his first term, had the luxury of focussing on specific goals he wanted to accomplish and using such newly fashionable rational tools as cost-effectiveness and systems analysis to attain those goals. His limited experience in working in large organizations could have made him somewhat uncomfortable in a bureaucratic environment. As a result, Trudeau wanted *competing sources of information* so that he did not have to rely solely on the traditional information sources of the operating departments. This was not evidence of distrust of the traditional organizational structures; rather, it was the logical desire to obtain more than one point of view on an issue before acting.

Thus, another major role for central agencies developed in addition to the coordinating role discussed above. Trudeau began to use these agencies as competing sources of information. As the agencies began to adopt a much more

Table 8.2
EMPLOYEES IN SELECTED DEPARTMENTS AND AGENCIES
FISCAL YEAR ENDING MARCH 31, 1989

Prime Minister's Office	85
Privy Council Office	182
Federal-Provincial Relations Office	59
Treasury Board Secretariat	749
Office of the Comptroller General	148
Department of Finance	784
Department of Labour	887
Department of Justice	1,516
Department of Transport	20,506
Department of Employment and Immigration	23,975
Department of National Defence	33,584

Source: Canada, *Estimates for the Fiscal Year Ended March 31, 1989* (Ottawa: Supply and Services Canada, 1988).

significant role in policy development, they began to attract to their ranks people who brought with them "rational" tools such as cost-benefit analysis, systems analysis, and economic modeling. The style of Prime Minister Trudeau, the need for competing sources of information, and the presence of, and confidence in, these rational techniques significantly increased the role of these central agencies in the 1970s.

When Prime Minister Mulroney came to office, he brought with him a different style of governing, which has been characterized as brokerage politics, focussing more on accommodating varying interests than Trudeau's search for rationality. Peter Aucoin argues that this different style is reflected in a different approach to the use of the Cabinet committee system and the central agencies. For example, Mulroney has been less interested in competing sources of information and more interested in bringing power closer to him so that he has the necessary levers to engage in accommodation. Specifically, this has resulted in the ascendancy of the Prime Minister's Office (the PM's personal political advisors) at the expense of the Privy Council Office composed of public servants "left over from the Liberal era."[21]

It is important to understand that each Prime Minister has placed his own personal stamp on the government bureaucracy, but there has been enough consistency that it is still possible to generalize about the duties of the central agencies. They have two related roles. They are responsible for the coordination of both political and administrative activities of line departments. They are also involved in advising the Prime Minister and Cabinet on policy initiatives and shepherding these initiatives through the decision-making and implementation processes. Van Loon argues that the ascendancy of central agencies

> derives from the continuing attempt within the federal government to impose financial and qualitative discipline and a notion of collective responsibility on what was hitherto a rather undisciplined policy process.[22]

These roles and responsibilities can be illustrated best by a discussion of the activities of each of these six agencies.

The Prime Minister's Office

The **Prime Minister's Office (PMO)** works directly for the Prime Minister and has an overtly partisan political role.[23] Its major responsibilities are to serve the Prime Minister by providing advice on how policy initiatives will be viewed politically in the country, and to assist in other ways that will cast the Prime Minister in the best political light. Specifically, these responsibilities include planning and coordinating major new policy initiatives, providing liaison with the party machinery in the provinces, maintaining good relations with the media, writing speeches, advising on appointments and nominations, and briefing the Prime Minister concerning issues that could come up during daily question period and debate.

Because these functions are all overtly political activities, Prime Minister Trudeau began the tradition of making the small number of people in the PMO who are involved in these activities overtly partisan appointees. This means that they are there to serve unabashedly the Prime Minister's political needs and that they hold their positions at the pleasure of the Prime Minister and always resign when there is a change of government.

Prime Minister Mulroney has returned to the previous tradition of dipping into the ranks of the permanent public service for some of his appointees. This has tended to blur the line between partisan appointees and the professional public service. This blurring and the problems it entails will be discussed in more detail in Chapter 13, but a continuation of this trend could damage Canada's public service traditions.

Trudeau's former principal secretary (head of the PMO) has argued that the PMO's role should be to establish a "strategic prime ministership."[24] By this, he means that the PMO must assist the Prime Minister in keeping new policy initiatives on track and avoiding being side-tracked. He describes how the Prime Minister and PMO are continually being confronted with urgent crises. It is imperative, but very difficult, to prevent the urgent from overwhelming the important. Axworthy feels that the role of the PMO is to assist the Prime Minister in identifying the five or six major initiatives that he or she wants to accomplish during a term of office, and then being certain that the Prime Minister's energies are expended in this direction rather than being dissipated on small matters. He describes this as the strategic prime ministership.

The PMO has other important activities of a "housekeeping" nature, such as making travel arrangements and answering the huge volume of mail for the Prime Minister. The largest number of employees in the PMO are employed in carrying out the latter function. The growth in the size of the Office has been severely criticized, but much of that growth has occurred in this correspondence function.

It is difficult to generalize about the relationship between the PMO and operating departments. The PMO has no statutory authority of its own; it derives its power from the fact that it is headed by the Prime Minister, through whom it must act in taking initiatives with departments. Its contact with departments is largely limited to consulting about new policy initiatives or dealing with political problems. There is some idea that the PMO would like to become more involved in policy matters, but its small size and other responsibilities prevent it from doing so. In sum, the PMO usually chooses not to become too involved with the activities of operating departments, but it has a significant amount of power that it can exercise on the authority of the Prime Minister.

The Privy Council Office

The **Privy Council Office (PCO)** is a relatively small organization that provides policy advice and administrative support to the Prime Minister, Cabinet, and Cabinet committees. The title of the office comes from the fact that the formal name for Cabinet is the Queen's Privy Council.[25] The status of the PCO is illustrated by the fact that the senior public servant in the agency, who is called the Clerk (ordinarily pronounced "clark," in the British tradition) of the Privy Council and the Secretary to the Cabinet, is considered to be the most senior federal public servant.

Unlike the PMO, the PCO is staffed by career public servants rather than political appointees. However, the kind of advice provided by PCO, while not overtly political in the partisan sense, is certainly sensitive to the political pulse of the nation. A former Clerk of the Privy Council described the roles of the PMO and the PCO in this manner:

> The Prime Minister's Office is partisan, politically oriented, yet operationally sensitive. The Privy Council Office is non-partisan, operationally oriented yet politically sensitive.[26]

The Privy Council Office has a number of different roles, including some that are assigned to it by the Prime Minister on a temporary basis. However, the major, continuing activities of the PCO fall into the two categories of support for the Cabinet and its committees, and advice on machinery of government.[27]

The PCO provides several different kinds of support for Cabinet committees. Organizationally, the office is divided so that there is a small secretariat attached to each Cabinet committee, except Treasury Board, which has its own secretarial arm. Each secretariat monitors the general policy environment in the area for which its committee is responsible. The secretariat advises on new policy initiatives or responses to ongoing problems and ensures that all proposals that go before a Cabinet committee are in good order. Among other things, this means that the interdepartmental aspects have been discussed and any problems resolved. This aspect of the PCO has prompted some to refer to it as a "gate-keeper," although this might be something of an overstatement. PCO also assists in the preparation of the agenda of Cabinet committee meetings, and in briefing the chairperson of the committee. At the housekeeping level, PCO also arranges for meeting space and maintains the minutes of the meetings.

The machinery of government group in the PCO advises the Prime Minister on the reallocation of programs between departments, and the reorganization of government departments and agencies. This also involves the handling of jurisdictional disputes between ministers or departments and an analysis of the operation of the Cabinet committee system.

The machinery of government section of the PCO also advises the Prime Minister and Cabinet about senior appointments within the federal bureaucracy. It is concerned with moving highly competent public servants through senior postings so that they are always employed in a capacity where their talents can be best used, and can gain experience for their next position. The PCO is involved in advising only about employment of public servants; advice about more political kinds of appointments comes from the PMO.

The PCO provides a good example of central agency activities and the general position of central agencies in the organizational structure. The duties of the PCO give it the legitimate right to become involved in the activities of every other department of government. It does not have line authority over those departments, but its position as "gate-keeper" and its proximity to Cabinet mean that operating departments always consider advice offered by the PCO very carefully. This helps to explain the very complex love-hate relationships that operating departments usually have with central agencies.

Federal-Provincial Relations Office

The **Federal-Provincial Relations Office (FPRO)** has a relatively long history as a unit within the PCO, but its existence as a separate unit dates only from the late 1970s. It was elevated in response to a growing concern over the general state of federal-provincial relations and to provide the federal government with a better way to manage its approach to dealing with the provinces.[28]

The FPRO maintains liaison with federal and provincial officials who are involved in the operation of federal-provincial programs. It is most concerned with policy issues and the overall operation of the federal-provincial structure, and not as concerned about the details of individual programs.

The status of the FPRO is clear from the fact that it reports directly to the Prime Minister and is headed by the Secretary to Cabinet (Federal-Provincial Relations) whose status is only slightly below that of the Clerk of the Privy Council.

Like the PCO, the FPRO has many opportunities to become involved in the activities of operating departments, i.e., in any area in which a department operates an intergovernmental program. This engenders some of the same love-hate relationships between departments and FPRO as was mentioned above in connection with PCO.

Treasury Board

Treasury Board (TB) is a Cabinet committee consisting of the President of Treasury Board, the Minister of Finance, and four other ministers appointed by the Prime Minister. TB differs from other Cabinet committees in two respects. It is the only Cabinet committee that is enshrined in legislation—the Financial Administration Act—and it is the only Cabinet committee that has a large bureaucracy reporting to it. In fact, it controls two administrative units— Treasury Board Secretariat (TBS) and the Office of the Comptroller General (OCG). A former Secretary of the Treasury Board has written that the board is one committee, but it has a dual role. It functions as both the Cabinet's committee on the expenditure budget and the Cabinet's committee on management.[29] The Treasury Board itself considers these matters in the final analysis, but in practice most of the preparatory work is done by TBS and OCG.[30]

Treasury Board Secretariat. TBS has gradually accumulated many seemingly diverse responsibilities. The one factor that ties them together is that they all relate to ensuring the efficient and effective use of government resources, both human and financial.

TBS is responsible for the preparation of the expenditure budget that the government proposes in the House of Commons each year. It receives general guidelines from the Cabinet Committee on Priorities and Planning and the Department of Finance, which allow it, in turn, to set guidelines for expenditure by operating departments. This requires TBS to negotiate with departments about starting new programs, or cutting-back or eliminating existing ones. The budget process will be described in greater detail in Chapter 26.

TBS is also responsible for certain aspects of human resource administration. When it was established as a separate organization in 1966, this was a very minor part of its activities, but it has grown so much that by 1988

> nearly 50 per cent of the Treasury Board Secretariat's staff currently works on human resource management functions. The Treasury Board is responsible for the development of personnel policies, the classification of positions, the application of the Official Languages Act, the coordination of the government's human resource planning process and for conducting negotiations and consultations with the unions.[31]

The introduction of collective bargaining in 1967 and the progressive establishment of a truly bilingual public service since the 1960s have imposed a tremendous workload on TBS. Societal and legislative changes in the 1980s have also made its responsibilities considerably more complicated. For example, Treasury Board policies have been affected by the application of the Charter of Rights to employment and union activity, human rights legislation, pay equity legislation, and access to information and privacy legislation.

On top of this, TBS has a special concern for reducing the deficit, which has caused it to, among other things, take the "lead role in defining the government's workforce adjustment policy."[32] "Workforce adjustment policy" is a government euphemism for layoffs—how they will be made, what rights to other government jobs people have, etc. It is a very complex and difficult chore to ensure that these adjustments occur at the rate promised by the government and that employees affected by them are dealt with fairly.

TBS has a shared role with the Office of the Comptroller General in ensuring that sound administrative principles are followed in all government activities. It is responsible for making regulations dealing with administrative matters such as purchasing, entering into contracts, and receiving and spending public funds. The general thrust of these duties is to ensure that proper controls are in effect concerning government assets and adequate safeguards are in place before funds are spent.

Office of the Comptroller General. The Comptroller General is considered the chief financial officer of the government of Canada. As mentioned above, the OCG shares certain duties with the TBS in making regulations concerning receipt and disbursement of public money, accounting procedures, and the form of financial statements. The OCG has a special interest in ensuring the quality of all departmental financial officers and the integrity of the internal audit function to help improve departmental management. As discussed in Chapter 7, evaluations are actually done by departments, but the OCG is responsible for providing the guidance and direction under which the evaluations are undertaken. It is then responsible for discussing the results of the evaluation with the department to help it improve its management and, with Treasury Board, to aid it in the budget process.

In sum, Treasury Board, supported by its two secretariats, has numerous responsibilities, but they all relate to ensuring the wise use of resources—both human and financial—within federal government departments. This involves determining that prudence and probity are always observed in government transactions and attempting to ensure uniformity in areas such as levels of pay across all government departments.

From the standpoint of operating departments, Treasury Board is easily the most active—some might say, intrusive—of the central agencies, simply because there are so many points of contact and so many specific activities for which TB clearance must be obtained.

Treasury Board officials are aware that

> program managers see uniform, government-wide rules and regulations as obstacles to efficient program delivery. Treasury Board fully recognizes that such rules can inhibit efficient program delivery.[33]

However, Veilleux and Savoie go on to say that this concern must be balanced against other, possibly more important, concerns. Because departments are dependent on public revenue, and because Cabinet is collectively responsible for actions of individual ministers, it is impossible to allow department officials a totally free hand in the use of assets and the implementation of policies.

However, Treasury Board does recognize the need to move away from the detailed, intrusive controls and toward more general guidelines that will allow for a reasonable level of control without stifling departmental initiatives. One of the mechanisms it is using to accomplish this is the system of Increased Ministerial Authority and Accountability (IMAA). IMAA involves a separate Memorandum of Understanding (MOU) between Treasury Board and each individual department that provides departments with more authority and flexibility in delivering programs, as long as they comply with the targets and performance expectations set out in the MOU. IMAA will be discussed in more detail in Chapter 16.

Department of Finance

The Department of Finance is responsible for advising Cabinet on matters of economic policy. Thus, the department has an exceedingly broad mandate. It advises on questions of fiscal policy, international trade policy (including tariffs), domestic industrial policy, taxation policy, and the preparation of the revenue and expenditure budgets.[34]

The Department of Finance could potentially intervene in the activities of any department involved in policies that touch upon any of the above areas. And, given the breadth of those areas, it is difficult to think of a department that does not. The role of Finance does not bring it into the same kind of obtrusive, day-to-day contact with operating departments as with TBS, but its concern with economic policy allows it to intervene at strategic points in the policy development process. Its role in the preparation of the expenditure budget helps determine whether the upcoming year will be a lean or a fat one for government agencies. Finance also has a role as the budgetary gate-keeper. Indeed, it has traditionally provided the strongest opposition to new spending programs.[35] This brings Finance into fairly frequent conflict with operating departments.

Central Agencies in the Provinces

It is obvious that the functions performed by central agencies in the federal government will also be necessary in provincial governments. However, the smaller size of the provincial governments usually means that organizational structures are less complex and differentiated. In most provinces, the functions of the PMO, the PCO, and sometimes the TB are all carried out in the Premier's Office. However, there is a general movement toward the establishment of a separate organization with duties similar to those carried out by TB at the federal level.[36] For example, the duties of the Management Board of Cabinet in Ontario are very similar to those of TB. The functions of the Department of Finance are carried out in most provinces by a Treasury Department headed by the Provincial Treasurer.

ORGANIZATION OF A TYPICAL OPERATING DEPARTMENT

Figure 8.1 is an organization chart of the federal Department of Public Works. The minister is at the top of the pyramid. The minister has a political staff reporting directly to him or her, but these people do not have direct line authority within the department. They advise the minister and frequently consult on the minister's behalf with public servants, but they must always act through the minister in seeking action by public servants.

The next link in the chain of accountability is the **deputy minister**. Deputy ministers are the administrative (as distinct from political) heads of depart-

Figure 8.1
ORGANIZATION OF PUBLIC WORKS

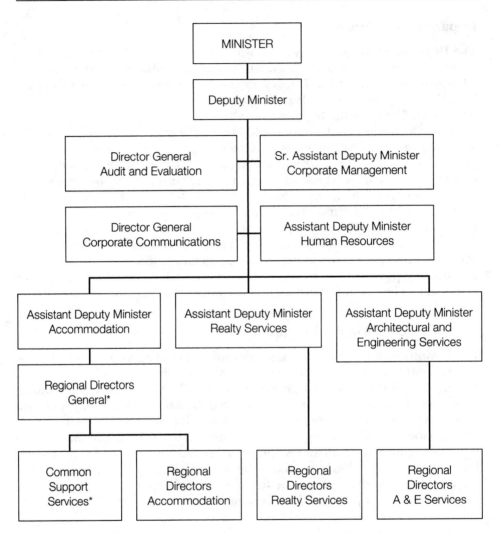

*Resources for these entities include Finance, Human Resources, Communications and other administrative and related functions in the Regions.
Source: Public Works Canada, *Annual Report, 1988-1989*, p. 3.

ments. They are permanent heads of departments in that they do not usually leave when governments change. Unlike ministers, who are politicians, deputy ministers usually work their way up through the ranks of the public service, although, in some cases, they are brought in directly from other governments or the private sector.

In some senses, deputy ministers have the most difficult position in the entire system, because they must act as a link between the political desires of the minister and the administrative concerns of the public servants in the departments. Of course, ministers are not totally insensitive to administrative concerns, any more than public servants are totally insensitive to political ones, but each side brings a different dimension to the issue at hand. Ministers, particularly if they represent a new government, often feel under pressure from colleagues to make changes in programs and activities. It would not be appropriate for public servants to oppose these changes, but public servants are frequently more attuned to the administrative problems posed by change than to its political benefits.

Good deputy ministers must stand between these two concerns and not be afraid either to impose change on a reluctant department, or to advise ministers fully and frankly if their actions will lead to serious administrative problems. However, if this advice is not delivered in a very sensitive and diplomatic manner, it can be taken for disloyalty. Because the role of the deputy minister is so important it is described in greater detail in Chapter 16.

One word of caution is necessary. The term "deputy minister" is not used consistently throughout departments. For example, in the Department of External Affairs, where the minister is referred to as the Secretary of State for External Affairs, the senior public servant is called the "undersecretary," while in Treasury Board where the minister is called the "president," the senior public servant is called the "secretary." Confused? In most government publications, the term "deputy head" is used to cover all of these senior people. In normal discussion around government offices, one frequently hears reference to "the deputy."

Beneath the level of deputy minister, the nomenclature can become even more confusing. Usually, there will be several "assistant deputy ministers" (ADMs) reporting to the DM. Sometimes the superior status of one of these positions will be established by designating it as associate deputy minister or senior assistant deputy minister. This is usually a sign that the position carries a heavier weight of duties or responsibilities than the other ADM positions.

Also, in this department, there are two directors general reporting directly to the DM—one responsible for audit and evaluation, and the other responsible for communications. These positions have almost the same status as the ADM in that they report directly to the DM, but their title indicates that their ranking is slightly lower, usually because they have less weighty responsibilities.

At this point, it is useful to relate this organization chart to some of the material about organizational behaviour covered in Chapter 3.

In terms of the line-staff distinction, there are three line units—Accommodation, Realty Services, and Architectural and Engineering Services—and four staff functions—Audit and Evaluation, Corporate Communications, Corporate Management, and Human Resources. A more complete organization chart would also illustrate the functional lines of authority between the line and staff functions.

CONCLUSION

This chapter has described the main characteristics of the departmental form of organization. This form is usually preferred when the situation calls for strong ministerial control. There are other cases in which it is better for an agency to function at arm's length from the direct control of the minister. The next two chapters will deal with two organizational forms that ensure this distance—the Crown corporation and the regulatory agency.

NOTES

1. G. Bruce Doern and Richard W. Phidd, *Canadian Public Policy: Ideas, Structures, Process* (Toronto: Methuen, 1983), p. 110.
2. Michael J. Trebilcock et al., *The Choice of Governing Instrument* (Ottawa: Minister of Supply and Services Canada, 1982), p. 1.
3. A more detailed treatment of these interactions is contained in Chapters 15-17.
4. R.S.C. 1985, c. F-11, s. 2.
5. R.S.C. 1985, c. P-33, s. 2.
6. *The Canadian Public Service: A Physiology of Government* (Toronto: University of Toronto Press, 1973), p. 89.
7. Ibid., ch. 5.
8. G. Bruce Doern, "Horizontal and Vertical Portfolios in Government," in G. Bruce Doern and V. Seymour Wilson, eds., *Issues in Canadian Public Policy* (Macmillan of Canada, 1974), pp. 310-29. This same idea is also developed in Doern and Phidd, *Canadian Public Policy*, pp. 206-209.
9. Doern, "Horizontal and Vertical Portfolios in Government," pp. 316-17.
10. R.S.C. 1985, c. C-35.
11. R.S.C. 1985, c. P-34.
12. For a description of how the Ontario Progressive Conservative Party managed this, see Vaughan Lyon, "Minority Government in Ontario, 1975-1981: An Assessment," *Canadian Journal of Political Science* 17 (December 1984): 685-705.
13. For a more complete discussion of ministerial responsibility, see Chapters15 and 17.
14. The general roles of these staff members and, in particular, their use under Prime Minister Mulroney is discussed in more detail in Chapter 16.
15. R.S.C. 1985, c. M-8.
16. Peter Aucoin and Richard French, *Knowledge, Power and Public Policy* (Ottawa: Information Canada, 1974), ch. 3 and passim.
17. John A. Chenier, "Ministers of State to Assist: Weighing the Costs and the Benefits," *Canadian Public Administration* 28 (Fall 1985): 400-403.
18. Ibid.: 403-11.
19. This list coincides with the list used in the most recent comprehensive study of central agencies: Colin Campbell and George J. Szablowski, *The Superbureaucrats* (Toronto: Macmillan, 1979).
20. G. Bruce Doern, "Recent Changes in the Philosophy of Policy-making in Canada," *Canadian Journal of Political Science* 4 (June 1971): 243-66.
21. Peter Aucoin, "Organizational Change in the Machinery of Canadian Government: From Rational Management to Brokerage Politics," *Canadian Journal of Political Science* 19 (1986): 22 and passim.

22. R. Van Loon, "Stop the Music: The Current Policy and Expenditure Management System in Ottawa," *Canadian Public Administration* 24 (Summer 1981): 176.
23. Marc Lalonde, "The Changing Role of the Prime Minister's Office," *Canadian Public Administration* 14 (Winter 1971): 509-37.
24. Thomas S. Axworthy, "Of Secretaries to Princes," *Canadian Public Administration* 31, no. 2 (Summer 1988): 247-64.
25. Technically, the Queen's Privy Council consists of all previous and present federal Cabinet ministers plus a limited number of others on whom the honour has been bestowed.
26. Gordon Robertson, "The Changing Role of the Privy Council Office," *Canadian Public Administration* 14 (Winter 1971): 506.
27. For a good discussion of the role of PCO, see Audrey D. Doerr, *The Machinery of Government in Canada* (Toronto: Methuen, 1981), pp. 30-34, and Richard D. French, "The Privy Council Office: Support for Cabinet Decision Making," in Richard Schultz, Orest Kruhlak, and John C. Terry, eds., *The Canadian Political Process* (Toronto: Holt, Rinehart and Winston, 1979), pp. 363-94.
28. For an interesting explanation of the creation of the FPRO, see Colin Campbell, *Governments Under Stress* (Toronto: University of Toronto Press, 1983), p. 90.
29. A. W. Johnson, "The Treasury Board of Canada and the Machinery of Government of the 1970's," *Canadian Journal of Political Science* 4 (September 1971): 346.
30. The duties of these two organizations will be discussed in more detail in Chapters 25 and 26.
31. Gérard Veilleux and Donald J. Savoie, "Kafka's Castle: The Treasury Board of Canada Revisited," *Canadian Public Administration* 31, no. 4 (Winter 1988): 527.
32. Ibid., 529.
33. Ibid., 532.
34. For a more detailed description of the responsibilities of the Department of Finance, see Richard W. Phidd and G. Bruce Doern, *The Politics and Management of Canadian Economic Policy* (Toronto: Macmillan, 1979), ch. 7.
35. Ibid., p. 224.
36. Marsha A. Chandler and William M. Chandler, *Public Policy and Provincial Politics* (Toronto: McGraw-Hill Ryerson, 1979), pp. 101-105.

BIBLIOGRAPHY

Aucoin, Peter, and Richard French. *Knowledge, Power and Public Policy*. Ottawa: Information Canada, 1974.

Axworthy, Thomas S. "Of Secretaries to Princes." *Canadian Public Administration* 31, no. 2 (Summer 1988): 247-64.

Borgeat, Louis, René Dussault, Lionel Ouellet avec la collaboration de Patrick Moran, Marcel Proulx. *L'administration québécoise: Organisation et fonctionnement*. Presses de l'Université du Québec, 1984.

Bryden, Kenneth. "Executive and Legislature in Ontario: A Case Study on Governmental Reform." *Canadian Public Administration* 18 (Summer 1975): 235-52.

Campbell, Colin. *Governments Under Stress*. Toronto: University of Toronto Press, 1983.

Campbell, Colin, and George J. Szablowski. *The Superbureaucrats*. Toronto: Macmillan, 1979.

Chandler, Marsha A., and William M. Chandler. *Public Policy and Provincial Politics*. Toronto: McGraw-Hill Ryerson, 1979.

Chenier, John A. "Ministers of State to Assist: Weighing the Costs and the Benefits." *Canadian Public Administration* 28 (Fall 1985): 397-412.

Doern, G. Bruce. "Horizontal and Vertical Portfolios in Government." In G. Bruce Doern and V. Seymour Wilson, eds., *Issues in Canadian Public Policy*. Toronto: Macmillan, 1974, pp. 310-36.

———. "Recent Changes in the Philosophy of Policy-making in Canada." *Canadian Journal of Political Science* 4 (June 1971): 243-66.

Doern, G. Bruce, and Richard W. Phidd. *Canadian Public Policy: Ideas, Structure, Process*. Toronto: Methuen, 1983.

Doerr, Audrey D. *The Machinery of Government in Canada*. Toronto: Methuen, 1981.

Fleck, James D. "Reorganization of the Ontario Government." *Canadian Public Administration* 15 (Summer 1972): 383-85.

———. "Restructuring the Ontario Government." *Canadian Public Administration* 16 (Spring 1973): 55-68.

French, Richard D. "The Privy Council Office: Support for Cabinet Decision Making." In Richard Schultz, Orest Kruhlak, and John C. Terry, eds., *The Canadian Political Process*. Toronto: Holt, Rinehart and Winston, 1979, pp. 363-94.

Hockin, Thomas A. *Apex of Power*. 2nd ed. Scarborough, Ont.: Prentice-Hall, 1977.

Hodgetts, J. E. *The Canadian Public Service: A Physiology of Government*. Toronto: University of Toronto Press, 1973.

Jackson, Robert J., Doreen Jackson, and Nicolas Baxter-Moore. *Politics in Canada: Culture, Institutions, Behaviour and Public Policy*. Scarborough, Ont.: Prentice-Hall Canada, 1986.

Johnson, A. W. "The Treasury Board of Canada and the Machinery of Government of the 1970's." *Canadian Journal of Political Science* 4 (September 1971): 346-66.

Lalonde, Marc. "The Changing Role of the Prime Minister's Office." *Canadian Public Administration* 14 (Winter 1971): 509-37.

Langford, John W. *Transport in Transition*. Montreal: McGill-Queen's University Press, 1976.

Loreto, Richard A. "The Structure of the Ontario Political System." In Donald C. MacDonald, ed., *The Government and Politics of Ontario*. 3rd ed. Scarborough, Ont.: Nelson Canada, 1985, pp. 17-47.

Lyon, Vaughan. "Minority Government in Ontario, 1975-1981: An Assessment." *Canadian Journal of Political Science* 17 (December 1984): 685-705.

Mallory, J. R. "Restructuring the Government of Ontario: A Comment." *Canadian Public Administration* 16 (Spring 1973): 69-72.

Ontario, Committee on Government Productivity. *Interim Report Number Three*. 1971.

Phidd, Richard W., and G. Bruce Doern. *The Politics and Management of Canadian Economic Policy*. Toronto: Macmillan, 1978.

Robertson, Gordon. "The Changing Role of the Privy Council Office." *Canadian Public Administration* 14 (Winter 1971): 506.

Trebilcock, Michael J., Douglas G. Hartle, J. Robert S. Prichard, and Donald N. Dewees. *The Choice of Governing Instrument*. Ottawa: Minister of Supply and Services Canada, 1982.

Van Loon, R. "Stop the Music: The Current Policy and Expenditure Management System in Ottawa." *Canadian Public Administration* 24 (Summer 1981): 175-99.

Van Loon, Richard J., and Michael S. Whittington. *The Canadian Political System: Environment, Structure, and Process*. 3rd ed. Toronto: McGraw-Hill Ryerson, 1981.

Veilleux, Gérard, and Donald J. Savoie. "Kafka's Castle: The Treasury Board of Canada Revisited." *Canadian Public Administration* 31, no. 4 (Winter 1988): 517-38.

CASES

In *Case Program in Canadian Public Administration* (Toronto: Institute of Public Administration of Canada):

Case Studies in Government Operations and Procedures. By R. H. McLaren

A Taxing Problem. By Roy S. Gunn

9

Public Enterprise

This chapter will focus on the form of government organization traditionally known as the Crown corporation or public enterprise. This organizational form is very commonly used by government to deliver commercial types of services. Crown corporations affect us virtually every day; for example, when we receive our mail, use electricity in our homes, or ride to work in a public transit vehicle operated or manufactured by a public enterprise. D. P. Gracey illustrates the importance of Crown corporations in the Canadian economy:

> [R]oughly 25 per cent of Canada's net fixed assets fall under the control of federal or provincial Crown corporations. Crown corporations' contribution to the gross national product (GNP) is somewhere between 10 and 12 per cent. Six federal Crown corporations and 4 provincial Crown corporations are listed in the *Financial Post's* top 100 corporations. All, or virtually all, of Canada's electrical generation and distribution, water and liquor distribution, mail distribution and overseas telecommunications, and a significant portion of all domestic telecommunications, railways and air transportation are provided by Crown corporations.[1]

This chapter first defines public enterprise and then discusses the rapid growth of this form of government structure. In keeping with the theme of this part of the book—the choice of organizational form—there will be an analysis of why the corporate form of organization is chosen over other forms. Then, concerns such as methods of control of the corporation and its internal structure and method of operation will be considered. Finally, some of the criticisms of the corporate form and related proposals for reform will be discussed.

DEFINITION OF PUBLIC ENTERPRISE

A number of different terms are used to denote the corporate form. The most common are "Crown corporation," "mixed enterprise," and "public enterprise." Sometimes, these terms are used interchangeably, but this section will provide different definitions for each.

Separating the corporate form from other forms of government organization is relatively easy.[2] Crown corporations are established either through their own legislation, or through incorporation under the federal or provincial companies legislation in exactly the same way as any private sector corporation. Determining what constitutes a corporate form, as distinct from other organizational forms, is not difficult; the difficult part is determining what constitutes a **Crown corporation.**

Patrice Garant suggests that

> Crown corporations are companies in the ordinary sense of the term, whose mandate relates to industrial, commercial or financial activities but which also belong to the state, are owned by the government or the Crown or whose sole shareholder is the government or the Crown. This also includes wholly owned subsidiaries. Such companies must be considered part of the governmental public sector: they belong to the state and are exclusively controlled by it.

> On the other hand, institutions that are really administrative bodies rather than companies should be excluded from the family of Crown corporations: for example, organizations concerned with economic or social regulation, administrative management and consultation. On the other hand, semi-public companies, that is, majority or even minority subsidiaries in which there is co-participation of public and private capital, are not Crown corporations, although they are often similar to them.[3]

This definition leaves out certain non-commercial entities that are defined as Crown corporations in the federal Financial Administration Act; these include the Canada Employment and Immigration Commission, the Agricultural Stabilization Board, and the Economic Council of Canada. While there are valid financial and political reasons for separating these organizations from their related departments, they are excluded from this definition because their *method of operation* is much more like an operating department than a corporation.

A **mixed enterprise** is a corporation "in which the federal government has taken a direct equity position in common with other participants for the purposes of implementing a public policy or satisfying a public need."[4] These "other participants" could be provincial or foreign governments or private sector organizations. Some examples of mixed enterprises are Telesat Canada, the Canada Development Corporation, and the Asian Development Bank. The mixed enterprise is not a unique organizational form; it is simply a standard business corporation in which governments own a certain number of the shares.

Public enterprise is the most general term and encompasses both Crown corporations and mixed enterprises.

This chapter will focus predominantly on Crown corporations, although there will be some discussion of mixed enterprises as well.

THE GROWTH OF PUBLIC ENTERPRISE

Governments grew very rapidly in the 1960s and 1970s, and it is not surprising that public enterprise followed suit.[5] In more recent times, the growth of government has slowed down, and the size of the corporate sector has declined as a result of a growing trend toward privatization.

Table 9.1
FEDERAL CROWN CORPORATIONS BY METHOD OF OWNERSHIP

	Parent Corporations	Subsidiaries	Total
Owned Directly and Solely	81	161	242
Owned Jointly with Other Governments, Private Organizations, and Individuals	20	174	194
Membership Interest	18	—	18
Total	119	335	454

Source: John W. Langford and Kenneth J. Huffman, "The Uncharted Universe of Federal Public Corporations," in J. Robert S. Prichard, ed., *Crown Corporations in Canada: The Calculus of Instrument Choice* (Toronto: Butterworths, 1983), pp. 233-73.

The Federal Scene

For the federal government, the first problem confronted in measuring the growth of Crown corporations stems from the somewhat embarrassing fact that there is no central listing of all government holdings of corporations.[6] Since this fact was first publicized by the Auditor General in 1976,[7] various agencies have attempted to assemble this information, and by 1980 a list of 464 "corporations in which the government has an interest" was prepared.[8] Langford and Huffman made some changes in this list and identified 454 corporations and subsidiaries, which they then grouped by degree of government ownership as illustrated in Table 9.1.

There is no definitive count of the number of Crown corporations; the figures presented by different commentators usually flow from the different definitions employed. The federal government produced a report in 1984 that identified 336 Crown corporations.[9] It seems unlikely that any widely acknowledged "right" number will emerge from this discussion. The most salient fact is that everyone agrees that the numbers are very high, the relationships generated are very complex, and the scope of their activities is very broad.

This complexity is indicated by the fact that in their listing of corporations, Langford and Huffman must use symbols such as [SSSSSS] to indicate "a subsidiary of a subsidiary of a subsidiary of a subsidiary of a sub-subsidiary corporation" and [SSSAS] "a subsidiary of a sub-subsidiary of an associate of a subsidiary corporation." The scope of these entities runs from the fairly well-known corporations, such as the Canada Mortgage and Housing Corporation and the Canadian Broadcasting Corporation, to such exotic organizations as the Canada-France-Hawaii Telescope Corporation.

Commenting on the growth of public corporations is very difficult because there are at least three measures of growth that could be used—number of corporations, assets owned, or number of employees.

Table 9.2 indicates that the majority of Crown corporations that were in existence when Langford and Huffman were doing their research (early

Table 9.2
FEDERAL CROWN CORPORATIONS BY METHOD OF OWNERSHIP AND
DATE OF INCORPORATION

	Sole		Joint		Membership		Total	
	N	%	N	%	N	%	N	%
1970-79	21	26	8	40	13	72	42	35
1960-69	18	22	8	40	3	17	29	24
1950-59	13	16	2	10	1	6	16	13
1940-49	13	16	1	5	0	0	14	12
1930-39	6	7	1	5	0	0	7	6
1908-29	10	12	0	0	1	6	11	9
	81	100	20	100	18	100	119	100

Source: John W. Langford and Kenneth J. Huffman, "The Uncharted Universe of Federal Corporations,"
in J. Robert S. Prichard, ed., *Crown Corporations in Canada: The Calculus of Instrument Choice* (Toronto:
Butterworths, 1983), p. 275.

1980s)[10] were incorporated since 1960, and over one-third were incorporated since 1970. The other interesting fact indicated in Table 9.2 is the shift in the type of corporation, from the traditional solely owned company to the jointly owned or membership type of entity.

The above information would suggest that the 1960s and 1970s were the golden age of Crown corporations, but a consideration of the other possible measures of growth—assets and employees—produces a different result.

Figure 9.1 illustrates the growth of public enterprise in Canada. The line showing corporate enterprise confirms what was discussed earlier, i.e., the *number* of enterprises grew fairly slowly in the early years, but increased rapidly during the 1960s and 1970s. The other two lines in Figure 9.1 indicate that the largest corporations (in 1978) are those created in the earlier years. Fifty percent of employees of Crown corporations work for corporations owned prior to 1938, and 50 percent of assets are held by corporations owned prior to 1946. The really large increments in these areas came as a result of the 1919 creation of Canadian National Railways and the 1934 takeover of the Bank of Canada. More recent acquisitions have not added as much in terms of assets or employees. Of course, this chart would look somewhat different if it were extended beyond 1979 to include the addition of more than 54,000 postal workers in 1981.

The activities in which federal Crown corporations have been involved have changed over the years. In the years immediately after Confederation, the federal government was most concerned with nation-building, and so focussed on transportation undertakings that would unify the diverse parts of the country. During the Second World War, the major theme of public policy changed from national unity to national defence, with the creation of many new corporations to supply the war effort. Since the end of the war, the federal Crown corporations have become more involved in the areas of finance, insurance, and real estate.

The question of which political party has employed the corporate form more frequently has always been contentious. Langford and Huffman point out

Figure 9.1

GROWTH OF CORPORATE ENTERPRISE, ASSETS AND EMPLOYMENT, 1911–1978

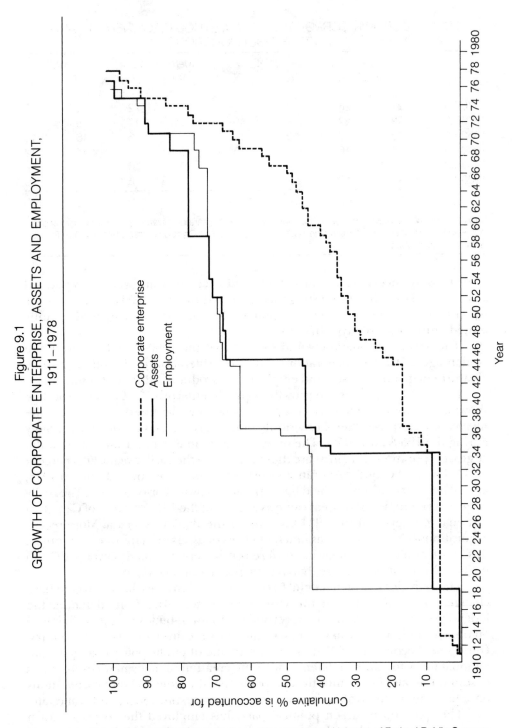

Source: John W. Langford and Kenneth J. Huffman, "The Uncharted Universe of Federal Public Corporations," in J. Robert S. Prichard, ed., *Crown Corporations in Canada: The Calculus of Instrument Choice* (Toronto: Butterworths, 1983), p. 298.

Table 9.3
PROVINCIAL CROWN CORPORATIONS BY PROVINCE

Province	N	%
Newfoundland	42	18
Prince Edward Island	10	4
Nova Scotia	10	4
New Brunswick	9	4
Quebec	35	15
Ontario	27	12
Manitoba	13	6
Saskatchewan	25	11
Alberta	20	9
British Columbia	36	15
Northwest Territories	2	1
Yukon	2	1
Regional	2	1
TOTAL	233	100

Source: Aidan R. Vining and Robert Botterell, "An Overview of the Origins, Growth, Size and Functions of Provincial Crown Corporations," in J. Robert S. Prichard, ed., *Crown Corporations in Canada: The Calculus of Instrument Choice* (Toronto: Butterworths, 1983), p. 325.

that the federal Liberals have created an average of two corporations for each year they have been in power, which is more than twice the average of the Conservatives.[11] And the Liberal years of the 1960s and 1970s certainly saw the creation of a large *number* of Crown corporations. However, the Conservatives have created such major corporations as the Canadian Broadcasting Corporation, the Bank of Canada, Canadian National Railways, and the Canadian Wheat Board. This topic is likely to remain a subject of lively partisan debate.

The Provincial Scene

Defining the public enterprise sector is even more difficult in the provincial than in the federal sphere. The ten jurisdictions each have slightly different definitions of Crown corporations, so that the data collection and comparability problems are significantly multiplied. However, it is usually suggested that provincial Crown corporations are both considerably larger and have grown more rapidly in recent years than federal Crown corporations.[12] Vining and Botterell have concluded an excellent survey in which they identified 233 provincial Crown corporations distributed geographically as illustrated in Table 9.3.

The timing of the growth of provincial Crown corporations has been similar to the federal trend. There has been a large growth in the *number* of corporations since 1960, but the major growth in assets occurred in the periods 1900 to 1920 and 1940 to 1960.[13]

Table 9.4

NUMBER OF PROVINCES EMPLOYING CROWN CORPORATIONS BY FUNCTION

Function	Number of Provinces
Industrial Development	10
Liquor	10
Housing	9
Power Utility	8
Research and Development	8
Forest Development and Manufacturing	7
Miscellaneous Marketing and Brokerage Facilities	7
Agricultural Development	6
Mineral Mining and Development	6
General and Auto Insurance	5
Municipal Finance Corporations	5
Oil and Gas Production	5
Telephones and Communications	5
Transport Facilities	5
Transport Systems	5
Banking, Saving, and Investment	4
Government Computer Services	4
Miscellaneous Manufacturing	4
Government Buildings	3
School and Hospital Financing	3
Lotteries (also two regional corporations)	2
Shipyards	2
Steel Production	2
Water Supply	2

Source: Aidan R. Vining and Robert Botterell, "An Overview of the Origins, Growth, Size and Functions of Provincial Crown Corporations," in J. Robert S. Prichard, ed., *Crown Corporations in Canada* (Toronto: Butterworths, 1983), pp. 328-34. (Note that this is the number of *provinces* that utilize Crown corporations in this area, not the number of corporations.)

Provinces have adopted the Crown corporation form in a number of different functional areas. Table 9.4 indicates that industrial development, liquor sales, housing, power generation, and research and development are the most popular, in terms of the number of provinces employing them. In terms of the total value of assets controlled, the two major fields are electrical power and banking, followed by housing, education, and telephone and communications. These five functions account for just over 80 percent of total assets.[14]

The major activities in which provincial Crown corporations have been involved have changed over the years. In the early years, one function was dominant—power generation.[15] This gave way to diversification into the trade, finance, insurance, and real estate sectors. More recently, provincial Crown corporations have become involved in industrial and resource development areas, with the newest area being insurance.[16]

Marsha Chandler's work suggests that this recent growth is the result of the presence of more left-wing (NDP and Parti Québécois) governments in provincial capitals. Her data indicate that left-wing governments not only use the corporate form more often, but they also use it for different purposes from those of their right-wing counterparts. "[N]on-socialist governments have used public ownership almost exclusively to facilitate economic development,"[17] e.g., hydroelectric and industrial development corporations. Left-wing governments have been more likely to use the corporate form for redistributive ends and to supplant private sector corporations, e.g., insurance and natural resources.

THE RATIONALE FOR THE CREATION OF PUBLIC ENTERPRISES

This section will consider some of the factors inherent in the structure of Crown corporations that make this organizational form superior to others in accomplishing certain goals.[18]

There is one important factor that distinguishes Crown corporations in Canada from similar entities in many other countries. In some countries, public enterprises are referred to as "nationalized industries" because they were at one time private sector corporations that have since been taken over as a result of some degree of coercion by the state. The phrase "nationalized industries" is not usually employed in Canada because this has not been the ordinary mode of establishing Crown corporations.

In most cases, Crown corporations have been started from scratch. In some recent cases, governments have taken over existing entities, but seldom with any overt coercion. In other cases, the takeover has involved picking up the pieces of a failed or near-failed company and continuing to operate it to provide jobs, or purchasing a publicly traded company on the open market, such as Alberta's purchase of Pacific Western Airlines[19] or the numerous purchases made by Petro-Canada.[20]

Corporations have been created for many different reasons. "It cannot be said that any unifying philosophy underlies the use of the public corporation in Canada: the whole development has been piece-meal and pragmatic."[21] However, several attempts have been made to categorize a few of the diverse reasons for employing the corporate form.[22]

Nation-building (or Province-building) and Community and Economic Development

Trebilcock and Prichard suggest that this is the most common rationale for the creation of public enterprises. They suggest that it usually involves two components:

1. integrating the country by making infrastructure investments and providing essential services, which private business is unable or unwilling to provide; and
2. promoting Canadian nationalism, i.e., developing a national identity and preserving Canadian control over certain services and sectors of the economy.[23]

There are numerous examples of both of these elements. The earliest Crown corporations were begun to develop infrastructure in areas where the private sector was unable or unwilling to become involved. Some of the more obvious examples are in transportation (canals, railways, and even Trans-Canada Airlines) and energy (the provincial hydro-electric utilities). In general, these projects either required large sums of money that were difficult to raise on the open market, or were sufficiently risky that private investors were reluctant to invest in them.

In some cases, public enterprise was chosen simply because the general populace had more confidence in government than in private sector investors. Ontario Hydro was a product of the desire of local business people to have assured power at low rates, something that they could not be assured of if private power magnates controlled the industry.[24]

Business people frequently complain about the Crown corporation form because they feel that it is inappropriate and unfair for government to compete with the private sector; there are many cases where this competition exists. However, Crown corporations have frequently been established to provide support to private sector corporations. The provincial power-generation utilities and the federal Export Development Corporation are prime examples.

Laux and Molot build on this economic development theme to explain the increase in government enterprises in the 1970s. They identify a world-wide trend to larger scale, even global, production and marketing units. Countries like the United States and Japan have adapted to this well, but

> [a] particular historical pattern of development distinguishes Canada from other advanced capitalist countries. Its special features are (1) a world economy in which Canada is highly trade-dependent and has a relatively weak manufacturing sector; (2) a pattern of truncated industrialization which makes Canada very reliant on foreign capital and technology; and (3) a federal system in which uneven regional development and high provincial autonomy make Canada appear a fragmented state.[25]

They argue that Canadian governments invested heavily in large commercial corporations in the 1970s because this was the only way there would be a Canadian presence in these fields. This same argument can be used to explain recent moves toward privatization. Only major government investment can establish such global entities, but after such a vehicle has been created, there is no reason why government must still be involved in it.

Provinces use the Crown corporation instrument to engage in province-building and to attain what they see as their rightful position in the national economic structure. Quebec's Caisse de dépôt et placement is an excellent example of this. The Caisse is the main depository of funds collected by the Quebec Pension Plan and some other large provincial pension plans and insurance funds. This money must be invested by the Caisse so that it earns a return adequate to pay these pensions in future years. Traditionally, fiduciary organizations such as the Caisse have been "passive investors," i.e., they have not attempted to control or influence the companies in which they have invested.

However, in recent years the Caisse has become a more active investor, attempting to obtain seats on the Boards of Directors of companies in which it invests. The Caisse has taken major positions in such well-known companies as Steinberg's food markets, Bell Canada Enterprises, Toronto-Dominion Bank, Canadian Pacific, Seagram Co., Noranda, and Imperial Oil.[26]

A different kind of economic development is the increasing number of cases that involve rescuing failed or floundering private companies to preserve jobs. This has been referred to as "hospitalization," because the theory is that these organizations have temporarily become ill, and that with some nurture provided by government funds they will be on their feet again and supporting themselves. The problem is that some of the corporations that have been rescued under this rationale are more in need of a hospice than a hospital.

Frequently, the real rationale for this kind of rescue is to support a company in a geographic area where unemployment is already a serious problem. This was the rationale for the creation of the Cape Breton Development Corporation and the Canadian Saltfish Corporation. Or it could mean providing a continuing Canadian presence in a sensitive industry such as transportation or resource development.

Economic development can be one of the soundest motives for creating a Crown corporation. There is little doubt that Canada has benefited from the presence of the large hydro-electric companies able to undertake huge capital projects and keep the cost of energy low. However, there is also some evidence that this argument is one of the most abused. Governments have usually not been very successful in "rescue efforts." Even referring to some of these as economic development is a misnomer; they frequently come about in areas where little development is likely to occur.

> The danger inherent in state rescues, whatever their form, is that, because they are designed to subvert market forces, they can lead to costly misallocation of economic resources. State intervention may prevent the shift of capital and labor away from unproductive activities to newer (and more productive) ones. In such circumstances the state may end up supporting increasingly inefficient enterprises—those that may have become obsolete because of technological and/or market changes. Moreover, by backing inefficient operations, the state makes them dependent on government aid, and this dependence can become progressively more difficult to break. In the eyes of dependent interests, government assistance becomes their social right.[27]

It is a very humane government policy to provide subsidies to continue jobs for workers about to become unemployed. However, it might be that using the corporate form to do something that is basically humanitarian rather than commercial puts the entire corporate sector under an unfortunate cloud.

Cultural nationalism has also had a role in the creation of some Crown corporations. Canada's proximity to the overwhelming magnetism of the United States has prompted a conscious desire to maintain a unique Canadian culture, but has simultaneously raised doubts about the ability of the private sector alone to accomplish this. The Canadian Broadcasting Corporation and some more recent initiatives in the film industry are examples of corporations geared to developing a national identity and promoting community development.

Herschel Hardin has argued in a similar, but more extreme, vein that, contrary to the popular myth, it has not been private enterprise that has been instrumental in the development of Canada, but rather such public enterprises as the canals, railways, and the CBC. He argues that the public corporation has been so important to Canada that it has spawned a "Canadian public enterprise culture."[28]

Separation from Political Control

It is important that an organization that carries out government policy is closely controlled by the political executive. However, when an organization has a predominantly commercial mandate, it is possible that political concerns could interfere with that commercial mandate. For example, it has been argued that the commercial objectives of Amtrack (the United States public passenger railway) have suffered because it has been forced to modify its route system as a result of political, not commercial, concerns.[29]

The Crown corporation form places the organization under the control of a board and at arm's length from government control. This is beneficial from the standpoint of assisting the corporation in furthering its commercial activities, but one of the problems discussed below is that Crown corporations can become too independent of legislative and government control.

Diverse Representation on the Board

Crown corporations are headed by Boards of Directors that allow for the presence of geographic, consumer, ethnic, language, and other types of representation. This differs from an operating department headed by a single minister. In the Crown corporation form, a number of people representing interested groups are actively involved in the decision-making process, thus ensuring that these diverse interests are considered in the making of important decisions. For example, it is traditional that the Board of Directors of the Canadian Broadcasting Corporation contain balanced representation from the various geographic areas of the country.

Provide a "Window" on the Private Sector

Some kinds of activities are usually carried out by the private sector, but are still immensely important to the overall public well-being. In these cases, governments sometimes feel a need to use the corporate form to obtain a "window" on this particular industry, so that the government can ensure that the industry will act in the national interest.

Prior to the creation of Petro-Canada, almost all petrochemical trading was done in the private sector. As a result of the energy crisis of the early 1970s, governments were urged to take a stronger hand in this field, but the solution was clearly not to nationalize the entire industry. Instead, Petro-Canada was established so that the federal government could enter the field in a fairly small way (initially), and develop an understanding of how the industry operated so that it could regulate the industry in a responsible manner. The presence of Petro-Canada as a source of information about the industry was important.

Freedom from Central Agency and Other Controls

Operating departments frequently complain that they experience difficulties in fulfilling their mandate because of the strict financial and personnel restrictions imposed by organizations such as the Treasury Board and the Public Service Commission. The argument is frequently made that entities engaging in commercial activities would be at a competitive disadvantage if they were subject to the same regulations. Thus, the corporate form is frequently employed in cases where competitive pressures require more flexibility than is provided in other organizational forms.

This freedom from controls is one reason the postal unions argued strongly in favour of the post office becoming a Crown corporation. Labour relations in departments are governed by the Public Service Staff Relations Act, which limits the items that are subject to bargaining. Crown corporations are governed by the same legislation as any other corporation, which allows for a broader scope of bargaining.

Attract Business People to Management

One of the most important keys to success for any organization is attracting good people as directors and managers. Successful business people frequently have much to offer to government organizations, but they are sometimes uncomfortable coming into an unfamiliar management structure such as an operating department with a political head, central agency controls, and the other trappings of government. These people feel more comfortable in a setting familiar to them, such as the corporate form. Therefore, it is sometimes suggested that one of the benefits of the Crown corporation is an increased ability to attract successful business people as managers.

Low Visibility Taxation

Crown corporations pay dividends to their shareholders, i.e., government, in the same manner as private sector corporations. In some cases, governments use Crown corporations as sources of income, which might be considered a form of scarcely concealed taxation. For example, the provincial liquor sales agencies make significant profits, which are passed along to provincial governments.

Joint Undertakings

Governments frequently engage in joint ventures. These could be between governments within Canada, such as the Western Canada Lottery, or internationally, such as the Asian Development Bank, or they could be between governments and private sector organizations, such as Telesat Canada (a joint undertaking of the federal government, CN/CP Telecommunications and a small number of other shareholders). The corporate form is the obvious one to employ in these cases because it creates an autonomous entity separate from any of the governments involved in the entity.

This is not a comprehensive list of the reasons for the use of the Crown corporation form. However, it does provide the major rationales that are usually put forward when a new corporation is being formed. Given the many different reasons for the creation of Crown corporations, it is not surprising that they exhibit many different characteristics. Therefore, not all Crown corporations are treated the same way for purposes of political accountability.

CLASSIFICATION OF FEDERAL CROWN CORPORATIONS

Most governments have a classification system that determines the type and amount of political control to which particular groups of corporations will be subject. For example, the federal Financial Administration Act has four schedules that define the accountability regime of federal organizations.[30] Schedule I lists the operating departments. Schedule II lists those entities that have separate corporate status, but which perform "administrative, research, supervisory, advisory or regulatory functions of a governmental nature."[31] These organizations, such as the Canada Employment and Immigration Commission and the National Research Council, do not meet the criteria of a Crown corporation specified at the beginning of this chapter. Some of the Schedule II organizations function in a manner almost identical to departments, and some are advisory councils that will be discussed in more detail in Chapter 11.

Schedule III - Part II lists the names of each corporation that "(a) operates in a competitive environment; and (b) is not ordinarily dependent on appropriations for operating purposes."[32] These are the high-profile corporations, such as Canadian National Railways, Canada Development Investment Corporation, and Petro-Canada.

Schedule III - Part I lists those corporations that do not meet one of the two criteria mentioned in the preceding paragraph. Some of these are not commercially-oriented, e.g., National Capital Commission; most fail to meet the second criterion—financial viability, e.g., VIA Rail Canada Inc.

The purpose of the classification system is to establish different accountability regimes for corporations in the different schedules. Moving from Schedule I to Schedule III-Part II is moving from the least to the most autonomous type of entity.

POLITICAL CONTROL OF CROWN CORPORATIONS

One of the reasons for the use of the Crown corporation form of organization is to separate the corporation from direct political control. However, a Crown corporation is a creature of the government, carries out government objectives, and, in many cases, uses government funds. Therefore, a Crown corporation cannot behave in a totally autonomous manner, but the precise method of political control is awkward because of the need for some limited amount of autonomy.

There is a detectable pendulum swing between emphasis on control and autonomy. The beginning of the latest swing toward greater control is usually identified as the Auditor General's Report for the fiscal year ending March 31, 1976.[33] In the first place, the Auditor General found that there was no focal point for the control of Crown corporations and therefore no single listing of all Crown corporations. Of the Crown corporations that he was able to identify and audit, his conclusion was devastating:

> In the majority of the Crown corporations audited by the Auditor General, financial management and control is weak and ineffective. Moreover, coordination and guidance by central government agencies of financial management and control practices in these Crown corporations are virtually nonexistent.[34]

This section will examine how the current system of political control of Crown corporations functions.

Establishing the Crown Corporation

Public enterprises can be established in three ways: by separate enabling legislation, under the relevant companies legislation, and through the purchase of the shares of a going concern.[35]

The first method provides the greatest legislative control and accountability. The legislature passes a separate law for each new corporation, specifying the mandate of the corporation, i.e., the activities in which it can engage, and its accountability regime to the legislature (e.g., annual reports and method of financing). Thus, the accountability relationship can be as tight or as loose as members of the legislature desire. In most cases, the corporations created in this manner do not have any share capital because they are controlled directly by the government. Some of the federal corporations that have been established by separate legislation are the Canadian Broadcasting Corporation[36] and the Canada Post Corporation.[37]

Alternatively, governments can incorporate companies under the relevant federal or provincial companies legislation in the same manner as any private citizen. A minister, or even a public servant, simply prepares the necessary documentation and, in due course, the Crown corporation is in business. These companies have share capital that is legally vested in either the minister or the Crown.

Finally, the government can enter into any sort of contract, which means that it may decide to purchase the shares of a company on the open market or through a private arrangement. The shares so obtained are then vested in either the minister or the Crown. This same heading covers those relatively rare situations in which governments have forcibly nationalized companies against the will of the previous shareholders. This requires enabling legislation and usually provokes a court challenge. The most recent examples of this are the actions of the Quebec government with regard to the asbestos industry[38] and the Saskatchewan government with regard to the potash industry.[39]

The creation of Crown corporations through the company's legislation and direct purchase has come under attack recently because of concerns about accountability. There have been occasions when a Crown corporation has been created by either a minister or a public servant deciding that this was desirable, finding available funding, and either establishing or purchasing a corporation. Parliamentary and even Cabinet approval was not necessary and in some cases was not obtained. The problem in these cases is that there is no established regime of accountability. This was a part of the cause of the embarrassing situation in which the federal government was not able to determine how many corporations it owned.

The 1984 amendments to the Financial Administration Act have changed this situation considerably. It is now illegal for any person to establish a new corporation or purchase the shares of a corporation without Cabinet approval,[40] and it is illegal for an existing Crown corporation to establish a subsidiary corporation without approval of the Governor in Council, i.e., the Cabinet.[41]

The Financial Administration Act

This Act establishes a general framework for the allowable activities and accountability of Crown corporations. The purpose of the Act is to provide some uniformity in the treatment of Crown corporations, but this uniformity is tempered by the provisions of the various Acts that created the corporations. The Crown corporation provisions of the Act changed little from its original proclamation in 1952 until the major amendments of 1984.[42] The specific provisions of these amendments are discussed elsewhere in this chapter, but their general thrust was to tighten considerably the accountability regime for Crown corporations. In one sense, this is clearly beneficial because there were certain problems with the accountability structure that needed improvement. However, there could be a negative side to this as well. Increasing accountability can lessen a corporation's autonomy and innovativeness. It might be less easy than some think to force all of the disparate kinds of Crown corporations into one mould.

Ministerial Responsibility

All corporations report to Parliament through a minister. In the case of corporations established by special legislation, this minister is specified in the legislation.

In the case of corporations with share capital, the minister usually holds the government's shares in trust for the Crown.

The concept of ministerial responsibility was discussed in the chapter on government departments because the ability to hold the minister accountable for bureaucratic actions is a very important control mechanism over operating departments. The concept of ministerial responsibility is not as strong with regard to the Crown corporation form of organization. It is clear that ministers are not accountable for the day-to-day activities of corporations that report to them; but when a Crown corporation has been created by the government, crucial appointments have been made by government, and subsidies are provided by government, then the government cannot escape some measure of responsibility for the actions of that corporation.[43]

This dilemma could present itself regarding almost any Crown corporation, but some examples from the Canadian Broadcasting Corporation highlight the nature of the problem. Most would agree that the government should not interfere with the operations of the CBC; this would smack of censorship or news management. Not only would it destroy the credibility of the CBC, but it would also open the government to severe criticism.

However, should the government step in when the CBC crosses over the boundaries of appropriate morality or good taste? Members of the Opposition have raised questions in the House of Commons concerning such matters as inappropriate conduct on a news show,[44] cancellation of a popular television series,[45] and even the broadcasting of the World Series in northern areas.[46] The minister's position in all of these cases is very difficult. On the one hand, the CBC cannot take public money and engage in activity that is repugnant to the general public. On the other hand, if the minister becomes too deeply involved in the activities of the CBC, he or she will be open to the charge of political interference, or even censorship. There is no obvious solution to this problem; ministers must simply learn to walk a tightrope on each issue.

Scrutiny of Corporate Plans and Annual Reports

As a result of the 1984 amendments to the Financial Administration Act, all federal Crown corporations are now required to submit an annual corporate plan for the minister's approval. This plan must include:

    (a) the objects or purposes for which the corporation is incorporated . . .
    (b) the corporation's objectives for the period . . .
    (c) the corporation's expected performance for the year . . . as compared to its objectives for that year. . . . [47]

After the plan is approved by the minister, it is tabled in Parliament in summary form for information purposes.

All Crown corporations are also required to submit year-end annual reports of their operations. These reports must include:

    (a) the financial statements of the corporation . . .

(b) the annual auditor's report. . . .
(c) a statement on the extent to which the corporation has met its objectives for the financial year,
(d) such quantitative information respecting the performance of the corporation, . . . relative to the corporation's objectives as the Treasury Board may require to be included in the annual report, and
(e) such other information as is required by this or any other Act of Parliament, or by the appropriate Minister, the President of the Treasury Board or the Minister of Finance, to be included in the annual report. . . . [48]

Members of Parliament have traditionally been dissatisfied with the lack of any method of reviewing the general operations of Crown corporations. The requirement for the corporate plan and the year-end report is certainly a step in the right direction, because they allow Parliament to assess the performance of the corporation against its stated objectives. It is too early to assess the real worth of these reports. In the private sector, it is fairly well understood that these kinds of reports are largely public relations exercises, frequently designed to hide as much as they reveal. The worth of these reports will depend on the goodwill of those preparing them, and on the desire of the legislators and members of the public to demand better accounting.

Power to Issue Directives

A directive issued to a corporation would require it to do something even if its Board of Directors and/or management was opposed. As a result of the 1984 amendments to the federal Financial Administration Act, the Governor in Council may issue *public* directives to any Crown corporation covered by the Act, after consultation with the board.[49] The requirement that the directive be public ensures that these directives will be tested in the court of public opinion and so will not be used for any nefarious purpose.

If the directive approach were used frequently and in anger, it would indicate heightened tension between the corporation and the government, and would likely provoke resignations from the Board of Directors and/or senior management of the corporation. The Lambert Commission suggests that the directive function will more likely be used in a friendly manner in two situations.[50] If the government wanted the corporation to act against its own economic interests for some political reason, the board might request that the government issue a directive to this effect so that the board would be absolved of any guilt for the consequences. The second way a directive could be used would be to clarify details of the corporation's mandate.

Method of Funding

Crown corporations receive their funding in a wide variety of ways.[51] In some cases, a corporation will need only a lump sum at its inception, similar to the amount provided by shareholders at the creation of a private corporation. In other cases, corporations will need start-up funds as well as periodic infusions of

Table 9.5
FINANCIAL ACCOUNTABILITY OF SCHEDULE III CROWN CORPORATIONS

	Part I	Part II
Corporate Plan	Approved by minister and Governor General in Council; summary tabled in Parliament	Same as Part I
Operating budget	Approved by minister and Treasury Board; summary tabled in Parliament	Not required by legislation
Capital budget	Approved by minister and Treasury Board; summary tabled in Parliament	Same as Part I
Borrowing	Approval of minister and Minister of Finance required	Same as Part I
Audit	Audit required by Auditor General	Audit required (not necessarily by Auditor General)

additional funds. These infusions could come directly from government, in the form of grants or loans, from the private sector in the form of loans guaranteed by the government, or from non-guaranteed loans.

The classification system of Crown corporations discussed earlier usually determines the type of financial control that the government and legislature have over particular Crown corporations. By way of illustration, Table 9.5 compares the accountability regime of Schedule III - Part I and Part II corporations, but the factor that probably has the greatest impact on a corporation's autonomy is whether it is self-financing. If the corporation must return to the public treasury on an annual basis and steer its request for funding through the surveillance of an operating department, the Treasury Board, a legislative committee, and ultimately the legislature, then it has little more autonomy than an operating department. On the other hand, if a corporation is self-funding, it has a much greater degree of autonomy.

Appointment and Removal of Directors

Like private sector corporations, a Crown corporation is under the control of a Board of Directors, which determines the general direction of the corporation. The board of a Crown corporation has a particular responsibility to act as a buffer between the corporation's management and the political concerns of the shareholder, i.e., the minister.

These directors are appointed (and removed) by the minister, after consultation with Cabinet.[52] There is no recent comprehensive analysis of the backgrounds of board members, but they seem to be mainly business and professional people. Public servants and, in some provinces, ministers also serve as board members.

These positions have also been used for purposes of political patronage. Directors appointed in this manner might lack expertise in the company's operation and might be so politically sensitive that they become unduly passive.[53] This situation also diminishes the status of the board and limits its credibility in policy-making.[54]

There is also a dilemma concerning the advisability of appointing public servants or ministers to be members of boards. The appointment of a public servant to a board could improve coordination between the corporation and the public servant's department, but it could also place the public servant in a conflict situation.[55] For example, should the public servant advise the corporation if his or her department is considering regulatory changes that will affect it?

However, even at best there can be problems with the operation of these boards. Just as in the private sector, there is some question about whether these part-time directors really effectively control the full-time, professional management of the corporation.[56] In the case of Crown corporations, this difficulty is exacerbated by the role of the minister. The minister (or full Cabinet) usually retains some of the powers that the Board of Directors in a private sector corporation would have. Chief among these are the power to issue directives and appoint senior management.

Scrutiny by Legislative Committees

Crown corporations are subject to the same kind of scrutiny by the various legislative committees as are the operating departments. Hearings are sometimes instituted as a result of information generated by the Auditor General or by public concerns about some controversial actions. This is an important element of control, but its usefulness is somewhat limited. Elected members have many responsibilities and little assistance in meeting them. This makes it very difficult for them to use the committee system in an optimal manner. This situation is exacerbated in the case of Crown corporations because they see themselves as somewhat removed from detailed political control, anyway. Furthermore, unless a corporation needs additional funding or a change in its legislation, there is no automatic mechanism to bring its affairs before a committee and no incentive on the part of the corporation to be totally forthcoming.

The Accountability-Autonomy Conundrum

Establishing the appropriate amount of control over the activities of a Crown corporation is an awkward dilemma. On the one hand, the corporation is an emanation of government and uses government funds, and so cannot be allowed to operate completely outside government control. On the other hand, too much control defeats the purpose of using the corporate form.

> Parliament and even the responsible Minister must show confidence in the corporation by refraining from breathing down the neck of management. On the other

hand, the Canadian system of parliamentary government can impose responsibility only on the Ministers of the Crown. Hence the public corporation cannot be used as a means of evading ultimate responsibility. Where to draw the line between the claims of managerial autonomy and the claims of parliamentary responsibility remains for Canada a problem that has been seriously posed rather than solved by contemporary use of the public corporation.[57]

Crown Management Board of Saskatchewan

Since 1946, Saskatchewan has had a unique way of dealing with this accountability-autonomy dilemma, which has leaned decidedly in the direction of accountability. It is based on the concept of the "holding company" borrowed from the private sector. A holding company is a company established for the sole purpose of holding the shares of other companies; it usually does not engage in any business activity of its own.

The Crown Management Board of Saskatchewan (CMB) is a holding company that owns the shares of thirteen companies (as of December 31, 1988) grouped in three sectors—resources, utilities, and financial and services.[58] These are such major provincial Crown corporations as Saskatchewan Power Corporation, Saskatchewan Telecommunications, and Saskatchewan Government Insurance.

Traditionally, the role of the CMB and its predecessors has been to enhance the *accountability* of Crown corporations to Cabinet. This has been done through three mechanisms.

First, Cabinet ministers have traditionally served as chairpersons or vice-chairpersons of the Boards of Directors of Crown corporations. This has provided a direct link between the corporation and Cabinet that is lacking in other governments. This has also created a direct linkage between the corporations and the legislature. In Saskatchewan, ministers do not escape responsibility for the actions of Crown corporations, as do their colleagues in other provinces.

Second, the Board of Directors of CMB is composed of a majority of Cabinet ministers, so that it functions as a Cabinet committee or as a kind of central agency concerned with Crown corporations. The board controls the capital budgets of subsidiary corporations and plays a major role in determining the amount of budgetary appropriation to those corporations that need them. The board also has a small staff that provides advice to Crown corporations in such areas as industrial relations, accounting policy, and public relations.

Third, there is a Crown Corporations Committee of the legislature that reviews the annual reports and financial statements of all Crown corporations. The committee can call ministers before it to discuss the activities of their corporations.

In the last few years, there has been a general trend toward appointing individuals with a private sector background to the boards of Crown corporations and a greater emphasis on business-like efficiency. This could have the effect of diminishing the direct lines of accountability that historically existed, but the holding company model as implemented in Saskatchewan remains a unique instrument of accountability.

STRUCTURE AND OPERATION OF CROWN CORPORATIONS

The internal structure and operation of Crown corporations resemble those of private sector corporations so much that little elaboration is necessary. As discussed above, the role of the minister and/or Cabinet complicates the picture somewhat, but the general direction of the corporation is the responsibility of the Board of Directors and the senior officials of the corporation. The members of the board, except sometimes the chairperson, serve on a part-time basis and their main involvement is attending meetings several times a year at which important policy issues are considered. The Governor in Council, i.e., Cabinet, appoints (and can remove) the Chief Executive Officer after consultation with the board, but all other senior appointments are the responsibility of the board and senior management. The senior officials of the corporation then carry on the activities of the corporation on a day-to-day basis, very much as they would if they were working for a private sector corporation.

SOME CRITICISMS OF CROWN CORPORATIONS

Many of the long-standing problems regarding federal Crown corporations were remedied by the 1984 amendments to the Financial Administration Act, but some problems have proven more resistant to easy solution. Also, the positions of the provinces vary. Some had enough foresight so that many of these problems were headed off in advance, but other provinces have not yet addressed the problems identified in the last few years by the federal government.

Proliferation of New Corporations and Subsidiaries

One of the most basic criticisms of the existing arrangement is that there are simply too many corporations, and many of them constitute an inappropriate use of the corporate form.

> A review of the list of Crown corporations reveals a bewildering array of corporations, including business corporations (Air Canada, CNR), cooperatives (Canadian Wheat Board), advisory bodies (Economic Council of Canada), regulatory agencies (Atomic Energy Control Board), granting councils (Canada Council), research organizations (National Research Council), theatres (National Arts Centre), museums (National Museums Corporation) and departmental corporate shells (the National Battlefields Commission). The business corporations can be further subdivided into monopolies, oligopolies and competitive corporations spanning the transportation, manufacturing, communications, insurance and banking sectors.[59]

The trend toward privatization, which will be discussed later in this chapter, has changed this situation somewhat, but there still remain a large number of Crown corporations, frequently in fields that could be explained more easily by history or accident than logic.

Inefficiency of Crown Corporations

There are frequent allegations that Crown corporations are less efficient than their private sector counterparts. Critics suggest that where Crown corporations have a monopoly position, there is no incentive for them to be efficient or innovative. Even when Crown corporations must compete in the marketplace, the fact that they can rely on government subsidies means that their managements do not have to be as disciplined as private sector managers.

Some of these criticisms might have more to do with ideology than fact, because the empirical evidence is unclear. Some criticisms are based on a single isolated incident, e.g., cost overrun on a project. Others flow from forgetting that Crown corporations have a public policy objective that frequently prevents them from maximizing efficiency. For example, the CBC might make as much money as the other networks if it did not have more stringent rules about Canadian content. Other criticisms are simply unfair on the surface: why can't Canada Post deliver a letter as fast as a courier that charges twenty-five times more for the service?

Empirical evidence on this point is very difficult to find. First, there are not many sectors in which both private and public corporations co-exist. Second, establishing comparability is difficult when the public corporation also has some public purpose objective. Borins and Boothman reviewed a number of sectoral studies that compared private and public sector corporations. Their conclusions were:

1. *There is no consistent evidence demonstrating that public enterprise is inherently less efficient than private enterprise.* At least in mature industries, the overwhelming bulk of the published research conducted in Canada and abroad, particularly the more sophisticated studies of productivity and cost efficiency, suggests that public and private firms have comparable performance levels when examined on an industry-by-industry basis . . .

2. *Environment appears to be a stronger determinant of efficiency than form of ownership.* A consistent pattern which has emerged in the case studies is that performance is conditional upon the intensity and form of competition . . . [60]

Unfair Competition with the Private Sector

Crown corporations receive financial support from government to become established, and, in some cases, to meet operating deficits. In other cases, the support is less direct; for example, the government may provide loan guarantees so that money can be borrowed at a lower interest rate or the Crown corporation could be the beneficiary of some regulatory preference. For example, for a number of years the Canadian Transport Commission ruled that Air Canada must have the majority of the transcontinental market, even though CP Air felt that it could have captured more of the market if this artificial restraint did not exist. These kinds of preferences can be very frustrating for independent entrepreneurs who are already in, or would like to enter, the same market as the Crown corporation.

Increasing Financial Power of Crown Corporations

The trend on the part of Crown corporations to be more involved in financial activities was discussed earlier. In some cases, the effect of this has been to create a very large pool of capital that could be used in any number of ways, some controversial.

Quebec's Caisse de dépôt et placement and the Alberta Heritage Savings Trust Fund are two examples of these kinds of corporations. The size and power of the Caisse in particular has raised concern on the part of some businesses that it could become a political tool of the Quebec government and so force these Crown corporations to make decisions based on political, rather than business, considerations.[61] When the owners of the Montreal Expos wanted to sell the team in 1990, there was some discussion that the Caisse should buy it so that it would definitely stay in Montreal. There is little evidence that the Caisse *has* used its power as a political tool,[62] but it is clear that it and similar organizations in other provinces *could* wield significant power if they chose to do so.

Profits or Public Purpose?—Problems of Accountability

One of the most basic problems facing a Crown corporation is whether it ought to function to make a profit or to serve a public purpose. There can easily be conflicts between these two. For example, VIA Rail can maximize profit by terminating long-distance runs and reducing services to smaller towns and instead focussing on high-volume routes, e.g., the Quebec-Windsor corridor. However, whenever it proposes this, various interests point out VIA's requirement to serve the public interest.

Determining the amount of control that the government should have over the activities of a Crown corporation is not an easy task.

> In the context of responsible government, the most telling questions turn around the problem of establishing a balance between the autonomy that the Crown corporation requires as an organizational form to perform the task it has been given, on the one hand, and the government's need to control and direct the corporation and Parliament's need to oversee or scrutinize it, on the other. This problem of balance runs through every aspect of the complex inter-relationships between Parliament, government..., and the Crown corporations.[63]

This problem engenders a number of difficulties. It is sometimes suggested that the managers of Crown corporations engage in activities which are contrary to the desires of politicians, and which later cause political embarrassment. This situation is frustrating to politicians who must bear criticism, even though they feel that in some cases they have very little control over these corporations. The managers of Crown corporations are also placed in a difficult position, because they are frequently ridiculed in the media for their inability to make a profit, or to operate more efficiently, when the problem is sometimes that profit and efficiency have been sacrificed deliberately to political concerns.

Accountability to Whom?

Not only is there this division between a concern for profits and public purpose, but there is also some concern that accountability is divided among a confusing number of different organizations.

Earlier in this chapter, it was suggested that Parliament has a number of ways of exerting its control, but a sober assessment of the role of Parliament would have to admit that its control is rather weak and sporadic. More effective control resides with the government, but even here there is significant division.

Legally, the shares of a Crown corporation are held by the minister, in trust for the Crown, but that does not mean that the minister can make unilateral decisions about Crown corporations. Members of the Board of Directors and the Chief Executive Officer can be appointed by the minister only after consultation with Cabinet. Then the roles are reversed, so that directives can only be given by Cabinet after consultation with the appropriate minister.

> [I]n attempting to respond to the demands for increased accountability, the government has resorted to building a complex web of multiple bureaucratic approvals which attempt to make Crown corporations accountable to everyone in sight. Parliament, Treasury Board, Department of Finance, various ministers, committees, officials and others now monitor Crown corporations. Although Crown corporations are nominally accountable to many people in Ottawa, they are, in fact, truly accountable to no one. At the same time, making the accountability process more bureaucratic threatens to stifle the very characteristic of Crown corporations that made them the chosen instrument in the first place: freedom from departmental bureaucracy.[64]

Problems of Mandate and Reporting

A part of the problem of ensuring accountability is the difficulty of specifying a mandate for the corporation. Cabinet and legislature are frequently reluctant to specify a corporation's mandate in such a narrow fashion that it could not engage in innovative behaviour to take advantage of a changing environment. After all, one reason for choosing the corporate form is to allow it to be more flexible and innovative. However, there have been allegations that some corporations have used this broad mandate to move into areas of activity that were not envisaged for them when they were created. Langford uses the phrase "mandate creep" to describe this phenomenon.[65]

This problem has been exacerbated by the uneven quality of reports that corporations provide to the government and legislature. These reports ought to make it possible to determine if the corporation actually followed the plan that was approved at the beginning of the year, but due to lack of information it is often difficult to do this. At any rate, the precise penalties for deviating from the approved plan are unclear. For example, the Auditor General pointed out that the budgets of approximately 25 percent of Crown corporations were not approved in 1982, yet this seems to have no impact on their operations.[66]

PROPOSALS FOR REFORM

The problems mentioned above cover a very wide range, but the most serious problems have been identified in the area of accountability. Thus most of the reforms discussed below will be geared to improving accountability. Patrice Garant, for one, applauds this trend, but he also sounds a note of caution:

> This awakening [to the need for better accountability] was necessary because Crown corporations are neither private companies nor "states within the state." But beware the pendulum! Some reform proposals, while well intended, are dangerous because they contradict both the raison d'être of the Crown corporation network and certain objectives inherent in this choice of instrument designed to ensure adequate intervention by the public authority.[67]

There are no simple solutions to the difficulties caused by the large and diverse agglomeration of Crown corporations. One of the more thoughtful students of the corporate form has suggested that a major rethinking of the whole sector is necessary:

> What is needed is a rethinking of Crown corporations' purpose and role that would result in a major reorganization of the Crown corporation sector. This would include the "de-incorporation" of many organizations and better organizational forms found or devised, the wind-up of several Crown corporations and the amalgamation of their activities with departments, and the privatization of all or parts of some corporations or their activities.[68]

Any proposals for reforms must deal with the fact that there is greater diversity than similarity in the field of Crown corporations. The Economic Council of Canada has grouped Crown corporations into a number of different categories and recommended different reform proposals for each type.[69]

Single-Window Approach

The main problem identified with the current accountability regime is that it is too complex, and involves too many different agents to whom corporations are supposed to be accountable. The single-window approach would streamline this system by making corporations accountable to only one body. Each corporation would be accountable only to its own minister or all corporations would be accountable to the same body, along the lines of the Crown Management Board in Saskatchewan.

While this idea seems to be beneficial, the likelihood of its adoption is fairly slim. Central agencies are well-entrenched in Ottawa and departments like Finance and Treasury Board jealously guard their prerogatives to control spending. These agencies feel that a weakening of control over Crown corporations would provide ministers with a loophole to do things through their corporations that they would not be allowed to do through their departments.

Privatization

Privatization has a number of meanings.

> In its narrowest sense privatization encompasses the whole or partial sale of state-owned companies but more broadly and importantly it also embraces actions to reduce the role of government and enhance market forces to produce a more competitive economy. In this larger sense, privatization includes deregulation, trade liberalization, and the increased contracting out of government services.[70]

This section will only discuss privatization in its narrow meaning. Other aspects of it will be discussed elsewhere in the book.

Privatization is a world-wide trend and the federal government has become very involved in it.[71] Most provinces have also considered this idea, but some have espoused it more whole-heartedly than others.[72]

The federal government currently has a Minister of State (Privatization and Regulatory Affairs) supported by an Office of Privatization and Regulatory Affairs. As of August 1, 1989, the federal government had sold thirteen Crown corporations, divested itself of partial holdings in five others and was actively pursuing three more privatization initiatives. The privatized corporations included such large and well-known companies as Air Canada, CN Hotels, de Havilland Aircraft, and Teleglobe Canada.[73]

The Office of Privatization and Regulatory Affairs lists the following benefits of privatization:

> Privatization reduces the size of government and makes room for private sector initiatives; it improves market efficiency and the allocation of resources and it improves the efficiency of the organization privatized, through market discipline and the reduction of political and bureaucratic impediments.

> Privatization can also offer the opportunity for individual Canadians to invest directly in major national corporations that they have supported as taxpayers.

> Privatization allows governments to concentrate on governing. It reduces government time and resources currently involved in the management of Crown corporations which no longer require government ownership. In addition, successful privatizations increase corporate earnings and employment, thus increasing the tax revenues available for allocation to other government priorities, including regional development, social policy concerns and many others.[74]

Some have questioned whether this is a carefully developed policy, or simply an ex post facto rationalization of a policy that the Conservative government adopted for ideological reasons.[75]

When the federal government first began its privatization efforts, there was some criticism that the process was disorganized and inefficient.[76] However, over time it has established a more orderly approach to the privatization process.

The first step is *initial assessment*. At this stage the following questions are asked:

- Does the corporation play a continuing role in support of national and regional public policy objectives?
- Does the company have the potential to be commercially viable?
- Is it ready to operate in the private sector?
- Will privatization be compatible with other federal government policies, such as bilingualism, competition, foreign investment and trade?
- What will be the effect on the employees, competitors, suppliers or customers of the corporation?[77]

When this initial review identifies a potential candidate for privatization, the second step is an *in-depth review* by teams of experts under the guidance of the Office of Privatization and Regulatory Affairs. These groups study not simply whether or not to privatize, but also what steps would need to be taken to get a corporation ready for privatization, if that is the decision made. Their recommendations might involve either winding up an unprofitable part of the operations, changing the company's industrial relations policy, or any number of other actions that would make the corporation more attractive to purchasers. These teams also consider any conditions that could be put on the sale such as location of head office, restrictions on non-resident ownership of shares, and continuity of pension plans. This comprehensive review is then examined by the Minister of State, who makes a recommendation to Cabinet.

The next step is the *passage of divestiture legislation* that defines how the transaction will take place, including any conditions that are to be imposed on purchasers.

After this legislative approval, the company is *prepared for sale*. This involves making the company more attractive to potential investors by following the recommendations of the earlier study teams.

The final stage is the *actual sale*. In ten of the federal government's thirteen privatizations, this has involved a bidding process that has resulted in one buyer taking over all shares of the company, e.g., Boeing's purchase of de Havilland Aircraft. In the remaining cases, e.g., Air Canada, underwriters have been used to sell the shares to the general public.

The funds generated by the sale can be used in two ways. They can go into federal government coffers as payment for the shares, or they can go to the company for use in future expansion. In some cases, funds have been divided between the two uses. The direction of the cash flow will obviously have a major impact on the attractiveness of the share issue.

Tupper and Doern have described the Mulroney government's record on privatization as

> one of slow and deliberate movement but with an approach that is very conscious of the pitfalls and of the underlying fact that Canadian public opinion is not overly critical of the current level and form of public enterprise.[78]

However, even this cautious approach has incited a number of criticisms.

Canadian nationalists have objected to sales of corporations to foreign purchasers. The most publicized case was the sale of de Havilland Aircraft (the manufacturer of the very popular Dash-7 and Dash-8 aircraft) to Boeing. This caused some concern about a reduction in the number of jobs in Canada, but it "raised a political storm as much for the loss of Canadian hopes as for the loss of taxpayers' investment."[79]

The federal government's tendency to sell companies to one large buyer, rather than make the shares widely available to the general public, could have the effect of increasing the market power of the purchaser over consumers. W. T. Stanbury has expressed concern about the sale of Teleglobe Canada, which has a monopoly on telecommunications services between Canada and areas outside North America, to Memotec, Inc., which is one-third owned by Bell Canada.[80] Borins and Boothman's review (mentioned earlier) indicated that intensity of competition in a sector is a better spur to efficiency than locus of ownership, i.e., private or public.[81] If privatization leads to greater concentration in certain sectors, then it might result in less, rather than more, efficiency.

Another criticism is that the government is "selling off the family silver to pay the rent." Critics have pointed out that many corporations pay regular dividends to the government. It could be very short-sighted to sell those companies for a one-time deficit reduction.

The reality is considerably more complex than either side states. When the government privatizes a profitable corporation it receives immediately a lump sum payment in exchange for the right to receive a steady flow of annual payments in future years. Whether the government receives full value depends on how one estimates the future flow of incomes, which requires making some very difficult assumptions.

Such a transaction can benefit both parties. The government will receive a large one-time payment for an entity that, as long as it was restricted by government policies, could never earn much money anyway. The purchaser receives an entity that will be a good money-maker when it is no longer constrained by government policies.

Workers are always concerned about jobs and security when corporations are privatized. Will jobs be eliminated? Will the geographic location of some jobs be changed? What about union agreements? What about pension plans?

The federal government's stock reply to this concern has been: "Privatization does not guarantee jobs, but neither does Crown ownership. As always, the best guarantee of job security is a successful, growing company."[82]

In fact, the federal government has usually attempted to provide some protection to workers. However, there is a trade-off here, because the more protection for workers and other conditions the federal government demands, the less attractive the corporation will be to purchasers. Also, there are inevitably time limits on any protection. When current union agreements expire, they must be renegotiated with the new purchaser. When expansion takes place, it will take place where the new owner wants it.

Just as Saskatchewan has a unique approach to organizing Crown corporations, it also has a unique approach to privatization, or what it refers to as "public participation." Saskatchewan sees its program as much broader than simply privatization, but even the privatization aspects of the program are different from the federal program. The federal government has tended to sell each of its corporations to one big purchaser. Saskatchewan prefers to sell its corporations as widely as possible to the Saskatchewan public so that as many people as possible have the opportunity to participate in the development of the local economy.

The Saskatchewan Department of Public Participation, which operated from 1988 to 1990, was very innovative in arranging for greater public participation. It relied on the tremendous pride that the people of Saskatchewan have always had in their Crown corporations and the fact that residents of Saskatchewan have a very high rate of savings, much of which is invested in Canada Savings Bonds and eastern banks. The Department of Public Participation wanted to make it as easy to invest in the Saskatchewan economy as it was to invest money in other ways. Thus, it arranged for shares to be purchased in banks or through payroll deductions.

But public participation goes beyond purchase of shares. Since 1985, the public participation program has arranged for bond and share offerings to the public; arranged the sale of the government's pulp company to a private company, after the company agreed to build a paper mill; enabled employees and Indian bands to purchase a sawmill; arranged for a local ski club to operate a ski hill in a provincial park; and provided for funding for the start-up of salt mines and peat bogs. The emphasis is on flexibility in helping local people develop their local economies in whatever way is best in the circumstances.

Compensation Principle

One of the major irritants to managers of Crown corporations is that they are frequently criticized for failure to make a profit when this failure comes about not as a result of their mismanagement, but because the government demands that the corporation do something that is in the broader national interest, but *not* in the corporation's economic interest. It has sometimes been suggested that when a corporation incurs expenses in this situation, it should be compensated out of general tax funds. This would allow the corporation to act in the national interest without suffering financially as a result.

A good example of this principle is the subsidy that the federal government pays to CN Rail to transport western grain to eastern Canada. For years, CN was simply expected to haul this grain at less than cost as a part of its public policy mandate, but the Western Grain Transportation Act of 1983 changed that, so that CN is now compensated by the federal government for providing this public service.[83]

A great deal of analysis and thought went into the 1984 amendments to the federal Financial Administration Act. The fact that the preceding list of possible reforms is much shorter now than it would have been before those revisions is testimony to the improvement it represented in the accountability regime for Crown corporations. However, it is clear that the role of Crown corporations is still a subject of heated debate. That debate can become particularly heated around the role of a relatively new type of entity called mixed enterprise.

MIXED ENTERPRISE

At the beginning of this chapter a mixed enterprise was defined as a Crown agency "in which the federal government has taken a direct equity position in common with other participants for the purposes of implementing a public policy or satisfying a public need."[84] It was mentioned earlier that there is some difficulty in deciding exactly which organizations fall within the definition of a Crown corporation; this task is even more difficult for mixed enterprise. However, there have been a number of listings[85] of these entities and there is some similarity in them. Using the more extensive listing of Langford and Huffman, it is possible to identify four general groupings of these enterprises.

International Development Funds. The Canadian government participates in a number of international organizations, such as the Asian Development Bank whose mandate is "to lend funds, promote investments and provide technical assistance to developing countries, and generally, to foster economic growth in the Asian Region."[86] These agencies usually require some financial contribution from Canada, but besides fulfilling some altruistic objectives, they provide the opportunity for Canadians to sell goods and services in the other member countries.

Domestic Development Activities. The federal government participates in a number of joint ventures with provincial governments and private groups, such as native peoples' organizations, to stimulate employment and economic development within Canada. For example, the Newfoundland and Labrador Development Corporation was established "to complement the regional development incentives program as a source of venture capital for manufacturing and resource development in the province."[87] Funding is provided jointly by the federal and Newfoundland governments.

Bridge Authorities. The federal government is also involved in joint ventures in bridge construction both domestically, e.g., Saint John Bridge Authority, and internationally, e.g., Thousand Islands Bridge Authority. There are not many of these ventures, but they are important in the areas in which they are located.

Commercial Ventures. The mixed enterprises with the highest profiles are the commercial ventures, most notably the Canada Development Corporation (CDC) and Telesat.[88]

The idea for something like the CDC came about in the nationalistic times of the 1960s, with the idea of a corporate vehicle to buy back Canada from foreign investors. However, when it was formed in 1971, its role was considerably more limited. Its major early purchases were in the energy and mining fields, although it has also invested in pharmaceutical, soft drink, and electronics companies. Originally, all of the company's shares were held by the government, but beginning in 1975 share offerings were made to the public. The short history of the CDC illustrates one of the major problems with mixed enterprise—accountability.

Problems of Accountability and Control

Presumably one reason governments enter into mixed enterprises, particularly commercial ventures, is because they want the best of both worlds. They want an organization that will be influenced by the business partners to operate in an efficient, business-like manner, but that the government will still be able to influence in order to implement public policy. Stephen Brooks has studied the activities of many mixed enterprises and his conclusion is that this simply does not work.

> [T]he MOC [mixed ownership corporation] involves an ambiguous form of organization that limits the ability of the government shareholder to impose its policy goals on that organization when these seriously conflict with those of management and/or private sector shareholders.[89]

When governments attempt to exercise *effective* control over mixed enterprises, they run into two arguments from company management. The first stems from the general pro-business, anti-government bias in society. Management will argue that business people know what is best for businesses and that the inefficiency caused by the imposition of political values is bad business. The second, more pragmatic, argument is that if the business does not act to maximize its income, the value of its shares will go down in the open market, which will cause shareholders to blame government for their losses. The result of this is that it will be more difficult to sell shares in future mixed enterprises, because potential shareholders will fear a repeat of previous government interference.

If this line of argument is accepted, management can have almost complete autonomy because of divisions of power on the Board of Directors and the inability of the minister to provide directives or other controls.[90] Stephen Brooks's analysis of the CDC situation leads him to the conclusion that a Crown corporation can function as *either* an engine for profit or an instrument of public policy, *but not both*.[91]

This chapter has focussed on the Crown corporation as an organizational form. Its main value is in carrying on commercial and financial operations at arm's length from the government of the day. The next chapter considers another organizational form that is also at arm's length—the regulatory agency.

NOTES

1. "The Real Issues on the Crown Corporations Debate," in Kenneth Kernaghan, ed., *Public Administration in Canada: Selected Readings*, 5th ed. (Toronto: Methuen, 1985), p. 122.
2. One of the most thoughtful considerations of the definition problem is found in M. J. Trebilcock and J. R. S. Prichard, "Crown Corporations: The Calculus of Instrument Choice," in J. Robert S. Prichard, ed., *Crown Corporations in Canada: The Calculus of Instrument Choice* (Toronto: Butterworths, 1983), pp. 8-15. John W. Langford also does an admirable job of grappling with this same difficult question in "The Identification and Classification of Federal Public Corporations: A Preface to

Regime Building," *Canadian Public Administration* 23 (Spring 1980): 76-104. For a different but equally plausible definition, see Royal Commission on Financial Management and Accountability, *Final Report* (Hull: Minister of Supply and Services Canada, 1979), ch. 16.

3. "Crown Corporations: Instruments of Economic Intervention—Legal Aspects," in Ivan Bernier and Andrée Lajoie, eds., *Regulations, Crown Corporations andAdministrative Tribunals*, Research study for the Royal Commission on the Economic Union and Development Prospects for Canada (Toronto: University of Toronto Press, 1985), p. 4. (Emphasis added.) Reprinted by permission of the University of Toronto Press in cooperation with the Royal Commission on the Economic Union and Development Prospects for Canada and the Canadian Publishing Centre, Supply and Services Canada.

4. Canada, Royal Commission on Financial Management and Accountability, *Final Report*, pp. 358-59.

5. A good history of the development of the public enterprise instrument in Canada is Economic Council of Canada, *Minding the Public's Business* (Ottawa: Minister of Supply and Services Canada, 1986), ch. 2.

6. By definition "Crown corporations" are those corporations listed in the Financial Administration Act, but the federal government holdings go far beyond these identified Crown corporations.

7. *Report of the Auditor General of Canada to the House of Commons for the Fiscal Year Ended March 31, 1976* (Ottawa: Minister of Supply and Services Canada, 1976), p. 51.

8. Canada, Office of the Comptroller General, "Corporations in which the Government Has an Interest" (photocopy.)

9. Treasury Board of Canada Secretariat, *Crown Corporations and Other Canadian Government Corporate Interests* (Ottawa: Minister of Supply and Services Canada, 1984), p. 3.

10. This excludes the large number of Crown corporations that were established during the Second World War to assist in supplying the war effort and were wound up shortly after the war. See Sandford F. Borins, "World War Two Crown Corporations: Their Wartime Role and Peacetime Privatization," *Canadian Public Administration* 25 (Fall 1982): 380-404.

11. John W. Langford and Kenneth J. Huffman, "The Uncharted Universe of Federal Public Corporations," in Prichard, ed., *Crown Corporations in Canada*, p. 276.

12. Marsha Gordon, *Government in Business* (Montreal: C. D. Howe Institute, 1981), pp. 11-12.

13. Aidan R.Vining and Robert Botterell, "An Overview of the Origins, Growth, Size and Functions of Provincial Crown Corporations," in Prichard, ed., *Crown Corporations in Canada*, p. 320.

14. Ibid., p. 340.

15. For a discussion of the early history of the hydro-electric companies and their uneven development in different provinces, see Aidan Vining, "Provincial Hydro Utilities," in Allan Tupper and G. Bruce Doern, eds., *Public Corporations and Public Policy in Canada* (Montreal: The Institute for Research on Public Policy, 1981), pp. 152-75.

16. Gordon, *Government in Business*, pp. 14-15.

17. "State Enterprise and Partisanship in Provincial Politics," *Canadian Journal of Political Science* 15 (December 1982): 735.

18. One of the best treatments of these factors is contained in Trebilcock and Prichard, "Crown Corporations: The Calculus of Instrument Choice," in Prichard, ed., *Crown Corporations in Canada*, pp. 39-75. Two other articles in this book are also useful in considering this area: Thomas A. Borcherding, "Toward a Positive Theory of Public

Sector Supply Arrangements," pp. 99-184; and Marsha A. Chandler, "The Politics of Public Enterprise," pp. 185-218.

19. The circumstances surrounding this acquisition are described in Allan Tupper, "The Nation's Businesses: Canadian Concepts of Public Enterprise," Ph. D. diss., Queen's University, 1977, pp. 99-113.

20. There have been a few exceptions to this happy picture in which government takeover attempts have been the subject of much consternation. Some are mentioned in Garant, "Crown Corporation," p. 6.

21. J. E. Hodgetts, "The Public Corporation in Canada," in W. Friedmann and J. F. Garner, eds., *Government Enterprise: A Comparative Study* (London: Stevens & Sons, 1970), p. 202. (Footnote omitted.)

22. V. Seymour Wilson, *Canadian Public Policy and Administration: Theory and Environment* (Toronto: McGraw-Hill Ryerson, 1981), pp. 365-70; C. A. Ashley and R. G. H. Smails, *Canadian Crown Corporations: Some Aspects of their Administration and Control* (Toronto: Macmillan, 1965), pp. 3-10; Tupper, "The Nation's Businesses," pp. ii-iv and passim; Chandler, "State Enterprise and Partisanship in Provincial Politics," pp. 727-35.

23. "Crown Corporations: The Calculus of Instrument Choice," p. 53.

24. H. V. Nelles, *The Politics of Development, Forests, Mines & Hydro-electric Power in Ontario, 1849-1941* (Toronto: Macmillan, 1974).

25. Jeanne Kirk Laux and Maureen Appel Molot, *State Capitalism: Public Enterprise in Canada* (Ithaca, N.Y.: Cornell University Press, 1988), p. 43.

26. "Fear, Envy of Caisse de Dépôt: Renewing Criticism of its Power," *The Globe and Mail*, August 28, 1989.

27. Gordon, *Government in Business*, p. 151.

28. *A Nation Unaware: The Canadian Economic Culture* (Vancouver: J. J. Douglas, 1974), part II.

29. Robert Kent Weaver, "The Politics of State Enterprise: Railroad Nationalization in The United States and Canada," Unpublished Ph.D. diss., Harvard University, 1982, pp. 505-508.

30. Seven Crown corporations are not covered by this new legislation. The Bank of Canada, the Canadian Wheat Board, the International Development Research Centre, and the Canada Council are each governed by their own legislation. The Canadian Broadcasting Corporation, the National Arts Centre, and the Canadian Film Development Corporation were not covered by the legislation because they were to be governed by a new "cultural agencies act" that was being prepared. This separate legislation was intended to recognize the importance of maintaining the independence of these cultural organizations from direct government control. The legislation was never passed and its current status is unclear.

31. R.S.C. 1985, c. F-11, s. 3(1) (a).

32. R.S.C. 1985, c. F-11, s. 3(5).

33. *Report of the Auditor General of Canada to the House of Commons for the Fiscal Year Ended March 31, 1976*, ch. 5.

34. Ibid., p. 49.

35. For a good overview of the legal and practical aspects of the use of these different methods, see Garant, "Crown Corporations," pp. 14-22.

36. R.S.C. 1985, c. B-9, s. 24(1).

37. R.S.C. 1985, c. C-10.

38. Pierre Fournier, "The National Asbestos Corporation of Quebec," in Tupper and Doern, eds., *Public Corporations and Public Policy*, pp. 353-64.

39. Jeanne Kirk Laux and Maureen Appel Molot, "The Potash Corporation of Saskatch-ewan," in ibid., pp. 189-219.

40. S.C. 1984, c. 31, s. 11. (Section 100, as amended.)

41. R.S.C. 1985, c. F-11, ss. 90-91.

42. S.C. 1984, c. 31.

43. This dilemma is not new; it was discussed extensively in Parliament in the 1920s. Ashley and Smails, *Canadian Crown Corporations*, ch. 5.

44. This can be a relatively common occurrence. For example, see the question by Mr. Cossitt in Canada, House of Commons, Debates, 1 June 1981, 10, pp. 119-20. The most tumultuous example of this kind of controversy surrounded the show, "This Hour Has Seven Days." The controversy is described in K. Kernaghan, *Canadian Cases in Public Administration* (Toronto: Methuen, 1977), pp. 48-54.

45. Canada, House of Commons, *Debates*, March 9, 1973, p. 2067.

46. Canada, House of Commons, *Debates*, October 13, 1983, p. 27986.

47. R.S.C. 1985, c. F-11, s. 122(3).

48. R.S.C. 1985, c. F-11, s. 150(3).

49. R.S.C. 1985, c. F-11, s. 89.

50. Royal Commission on Financial Management and Accountability, *Final Report*, pp. 337-38.

51. See Garant, "Crown Corporations," p. 18.

52. R.S.C. 1985, c. F-11, s. 105(1).

53. Sandford F. Borins and Lee Brown, *Investments in Failure: Five Government Corporations that Cost the Canadian Taxpayer Billions* (Toronto: Methuen, 1986), p. 63 and passim.

54. John Langford, "Crown Corporations as Instruments of Policy," in G. Bruce Doern and Peter Aucoin, eds., *Public Policy in Canada* (Toronto: Macmillan, 1979), p. 257.

55. Borins and Brown, *Investments in Failure*, pp. 151-53.

56. Michael J. Hatton, *Corporations & Directors: Comparing the Profit and Not-for-Profit Sectors* (Toronto: Thompson Educational Publishing, 1990), chs. 3 and 4.

57. Hodgetts, "The Public Corporation in Canada," p. 226.

58. Crown Management Board of Saskatchewan, *Annual Report 1988*, p. 6.

59. Gracey, "The Real Issues in the Crown Corporations Debate," p. 132.

60. Sandford F. Borins and Barry E. C. Boothman, "Crown Corporations and Economic Efficiency," in D. G. McFetridge, ed., *Canadian Industrial Policy in Action* (Toronto: University of Toronto Press, 1985), p. 121. Reprinted by permission of the University of Toronto Press in cooperation with the Royal Commission on the Economic Union and Development Prospects for Canada and the Canadian Publishing Centre, Supply and Services Canada.

61. This controversy is described in Allan Tupper, *Bill S-31 and the Federalism of State Capitalism* (Kingston, Ont.: Queen's University, Institute of Intergovernmental Rela-tions, 1983). For a general discussion of the Caisse, see Claude Forget, ed., *La Caisse de dépôt et placement du Québec: Sa mission, son impact et sa performance* (Montreal: Institut C. D. Howe, 1984).

62. Stephen Brooks and A. Brian Tanguay, "Quebec's Caisse de dépôt et placement: Tool of Nationalism?" *Canadian Public Administration* 28 (Spring 1985): 99-119.

63. John Langford, "Crown Corporations as Instruments of Policy," p. 240.

64. J. Robert S. Prichard, "Challenges Facing the Boards of Crown Corporations: Diagnosis and Prescription," in Thomas H. Mitchell, Executive Bulletin #30, *Cana-dian Directorship Practices: The Role of the Board of Directors in Crown Corporation Accountability* (Ottawa: The Conference Board of Canada, 1985), p. 4.

65. "Crown Corporations as Instruments of Policy," p. 256.
66. *Annual Report of the Auditor General of Canada to the House of Commons for the Fiscal Year Ending March 31, 1982.* (Ottawa: Minister of Supply and Services Canada, 1982), pp. 75-76.
67. "Crown Corporations," pp. 39-40. (Footnote omitted.)
68. Gracey, "The Real Issues in the Crown Corporations Debate," p. 132.
69. *Minding the Public's Business*, chs. 4-7.
70. Allan Tupper and G. Bruce Doern, "Canadian Public Enterprise and Privatization," in Allan Tupper and G. Bruce Doern, eds., *Privatization, Public Policy and Public Corporations in Canada* (Halifax: The Institute for Research on Public Policy, 1988), p. 1.
71. Discussion of the extent of this movement is found in "A Better Life Is Objective of Worldwide Privatization Push," *The Globe and Mail*, March 3, 1987. The trends that lie at the root of this worldwide movement are discussed in Lionel Ouellet, "La privatisation: un instrument de management public?" *Canadian Public Administration* 30, no. 4 (Winter 1987): 567-69.
72. Maureen Appel Molot, "The Provinces and Privatization: Are the Provinces Really Getting Out of Business?" in Tupper and Doern, eds., *Privatization, Public Policy and Public Corporations in Canada*, pp. 399-425.
73. "Federal Privatizations To Date," News Release of the Office of Privatization and Regulatory Affairs, August 1, 1989.
74. "Privatization in Canada," News Release of the Office of Privatization and Regulatory Affairs, August 1989.
75. W. T. Stanbury, "Privatization and the Mulroney Government," in Andrew W. Gollner and Daniel Salée, eds., *Canada Under Mulroney: An End-of-Term Report* (Montréal: Véhicule Press, 1988), pp. 130-32.
76. "Tory-Style Privatization Process Test Bidders' Stamina, Corporate Coffers," and "Privatization Trend Faces Test Over Big 3," *The Globe and Mail*, February 28, 1987; "Ottawa's Handling of Crown-Sale Talks Criticized by Study," *The Globe and Mail*, June 8, 1987.
77. "How Privatization Works," News Release of the Office of Privatization and Regulatory Affairs, n.d.
78. "Canadian Public Enterprise and Privatization," in Tupper and Doern, eds., *Privatization, Public Policy and Public Corporations in Canada*, p. 32.
79. Ron Graham, *One-Eyed Kings* (Toronto: Collins, 1986), p. 371.
80. "Privatization and the Mulroney Government," p. 128.
81. "Crown Corporations and Economic Efficiency," p. 121.
82. "Privatization in Canada," News Release of the Office of Privatization and Regulatory Affairs, August 1989, p. 6.
83. Garth Stevenson, "Canadian National Railways and Via Rail," in Tupper and Doern, eds., *Privatization, Public Policy and Public Corporations in Canada*, pp. 54-55.
84. Canada, Royal Commission on Financial Management and Accountability, *Final Report*, pp. 358-59.
85. Treasury Board of Canada Secretariat, *Crown Corporations and Other Canadian Government Corporate Interests*, p. 13 and pp. 36-39; Langford and Huffman, "The Uncharted Universe of Federal Public Corporations," pp. 258-69.
86. Treasury Board of Canada Secretariat, *Crown Corporations and Other Canadian Government Corporate Interests*, p. 36.
87. Canada, Department of Regional Economic Expansion, *Annual Report 1981-1982* (Minister of Supply and Services Canada, 1983), p. 9.

88. Only the former company will be discussed here. A good overview of the activities of Telesat is contained in G. Bruce Doern and James A. R. Brothers, "Telesat Canada," in Tupper and Doern, eds., *Public Corporations and Public Policy in Canada*, pp. 221-449.
89. *Who's in Charge?* (Halifax: The Institute for Research on Public Policy, 1987), p. 3.
90. For a catalogue of cases in which management has not followed the obvious desires of government, see Stephen Brooks, "The Mixed Ownership Corporation as an Instrument of Public Policy," *Comparative Politics* (January 1987): 173-91.
91. "The State as Entrepreneur: From CDC to CDIC," *Canadian Public Administration* 26 (Winter 1983): 541-43.

BIBLIOGRAPHY

Ashley, C. A., and R. G. H. Smails. *Canadian Crown Corporations: Some Aspects of their Administration and Control.* Toronto: Macmillan, 1965.

Auditor General of Canada. *Report of the Auditor General of Canada to the House of Commons for the Fiscal Year Ended March 31, 1976.* Ottawa: Minister of Supply and Services Canada, 1976.

——. *Annual Report of the Auditor General of Canada to the House of Commons for the Fiscal Year Ending March 31, 1982.* Ottawa: Minister of Supply and Services Canada, 1982.

Borins, Sandford F. "World War Two Crown Corporations: Their Wartime Role and Peacetime Privatization." *Canadian Public Administration* 25 (Fall 1982): 380-404.

Borins, Sandford F., and Barry E. C. Boothman, "Crown Corporations and Economic Efficiency." In D. G. McFetridge, ed., *Canadian Industrial Policy in Action.* Toronto: University of Toronto Press, 1985, pp. 75-129.

Borins, Sandford F., and Lee Brown. *Investments in Failure: Five Government Corporations that Cost the Canadian Taxpayer Billions.* Toronto: Methuen, 1986.

Brazeau, Jean, and Cathy Schutz. "Crown Corporations and Competition Policy." In *Government Enterprise: Roles and Rationale.* Papers presented at a symposium sponsored by the Economic Council of Canada in Ottawa. (September 1984): pp. 424-46.

Brooks, Stephen. "The Mixed Ownership Corporation as an Instrument of Public Policy." *Comparative Politics* (July 1986).

——. "The State as Entrepreneur: From CDC to CDIC." *Canadian Public Administration* 26 (Winter 1983): 525-43.

——. *Who's in Charge?* Halifax: The Institute for Research on Public Policy, 1987.

Brooks, Stephen, and A. Brian Tanguay. "Quebec's Caisse de dépôt et placement: Tool of Nationalism?" *Canadian Public Administration* 28 (Spring 1985): 99-119.

Canada. House of Commons. Standing Committee on Public Accounts. *Minutes of Proceedings and Evidence,* no. 22, 11 April 1978.

Canada. Office of the Comptroller General. "Corporations in Which the Government Has an Interest." Photocopy, 1980.

Canada. Privy Council Office. *Crown Corporations: Direction–Control–Accountability.* Minister of Supply and Services Canada, 1977.

Canada. Royal Commission on Financial Management and Accountability. *Final Report.* Hull: Minister of Supply and Services Canada, 1979.

Carter, Richard. "Les enterprises publiques: pourquoi et pour qui?" *Canadian Public Administration* 26 (Summer 1983): 239-54.

Chandler, Marsha A. "State Enterprise and Partisanship in Provincial Politics." *Canadian Journal of Political Science* 15 (December 1982): 711-40.

Economic Council of Canada. *Minding the Public's Business.* Ottawa: Minister of Supply and Services Canada, 1986.

Eichmanis, John, and Graham White. "Government by Other Means: Agencies, Boards and Commissions." In Donald C. MacDonald, ed., *The Government and Politics of Ontario.* 3rd ed. Scarborough, Ont.: Nelson Canada, 1985, pp. 82-99.

Elford, E. Craig, and W. T. Stanbury. "Mixed Enterprises in Canada." In D.G. McFetridge, ed., *Canadian Industry in Transition.* Research study for the Royal Commission on the Economic Union and Development Prospects for Canada. Toronto: University of Toronto Press, 1986, pp. 261-303.

Forget, Claude, ed. *La Caisse de dépôt et placement du Québec: Sa mission, son impact et sa performance.* Montreal: Institut C. D. Howe, 1984.

Garant, Patrice. "Crown Corporations: Instruments of Economic Intervention–Legal Aspects." In Ivan Bernier and Andrée Lajoie, eds., *Regulations, Crown Corporations and Administrative Tribunals,* pp. 1-79. Research study for the Royal Commission on the Economic Union and Development Prospects for Canada, vol. 48. Toronto: University of Toronto Press, 1985.

Gélinas, André, ed. *Public Enterprise and the Public Interest.* Toronto: The Institute of Public Administration of Canada, 1978.

Gordon, Marsha. *Government in Business.* Montreal: C. D. Howe Institute, 1981.

Gracey, D. P. "The Real Issues in the Crown Corporations Debate." In Kenneth Kernaghan, ed., *Public Administration in Canada: Selected Readings.* 5th ed. Toronto: Methuen, 1985, pp. 122-40.

Hardin, Herschel. *A Nation Unaware: The Canadian Economic Culture.* Vancouver: J. J. Douglas, 1974.

Hatton, Michael J. *Corporations & Directors: Comparing the Profit and Not-for-Profit Sectors.* Toronto: Thompson Educational Publishing, 1990.

Hodgetts, J. E. "The Public Corporation in Canada." In W. Friedmann and J.F. Garner, eds., *Government Enterprise: A Comparative Study.* London: Stevens & Sons, 1970, pp. 201-26.

Hogg, Peter W. *Constitutional Law of Canada.* Toronto: Carswell, 1985.

Langford, John. "Crown Corporations as Instruments of Policy." In G. Bruce Doern and Peter Aucoin, eds., *Public Policy in Canada.* Toronto: Macmillan, 1979, pp. 239-74.

———. "The Identification and Classification of Federal Public Corporations: A Preface to Regime Building." *Canadian Public Administration* 23 (Spring 1980): 76-104.

———. "Privatization: A Political Analysis." In Thomas E. Kierans and W. T. Stanbury, eds., *Papers on Privatization.* Montreal: Institute for Research on Public Policy, 1985.

Langford, John W., and Neil A. Swainson. "Public and Quasi-Public Corporations in British Columbia," in O.P. Dwivedi, ed., *The Administrative State in Canada.* Toronto: University of Toronto Press, 1982, pp. 63-87.

Laux, Jeanne Kirk, and Maureen Appel Molot. *State Capitalism: Public Enterprise in Canada.* Ithaca, N.Y.: Cornell University Press, 1988.

Mitchell, Thomas H., ed. *Canadian Directorship Practices: The Role of the Board of Directors in Crown Corporation Accountability.* Ottawa: The Conference Board of Canada, 1985.

Nelles, H. V. *The Politics of Development: Forests, Mines & Hydro-electric Power in Ontario, 1849-1941.* Toronto: Macmillan of Canada, 1974.

Ohasi, Theodore M., T. P. Roth, Z. A. Spindler, M. L. McMillan, and K. H. Norrie. *Privatization: Theory & Practice.* Vancouver: The Fraser Institute, 1980.

Ontario. Agencies, Boards and Commissions Project. *First Report.* 1985.

———. *Second Report: Privatization of Ontario Crown Corporations.* Report prepared for the

Ministry of Treasury and Economics and the Management Board of Cabinet, n. d., 1985?

Ouellet, Lionel. "La privatisation: un instrument de management public?" *Canadian Public Administration* 30, no. 4 (Winter 1987): 566-84.

Prichard, J. Robert S. ed. *Crown Corporations in Canada: The Calculus of Instrument Choice.* Toronto: Butterworths, 1983.

Stanbury, W. T. "Privatization and the Mulroney Government." In Andrew W. Gollner and Daniel Salée, eds., *Canada Under Mulroney: An End-of-Term Report.* Montréal: Véhicule Press, 1988, pp. 119-57.

Treasury Board of Canada Secretariat. *Crown Corporations and Other Canadian Government Corporate Interests.* Ottawa: Minister of Supply and Services Canada, 1984.

Tupper, Allan. *Bill S-31 and the Federalism of State Capitalism.* Kingston, Ont.: Queen's University, Institute of Intergovernmental Relations, 1983.

——. "The Nation's Businesses: Canadian Concepts of Public Enterprise." Ph.D. diss., Queen's University, 1977.

Tupper, Allan, and G. Bruce Doern, eds. *Privatization, Public Policy and Public Corporations in Canada.* Halifax: The Institute for Research on Public Policy, 1988.

——. *Public Corporations and Public Policy in Canada.* Montreal: The Institute for Research on Public Policy, 1981.

Weaver, Robert Kent. "The Politics of State Enterprise: Railroad Nationalization in the United States and Canada." Ph.D. diss., Harvard University, 1982.

Wilson, V. Seymour. *Canadian Public Policy and Administration: Theory and Environment.* Toronto: McGraw-Hill Ryerson Limited, 1981.

CASES

In *Case Program in Canadian Public Administration* (Toronto: Institute of Public Administration of Canada):

    Canadian Cellulose Company, Limited. By Robert W. Sexty

    Housing Corporation of British Columbia. By Robert W. Sexty

    Saskatchewan Oil and Gas Corporation. By Robert W. Sexty

    The Saskatchewan Government Insurance Office. By Robert W. Sexty

Cases developed by the Canadian Centre for Management Development and distributed by the Case Program in Canadian Public Administration:

    Privatizing the Canadian Maple Products Corporation. By Claire E. McQuillan and Cynthia Williams

10

Regulatory Agencies

This chapter will discuss the large and diverse group of governmental units commonly referred to as regulatory agencies. These units are probably the most misunderstood agencies of government because few ordinary citizens come into direct contact with a regulatory agency on a recurring basis. Compared to the Crown corporations discussed earlier, which deliver the mail, provide transportation, generate electrical power, and employ large numbers of people in fields such as fishing and mining, regulatory agencies have a much lower profile.

However, this lack of *direct* contact between citizens and regulatory agencies masks the very great influence that these agencies have over our everyday lives. They influence the content of programs broadcast on radio and television through Canadian content and other regulations; they control the rates charged for transportation and telephone services, the rents charged for apartments in some provinces, and even the importation of hog-bristle paint brushes. The ongoing discussion about the proper form and scope of regulation is a reflection of the very significant, if indirect, impact that the actions of these agencies have on all of us, and the very direct impact that they have on most businesses.

This chapter begins by establishing the definition of a regulatory agency. In keeping with the theme of this section of the book—the choice of organizational form—there will then be a discussion of some of the reasons politicians choose regulatory agencies to accomplish particular objectives. This relates to the following section, which describes the powers of regulatory agencies. Next, the important aspects of political and judicial control of regulatory agencies will be discussed. Then, the operating procedures and organizational structure of a typical regulatory agency will be described. Finally, two very important policy issues concerning regulatory agencies will be addressed—the current problems associated with regulatory agencies, and the solutions to these problems.

While this chapter deals with the general phenomenon of government regulation, it focusses specifically on regulation by regulatory agency rather than government department. A significant amount of regulation does emanate from government departments, and a lesser amount from other government organizations such as Crown corporations. Some obvious examples are the consumer protection regulations administered by the various federal and provincial departments responsible for consumer affairs, and the regulation of technical aspects of aviation by the federal Ministry of Transport. This chapter focusses solely on regulatory agencies, not only because they perform extremely important regulatory functions, but also because they differ in structure and operation from operating departments.

DEFINITION OF A REGULATORY AGENCY

Defining the phrase "regulatory agency" is a bit like trying to describe the shape of an amoeba. Regulatory agencies come in so many sizes and shapes with such a variety of duties that it is difficult to generalize about them. In spite of this difficulty, one expert defined a **regulatory agency** as:

> A statutory body charged with responsibility to administer, to fix, to establish, to control, or to regulate an economic activity or market by regularized and established means in the public interest and in accordance with government policy.[1]

Two phrases in this definition—"regularized and established means" and "the public interest"—deserve special attention. First, regulatory agencies must set out specific rules of procedure and must follow those rules in working toward a decision. Although regulatory agencies are different from the ordinary law courts in ways that will be discussed later, these agencies do have certain judicial-like trappings, and the emphasis on "regularized and established means" of acting is one of them. This is one of the main characteristics that separates regulatory agencies from operating departments and Crown corporations. Of course, these latter two types of organization also have restrictions on their actions, but, in general, they are able to make decisions in a manner that is considerably more flexible, and sometimes more secretive, than that of regulatory agencies.

Second, regulatory agencies are frequently directed to act in "the public interest," but it can be very difficult to define exactly what that means. When an agency is making a decision on rate setting, it must decide between the interests of consumers, who are members of the public, and shareholders of the company, who are also members of the public. In this situation, the strongest and most principled adherence to the public interest is not a very helpful guide to action. Still, a commitment to the public interest, however defined, is an important influence on the work of regulatory agencies.

Two improvements might be made in the definition given above. First, the emphasis on "economic activity or market" has more to do with traditional forms of regulation than with some of the newer forms of regulation in cultural, environmental, and social areas. A distinction is sometimes made between economic or direct regulation and social regulation:

> *Economic [or direct] regulation* is a term that has been used to describe the early type of government regulation, which of course continues to be applied, where regulations were concerned with industry practices involving pricing, marketing and competition. The regulations had a direct impact on industry structure and practices and were frequently aimed at specific industries or markets. From the characteristics of this type of regulation, it also became known as direct regulation and "old style" regulation.

Social regulation is the term which has been applied to describe that category of regulations which has become prominent in the last few decades and relates to the welfare of society. Regulations in this category tend to focus on the conditions under which goods and services are produced and distributed and on the attributes or physical properties of the products. They are primarily in the form of standards described above and relate to issues of safety, health, employment, the environment and a variety of social or welfare-related issues. The regulations for the most part are not directed at any one specific industry or market but tend to cut across industries. Pressure for these regulations generally originated from social groups including consumer interest groups, environmentalists, labour unions and others, and stem from social considerations related to improving the quality of life. This category of regulations has sometimes been referred to as the "new style" regulation or "new wave" regulation.[2]

One of the major changes in the regulatory environment in recent years has been the movement toward more social regulation, e.g., regulation in areas of culture, such as more stringent rules on Canadian content in broadcasting, and environmental and social concerns such as pollution control, occupational health and safety, and consumer protection.

The second problem with the above definition is that it does not mention the fact that a regulatory agency is insulated from direct political intervention when it is making decisions in specific cases, although there is some political control over its general policy direction.

The question of the appropriate role of the minister raises a conundrum. He or she is responsible for the policy outcomes of the activities of the agency, but cannot interfere in the making of individual decisions. The purpose of this apparent contradiction is to balance accountability to the minister in policy matters and autonomy in the making of specific decisions. As will be seen later, this need for balance poses one of the more awkward dilemmas in regulatory reform.

These considerations bring about some changes in the definition presented above. The main advantage of this revised definition is its emphasis on the lack of direct ministerial control over individual decisions made by the regulatory agency. The legislature and the minister set the overall policy of the regulatory agency, but the concept of ministerial responsibility does not have the same meaning with regard to regulatory agencies as it does in the case of operating departments. In fact, it would be inappropriate for a minister to intervene when the agency is making a decision on a specific case.

Thus, a **regulatory agency** may be defined as a statutory body charged with responsibility to administer, to fix, to establish, to control, or to regulate an economic, cultural, environmental, or social activity by regularized and established means in the public interest and in accordance with general policy guidelines specified by the government. This body is under the general direction of the legislature and a responsible minister with regard to policy matters, but possesses relative autonomy of action in making individual decisions within those policy guidelines.

FUNCTIONS OF REGULATORY AGENCIES

It is difficult to generalize about the functions of regulatory agencies because the powers and duties assigned to them by their enabling statutes vary widely. Richard Schultz has identified the five most common functions, each of which is examined below.

Adjudicative

This function is performed by all regulatory agencies. It involves "the determination of outcomes in individual cases which typically deal with control over entry, the setting of prices or rates of return, and the setting of standards or rules of conduct by regulated enterprises."[3]

To understand the adjudication function, it is necessary to distinguish a regulatory agency from an ordinary court of law. The law courts are called upon to make a finding of fact and to relate that finding to a relatively precise piece of legislation. If the legislation is not precise in some area, there is usually some precedent set out in a decision on a similar case that can be used to assist in the application of the law.

In the case of a regulatory agency, the terms of the law that must be applied are considerably more vague. Statutes containing phrases such as "the public interest" or "public convenience and necessity" are very imprecise guides to action. Therefore, the regulatory agency must act much more on its own initiative in shaping policy than an ordinary court does.

> Granting that the [regulatory agency] which applies these legislative standards should maintain a judicial attitude, it cannot give a decision which is judicial in the narrow sense because there is no law for it to apply. If a decision is to be made at all, it must be made on grounds of policy and therefore the function in question is primarily legislative rather than judicial.[4]

There is a paradox here in that regulatory agencies are required to behave in a judicial-like manner in considering a case, but they actually make the decision based on policy considerations. This latter point explains why agencies are not bound by precedent. In the many cases in which agencies are allocating scarce resources, they simply could not follow precedent anyway. If all of the available slots on the radio dial have already been assigned, then the quality of the next application received is not relevant. The scarcity of slots on the dial precludes approval on the basis of precedent.

The adjudicative function tends to be the core activity of most regulatory agencies, but there are several other activities that are also a part of the responsibilities of many agencies.

Legislative

This function comprises "the ability to make general rules or regulations, in the form of delegated legislation, that have the force of law."[5] Most legislation that establishes regulatory agencies gives them some power to prescribe more specific regulations within the guidelines set out in the legislation. These regulations are referred to as delegated legislation because they are made pursuant to powers delegated to the agency in the legislation. They could relate to either policy matters, i.e., specify the agency's approach to particular issues, or procedural matters, i.e., specify how applications are to be filed and hearings conducted.

Research

Most agencies employ some staff to conduct general research in the policy area that it regulates. The purpose of this research is to allow members to remain conversant with recent trends in the field. For example, it could provide them with an early warning when there is a need for a shift in policy. The research staff is also sometimes used to evaluate applications, and to provide advice to the members of the agency in making specific decisions.

Advisory

In many ways, this function follows from the research function. As a result of the research conducted and the findings flowing from hearings, the members and staff of the agency are frequently able to advise the minister and/or the operating department about the need for a fresh consideration of certain policy issues. The regulatory agencies are close to the regulated industry and its clientele, and therefore they have a good knowledge of emerging problems.

Administrative

Some agencies also have direct administrative responsibility for operating programs. For example, the National Transportation Agency provides subsidies to railways under the Western Grain Transportation Act and to railways, marine, and truck lines under the Atlantic Region Freight Assistance Act. This function is not found very frequently in regulatory agencies because it could create a conflict situation for an agency when it must both operate a program affecting an industry and regulate that industry.

This listing of some of the duties of regulatory agencies provides an idea of the rather broad scope and diversity of this organizational form. Therefore, it should not be surprising that there are many varied reasons given for employing the regulatory agency form of organization.

THE RATIONALE FOR REGULATORY AGENCIES

The administrator, the economist, and the politician frequently see regulation in somewhat different lights.[6] The practicing administrator frequently sees regulation as the easiest and cheapest method of attaining a particular objective. The economist is usually opposed to regulation, except in those relatively rare cases where it corrects some market imperfections.[7] The politician must respond to the frequently conflicting demands of electors, and so sometimes views regulation as an easy method of farming out complex problems to independent agencies to be dealt with over the long term. It is not surprising, therefore, that there are many different reasons for the creation of regulatory agencies. Those discussed below constitute only a partial list.

Remove an Issue from "Politics"

The word politics is used here in the negative sense of relying too much on partisanship, compromise, and expediency, and not enough on fairness and hard economic facts.

Many of the decisions made by regulatory agencies are in rather delicate areas. In cases such as the regulation of broadcasting, there was a fear that one political party would attempt to use the media for partisan advantage. There are also cases in which regulatory agencies are rationing scarce resources. These resources could be slots on a radio or television dial or the right to develop a particular piece of land.

Not only is there usually a large amount of money at stake in these cases, but they also frequently involve highly technical questions that require the attention of experts. For example, the question of whether an applicant has the engineering expertise and financial support to operate a radio station is a technical question best addressed by engineers and accountants. In this sense, it is sometimes reassuring to have decisions removed from the partisan political process so that they can be viewed more objectively.

However, this argument must be put in perspective. Most delicate issues of this kind consist of not only technical questions, but also contentious political ones. In the broadcasting case, the questions of engineering competence and financial support are predominantly technical ones, but questions of Canadian content, pornography, or appropriate programming mix are inherently political ones.

For this reason, the idea of using the vehicle of the regulatory agency to remove an issue from politics must be approached carefully. If it means providing experts with some scope to review technical problems outside the vagaries of the political process, then it is probably highly beneficial. If it implies that mixed technical and political questions can be resolved by technical experts, then it is not only naive, but dangerous, because it would suggest that politicians should not be held accountable for certain decisions simply because those decisions contain some technical element.

Provide an Impartial, Judicial-Like Hearing

This reason is related to the previous one. It is the nature of parliamentary governments that Cabinet decisions are made in closed sessions and rely on information that is not necessarily available to the public. In this context, it is difficult for someone submitting an issue to Cabinet to know whether all important arguments have been considered before a Cabinet decision is made.

Thus, it is sometimes considered important to have a public forum such as a regulatory agency where all the facts in a case can be presented. The forum usually involves a relatively formal hearing in which petitioners can present their arguments and cross-examine one another. This process ensures that all parties have a fair opportunity to state their case as well as they can. Since the members of the agency presiding over the hearing and making the decision must be free from bias, it also ensures that a decision that takes account of the arguments of all sides will be rendered.

If the decisions were made in an overtly political arena, it might be difficult for politicians to escape at least the appearance of bias. For example, some people who own companies that hold broadcast licenses are prominently identified with a particular political party. There could be an appearance of bias in either the renewal or the refusal to renew a license depending on the political stripe of the government.

Apply Specialized Expertise

Many kinds of concerns assigned to regulatory agencies could be handled in the ordinary courts. After all, judges become very proficient at sorting through conflicting arguments, separating the important from the trivial, and rendering an impartial decision. These are all activities performed by members of regulatory agencies.

However, while judges are learned in the law, they are not expected to have detailed knowledge of the activities of a particular industry. Also, one cannot expect different judges to apply an integrated, coherent policy in making decisions about an industry; judges decide individual cases based on the law.

By way of contrast, the members of a regulatory agency develop specialized knowledge over the years and so are capable of making decisions reflecting consciously conceived policies. It is also important that these specialized decision-makers can arrive at decisions more quickly than someone who must apply himself or herself to a new issue from the ground up, such as judges would be required to do.

Deal with Future Conditions that the Legislature Could Not Foresee

Frequently, technical and economic conditions are changing so rapidly that it is dysfunctional for the legislature to prescribe hard-and-fast rules in legislation that can only be changed by new legislation. It is preferable for the legislature to specify general principles and to allow the regulatory agency flexibility within those principles to respond to changing conditions.

Regulate a Natural Monopoly

A natural monopoly exists when the lowest cost for a good or service is obtained when there is only one producer of that good or service,[8] i.e., certain technical aspects of production mean that competition would increase its cost. For example, the delivery of electricity in a particular geographic area is a natural monopoly. The capital cost of installing two or more electrical service lines into every area of a city would be such that the costs could not possibly be lower than with one monopoly supplier.

The problem with a natural monopoly is that the discipline of the market is not available to force the supplier to deal fairly with consumers. In the absence of that discipline, most economists argue that the situation of natural monopoly is one of the few cases in which government regulation is justified to ensure appropriate price and adequate service.

Smooth Market Instability

In recent years, there has been a trend toward the use of regulatory agencies for "supply management." The best examples are the marketing boards for such farm products as eggs, milk, and chickens. These agencies work by setting quotas on the overall quantity of the product that can be produced and allocating this quota among specific producers. The effect of this is to ensure that an excess of supply does not reduce prices paid to producers.

Marketing boards have been criticized on the grounds that they increase the price that must be paid by consumers. However, they also assure reasonable security of supply by preventing injurious competition that would force some suppliers from the market. In other words, consumers must pay a premium for eggs every time they buy to ensure that there will always be some eggs available at a reasonable price. Whether the cost is worth the benefit is something that each voter must decide.

Prevent Discrimination Where a Situation of Inequality Exists

This rationale bears some similarity to the natural monopoly argument in that there is some perceived inequality of bargaining power that government feels should be corrected. Most of the new kinds of social regulatory agencies in fields such as human rights, occupational health and safety, and rent control were created for this reason. The role of the regulatory agency in this case is to protect the weaker party, by preventing the stronger party from taking unfair advantage of its position.

The agencies created as a result of this rationale have been the most controversial, because the existence of a perceived inequality that requires government intervention is frequently in the eye of the beholder. The controversy surrounding the need for rent control is one obvious example of an area in which not everyone is agreed on the need for protection.

Control Externalities or "Spill-overs"

A non-technical definition of an externality is a cost imposed by one person on another person, or on society as a whole, when the person imposing the cost has no market incentive to minimize or control the cost. The most common example is pollution. The obvious market incentive is for polluters to minimize their expenditure on pollution-control equipment so that the entire cost of pollution will be borne by society as a whole. In this situation, a regulatory agency with the power to enforce particular standards is the obvious solution.

Low-Cost Option from the Standpoint of Government

As discussed in Chapter 6, when a government wants to have an impact on a particular kind of behaviour, it has a number of options, ranging from exhortation, through tax incentives and grants, to coercive legislation. One of the lowest-cost options from the standpoint of the government is simply to say: Thou shalt not. There is a cost to the government of establishing and operating a regulatory agency, but the impact per dollar spent of a regulatory agency is usually greater than that of an operating department or Crown corporation because of the regulatory agency's coercive powers.

A classic example of the use of this rationale is the treatment of the Niagara escarpment in southern Ontario. The escarpment is a unique geological formation and prime recreation area for people living in the area. In the 1960s, there was considerable pressure on the Ontario government to control development in this area. A number of options were considered, including buying the entire escarpment or strategic portions of it. Not surprisingly, the Ontario government decided to establish a regulatory agency, the Niagara Escarpment Commission, and give it the power to say: Thou shalt not develop here without prior permission. This was clearly the low-cost option from the standpoint of the government.

Regulation is the low-cost option *only* from the standpoint of the government. As will be discussed in more detail later, regulation can impose significant costs on others. In the Niagara escarpment example, many people saw the value of their land plummet when it became unlikely that it could be used for subdivisions or resorts. It has been suggested that the low cost of regulation makes it particularly attractive to governments facing simultaneous demands for decisive action and financial restraint.[9]

The reasons noted above constitute only a partial listing of the reasons for establishing and preserving regulatory agencies. This diversity of reasons demonstrates why these agencies have such a wide variety of roles. However, the main characteristics that cut across all agencies are their relative autonomy from direct political control, and their judicial-like methods of operation. These characteristics will be examined in the next two sections.

POLITICAL CONTROL OF REGULATORY AGENCIES

A central feature of parliamentary control of regulatory agencies is that the legislature, the Cabinet, and individual ministers set general policies and guidelines for their activities, but are kept at arm's length from their day-to-day operations. This section will discuss the method of accomplishing this balancing act.

Enabling Statutes and Other Legislation

Regulatory agencies are similar to operating departments and most Crown corporations in that they are formed as a result of enabling legislation, which specifies the structure of the agency, the procedures it must follow in considering cases, the limits of its authority, and the general policies it must apply in making decisions. In some instances, all of these components are specified in one statute; in others, they are divided among a number of pieces of legislation. For example, the National Transportation Agency was created by the National Transportation Act,[10] but it draws many of its powers from the Aeronautics Act,[11] the Railway Act,[12] and the Canada Shipping Act,[13] among others.

Legislative committees also check the work of regulatory agencies. They scrutinize the operation of regulatory agencies in the same manner as that of operating departments and Crown corporations. Thus, the committee members can question the minister responsible for an agency and/or the members of the agency about its implementation of policies or its operating procedures.

Standing Joint Committee for the Scrutiny of Regulations

In addition to the policy-oriented legislative committees that oversee the activities of regulatory agencies, there can be specialized committees that review *all* regulations and delegated legislation. This was first employed in Saskatchewan in the early 1960s and came to the federal government in 1971 in the form of the Senate and House of Commons Standing Joint Committee on Regulations and Other Statutory Instruments,[14] which has now been retitled the Standing Joint Committee for the Scrutiny of Regulations.[15]

All regulations made under delegated legislation by either operating departments or regulatory agencies are referred to this committee. Its mandate includes determining that the regulation is in line with the authorizing legislation, that it does not violate the Charter of Rights and Freedoms, and that it does not intrude into an area that is the prerogative of Parliament.

Appointment of Members

The decisions of regulatory agencies are made by a panel of members who are appointed by the Governor in Council, usually after consultation with the minister responsible for the agency. The minister will normally recommend the appointment of persons who share his or her views on the policy area.

This role in the appointment of members provides the minister with real power in setting the overall tone of the agency. However, when these appointments are for lengthy fixed terms of office and members can be removed only "for cause," the members have considerable autonomy. Therefore, the ability of anyone, including the minister, to interfere in a specific decision is limited.

The allegation has often been made that this power of appointment has been used for patronage purposes. Clearly, there have been instances in which ministers have appointed people of their own political stripe, but allegations of patronage must be considered carefully. Evidence provided later in this chapter indicates that political appointments are not as common as popular opinion suggests.

Policy Statements and Directives

As noted above, it is inappropriate for a minister to intervene in specific cases before an agency. However, a minister, or the Cabinet collectively, can issue policy statements or directives to inform the regulatory agency of the government's desires in a particular area. For some agencies, it is not clear whether these are binding,[16] but for other agencies the legislation makes it clear that they are binding. These must be general policy statements and not directions concerning specific cases. Thus, it would be inappropriate for a minister to tell an agency: You must grant this broadcast license to person A instead of person B. However, it would be quite appropriate for the minister to direct the agency that: The only applicants who should be considered for this broadcast license are those who will agree to provide X percent of Canadian content.

These policy statements or directives can be made secretly to the agency, but it is usually considered important that they be made publicly. This gives all parties appearing before the agency the right to know what policy statements and directives have been made, and it acts as a constraint on any potential abuse of power by the minister.

Prior Approval of Decisions

In some instances, the decision of a regulatory agency does not become binding until it is approved either by the responsible minister or by the Cabinet collectively.[17] The role of the agency in this situation is to provide an impartial hearing to all concerned and to apply its specialized expertise in arriving at a recommendation for a decision. These recommendations are usually given publicly so that the Cabinet must consider very carefully both the recommendations and the supporting documentation. If this advice is ignored, allegations of inappropriate political influence can be made.[18]

Appeal

Some legislation dealing with regulation provides the right of appeal to the minister or to the Governor in Council, i.e., the Cabinet. Where this provision exists, the appellant usually has no right to appear personally before the minister or Cabinet, but must state in writing the reasons why the decision should be overturned. The minister or Cabinet considers these appeals carefully, but is somewhat reluctant to overturn a decision, partly to preserve the morale and integrity of the agency and partly to prevent a flood of similar appeals. It is probably this reluctance to overturn decisions that explains the small number of appeals made to Cabinet.

However, this appeal mechanism is still a valuable safety valve. At the extreme, it prevents the members of the agency from behaving in some entirely inappropriate manner, because they know that their decision could be appealed to a higher level. In a less extreme vein, the minister or Cabinet can use the selective acceptance of certain appeals to signal changes in policy at the political level.[19] Members of regulatory agencies are usually sensitive to this sort of signal.

Political control of regulatory agencies is geared to ensuring that the agencies follow the policy guidelines set out by the government. Judicial control of regulatory agencies, which is discussed in the next section, is geared to ensuring fairness in the handling of individual cases.

JUDICIAL CONTROL OF REGULATORY AGENCIES

Chapter 18 contains a full treatment of judicial control of administrative actions in general, and of regulatory decision-making in particular. It is useful to note here that there is usually much discussion about which type of redress is more effective—political or judicial. The answer depends on a number of factors. First, a court rarely *changes* the decision of a regulatory agency. The court considers only the *process* followed by the agency, not the *merits* of its decision. A court can find that an agency followed an improper procedure, and so overturn the decision. At this point, the agency is free to reconsider the matter, follow the proper procedure, and arrive at exactly the same decision. The court would then be satisfied. Of course, there is also the possibility that a different procedure will produce a different result.

If it is clear that the agency has followed the proper procedure, but there is still dissatisfaction with the decision reached, then the most likely source of redress lies at the political level. It is usually only the minister or Cabinet who can consider the *merits* of the decision and substitute another final and binding decision.

STRUCTURE AND OPERATION OF REGULATORY AGENCIES

It is very difficult to generalize about the structure and operation of regulatory agencies, because each agency is somewhat different. However, this section will describe some of the usual structures and procedures.

Organizational Structure

Regulatory agencies are virtually always headed by a panel of members. The panel usually consists of five to ten members, but the number can vary quite widely. In 1989, the Ontario Municipal Board was composed of thirty members.[20] Panel members are collectively responsible for the agency's operation.

The method of appointment and removal of panel members obviously has an impact on the independence of the agency from political control. To maximize independence, members should be appointed for relatively lengthy terms, and should be removable only for cause. This is the situation that exists for most federal agencies, but Brown-John found that many members of regulatory agencies do not have the security of tenure needed for independence.[21]

One member of the panel is designated as the chairperson or president of the agency. This individual is considered the administrative head of the agency and usually has the responsibility for assigning fellow panel members to cases, as well as supervising the public servants who work for the agency.

The fact that the agency is headed by a panel means that there is scope for the representation of diverse interests on the panel, e.g., geographic regions, special interest groups. Members of the Canadian Radio-television and Telecommunications Commission are traditionally appointed from different regions of the country, and labour relations boards contain a roughly equal balance between members sympathetic to the union and employer sides.

The background of panel members obviously has some impact on agency decisions. The specialized knowledge possessed by former employees of the regulated industry makes them choice candidates for appointment to the agency. It has sometimes been suggested that a preponderance of these people as panel members will make the agency "soft" on the industry.

However, a now somewhat dated Canadian survey indicates that members of regulatory agencies are more likely to be former public servants than former employees of the regulated industry.[22] This same survey found that there were not large numbers of former politicians serving as members of regulatory agencies, thus negating somewhat the image of these agencies as repositories of patronage appointees. However, a recent report of the Law Reform Commission of Canada suggests that the highly political nature of the appointments to these agencies can have a detrimental effect on their operations.[23] The commission recommends that the process be opened up considerably by advertising for interested candidates for open positions and by consulting with interested groups about potential members.

The members preside over hearings and make decisions, but it is unusual for all members to be present at any one hearing. Thus, several hearings can be held at the same time, and the work of the agency can be accelerated. Members can be assigned to cases by the chairperson on a random basis, or there can be a committee system that allows members to specialize.

All regulatory agencies have a fairly extensive staff of experts in law, economics, accounting, engineering, and whatever other specialty is required. The main functions of this staff involve supporting the work of the members in arranging hearings, conducting both general research and specific investigations concerning individual applications, and advising members on legal and/or technical aspects of their work.

Operating Procedures

This review of the operating procedures of regulatory agencies will focus on the legislative and adjudicative functions; these are the most important and visible of the five functions discussed earlier.

Legislative function. The enabling legislation usually gives the agency some discretion in establishing specific regulations within the guidelines set out in the Act. After new legislation (or a major amendment to existing legislation) is passed, the agency begins to consider the specific rules and regulations it needs to adopt to give effect to this legislation. The agency also periodically reconsiders its substantive policy in a particular area. These are very important opportunities for the regulated industry and consumer interest groups to affect the agency's policies.

When the agency is making or amending its policy or regulations, it usually notifies all interested parties through such measures as formal legal letters, advertisements in newspapers or trade publications, and news announcements in the media. In some cases, this notice is an open-ended request for any comments that interested parties want to tender. In other cases, the staff of the agency prepares some tentative working documents on which comments are invited.

Interested parties are usually requested to submit written comments first. On the basis of these comments, some people will be invited to attend a hearing to present their views and be questioned by the members of the agency. In some cases, these hearings are held at the home base of the agency, but in others, the members travel to major cities across the country or province to obtain a wide cross-section of views. Then the members prepare a formal set of regulations or a formal policy statement that will be binding in all future cases.

Adjudicative function. The adjudication process—the consideration of individual cases—can begin in a number of ways. Usually, an individual case begins when an application is submitted to the agency requesting, for example, a rate increase or a change in service level. The process can also be initiated by the agency or a third party where, for example, there is concern that a regulated company is not meeting some obligation.

In accordance with the requirements of natural justice,[24] there is usually a requirement that *notice* be provided to all interested parties that an application is under review. Any party who comes forward at this time is called an *intervener*. An intervener can prepare a submission supporting or opposing the application or proposing some middle ground. Typically, the interveners will be individual consumers, consumers' groups, or companies in the industry affected by the application. However, even government departments or other governments can intervene before a regulatory agency.

As interventions are received, the public servants who work for the regulatory agency will begin to analyze both the original application and the comments provided by interveners. They will then prepare a summary of the relevant issues for the panel, and possibly even a recommendation concerning the final disposition of the application.

Whether a full hearing will then be held depends on the requirements in the legislation and regulations, and the importance of the case. When there is a full formal hearing, the process begins with a presentation explaining the applicant's position. Then the agency will usually invite some of the interveners to explain their positions.

The hearings of some agencies are very formal, almost judicial, procedures held in settings that resemble a courtroom and involve the presence of lawyers, formal presentation of evidence, and cross-examination of witnesses. Other agencies strive to keep their proceedings as simple and informal as possible. In this situation, the members might only leave the room for a few minutes and return to present their decision verbally. In more complex cases, several months could be required for members to deliver a lengthy, written decision with reasons.

These procedures are carefully worked out to ensure fairness to all sides and a thorough consideration of the issue. A survey has indicated that most of those involved in the regulatory process are quite satisfied with the process,[25] but some commentators have identified flaws in the system.

PROBLEMS IDENTIFIED WITH REGULATION

The role of regulation and regulatory agencies in society is currently the subject of much debate. Agencies are attacked on one side for being too assertive and intrusive, and on the other for being "captive" of the interests that they were established to regulate. In this section, some of the main criticisms of regulatory agencies will be considered and in the next section some of the possible reforms will be discussed.[26]

Cost of Regulation

Although regulation is usually seen as the low-cost option from the standpoint of government, it can impose sizable costs on other parties. The most obvious examples are the direct costs incurred by the regulated industry and by other affected parties. The firms in the regulated industry must maintain extensive records in a format specified by the regulatory agency. All parties affected by regulatory agencies incur substantial information costs to keep themselves abreast of initiatives by the agency and by other groups affected by the agency.

Then there are legal and other costs involved in preparing a case and actually appearing before the regulatory agency.

However, these direct costs might be only the tip of the iceberg.[27] The major costs of regulation could come from a slowdown in the introduction of innovations as a result of the need for clearance from a regulatory agency. The pharmaceutical industry has long made this claim, but there are numerous other examples.

It is important to emphasize that benefits as well as costs arise from regulation. The record-keeping required of regulated industries allows the regulatory agency to consider intelligently requests for rate increases. The slowness in the introduction of new innovations sometimes keeps dangerous products off the market. This is not to suggest that all forms of regulation are justified. Clearly, there are cases in which legislators or regulators have become over-zealous.

There are also *hidden* costs of regulation. Economists argue that the optimum competitive situation occurs when barriers to entering an industry are low. Easy entry for new firms forces existing firms to be competitive in both price and quality of product. Regulatory agencies virtually always raise barriers to entry in the regulated industry. Barriers can be direct, such as the need for prior approval from the regulatory agency, or indirect, but equally effective, such as residence or minimum capitalization requirements. Still other barriers can be psychological in that entrepreneurs will simply choose not to enter an industry in which the regulations are seen as intrusive, particularly if the barriers are felt to be unfair or unreasonable.

The Empty Consumers' Chair

It is sometimes said that the purpose of a regulatory agency is to protect the consumer. While some legislators might intend this, it is not, strictly speaking, legally correct. The members of a regulatory agency listen to the arguments presented by the various parties and attempt to arrive at an optimum decision based on those arguments. They are clearly restrained from favouring one side or the other; they must decide on the basis of the arguments presented. If one side is able to present its arguments more persuasively or more forcefully, then, other things being equal, it is likely to win.

This premium on the ability to make one's case well is significant, because it has been suggested that producers have an advantage over consumers in the regulatory process.[28] There is usually a relatively small number of producers (sometimes, only one), and in actions such as rate increase applications, each producer has a large amount at stake. This makes it easy for producers to work together and spend large sums of money to defend their claims.

On the other hand, there are a large number of consumers, each of whom has a fairly small amount at stake in any given rate increase. Therefore, it is difficult for consumers to band together to fight rate increases. To put it directly: How much would you be willing to spend to prevent your telephone bill from increasing by fifty cents per month? Probably considerably less than a telephone company would be willing to spend to gain the several million dollars that it has at stake in the same application.

Captive Agency Theory

The **captive agency theory**, in many ways complementary to the above arguments about the lack of consumer power in the regulatory process, suggests that, over time, the agency is captured by the industry that it was set up to regulate, and so becomes supportive of that industry. This is a gradual process in which the agency develops a concern for the orderly development of the industry; this concern gradually comes to mean the protection of the companies currently in the industry from any disruptive forces, such as excessive competition from new entrants.

Marver H. Bernstein has developed a life cycle theory of regulatory agencies that explains this capture.[29] An agency is usually born as the result of political activism by groups concerned about some perceived problem. These groups work long and hard against difficult odds to encourage legislators to introduce some regulatory legislation.

However, when the necessary legislation is passed, these groups run out of steam, partly because it is innately difficult to hold such large and diverse groups together, and partly because people drift away when they feel that the battle is over. Paradoxically, it is at precisely this time, when the fledgling agency is just beginning its operations and drafting its regulations, that it needs public input the most.

The people staffing the new agency are unlikely to be knowledgeable about the industry since it has never been regulated before. Where should they turn for assistance and advice? The groups that agitated for the legislation in the first place are no longer strong and active. The only other source of knowledge about the industry is the industry itself. Therefore, the new regulators seek the advice of the regulated industry about how it wants to be regulated. This close contact allows the regulated industry to have a subtle, but effective, impact on the regulatory agency at its crucial formative stage. Once the pattern of close consultation between regulator and regulatee—with limited public involvement—is established, then it simply continues and becomes closer over the years.

At the same time, politicians tend to lose interest in the agency. They feel that the problem has been solved by the mere creation of the agency, and would rather not become involved in the sometimes very antagonistic atmosphere that exists when specific decisions are made. This is more likely to happen in the American situation, in which agencies are truly independent of executive control, than in the Canadian situation, where there is some element of ministerial responsibility. However, there is some evidence that this occurs in Canada as well.[30]

According to Bernstein's theory, over time the agency becomes highly judicialized and totally unwilling to take any policy initiatives. When people making budgeting decisions see the organization in this state, they are likely to decrease the agency's budgetary allocation, thus driving away good employees and worsening the downward spiral. The organization can continue in this spiral almost indefinitely unless some crisis snaps it out of its lethargy. It simply no longer possesses the drive and initiative to regulate the industry effectively.

Most discussion of the captive agency theory has been anecdotal, rather than more rigorous, because of the problems involved in testing it . For example, how does one determine that agency decisions are favouring the industry? One serious consideration of the theory for a Canadian regulatory agency suggests that the capture hypothesis does not hold and that the process is much more complex than the hypothesis suggests.[31]

The Conundrum of Accountability and Autonomy

A major characteristic of a regulatory agency is that it operates at arm's length from direct political control. This creates a conundrum in that the agency must be accountable to the minister and the legislature, but at the same time it must have autonomy in making individual decisions. Some of the problems that this raises were identified by a report of the Economic Council of Canada:

> This form of compromise between regulatory independence and political control has led in recent years to a great deal of tension, confusion and compromise. The record of both the federal and provincial governments' relationships with their regulatory agencies raises a number of challenging questions. Who should make regulatory policy? How should such policy be made—through open, participatory hearings in advance of specific cases or as a result of appeals to the cabinet following a specific case? Should [regulatory agencies] perform *both* adjudicative functions, for which they appear to be well suited, as well as policy advisory, research, and administrative functions, for which they may be less well suited. In particular, if a policy advisory role is retained, should the agency's advice to the government be confidential or made only in public documents? Finally, is it realistic to expect a government to be able to clearly articulate its policy positions, except in rather general terms, in advance of specific choices that embody the means of implementing them?[32]

Weak political control of the agency might allow it to act at cross-purposes with other government agencies, or to make decisions that are not in the overall public interest. However, excessive political control deflates the morale of the agency and could lead to dominance by powerful interest groups. The conundrum of accountability and autonomy is one of the most difficult problems to handle in discussing regulatory reform.[33]

Regulatory Agencies and Federalism

In recent years, regulatory agencies have made decisions that have a substantial impact on federal-provincial relations. In some cases, decisions by federal regulatory agencies have allowed the federal government to intervene in provincial areas in a manner that ignored the concerns of provincial governments about both the content of decisions, and the process by which the decisions were made.

> Aside from their predictable opposition in principle to federal-led economic decision-making, there are three specific reasons for provincial concerns. The first is the now commonplace and widespread provincial criticism that federal economic policy making is unfairly discriminatory in favour of some regions and industries, at the expense of others. This argument has long been routinely invoked, not without some justification, in battles, for example, over transportation and energy policies.

> Secondly, in the past three decades especially, provincial opposition to federal economic dominance has been based on doubts about the capacity of the federal government to perform effectively as an economic decision maker. Provinces are simply not prepared to accept that the federal government possesses greater competence than they as justification for it having more power or influence over economic decision making . . . [34]

The third reason relates to the use of the regulatory agency form and the fact that the "distinguishing feature of these agencies is their exceptionally high degree of independence within the federal parliamentary system."[35]

Schultz has described this sort of situation as being characterized by regulatory agency independence and federal-provincial interdependence.[36] Federal and provincial governments frequently enter into agreements to share authority in particular policy areas. However, regulatory agencies, asserting their independence of executive control, can take the position that they are not bound by such agreements. This is exactly what the CRTC did with regard to an agreement between the federal and Manitoba governments in the field of cable television.[37]

The federal government and the three prairie provinces have been feuding over telecommunications regulation in recent years. In the past, the federal government has regulated telecommunications in most of Canada, but each of the three prairie provinces has had its own telephone company that was not subject to federal regulation. This has been very important to these provinces partly because telecommunications have been a good source of revenue, but mostly because the companies have taken advantage of cross-subsidies to provide a high standard of relatively inexpensive service to rural areas. Politically, this is very important to those three governments.

The federal government has now moved to create one regulatory regime for all Canada. This will also effectively create one market across the entire country for long-distance and other specialized services. The Minister of Communications has explained that there are very good economic and technological reasons for this.[38] The fact that it happens to benefit private companies located in eastern Canada is simply a coincidence.

The prairie provinces fear these moves for two reasons.[39] If the federal regulatory agency demands an end to the cross-subsidies, then rural rates could rise. However, the more serious problem would occur if the regulatory agency allowed the large (eastern-dominated) companies such as Bell Canada and CN/CP Telecommunications to compete for long-distance and other services in the prairie provinces. For practical reasons, the smaller prairie companies would have no way of reciprocating by moving into Ontario and Quebec to compete against Bell Canada.

Sometimes the conflict is less direct, but no less significant. Both energy-producing and energy-consuming provinces have a real stake in certain decisions of the National Energy Board. Provincial governments feel that they should have some sort of special status in board hearings because they are the legitimate governments representing the people of their province. However, most regulatory agencies adopt the position that provincial governments have the same status as any other intervener.

It would be inappropriate to leave the impression that regulation always results in federal-provincial clashes. There are reported cases in which the presence of the federal and provincial governments in the same regulatory arena results in a complementary and mutually supportive arrangement,[40] but these cases seem to be fewer in number than the more contentious ones.

Compliance

Traditionally, it has been assumed that regulatees will automatically comply with the rulings of regulatory agencies. Agencies have a number of mechanisms, such as the imposition of fines or the lifting of licenses, that tend to ensure compliance. For this reason, the question of compliance has received little study. However, there is a growing understanding that ensuring compliance can be a real problem because regulatees can circumvent rulings in both subtle and overt ways.

Some of the best examples of subtle evasion are in the area of broadcasting regulation. The CRTC usually issues a license to a broadcasting company with the condition that it provide a certain level of Canadian content. After a period of operation, the licensee sometimes argues that it has not quite fulfilled its obligation for economic or practical reasons. The CRTC is then confronted with a difficult dilemma. It can either lift the license of the company and leave an area with reduced or, in some cases, no service, or it can slap the company on the wrist and ask it to do better in the future. So far, the CRTC has usually pursued the latter course and been subjected to some criticism for being too weak.[41] It would likely be subjected to equal criticism from other quarters if it pursued the firmer course. Thus, in the real world, compliance is not as automatic as some assume.

There are also examples of more overt refusals to comply with agency directives. Some of the most awkward examples of overt refusals have occurred as a result of federal-provincial disputes,[42] but the most colourful incidents occurred in the mid-1970s when the dish-type satellite-receiving antennas were illegal. On numerous occasions when RCMP officers attempted to seize these devices at remote mining or lumber camps, they were simply chased away by the irate residents, thus prompting one commentator to suggest that while the Mounties may always get their man, they don't always get their dish.[43]

PROPOSALS FOR REFORM

These perceived problems with regulation have generated many proposals for changes in the regulatory process. The most important of these are discussed below.

The Mulroney Government's Regulatory Reform Strategy

In 1986, the Mulroney government articulated its "Regulatory Reform Strategy." This has some characteristics in common with deregulation in other jurisdictions. However, the Mulroney government has been careful never to use the word deregulation because, in Canada, the word is seen as somewhat ideologically charged in that it is associated with the right-wing governments of Margaret Thatcher and Ronald Reagan. Mulroney would also argue that both his general approach and his specific initiatives are somewhat different from Thatcher's and Reagan's.

Shortly after coming to office in 1984, the Mulroney government appointed an agency to examine regulatory reform. This agency has since become the Office of Privatization and Regulatory Affairs with its own Minister of State. In 1986, the government promulgated its ten guiding principles of regulatory policy:

1. *Regulation is and will remain a necessary and important instrument for achieving the government's social and economic objectives. But the government intends to "regulate smarter."*
2. The government recognizes the vital role of an efficient marketplace and dynamic entrepreneurial spirit in generating the ongoing economic growth needed to improve the standard of living for Canadians, and it recognizes that regulation should not impede those values without the most persuasive justification.
3. The government intends to limit, as much as possible, the overall rate of growth and proliferation of new regulation. It will proceed on a pragmatic basis with increased emphasis on economic efficiency but with continuing protection of the public where appropriate.
4. With regard to existing regulatory programs, *priority is to be placed on reforming ineffective and economically counterproductive regulation, but there will be no program of wholesale deregulation.* On a case-by-case basis, there will be reduced regulation where the practical interests of the economy and job creation call for it, just as there will be improved and intensified regulation where public protection requires it.
5. Regulation entails social and economic costs, and the government will evaluate those costs to ensure that benefits clearly exceed costs before proceeding with new regulatory proposals.
6. Regulation is legislation and, as such, will be brought more fully under the control of elected government representatives and subjected to more effective review by Parliament.
7. The public has an important role to play in the development of regulation, and the government will increase public access and participation in the regulatory process while simplifying procedures and restricting legalities to the minimum.

8. The federal regulatory system will be streamlined and made more efficient and effective to reduce costs, uncertainties and delays.

9. The government will place priorities on increased regulatory cooperation with the provinces with a view to addressing the overall regulatory burden on Canadians, and eliminating wasteful duplication.

10. A minister will be assigned specific responsibility for regulatory affairs, including improved management of the system and overall implementation of the government's regulatory policy and reform strategy. Individual ministers with regulatory mandates will be responsible for implementing and exercising their responsibilities in conformity with the spirit and objectives of this policy.[44]

This has resulted in the establishment of a defined process for the creation of new regulations. When a minister feels that a new regulation is needed, he or she will convey this to the Minister of State for Privatization and Regulatory Affairs. If the Minister of State concurs, plans to establish the regulation will be announced in the *Federal Regulatory Plan*, which is published each December. As the department consults with interested parties, it prepares the precise text of the regulation and a *regulatory impact analysis statement* (RIAS). This statement "explains the purpose of the proposed regulation and sets out the impact it is expected to have."[45] The regulation is then reviewed by the Minister of State for Privatization and Regulatory Affairs to ensure that it conforms to the government's regulatory policy, and by the Minister of Justice to check legal drafting. When they approve the regulation, it is then submitted to a special Cabinet committee. If the regulation clears this hurdle, it is published in the *Canada Gazette* to invite public input. After time for public input, the regulation, possibly with revisions, will then be published again in the *Gazette,* at which time it will be binding.

In addition to this system that deals with new regulations, the government decided to subject each regulatory program to a systematic review and evaluation on a seven-year cycle.

The general idea of the program is to introduce just enough procedural impediments to the establishment of new regulations that ministers will think twice about whether they really need a particular regulation. Indications are that the program is having the desired impact. "There are about 25 per cent fewer regulations in 1987 than in 1986, and projections based on the number of regulations passed by August 1988 indicate a further reduction."[46]

Some of the initiatives undertaken by the Office of Privatization and Regulatory Affairs could be described as deregulation, in that they have resulted in decreasing and/or streamlining regulations. One example is the federal government's new "Freedom to Move" policy in transportation. However, the program is much broader than that. Some other activities of the program have included:

• improving the regulatory process by encouraging broader participation in it;

• putting inspection procedures on a full cost recovery basis as a movement toward possibly having them taken over by the private sector;

- combining several related agencies into one; and
- improving appeal procedures.[47]

The public reception of the program has been mixed. The parts of the program that deal with streamlining regulations and easing administrative processes have been uniformly praised by diverse groups.[48] However, the deregulation aspects of the program have not received the same uniform praise. For example, airline deregulation has benefited the consumer in the short run by encouraging lower fares. However, there is concern that those lower fares have caused some airlines to fail, which could result in a smaller number of carriers and less price competition in the long run.[49]

Companies in the regulated industries have frequently criticized deregulation because they feared "the adjustments and upheaval that could conceivably result. This lent credence to the charge that regulation benefitted the regulated and produced cartelization of the industry."[50]

Sunset Legislation

Sunset legislation has some of the same characteristics as deregulation. The basic idea is that regulatory agencies would be established for a certain finite period of time, and if they were unable to prove their worth over that period, they would be allowed to die.[51] This is a remedy for the frequently discussed phenomenon that a government agency seldom dies, even when its *raison d'être* seems to have passed. Under sunset legislation, the onus would be on the agency to prove its continued value.

More Consumer Involvement

The significance of greater consumer involvement in the regulatory process is clear, but there are so many specific proposals to accomplish this that it is impossible to cover more than a few of them here. They are all designed to put the consumer on a more even footing with the producer.

Consumers' Associations. Among the associations representing Canadian consumers are the broad-based Consumers' Association of Canada and specific associations representing such groups as automobile owners and airline travelers. For reasons discussed earlier, these associations are usually weaker than the producers and producers' associations with which they must do battle. Therefore, it is sometimes suggested that the strength of these consumers' groups ought to be bolstered. The usual suggestions include an infusion of government funding, tax incentives, or some payments from the regulated industry.

Funding for Interveners. Another proposal is that the government, the regulated industry and/or its association should provide funding to all legitimate interveners in regulatory proceedings. Regulated industries point to the difficulties of controlling costs, and of distinguishing legitimate from nuisance interveners.

The Agency as Advocate. The current legal situation of the agency makes it an impartial referee between the various interests before it. It has been proposed that the agency should instead be charged with defending the interests of the consumer. This proposal would weight the regulatory process in favour of the consumer, and so place the onus on the industry to prove the efficacy of its claim for higher rates or different service levels.

Resolving the Accountability-Autonomy Conundrum

A number of different proposals have been made to resolve the apparent conflict between the need for accountability to political forces, and the need for some autonomy from the vagaries of partisan politics.

Douglas G. Hartle has recommended that all agencies be designated as either *advisory agencies* or *decision-making agencies*.[52] The *advisory agencies* would emphasize accountability in that they would conduct research in their policy field and *advise* the government concerning new policy initiatives. These agencies would differ from operating departments in that they would have an element of independence in the manner in which they gathered evidence and prepared recommendations. They could hold public hearings and present their advice to the minister publicly. However, accountability would be emphasized with these kinds of agencies because the minister would be able to accept or reject the advice offered.

Decision-making agencies would emphasize autonomy. These agencies would be guided by government policy directives in making decisions on individual cases, but their decisions could not be overturned by politicians, except in unusual circumstances. This is similar in some ways to a proposal made earlier by the Ontario Committee on Government Productivity, which would also have had the effect of classifying agencies according to their major function and assigning different amounts of independence to them accordingly.[53]

These classification schemes possess the virtues of simplicity and clarity. However, they might be too abstracted from the real world to be very useful. The accountability-autonomy conundrum simply reflects the love-hate relationship that many Canadians have with politicians. On one hand, we mistrust politicians and fear that they will act for improper, self-serving motives; on the other hand, we sometimes see appeal to politicians as a way of escaping the tyranny of the bureaucracy. It might well be that there is no simple way out of this accountability-autonomy dilemma. The ideal arrangement might involve a continued balancing of the two to ensure both are present in appropriate levels in the decision-making process.

Policy Directives

One recommendation that would modify the current accountability regime suggests that Cabinet should be able to issue policy directives to regulatory agencies.[54] Through this means, the government could convey its desires regarding particular policy areas to the regulatory agency before the agency made any specific decisions. This would allow the regulated industry, consumers, and other interested parties to know what the rules of the game were before they started to play. It would also improve accountability, because it would make it clear when the agency was acting at the request of the government and when the agency was making its own policy.

The fear about this proposal is that it would "enhance the power of those with greater access to Cabinet, namely the large regulated firms and departmental officials."[55]

Better Accountability to Parliament

There is also a perceived need for better accountability to Parliament, which is the ultimate source of the authority of all regulatory agencies. The House of Commons Special Committee on Regulatory Reform has pointed out that

> [t]he Standing Joint Committee on Regulations and other Statutory Instruments reviews regulations and other published statutory instruments using criteria that relate to the legality and propriety of the measures examined. There is, however, no analogous arrangement facilitating parliamentary examination of subordinate legislation from the point of view of policy or merit.[56]

The committee went on to recommend a considerably enhanced parliamentary committee system in which each of the standing committees would review the activities of regulatory agencies in its substantive area. Specifically, the committees would monitor the regulatory process in general, review the merits of specific regulations, and review the activities of the agency itself using the program evaluations prepared under the auspices of the Office of the Comptroller General. These and other recommendations of the committee were all geared to improving the accountability of regulatory agencies to Parliament.

The Provincial Role in the Federal Regulatory Process

As mentioned earlier, one of the sore points with provincial governments is that their interests are sometimes very directly affected by the actions of federal regulatory agencies, yet they have no special status with those agencies. The federal government also experiences embarrassment in this area because it is sometimes unable to issue directives to its regulatory agencies, even in areas in which it has entered into an agreement with a province.[57]

One of the most radical remedies suggested is that there should be "joint regulatory mechanisms" involving the federal and provincial governments, or several provincial governments, as the case may be. This could be accomplished in a number of ways. One way would have existing regulatory agencies, federal or provincial, meet together to conduct a joint hearing and possibly even issue one joint decision.[58]

This would pose some obvious practical problems in agreeing on common rules of procedures, not to mention the tension involved in working out a joint decision. This arrangement might be difficult at first, but over time the agencies would learn how to work with one another. Ontario already has a provision for several agencies within its jurisdiction to hold one consolidated hearing on a proposal.

"A second major variant would entail the power of appointment by one level of government of members of a regulatory agency established by another level."[59] This would produce some of the same tensions as the previous proposal and it raises the difficult issue of which governments appoint how many members.

Another proposal is what has been called "political regulation." This "option involves a fully politicized model of regulation without recourse to independent authorities."[60] This would require Cabinet or the minister to make decisions that are currently delegated to a regulatory agency. This is clearly not a panacea. Recent events make it clear that federal and provincial politicians have a great deal of difficulty arriving at agreements. However, it might be an improvement on the status quo because it would convert an odd trilateral relationship involving two politicians and a somewhat independent agency into a bilateral relationship. This simplified structure ought to make it easier to resolve problems.

Some of these proposals are radical and/or highly problematic, but the tensions caused by the existing system are so serious that some better arrangement must be found. The impact of regulatory agencies on federalism (and vice versa) is an area that bears watching over the next few years, because federal-provincial relations could become extremely tense if federal regulatory agencies do not deal with provincial concerns in a sensitive manner.

More Co-participation and Fewer Binding Decisions

Traditionally, the economic kinds of regulatory agencies have borrowed some trappings from the courts in that they hear arguments concerning an issue, go away to discuss it, and return with a decision that is binding on all parties. There is no room for negotiation or compromise between the parties after the process has started.

The newer cultural, environmental, and social agencies sometimes behave a bit differently. The Foreign Investment Review Agency, in its original form, was a classic example of this. The main part of the application process involved detailed negotiations between the agency and the investor to determine what benefits the investor would be willing to provide to Canada in exchange for the right to do business in the country. Thus, rather than presenting an all-or-nothing decision, the agency was free to discuss the overall situation with the applicant and work out an arrangement that was beneficial to all. It is sometimes argued that this co-participative style is likely to be the style of the future.

CONCLUSION

The most common organizational forms used by governments are the operating department, the Crown corporation, and the regulatory agency. In this and the previous two chapters, these forms have been discussed and the reasons for choosing one to accomplish a particular objective have been considered. However, the story is not quite complete. There are a number of other organizational forms that are used less frequently, but are still important for an overall understanding of the operations of government. The next chapter will consider some of these other forms, namely, Royal commissions, task forces, and advisory councils.

NOTES

1. C. Lloyd Brown-John, *Canadian Regulatory Agencies* (Toronto: Butterworths, 1981), p. 35.
2. John C. Strick, *The Economics of Government Regulation* (Toronto: Thompson Educational Publishing, 1990), p. 7. (Emphasis added.) This distinction is also made in Economic Council of Canada, *Reforming Regulation* (Ottawa: Minister of Supply and Services Canada, 1981), p. 7.
3. "Regulatory Agencies and Accountability," a study prepared for the Royal Commission on Financial Management and Accountability, May 1978, unpublished manuscript, as referred to in Economic Council of Canada, *Responsible Regulation: An Interim Report* (Hull: Minister of Supply and Services Canada, 1979), p. 56. For a similar but slightly different list of functions, see Canada, Privy Council Office, *Submissions to the Royal Commission on Financial Management and Accountability* (Minister of Supply and Services Canada, 1978), 2-77 to 2-93.
4. J. A. Corry, "Introduction: The Genesis and Nature of Boards," in John Willis, ed., *Canadian Boards at Work* (Toronto: Macmillan, 1941), p. xxxvi.
5. Economic Council of Canada, *Responsible Regulations: An Interim Report*, p. 56.
6. Roderick A. Macdonald, "Understanding Regulation by Regulations," in Ivan Bernier and Andrée Lajoie, eds., *Regulations, Crown Corporations and Administrative Tribunals* (Toronto: University of Toronto Press, 1985), pp. 84-89.
7. A good discussion of the economic rationales for regulation is contained in Strick, *The Economics of Government Regulation*, ch. 2
8. Economic Council of Canada, *Responsible Regulation: An Interim Report*, p. 46.
9. G. Bruce Doern, "Introduction," in G. Bruce Doern, ed., *The Regulatory Process in Canada* (Toronto: Macmillan, 1978), pp. 17-18.
10. S.C. 1987, c. 34.
11. R.S.C. 1985, c. A-2.
12. R.S.C. 1985, c. R-3.
13. R.S.C. 1985, c. S-9.
14. Macdonald, "Understanding Regulation by Regulations," p. 96.
15. The role of this committee will be discussed further in Chapter 15.
16. Lucinda Vandervort, *Political Control of Independent Administrative Agencies* (Ottawa: Law Reform Commission of Canada, 1979), pp. 12-13.
17. This is the case with certain decisions of the National Energy Board. R.S.C. 1985, c. N-7, s. 52.

18. "PC Backers Win Review of TV-Station Licences," *The Globe and Mail,* November 13, 1985.
19. Vandervort, *Political Control of Independent Administrative Agencies,* pp. 35, 59-60.
20. The Ontario Municipal Board, *79th Annual Report* (1985), p. 15.
21. *Canadian Regulatory Agencies,* p. 118.
22. Caroline Andrew and Rejean Pelletier, "The Regulators," in Doern, ed., *The Regulatory Process in Canada,* pp. 150-52; Brown-John, *Canadian Regulatory Agencies,* pp. 114-16.
23. *Report on Independent Administrative Agencies: A Framework For Decision Making,* Report 26 (Ottawa: Law Reform Commission of Canada, 1985), p. 77.
24. Natural justice is described in more detail in Chapter 18.
25. Brown-John, *Canadian Regulatory Agencies,* p. 143.
26. An excellent recent review of problems and reforms is contained in David J. Mullan, "Administrative Tribunals: Their Evolution in Canada from 1945 to 1984," in Bernier and Lajoie, eds., *Regulations, Crown Corporations and Administrative Tribunals,* pp. 155-201.
27. A good discussion of the nature of some of these costs is contained in Economic Council of Canada, *Responsible Regulation: An Interim Report,* pp. 34-38.
28. Anthony Downs, *An Economic Theory of Democracy* (New York: Harper & Row, 1957), ch. 13, esp. 254ff; Michael J. Trebilcock et al., *The Choice of Governing Instrument* (Ottawa: Minister of Supply and Services Canada, 1982), pp. 7-10.
29. *Regulating Business by Independent Commission* (Princeton, N.J.: Princeton University Press, 1955), ch. 3.
30. W.H.N. Hull, "Captive or Victim: The Board of Broadcast Governors and Bernstein's Law, 1958-68," *Canadian Public Administration* 26 (Winter 1983): 560.
31. Ibid.
32. Economic Council of Canada, *Responsible Regulation: An Interim Report,* p. 57. (Emphasis in original; footnote omitted.)
33. Richard Schultz, "Regulatory Agencies and the Canadian Political System," in Kenneth Kernaghan, ed., *Public Administration in Canada: Selected Readings,* 4th ed. (Toronto: Methuen, 1982), pp. 70-80.
34. Richard Schultz and Alan Alexandroff, *Economic Regulation and the Federal System* (Toronto: University of Toronto Press, 1985), p. 29. Reprinted by permission of the University of Toronto Press in cooperation with the Royal Commission on the Economic Union and Development Prospects for Canada and the Canadian Publishing Centre, Supply and Services Canada.
35. Ibid., p. 30.
36. Richard Schultz, "The Regulatory Process, and Federal-Provincial Relations," in Doern, ed., *The Regulatory Process in Canada,* pp. 128-31 and passim.
37. Vandervort, *Political Control of Independent Administrative Agencies,* pp. 40-42
38. "Debalkanizing Telecom," *The Globe and Mail,* November 11, 1989.
39. "Federal Phone Takeover Infuriates 3 Provinces," *Toronto Star,* October 20, 1989.
40. Peter N. Nemetz, "The Fisheries Act and Federal-Provincial Environmental Regulation: Duplication or Complementarity?" *Canadian Public Administration* 29, no. 3 (Fall 1986): 401-24.
41. Robert Fulford, "Promises, Promises," *Saturday Night,* July 1987, pp. 5-7; "CBC Program Cuts 'Dismaying' Says Author of Task Force Report," *The Globe and Mail,* March 5, 1987.

42. Richard Schultz, "Regulation and Public Administration," in Kenneth Kernaghan, ed., *Canadian Public Administration: Discipline and Profession* (Toronto: Butterworths, 1983), p. 209.
43. Ibid.
44. Office of Privatization and Regulatory Affairs, *Regulatory Reform Strategy* (n.d., 1986?), pp. 3-4. (Emphasis added.)
45. "Life Cycle of a Regulation," News Release of the Office of Privatization and Regulatory Affairs, n.d., p. 1.
46. Office of Privatization and Regulatory Affairs, *Regulatory Reform: Making It Work* (Ottawa: The Office of Privatization and Regulatory Affairs, 1988), p. 11.
47. Ibid., pp. 15-64.
48. "Putting out a Red Alert to Voters on Red Tape," *The Globe and Mail*, October 14, 1988.
49. "Deregulation Opened Door to Airline Price Woes, Failures," *The Globe and Mail*, May 4, 1990; "Remaining Airline Giants Taking Control," *The Globe and Mail*, August 6, 1990.
50. Strick, *The Economics of Government Regulation*, p. 14.
51. Economic Council of Canada, *Responsible Regulation: An Interim Report*, pp. 78-81.
52. *Public Policy Decision Making and Regulation* (Toronto: Institute for Research on Public Policy, 1979), pp. 131-33.
53. *Report Number Nine* (1973), pp. 40-45.
54. Canada, House of Commons, Special Committee on Regulatory Reform, *Report*, pp. 15-17.
55. Richard Schultz, "Regulatory Agencies," in Michael S. Whittington and Glen Williams, eds., *Canadian Politics in the 1990s*, 3rd ed. (Scarborough, Ont.: Nelson Canada, 1990), p. 475.
56. Canada, House of Commons, *Report*, p. 24.
57. Vandervort, *Political Control of Independent Administrative Agencies*, pp. 91-92.
58. Schultz and Alexandroff, *Economic Regulation and the Federal System*, p. 149.
59. Ibid. (Footnote omitted.)
60. Ibid., p. 152.

BIBLIOGRAPHY

Bernier, Ivan, and Andrée Lajoie, eds. *Regulations, Crown Corporations and Administrative Tribunals.* Research study for the Royal Commission on the Economic Union and Development Prospects for Canada, vol. 48. Toronto: University of Toronto Press, 1985.

Bernstein, Marver H. *Regulating Business by Independent Commission.* Princeton, N.J.: Princeton University Press, 1955.

Brown-John, C. Lloyd. *Canadian Regulatory Agencies.* Toronto: Butterworths, 1981.

Canada. House of Commons. Special Committee on Regulatory Reform. *Report.* Ottawa: Minister of Supply and Services Canada, 1981.

Canada. Office of Privatization and Regulatory Affairs. *Regulatory Reform: Making It Work.* Ottawa: The Office of Privatization and Regulatory Affairs, 1988.

——. *Regulatory Reform Strategy.* n. d., 1986?

Canada. Office of Regulatory Reform. *Report on Regulatory Reform.* Various issues.

Canada. Privy Council Office. *Submissions to the Royal Commission on Financial Management and Accountability.* Minister of Supply and Services Canada, 1978.

· Canada. Senate and House of Commons. Standing Joint Committee on Regulations and other Statutory Instruments. *Minutes and Proceedings*, no. 1, February 16, 1984.

Doern, G. Bruce, ed. *The Regulatory Process in Canada*. Toronto: Macmillan, 1978.

Economic Council of Canada. *Reforming Regulation*. Ottawa: Minister of Supply and Services Canada, 1981.

——. *Responsible Regulation: An Interim Report*. Hull: Minister of Supply and Services Canada, 1979.

Hartle, Douglas G. *Public Policy Decision Making and Regulation*. Toronto: Institute for Research on Public Policy, 1979.

Hull, W. H. N. "Captive or Victim: The Board of Broadcast Governors and Bernstein's Law, 1958-68." *Canadian Public Administration* 26 (Winter 1983): 544-62.

Law Reform Commission of Canada. *Report on Independent Administrative Agencies: A Framework For Decision Making*, Report 26. Ottawa: Law Reform Commission of Canada, 1985.

Nemetz, Peter N. "The Fisheries Act and Federal-Provincial Environmental Regulation: Duplication or Complementarity?" *Canadian Public Administration* 29, no. 3 (Fall 1986): 401-424.

Ontario. Committee on Government Productivity. *Report Number Nine* (1973).

Reschenthaler, Gil, Bill Stanbury, and Fred Thompson. "Whatever Happened to Deregulation?" *Policy Options* (May-June 1982): 36-42.

Saskatchewan. *General Framework for Regulatory Reform*. Photocopy.

Schultz, Richard J. *Federalism and the Regulatory Process*. Montreal: Institute for Research on Public Policy, 1979.

——. *Federalism, Bureaucracy, and Public Policy: The Politics of Highway Transportation Regulation*. Montreal: McGill-Queen's University Press, 1980.

——. "Regulation and Public Administration." In Kenneth Kernaghan, ed., *Canadian Public Administration: Discipline and Profession*. Toronto: Butterworths, 1983, pp. 196-210.

——. "Regulatory Agencies." In Michael S. Whittington and Glen Williams, eds., *Canadian Politics in the 1990s*. 3rd ed. (Scarborough, Ont.: Nelson Canada, 1990), pp. 468-80.

——. "Regulatory Agencies and the Canadian Political System." In Kenneth Kernaghan, ed., *Public Administration in Canada: Selected Readings*. 4th ed. Toronto: Methuen, 1982, pp. 70-80.

Schultz, Richard, and Alan Alexandroff. *Economic Regulation and the Federal System*. Toronto: University of Toronto Press, 1985.

Strick, John C. *The Economics of Government Regulation*. Toronto: Thompson Educational Publishing, 1990.

Trebilcock, Michael J., Douglas G. Hartle, J. Robert Pritchard, and Donald N. Dewees. *The Choice of Governing Instrument*. Ottawa: Minister of Supply and Services Canada, 1982.

Tupper, Allan. "Pacific Western Airlines." In Allan Tupper and G. Bruce Doern, eds., *Public Corporations and Public Policy in Canada*. Montreal: The Institute for Research on Public Policy, 1981, pp. 285-317.

Vandervort, Lucinda. *Political Control of Independent Administrative Agencies*. Ottawa: Law Reform Commission of Canada, 1979.

Willis, John, ed. *Canadian Boards at Work*. Toronto: Macmillan, 1941.

CASES

In *Case Program in Canadian Public Administration* (Toronto: Institute of Public Administration of Canada):

  The Grain Dust Case: Public Policy Analysis and Regulation. By G. Bruce Doern and
    John Kowalski

  Regulatory Decision: Airlines. By Peter Clancy

Cases developed by the Canadian Centre for Management Development and distributed
by the Case Program in Canadian Public Administration:

  Triple A: The Acquisitions Assessment Agency. By Richard Paton, Dave Ouimet and
    John William Pullen

  The Natural Gas Deregulation Case. By G. Bruce Doern

11

Other Non-Departmental Organizations

The most commonly used forms of government organization are the operating department, the regulatory agency, and the Crown corporation, discussed in detail in the previous chapters. However, a number of other organizations and instruments that are used less widely are still very important. These include Royal commissions, task forces, and advisory councils. These forms of organization provide the Cabinet and individual ministers with alternative sources of policy advice beyond that provided by public servants. Some other important types of organization, such as interdepartmental task forces and intergovernmental committees, are dealt with in Chapters 16 and 19, respectively.

The dominant theme of Part III of this book is the choice of organizational form—why governments choose particular organizational forms to respond to particular problems. A common characteristic of all of the forms discussed in this chapter is that they are more involved in *advising, consulting* or *researching* than in *implementing* or *doing*. Frequently, the problems faced by a government are so severe and far-reaching that the government must study the situation carefully and seek policy advice widely before it acts, so that it does not act unwisely. Cynics would likely argue that some of the instruments discussed below are really "non-responses" geared to distracting people's attention and making it appear that government is interested, when in fact the desire is simply to defer consideration of something until later, possibly after the next election.

> Even where such comment has been perceptive, its implied criticism may have been misplaced. Institutionalized delay may have its merits where no adequate consensus for action exists. Grasping a nettle firmly is a fairly reliable formula for experiencing pain, but not necessarily for making progress. In any event, it is clear that in the case of a large majority of Royal commissions and task forces of recent years the object has been enlightenment, not evasion. Their aim has been to achieve more widespread public understanding of questions at issue and a more informed basis for policy choices by the decision-makers.[1]

ROYAL COMMISSIONS AND TASK FORCES

The federal Inquiries Act provides for three types of inquiries. Part II of the Act allows a departmental minister to appoint a commissioner or commissioners for the purposes of a departmental investigation. These kinds of commissions are more limited in scope, and are less formal and public than the Royal commissions and task forces discussed in this chapter. Part IV of the Act empowers the Governor in Council to allow an international commission to carry on a portion of its work in Canada. This is a very specialized kind of arrangement and will not be discussed in this chapter.

Part I of the Inquiries Act governs those commissions with a much higher profile, such as Royal commissions and task forces. It stipulates that the Governor in Council, i.e., Cabinet, may "cause inquiry to be made into and concerning any matter connected with the good government of Canada or the conduct of any part of the public business thereof."[2]

Royal commissions and **task forces** are temporary organizations constituted to investigate either specific incidents or general policy concerns and report to government. They usually go out of business after the delivery of their report and so are not involved in the implementation of any of their recommendations.

There are more similarities than differences between task forces and Royal commissions. The Law Reform Commission of Canada has suggested that there is little reason to make a distinction between the two. "The adjective 'royal' is much abused, with some commissions technically entitled to its use not employing it, and others appropriating it when they have no business doing so. In our view, the term is best ignored."[3] In this chapter, the advice of the commission will be followed and there will be a discussion of commissions appointed under Part I of the Inquiries Act without regard to the term used to describe any particular commission. However, there are some statements of tendency that can be made about the two forms.[4]

Royal commissions tend to be more formal in their organization. For example, the members of the commission are appointed, and its mandate is assigned, by an Order in Council. A task force might receive its mandate by a letter from the Prime Minister or another minister. Royal commissions tend to be used for major tasks requiring lengthy analysis; task forces emphasize speed of reply. Royal commissions tend to conduct most of their proceedings in public and produce *public* reports containing recommendations to the government. Task forces can report publicly, but are frequently asked to report privately. Public reports are harder for the government to ignore than private ones. As noted above, one should not make too much of these differences; there is wide variance in individual cases and the statements of tendency mentioned above do not always apply.

Commissions appointed under the Inquiries Act have been a very popular device in Canada; between 1867 and 1979, 425 of them were established.[5] In the Trudeau era, the task force appointed under Part I or Part II of the Inquiries Act became more popular than the full-blown Royal commission in terms of numbers, but Trudeau is responsible for the largest Royal commission by almost any measure—the Royal Commission on the Economic Union and the Development Prospects for Canada (Macdonald Commission). Mulroney seems less inclined to use the Royal commission, but he has appointed some high-profile commissions such as the Dubin Commission of Inquiry into the Use of Drugs and Banned Practices Intended to Increase Athletic Performance, and the very important, but lesser-known Royal Commissions on New Reproductive Technologies, and Electoral Reform and Party Financing.

Commissions can be appointed to delve into any area which the government desires, but Hodgetts has identified four major areas in which commissions have been active.[6]

- catastrophic incidents—train wrecks, air disasters, bridge collapses;
- social or cultural problems of national importance—broadcasting, arts and sciences, bilingualism and biculturalism;
- economic matters—transportation, banking and finance, corporate concentration, economic future of the country; and
- government organization—financial and personnel management, morale in the foreign service.

The purposes for which commissions have been used have changed over time. Writing in 1964, John Courtney identified a trend that continues to this day:

> The trend, therefore, of recent royal (sic) commissions has been away from investigations important only to a limited number of people or a restricted geographic area and toward examinations of importance to the Canadian people as a whole. The changing pattern may be characterized as one away from "intensive" inquiries, of only limited significance, to one of "extensive" inquiries, of national significance. The effect of the changing pattern has been to turn the royal commission of inquiry into an investigatory technique suitable for publicizing group sentiments on a national basis and for formulating national objectives. The modern royal commission has become, in effect, a vehicle by which individuals, groups and governments are permitted to state their views on matters of concern to the nation as a whole.[7]

Reasons for Use

Several reasons why governments use the Royal commission or task force form of organization, rather than some of the more permanent structures discussed in earlier chapters, are discussed below. All of the organizations and instruments discussed in this chapter have in common a concern with study and consultation rather than implementation. As will be discussed later, this is both the strong and the weak point of the commission form.

Tool for Objective Policy Analysis. Peter Aucoin provides three general reasons why commissions are very good instruments for policy analysis:

> First, their establishment enables decision-makers in government to delay or postpone decisions without being criticized for doing nothing at all. Policy analysis in this circumstance may be an excuse for a "non-decision", (sic) but at least it ensures that the issue at hand stays on the policy agenda in a certain fashion. Second, such commissions provide for a process whereby the views of special interest groups and the interested public can be presented in a forum that is not subject to direct government control... Third, and perhaps most relevant, commissions of inquiry of this sort represent the most effective option available to government for policy

analysis undertaken by an independent and objective, and yet official, organization. Commissions are the most effective option in this regard because they have a greater capacity to be, and to be seen to be, independent and objective than other governmental instruments of public policy analysis.

Each of these characteristics is important to policy analysis as an activity of governance. The first provides time for analysis as an intellectual exercise; the second provides the opportunity to examine and assess demands and support for various policy options; and the third provides for analysts who are able to evaluate policy options free from the constraints of partisan controls or institutional limitations extant in other government organizations which conduct policy analysis.[8]

Identify Innovative Approaches. Commissions usually employ people from outside the public service. It is hoped that they will be able to take a fresh look at some problem and propose an innovative solution. The Royal Commission on Financial Management and Accountability (Lambert Commission) was composed of a bank president, a political scientist, a former public servant, and an accountant with both business and public sector experience. In this case, the combination of members with public service experience and outsiders with a fresh view produced some innovative ideas about changes in government structures.

This positive point highlights a potential problem for the government. Governments do not have as much control over the activities or final conclusions of Part I commissions as they have over departmental, or Part II, task forces. Independent commissions report publicly, and their recommendations cannot be ignored by the government. Politicians are aware that they are unleashing a potentially very powerful force by creating an independent commission, and so are reluctant to use this device in circumstances where they feel a need to control, or at least influence, the outcome.

On the other hand, where governments can make a valid case against the proposals of a commission, they are somewhat freer to reject advice from an independent commission than they would be from a body more closely related to the government.

> This lack of accountability then preserves flexibility for the politician at the conclusion of the inquiry, in that at that point he is free either to embrace warmly the results or to indicate that he is not bound to accept the inquiry results. In contrast to this, in those situations where the inquiry is directly accountable to the politician, he is less able to disown the results.[9]

Fact-finding. Royal commissions and task forces are frequently established to investigate disasters or questionable activities, to determine exactly what happened and recommend measures to prevent their recurrence. The Dubin Commission of Inquiry into the Use of Drugs and Banned Practices Intended to Increase Athletic Performance, and the Hughes Royal Commission on the Donald Marshall, Jr., Prosecution are examples of these kinds of Royal commissions.

Postpone an Embarrassing Problem. It is sometimes suggested that governments have established commissions merely to ensure that a problem is temporarily placed on the back burner, and that, with luck, the problem might go away altogether. The Royal Commission on Corporate Concentration was appointed when Paul Desmarais of Power Corporation was attempting to take over the giant Argus Corporation. The takeover bid was unsuccessful, and no action was taken on the recommendations of the Royal commission.

The delay caused by the use of the commission form is a frequent source of criticism:

> One can almost predict that nothing will be done without a Commission and in fact often not much is done with a Commission except to pass it on to the next Commission. It is a kind of commission chain letter process. Governments have been known to avoid a head-on collision with an issue for upwards of fifty years as was the case with the nationalization of wheat marketing.[10]

Stimulate Interaction With the Public. Royal commissions are frequently established as a two-way communications link—both obtaining the views of members of the public on an issue and communicating important facts to them. Some commissions invite the participation of the public through the presentation of written briefs or appearances before the commission.[11] The Task Force on National Unity (Pépin-Roberts Commission) travelled extensively and heard the views of many Canadians on this very emotional issue.

Commissions also arrange for research to be done on the problem at hand, and prepare interim reports in an attempt to improve the level of discussion of the issue. These reports are frequently used to begin to sell the ultimate conclusions of the commission to the public and politicians.

Low-cost Way of Showing Concern. Governments are frequently under great pressure to prove that they recognize a particular problem and are striving to resolve it. A full-scale attempt to solve the problem will likely be expensive; commissions are often somewhat expensive, but the expense is almost certainly less than the expense of actually solving the problem.

> In sum, all public inquiries offer to politicians the opportunity to demonstrate concern about a policy issue and to indicate that action is being taken upon it, while deferring the need to expend substantial resources in response to a perceived policy concern . . . [12]

Operation

The Order in Council that establishes a commission sets out the mandate of the commission, the names of the commissioners, and, sometimes, the date by which it must report.

In the past, it was common for commissions to be headed by a single commissioner, frequently a judge. This reflects the investigatory nature of some commissions. Even today, commissions with an investigative role are frequently headed by a judge. The benefits of having someone with the expertise and prestige of a judge as a commissioner are fairly clear, particularly where the major role of the commission is investigative. However, where the commission is delving into political matters, the involvement of judges is more problematic.

When Justice Willard Estey of the Supreme Court of Canada was appointed to investigate the causes of the collapse of the Canadian Commercial and Northland Banks, James Snell and Frederick Vaughan were strongly critical:

> The use of the judiciary, particularly members of the Supreme Court, to deal with political problems is a practice which should be ended for several reasons. First, it draws judges into political controversy. In taking advantage of the judicial reputation for non-partisanship, governments are actually maintaining a practice which tarnishes that reputation. The judiciary itself can be, and certainly has been, brought into disrepute through this process.

> Second, inquiries such as Judge Estey's are essentially being asked to examine and comment upon the political judgment of a government...

> ... Why should judges be asked to assess political decisions? Surely that is the job of the electorate or of its elected representatives.[13]

The authors also mention the great amount of work facing the court as a result of the large number of Charter cases coming up in the next few years.

In recent years, the size of commissions has been expanding and there has been a tendency to appoint people with a diversity of backgrounds including, but not limited to, law.[14] The argument is sometimes made that the commissioners should be representative of the various interests affected by the commission, but this view has been criticized:

> The proper place for special interests is in the witness box, not on the Commission. The generous representation accorded various interests in Britain has, it seems to me, unfortunate consequences. Most members have firmly rooted convictions which no amount of evidence is likely to shake. Unanimous reports for that reason are seldom obtained. But, what is more serious to my mind, minority reports can be used as vehicles for carrying to the public the prejudices of special interests (at the public's expense of course).[15]

The actual activities of the commissions vary considerably depending on their mandate, but they usually involve both public input and academic research components.

The public input aspect also varies widely, depending on the nature of the commission. Fact-finding commissions usually focus on input from the people involved in the incident and experts in the field. Commissions appointed under Part I of the Inquiries Act even have the power to compel reluctant witnesses to attend.[16] Sometimes, commissions will cast their net considerably wider to seek the views of a cross-section of the public. The Royal Commission on Electoral Reform and Party Financing has held public meetings from coast to coast to hear public opinion.

Commissioners also usually arrange for academic research to provide them with some background on the issue under review, e.g., the history of the issue, how it is handled in other countries. This usually involves hiring academics or consultants to produce background papers, which may or may not be published and made available to the public. The Macdonald Royal Commission on the Economic Union and the Development Prospects for Canada employed several study teams that produced almost three hundred studies, ultimately published in seventy-two volumes.[17]

Some commissions produce interim reports to advise the public of the direction in which their thinking is going; this could incite some additional public participation. The commission always produces a final report containing its analysis of the situation and some recommendations. The commission's final report can sometimes be accompanied by a minority report, or a dissent from some part of the majority report if all commissioners are not in full agreement.

The Provincial Scene

This section has focussed mainly on federal Royal commissions and task forces, partly because these are the most widely known and partly because there has been little systematic study of provincial commissions.[18] However, provincial governments have legislation similar to the federal Inquiries Act that provides for the establishment of these kinds of bodies. Some of the areas investigated by provincial bodies seem very similar to those investigated by federal bodies, such as the Nova Scotia Royal Commission on Pensions (reported 1983) and Manitoba's Task Force on Government Organization and Economy (reported 1978).

Criticisms

The most common criticisms of the commission form of organization relate to cost, delay, and the lack of any implementation mechanism. For a device that was supposed to provide an ad hoc review of a specific problem, modern-day commissions can appear incredibly bureaucratic. Large numbers of people are hired and masses of literature are produced over the several-year life of the commission. When the commissioner is a high-profile person receiving a large per diem payment, the criticism can be even stronger.[19]

Delay can also be a problem in a situation where people want change quickly. They become very frustrated with another study and more paper about an issue that they regard as urgent.

These criticisms must be weighed against the quality of the recommendations and other output of the commission. Even the largest commissions cost considerably less than ordinary operating departments. Commissions have the further benefit of being finite; the costs incurred will continue for only a limited period. Even the delay caused by commissions is frequently beneficial. Commissions are sometimes used to show a government's concern, while simultaneously marking time to see how a situation will develop. The Task Force on National Unity appointed shortly after the election of the Parti Québécois in 1976 is one example of this. Commissions are sometimes used to delay decisions, but it is better to delay and adopt a good solution than to act quickly and do the wrong thing.

The fact that there is usually no mechanism to ensure implementation of commission recommendations is a cause for some concern. This lack of responsibility for implementation could cause commissions to propose utopian recommendations that are effectively useless.

However, the opposite tendency is also possible. Wilson has argued that structural constraints make it very difficult for these commissions to do more than "administrative tinkering."

> Critics of staged inquiries into the policy process argue that these exercises must fall into two categories: (a) validating stamps of approval on changes already effected or sanctioned by the bureaucracy, and (b) reports that will never be implemented because they lack a powerful constituency. To attempt more is to ask for serious trouble. Tinkering with improving the inputs into the policy process is a very safe exercise. However, once task forces or other forms of inquiries start interfering or fundamentally questioning how resources are utilized, they challenge administrative competence. Should they be bold enough to question outputs, then they challenge political competence. Therefore, inquiries into the policy process in today's climate which construe their missions as being much wider than mere technical administrative exercises will end up as embarrassing political trials.[20]

Liora Salter refers to this as one of the contradictions of inquiries. On the one hand, these commissions can encourage radical debate about very innovative ideas that raise the hopes of people dissatisfied with the status quo. However, when the commission actually makes its recommendations, it usually opts for incremental reforms because it knows that nothing else will be accepted.[21]

Another criticism of commissions has been that, even after all the resources that have been poured into their work, governments tend not to accept their recommendations if they do not fit their preconceived ideas. Sylvia Bashevkin found that Royal commissions and task forces that have dealt with issues of economic and cultural nationalism have not had much success in having their recommendations implemented. Her explanation for this is that usually these recommendations have had only lukewarm support from the general public and very little support from elites.[22] The lesson would seem to be that the logical arguments made by Royal commissions do not carry much weight when they are out of line with general public, or more important, elite, opinion.

However, it is very difficult to evaluate the real impact of a Royal commission. Some people have a scoreboard mentality about commission recommendations in that they record the number of recommendations implemented versus the total number of recommendations. By this measure, few commissions look good. However, a more thoughtful analysis of the *general tone* of commission recommendations suggests that governments have usually taken the recommendations very seriously and implemented at least some portion of them.[23] Also, certain commissions have set a tone for change that goes far beyond any specific recommendation.[24] The classic example of this is the Royal Commission on Bilingualism and Biculturalism, which operated in the late 1960s. There is no question that the status of the French language was considerably enhanced as a result of the attention devoted to the activities of the commission. Counting recommendations in this situation is meaningless.

One of the most serious problems that commissions will have to face in the Charter of Rights era is the clash between policy-makers' values and lawyers' values.

> The policy-maker sees commissions of inquiry as stepping-stones to policy. In this guise, inquiries serve several functions, of which the most important are the elucidation and education of public opinion, the discovery and exploration of policy options and the making of recommendations for action.[25]

Thus, the policy-maker wants a process that is relatively simple and allows all interested parties to have their say with a minimum of complication. Policy-makers recognize, and are usually not bothered by the idea, that obtaining the ultimate "truth" is probably not possible. One simply listens to all sides of the issue and uses one's judgment to make what seems like a satisfactory decision.

Commissions that deal with general policy issues work very well this way, but there are some commissions in which people's actions will be discussed in such a way that their reputations could be tarnished, or their right to a fair trial could be limited. In these cases, lawyers will want to intervene to ensure that their clients' rights are protected and proper procedures are followed by the commission.

The dilemma is that this emphasis on procedure will undoubtedly slow down the workings of the commission and could shift the focus of debate to procedural rather than substantive questions, and thus defeat the purpose of appointing a commission. However, when people's names are thrown about in a public forum and serious accusations are made, some mechanisms for their protection must be introduced.

This has always been a problem, but it will become a more serious problem in the post-Charter era. If governments are not sensitive to this problem, it could destroy the benefits of the commission form of organization. In particular, governments must be more careful in the future about the issues they assign to commissions, and how widely they draw their terms of reference.

ADVISORY COUNCILS

Advisory councils come in such a wide variety that it is very difficult to generalize about them. This section will first discuss some of their general characteristics and then illustrate their activities and functions through a more detailed discussion of two councils.

An **advisory council** is an organization composed of private citizens, created by the government to provide an independent source of advice to a minister. It is established outside the normal departmental bureaucracy and does not ordinarily have responsibility for administering programs.[26]

The members of these councils are private citizens; neither politicians nor public servants ordinarily serve as members. This ensures the council's independence. Another assurance of independence comes from the fact that the council ordinarily provides its advice to the minister publicly, free of any potential laundering by the public service. However, the independence of these advisory councils is limited by the fact that they obtain most, if not all, of their funding from government.

The people who serve on these bodies are sometimes representatives of particular interest groups in that they are asked to serve by the minister after consultation with certain relevant groups. Members are also chosen because of their personal status and expertise. There seems to be no recent study of the characteristics of members of advisory councils, but a somewhat dated study suggested that members of these councils do not exactly constitute a cross-section of society. Managerial and professional types each accounted for about 30 percent of the membership of the large number of councils surveyed, while "homemakers" accounted for 8 percent and "factory/industrial workers" accounted for 5 percent.[27]

Audrey D. Doerr has identified four broad categories of councils:

- central advisory bodies, e.g., Economic Council of Canada;
- functional advisory councils, e.g., Fisheries and Oceans Research Advisory Council;
- granting councils, e.g., Social Sciences and Humanities Research Council; and
- consultative bodies, e.g., Canadian Advisory Council on the Status of Women.[28]

She goes on to suggest that this diversity means that advisory councils can combine a number of different functions.

> As bodies composed of representatives from the private sector, they serve as vehicles for channelling public opinion on particular issues. Conversely, they assist the government in this capacity by generating support for the latter's policies. As independent research centres, they can serve as counterweights to bureaucratic expertise in the departments. Thus, they can serve as critics and consensus builders in the policy process. In providing a link between governmental and private interests, advisory councils can become engaged in the reciprocal exchange of information and opinions. In the case of granting councils, such bodies also serve to define and focus policy issues in applied research and provide technical knowledge in pure research undertakings.[29]

Advisory councils in some form have been around for a long time, but Prime Minister Trudeau established more of them than his predecessors. One of Trudeau's main concerns was to cultivate competing sources of information outside the normal government bureaucracy. Advisory councils are also an example of participatory democracy, which was one of the trappings of the Trudeau era. However, the fact that the Mulroney government has abolished virtually none of these organizations, and uses them quite widely, indicates that they are more than the whim of one Prime Minister.

Advisory councils are found along a continuum. At one end are the very formal, high-profile, well-staffed advisory councils, such as the Science Council of Canada, which have many of the trappings of a bureaucracy. At the other end of the continuum are the very small, low-profile organizations, such as the

Canada Employment and Immigration Advisory Council, which have a very small staff, frequently seconded from the department. It is easy to illustrate the role of advisory councils by focussing on one organization that fits at the highly organized extreme of the spectrum—the Economic Council of Canada—and one that fits closer to the opposite end—the Canadian Advisory Council on the Status of Women.

Economic Council of Canada

The Economic Council of Canada was founded in 1963 to function as a sort of "permanent Royal commission,"[30] with the objective of improving Canada's economic performance. It operates outside the regular government bureaucracy, with no administrative or program responsibilities. Its major roles are, first, to consider economic policies in the medium and long term and provide advice to the government and, second, to educate the general public about economic issues. It was originally intended to have a consensus-building role as well, but this has fallen on hard times, as will be discussed below.

The council is independent in that it sets its own research agenda and publishes anything it desires, without the need to obtain prior government approval. However, it does sometimes receive requests from the Prime Minister to investigate particular areas. It has received such references in the areas of competition policy and regulation, among others. Even in these cases, the council publishes its findings without prior government approval.

The council's main activity is publishing various kinds of economic studies. In the period covered by the council's 1988-89 *Annual Report*, it published its twenty-fifth annual review of the Canadian economy, *Back to Basics*, two other council publications, *Venturing Forth: An Assessment of the Canada-U.S.A. Trade Agreement* and *Perspective 2000*, an overview of public policy issues that Canada is likely to face in the year 2000. It also published a series of other research reports dealing with such diverse areas as the prairie grain economy, competition policy, new technology, and tax reform. The council also publishes the magazine *Au Courant*, which discusses current economic issues in a very readable fashion.

The council is composed of a full-time chairman, two full-time vice-chairmen,[31] and up to twenty-five other directors, all appointed by the Governor General in Council, the chairman for seven years, the other members for three-year terms.[32]

The directors meet four times per year to decide on the general direction of the council's research and the specific content of its *Annual Review* and other publications. In the council's early years, there was an attempt to have directors who represented a reasonable cross-section of the Canadian economy. However, by 1988, the council was composed entirely of business people and academics. Politicians, public servants, or other government representatives have never been appointed to the council.

When the council was created, it was hoped that it could engage in consensus-building. This was to be done in general by educating the public about economic issues, and more specifically by being a forum for *tripartitism*—

discussion between business, government, and labour leaders to increase mutual understanding and improve productivity. In the past, the membership of the council included labour leaders, but in recent years they have refused to serve, as a protest against various government policies. Thus, through no fault of its own, the council has not fulfilled its expectations as a consensus-builder.

Most assessments of the value of the council point out that its position outside the government bureaucracy with no program responsibilities is a double-edged sword.[33] On the one hand, the council has the freedom to examine government policy in an independent fashion and comment without prejudice. On the other hand, this very freedom means that the council has no levers to implement its recommendations.[34]

Canadian Advisory Council on the Status of Women (CACSW)

The CACSW was formed in 1973 as a result of a recommendation of the Royal Commission on the Status of Women. The mandate of the council is:

(a) to bring before the government and the public matters of interest and concern to women; and
(b) to advise the Minister [Responsible for the Status of Women] on such matters relating to the status of women as the Minister may refer to the Council for its consideration or as the Council may deem appropriate.[35]

The council consists of a maximum of thirty members appointed by Order in Council to serve three-year terms. Three members work full-time for the council; the others are part-time appointees. According to the *Annual Report*, they are chosen "so that the Council collectively represents the regional, cultural, occupational, and ethnic diversity of Canada as well as both official languages."[36] While the members of the council are not quite as elitist as the members of male-dominated councils, they are not exactly a cross-section of Canadian society. Their backgrounds tend to be in law, business, teaching, nursing, or social service agencies. In 1988-89, two of the members were men.

The CACSW is a much smaller organization than the Economic Council. It has a budget of just over three million dollars, all of which comes from the federal government.

The council attempts to influence government in a number of ways. For example, during 1988-89, the President appeared before parliamentary committees to discuss post-secondary education and the proposed Child Care Act. The council also submitted a brief to the Minister of Justice on proposed pornography legislation. The council's *Annual Report* takes the unusual step of publishing recommendations made by the council. In 1988-89, there were recommendations concerning mandatory retirement, women in agriculture, appointments to the Supreme Court of Canada, and the Canadian Jobs Strategy.

The council produced a number of publications geared to showing the impact of laws and government policies on women. Some of these publications were *The Equality Game: Women in the Federal Public Service (1908-1987)*, *The Reality Gap: Closing the Gap Between Women's Needs and Available Programs and Services*,

Women, Paid/Unpaid Work, and *Stress: New Directions for Research.* Like the Economic Council, the CACSW has an independent publication policy in that it does not consult with the government before publishing.

Also in 1989, the council held a two-day symposium on *Women and Well-Being* to which representatives of sixty-five women's group were invited. The meeting discussed such issues as stress, reproductive technology, and freedom from violence.[37]

The Provincial and Local Government Scene

These advisory councils are also very widely used in other spheres of government. Some of the provincial councils, such as the Manitoba Advisory Council on the Status of Women and the Ontario Law Reform Commission, mirror federal councils. Others, such as Alberta's Irrigation Council and New Brunswick's Fisheries Development Board, are concerned with uniquely provincial concerns. Organizations such as heritage advisory councils and economic development councils play an important role in local governments.

Criticisms

One of the most difficult roles for these councils is to maintain their independence from government, while at the same time maximizing their influence on government policy. The fact that appointments to these councils are made by government and most (if not all) funding comes from government means that a council that becomes too critical of government policy could jeopardize its existence. However, the government is not well served by a panel of sycophants; such a council would have no credibility with its community, and so could not serve its purpose of being a two-way communications link.

This problem is well illustrated by a controversy that developed between the government and the Canadian Advisory Council on the Status of Women during the debate over the new constitution in the early 1980s. The CACSW wanted to hold a major national conference on the effect of the new constitution on women. It was likely that this would develop into a session that would be critical of the constitution and, by extension, of the Liberal government that proposed it.

Lloyd Axworthy, the Minister Responsible for the Status of Women, asked the president of the council, Doris Anderson, to postpone the conference. She opposed this, but a majority vote of the council decided to delay it anyway. She then charged that the vote was influenced by inappropriate political interference by Axworthy, and resigned from the council along with some other members. She was replaced as president by a woman who had actively campaigned for Axworthy in the previous election.[38] This immediately caused a number of women's groups to suggest that this was inappropriate political meddling and destroyed the credibility of the council. *The Globe and Mail* editorialized that: "The effectiveness of the council appears to have been seriously undermined, if not fatally wounded."[39]

A related problem is that it can be very difficult to determine whether accommodative or assertive tactics will maximize a council's influence. Some constituents of a council will argue that it should pursue a low-profile policy of influencing the government by friendly persuasion, while other constituents will suggest that the best tactic is one of "going public" and bringing overt pressure to bear on the government. Members of councils suggest that the balancing of these two concerns is one of their most difficult tasks.

Advisory councils are also frequently criticized for being captive of one part of their constituency, rather than speaking in the interests of all members of that constituency. The larger and more diverse the constituency group, the greater this problem becomes. The Canadian Advisory Council on the Status of Women has been attacked from both ends of the political spectrum on this issue.

Advisory councils clearly *can* serve a useful purpose, although they are in an innately difficult position. They must tread a middle course so that they retain credibility with the government, while not being captured by it. They must also be very skillful in balancing the interests of their constituents so that they are not captured by any one group. Maintaining these several different balancing acts is obviously a very difficult exercise.

NOTES

1. Ronald S. Ritchie, *An Institute for Research on Public Policy* (Ottawa: Information Canada, 1971), p. 8.
2. R.S.C. 1985, c. I-11, s. 2.
3. *Commissions of Inquiry* (Ottawa: Minister of Supply and Services Canada, 1977), p. 5.
4. These differences in form and tone are discussed in M. J. Trebilcock et al., *The Choice of Governing Instrument* (Ottawa: Minister of Supply and Services Canada, 1982), p. 40; and V. Seymour Wilson, "The Role of Royal Commissions and Task Forces," in G. Bruce Doern and Peter Aucoin, eds., *The Structures of Policy-Making in Canada* (Toronto: Macmillan 1971), pp. 115, 121-26.
5. George Fletcher Henderson, *Federal Royal Commissions in Canada, 1867-1966: A Checklist* (Toronto: University of Toronto Press, 1967). This has been updated by Denise Ledoux, *Commissions of Inquiry Under the Inquiries Act, Part I: 1967 to Date* (Ottawa: Library of Parliament, 1980). These figures are reasonably accurate, but exact numbers are virtually impossible to confirm. Law Reform Commission of Canada, *Commissions of Inquiry*, p. 10.
6. J. E. Hodgetts, "The Role of Royal Commissions in Canadian Government," in *Proceedings of the Third Annual Conference of the Institute of Public Administration of Canada* (1951), pp. 354-55.
7. John Childs Courtney, "Canadian Royal Commissions of Inquiry, 1946 to 1962: An Investigation of an Executive Instrument of Inquiry," Ph.D. diss., Duke University, 1964, p. 121. J. E. Hodgetts makes a similar distinction in "Public Power and Ivory Tower," in Trevor Lloyd and Jack McLeod, eds., *Agenda 1970: Proposals for a Creative Politics* (Toronto: University of Toronto Press, 1968), pp. 271-78.
8. "Contributions of Commissions of Inquiry to Policy Analysis: An Evaluation," in A. Paul Pross, Innis Christie, and John A. Yogis, eds., *Commissions of Inquiry* (Toronto: Carswell, 1990), pp. 197-98. (Footnote omitted.)
9. Trebilcock, *The Choice of Governing Instrument*, p. 45.

10. Meyer Brownstone, "To Commission or not to Commission: As An Advisory Body," *Canadian Public Administration* 5 (Fall 1962): 261.
11. For an analysis of the extent of this kind of participation, see Hugh Whalen, "Public Participation and, (sic) the Role of Canadian Royal Commissions and Task Forces: 1957-1969," Paper presented to the Annual Conference of the Institute of Public Administration of Canada (September 1981), p. 15.
12. Trebilcock, *The Choice of Governing Instrument*, p. 44.
13. "Putting Judges in the Political Hot Seat," *The Globe and Mail*, October 10, 1985, p. A7.
14. Henderson, *Federal Royal Commissions in Canada, 1867-1966* and Ledoux, *Commissions of Inquiry Under the Inquiries Act, Part I: 1967 to Date.*
15. Hodgetts, "The Role of Royal Commissions in Canadian Government," p. 358.
16. R.S.C. 1985, c. I-11, s. 4.
17. For a list of the published reports, see Canada, Royal Commission on the Economic Union and Development Prospects for Canada, *Report: Volume Three* (Ottawa: Minister of Supply and Services Canada, 1985), pp. 679-90.
18. For a listing of provincial Royal commissions, see Lise Maillet, *Provincial Royal Commissions and Commissions of Inquiry* (Ottawa: Minister of Supply and Services Canada, 1986).
19. Editorial, "A Royal Waste," *Vancouver Sun*, September 9, 1983; "Macdonald Commission Members Get $350 a Day," *Toronto Star*, May 3, 1983; "Macdonald Commission: Chairman Eager to Demonstrate He's Worth His Wages," *Calgary Herald*, November 10, 1983.
20. V. Seymour Wilson, "What Legacy? The Nielsen Task Force Program Review," in Katherine A. Graham, *How Ottawa Spends—1988/89* (Ottawa: Carleton University Press, 1988), p. 25.
21. "The Two Contradictions in Public Inquiries," in Pross, Christie, and Yogis, eds., *Commissions of Inquiry*, p. 177 and passim.
22. "Does Public Opinion Matter? The Adoption of Federal Royal Commission and Task Force Recommendations on the National Question, 1951-1987," *Canadian Public Administration* 31, no. 3 (Fall 1988): 390-407.
23. Courtney, "Canadian Royal Commissions of Inquiry," pp. 140-55.
24. G. Bruce Doern and Richard W. Phidd, *Canadian Public Policy: Ideas, Structure, Process* (Toronto: Methuen, 1983), pp. 543-44.
25. Innis Christie and A. Paul Pross, "Introduction," in Pross, Christie, and Yogis, eds., *Commissions of Inquiry*, p. 4.
26. A few advisory councils do have program responsibilities that can pose some difficulties for them; see Peter Aucoin, "The Role of Functional Advisory Councils," in Doern and Aucoin, eds., *The Structures of Policy-Making in Canada*, pp. 154-78.
27. C. Lloyd Brown-John, "Advisory Agencies in Canada: An Introduction," *Canadian Public Administration* 22 (Spring 1979): 87.
28. *The Machinery of Government in Canada* (Toronto: Methuen, 1981), p. 121.
29. Ibid.
30. A good description of the rationales for the creation of the council and its early years of operation is contained in R. W. Phidd, "The Role of Central Advisory Councils: The Economic Council of Canada," in Doern and Aucoin, eds., *The Structures of Policy-Making in Canada*, pp. 204-45.
31. The council uses the words chairman and vice-chairman even though two of the three officers are currently women.
32. Economic Council of Canada, R.S.C. 1985, c. E-1, s. 4.

33. Ritchie, *An Institute for Research on Public Policy,* pp. 10-12.
34. Richard W. Phidd and G. Bruce Doern, *The Politics and Management of Canadian Economic Policy* (Toronto: Macmillan of Canada, 1978), pp. 478-80.
35. Canadian Advisory Council on the Status of Women, *Annual Report, 1988-89,* p. 2.
36. Ibid.
37. Canadian Advisory Council on the Status of Women, *Fine Balances* (Fall 1989).
38. "And the Minister Will Sing My Way," *The Globe and Mail,* January 23, 1981, p. 6. Editorial.
39. Ibid.

BIBLIOGRAPHY

Bashevkin, Sylvia. "Does Public Opinion Matter? The Adoption of Federal Royal Commission and Task Force Recommendations on the National Question, 1951-1987," *Canadian Public Administration* 31, no. 3 (Fall 1988): 390-407.

Brown-John, C. Lloyd. "Advisory Agencies in Canada: An Introduction." *Canadian Public Administration* 22 (Spring 1979): 72-91.

Brownstone, Meyer. "To Commission or not to Commission: As An Advisory Body." *Canadian Public Administration* 5 (Fall 1962): 261-68.

Clokie, Hugh McDowell, and J. William Robinson. *Royal Commissions of Inquiry.* Stanford: Stanford University Press, 1937.

Courtney, John Childs. "Canadian Royal Commissions of Inquiry, 1946 to 1962: An Investigation of an Executive Instrument of Inquiry." Ph.D. diss., Duke University, 1964.

——. "In Defense of Royal Commissions." *Canadian Public Administration* 12 (Summer 1969): 198-212.

Doern, G. Bruce, and Peter Aucoin, eds. *The Structures of Policy-Making in Canada.* Toronto: Macmillan, 1971.

Doern, G. Bruce, and Richard W. Phidd. *Canadian Public Policy: Ideas, Structure, Process.* Toronto: Methuen, 1983.

Doerr, Audrey D. *The Machinery of Government in Canada.* Toronto: Methuen, 1981.

Hanson, Hugh. "Inside Royal Commissions." *Canadian Public Administration* 12 (Fall 1969): 356-64.

Henderson, George Fletcher. *Federal Royal Commissions in Canada, 1867-1966: A Checklist.* Toronto: University of Toronto Press, 1967.

Hodgetts, J. E. "Public Power and Ivory Tower." In Trevor Lloyd and Jack McLeod, eds., *Agenda 1970: Proposals for a Creative Politics.* Toronto: University of Toronto Press, 1968, pp. 256-80.

——. "The Role of Royal Commissions in Canadian Government," in *Proceedings of the Third Annual Conference of the Institute of Public Administration of Canada* (1951): pp. 351-67.

——. "Should Canada Be De-Commissioned? A Commoner's View of Royal Commissions." *Queen's Quarterly* 70 (Winter 1964): 475-90.

Law Reform Commission of Canada. *Commissions of Inquiry.* Ottawa: Minister of Supply and Services Canada, 1977.

Ledoux, Denise. *Commissions of Inquiry Under the Inquiries Act, Part I: 1967 to Date.* Ottawa: Library of Parliament, 1980.

Maillet, Lise. *Provincial Royal Commissions and Commissions of Inquiry.* Ottawa: Minister of Supply and Services Canada, 1986.

Phidd, Richard W. "The Economic Council of Canada: Its Establishment, Structure, and Role in the Canadian Policy- Making System, 1963-74." *Canadian Public Administration* 18 (Fall 1975): 428-73.

Phidd, Richard W., and G. Bruce Doern. *The Politics and Management of Canadian Economic Policy.* Toronto: Macmillan, 1978.

Pross, A. Paul, Innis Christie, and John A. Yogis, eds. *Commissions of Inquiry.* Toronto: Carswell, 1990.

Trebilcock, M. J., Douglas G. Hartle, J. Robert S. Prichard, and Donald N. Dewees. *The Choice of Governing Instrument.* Ottawa: Minister of Supply and Services Canada, 1982.

Whalen, Hugh. "Public Participation and, (sic) the Role of Canadian Royal Commissions and Task Forces: 1957-1969." Paper presented to the Annual Conference of the Institute of Public Administration of Canada, September 1981.

IV

POLITICS, VALUES, AND PUBLIC ADMINISTRATION

12

Institutional and Value Frameworks

Part III of this book described the forms of organization in the executive-bureaucratic sphere of government. However, reading a description of the central components of the machinery of government is somewhat akin to visiting a silent factory in the dead of night. You can see the machinery and be told how it is supposed to operate, but you cannot understand how it really works until you see it humming, whirring, clanking and, occasionally, breaking down. Moreover, you need to see how the operators use the machinery and how they relate to one another.

Thus, the primary purpose of Parts III and IV is to explain the ways in which the machinery of government operates in practice. This part focusses on the role of the administrative bodies (departments, agencies, boards, and commissions) discussed in Part III, and on the bureaucrats who manage them. It examines interaction in the executive-bureaucratic sphere among bureaucrats, and between bureaucrats and Cabinet ministers; it also examines interaction between bureaucrats and actors outside this sphere, namely legislators, the courts, provincial governments, pressure groups, journalists, and the general public.

To facilitate a coherent treatment of the many interactions between bureaucrats and other political actors, this chapter sets out two complementary frameworks—the institutional framework and the value framework. These frameworks are based on concepts and insights provided by scholarly writings in public administration, political science, and organization theory. The final section of this chapter deals with the concept and practice of coordination, which is an extremely important and pervasive process in Canadian governments.

THE INSTITUTIONAL FRAMEWORK

Such a large number of actors is involved in the public policy process that it is essential to provide a means of identifying and classifying them. Moreover, since this book is concerned with the role of *the bureaucracy* in the policy process, it is necessary to devise a framework that permits a focus on administrative organizations.[1] Thus, we have set out below an institutional framework that facilitates an examination of interactions:

1. within administrative organizations;
2. between and among administrative organizations; and
3. between administrative organizations and actors outside the bureaucracy.

The term administrative organization is used here to refer to either a department or a non-departmental body (e.g., Crown corporation, regulatory agency, advisory council).

The Concept of Power

The key concept underlying the institutional framework, as well as the value framework discussed later, is one that is central to scholarly writings in political science, organization theory, and public administration, namely the concept of power. Social science literature contains various definitions and usages of power and the closely related concepts of influence, control, and authority.[2] It is generally agreed that power is a relational concept. It is, therefore, extremely useful for describing and explaining relations between and among organizations, groups, and individuals—and indeed, as we shall see, between and among governments. **Power** is defined here as "the capacity to secure the dominance of one's values or goals."[3] This definition is very similar to that of R.H. Tawney, who defined power as "the capacity of an individual, or group of individuals, to modify the conduct of other individuals or groups in the manner in which he desires, and to prevent his own being modified in a manner which he does not."[4]

Control and Influence

There are two forms of power, namely control and influence. **Control** refers to that form of power in which A has authority to direct or command B. For example, a deputy minister wields control over a subordinate when he or she exercises statutory or other authority to order the subordinate to act in a certain way. **Influence** is a more general and pervasive form of power than control. When B conforms to A's desires, values, or goals by suggestion, persuasion, emulation, or anticipation, then A exercises influence over B. For example, a deputy minister may influence another deputy minister by persuading him or her to take a particular action. Influence can sometimes cause power to flow in unexpected directions when administrative subordinates who possess special expertise in some field can exercise influence over hierarchical superiors in the form of "authority of expertise" or "expert power." Bachrach and Lawler assert that influence "is the mode of power that both gives subordinates the capability of manipulating superiors and gives superiors the capability of getting more from their subordinates than is specified in the formal role obligations."[5] They state also that "influence is two-directional in hierarchical relations, but it also applies to horizontal relations not lodged in an authority structure."[6] Thus, for example, influence is at work in interdepartmental and intergovernmental relations.

To exercise control, A must have authority in the sense of having access to the inducements, rewards, and sanctions necessary to back up commands. This is "authority of position" or "position power." A may also exercise influence over B through "authority of leadership" or "personal power," which involves the use of such means as persuasion, suggestion, and intimation rather than direction, supervision, and command. Moreover, authority of position puts A in a favourable position to exercise influence as a result of "the rule of anticipated reactions."[7] Application of this rule is evident in the innumerable instances in which administrative officials "anticipate the reactions" of those who have power to reward or constrain them. Officials tend to act in a fashion that would be applauded—or at least approved—by those whose favour they seek. Thus, those actors ordinarily perceived as exercising control (e.g., hierarchical superiors) can also exercise influence by affecting another actor's decisions in an informal, unofficial—even in an unintentional—way.[8] Heclo and Wildavsky's observation about the British government is equally applicable to Canada: "Most of the time on most issues, ministers, sitting alone at the top of their departmental empire, can exercise their political leadership only through civil servants' second-, third-, or fourth-hand anticipation of ministers' likely reactions."[9]

What distinguishes actors with the capacity to exercise both control and influence from those possessing only influence is that the former have at their disposal sanctions and inducements formalized by law and the organization chart. Influence over administrative organizations and over bureaucrats within these organizations can be exercised by those who do not have legally or formally sanctioned power to command or supervise. For example, pressure groups may seek favours from bureaucrats by offering inducements (e.g., gifts) or imposing penalties (e.g., criticism), but they have no legal or formal capacity to compel compliance to their wishes. This does not mean, however, that such influence cannot be as effective as control or, in some instances, even more effective. A bureaucrat may well grant special favours to pressure groups despite formal directions to the contrary from an administrative superior. Thus, influence can be exercised by those without either authority of position or authority of leadership through a variety of means, including persuasion, friendship, knowledge, and experience.

Internal and External Interactions

The preceding analysis provides the basis for the development of a framework showing the patterns of interaction both within administrative organizations and between these organizations and other participants in the public policy process. These interactions involve in large part the reciprocal exercise of power in the form of control and/or influence. From the perspective of any one organization, these interactions can be classified as internal, external-within government, and external-outside government. This classification is depicted in Figures 12. 1 and 12. 2.

Figure 12.1 consists of five concentric circles with the major actor—an

Figure 12.1
INTERNAL AND EXTERNAL INTERACTIONS OF
ADMINISTRATIVE ORGANIZATIONS

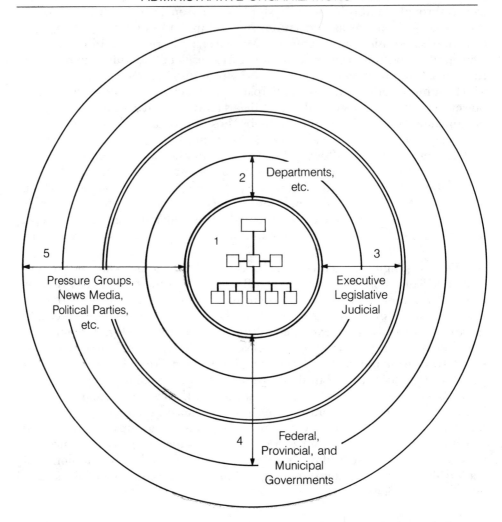

administrative organization—at the centre. The order in which these circles are labelled from the centre outward represents the organizational proximity of other actors to the organization. Proximity to the centre does not, however, indicate the extent of power exercised over the organization or over officials within the organization. For example, in some situations, a pressure group can exert more power over a department than a central agency can.

The innermost circle (circle one) depicts the internal pattern of interaction, that is, the administrative organization and its sub-units. For the sake of simplicity, the organization's administrative pyramid has been greatly compressed to indicate merely the major lines of interaction within the organization.

Circles two and three portray the external-within government pattern of interactions; this pattern includes those actors outside the organization but within the particular government under consideration (e.g., other administrative organizations, political executives, legislators, the courts).

The outer limit of circle three is the boundary between actors within and outside government—the external-outside government pattern of interaction. Circle four includes actors in other governments, either in the same sphere or in different spheres of government. Finally, circle five contains the broad range of non-governmental actors (e.g., pressure groups, political parties, journalists). Each of these categories of interaction is covered in later chapters of this part of the book.

This framework for classifying interactions involving bureaucrats and other policy actors is explained in greater detail in Figure 12.2. Here the framework is specifically applied to the parliamentary-Cabinet form of government as it operates in Canada's federal and provincial governments. The framework can be modified slightly to apply to the municipal sphere of government as well. In addition, the framework can be used to examine systematically the vertical and horizontal relations of administrative organizations with other relevant actors and to identify the participants and their interactions in a particular policy field.[10]

In Figure 12.2, the three broad patterns of interaction in the first column are subdivided to show the major categories of interaction in which an administrative organization may be involved, namely:

1. intraorganizational (e.g., intradepartmental)
2. interdepartmental
3. executive-bureaucratic
4. legislative-bureaucratic
5. judicial-bureaucratic
6. intergovernmental, and
7. governmental-non-governmental

These various categories of interaction are discussed in Chapters 15 to 21. Thus, the institutional framework provides the basis for organizing much of this part of the book.

Column three contains a further refinement of these categories into the potential actors in each category. Then column four lists the most significant means by which these actors can exercise control and influence (i.e., power) over one another. The interaction of these actors can be explained largely in terms of power relations, that is, relations between actors for the purpose of, or with the result of, affecting behaviour in a specific direction.

There is insufficient space in Figure 12.2 to provide a detailed list of the actors involved in the policy process and of their power resources (i.e., the means of control and influence available to them). It is evident, however, that column three could be subdivided to show the sub-units of the various actors (e.g., departmental divisions and sections, Cabinet committees, legislative committees). Further, an even finer subdivision could be achieved by identifying

Figure 12.2
INTERNAL AND EXTERNAL INTERACTIONS OF ADMINISTRATIVE ORGANIZATIONS

1 Broad Patterns of Interaction	2 Major Categories of Interaction	3 Actors	4 Power Resources
Internal	Intradepartmental	Line units Staff units Field units	
External (within government)	Interdepartmental	Administrative organization Other administrative organizations	
	Executive-bureaucratic	Administrative organization Prime Minister Cabinet Central Agencies	Expertise Experience Discretionary power Clientele support Appointment/removal powers Information and advice from central agencies Chairmanship of Cabinet
	Legislative-bureaucratic	Administrative organization Parliament Auditor General	
	Judicial-bureaucratic	Administrative organization Federal courts Provincial courts	
External (outside government)	Intergovernmental	Administrative organization Institutions and organizations of other levels of government Intergovernmental bodies	
	Governmental-non-governmental	Administrative organization Non-governmental organizations	

individual roles associated with each of the organizations or groups listed in column three (e.g., bureaucrats, ministers, legislators). The effective application of the framework to a particular administrative organization in a specific policy field (e.g., Health and Welfare in aging policy) would require these more detailed subdivisions. In column four, some elaboration is provided of the interaction between the administrative organization and the Prime Minister or a provincial Premier.

Power relations between administrative organizations and other actors flow in two directions. Bureaucrats are not defenceless against pressures brought to bear on them by actors outside the bureaucracy. An examination of the real or potential impact of controls and influences over the bureaucracy must take account of the potent resources that bureaucrats can use to resist pressure and to exert power over others. Among the resources that bureaucrats possess to control and/or influence other actors are expertise, experience, budgetary allocations, confidential information, and discretionary powers to develop and implement policies and programs. These resources may be utilized in various ways. For example, bureaucrats may prevail over political superiors by virtue of special knowledge of a policy area (authority of expertise); they may feed selected bits of information to journalists to enhance support for a certain program; or they may disarm external critics by organizing them into advisory bodies.

In summary, the institutional framework can serve several purposes. First, it provides a means of examining interactions among participants in the public policy process and it places administrative organizations at the centre of these interactions. Second, it can be applied at any level of government and can focus attention on a specific administrative body or a specific policy field. Third, it is a heuristic device in that it portrays and suggests relationships that might otherwise be overlooked. Fourth, it is based on a concept in the social science literature that is central to understanding relations between and among governments, institutions, organizations, groups, and individuals, namely the concept of power. Fifth, it utilizes insights from conceptual and theoretical writings in organization theory and provides a linkage between intra- and interorganizational relations. Finally, it provides a systematic way of collecting, ordering, and analyzing data.

THE VALUE FRAMEWORK

Values are enduring beliefs that influence the choices made by individuals, groups, or organizations from among available means or ends. Values are organized into value systems, in which values are ranked in terms of their relative importance. Thus, the bureaucrat has a value system or value framework in which various social, political, administrative, and personal values are ranked, admittedly very roughly, even unconsciously, in order of importance. The focus here is on *administrative*, or *public service*, values.

A review of Canadian administrative history shows that among the most important administrative values are neutrality, accountability, efficiency, effectiveness, responsiveness, representativeness, and integrity. Moreover, in the past few decades, equity (or fairness) has become an increasingly central administrative value. Since each of these values is discussed in one or more of the subsequent chapters, only a brief explanation of them is provided here.

Neutrality

As explained in the next chapter, it is essential to distinguish between political neutrality, in the sense of non-partisanship, and value neutrality. Most bureaucrats preserve their neutrality in terms of partisan politics; they cannot, however, reasonably be expected to be value neutral because they are actively involved in politics in the broad sense of the authoritative allocation of values for society. The value system of individual bureaucrats is central to an analysis of bureaucratic behaviour and bureaucratic power, because they *cannot* be completely value neutral in making and recommending decisions. Indeed, bureaucrats have never been value neutral and they have become less so as their discretionary powers have increased. Many of the decisions they make oblige them, or give them the opportunity, to inject their own views as to which values should take priority. The difficulty of ensuring the responsible exercise of power under these circumstances helps to explain the importance of accountability.

Accountability

The quest for **administrative accountability** arises largely from the fact that bureaucrats are not value neutral. Accountability involves concern for the legal, institutional, and procedural means by which bureaucrats can be obliged to answer for their actions. It is a pervasive theme in this book both because it has been one of the major values in the evolution of Canadian public administration and because of its current importance. Indeed, the present emphasis on accountability threatens to minimize the importance of such other administrative values as effectiveness and responsiveness.

Efficiency and Effectiveness

Despite the current concern with accountability, the most consistently dominant value in Canadian public administration over the broad sweep of the twentieth century has been efficiency. Moreover, much of the emphasis on accountability has really been directed to holding public bureaucrats accountable for the efficient and effective use of public funds. The values of efficiency and effectiveness are interdependent but distinct in meaning. **Efficiency** is a measure of performance that may be expressed as a ratio between input and output. **Effectiveness** is a measure of the extent to which an activity achieves the organization's objectives. Thus, efficiency and effectiveness may complement one another, but they may also conflict. For example, the construction of a thousand houses for native people at an appropriate cost and quality, and on schedule, may be an efficient and effective operation. The completion of these houses long after they are needed is efficient, but ineffective. The timely construction of adequate homes at very high cost is effective but inefficient.

There has been increasing emphasis, especially since the late 1960s, on the so-called three E's—economy, efficiency, and effectiveness. During this period, however, effectiveness has gradually superseded economy as the major companion value of efficiency. The Treasury Board has been the prime mover in promoting efficiency and effectiveness throughout the public service. The board has supported the introduction of more sophisticated techniques of achieving and assessing efficiency and effectiveness, including the planning-programming-budgeting system, cost-benefit analysis, the operational performance measurement system, management by objectives, and program evaluation. The Office of the Comptroller General, which was established in 1978, has the responsibility of developing systems to stimulate the efficiency and effectiveness of government operations, in part by designing and promoting procedures for program evaluation. Moreover, the Auditor General Act of 1977 broadens the Auditor General's powers to include reporting on instances where money has been spent without "due regard to economy or efficiency" or where "satisfactory procedures have not been established to measure and report the effectiveness of programs, where such procedures could appropriately and reasonably be implemented." Elaboration on the role of these various managerial techniques and administrative organizations, in relation to the pursuit of efficiency and effectiveness, is provided in Chapters 26 and 27.

Responsiveness

Administrative responsiveness refers to the inclination and the capacity of public servants to respond to the needs and demands of both political institutions and the public. Thus, public servants are expected to be responsive to two major groups of participants in the political system. The first group includes political executives and legislators; the second includes the general public as well as various "publics," that is, groups and individuals affected by the decisions and recommendations of public servants.

Administrative responsiveness is usually discussed in relation to the second group of participants. The Royal Commission on Government Organization (the Glassco Commission) concluded that "the importance to the public of efficiency and integrity in the machinery of government . . . is unquestionably great. . . . But even greater is the importance of a service responsive to public wants and expectations."[11] As noted in Chapter 21, a major purpose of the movement for increased public participation is greater government responsiveness to the public's wants and needs. Public servants may be required to reconcile responsiveness with such other values as accountability and efficiency. For example, the emphasis on these latter two values during times of financial restraint in government is usually to the detriment of administrative responsiveness to the public.

Representativeness

A representative public service is one in which employees are drawn proportionately from the major ethnic, religious, socio-economic, and other groups in society. Representativeness in the public service is closely tied to several other administrative values. For example, the argument is frequently made that a more representative public service is a more responsive public service. In the belief that the attitudes of representatives of a group will be similar to the attitudes of the whole group, a representative public service is deemed to be more responsive to the needs of the public and more effective in giving policy advice. However, it is also argued that if efforts to achieve a representative public service mean that the most meritorious persons are not hired, the efficiency and effectiveness of the service will be adversely affected. Thus, as we shall see in Chapter 24, the representativeness of the public service is tightly tied to the issues of equal opportunity, affirmative action, and employment equity.

Integrity

Integrity refers here to ethics in public administration. The integrity of public servants is extremely important to the preservation of public trust and confidence in government. Recent experience in Canada and elsewhere indicates that increased vigilance is required to ensure that public servants adhere to high ethical standards. Chapter 14 provides evidence that the ethical dimension in public administration is a very pervasive one, and that governments are paying increased attention to the various means by which ethical conduct can be maintained and nurtured.

Equity

For most practical purposes, the terms equity and fairness can be used interchangeably. We shall see in Chapter 13 that equity is a central theme in the new public administration movement, and in Chapter 23 that it is one of the major values to be balanced in determining the merit of persons seeking appointment to the public service. As explained in Chapter 18, the courts and governments are increasingly putting greater emphasis on procedural fairness. Considerations of procedural fairness have gradually expanded beyond the boundaries of administrative law to the administrative processes of the public service. Public servants are increasingly expected—or required—to consider whether their decisions and recommendations are fair both in substance and procedure. This heightened emphasis on fairness and equity is based largely on recognition of the significant power that public servants exercise over the rights and livelihood of individual citizens.

There is a complementary relationship between the values of fairness and responsiveness in that procedural fairness could be said to require that public servants be responsive to the public through various mechanisms for public participation. It is equally obvious that fairness can clash with such values as efficiency and effectiveness.

The Clash of Values

The relative importance of administrative values varies according to "the situation," that is, according to the particular circumstances of time, place, and policy within which value choices are made. The bureaucrat seeking guidance as to the appropriate content of his or her administrative value system will find much advice, but little solace, in scholarly writings. Different authors single out different administrative values.

The dominant administrative values of a society, which will be reflected in administrative performance, depend on political, economic, and social conditions in that society. Moreover, the relative importance of these values alters with changes in these conditions. For example, the administrative values of representativeness and responsiveness may become predominant during a period when the general public or the government feels that the interests of certain disadvantaged minority groups must be better represented, and their needs and demands better understood and satisfied. During such a period, considerations of efficiency and neutrality may be relegated to a secondary order of importance.

Facts and Values

If an administrative issue is significant enough to require the conscious preparation of alternative solutions and the evaluation of their possible consequences, each alternative will be an amalgam of what Herbert Simon refers to as the value and factual elements in any decision.[12] The mix of fact and value will, of course, vary greatly from one decision-making circumstance to another. Many decisions of a very routine and repetitive nature (programmed decisions) require little, if any, conscious value selection. Other decisions of a unique or novel nature (nonprogrammed decisions) may contain a substantial mix of value and factual elements. As Simon contends:

> Decisions are something more than factual propositions. To be sure, they are descriptive of a future state of affairs, and this description can be true or false in a strictly empirical sense; but they possess, in addition, an imperative quality—they select one future state of affairs in preference to another and direct behaviour toward the chosen alternative. In short, they have an *ethical* as well as a factual content.[13]

Sources of the Bureaucrat's Values

A focus on the bureaucrat's values is especially important in that bureaucratic behaviour may be explained or interpreted in terms of the interplay (1) among the individual bureaucrat's values, and (2) between the bureaucrat's values and the values of those with whom he or she interacts. Before an individual joins the public service, his or her general value system, as well as particular attitudes and orientations toward the public service, are moulded by powerful and enduring forces. This is accomplished through the process of **socialization**, i.e., "an individual's learning from others in his environment the social patterns and values of his culture."[14] The socializing "agencies" involved in this process include family, peer groups, schools, prior employment, and adult organizations. As a result of this socialization experience, an individual does not take up government employment with a *tabula rasa* so far as values relevant to bureaucratic decision-making are concerned. In varying degrees, the several socializing agencies continue to affect the bureaucrat's values during his or her public service career.

However, the bureaucratic organization that employs the individual is itself a powerful socializing agent. The individual's personal values and perceptions of the public service are altered by a process of **organizational socialization** that begins the very day he or she is recruited for a public service position. Organizational socialization refers to the process through which the individual learns the expectations attached to the position he or she occupies in the organization, and selectively internalizes as values some of the expectations of those with whom he or she interacts.

THE CRUCIAL LINK

It is at this juncture that the theoretical link between the value framework and the institutional framework can be demonstrated. The bureaucrat is expected to be responsive to the values of the various policy participants as these values are expressed through the exercise of specific controls and influences. The policy participants shown in Figure 12.2 are then the primary sources of the official's administrative values.

Since various policy participants pursue different, and sometimes mutually exclusive, ends in their relations with bureaucrats, the bureaucrat will be the object of conflicting expectations and pressures as to his or her behaviour. The purpose of each participant's interaction with the bureaucrat will usually be the dominance of the participant's particular values and goals over those of both the bureaucrat and other participants. The problem for the bureaucrat is clearly posed—how can he or she be responsive to the multiplicity of values expressed?

The linkages between the institutional and the value frameworks help to explain the means by which the number and assortment of variables impinging on the bureaucrat may be reduced to more manageable proportions.

Over a considerable period of time, and in a variety of bureaucratic positions, an official might conceivably interact with virtually the whole range of policy participants, and be subjected to a wide variety of controls and influences. As the incumbent of a specific position over a shorter period, an official will, however, only interact with, and be subjected to the power resources of, a limited number of actors. The range of these actors will be confined to those with a stake in either the activities of the official or the issue at hand. For example, a deputy minister of consumer and corporate affairs is the object of much greater pressure from outside the public service (e.g., interest groups and journalists) than a deputy minister of supply and services. More importantly, during the process of organizational socialization, the bureaucrat learns what kinds of behaviour will bring reward or punishment from various policy actors and what values they are seeking to realize. The bureaucrat's value system is usually most directly moulded by the values of those hierarchical associates on whom he or she relies most heavily for approval and reward, that is, political and administrative superiors and peers and subordinates. The bureaucrat is also expected, of course, to be responsive to the values of such other policy actors as legislators, interest group representatives, and the general public. Faced with complementary, conflicting, and contradictory expectations issuing from various sources, the bureaucrat can inculcate only some of the values manifested by those with whom he or she interacts.

This socialization experience can provide enormous practical and psychological benefits for the bureaucrat. Over time, the bureaucrat internalizes not only a commitment to certain administrative values, but also a commitment to the correctness of applying a value or a set of values to specific situations. He or she develops a value framework that facilitates the making of decisions because there is a point beyond which he or she will not go in contemplating, much less yielding to, pressures in his or her decision-making environment. The bureaucrat will refuse to examine the pre-set value system *a priori* in each decision situation and will be predisposed to accept or reject the exercise of power (i.e., control and influence) from certain directions.

The existence of this value framework for individual decision-making relates also to the earlier discussion of the resources available to bureaucrats to withstand the exercise of power by other policy participants. The situation in which the official chooses to wield countervailing power and the resources he or she selects to control or influence others are, in very large measure, determined by this value system.

Value Conflict

Despite efforts to minimize the number of variables involved in any given decision-making situation, value conflict is a frequent condition, especially for senior bureaucrats. Herbert Simon contends that at the lower levels of the organization, the framework for decision-making is usually well established in that "the factors to be evaluated have already been enumerated, and all that remains is to determine their values under the given circumstances."[15] At the senior levels of the organization, however, "the task is an inventive one. New values must be sought out and weighed; the possibilities of new administrative structures evaluated. The very framework of reference within which each decision is to take place must be constructed."[16]

The major categories of value conflicts that bureaucrats encounter are those

1. between personal values and administrative values;
2. between and among administrative values; and
3. between administrative values and the values of other policy participants.

The resolution of value conflicts involving personal and administrative values (e.g., ambition vs. accountability or avarice vs. integrity) depends on the personality and character of the particular bureaucrat. Anthony Downs contends that "most officials are significantly motivated by self-interest when their social function is to serve the public interest."[17] He provides a typology of public servants ranging from "purely self-interested officials" (i.e., climbers and conservers) through to "mixed-motive officials" (i.e., zealots, advocates, and statesmen). Statesmen are the least self-seeking and most public-oriented of bureaucrats. They are "motivated by loyalty to society as a whole and a desire to obtain the power necessary to have a significant influence upon national policies and actions. They are altruistic to a high degree because their loyalty is to the 'general welfare' as they see it."[18] The "statesman" type of public servant will have comparatively little difficulty reconciling personal and administrative values, but will occasionally be obliged to choose between and among administrative values he or she holds equally dear (e.g., accountability vs. integrity or accountability vs. responsiveness). Similarly, bureaucrats' values come into conflict with the values held by those with whom they interact (e.g., accountability vs. responsiveness to an interest group's request or accountability vs. efficiency expected by a professional colleague).

Bureaucrats may conceivably pass through one, two, or all three stages of value conflict. In practice, of course, these stages are not chronological; rather, they overlap and interact with one another. Thus, a choice between the administrative values of accountability and responsiveness is likely to be made in conjunction with, and to be affected by, controls and influences reflecting the values of other policy actors. We shall see in Chapter 14 that there is an intimate connection between the resolution of value conflicts and the concept of the public interest.

In summary, the role of the bureaucracy in the public policy process can be illuminated by using the institutional and value frameworks outlined above. The institutional framework may be used separately to examine relationships among bureaucratic actors and between these actors and other participants in the policy process. The value framework complements the institutional framework by showing that the values of individual bureaucrats are significantly affected by the values of those actors who exercise power over them. Thus, the frameworks facilitate the study of issues and concepts in public administration, where an essential basis for further analysis is knowledge of interactions within the bureaucracy and between the bureaucracy and other policy actors. The frameworks are especially useful for examining the nature and extent of coordination within and between governments.[19]

COORDINATION

The foregoing analysis provides a useful basis for examining the concept of **coordination**, which is critically important in the making and administration of public policy in Canada. The Prime Minister, at the centre of the machinery of government, looks out on a vast constellation of administrative organizations ranging from operating departments through central agencies, Crown corporations, and regulatory agencies to advisory councils and Royal commissions. Moreover, beyond the bounds of the federal government is an even larger number of administrative organizations in the provincial and municipal spheres of government with which the federal government must deal. Provincial Premiers face a similar but somewhat smaller array of organizations.

Coordination of both the formulation and implementation of public policy is widely viewed as essential to efficient, effective, and responsive government, and is considered especially desirable during periods of financial restraint. Also, public officials (whether politicians or bureaucrats) have become actively involved in coordination through consultative processes with persons and groups affected by official decisions. Consequently, in recent years greater attention has been paid to the coordination of the activities of administrative organizations and to coordination between governments and policy actors outside government. In addition, the challenge of managing intergovernmental relations, especially in federal states, requires increasingly vigorous efforts to coordinate the activities of organizations and officials in two or more orders of government.

Both the general public and public officials frequently bewail the absence or inadequacy of coordination in government. Coordination is often viewed as a means of ensuring that appropriate policy and program decisions are made, duplication and overlap are avoided, and effective and responsive services are provided. It is important, therefore, to dash false hopes and unrealistic expectations about the nature and utility of coordination. It is not a panacea for such government ills as inefficiency, ineffectiveness, and unresponsiveness. Nor is it a substitute for shared values and goals among participants in the policy process. It is evident that coordination can be used to achieve different and sometimes conflicting values and goals (for example, efficiency and responsiveness).

The Meaning of Coordination

Coordination is an extremely elusive and pervasive concept. It is a process in which two or more parties take one another into account for the purpose of bringing their decisions and/or activities into harmonious or reciprocal relation. Thus, policy coordination is a process in which two or more policy actors take one another into account for the purpose of bringing their decisions and/or activities with respect to policy development and implementation into harmonious or reciprocal relation. This process can be formal or informal, and it can be pursued both within administrative organizations and between these organizations and other policy actors.

Virtues and Limitations of Coordination

The curative effects of coordination can be impressive but they are limited. Requirements that coordination be sought through time-consuming consultative techniques (for example, through extensive citizen participation) can lead to delay and indecision that may aggravate, rather than remedy, a problem. Also, the process of coordination can lead to over-coordination. A convincing case can be made that redundancy in the form of duplication and overlap often serves a valuable purpose.[20] Landau contends that " 'streamlining an agency,' 'consolidating similar functions,' 'eliminating duplication,' and 'commonality' are powerful slogans . . . But it is just possible that their achievement would deprive an agency of the properties it needs most—those which allow rules to be broken and units to operate defectively without doing critical injury to the agency as a whole."[21]

Coordination is sought and attained not simply through formal structures and processes, but also through informal relations between and among policy actors. Moreover, it is often difficult to know when coordination is actually taking place. Charles Lindblom argues persuasively that through a process of **partisan mutual adjustment** a very large measure of coordination in government occurs without any deliberate, conscious attempt to coordinate. He contends that there are no coordinators in this process; rather, coordination comes about as "a by-product of ordinary decisions, that is, of decisions not specifically intended to coordinate."[22] He distinguishes this process from that of central coordination whereby, for the most part, "decision makers adapt to one another on instruction from a central decision maker."[23] He acknowledges also the existence of situations characterized by a mixture of central coordination and partisan mutual adjustment "where somebody can be both a central supervisor to a degree and a mutual adjuster."[24]

While central coordination is sought primarily through the exercise of control, partisan mutual adjustment is pursued through a broad range of techniques, most of which (e.g., negotiation, bargaining) require the exercise of influence. Lindblom's mixture of central coordination and mutual adjustment, which is commonly found within public organizations and frequently within government as a whole, involves the use of both control and influence. In a later work, Lindblom states that some political systems, such as the British, "rely more heavily on central coordination" whereas other systems, such as the American, depend "more heavily on mutual adjustment."[25] Canada's political system, like that of Britain, relies more on central coordination than mutual adjustment. His analysis, which has been greatly simplified here, indicates the large extent to which coordination is achieved as a result of the exercise of power for other purposes.

Lindblom acknowledges the utility of central coordination and recognizes that governments cannot rely solely on partisan mutual adjustment. We shall see in subsequent chapters that formal coordinating activities by governments are often needed to supplement coordination sought or attained by other means.

NOTES

1. Although it is analytically convenient to speak of decisions being made by institutions and organizations, decisions are in reality made by individuals and groups within these institutions and organizations.
2. For example, some writers use the terms power and influence interchangeably; other writers distinguish power from influence by interpreting power as a force backed by coercive authority. Note that Max Weber "used *power* to refer to the ability to induce acceptance of orders; *legitimation* to refer to the acceptance of the exercise of power because it is in line with values held by the subjects; and *authority* to refer to the combination of the two—i.e., to power that is viewed as legitimate." Amitai Etzioni, *Modern Organizations* (Englewood Cliffs, N.J.: Prentice-Hall, 1964), p. 51.
3. John F. Pfiffner and Frank P. Sherwood, *Administrative Organization* (Englewood Cliffs, N.J.: Prentice-Hall, 1960), p. 77.
4. *Equality* (London: G. Allen and Unwin, 1931), p. 229.
5. Samuel B. Bachrach and Edward J. Lawler, *Power and Politics in Organizations* (San Francisco: Jossey-Bass Publishers, 1980), p. 41.
6. Ibid.
7. The best single treatment of this concept may be found in Carl J. Friedrich, *Man and His Government* (New York: McGraw Hill, 1963), ch. 11.
8. Some organizational theorists distinguish between "formal" and "informal" controls. In the context of our definition of control and influence and throughout this book, all controls are of a formal nature; informal controls are subsumed under the broad definition of influences.
9. *The Private Government of Public Money: Community and Policy Inside British Politics* (Berkeley: University of California Press, 1974), p. 376.
10. For an application of the framework to the policy field of aging, see Kenneth Kernaghan and Olivia Kuper, *Coordination in Canadian Governments: A Case Study of Aging Policy* (Toronto: Institute of Public Administration of Canada, 1983).
11. Canada, Royal Commission on Government Organization, *Report* 1: 63 (Ottawa: Queen's Printer, 1962).
12. Herbert A. Simon, *Administrative Behaviour*, 2nd ed. (New York, The Free Press, 1957), pp. 45-60.
13. Ibid., p. 46.
14. Kenneth P. Langton, *Political Socialization* (New York: Oxford University Press, 1969), p. 3.
15. Herbert Simon, *Administrative Behaviour*, 2nd ed. (New York: The Free Press, 1957), p. 217.
16. Ibid.
17. Anthony Downs, *Inside Bureaucracy* (Boston: Little, Brown, 1967), p. 87.
18. Ibid., p. 88.
19. See, for example, Kernaghan and Kuper, *Coordination in Canadian Governments*.
20. See Martin Landau, "Redundancy, Rationality and the Problem of Duplication and Overlap," *Public Administration Review* 29 (July-August 1969): 346-358.
21. Ibid., 356.
22. *The Intelligence of Democracy* (New York: The Free Press, 1965), p. 9.

23. Ibid., p. 25.
24. Ibid., p. 27.
25. *The Policy-Making Process* (Englewood Cliffs, N.J.: Prentice-Hall, 1968), p. 82.

BIBLIOGRAPHY

Aucoin, Peter. "Portfolio Structures and Policy Coordination." In G. Bruce Doern and Peter Aucoin, eds., *Public Policy in Canada*. Toronto: Macmillan, 1979.

Bachrach, Samuel B., and Edward J. Lawler. *Power and Politics in Organizations*. San Francisco: Jossey-Bass Publishers, 1980.

Downs, Anthony. *Inside Bureaucracy*. Boston: Little, Brown, 1967.

Dunsire, Andrew. *Control in a Bureaucracy*. Oxford: Martin Robertson, 1978.

Gilbert, Charles. "The Framework of Administrative Responsibility." *The Journal of Politics* 21 (August 1959): 373-407.

Kernaghan, Kenneth, and Olivia Kuper. *Coordination in Canadian Governments: A Case Study of Aging Policy*. Toronto: Institute of Public Administration of Canada, 1983.

Landau, Martin. "Redundancy, Rationality and the Problem of Duplication and Overlap. *Public Administration Review* 29 (July-August 1969): 346-58.

Lindblom, Charles E. *The Policy-Making Process*. Englewood Cliffs, N.J.: Prentice Hall, 1968.

Lindblom, Charles E. *The Intelligence of Democracy*. New York: The Free Press, 1965.

Litwak, Eugene, and Lydia F. Hylton. "Interorganizational Analysis: A Hypothesis on Coordinating Agencies." *Administrative Science Quarterly* 6 (1962): 395-420.

Marrett, Cora Bagley. "On the Specification of Interorganizational Dimensions." *Sociology and Social Research* 56 (1971): 39-97.

Simon, Herbert A. *Administrative Behaviour*. 2nd ed. New York: The Free Press, 1957.

Wamsley, Gary L., and Mayer N. Zald. *The Political Economy of Public Organizations* Bloomington, Ind.: Indiana University Press, 1976. p. 83.

13

Power, Politics, and Bureaucracy

BUREAUCRATIC POWER

Power was defined in the previous chapter as "the capacity to secure the dominance of one's values or goals." In this sense, public servants wield substantial power by virtue of their role in policy development and execution. If the machinery of government could be arranged so that bureaucrats simply implemented laws spelled out in very specific terms by the legislature, enforced judicial decisions interpreting these laws, and administered policies and programs under the close supervision of political executives, few value problems would exist for most bureaucrats. The realm of politics and policy would belong to elected representatives and would be sharply delineated from the administrative sphere. The value issues in any situation would be worked out by others so that the bureaucrat's primary concern would be to adhere to those values emerging from the executive, legislative, and judicial spheres of government.

The historical record shows that an era of such bureaucratic innocence has never existed in modern democratic states. There is, in reality, much room for the injection of the public servants' values into decisions and recommendations. It is generally acknowledged that public servants exercise significant power in both the development and execution of policy. In a lecture on the threat to parliamentary responsible government, Robert Stanfield, a former leader of the Progressive Conservative Party, stated that "while the House of Commons has been losing control, so also has the Government. The ministers just do not have the time to run such a vast show and make such a vast range of decisions. Consequently, more and more is for all practical purposes being decided by and implemented by the bureaucracy."[1] And in a reminiscence on thirty years as a senior public servant and a minister, Mitchell Sharp observed that

> top public servants are powerful persons in the machinery of government at the federal level. They wield great influence. They do so because they are, in the main, professionals who have been selected for their proven administrative ability and who devote their full time to government. In many cases, they have a greater influence upon the course of events than have Ministers, particularly the weaker and less competent."[2]

The extent of this bureaucratic power clearly varies in accordance with such factors as the government's view of the proper role of public servants in the political process, the policy or program under consideration, the department or agency involved, and the style and competence of ministers and their officials.

The Concept and Practice of Political Neutrality[3]

A framework for examining the power of public servants may be devised by utilizing the concept of political neutrality. **Political neutrality** is a constitutional doctrine or convention according to which public servants should avoid activities that are likely to impair—or seem to impair—their political impartiality or the impartiality of the public service. The several interrelated ideas traditionally associated with the notion of political neutrality provide a useful model for examining the nature of interaction between public servants and other actors in the political system. The model also permits a consideration of the changing nature of bureaucratic power and of the role of public servants in the policy process. The major elements of the traditional doctrine may be summarized as follows:

1. politics and policy are separated from administration: thus politicians make policy decisions; public servants execute these decisions;
2. public servants are appointed and promoted on the basis of merit rather than of party affiliation or contributions;
3. public servants do not engage in partisan political activities;
4. public servants do not express publicly their personal views on government policies or administration;
5. public servants provide forthright and objective advice to their political masters in private and in confidence; in return, political executives protect the anonymity of public servants by publicly accepting responsibility for departmental decisions; and
6. public servants execute policy decisions loyally, irrespective of the philosophy and programs of the party in power and regardless of their personal opinions; as a result, public servants enjoy security of tenure during good behaviour and satisfactory performance.

As a means of explaining the nature and extent of bureaucratic power in the Canadian political system, each of these six elements will be examined separately below. Special attention is centred on the degree to which actual practice has departed from the requirements of the model. Note that this is an ideal-type model in that it describes the relations between politicians and bureaucrats in a government characterized by absolute political neutrality.

(1) Politics and Administration

The politics-administration dichotomy. The political neutrality of public servants has traditionally rested on the possibility of a separation between politics and administration, and on a related distinction between policy and administration.

Frequently, the two dichotomies are treated as synonymous—as if the terms politics and policy are interchangeable. The scope of activity covered by the term politics is, however, much broader than that embraced by the term policy. "*Politics* is concerned, throughout the sphere of government, with the whole business of deciding what to do and getting it done. *Policy* is the decision as to what to do; *administration* is getting it done."[4] According to the **politics-administration dichotomy,** political executives and legislators are concerned with the formation of policy, and public servants are concerned with its implementation. Policy decisions are political; administrative decisions are non-political. However, abundant evidence points to the important political and policy-advisory roles of public servants.

The distinction between politics and policy on the one hand and administration on the other has been central to the evolution of both the study and the practice of public administration. V. Seymour Wilson, who uses interchangeably the terms politics-administration dichotomy and policy-administration dichotomy, states that the dichotomy

> remains a powerful philosophy...It has guided, and will continue to guide, many aspects of the actions and perceptions of politicians, public servants and the public...The policy/administration dichotomy has a profound influence on just about every aspect of theory and practice in public policy and administration.[5]

From 1887 to the end of the Second World War, most prominent writers on public administration wrote within a framework of a dichotomy between politics and administration. Woodrow Wilson's celebrated essay of 1887 on "The Study of Administration" is usually taken as the point of departure for academic and theoretical writing on public administration in North America. In his essay, Wilson asserted that

> the field of administration is a field of business. It is removed from the hurry and strife of politics...administrative questions are not political questions..."Policy does nothing without the aid of administration," but administration is not therefore politics.[6]

Wilson's distinction between politics and administration was accepted and perpetuated by such other pioneers as Frank Goodnow (1914), L.D. White (1926), and W.F. Willoughby (1927). In their writings, "the politics-administration dichotomy was assumed both as a self-evident truth and a desirable goal; administration was perceived as a self-contained world of its own, with its own separate values, rules and methods."[7] Set in proper historical perspective, these questionable views are more comprehensible.

During the late nineteenth and early twentieth centuries, administrative reform efforts in both the United States and Canada were devoted to eradicating patronage from the government service, with a view to promoting efficient administration. A separate but overlapping development that had its origins in industrial organization in the United States was the "scientific management" movement described in Chapter 3. This movement, which pursued efficiency in large-scale organizations by seeking the most rational means—the "one best way"—of performing any organizational task, had an enormous impact on the civil service reform movement in the United States. The tenets of the scientific management movement spread not only throughout the United States but also to Canada and several European countries.

In both the United States and Canada, the two elements of the reform movement—efficiency through the elimination of patronage and efficiency through scientific management—reinforced one another and became integral components of the merit system. In Canada, the 1917-18 Report of the Civil Service Commission noted that the merit system in the Canadian civil service "consisted of two distinct parts: the first is concerned with the selection and appointment of individuals 'without regard to their politics, religion or influence'; the second is concerned with 'applying the methods of scientific employment to maintain the efficiency of these selected employees after they enter the service.' "[8] While the Civil Service Act of 1918 was a landmark event in establishing a merit system for the Canadian public service, political interference with the application of the system hindered efforts to eliminate patronage appointments.

Although there were no Canadian counterparts to American writers on public administration who articulated the notion of a separation between politics and administration, Canadian reformers operated within a similar framework. Implicit in their efforts to remove partisan political considerations from appointments to the public service was acceptance of the possibility and desirability of separating politics from administration—at least insofar as staffing the service was concerned. For example, the 1917-1918 Report of the Civil Service Commission stated that the purpose of the 1918 Civil Service Act was to promote "efficiency and economy in the *non-political* Civil Service."[9]

Concurrent with this pursuit of impartial and efficient administration was a steady growth in the discretionary powers of public servants. While efficient staffing of the service required the separation of politics and administration, the need for effective development and execution of public policy drew administrative officials into the political maelstrom—not in the sense of partisan activity but in the sense of involvement in the authoritative allocation of values for society. Public servants formulated rules and regulations to put flesh on the skeleton of vaguely worded statutes, enforced these rules and regulations, and adjudicated disputes arising from this enforcement. Moreover, the complicated and technical nature of public policy issues meant that political executives had to rely increasingly on public servants for policy advice and for the management of large-scale public organizations.

During the 1930s, writers on public administration who recognized the significant and growing political role of the bureaucracy lived uncomfortably with the textbook dichotomy between politics and administration.[10] The dichotomy came under increasing attack during the war years as many scholars gained practical administrative experience in government. Shortly after the war, a number of political scientists launched a devastating assault on the notion that politics and administration were, or could be, separated. Among this group of post-war authors, Paul Appleby stands out for his defence of the proposition that "public administration is policy making... Public administration is one of a number of basic political processes."[11] In less celebrated and more broadly focussed works than those written by American authors, British and Canadian writers during this same period demonstrated a growing recognition of the blurring of the traditional constitutional line between politicians and bureaucrats in the parliamentary-Cabinet system of government.

By 1960, the interdependence of politics and administration had been enshrined in the theoretical literature on public administration and accepted by the major actors in the political system. By this time, however, recognition of the reality of bureaucratic power in the political process led to suggestions that public servants should assume the task and the orientation of "agents of social change." Public servants were encouraged to promote new and creative innovations and solutions in social policy by aggregating and articulating the needs of unorganized and disadvantaged groups (for example, consumers, the poor), and by stimulating groups and individuals to make demands on government for remedies to their social and economic ills. It was clear that public servants who undertook such activities were likely to clash on occasion with political and administrative superiors who did not perceive the proper role of a public servant to be an active initiator of social change. The basic question was the extent to which appointed public officials could, or should, share with elected representatives the responsibility for stimulating and responding to social change. Discussion of public servants as social change agents was intermingled with the movement for increased citizen participation in government decision-making. This movement brought both politicians and public servants into more direct contact and confrontation with the general citizenry.

In the United States, these and other developments culminated in the late 1960s in a loose confederation of scholars and practitioners seeking a **new public administration**.[12] Among the major concerns of the advocates of this movement were social equity, sensitivity to, and representation of, disadvantaged minority groups, increased citizen participation in government decision-making, and new forms of public organization.

The relevance of the new public administration movement for the relation between politics and administration was that some of its supporters called for a reformulation of the traditional roles of politicians and public servants.[13] It was argued that public servants, because of their expertise and experience, and their close contacts with members of the public, are better qualified than political executives or legislators to determine the public interest. Public servants must, however, establish a value system with a focus on human dignity or administrative humanism; they should not simply reflect the values of their political masters. Implicit also was a resistance to political control over public administration. The new public administration movement drew attention to the actual and potential power of public servants, and to the importance of their value system for decision-making in government; however, it did not resolve—indeed, it complicated—the issue of finding an appropriate balance between the power of public servants and that of elected representatives.

Thus, the scholarly literature on public administration records an evolution since 1945 from a situation where only a few writers recognized the necessary involvement of public servants in politics to a situation where a few writers suggested that leadership in policy development rightly belongs to public servants rather than to politicians. The new public administration movement had little spillover effect on the study and practice of public administration in Canada. Nevertheless, scholars and practitioners in Canada are acutely aware that the line between politics and administration has become increasingly indistinct as both politicians and public servants participate actively in policy development. Moreover, the line is a fluctuating one, characterized by the expansion of bureaucratic power and the gradual politicization of the public service.

Policy development and policy implementation. Since the political role of public servants is attributed primarily to their contribution to policy development, much attention in the literature has focussed on the intermingling of policy and administration. The conventional view that a clear division may be made between policy and administration has always been a fiction, but has become increasingly untenable with the continuing growth of government activities and bureaucratic power. The terms policy and administration are of limited use in distinguishing between the roles of political executives (i.e. Cabinet ministers) and public servants because political executives and public servants are jointly involved in the administration of policy. Gordon Robertson, former Clerk of the Privy Council, observed:

> I can hardly claim to be capable of complete objectivity. It would be easier to achieve such detachment if I could shelter behind the dictum so solemnly delivered from editorial pages and professorial podia that politicians, and not civil servants, make policy and civil servants, and not politicians, apply it. It is unfortunate that so clear and helpful a distinction should have so little truth about it.[14]

In the late 1970s, public administration scholars began to study more vigorously "the missing link" in the policy-making process, namely policy implementation.[15] It is now widely recognized that the power of bureaucrats is greatly enhanced by their dominant role in program implementation and service delivery. Subsequent discussion will, therefore, examine the exercise of bureaucratic power in both policy formation and policy implementation.

Writers on bureaucratic power have long recognized the enormous influence of bureaucrats on policy *formation*. Senior public servants in particular make significant discretionary decisions as to the policy options to be set before their political masters. Moreover, in the development and presentation of policy proposals, these public servants are expected to be attuned to the *political*, as well as the administrative, financial, and technical implications of their recommendations. By the late 1960s, the power of public servants in policy development was perceived to be so great that Prime Minister Trudeau endeavoured to place more policy-making power in the hands of politically accountable authorities, especially Cabinet ministers. To this end, the Cabinet committee system and the parliamentary committee system were reformed, the coordinating capacity of the Privy Council Office was strengthened, and the policy influence of the Prime Minister's Office was expanded. The use of such alternative sources of policy advice as task forces, white papers, and advisory councils provided a competing influence to departmental advice. The impact of these changes is discussed at various points throughout this book. However, it is notable that these changes did increase the role of ministers in policy formation. Moreover, since the late 1960s, the power of the so-called "public service mandarins" (a small group of influential senior bureaucrats) was diffused among a broader range of political actors and among a greater number of senior public servants.[16]

Despite these reforms, certain public servants continue to exercise significant power by virtue of their central positions in the policy process (e.g., the Deputy Minister of Finance, the Clerk of the Privy Council). Furthermore, despite the greater variety of available sources of policy advice, the very technical, complex, and time-consuming nature of certain policy issues obliges ministers to continue to rely heavily on the advice of their officials.

In the sphere of policy implementation, public servants also exercise substantial power. The extent of bureaucratic power in policy implementation depends largely on the specificity of the statute enacted by the legislature. In an early, but very perceptive, discussion of **administrative discretion**, the philosopher Wayne A.R. Leys developed a threefold classification of discretion depending on the willingness and capacity of elected representatives to set down in statutes the criteria on which administrative decisions are to be based. Ley's classification of discretionary powers distinguishes among:

1. merely technical discretion, where the legislature has stated or assumed that the administrator knew the results which it desired;
2. discretion in social planning, where the legislature does not know exactly what it will ultimately want in the way of results; and
3. discretion in the work of reconciliation, where the legislature has, in effect, asked the administrator to break a political deadlock.[17]

The first category, where discretionary judgment is limited, illustrates that care must be taken not to exaggerate the number of value-laden issues confronting officials. A large percentage of the thousands of administrative decisions made each day present value problems of such minor significance that officials are scarcely aware of any value content in the decisions made. The second and third categories demonstrate the discretionary powers exercised by officials, either because of the complexity of the issue or the inability of the executive or legislature to resolve the political conflicts involved. Both situations shift the burden of decision-making from political executives, legislators, and judges to public servants. The making of decisions and recommendations on complex and technical matters of "social planning" requires the exercise of discretionary powers of a legislative and judicial nature. And the participation of officials in negotiation, bargaining, compromise, and reconciliation in order "to break a political deadlock" is undeniably *political* activity.

In the course of interpreting, clarifying, and applying policy, public servants can significantly influence the success of policy decisions made by ministers and legislators. The care and enthusiasm with which public servants administer policy determine to a large extent the success of that policy. A series of individual, relatively minor decisions in a particular policy area can have a significant cumulative impact on the extent to which the original intent of Cabinet and Parliament is realized. Moreover, such decisions can help to determine the content of subsequent changes in existing policy. In wielding such discretionary powers, public servants are, of course, expected to ensure that their decisions are broadly attuned to the general policy of their minister and their department.

The discretionary powers of public servants in policy implementation are especially evident in the making and enforcement of regulations under authority delegated to them by Parliament, or subdelegated to them by a minister or by Cabinet.[18] The statutory provisions authorizing the making of regulations are often phrased in general or imprecise language that permits public servants to exercise significant discretion both in the wording of the regulations and in the application of their provisions to particular cases. Eric Hehner has repeatedly warned of the danger of "dispersed discretions." He argues:

> If regulations extend only to details of mechanical procedures, no real discretionary powers are delegated. However, where the statutory provisions are only a skeleton and it is left to regulations to say "what, where, when, why, how and who," then we have created meaningful discretionary powers... When regulations are issued by the governor-in-council, or even by a minister of the Crown, there is at least a degree of accountability for this first step. Where the power is conferred upon a board or commission, review of its exercise becomes more difficult and remote... If persons or bodies possessed of delegated powers redelegate them, we come to a state that may be described as "dispersed discretions."[19]

The delegation by Parliament of power to make regulations is now very common and a large number of regulations have been made. The Special Committee on Statutory Instruments reported in 1969 that 420 of 601 statutes perused by the committee provided for delegated legislation, and that an annual average of 530 regulations had been passed between 1956 and 1968.[20] Then, in 1977, the Joint Standing Committee on Regulations and Other Statutory Instruments (now the Joint Standing Committee on Regulatory Scrutiny), on the basis of its inquiry into "the subordinate law made by delegates of Parliament," provided examples not only of the substantial volume of subordinate law but also of cases where public servants had exceeded the regulation-making authority granted to them by Parliament.[21] The committee recognizes the need for subordinate legislation, but it continues to make recommendations to ensure more effective parliamentary scrutiny of this legislation and more attention to the rights of individuals affected by it.

The exercise of discretionary powers is also pervasive in that these powers are dispersed to various levels of the hierarchy. Both the scope and importance of discretionary powers increase, however, as one moves up the administrative pyramid into the upper echelons of the bureaucracy. It is, therefore, among senior public servants that value problems and priorities are most crucial for the determination of public policy and the state of administrative responsibility. It is important, however, not to overestimate the value problems of the most senior bureaucrats and thereby to minimize the substantial, sometimes critical, significance of value choices made by professional, technical, and administrative personnel at lower levels of the hierarchy. The failure of such officials to act responsibly, particularly by making decisions that are efficient, effective, and responsive, may seriously jeopardize policies and programs determined at the top executive levels of the organization. Decisions judged to be irresponsible may be taken with the best of personal intentions; other irresponsible decisions may constitute deliberate efforts to obstruct or sabotage the implementation of government policies. Instances of this latter type of irresponsible administrative conduct are difficult to document, but there are numerous opportunities for such conduct. In a large organization—whether in the public or the private sector—the decision-making process may involve inputs and judgments by so many individuals that the person or persons guilty of irresponsible behaviour, whether unintentional or deliberate, are extremely difficult to pinpoint. This is the condition Robert Presthus describes as "organized irresponsibility."[22]

The role of provincial public servants in policy development and implementation is very similar to that of federal public servants. Kornberg et al. have noted that "provincial bureaucracies exercise legislative powers in various ways. Some bureaucratic officials identify problem areas requiring the action of cabinets. They marshall the information ministers require to decide among competing priorities ... and they either draft or assist in the drafting of legislation." In addition, these provincial public servants "formulate general and specific rules having the force of law as part of the process of implementing legislation which assemblies have enacted."[23] Clearly, policy implementation has a significant effect on the development and content of policy in all spheres of government.

Despite the fact that politics and policy cannot be easily separated from administration, the distinctions commonly made between politics and administration, policy and administration, and policy formation and implementation serve an extremely useful analytical and practical purpose. They enable political theorists to distinguish—not in an absolute sense but as a matter of degree and emphasis—between the constitutional and legal functions of political executives and public servants. While the policy role of public servants has led some writers to refer to them as "permanent politicians" and "ruling servants," they remain, in fact and in democratic theory, subject to the overriding authority of elected representatives and the courts. It is useful, then, to refer to the *predominance* of ministers in policy formulation and the *predominance* of public servants in policy implementation, while acknowledging that both ministers and public servants are involved in both policy formation and implementation.

These dichotomies also serve a very practical end in that they enable politicians to preserve the appearance before the public that they, not the public servants, are the policy-makers. Elected representatives have a stake in preserving the notion that public servants are neutral instruments of political masters. This notion in turn supports the doctrine that ministers must accept responsibility for the decisions of their administrative subordinates. Public servants also have an interest in preserving these convenient fictions so that they may retain their anonymity and be sheltered from public attack.

(2) Political Appointments

Merit and patronage. A second component of the ideal model of political neutrality is the practice whereby "public servants are appointed and promoted on the basis of merit rather than of party affiliation or contributions." Political **patronage** involves the appointment of people to government service on the grounds of contributions, financial or otherwise, to the governing party; it is a blatant violation of the doctrine of political neutrality.[24] Indeed, the appointment is made on the basis that the appointee is *not* politically neutral but rather is politically partisan. Such appointments clash with the **merit principle** according to which:

1. Canadian citizens should have a reasonable opportunity to be considered for employment in the public service;
2. selections must be based exclusively on merit, or fitness to do the job.[25]

The **merit system**, on the other hand, "is the mechanism in use at any time by which these goals are achieved." It is "an administrative device which can and should be adapted to changing circumstances."[26]

The merit system established by the Civil Service Act in 1918 greatly diminished, but by no means eliminated, patronage appointments. As late as 1944, H.M. Clokie claimed that Canada had not "fully emancipated herself from the laxness of appointment by favour which tends to paralyze all efforts to attain a sound merit system."[27] By 1945, however, the number of patronage appointments had been greatly reduced, and by 1962 the Glassco Commission was able to conclude that "for all practical purposes . . . the Civil Service Commission [now the Public Service Commission] has managed to eliminate political patronage appointments to those positions falling within its jurisdiction."[28]

Recipients and effects of patronage. Patronage appointments have certainly not disappeared altogether. A review of debates in the House of Commons in recent decades reveals numerous allegations and denials regarding the use of patronage in staffing the public service. Many of the alleged patronage appointments have been to lower-level or part-time positions where the appointees are so far removed from policy development that their appointment has negligible effect on the status of political neutrality. Opposition parties, the news media, and the general public have shown greater interest in *senior* positions that are filled by patronage appointees rather than on a competitive basis by persons from within or outside the public service. The Prime Minister and the Cabinet have the authority to appoint deputy ministers, heads and members of agencies, boards and commissions, ambassadors, high commissioners, consuls general and certain other diplomatic representatives, and federal judges. Moreover, officials in the Prime Minister's Office are selected by the Prime Minister, and Cabinet ministers choose their assistants. All these appointments are exempt from the appointing power of the Public Service Commission.

Among the persons who may be, and frequently are, appointed to exempt positions are retired legislators, defeated candidates of the governing party, and party supporters who have made significant financial or other contributions to the party's fortunes. For example, in the period following the 1972 general election, more than two-thirds of the thirty-eight retired or defeated Liberal politicians were appointed as heads or members of government agencies, contract employees in government departments, judges, or assistants to the Prime Minister or to ministers. An Opposition member was provoked into proposing a motion to the House of Commons "that this House request the government to table a list of all Liberal candidates defeated in the last election who have not yet been appointed to government positions, together with a list of the positions to which they will be appointed."[29] Defeated or retired Cabinet ministers have enjoyed particular success in finding a comfortable niche in government service.[30] Finally, the expansion of the personal staff of Cabinet ministers since 1960 has increased the importance of this group as a source of patronage appointments.[31]

Such appointments are often denounced on the grounds that they are made more on the basis of partisanship than merit. Nevertheless, the government has the authority to make these appointments on whatever basis it deems appropriate. A measure of merit is achieved with respect to the most senior posts because the government is not usually willing to bear the embarrassment that the appointment of an incompetent partisan may bring. Moreover, party supporters are more likely to find their reward in appointments to Crown agencies, boards, and commissions than to the regular departments of government. There are few partisan appointments to deputy ministerial posts.

The number of patronage appointments in each of the categories examined above is relatively small, but, taking all the categories together, the number of *senior* positions filled by patronage appointees is substantial. The impact of these appointments on bureaucratic power is difficult to measure with any precision. Appointments to public service posts without competitive examination and on grounds of partisanship violate the merit principle but not the merit system. Such appointments limit the influence of career public servants by blocking their access to some of the highest positions in government. Moreover, long-serving officials are obliged to share their influence in the policy process with newcomers who may have fresh ideas and unorthodox approaches, and who may not share the administrative values to which most public servants have become socialized.

Patronage in the provinces. The evolution of political patronage in Canada's provinces has been very similar to that in the federal government. Civil service acts were passed and civil service commissions or their equivalent were created to promote public service neutrality and efficiency through a merit system of personnel management.[32] The timing of these reforms varied greatly from province to province but in all cases effective reforms occurred more slowly than on the federal scene. Hodgetts and Dwivedi note that "until the early '60s, most provinces continued to present only the facade of a merit system, while combatting charges of patronage and personal favouritism in their public services." However, "by the mid-'60's nearly all provinces had made their central personnel agencies powerful enough to implement the merit principle."[33] Patronage appointments to agencies, boards, and commissions, and to lower-level positions in certain operating departments, remain a common practice in provincial governments.[34] The Ontario government has available for political appointments more than 2500 full-time and part-time positions in agencies, boards, and commissions.[35] Some provinces (e.g., Saskatchewan)[36] are more inclined than others to make political appointments to senior posts in *departments* as well as in semi-independent bodies.

(3) Political Partisanship

Political sterilization. The ideal model of political neutrality requires that public servants not "engage in partisan political activities."[37] During the first fifty years of Canada's political history, the issues of political partisanship and political patronage were intimately linked. Patronage appointments were rewards for service to the governing party. Many of the appointees sought to enhance their progress within the public service by continuing their partisan support of the governing party after their appointment. Thus, when a new party came into power, it replaced these persons with its own supporters.

In an effort to eliminate this practice, legislators provided in the 1918 Civil Service Act that no public servant could "engage in partisan work in connection with any. . . election, or contribute, receive or in any way deal with any money for any party funds." Violations were punishable by dismissal. The penalty was so severe and so clearly stated that, with the exception of the right to vote, the impact of the Act was the political sterilization of Canada's federal public servants. Despite this effective weakening of the link between patronage and political activity, the rigid restraints imposed in 1918 remained virtually unchanged until 1967. The primary explanation for those enduring restraints was the desire to ensure the political impartiality of public servants in the performance of their advisory and discretionary powers.

The Public Service Employment Act of 1967 liberalized the long-standing restrictions on political activity. Section 33 of the Act provides that public servants, unless they are deputy heads, may stand for election to public office if the Public Service Commission believes that their usefulness would not be impaired by their candidacy. They must, however, take a leave of absence during the campaign and, if they are elected, they must resign from the public service. The decisions of the Public Service Commission suggest that roughly 90 percent of all public servants will be permitted to seek election if they wish. This liberalization of restraints on political candidacy has attracted a small number of public servants to the hustings for each federal election. Employees are not permitted to work for or against a candidate for election to a federal or provincial office, or for or against a political party; they are permitted, however, to attend political meetings and to make contributions to the funds of a political candidate or party.

Political activity in the provinces. In provincial governments, a common pattern has emerged with respect to public servants who wish to become candidates for public office. Although the number of senior and other officials who are prohibited from such activity varies from province to province, most public servants seeking candidacy and election may receive a leave of absence for a period preceding the date of the election. Employees who are elected must resign their public service position. In several provinces, however, an employee who is elected but who ceases to be a representative within five years will be reinstated to government service.

In regard to other forms of political activity (e.g., membership in political parties; attendance at political meetings, rallies, and conventions; making and soliciting financial contributions; canvassing for a political candidate), provincial governments vary greatly in their rules. In virtually every province, the right of public servants to support the party of their choice or no party at all is specifically protected by statute. For example, the Saskatchewan Public Service Act provides that no public servant:

1. shall be obliged to contribute to a political party or to participate in political activities;
2. use his or her authority or influence to "control or modify" political action of another person;
3. engage in political activities at the workplace; or
4. participate in political activities likely to impair his or her usefulness in the public service.

The fact that most public servants may now stand for election and engage in a broader spectrum of political activities has heightened the general level of partisan activity and consciousness in Canada's public services, especially among younger employees. However, officials in senior and sensitive posts are usually required to refrain from partisan activity; thus, those officials most actively involved in policy formation and in the discretionary application of policy retain their impartiality. Also, officials with many years of government experience seem to have difficulty overcoming their ingrained avoidance of political activity. Some public servants may justifiably perceive overt partisanship as an obstacle to promotion to the senior ranks of what is, substantially, a politically neutral public service. Moreover, one of the attractions of government employment at the senior levels is the opportunity to exercise influence in relative privacy and anonymity. While there have been some notable examples of public servants being transformed into Cabinet ministers, a Cabinet post is by no means a sure reward for a public servant who is elected to public office. Thus, the broadening of the permissible limits of political activity has modified the traditional doctrine and practice of political neutrality but it has not had a significant effect on the exercise of bureaucratic power.

Restrictions on the political partisanship of public servants, in both the federal and provincial spheres of government, have been challenged in the courts under the Canadian Charter of Rights and Freedoms. The issue is, for the most part, framed in terms of the need to strike the most appropriate balance between the political rights of public servants and the political neutrality of the public service. Section 2 of the Charter guarantees the fundamental freedoms of expression, peaceful assembly and association, and section 1 provides that the guarantees to rights and freedoms under the Charter are subject to "such reasonable limits prescribed by law as can be demonstrably justified in a free and democratic society." The issue before the courts, then, is whether the limits on the political partisanship of public servants can be demonstrably justified to be reasonable limits in contemporary Canadian society. Recent court decisions indicate that there is a clear trend in the direction of extending the political rights of public servants.

(4) Public Comment

Restrictions. The admonition that public servants "not express publicly their personal views on government policies or administration" is an integral component of the ideal model of political neutrality. The prime reason given by contemporary governments for restrictions on public comment is the need to preserve the confidence of the public and of political superiors in the impartiality of public servants.

Strict interpretation of this rule of official reticence requires that public servants not express personal opinions on government policies, whether they are attacking or supporting those policies. As explained below, this convention has been supplemented by statutory prohibitions relating to political partisanship and to the use of confidential information, by decisions of administrative tribunals, and by written guidelines.

A few provincial governments accompany their regulations on political activities with guidance on partisan public comment. Section 14 of the Ontario Public Service Act, for example, states that "except during a leave of absence . . . a civil servant shall not at any time speak in public or express views in writing on any matter that forms part of the platform of a provincial or federal political party." Public servants on leave of absence to seek election are of course obliged to express personal and partisan views on campaign issues. Those who wish to return to government service if they are defeated may find it prudent to show discretion in their public statements, especially with respect to the policies and programs of the department to which they may wish to return.

Public servants, whether seeking election or not, are normally prohibited by an oath of office and secrecy, and by the Official Secrets Act, from disclosing or using for personal gain confidential information acquired by virtue of their government position. It is a serious offence to criticize government policy or administration; the use of confidential information for this purpose would greatly compound the offence.

Formal written guidelines on public comment are so sparse that considerable uncertainty exists as to the rights of public servants in this area. It is well established in the civil service legislation of modern democratic states that the role of public servants in policy development and implementation requires that they enjoy fewer political rights than other citizens. In the area of public comment, the difficulty is to strike an appropriate balance between freedom of expression and political neutrality. The dilemma for a public servant who engages in public criticism of government is illustrated well by the celebrated Fraser case.

Mr. Fraser, an employee of the Department of National Revenue, began his public protest with attacks on the government's compulsory imposition of the metric system; he then extended his criticism to the proposed Charter of Rights. When Mr. Fraser's appeal against his subsequent dismissal was being heard by an adjudicator of the Public Service Staff Relations Board, Mr. Fraser said that if he discontinued his protests, he would be breaking "the common law that the citizen has a duty to speak out against a Government that lies to the people."[38] The adjudicator's decision that Mr. Fraser's dismissal was appropriate was upheld by the Supreme Court of Canada. The Court stated that:

> public servants have some freedom to criticize the government. But it is not an absolute freedom... In some circumstances a public servant may actively and publicly express opposition to the policies of a government. This would be appropriate if, for example, the government were engaged in illegal acts, or if its policies jeopardized the life, health or safety of the public servant or others, or if the public servant's criticism had no impact on his or her ability to perform effectively the duties of a public servant or on the public perception of that ability.[39]

Beyond public criticism. The decisions of the adjudicator and of the Supreme Court are of limited value in dealing with forms of public comment other than criticism of government. The issue of public comment is much more complex than the conventional rule suggests. This rule does not take adequate account of the extent to which public servants are inescapably involved in public comment in the regular performance of their duties. In speaking or writing for public consumption, public servants may serve such purposes as:

1. providing information and analysis of a scientific or technical nature for consideration primarily by their professional colleagues within and outside government;
2. describing the administrative process and departmental organization and procedures;
3. explaining the content, implications, and administration of specific government policies and programs;
4. discussing, within the framework of governmental or departmental policy, the solution of problems through changes in existing programs or the development of new programs;
5. discussing issues on which governmental or departmental policy has not yet been determined;
6. explaining the nature of the political and policy process in government;
7. advocating reforms in the existing organization or procedures of government;

8. commenting in a constructively critical way on government policy or administration;
9. denouncing existing or potential government policies, programs, and operations; and
10. commenting in an overtly partisan way on public policy issues or on government policy or administration.[40]

This list moves from types of public comment that are generally expected, required, or permissible, to those that are questionable, risky, or prohibited. Few public servants have ventured beyond the first four categories. The fourth category often involves public servants in bargaining, accommodation, and compromise on behalf of their political superiors. It is on these occasions that members of the public may see most clearly the nature and extent of bureaucratic power in the policy process. These meetings usually take place in private, but public servants are sometimes required to make presentations and answer questions in public forums where a larger measure of risk exists.

The extent to which public servants may venture beyond the first four categories of public comment was clarified in 1979 by the Clark government. To complement the government's freedom of information bill, Prime Minister Clark issued guidelines on communications between public servants and the public.[41] Public servants were advised that they "should be prepared to discuss frankly information within their areas of responsibility that describes or explains programs that have been announced or implemented by the government." Public servants were counselled not to "go beyond this discussion of factual information" and not "to discuss advice or recommendations tendered to Ministers, or to speculate about policy deliberations or future policy decisions." The guidelines stated that "it will be normal for public servants to be quoted by name, and to be interviewed" for both the electronic and print media. Finally, the guidelines prohibited the disclosure of information that was specifically prohibited by law. However, public employees "*acting in good faith*"[42] under the guidelines were not to "be considered as having violated their oaths of secrecy." The new Trudeau government elected in 1980 retained these guidelines, but the Mulroney government elected in 1984 amended the guidelines by requiring that interviews with the public or the media "shall be on the record and for attribution by name."[43] While this amendment was made in the name of "open government," the view was widely expressed that it would have the effect of discouraging public servants from giving out even factual information.

As a result of the intimate links among politics, policy, and administration described earlier, public servants often enhance understanding of the political and policy process through their speeches and writings on the machinery of government and the administrative process. The major burden of explaining the political system to the public is, however, likely to remain with politicians and academic scholars.

Public advocacy of administrative reform and constructive criticism of government activities may complement the public servants' information and conciliation functions. However, the participation of public servants in these forms of public comment is restricted by their political superiors, who bear public responsibility for the operations of government.

Denunciations and overtly partisan assessments of government policy or administration tend to be clearer than other forms of public comment in their manifestation and in the certainty of their punishment. Both the traditional admonition against public comment and recent decisions by administrative tribunals prohibit such activity unless public servants are on leave of absence to seek election.

The unwritten rule against public comment is subject to varying interpretations and applications in contemporary society. Public servants are now involved in forms of public comment not explicitly covered by the conventional rule and the nature of this involvement constitutes a significant departure from a position of political neutrality. It appears that public servants will increasingly be required to attend public meetings to provide information about the substance and implementation of government policies and programs. As a result, the public will become more aware of the influence that public servants bring to deliberations on public policy matters. It is often difficult for public servants to discuss government policy without indicating, inadvertently or otherwise, some measure of the influence they have—or could have—over the content of policy.

(5) Anonymity and Ministerial Responsibility

As noted early in this chapter, the ideal model of political neutrality requires that "public servants provide forthright and objective advice to their political masters in private and in confidence; in return, political executives protect the anonymity of public servants by publicly accepting responsibility for departmental decisions." The anonymity of public servants depends, in large measure, on the vitality of the doctrine of individual ministerial responsibility according to which ministers are personally responsible to the legislature both for their own actions and for those of their administrative subordinates. Thus, public servants are not directly answerable to the legislature and their minister protects their anonymity. Recent events have shown, however, that ministers will not invariably protect the anonymity of their officials by refusing to name or blame them publicly. This issue and the relationship of ministerial responsibility to political neutrality and anonymity are discussed in Chapter 17.

The decline of official anonymity. Public service anonymity depends significantly on factors other than the operation of ministerial responsibility. Departures from political neutrality in the areas of patronage and political activity also diminish official anonymity, but the greatest threat is probably the expansion of public comment described earlier. The increased interaction of public servants with both individual citizens and specific "publics," or clientele groups, reveals the nature of official involvement in policy development. The cumulative impact of the growing information and conciliation functions performed by public servants is a gradual, but significant, decline in official anonymity.

The anonymity of public servants has also been diminished by their more frequent appearances before legislative committees. Their diplomatic skills are often severely taxed as they strive to describe and explain their department's programs fully and frankly, while preserving their loyalty to their minister and their reputation for impartiality. On occasion, however, legislators, pressure groups, journalists, and others concerned with the committees' deliberations can discern the actual or potential power of public servants in the policy process. Elaboration on the interaction between public servants and legislators is contained in Chapter 17.

The pervasive role of the news media in contemporary society has been reflected in increased media coverage of the activities and identities of public servants. As explained in Chapter 21, the media and public servants share a mutual desire to inform the public about government programs. Public servants utilize the media for public relations and publicity—to tell their department's story and to sell their department's programs. The media serve as excellent channels of communication to the public for officials engaged in public comment that requires the description and explanation of government programs. The media, in turn, analyze the purposes and, whenever possible, identify the personalities involved in the development and administration of programs. This media coverage helps to limit bureaucratic power by exposing the activities of public servants to public questioning and criticism.

The extent to which public servants are exposed to the public's gaze through the news media depends largely on the position they occupy, on current interest in their department's activities, and on their personal views and their minister's views on anonymity. Certain public servants (for example, a deputy minister of finance) are better known because of the enduring importance of their position; others receive publicity during periods of public controversy in their sphere of responsibilities.

Although the tradition of anonymity remains strong among public servants, their visibility has been heightened by changes in political institutions and practices, and by the media's response to demands for more public information. This gradual decline in official anonymity is likely to continue, revealing the significant role of public servants in the political process.

(6) Permanency in Office

The case for security of tenure. The preservation of political neutrality, as previously noted, requires that "public servants execute policy decisions loyally, irrespective of the philosophy and programs of the party in power and regardless of their personal opinions. As a result, public servants enjoy security of tenure during good behaviour and satisfactory performance." Thus, in the event of a change of government, official neutrality helps to ensure continuity of administration by competent and experienced public servants, as well as the provision of impartial advice on policy options and the loyal implementation of policy decisions. Security of tenure enables a career public servant not only to establish and wield influence in the policy process but also to continue to exercise such influence even if there is a change in the governing party. Long tenure in office enables public servants to acquire knowledge and experience, both in specific policy fields and in the political-administrative system within which policy decisions are made. Permanence in office for public servants increases their power vis-à-vis politicians. Ministers cannot match the expertise of their senior officials, and the frequent rotation of ministers among departments prevents them from accumulating much experience in particular policy areas.

As public servants, especially at the senior levels, become more overtly or apparently political, the argument for political appointments to senior posts is strengthened. Thus, permanence in office depends largely on adherence to the elements of political neutrality already described. The merit system is designed to bring about a career public service by minimizing the number of patronage appointments and avoiding a turnover of personnel following a change of government. Senior public servants are not permitted to engage in partisan political activity or public criticism of government. Finally, the preservation of ministerial responsibility and public service anonymity helps to protect officials from public identification as supporters or opponents of particular policies.

Despite these efforts to achieve the fact and the appearance of administrative impartiality, Opposition party leaders have frequently promised, if elected, to turf out senior officials because of their assumed contribution to government policies to which these leaders are opposed. Public servants must be able to demonstrate, therefore, the capacity to adapt quickly and effectively to the requirements of a new governing party. The best test of these adaptive qualities is the behaviour of public servants when a different political party comes into power.

When permanence in office for public servants has been combined with longevity in office by a particular political party, a change of government presents an especially difficult challenge to the capacity of public servants to serve different political masters impartially. It is understandable that senior officials who have worked closely with ministers in the development of existing policies should be apprehensive about the arrival of a new governing party. Shortly before Mr. Diefenbaker and the Progressive Conservatives ended the twenty-two-year reign of the Liberal Party in 1957, J.E. Hodgetts wondered about the effects of such a change: "Could we expect impartial service from the permanent servants or would we have to face some form of the American system of turning out the top ranking officials?"[44] During the Diefenbaker period, unhealthy tension often existed between senior public servants and the government. J.R. Mallory has observed, however, that "there were few resignations and few drastic changes in policy. The new ministers soon discovered that a good civil servant conceives it his duty to serve his political master to the best of his ability, and that the higher civil service was as effective at advising the new government as it had been the old."[45] In general, subsequent new governments have come to the same conclusion.[46]

During the brief Clark period, few senior officials were invited or decided to resign. But ministers in the Clark government disagree as to whether they were well and faithfully served by senior bureaucrats. Flora MacDonald, the Secretary of State for External Affairs, stated[47] that her efforts to seek advice from persons outside government were resisted almost entirely by "those who really have their hands on the levers of power—the senior mandarins." She also complained about the use by senior bureaucrats of such "entrapment devices" as the many "crisis corridor decisions" with which she was faced, unduly lengthy and numerous memos, the late delivery of her submissions to Cabinet, and "the one-dimensional opinions put forward in memos." She noted that she "was expected to accept the unanimous recommendation of the Department" and that she was "seldom, if ever... given the luxury of multiple-choice options on matters of major import."

The experience of other ministers was different.[48] One minister stated that his experience with officials in his own department and "indeed, generally, was not similar to Miss MacDonald's. I am not suggesting there might not have been some incidents where public servants with deep political or policy convictions which differ from mine might have endeavoured to frustrate or mislead me. However, generally I found them to be hard-working, dedicated and professional."[49]

These differing views support the argument earlier in this chapter that the extent of bureaucratic power varies according to such factors as "the policy or program under consideration, the department or agency involved, and the style and competence of ministers and their officials." Prime Minister Clark stated that he and his government had no complaint regarding the treatment they received from the senior public service. He did ask, however, whether "a large and diverse country like ours can be as well served as Britain is by the exclusive reliance upon a professional Public Service, or whether we should be leaning more towards elements of the American system which allow a new government to bring in people who agree with its point of view."[50]

The case for politicization. There is some support in Canada for a system of political appointments similar to that in the United States. Supporters of a politicized public service usually cite the following benefits from political appointments to senior public service posts:

- a strong commitment to implementing the policies of the new government;
- a breath of fresh air in the form of new ideas and approaches toward government policies and processes;
- the restoration and preservation of political (ministerial) control over permanent officials and the decision-making processes of government;
- advice on policy issues that is more sensitive to their partisan political implications;
- greater trust by ministers in their policy advisors.

Under this system, the incumbents of the most senior public service positions would be replaced whenever a change in government occurred. Some senior appointments would thus be held on a temporary, rather than a permanent, basis. The power of career public servants would be reduced because they would not normally be appointed to the highest administrative posts in government. However, assuming regular changes in the governing party, the tenure in office of senior political appointees would be too brief to enable them to exercise as much power based on experience and expertise as career public servants do.

At present, a shift to a system of political appointments either in the federal government or in most provincial governments is unlikely. Career public servants in Canada can normally expect security of tenure during good conduct, adequate performance, and political neutrality. Note must be taken, however, of a gradual politicization of the senior bureaucracy in a few provinces and of the fact that the Conservative government that came to power in Saskatchewan in 1982 dismissed about two hundred senior public servants. The Saskatchewan experience appears to be an aberration. Certainly the rationale for the sweeping nature of the dismissals is unclear; many of those dismissed were career public servants with no partisan affiliation.

Political Neutrality and Bureaucratic Power

The present operations of Canada's public services are not in accord with a strict interpretation of the traditional doctrine of political neutrality. Some of the requirements of the traditional doctrine remain substantially unchanged, but some have never been met and others have been altered to keep pace with changing political, social, and technological circumstances. The elements of the doctrine may be updated and restated as follows:

1. Policy, politics, and administration are intertwined.
2. Most public servants are selected and promoted on the basis of merit, but some positions are filled by partisans of the governing party.
3. Public servants may participate in a number of partisan political activities, unless they occupy senior or sensitive positions.
4. Public servants are not usually permitted to criticize their government's actions publicly, but are involved in various other forms of public comment in the normal course of their duties.
5. Public servants provide confidential advice to ministers; ministers usually protect the anonymity of public servants, but this anonymity is gradually declining for other reasons.
6. Public servants usually execute policy decisions loyally, regardless of their personal views and of the political complexion of the governing party.

Thus, public servants are actively involved in the political system both by necessity in the areas of policy development and execution, and by choice in the sphere of political partisanship. This involvement accounts, in large part, for the nature and extent of bureaucratic power in contemporary Canadian governments. The next chapter assesses the implications of this bureaucratic power for the concept and practice of administrative responsibility.

NOTES

1. The George C. Nowlan Lecture, Acadia University, February 7, 1977. Reprinted in *The Globe and Mail*, February 8, 1977.

2. Mitchell Sharp, "Reflections of a Former Minister of the Crown," address to the Toronto Regional Group of the Institute of Public Administration of Canada, November 29, 1976, pp. 6-7.

3. See the chapter on "The Politically Neutral Public Servant," in Kenneth Kernaghan and John Langford, *The Responsible Public Servant* (Toronto: Institute of Public Administration of Canada and Halifax: Institute for Research on Public Policy, 1990).

4. R.J.S. Baker, *Administrative Theory and Public Administration* (London: Hutchison, 1972), p. 13.

5. *Canadian Public Policy and Administration* (Toronto: McGraw-Hill Ryerson, 1981), p. 99.

6. Woodrow Wilson, "The Study of Administration," reprinted in Peter Woll, ed., *Public Administration and Policy* (New York: Harper and Row, 1966), pp. 28-29.

7. Wallace S. Sayre, "Premises of Public Administration: Past and Emerging," *Public Administration Review* 18 (1958): 103.

8. Quoted in J.E. Hodgetts et al., *The Biography of an Institution; The Civil Service Commission of Canada, 1908-1967* (Montreal: McGill-Queen's University Press, 1972), p. 56.

9. Ibid. (Emphasis added.)

10. See, for example, Luther Gulick's "Politics, Administration and the New Deal," *Annals of the American Academy of Political and Social Science* (1933), and Pendleton Herring, *Public Administration and the Public Interest*, 1936. (Reprinted in 1967 by Russell, New York.)

11. Paul Appleby, *Policy and Administration* (University, Ala.: University of Alabama Press, 1949), p.170. See also Dwight Waldo, *The Administrative State* (New York: Ronald Press, 1948) and Harold Stein, *Public Administration and Policy Development: A Casebook* (New York: Harcourt, Brace and Co., 1952).

12. See Frank Marini, ed., *Toward a New Public Administration: The Minnowbrook Perspective* (Scranton, Pa.: Chandler, 1971).

13. See especially Eugene P. Dvorin and Robert H. Simmons, *From Amoral to Humane Bureaucracy* (San Francisco: Canfield Press, 1972) and Louis C. Gawthrop, *Administrative Politics and Social Change* (New York: St. Martin's Press, 1971).

14. "The Coming Crisis in the North," *Journal of Canadian Studies* 2 (February 1967): 3.

15. See Chapter 7.

16. See Kenneth Kernaghan and T.H. McLeod, "Mandarins and Ministers in the Canadian Administrative State," in O.P. Dwivedi, ed., *The Canadian Administrative State* (Toronto: University of Toronto Press, 1982), pp. 17-30.

17. Wayne A.R. Leys, "Ethics and Administrative Discretion," *Public Administration Review* 3 (Winter 1943): 23.

18. See Denys C. Holland and John P. McGowan, *Delegated Legislation in Canada* (Toronto: Carswell, 1989), chs. 1-6.

19. Eric Hehner, "Growth of Discretions—Decline of Accountability," in Kenneth Kernaghan, ed., *Public Administration in Canada: Selected Readings*, 5th ed. (Toronto: Methuen, 1985), p. 342.

20. House of Commons, Special Committee on Statutory Instruments, *3rd Report* (Ottawa: Queen's Printer, 1969), p. 4.

21. Senate and House of Commons, Standing Joint Committee on Regulations and Other Statutory Instruments, *2nd Report* (Ottawa: Queen's Printer, 1977), esp. pp. 2-12.

22. Robert Presthus, *The Organizational Society* (New York: Vintage Books, 1962), p. 53.

23. Allan Kornberg, William Mishler, and Harold D. Clarke, *Representative Democracy in the Canadian Provinces* (Scarborough, Ont.: Prentice-Hall, 1982), p.184.

24. For an account of the evolution of patronage in the federal and provincial spheres of government, see Jeffrey Simpson, *Spoils of Power: The Politics of Patronage* (Toronto: Collins, 1988).

25. R.H. Dowdell, "Public Personnel Administration," in Kenneth Kernaghan, ed., *Public Administration in Canada*, 4th ed. (Toronto: Methuen, 1982), p. 196.

26. Ibid.

27. Clokie, *Canadian Government and Politics* (Toronto: Longmans, Green, 1944), p. 190.

28. Canada, Royal Commission on Government Organization, *Report*, vol. 1 (Ottawa: Queen's Printer, 1962), p. 371

29. Stanley Knowles, House of Commons, *Debates*, April 11, 1973, p. 3176.

30. Between 1948 and 1972, 12.1 percent of retiring or defeated ministers were appointed to patronage positions. See W. A. Matheson, *The Prime Minister and the Cabinet* (Toronto: Methuen, 1976), p. 121.

31. See Chapter 16 for elaboration on the role of ministerial staff.

32. See J.E. Hodgetts and O.P. Dwivedi, *Provincial Governments as Employers* (McGill-Queen's University Press, 1974), ch. 2.

33. J.E. Hodgetts and O.P. Dwivedi, "Administration and Personnel," in David J. Bellamy, Jon H. Pammett, and Donald C. Rowat, eds., *The Provincial Political Systems: Comparative Essays* (Toronto: Methuen, 1976), p. 347.

34. See Doug Love, "The Merit Principle in the Provincial Governments of Atlantic Canada," *Canadian Public Administration* 31 (Fall 1988): 335-81.

35. *The Globe and Mail*, April 11, 1988, p. A4.

36. See S.M. Lipset, *Agrarian Socialism: The Cooperative Commonwealth Federation in Saskatchewan* (Berkeley: University of California Press, 1959), Evelyn Eager, *Saskatchewan Government* (Saskatoon: Western Producer Prairie Books, 1980), pp.164-67, and Hans J. Michelmann and Jeffrey S. Steeves, "The 1982 Transition in Power in Saskatchewan: the Progressive Conservatives and the Public Service," *Canadian Public Administration* 28 (Spring 1985): 1-23.

37. For a definition of political activity and an account of the arguments usually raised for and against the political activity of government employees, see Kenneth Kernaghan, *Ethical Conduct: Guidelines for Government Employees* (Toronto: Institute of Public Administration of Canada, 1975), pp. 26-28.

38. *Neil A. Fraser, Grievor, v. Treasury Board (Department of National Revenue, Taxation), Employer*, Public Service Staff Relations Board Decision, May 31, 1982, p. 16.

39. Supreme Court of Canada, *Neil Fraser and Public Service Staff Relations Board*, [1985] 2 S.C.R., pp. 468, 470.

40. This classification is an expansion of that set out in Kernaghan, *Ethical Conduct*, p. 36.

41. *Policy Guidelines for Public Servants: Communications with the Public*, November 23, 1979, reproduced in *Debates* (Commons), November 29, 1979, p. 1875.

42. Emphasis added.

43. Office of the Prime Minister, *Policy Guidelines for Public Servants: Communications with the Public*, November 23, 1984.

44. J.E. Hodgetts, "The Liberal and the Bureaucrat," *Queen's Quarterly* 62 (1955): 176-83. Following the 1957 election, John Meisel observed that the Liberal program "had, in

the main, evolved gradually as the consequence of the continuous interaction of the cabinet and the leading experts in the civil service ... Much of what had, in the years immediately before the election, been called Liberal policies or the Liberal pro-gramme was actually the product of the intimate co-operation of leading civil servants and their ministers." John Meisel, *The Canadian General Election of 1957* (Toronto: University of Toronto Press, 1962), pp. 37-38.

45. J.R. Mallory, *The Structure of Canadian Government* (Toronto: Macmillan, 1971), p. 116.

46. Jacques Bourgault and Stéphane Dion conclude that the Mulroney government did not politicize the role of deputy ministers. See "Brian Mulroney a-t-il politisé les sous-ministres?" *Canadian Public Administration* 32 (Spring 1989): 63-83.

47. See "The Ministers and the Mandarins," *Policy Options* 1 (September-October, 1980): 29-31.

48. Reported in confidential communications with Professor Kernaghan in October 1980.

49. Ibid.

50. Transcript of An Address (Including Question and Answer Period) to the 11th Annual Leadership Conference Sponsored by the Centre for the Study of the Presidency, Ottawa, October 19, 1980, p. 14.

BIBLIOGRAPHY

Atkinson, Michael M., and William D. Coleman. "Bureaucrats and Politicians in Canada: An Examination of the Political Administration Model." *Comparative Political Studies* 18 (April 1985): 58-80.

Baker, Walter. "Power and the Public Service." *Canadian Public Administration* 30 (Spring 1987): 14-33.

Campbell, Colin. *Governments Under Stress: Political Executives and Key Bureaucrats in Washington, London and Ottawa.* Toronto: University of Toronto Press, 1983.

Cassidy, Michael. "Political Rights for Public Servants: A Federal Perspective I." *Canadian Public Administration* 29 (Winter 1986): 653-64.

D'Aquino, Thomas. "The Public Service of Canada: The Case for Political Neutrality." *Canadian Public Administration* 27 (Spring 1984): 14-23.

Dawson, R. M. "The Civil Service of Canada." *Canadian Journal of Economics and Political Science* 2 (August 1936): 291.

Dvorin, Eugene P., and Robert H. Simmons. *From Amoral to Humane Bureaucracy.* San Francisco: Canfield, 1972.

Hodgetts, J. E. "The Civil Service and Policy Formation." *Canadian Journal of Economics and Political Science* 23 (November 1957): 467-79.

Hodgetts, J. E., William McCloskey, Reginald Whitaker, and V. Seymour Wilson. *The Biography of an Institution: The Civil Service Commission of Canada, 1908-1967.* Montreal: McGill-Queen's University Press, 1972.

Kernaghan, Kenneth. "Changing Concepts of Power and Responsibility in the Canadian Public Service." *Canadian Public Administration* 21 (Fall 1978): 389-406.

Kernaghan, Kenneth. "Politics, Policy and Public Servants: Political Neutrality Revisited." *Canadian Public Administration* 19 (Fall 1976): 432-56.

Kernaghan, Kenneth. "Political Rights and Political Neutrality: Finding the Balance Point." *Canadian Public Administration* 29 (Winter 1986): 639-52.

Kernaghan, Kenneth. "Power, Parliament and Public Servants: Ministerial Responsibility

Reexamined." *Canadian Public Policy* 5 (Autumn 1979): 383-96.

Kernaghan, Kenneth, and John Langford. *The Responsible Public Servant.* Toronto: Institute of Public Administration of Canada, and Halifax: Institute for Research on Public Policy, 1990, ch. 3.

Kernaghan, Kenneth, and T.H. McLeod. "Mandarins and Ministers in the Canadian Administrative State." In O.P. Dwivedi, ed., *The Administrative State in Canada.* Toronto: University of Toronto Press, 1982.

Love, Doug. "The Merit Principle in the Provincial Governments of Atlantic Canada." *Canadian Public Administration* 31 (Fall 1988): 335-51.

MacDonald, Flora. "The Ministers and the Mandarins." *Policy Options* 1 (September-October 1980): 29-31.

Nakamura, Robert. T., and Frank Smallwood. *The Politics of Policy Implementation.* New York: St. Martin's Press, 1980.

Peters, B. Guy. *The Politics of Bureaucracy.* 2nd ed. New York: Longman, 1984.

Pressman, Jeffrey L., and Aaron Wildavsky. *Implementation.* Berkeley: University of California Press, 1965.

Sharp, Mitchell. "The Bureaucratic Elite and Policy Formation," in W. D. K. Kernaghan, ed., *Bureaucracy in Canadian Government.* Toronto: Methuen, 1973, pp. 82-87.

Simpson, Jeffrey. *Spoils of Power: The Politics of Patronage.* Toronto: Collins, 1988.

Wilson, V. Seymour. *Canadian Public Policy and Administration.* Toronto: McGraw-Hill Ryerson, 1981, ch. 4.

Zussman, David. "Walking the Tightrope: The Mulroney Government and the Public Service," in Michael J. Prince, ed., *How Ottawa Spends, 1986-87: Tracking the Tories.* Toronto: Methuen, 1986, pp. 25-82.

CASES

In *Case Program in Canadian Public Administration* (Toronto: Institute of Public Administration of Canada):

The Draft Memorandum to Cabinet. By Douglas G. Hartle

14

Responsibility, Accountability, and Ethics

It is not simply the existence of bureaucratic power that arouses public concern; it is also the irresponsible exercise of that power. This chapter examines the responsibility of public servants for the power they exercise, and assesses the ethical standards that they bring to their recommendations and decisions. The chapter begins by explaining the importance of administrative responsibility. This is followed by a summary of various theories of administrative responsibility and an examination of the interrelated issues of administrative accountability, public service ethics, and the public interest.

It is notable that the administrative values outlined in Chapter 12 are central not only to the evolution of Canadian public administration but to the theoretical literature on administrative responsibility as well. The "responsible" bureaucrat is commonly perceived as the one who pursues such values as accountability, integrity, neutrality, efficiency, effectiveness, responsiveness, representativeness, and equity. This chapter focusses on accountability and integrity.

THE IMPORTANCE OF ADMINISTRATIVE RESPONSIBILITY

During the past twenty-five years in particular, public concern about responsibility in government has been stimulated in western democratic states, including Canada, by events involving illegal or unethical activities by both politicians and bureaucrats. Discussion of incidents of political espionage, conflicts of interest, and disclosures of confidential information have revealed that both the general public and students of government disagree among themselves as to what constitutes irresponsible conduct, who should assume blame in particular cases, and what penalty should be paid.

The scope and complexity of government activities have become so great that it is often difficult to determine the actual—as opposed to the legal or constitutional—locus of responsibility for specific decisions. Although political executives (i.e., Cabinet ministers) are held responsible for personal wrong-doing, they are not expected to assume responsibility by way of resignation or demotion for acts of administrative subordinates about which they could not reasonably be expected to have knowledge. Yet it is frequently impossible to assign individual responsibility to public servants for administrative transgressions because so many public servants have contributed to the decision-making process. The allocation of responsibility in government has been complicated even further by the interposition of political appointees or temporary officials between political executives and permanent public servants.

While the involvement of political executives in unlawful or questionable activities has drawn much public attention to the issue of *political* responsibility, the status of *administrative* responsibility has also become a matter of increasing anxiety. As noted in the previous chapter, elected officials make the final decisions on major public policy issues, but public servants have significant influence on these decisions and have authority to make decisions on their own that affect the individual and collective rights of the citizenry.

Concern about the preservation of administrative responsibility is shared in varying degrees by all major actors in the political system—whether political executives, legislators, judges, interest group and mass media representatives, members of the general public, or public servants themselves. In an effort by these various actors to promote responsible administrative conduct, the decisions of public servants are subject to an almost bewildering assortment of controls and influences, many of which are examined in Chapters 15 to 21.

THEORIES OF ADMINISTRATIVE RESPONSIBILITY

The Conventional Theories

The traditional concepts of administrative responsibility may be explained by reference to the celebrated debate between Carl Friedrich and Herman Finer during the period 1935-1941.[1]

Both Friedrich and Finer correctly identified the source of burgeoning bureaucratic power as the rapid expansion of government's service and regulatory functions. They disagreed vehemently, however, on the most effective means of guarding against abuse of administrative discretion so as to maintain and promote responsible administrative conduct. Their disagreement was, in large part, an outgrowth of their differing conceptions of the capacity of political systems to adapt to change, and of the proper role of public servants. To achieve administrative responsibility, Finer placed primary faith in controls and sanctions exercised over public servants by the legislature, the judiciary, and the administrative hierarchy. In his insistence on the predominant importance of political responsibility (that is, responsibility to elected officials), he claimed that "the political and administrative history of all ages" had shown that "sooner or later there is an abuse of power when external punitive controls are lacking."[2]

Friedrich relied more heavily on the propensity of public servants to be self-directing and self-regulating in their responsiveness to the dual standard of technical knowledge and popular sentiment. While he admitted the continuing need for political responsibility, he argued that a policy was irresponsible if it was adopted without proper regard to the existing sum of human knowledge concerning the technical issues involved ... [or] without proper regard for existing preferences in the community, and more particularly its prevailing majority. Consequently, the responsible administrator is one who is responsive to these two dominant factors: technical knowledge and popular sentiment.[3]

Friedrich asserted also that "parliamentary responsibility is largely inoperative and certainly ineffectual"[4] and that "the task of clear and consistent policy formation has passed ... into the hands of administrators and is bound to continue to do so."[5]

Finer admitted the difficulty, but stressed the necessity, of remedying the several deficiencies of political control over administrative officials. He believed that the means of legislative control should be improved.[6] He argued further that officials should not determine their own course of action. Rather, the elected representatives of the people should "determine the course of action of public servants to the most minute degree that is technically feasible."[7] Finer presented an excellent summary of both his position and his critique of Friedrich's stand in his explanation of "the two definitions" of administrative responsibility:

> First, responsibility may mean that X is accountable for Y *to* Z. Second, responsibility may mean an inward personal sense of moral obligation. In the first definition the essence is the externality of the agency or persons to whom an account is to be rendered, and it can mean very little without that agency having authority over X, determining the lines of X's obligation and the terms of its continuance or revocation. The second definition puts the emphasis on the conscience of the agent, and ... if he commits an error it is an error only when recognized by his own conscience, and ... the punishment of the agent will be merely the twinges thereof. The one implies public execution; the other hara-kiri.[8]

Finer described the sum of Friedrich's arguments as *moral* responsibility, as opposed to his own emphasis on *political* responsibility.

Friedrich's contention that administrative responsibility can be more effectively elicited than enforced raises a critical issue for contemporary discussion of administrative responsibility. He believed that responsible conduct depended to a large extent on "sound work rules and effective morale."[9] To this end, he suggested that the environment of government employment be changed. Public servants were to be granted the right to organize into staff associations, and to bargain collectively with the government. Furthermore, responsibility to technical knowledge could not be assured unless public servants were permitted to discuss policy issues publicly. He noted that "in matters of vital importance the general public is entitled to the views of its permanent servants."[10] Finer argued for the preservation of the official's anonymity in order to avoid "bringing himself and his colleagues into partisan contempt"[11] and making him "the instrument of conflict between 'the general public' ... and the legislature."[12]

An understanding of the Friedrich-Finer debate is an essential foundation on which to construct subsequent discussion. It raises several of the major issues of administrative responsibility still being debated by contemporary scholars, albeit in a vastly different social and political environment. The strength of Finer's approach lay in his recognition of the continuing need for political controls over the bureaucracy. Its primary weakness lay in his failure to antici- pate the inadequacy of these controls to ensure administrative responsibility in a period of ever-accelerating political and social change. The strength of Friedrich's argument rested on his awareness of the deficiency of solely political controls. Its major weakness lay in the difficulty of reconciling conflicts between the two criteria of technical knowledge and popular sentiment.

Although the Friedrich-Finer controversy preceded the post-war assault on traditional principles and tenets of public administration, the seeds of change had already borne enough fruit for Friedrich to see the emerging trends. Among the developments he foresaw were the rejection of the politics-administration dichotomy, with the acceptance of the role of public servants in policy develop- ment; the increased need to delegate to public servants powers of a legislative and judicial nature; the strikingly rapid growth and significance of professional- ism in the public service; recognition of the effect of employee morale on work performance; agitation for the extension to public employees of the rights to bargain collectively and to speak publicly on issues of public policy; and finally, demands for direct citizen participation in the administrative process.

Criticisms of the Conventional Theories

During the past five decades, the Friedrich and Finer approaches have been subject to a number of critiques, and alternative interpretations have been formulated.[13] Their approaches have remained the dominant contending ones, however, and most writers on administrative responsibility have referred to the Friedrich-Finer debate with a view to supporting, attacking, or updating one or both sides of the argument. In more recent years, these traditional notions of administrative responsibility have come under attack.

Michael Harmon, for example, argues that both Finer and Friedrich, despite their differences, take a negative view of the nature of "man," and of administrative man in particular, because they agree that "without the checks provided by either the law or the processes of professional socialization, the resultant behaviour of administrators would be both selfish and capricious."[14] Harmon looks to the existentialist's notion of self-development and self-actuali- zation as a basis for a new theory of administrative responsibility. Officials are expected to become much more actively engaged in the initiation and promo- tion of policy. Harmon fails, however, to reconcile this increased participation with the conventional idea that administrators' decisions should be guided by the values and goals of elected politicians within the constraints of the law and the administrative hierarchy.[15]

Theodore Lowi, writing in the context of the United States, recommends that the Supreme Court declare "invalid and unconstitutional any delegation of powers to an administrative agency that is not accompanied by clear standards of implementation."[16] This call to the legislature to specify the course of action of public servants in more precise terms is complemented by a plea for "early and frequent *administrative rule-making*."[17] Rather than relying primarily on case-by-case adjudication under a statute delegating broad powers in vague language, bureaucrats should formulate rules that provide standards for the adjudication of cases under that statute. Harmon and Lowi offer a different but related version of the Finer-Friedrich debate.

Objective and Subjective Responsibility

Frederick Mosher provides a broader, more inclusive classification than the Friedrich-Finer categories by making a distinction between objective responsibility (or accountability) and psychological or subjective responsibility. According to his widely accepted definition, **objective responsibility** "connotes the responsibility of a person or an organization *to* someone else, outside of self, *for* some thing or some kind of performance. It is closely akin to *accountability* or *answerability*. If one fails to carry out legitimate directives, he is judged *irresponsible*, and may be subjected to penalties."[18]

Psychological or **subjective responsibility**, by way of contrast, focusses

> not upon to whom and for what one *is* responsible (according to law and the organization chart) but to whom and for what one *feels* responsible and *behaves* responsibly. This meaning, which is sometimes described as *personal* responsibility, is more nearly synonymous with identification, loyalty and conscience than it is with accountability and answerability.[19]

Thus, Mosher views administrative responsibility as a broad concept that includes administrative accountability.

The presence of subjective or psychological responsibility is more difficult to discern than that of objective responsibility, but there is some evidence of its existence and its influence. The deputy ministers surveyed by the Lambert Commission were in complete agreement that they felt "personally responsible" for ensuring that they had good financial controls.[20] Moreover, when asked to what persons and organizations they considered themselves *most* responsible for specific subjects, a large number of deputies answered "myself" in regard to performing the role of leader for the department's employees, managing their executive team, and building their department's management capability.[21] Despite the importance of this notion of subjective responsibility, it is accountability (objective responsibility) that has received by far the most public and scholarly attention.

ADMINISTRATIVE ACCOUNTABILITY

The questions commonly asked about the accountability of public servants are: *Who* is accountable? *To whom* is accountability owed? *For what* is accountability owed? *By what means* can accountability be achieved?[22] These questions are dealt with in Chapters 15 to 21 as an integral part of an examination of interactions between public servants and other actors in the political system.

The current emphasis on accountability is a result not only of the need to strengthen accountability in government generally; it is also a result of the very broad interpretations that the word accountability has gradually acquired. For example, the Royal Commission on Financial Management and Accountability (the Lambert Commission) viewed accountability as "the activating, but fragile, element permeating a complex network connecting the government upward to Parliament and downward and outward to a geographically dispersed bureaucracy grouped in a bewildering array of departments, corporations, boards and commissions."[23] This definition portrays well the breadth of meaning currently given to the notion of accountability in government. It is, however, too sweeping a definition to be very useful in operational terms; moreover, it covers the accountability of both politicians and public servants, whereas our primary concern is with public service accountability. A narrower and, for our purposes, a more useful definition of **administrative accountability** is:

> the obligation of public servants to be answerable for fulfilling responsibilities that flow from the authority given them. . . . Internal accountability holds public servants answerable to their line superiors for their own actions and the actions of their subordinates. . . . External accountability holds public servants answerable to the public as well. The normal channel through which this requirement is satisfied is the minister.[24]

This definition draws attention to the critical fact that public servants are directly accountable only to a limited number of political actors, and that to hold public servants accountable one must be able to exercise authority over them. Indeed, a more useful distinction than that between internal and external accountability is that between direct and indirect accountability. Public servants are directly accountable only to political and administrative superiors, to the courts, and to any internal governmental authorities (e.g., central agencies) to which accountability is required by law or the administrative hierarchy. They are not directly accountable to the legislature, to pressure groups, to the news media, or to the general public. However, they are generally required to explain their decisions and actions to these entities, and they may feel a sense of psychological or personal responsibility toward them.

Enforcing accountability for the exercise of bureaucratic power has become more difficult as our public services have continued to grow in size and as their responsibilities have grown in complexity. The decision-making process in government is often so lengthy and complicated that it is difficult to single out those public servants who should be held responsible for specific recommendations and decisions. Moreover, as explained in Chapter 17, the present application of the doctrine of ministerial responsibility does not ensure that ministers will be held responsible for maladministration in their departments.

Another obstacle on the road to accountability is the wide range of authorities to which public servants are deemed to be accountable. While, in general, it is agreed that public servants are accountable first of all to their minister, in practice public servants receive directions, rewards, and penalties from a variety of sources. This is one of the major differences between public and private sector administration.

Subsequent chapters will show that governments have an impressive array of mechanisms to promote administrative accountability. Reforms in these mechanisms over the past two decades have included the restructuring of the Cabinet committee system (e.g., the use of policy committees with substantial decision-making powers); an expansion in the number and size of central agencies (e.g., Cabinet secretariats, treasury and management boards, and intergovernmental relations units); changes in the legislative committee system (e.g., new committees and revised procedures); strengthening the role of auditors and adopting a comprehensive auditing system; establishing the Federal Court to hear appeals against administrative decisions; and introducing the system of Increased Ministerial Authority and Accountability (IMAA) to expand the authority and accountability of departments while reducing central agency controls over them.

ADMINISTRATIVE ETHICS[25]

As noted in Chapter 12, *integrity* is a primary administrative value. It can be interpreted to cover a broad range of bureaucratic behaviour, but it is used here in a limited sense to refer to **administrative ethics**, that is, to principles and standards of right conduct for public servants. Certain principles and standards of ethical behaviour (e.g., honesty, truthfulness, fairness) are of such enduring importance in all walks of life that they can be described as *ethical* values. These ethical values can be used to resolve conflicts between such administrative values as accountability and efficiency; they can also be applied to clashes between administrative values on the one hand, and social values like liberty and equality, or personal values like success and wealth, on the other. Consider, for example, public servants whose political superiors direct them to conceal information about a threat to the public's health. The conflict between accountability to their superiors and their sense of responsiveness to the public could be resolved according to the ethical value of truthfulness. Integrity in the sense of ethical behaviour can in some instances override all other values.

Opportunities for public servants to become involved in unethical conduct arise from the power they exercise in the development and administration of public policy. Senior public servants with discretionary authority and confidential information have the greatest opportunities to benefit from unethical conduct. But temptations to engage in unethical behaviour exist at all levels of the administrative hierarchy and at all levels of government (e.g., a senior official with contracting authority in a federal department or a secretary in a municipal government with access to confidential development plans).

Historically, the public's interest in the ethical conduct of government officials, whether politicians or public servants, has waxed and waned as instances of wrongdoing have been exposed, publicized, debated, punished, and then forgotten. But since the early 1970s, there has been continuing anxiety among the public and within governments about the ethical standards of public officials. There is increasing recognition that the ethical dimension of public administration has been unduly neglected in the past.

Much of the recent public and media concern about public service ethics has centred on conflicts of interest and, to a lesser extent, on issues of political partisanship, public comment, and confidentiality. Among the many questions of current concern in these problem areas are the following: What kinds of gifts or entertainment should public servants accept from someone with whom they do business? Under what circumstances is moonlighting acceptable? Is an apparent conflict of interest as serious as an actual conflict? To what extent should public servants participate in partisan political activity? To what extent should public servants criticize government policies and programs in public? Under what circumstances, if any, are public servants justified in leaking government documents?

The effective management of these issues is generally considered to be essential to public trust and confidence in government. Over the past two decades, governments have responded to heightened public concern about these issues by drafting statutes, regulations, guidelines, and codes dealing with ethical conduct. However, these high-profile issues constitute only a small proportion of the total field of ethical problems. Many other ethical issues of enormous importance receive comparatively little public attention. These are issues that relate less to the use of public office for private, personal, or partisan gain and more to ethical and value conflicts and dilemmas that arise in the performance of administrative duties. Among these issues are the following: Under what circumstances, if any, should public servants lie to the public? Should public servants zealously implement a policy that they think is misguided? Do public servants owe their ultimate loyalty to their political superiors? To the public? To their perception of the public interest? To their conscience? Is it appropriate to bend the rules to assist a member of the public who is especially needy or especially deserving? Is the public interest the same thing as the interest of the government in power? What level of risk should a public servant take with the public? Where should the balance be struck between a representative public service and an efficient and effective public service?

It is notable that these issues, compared to issues like conflict of interest and confidentiality, have not only received less public attention but are less amenable to management by written ethics rules. Thus, the effective management of these issues requires that ethics rules in general and ethics codes in particular be supplemented by other means of promoting ethical behaviour, for example, reliance on the role model provided by political and administrative superiors, and on education, training, and development.

The remainder of this section examines, in turn, the costs and benefits of codes of ethics; the form, content, and administration of these codes; and the implications for administrative responsibility of codes of ethics and other means of promoting ethical behaviour.

Costs and Benefits of Codes of Ethics

Disclosures of unethical conduct by government officials during the early 1970s prompted several governments to assess the desirability of providing or improving ethics rules. By the end of the decade, most provincial governments had adopted written rules, often in the form of codes of ethics, to regulate the ethical behaviour of public servants. Developments in the municipal sphere of government have been much slower.

A code of public service ethics is a statement of principles and standards about the right conduct of public servants. It normally contains only a portion of a government's rules on public service ethics and is, therefore, a more narrow term than ethics rules, which refer to statutes, regulations, and guidelines. The form, content, and administration of ethics codes differ significantly from one government to another. Indeed, much of the dispute over the usefulness of codes of ethics arises from the fact that such a wide variety of instruments are described as codes. The situation is further complicated by the fact that public servants may be subject not only to their government's code of ethics but also to codes developed for their own profession (e.g., law, engineering).

Even the most vigorous advocates of codes of ethics for public servants acknowledge that codes are not a panacea for preventing unethical behaviour. There is, however, much disagreement over how useful codes actually are.

Perhaps the most common criticism of codes is that the broad ethical principles contained in many codes are often difficult to apply to specific situations. For example, what precisely does it mean in practice to "put loyalty to the highest moral principles and to country above loyalty to persons, party, or Government department"?[26] A second and related concern is that codes of ethics, even if they contain detailed provisions, are difficult to enforce; indeed, many codes contain no provision for their enforcement. Third, the large scale and complexity of government makes it difficult to draft a code that can be applied fairly and consistently across a large number of departments. Fourth, codes can adversely affect the individual rights and private lives of public servants whose ethical behaviour is beyond reproach. Consider the effect on individual privacy of the requirement in some governments that public servants disclose not only their own financial interests but also those of their spouses and dependent children. Finally, certain ethical and value issues (e.g., determining what measure of risk to the public is acceptable) are not easily amenable to management by ethics rules in general or ethics codes in particular.

On the other hand, codes can reduce uncertainty among public servants as to what constitutes ethical and unethical behaviour. Unwritten rules in the form of understandings and practices leave much room for argument as to what the content of the rules actually is, and what penalties must be paid for violating rules. Second, codes can promote public trust and confidence in the ethical behaviour of public servants. Taxpayers can be better assured, for example, that they will be treated fairly and impartially, and that public servants are less likely to use their position for personal gain. Third, codes can reduce unethical practices by discouraging and punishing them. They provide one of several means by which political leaders and senior managers can hold public servants accountable for their activities. Fourth, codes can sensitize public servants to the fact that the ethical and value dimensions of their decisions and recommendations are as important as, and often more important than, the technical, legal, and political dimensions. Finally, the development of a code of ethics may prompt governments to reassess their existing written or unwritten rules so that the rights and participation of public servants in regard to certain activities (e.g., political partisanship, outside employment) may be enhanced.

The Style and Substance of Ethics Rules

Although Canadian governments have taken varying approaches to the form, content, and administration of their ethics rules, it is widely acknowledged that the best approach is a code of ethics that contains comprehensive coverage of the major ethical problem areas and effective means for the code's administration. It is useful to codify existing rules by bringing them together in a single document, or at least incorporating in that document reference to service-wide rules already existing in statutes and regulations.

Safeguards against unethical conduct can take the *form* of statutes providing for prosecution and punishment by the regular courts (e.g., Criminal Code provisions on bribery and corruption) or of statutes, regulations, or guidelines administered within the government itself. Prosecution by the courts (e.g., under the Criminal Code) is too blunt an instrument to apply to most unethical practices. Many instances of unethical conduct fall into a "grey zone," in that they are unacceptable but cannot be effectively handled by the courts. In other cases, it is debatable whether an offence has actually been committed, since many ethical issues are very complex and the offence may be more apparent than real. In such circumstances, governments are required to exercise judgment as to what penalty, if any, is appropriate. Penalties can range from a reprimand to dismissal.

The *content* of codes of ethics has focussed so heavily on conflicts of interest that it is useful to elaborate on this problem area. A **conflict of interest** may be defined as a situation in which a public employee has a private or personal interest sufficient to influence, or to appear to influence, the objective exercise of his or her official duties. Conflicts of interest receive a great deal of public attention not only because of the prospect of financial gain from such activities but also because of the many varieties of the offence.[27] Among the varieties of conflict of interest are accepting benefits, outside employment, and post-employment.

Accepting benefits of significant value from individuals, groups, or firms with whom the employee has official dealings sometimes borders on bribery and corruption, which is punishable under the Criminal Code. However, the propriety of accepting gifts or hospitality is usually judged on the basis of whether the benefit to the employee is of sufficient value to be likely to influence or *appear* to influence the objective discharge of that person's responsibilities. Twenty-five employees of the Ontario Housing Corporation were charged under the Criminal Code with having accepted gifts from developers. The gifts included colour television sets, Caribbean trips, and amounts of money ranging from $200 to over $12,000.[28] However, employees of the Central Mortgage and Housing Corporation who accepted developers' gifts in the form of liquor, cheese, chocolates, and lunches were simply reprimanded.[29] A less obvious example involves public servants who accept free lunches or dinners from persons in a position to benefit from the public servants' official decisions.

Outside employment, or "moonlighting," constitutes a conflict of interest when that employment reduces significantly the time and effort that public servants devote to their official duties, or when that employment is incompatible with their duties. Thus, a public servant who slept all day on the job after driving a taxi all night would be in a conflict of interest situation; so would a public servant responsible for regulating marine safety who worked for, or owned, a company selling marine safety equipment. A similar example would be a government plumbing inspector with a part-time plumbing business who offers to come back after hours to fix, for a price, some plumbing he or she has just inspected.

The *post-employment* problem arises when a public servant resigns or retires from government to join a firm with which he or she has had official dealings, or that could benefit unduly from information that the public servant acquired while in government. There is often concern that this person may have conferred benefits on the firm in the hope of future employment, or that the firm might gain a competitive advantage by gaining access to confidential information, including trade secrets.

The effective *administration* of ethics rules in these several problem areas is critical to their success in promoting high ethical standards. Provisions for administration of the rules ideally should include publicity, enforcement, and grievance procedures. In governments with a large number of employees and administrative units, it is usually necessary to delegate to individual departments and agencies responsibility not only for elaborating on service-wide rules but also for administering the rules for their own employees.

Most varieties of conflict of interest are covered in the federal government's *Conflict of Interest and Post-Employment Code for the Public Service*.[30] Both new and current employees are required to certify that they have read and understood the code, and that they will observe it as a condition of appointment and employment.

Are the tasks of drafting and administering a code of ethics worth the effort? Governments provide little or no data on the number and nature of ethical offences committed, but it appears that the percentage of public servants involved in unethical conduct is very small. Ethics rules are, however, not designed simply to catch offenders but to provide guidance to public servants who are uncertain as to what activities are permissible and what activities are prohibited. Moreover, a comparatively large cost in time and effort may be justified by the benefit of increased public confidence in government and in the responsibility of public servants.

Ethics Rules and Administrative Responsibility

Written rules can be useful in promoting the high ethical standards required of responsible public servants. However, as noted above, not all ethical problems can be handled by ethics rules. Such rules are of limited assistance in helping public servants to develop skills in the analysis of ethical and value issues and in the resolution of these issues. It is desirable to complement formal rules with formal education, training programs, and exemplary role models.

An increasingly important means of promoting ethical behaviour is to sensitize public servants to the ethical and value dimensions of public service during their pre-employment education and in-service training. Recognition of the importance of this approach can be seen in the growing number of courses on public service ethics in universities and of staff development courses on ethics for those already in the public service.

The influence of administrative superiors is also an extremely important means of promoting ethical behaviour. However, some contemporary governments, and many individual departments, are so large that even senior officials have personal contact with a relatively small percentage of their employees. There is, therefore, less assurance than there used to be that the influence of bureaucratic leaders on ethical matters will flow down the administrative pyramid. This explains in part why many senior public servants support the codification of ethical standards as a means of nurturing responsible administrative behaviour.

THE PUBLIC INTEREST

The Meaning of the Public Interest

The concept of the public interest is very closely related to the issues of administrative responsibility and administrative ethics. Indeed, responsible bureaucratic behaviour is frequently assessed in terms of the bureaucrat's ability to resolve conflicts among administrative and other values according to the criterion of the public interest. Moreover, the public interest has been proposed as the dominant ethical principle or standard for bureaucratic behaviour. One author describes the public interest as "the highest ethical standard applicable to political affairs."[31]

The concept of the public interest, like that of administrative responsibility, has been interpreted in various ways.[32] It has been defined as "the general will," "the wisest and most foresighted interest," a moral imperative "resting on natural law foundations," and "compromise ... as the optimum reconciliation of the competing claims of special and private interests."[33] Each of these definitions is, to some extent, partial or deficient. In the context of administrative decision-making, for example, the first three definitions are too nebulous to provide sufficient guidance to the bureaucrat. However, the interpretation of the public interest as the best possible accommodation of conflicting particular interests provides an essential element of specificity.

The accommodation of the claims of special and private interests connotes a power struggle among competing groups, each possessing approximately equal access to the decision-maker and devoting roughly equivalent resources to the struggle. In reality, as explained in Chapters 20 and 21, both access and resources in money, organization, supporters, and research capacity are uneven among various groups. Moreover, the interests of some segments of the population may not be represented because these segments are underprivileged, uneducated, uninformed, inarticulate, unorganized, underfunded, or simply uninterested. Even if the whole range of relevant special interests is taken into account, the definition is still incomplete. Public interest theorists commonly assert that the public interest is not the mere sum of special interests, no matter how evenly and equitably these interests are represented. Frequently, these special interests are too short-sighted or are unable, on their own, to reach an accommodation of their various interests. In these cases, the critical contribution to the determination of the public interest comes from the decision-maker.

However, as explained in Chapter 12, the avenue to some decisions runs through a myriad of conflicting and complementary values. Among the obstacles along the road is the temptation to succumb to personal or narrow interests when a decision in the broader interest of the general public or of substantial segments of the general public is required. The extent to which bureaucrats are likely to suppress self-interest in a quest for the public interest is a matter for debate. Should the ultimate aim be the development of officials who, like Downs's *statesmen*, have a broad, altruistic, and idealistic devotion to government policies and programs? Or is the inculcation of loyalty to specific programs or administrative units, as in the case of Downs's *zealots* and *advocates*,[34] a sufficient and more realistic goal? Do those who envisage the eventual predominance of self-directing bureaucrats actively pursuing human dignity in every decision[35] have an unduly optimistic view of human nature? Downs contends that, with rare exceptions, "bureaucracies have few places for officials who are loyal to society as a whole" (e.g., for statesmen), and that "this is true even though all administrative textbooks and nearly all administrators at least verbally exhort all officials to exhibit such loyalty."[36]

Determining the Public Interest[37]

The resolution of value conflicts in the light of the public interest is sometimes a difficult challenge for public servants. This is demonstrated well by the following letter to the editor of the *Journal* of the Professional Institute of the Public Service:

> I have been concerned that too rigid an application of... "the Oath of Secrecy" conflicts with professional integrity. Now that environmental concerns, which are frequently matters of opinion, not fact, are being accorded increasing attention, the question becomes more urgent. Many... of Canada's professional biologists who

are well-qualified to speak on environmental matters are muzzled because they are Civil Servants and so any environmental debate is frequently left to extremist and partisan voices.

If one considers a hypothetical case where pressure is being applied, perhaps from ministerial level, to have a contract awarded to a firm which, for professional reasons, is deemed unsatisfactory, how far dare a Civil Servant go in opposing such seemingly unethical practices? What of an employee who is sufficiently troubled by such an incident to discuss it with a priest under "Seal of the Confessional?"

... surely, our responsibility to Canada is greater than any duty we owe to our political masters of the day. We have standards of professional integrity to maintain and a moral position to uphold. The glib, cynical retort, "Well, you can always resign," is hopelessly inadequate. . . .

(Name withheld by request)[38]

Except in situations where bureaucrats have been given complete discretionary authority, they may be able to shift the burden of choice among contending values to their hierarchical superior. *Hierarchy* in administration is a prime safeguard of administrative responsibility in that it forces "important decisions to higher levels of determination or at least higher levels of review where perspectives are necessarily broader, less technical and expert, more political."[39] At the highest policy-making levels of government, it may be argued that, in the final analysis, the determination of the public interest is the task of the elected representatives. Bureaucrats cannot, however, escape the responsibility of providing their political masters with the best possible advice. Moreover, if only in the cause of personal survival, bureaucrats cannot evade the responsibility of pointing out the political, economic, and social costs and benefits of selecting one course of action over another.

Scholarly writings on the public interest demonstrate the difficulty of establishing specific and immutable criteria for how the public interest is determined in any given situation. The public interest may fruitfully be viewed as a dynamic concept. Its content changes from one situation to another, and depends, in large part, on the values of both the decision-maker and the interests whose claims are considered. Nevertheless, public servants can be provided with some guidelines for acting in the public interest. They need to recognize their biases to ensure that they do not ignore important considerations and interests, and to ask the right questions of themselves and others before making a decision. Among the questions to be asked are these: Am I certain that my personal values—and my self-interest—are not overwhelming all other values? Have I identified and consulted "all stakeholders likely to be affected" by my decision? Have I ensured that "the procedures followed in obtaining information and consulting those affected are fair and open?" Have I done "the most comprehensive analysis of the costs and benefits that is possible in the circumstances?"[40]

An important distinction may be made between a *passive* as opposed to an *active* pursuit of the public interest. The public servant who considers the claims only of *organized* special interests, and whose range of values is narrow and inflexible, is passive in the search for the public interest. By way of contrast, the public servant who seeks the views of *all relevant interests*, and whose value framework is comparatively broad and flexible, is in active pursuit of the public interest. Each orientation has its virtues and drawbacks, depending on the issue at hand and the level of the organizational pyramid at which the decision is being made.

ADMINISTRATIVE RESPONSIBILITY AND THE PUBLIC INTEREST

The passive and active orientations toward the public interest may be linked with our earlier distinction between objective and subjective (psychological) responsibility. In a brief and admittedly oversimplified fashion, the main characteristics of two hypothetically extreme types of bureaucrat—the objectively responsible and the subjectively responsible official—are suggested here.

Objectively responsible bureaucrats feel responsible primarily to the legal or formal locus of authority, and take a passive approach to the determination of the public interest. Their most prominent characteristic and value is accountability to those who have the power to promote, displace, or replace them. The controls and influences that they internalize in the form of administrative values are those expressed by their hierarchical superiors. In making and recommending decisions, they anticipate and reflect the desires of their superiors. It is these superiors who have legitimate authority and who may most easily threaten or impose penalties to ensure compliance. Bureaucrats of this type do not actively seek the views of policy actors other than their superiors unless they are required to do so. For example, they consult parties with an interest in impending regulations only if such consultation is required by law or expected by their superiors. Their foremost administrative values include accountability and efficiency. They do not take initiatives or risks that may get them or their superiors into trouble. They are, for example, likely to err on the side of caution in their communications with the media. They also prefer, if possible, that their political and administrative superiors resolve any value dilemmas and determine the content of the public interest for them.

Objectively responsible bureaucrats perceive themselves as ultimately responsible to the general public through the administrative hierarchy, the political executive, and the legislature. Their behaviour is based on the possibility and the desirability of separating policy and administration—even at the senior levels of the public service. In Finer's terminology, they are, therefore, "politically" responsible.

Subjectively responsible bureaucrats are a striking contrast. They feel responsible to a broad range of policy participants and are active in the pursuit of the public interest. Their most outstanding characteristic and value is commitment to what they perceive to be the goals of their department or program. Since they view the expectations of a variety of policy actors as legitimate, the sources of their administrative values are numerous and diverse. Subjectively responsible public servants are frequently in conflict with their superiors, but they are not influenced much by the threat of negative sanctions. They seek the views of interests affected by their decisions and recommendations in the absence of, and even in violation of, any legal or formal obligation to do so. Their primary administrative values include responsiveness and effectiveness. They are innovative, take risks, and bend the rules to achieve their objectives. They urge their superiors to follow certain courses of action and are prepared to resolve by themselves the value dilemmas they encounter in their search for the public interest. Subjectively responsible bureaucrats are, for example, more likely than others to engage in "whistle-blowing," that is, exposing actions of political and administrative superiors that are illegal, unethical, or unduly wasteful of public funds.

The subjectively responsible bureaucrat rejects the possibility and desirability of separating policy and administration—especially at the senior echelons of the bureaucracy. To use Finer's language again, officials of this type are "morally" responsible in that they look to their own conscience rather than to "external punitive controls" for guidance.

Neither the purely objective nor the purely subjective type is appropriate as a model of the responsible bureaucrat. Some characteristics of both types produce conduct that scholars and public officials generally view as undesirable. Undue emphasis on certain elements of objective responsibility may lead to behaviour that is unresponsive or ineffective. At the other extreme, too great an emphasis on particular aspects of subjective responsibility may bring equally undesirable results in the form of behaviour that is unaccountable or inefficient.

If the public service was composed predominantly of either objectively or subjectively responsible bureaucrats, it would tend to manifest the same objectionable features. The "ideal" situation, then, would be a public service in which each public servant strikes that balance between the objective and subjective elements of responsibility that is appropriate to his or her responsibilities and level in the hierarchy.

A recurring theme in many of the remaining chapters of this book is the extent to which controls and influences over the exercise of bureaucratic power promote administrative responsibility. Keep in mind that in popular discussion the terms administrative responsibility and administrative accountability are frequently used interchangeably.

NOTES

1. Carl J. Friedrich, "Responsible Government Service Under the American Constitution," in *Problems of the American Public Service* (New York: McGraw-Hill, 1935), pp. 3-74, and "Public Policy and the Nature of Administrative Responsibility," in Carl J. Friedrich and Edward S. Mason, eds., *Public Policy* (Cambridge: Harvard University Press, 1940), pp. 3-24. Herman Finer, "Better Government Personnel," *Political Science Quarterly* (1936): 569 ff. and "Administrative Responsibility in Democratic Government," *Public Administration Review* 1, no. 4 (1941): 335-50. The most compre-

hensive statements of the opposing positions are found in the 1940-1941 exchange of articles.

2. Finer, "Administrative Responsibility in Democratic Government," p. 337.
3. Friedrich, "Public Policy and the Nature of Administrative Responsibility," p. 12.
4. Ibid., p. 10.
5. Ibid., p. 5.
6. Finer, pp. 339-40.
7. Ibid., p. 336.
8. Ibid., p. 336. (Emphasis added.)
9. Friedrich, p. 19.
10. Ibid., p. 23.
11. Finer, p. 349.
12. Ibid.
13. See, for example, the excellent summary and critique of five major interpretations in Arch Dotson, "Approaches to Administrative Responsibility," *Western Political Quarterly* 10 (September 1957): 701-27.
14. Michael M. Harmon, "Normative Theory and Public Administration: Some Suggestions for a Redefinition of Administrative Responsibility," in Frank Marini, ed., *Toward a New Public Administration: The Minnowbrook Perspective* (Scranton, Pa.: Chandler, 1971), p. 173.
15. See John Paynter, "Comment: On a Redefinition of Administrative Responsibility," ibid., p. 187.
16. Ibid., p. 298.
17. Ibid., p. 299.
18. Ibid., p. 7. (Emphasis added.)
19. Frederick C. Mosher, *Democracy in the Public Service* (New York: Oxford University Press, 1968), pp. 7-10.
20. Royal Commission on Financial Management and Accountability, *Final Report* (Ottawa: Supply and Services, 1979), p. 458.
21. Ibid., p. 471.
22. See Kenneth Kernaghan and John Langford, *The Responsible Public Servant* (Toronto: Institute of Public Administration of Canada and Halifax: Institute for Research on Public Policy, 1990), ch. 7.
23. Royal Commission on Financial Management and Accountability, *Final Report*, p. 9.
24. Government of Ontario, Management Board of Cabinet, *Accountability*, OPS Management Series (Toronto: Queen's Printer, 1982).
25. For a detailed treatment of administrative ethics in Canada, see Kernaghan and Langford, *The Responsible Public Servant.*
26. United States, *Code of Ethics for Government Service*, House Concurrent Resolution 175, 85th Congress, 2nd session (1985).
27. For an explanation and illustrations of eight varieties of conflict of interest, see Kernaghan and Langford, *The Responsible Public Servant*, ch. 6.
28. *The Globe and Mail*, October 2, 1974.
29. *The Globe and Mail*, May 4, 1979.
30. (Ottawa: Supply and Services, 1985).
31. C. W. Cassinelli, "The Public Interest in Political Ethics," in Carl J. Friedrich, ed., *Nomos V: The Public Interest* (New York: Atherton Press, 1962), p. 46.
32. See especially Pendleton Herring, *Public Administration and the Public Interest* (New York: McGraw Hill, 1936); Frank Sorauf, "The Public Interest Reconsidered," *Journal of Politics* 19 (November 1957): 616-39; Glendon Schubert, *The Public Interest:*

A *Critique of a Political Concept* (Glencoe, Ill.: The Free Press, 1960); Friedrich, ed., *Nomos V: The Public Interest*; Herbert J. Storing, "The Crucial Link: Public Administration, Responsibility and the Public Interest," *Public Administration Review* 24 (March 1964): 39-46; and Richard E. Flathman, *The Public Interest* (New York: John Wiley & Sons, 1966). For a list of definitions of the public interest and a bibliography on this subject, see W.T. Stanbury, "Definitions of the Public Interest," in Douglas G. Hartle, *Public Policy Decision Making and Regulation* (Montreal: Institute for Research on Public Policy, 1979), pp. 213-18.

33. Rowland Egger, "Responsibility and Administration: An Exploratory Essay," in Roscoe Martin, ed., *Public Administration and Democracy: Essays in Honor of Paul H. Appleby* (Syracuse: Syracuse University Press, 1965), pp. 311-13.

34. A. Downs, *Inside Bureaucracy* (Boston: Little, Brown, 1967), p. 88. "*Zealots* are loyal to relatively narrow policies or concepts, such as the development of nuclear submarines. They seek power both for its own sake and to effect the policies to which they are loyal ... *Advocates* are loyal to a broader set of functions or to a broader organization than zealots. They also seek power because they want to have a significant influence upon policies and actions concerning those functions or organizations."

35. See especially Eugene P. Dvorin and Robert H. Simmons, *From Amoral to Humane Bureaucracy* (San Francisco: Canfield, 1972).

36. Downs, *Inside Bureaucracy*, p. 111.

37. For an examination of four major approaches to operationalizing the public interest, see Kernaghan and Langford, *The Responsible Public Servant*, ch. 2.

38. *Journal*, 52 (November 1973): 9-10

39. Mosher, *Democracy and the Public Service*, p. 212.

40. Kernaghan and Langford, *The Responsible Public Servant*, pp. 49-50.

BIBLIOGRAPHY

Appleby, Paul. *Morality and Administration in Democratic Government*. Baton Rouge, La: Louisiana State University Press, 1952.

Baker, Walter A. "Accountability, Responsiveness and Public Sector Productivity." *Canadian Public Administration* 23 (Winter 1980): 542-47.

Bok, Sissela. *Lying*. New York: Pantheon, 1978.

Canada. Royal Commission on Financial Management and Accountability. *Final Report*. Ottawa: Supply and Services, 1979.

Canada. Privy Council Office. *Responsibility in the Constitution*. Submission to the Royal Commission on Financial Management and Accountability, March 1979.

Cameron, D. M. "Power and Responsibility in the Public Service: Summary of Discussions." *Canadian Public Administration* 21 (Fall 1978): 359-72.

Cooper, Terry L. *The Responsible Administrator*. Port Washington, New York: Kennikat Press, 1982.

Denhardt, Kathryn G. *The Ethics of Public Service*. Westport, Conn.: Greenwood Press, 1988.

Dotson, Arch. "Approaches to Administrative Responsibility." *Western Political Quarterly* 10 (September 1957): 701-27.

Finer, Herman. "Administrative Responsibility in Democratic Government." *Public Administration Review* 1 (Summer 1941): 335-50.

Finer, Herman. "Better Government Personnel." *Political Science Quarterly* (1936): 569ff.

Friedrich, Carl J. "Public Policy and the Nature of Administrative Responsibility." In Carl J. Friedrich and Edward S. Mason, eds., *Public Policy*. Cambridge, Mass.: Harvard University Press, 1940, pp. 3-24.

Friedrich, Carl J. "Responsible Government Service Under the American Constitution." In *Problems of the American Public Service*. New York: McGraw-Hill, 1935, pp. 3-74.

Friedrich, Carl J. *Nomos V: The Public Interest*. New York: Atherton Press, 1962.

Herring, Pendleton. *Public Administration and the Public Interest*. New York: McGraw-Hill, 1936.

Hodgetts, J. E. "Government Responsiveness to the Public Interest: Has Progress Been Made?" *Canadian Public Administration* 24 (Summer 1981): 216-31.

Hodgetts, J. E. "Implicit Values in the Administration of Public Affairs." *Canadian Public Administration* 25 (Winter 1982): 471-83.

Jabbra, Joseph G., and O.P. Dwivedi, eds. *Public Service Accountability: A Comparative Perspective*. West Hartford, Conn.: Kumarian Press, 1988.

Kernaghan, Kenneth. "Codes of Ethics and Administrative Responsibility." *Canadian Public Administration* 17 (Winter 1974): 527-41.

Kernaghan, Kenneth. "Codes of Ethics and Public Administration: Progress, Problems and Prospects." *Public Administration* 58 (Summer 1980): 207-24.

Kernaghan, Kenneth. *Ethical Conduct: Guidelines for Government Employees*. Toronto: Institute of Public Administration of Canada, 1975.

Kernaghan, Kenneth. "Responsible Public Bureaucracy: A Rationale and a Framework for Analysis." *Canadian Public Administration* 16 (Winter 1973): 572-603.

Kernaghan, Kenneth. "The Conscience of the Bureaucrat: Accomplice or Constraint?" *Canadian Public Administration* 27 (Winter 1984): 576-91.

Kernaghan, Kenneth, and John Langford. *The Responsible Public Servant*. Toronto: Institute of Public Administration of Canada, and Halifax: Institute for Research on Public Policy, 1990.

Laframboise, H. L. "Conscience and Conformity: The Uncomfortable Bedfellows of Accountability." *Canadian Public Administration* 26 (Fall 1983): 325-43.

Mosher, Frederick. *Democracy and the Public Service*. New York: Oxford University Press, 1968.

Osbaldeston, Gordon. *Keeping Deputy Ministers Accountable*. Toronto: McGraw-Hill Ryerson, 1989.

Rohr, John A. *Ethics for Bureaucrats: An Essay on Law and Values*. New York: Marcel Dekker, 1978.

Schubert, Glendon. *The Public Interest: A Critique of a Political Concept*. Glencoe, Ill.: The Free Press, 1960.

Spiro, Herbert. *Responsibility in Government: Theory and Practice*. New York: Van Nostrand Reinhold, 1969.

Thompson, Dennis F. "Moral Responsibility of Public Officials: The Problem of Many Hands." *The American Political Science Review* 74 (1980): 905-16.

CASES

In *Case Program in Canadian Public Administration* (Toronto: Institute of Public Administration of Canada):

A Conflict of Loyalties. By Kenneth Kernaghan

The Four Million Dollar Typo: A Case About Accountability. By Laurence E. St. Laurent and Sandford F. Borins

The Alan Jeffrey Affair. By Kenneth Kernaghan

Perceiving Conflict of Interest: Bureaucratic Discretion in Contracting. By S. L. Sutherland

V

THE BUREAUCRACY IN THE POLITICAL SYSTEM

15

The Executive and the Bureaucracy

In Canada, the executive part of government is composed of the *formal* executive (the Governor General, provincial Lieutenant Governors) and the *political* executive (the Prime Minister or provincial premiers and the Cabinet). The term *executive* is often used to encompass both the Cabinet and the bureaucracy, but a more descriptive term is *the executive-bureaucratic sphere* of government. This sphere includes three of the major categories of interaction shown in Figure 12.2 in Chapter 12, namely executive-bureaucratic, interdepartmental, and intra-departmental. The main actors involved in these categories are the Prime Minister (or Premier), Cabinet, Cabinet ministers, central agencies, departments, and other administrative units. The functions of these actors were outlined in Chapters 8 to 10. This chapter focusses on relations between the political executive and the bureaucracy; the next chapter deals with interdepartmental and intradepartmental relations. Two concepts of special use in explaining these relations between and among political executives and bureaucrats are coordination and ministerial responsibility.

COORDINATION AND MINISTERIAL RESPONSIBILITY

Chapter 12 explained the importance and pervasiveness of coordination in Canadian governments. In this chapter, we will see that the Cabinet and the bureaucracy are the primary instruments for coordinating the development and implementation of public policy. Moreover, coordination is closely related to the principles of collective ministerial responsibility (or Cabinet responsibility) and individual ministerial responsibility, which were discussed briefly in Chapter 8.

Ministerial Responsibility

According to the principle of **collective ministerial responsibility**, ministers are responsible as a group (that is, as members of the Cabinet) for the policies and management of the government as a whole. The Cabinet must resign if it loses the confidence of the legislature, that is, if it loses the support of the majority of the members of the House of Commons (or of a provincial legislature). Individual ministers must, in public, support the decisions of the Cabinet, acting as a collectivity, so as to maintain at least the appearance of Cabinet solidarity. More specifically, ministers are required, in private, to work out a consensus on the content of public policies and on the allocation of resources for the development and implementation of these policies. Ministers who cannot support a Cabinet decision in public are expected to resign from the Cabinet.

The principle of **individual ministerial responsibility**, which is explained at length in Chapter 17, is subject to varying interpretations. In general, however, it refers to the responsibility of the minister, as the political head of a department, to answer to the legislature and, through the legislature, to the public both for his or her personal acts and for the acts of departmental subordinates. The minister is also legally responsible for the policies, programs, and administration of his or her department.

Coordination and Hierarchy

The principles of collective and individual ministerial responsibility significantly determine the nature of power relations not only between politicians and bureaucrats but also among the bureaucrats themselves. The principles have an especially important effect on the organizational design of the executive sphere of government. Organizational charts of the Government of Canada typically depict this sphere as an hierarchical arrangement of offices. It is evident from the fold-out organizational chart in this book that, aside from the Governor General, the Prime Minister and the Cabinet stand at the pinnacle of the hierarchy from which lines of authority flow down to departments headed by Cabinet ministers and to Crown agencies reporting to Cabinet ministers. Those central agencies that have departmental form and that report to a minister (e.g., Finance, Treasury Board Secretariat) are normally portrayed as equal in status to the regular operating departments and ministries of state strung horizontally across the chart. Other central agencies (e.g., the Prime Minister's Office and the Privy Council Office) are shown in a staff (advisory) relationship to the Prime Minister and the Cabinet.

However, the organizational chart discloses little about the complex pattern of power relations in the executive realm, especially insofar as these relations involve the exercise of influence rather than control. The organizational chart exposes only the bare bones of political-bureaucratic interaction. This organizational skeleton reveals simply the formal lines of authority through which control moves down the governmental pyramid and accountability moves up. The "informal organization" is hidden from view. Similarly, an organizational chart of a single department or agency that purports to describe the reality of administrative life simply as a hierarchy of superior-subordinate relationships or as a "chain of command" is misleading.

The deficiencies or "pathologies" of bureaucracy in general, and of its hierarchical feature in particular, have been discussed at length elsewhere.[1] Hierarchy does, however, serve several important purposes. One of these is particularly relevant to a discussion of ministerial responsibility in that hierarchy provides for unity of command and of direction both at the top of the government (by the Prime Minister or Premier and the Cabinet) and at the top of government departments (by ministers). In other words, hierarchy promotes accountability. Hierarchy also facilitates coordination. Beginning with the Cabinet as the central coordinating mechanism of government, various means of pursuing policy and administrative coordination permeate the executive-bureaucratic arena. We shall see that ministers, in fulfilling both their collective responsibility for coordinating government as a whole and their individual responsibility for coordinating their departments, are obliged to rely heavily on senior bureaucrats in central agencies and departments.

Aside from hierarchical control, power in the executive sphere is exercised in the form of influence. This fact is demonstrated well by the literature on the **bureaucratic politics** approach to policy-making.[2] Allison and Halperin note that the bureaucratic politics approach focusses "primarily on the individuals within a government, and the interaction among them, as determinants of the actions of a government."[3] The interaction of these individuals, either within or between administrative units, may involve conflict, bargaining, compromise, and persuasion rather than hierarchical control. However, in a parliamentary system, like that of Canada, bureaucratic politics tends to be *muted* because: "(i) there is a conscious effort to coordinate policy; (ii) this coordination is made easier by the 'casual processes of intra-bureaucratic consultation and exchange'; and (iii) Cabinet is able, where necessary, to settle serious conflicts among departments with divergent interests and preferences."[4] Nevertheless, the bureaucratic politics model does indicate that, in executive-bureaucratic relations, power is exercised not only in the form of control through the governmental hierarchy but also in the form of influence through bargaining and negotiation.

The Key Role of the Deputy Minister

Easily the most dominant *bureaucratic* actors in these relations are the deputy ministers of government departments[5] and their central agency equivalents (e.g., the Clerk of the Privy Council and Secretary to the Cabinet, the Secretary of the Treasury Board). Indeed, deputy ministers play such a pivotal role in the decision-making process that an effective means of understanding the place of the bureaucracy in the Canadian political system is to view the system from the perspective of a deputy minister.

Ministers play the leading roles in the political system as a whole, but they share centre stage with their deputies in the executive-bureaucratic theatre of government. The Royal Commission on Financial Management and Accountability treated the deputy as a critical link in the chain of accountability and concluded that "any defence of ministerial responsibility that did not take into account the real and independent role of the deputy in the administration of government would ultimately prove destructive to the doctrine itself."[6] Deputies yield the spotlight to ministers on policy decisions, but as supporting actors they perform onerous advisory and administrative roles. In carrying out these responsibilities, deputies must be sensitive not only to administrative, technical, and financial considerations but also to the partisan political implications of their advice and actions. They are, in addition, entangled in the net of bureaucratic politics within their departments, and between their departments and other administrative units. In short, deputies are challenged to perform the difficult feat of keeping their nose to the grindstone, their ear to the ground, and their back to the wall. Moreover, in the executive-bureaucratic sphere, deputies are required to look in three directions to find the audience for their performance. They must look upward to their political superiors, laterally to their administrative peers, and downward to their departmental subordinates. The pervasive role of deputy ministers will be evident in subsequent discussion of relations between and among bureaucrats, the Prime Minister, and the Cabinet.

THE PRIME MINISTER AND THE CABINET

The Prime Minister

In the Canadian political system, the Prime Minister (or a provincial Premier) and his or her Cabinet colleagues possess the foremost power and responsibility for making and implementing public policy. In very large part, they determine the political and policy parameters within which the many participants in the political system interact. In the executive realm of government, the Cabinet, acting primarily through Cabinet committees, provides the general framework of policies for which public servants must devise programs and for which resources must be allocated through the many departments and agencies.[7] Given their individual and collective responsibility for the performance of the public service, ministers must strive to control and influence bureaucratic behaviour. They evaluate and coordinate policy and program proposals emanating from departments and bring partisan political considerations to bear on these proposals. They also initiate policy proposals of their own. In their capacity as Cabinet members, federal ministers receive a great deal of political, policy, and administrative support, primarily from the central agencies described in Chapter 8 (the Prime Minister's Office, the Privy Council Office, the Federal-Provincial Relations Office, the Treasury Board Secretariat, the Department of Finance). This central agency support is generally channelled to ministers in their capacity as chairpersons of Cabinet committees. In their capacity as political heads of government departments, ministers receive this assistance primarily from their deputy ministers and from the staff in their ministerial offices.

The federal Cabinet is located at the centre of a complicated network of political-bureaucratic relations, and the Prime Minister is the central figure in that network. It is generally acknowledged that the Prime Minister is much more than "first among equals" in relation to Cabinet colleagues. In fact, several scholars have argued in recent years that the Prime Minister's power has been aggrandized to the point where Canada has "prime ministerial" rather than Cabinet government. One author has even suggested that we "seem to have created in Canada a presidential system without its congressional advantages."[8]

Similar arguments have *not* been made so strongly about the role of provincial Premiers. In any event, it is generally agreed that the claims about the expansion of prime ministerial power have some basis in reality, but have been overstated.

The power of the Prime Minister in the political system generally, and in relation to government departments specifically, is often exaggerated. Certainly the Prime Minister is a dominant figure by virtue of his or her responsibilities for leading the governing political party, chairing the Cabinet and key Cabinet committees, acting as chief spokesperson for the government, and appointing and removing both ministers and deputy ministers. Moreover, the Prime Minister can control and influence government departments (and individual bureaucrats) both indirectly through ministers and directly.

There are, however, severe constraints on the ability of the Prime Minister and, indeed, of most provincial Premiers to exercise their powers fully. Their time is so precious that they can afford to become actively involved only in those few policy areas or issues in which they have a personal interest or that command attention on the grounds of urgency or partisan politics. Certainly, as chairperson of Cabinet, the Prime Minister is the key actor in the central policy-making and coordinating institution of government, but he or she alone cannot direct or coordinate the activities of the vast number of bureaucratic actors in government. The Prime Minister must rely on the assistance of Cabinet colleagues and central agencies.

Over the past two decades, Canadian Prime Ministers as well as several provincial Premiers have made vigorous efforts to strengthen political control, especially Cabinet control, over the making and coordination of public policy. Among the primary means of pursuing this objective have been the reform of the Cabinet committee system and the expansion of the role of central agencies. The development and current status of each of these is discussed below. Table 15.1 provides a chronology of the evolution of Cabinet committees and central agencies from the beginning of the Diefenbaker government in 1957.

Cabinet Committees

Taken together, Cabinet committees are responsible for coordinating policies and programs, allocating human and financial resources, and controlling the bureaucracy. Except for the Treasury Board, which is a Cabinet committee provided for in the Financial Administration Act, the existence and responsibilities of Cabinet committees are determined by the Prime Minister.

The significance and sophistication of the Cabinet committee system in the federal government have increased greatly since the late 1930s, and especially since the mid-1960s. Before the Second World War, there were only three Cabinet committees. In 1939, ten new committees were created to facilitate and coordinate Canada's war operations; the most important of these committees was the War Committee chaired by the Prime Minister. Between 1945 and 1964, Cabinet committees were largely of an ad hoc nature; they were usually created to consider specific issues referred to them by Cabinet, and they were abolished when their job was done.[9]

Table 15.1
EVOLUTION OF CABINET STRUCTURES AND CENTRAL AGENCIES

Prime Minister	Ministry Size	Cabinet and Central Agencies
Diefenbaker (1957-1963)	17-23	• infrequent meetings of committees • several Cabinet meetings weekly
Pearson (1963-1968)	25-26	• 9 standing committees 1968; issues generally to committee before Cabinet • Cabinet meetings weekly • Priorities and Planning (1968) • TBS split from Finance (1966) with separate minister
Trudeau (1968-1979)	27-33	• fewer committees with more authority • FPRO split from PCO (1975) • OCG split from TBS (1977) • MSED established (1979)
Clark (1979-1980)	30	• Inner Cabinet plus 12 committees • PEMS established • MSSD set up (proclamation 1980)
Trudeau (1980-1984)	32-37	• Priorities and Planning with authority to issue decisions • PEMS elaborated • MSERD with FEDCs (1982)
Turner (1984)	29	• Communications, Labour Relations, and Western Affairs Committees wound up • MSERD and MSSD wound up; FEDCs to DRIE • "mirror committees" wound up
Mulroney (1984-1988)	40	• Envelopes consolidated • PEMS rules simplified • Cabinet papers further streamlined • Communications Committee set up • Privatization, Regulatory Affairs and Operations established
Mulroney (1988-)	40	• PEMS abolished • sectoral committees abolished • Environment, Economic Policy, Human Resources, and National Identity Committees set up • ERC created • size of committees reduced

Source: Updated and abridged from Ian D. Clark, "Recent Changes in the Cabinet Decision-Making System in Ottawa," *Canadian Public Administration* 28 (Summer 1985): 188-89.

In 1968, however, Prime Minister Lester Pearson modified the Cabinet committee system by replacing the ad hoc committees with nine standing committees so as "to obtain, under the Prime Minister's leadership, thorough consideration of policies, co-ordination of government action, and timely decisions in a manner consistent with ministerial and Cabinet responsibility."[10] Special committees and additional standing committees were subsequently established according to need. In 1968, Mr. Pearson created the Priorities and Planning Committee, which he chaired, to set overall government priorities as a framework for expenditure decisions. The practice of requiring that matters be considered by Cabinet committees before coming to the full Cabinet was initiated, and public servants were permitted to attend Cabinet committee meetings on a more regular and frequent basis.

The general configuration of the existing Cabinet system dates from the election of Pierre Elliott Trudeau as Prime Minister in 1968. He reorganized the Cabinet committee system "to permit a greater centralization of functions and the delegation of certain powers of decision to the committees."[11] The reduction of the number of standing committees to eight and the setting of regular times for the weekly meeting or meetings of each committee improved the attendance of ministers. An extremely important innovation was to expand the powers of the committees from making recommendations to Cabinet to allowing them to take certain "decisions" on their own. These decisions, called "committee recommendations," were annexed to the agenda for Cabinet meetings and were routinely ratified unless a minister specifically requested that they be discussed in full Cabinet. As a result of these changes, the number of Cabinet meetings declined considerably while the number of Cabinet committee meetings increased dramatically. The nature and responsibilities of Cabinet committees evolved over time but, by 1978, there were still eight committees; five of these dealt with major policy sectors (Economic Policy, Social Policy, Culture and Native Affairs, External Policy and Defence, and Government Operations) and three were co-ordinating committees (Priorities and Planning, Treasury Board, and Legislation and House Planning). Secretariat support for these committees (except for Treasury Board) was provided by the PCO. However, a special Cabinet committee called the Board of Economic Development Ministers (BED) was established in 1978 with a secretariat independent of the PCO.

Further changes in the Cabinet committee system were made by Prime Minister Clark in 1979. The Priorities and Planning Committee was replaced by an Inner Cabinet of twelve ministers that had final decision-making authority; the full Cabinet, which met less frequently than under Mr. Trudeau, confined its deliberations primarily to coordination and to politically sensitive or controversial questions. (The inner Cabinet was abolished and the Planning and Priorities Committee was restored when Mr. Trudeau was returned to office in early 1980.) The secretariat for BED was enlarged and formalized in the form of a new central agency called the Ministry of State for Economic Development which, in 1982, under the Trudeau Government, became the Ministry of State for Economic and Regional Development (MSERD); still another central agency was created under the name of the Ministry of State for Social Development to provide staff support for the Cabinet Committee on Social and Native Affairs. The most important organizational initiative of the Clark Government was the introduction of the Policy and Expenditure Management System (PEMS), also called the "envelope" system, which is discussed below.

During his brief tenure, Prime Minister Turner abolished three Cabinet committees and dismantled the two "new" central agencies—the Ministries of

State for Economic and Regional Development and for Social Development—so that public service support for Cabinet committees could be consolidated within the traditional central agencies—the PCO, the TBS, and the Department of Finance. He also eliminated the "mirror committees," which were composed of deputy minsters and were public service counterparts to the policy committees of Cabinet.

The Policy and Expenditure Management System (PEMS)

The overall aim of PEMS was to give Cabinet greater control over the management of both policies and expenditures. This objective was pursued by integrating the processes of policy-making and fiscal and expenditure planning within the Cabinet committee system. More specifically, PEMS was designed to ensure that the government's decisions on priorities and policies were closely integrated with the allocation of resources. Thus, policy decisions and related expenditure decisions were made by the same Cabinet committee and at the same time. With the intent of increasing ministerial direction and control, PEMS decentralized decision-making authority for both policies and expenditures from Cabinet to Cabinet committees. In addition, PEMS provided for the setting of priorities and expenditure *limits* before developing expenditure *plans*. This was intended to allow sufficient time in the planning process for ministers to review and change policies and to reallocate resources.

A central feature of this system was that specific expenditure limits, called resource envelopes, were set. Total expenditures covering a five-year period were divided into eight envelopes for eight policy sectors. Responsibility for managing the eight policy sectors within the expenditure limits was assigned to five Cabinet policy committees. For example, the Social Development envelope was assigned to the Cabinet Committee on Social Development, which allocated funds to various departments and agencies in that policy sector. The prominent role played by central agencies in the Cabinet decision-making system since the late 1960s was preserved under PEMS.

Prime Minister Mulroney made several changes to the Cabinet decision-making system during his first term of office, including the simplification of the procedures of PEMS. All these changes made by successive Prime Ministers resulted, by 1988, in a Cabinet committee structure under Prime Minister Mulroney that consisted of six committees connected with PEMS (Priorities and Planning, Treasury Board, Social Development, Economic and Regional Development, Foreign and Defence Policy, and Government Operations), and four other committees (Communications, Legislation and House Planning, Security and Intelligence, and the Special Committee of Council).

The 1988-89 Mulroney Reforms and the Death of PEMS

The demise of PEMS accompanied the major changes in the Cabinet decision-making system made during Mr. Mulroney's second term of office (shown in Figure 15.1). These changes were designed, in large part, to centralize and

Figure 15.1
CABINET STRUCTURE FOR POLICY COORDINATION AND MANAGEMENT

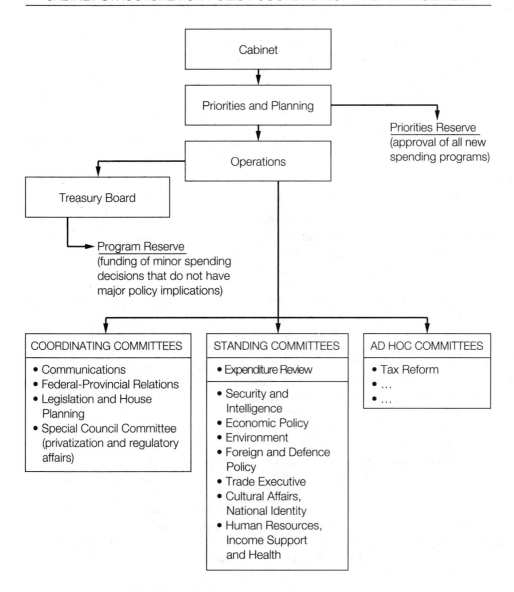

strengthen control over expenditure decisions. The central role of the Priorities and Planning Committee was further enhanced. It not only has authority to review the decisions of the other Cabinet committees; it is now the sole Cabinet committee with authority to approve expenditures on new "big ticket" items.

Treasury Board has been given responsibility for approving expenditures on smaller items.

Thus, the policy committees of Cabinet no longer determine the allocation of funds from the resource envelopes; rather, they are expected to focus their attention on policy. To this end, the committee system has been further restructured. The former broad sectoral committees (e.g., Social Development, Economic and Regional Development) have been abolished. However, the number of committees has increased from ten to fourteen because four new policy committees have been created, namely, the committees on the Environment; Economic Policy; Human Resources, Income Support and Health; and Cultural Affairs and National Identity. Moreover, membership on each Cabinet committee has been reduced from 22–23 ministers to 8–12 ministers.

The Priorities and Planning Committee

During the whole period from 1968, the Priorities and Planning Committee has been the leading Cabinet committee. Until early 1989, it was composed of the Prime Minister, as chairperson, and sixteen ministers, including the chairpersons of the other Cabinet committees and the Minister of Finance. A few additional ministers were chosen because of the Prime Minister's respect for their views or to achieve regional representation. The committee is responsible for deciding upon the fiscal framework, for establishing overall government priorities, for detailed consideration of major policy issues, for federal-provincial matters of general import and problems of a cross-cutting nature that involve more than one Cabinet committee, and for managing the expenditure of public funds in several policy sectors. The committee can ratify decisions made by other Cabinet committees and can make final decisions on most other matters. In practice, "most items of general interest (e.g., Throne Speech preparation, major foreign policy initiatives) that are brought initially to Priorities and Planning are subsequently taken to cabinet for discussion."[12] This ensures that "all ministers have a chance to express their views on virtually all matters of general interest."[13] Under the Mulroney government, the concentration of governmental power in the hands of the Prime Minister has been accompanied by an enhanced role for the Priorities and Planning Committee and the PMO.

The size of the Priorities and Planning Committee has been expanded and its membership has been made more representative of the various regions of the country. This is appropriate because the committee has effectively replaced the Cabinet as the executive decision-making body of the government. Cabinet has become largely a forum for partisan political discussion. Moreover, since the present Priorities and Planning Committee is about the same size as the full Cabinet was thirty years ago, the Operations Committee, which emerged as an informal committee early in 1988, now has formal authority "to review the Government's weekly agenda to ensure proper coordination in responding to issues and developing new policies."[14] It is an extremely influential committee in that it reviews the agendas of the policy committees and examines any policy proposals that may create expenditure problems before these proposals are considered by the policy committees. In effect, it acts as a gatekeeper to the Priorities and Planning Committee and sets the Cabinet agenda. This committee is composed of the Deputy Prime Minister as chairperson and seven other influential ministers.

The final reform was the creation of the Expenditure Review Committee, which is chaired by the Prime Minister and has seven other members. This committee is responsible for ensuring "that the government's expenditures continue to be directed to its highest priorities, and that expenditure control continues to contribute to deficit reduction."[15] Like the Operations Committee, this committee is extremely influential. It reviews government expenditures as a basis for the annual budget.

Central Agencies

As noted earlier, there is much debate as to which administrative units should be described as central agencies. In this chapter, the focus is on the Prime Minister's Office (PMO) and the so-called "traditional" central agencies, that is, the Department of Finance, the PCO, and the Treasury Board Secretariat (TBS). The senior officials of these agencies, together with those in the Federal-Provincial Relations Office (FPRO), have been described in a major study of federal central agencies as "superbureaucrats" because they "are among the most powerful public servants in government" and because "in performing their duties they often cross the line between bureaucrat and policy maker...."[16] The detailed description of the functions of these agencies provided in Chapter 8 will not be repeated here. This chapter is concerned with the interaction between these central agencies and other actors in the executive-bureaucratic sphere of government.

Over the past two decades, the role of central agencies in assisting political executives to control and coordinate government policies and programs has expanded. In serving both the Prime Minister and the Cabinet, central agency officials control and influence departmental officials by affecting the allocation of human and financial resources, the organization of governmental and departmental machinery, and the coordination of intergovernmental relations. Central agencies thereby help to promote such administrative values as efficiency, effectiveness, and accountability.

During the early years of the first Trudeau government, elected in 1968, the PMO and the PCO were reorganized and expanded so as to improve their advisory and coordinating functions. The growth in the staff and expenditure of these offices led some commentators to compare them to the White House Staff and the Executive Office of the President in the United States, and to suggest that the expansion of these offices was part of the Prime Minister's objective of "presidentializing" the Canadian political system and enhancing prime ministerial power. This suggestion is now seen to have been greatly exaggerated. Moreover, there is wide recognition that "political executives require elaborate machinery and large staffs devoted to coordination and control just to get on with the job of governing."[17]

The relative importance of the PMO and the traditional central agencies has shifted since 1968, but all have continued to play a prominent role in supporting the Prime Minister and the Cabinet. The interaction and shifts in relative power among the central agencies themselves will be explained in the next chapter on interdepartmental and interagency relations. It is sufficient to note here that the balance of power among the agencies was altered as a result of the creation in 1979 of two new central agencies—the Ministry of State for Social Development (MSSD) and the Ministry of State for Economic Development, which, in 1982, became the Ministry of State for Economic and Regional Development (MSERD). As noted above, these two agencies were abolished by Prime Minister Turner in 1984 as part of an effort to simplify the Cabinet decision-making system.

It is notable that the PMO is a central agency unlike the others in that it is primarily a partisan instrument of the Prime Minister. The overriding concern of PMO officials, who are political appointees rather than career public servants, is the political fortunes of the Prime Minister and the governing party. While they owe their first loyalty to the Prime Minister, these officials also serve the political interests of the Cabinet as a whole. The PMO helps to ensure that the Prime Minister is knowledgeable about major policy issues, especially their political implications, and that he or she has an alternative source of policy advice to that provided by departmental ministers and officials.

In contrast to the PMO, officials in the PCO are generally career public servants who are non-partisan; they are, however, highly sensitive to political considerations. The Department of Finance and TBS are also composed of career public servants. The Prime Minister and Cabinet rely heavily on the central agencies to control and influence the behaviour of departmental public servants. This is especially evident in the sphere of financial management. We shall see in Chapters 26 and 27 that the Department of Finance and the TBS are critical forces in influencing and facilitating Cabinet decisions on the management of financial resources.

The Prime Minister and, to a lesser extent, Cabinet ministers, with the assistance of central agencies, exercise important functions in the sphere of human resource management, particularly in the staffing area. The Prime Minister and the Cabinet make what are called Governor in Council appointments to the senior levels of the bureaucracy. The choice of deputy ministers is, by convention, the prerogative of the Prime Minister who receives advice from the Secretary to the Cabinet and normally discusses possible candidates with the minister of the department in question. With respect to the several hundred senior positions in agencies, boards, and commissions, the Prime Minister usually consults with those ministers whose portfolio or region of the country is affected by an appointment. These appointments are made by the Governor in Council, that is, by the Governor General upon the recommendation of the Prime Minister and his colleagues. Under Prime Minister Mulroney, control over these appointments has been centralized in the PMO.

The Prime Minister wields substantial power not only in expenditure and human resource management, but also in the organization of the machinery of government. He is advised in this function by the Clerk of the Privy Council and Secretary to the Cabinet, who is supported by the PCO's Machinery of Government Secretariat. This advice can involve the allocation of new policy and program responsibilities to specific departments, as well as major reallocations of existing responsibilities. The Prime Minister's control in this area is beneficial because it helps to avoid clashes among Cabinet ministers over the allocation of governmental responsibilities. The Prime Minister creates new departments as part of his machinery of government responsibilities. Moreover, the Prime Minister and Cabinet have frequently made substantial modifications in existing government organizations under the authority of the Public Service Rearrangement and Transfer of Duties Act, which provides that the Governor in Council may:

(a) transfer any powers, duties or functions or the control or supervision of any part of the public service of Canada from one minister of the Crown to any other minister of the Crown, or from one department or portion of the public service to any other department or portion of the public service; or

(b) amalgamate and combine any two or more departments under one minister of the Crown and under one deputy minister.[18]

The Prime Minister is still the dominant decision-maker with respect to the machinery of government.

Cabinet Approval and Cabinet Documents

Figure 15.2 shows the process by which proposals from government departments for new policies are approved, amended, or rejected by Cabinet committees and by Cabinet, and how the Cabinet's decision, in the form of a record of decision, serves as authority for the allocation of resources for the implementation of those policies. Also, it illustrates the formal and informal interaction among the major players in the executive-bureaucratic arena. Cabinet committees and central agencies clearly play an important role, but policy proposals are formally prepared by government departments and are presented by a minister to the appropriate Cabinet committee, usually in the form of a document called a Memorandum to Cabinet. A minister's policy proposals can, of course, be influenced by a variety of sources, including political parties, interest groups, and individual citizens.

The two principles on which the Cabinet approval process is based are that "all ministers have the right to bring to their colleagues proposals for government action in their area of policy responsibility" and that "all ministers should have the opportunity to express an informed view within the cabinet process on a proposal for which they will share collective responsibility."[19] The **Memorandum to Cabinet** is the key mechanism by which policy proposals are brought

Figure 15.2
PROCESS OF CABINET APPROVAL

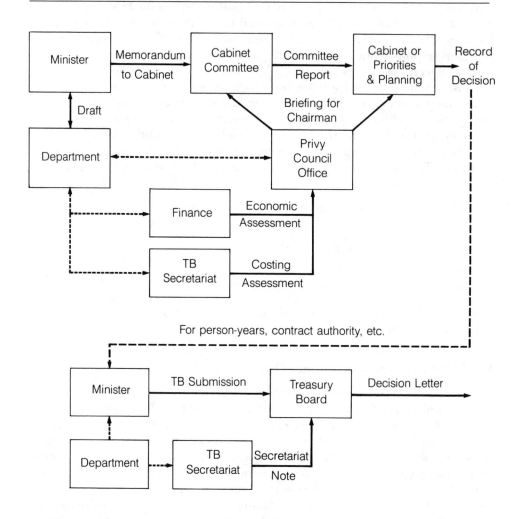

forward by ministers for consideration and approval by their Cabinet colleagues. It is also the formal means by which deputy ministers provide confidential policy advice to their ministers. Cabinet memoranda, which are normally based on extensive research and interdepartmental consultations, set out as briefly as possible the issues associated with a particular problem or proposal, alternatives for dealing with these issues, the implications of these various alternatives for such concerns as finances, public relations, interdepartmental relations, federal-provincial relations and the party caucus, and recommendations for action. A Cabinet memorandum has two parts—a three-page "Ministerial Recommendations" (MR) section, which contains key information for ministers, and an "Analysis" section, which contains a much lengthier treatment of substantially the same matters covered in the MR, with the exception of the recommendations and politically sensitive matters.

Following its consideration of a Cabinet memorandum, a Cabinet committee makes a recommendation that is passed on to the Priorities and Planning Committee or to Cabinet in the form of a committee report. Formal approval takes the form of a record of decision that is circulated to all ministers for whatever follow-up is required. PCO officials play a very sensitive and influential role both in briefing committee chairpersons and in drafting committee reports and records of decision. Note the important role of the Department of Finance and the TBS in providing Cabinet committees, through the PCO, with an economic and a costing assessment of policy proposals contained in Cabinet memoranda.

The record of decision serves as a basis for ministers, on behalf of their departments, to request approval from Treasury Board and the TBS for the human and financial resources needed to implement approved policies. The source of funding, however, has already been identified during Cabinet committee discussion of the policy or program in question. Ministers seek Treasury Board approval through what is called a Treasury Board submission. Each submission is assessed by one of the several branches of the Treasury Board Secretariat (e.g., the Program Branch, the Administrative Policy Branch), and the Secretariat recommends to the board whether submissions should be approved, rejected, or altered. The decision to approve or reject is provided in the form of a "decision letter." Figure 15.2 indicates, by dotted lines, the consultation between departments and central agencies that accompanies the preparation and processing of both Cabinet memoranda and Treasury Board submissions.

A primary purpose of the several reforms of the Cabinet decision-making system since the mid-1960s has been to enhance the power of political executives over bureaucrats in the making of public policy. Yet, even after these changes, senior officials from departments and central agencies were permitted to attend Cabinet committee meetings to provide advice and support to their ministers or the Prime Minister. This participation provided an opportunity for bureaucrats to use their knowledge and experience to influence policy at a critical stage of its development. The Mulroney government decided in 1985 to limit strictly the attendance of bureaucrats at Cabinet committee meetings to ensure the predominance of ministers in the making of policy decisions.

Reforms in the structures and processes of provincial Cabinet decision-making systems followed a pattern very similar to the federal reforms discussed above[20] and aimed to achieve the same objectives of Cabinet coordination and control of policy-making. In most provinces, these objectives were pursued through an expanded Cabinet committee system dominated by planning and priorities committees, treasury boards or management boards, and standing policy committees. As on the federal scene, Cabinet secretariats and other central agencies were established or upgraded to support the Premier, the Cabinet, and Cabinet committees.

The emphasis in this chapter has been on interaction between the Prime Minister and the Cabinet on the one hand, and central agencies and departments on the other. We turn now to an examination of interaction between government departments, between departments and central agencies, and among the central agencies themselves.

NOTES

1. See, for example, J. March and H. Simon, *Organizations* (New York: John Wiley & Sons, 1958); Victor A. Thompson, *Modern Organization* (New York: Knopf, 1961); and Robert K. Merton, "Bureaucratic Structure and Personality," in Robert K. Merton, ed., *Reader in Bureaucracy* (New York: The Free Press, 1952).
2. See the explanation of the bureaucratic politics approach in Chapter 5.
3. Graham T. Allison and Morton H. Halperin, "Bureaucratic Politics: A Paradigm and Some Policy Implications," *World Politics* 24 (Supplement, 1972): 43.
4. Denis Stairs, "The Foreign Policy of Canada," in James N. Rosenau, Kenneth W. Thompson, and Gavin Boyd, eds., *World Politics: An Introduction* (New York: The Free Press, 1976), pp. 185-86.
5. See the discussion of deputy ministers in Chapter 16.
6. Royal Commission on Financial Management and Accountability, *Final Report* (Ottawa: Supply and Services, 1979), p. 42.
7. For an examination of the impact of the Mulroney government on the public service, see David Zussman, "Walking the Tightrope: The Mulroney Government and the Public Service," in Michael J. Prince, ed., *How Ottawa Spends: 1986-87: Tracking the Tories* (Toronto: Methuen, 1986), pp. 250-82.
8. Denis Smith, "President and Parliament: The Transformation of Parliamentary Government in Canada," in Thomas A. Hockin, ed., *Apex of Power*, 2nd ed. (Scarborough, Ont.: Prentice-Hall, 1977), p. 323.
9. See W. A. Matheson, *The Prime Minister and the Cabinet* (Toronto: Methuen, 1976), pp. 83-91.
10. Lester B. Pearson, Press Release, Office of the Prime Minister, January 20, 1968.
11. Pierre Elliott Trudeau, Press Release, Office of the Prime Minister, "Statement by the Prime Minister on Cabinet Committee Structure," April 30, 1968.
12. Ian D. Clark, "Recent Changes in the Cabinet Decision-Making System in Ottawa," *Canadian Public Administration* 28 (Summer 1985): 199. As updated by Mr. Clark to April 20, 1988.
13. Ibid.
14. Government of Canada, Privy Council Office, *Background Paper on the New Cabinet Decision-Making System* (Ottawa: Privy Council Office, 1989).
15. Ibid.
16. Colin Campbell and George J. Szablowski, *The Superbureaucrats: Structure and Behaviour in Central Agencies* (Toronto: Macmillan, 1979), p. 1.
17. Colin Campbell, "Central Agencies in Canada," in Kenneth Kernaghan, ed., *Public Administration in Canada: Selected Readings* (Toronto: Methuen, 1985), p. 13.
18. Canada, *Statutes*, 1918, c. 6 as amended in 1925, c. 23.
19. Clark, "Recent Changes in the Cabinet Decision-Making System in Ottawa," p. 198.
20. See Marsha A. Chandler and William M. Chandler, *Public Policy and Provincial Politics* (Toronto: McGraw-Hill Ryerson, 1979), ch. 4 and "Public Administration in Can-

ada's Provinces," in Kenneth Kernaghan, ed., *Canadian Public Administration: Practice and Profession* (Toronto: Butterworths, 1983), pp. 145-50. On the evolution of the Cabinet system in Ontario, see Richard A. Loreto and Graham White, "The Premier and the Cabinet," in Graham White, ed., *The Government and Politics of Ontario*, 4th ed. (Scarborough, Ont.: Nelson, 1990), pp. 79-102.

BIBLIOGRAPHY

Aucoin, Peter. "Portfolio Structures and Policy Coordination." In G. Bruce Doern and Peter Aucoin, eds., *Public Policy in Canada*. Toronto: Macmillan, 1979.

Aucoin, Peter. "Organizational Change in the Machinery of Canadian Government: From Rational Management to Brokerage Politics." *Canadian Journal of Political Science* 19 (March 1986): 3-27.

Balls, Herbert R. "Decision-Making: The Role of the Deputy Minister." *Canadian Public Administration*19 (Fall 1976): 417-31.

Campbell, Colin. *Governments Under Stress: Political Executives and Key Bureaucrats in Washington, London and Ottawa*. Toronto: University of Toronto Press, 1983.

Campbell, Colin, and George Szablowski. *The Superbureaucrats: Structure and Behaviour in Central Agencies*. Toronto: Macmillan, 1979.

Canada. Royal Commission on Financial Management and Accountability. *Final Report*. Ottawa: Supply and Services, 1979, ch. 4.

Chandler, Marsha A., and Chandler, William M. *Public Policy and Provincial Politics* (Toronto: McGraw-Hill Ryerson, 1979): ch. 4.

Clark, Ian. "Recent Changes in the Cabinet Decision-Making System in Ottawa." *Canadian Public Administration* 28 (Summer 1985):185-201.

Doern, G. Bruce, and Richard W. Phidd. *Canadian Public Policy*. Toronto: Methuen, 1983, ch. 7.

Doerr, Audrey. *The Machinery of Government in Canada*. Toronto: Methuen, 1981, chs. 2-3.

French, Richard. *How Ottawa Decides: Planning and Industrial Policy Making, 1968-1984*. 2nd ed. Toronto: James Lorimer, 1984.

Johnson, A. W. "The Role of the Deputy Minister." *Canadian Public Administration* 4 (December 1961): 363-69.

Kernaghan, Kenneth, and Olivia Kuper. *Coordination in Canadian Governments: A Case Study of Aging Policy*. Toronto: Institute of Public Administration of Canada, 1983.

Lalonde, Marc. "The Changing Role of the Prime Minister's Office." *Canadian Public Administration* 14 (Winter 1971): 538-55.

Leger, Paul. "The Cabinet Committee System of Policy-Making and Resource Allocation in the Government of New Brunswick." *Canadian Public Administration* 25 (Spring 1983): 16-35.

Loreto, Richard. "The Structure of the Ontario Political System." In Donald C. MacDonald, ed., *The Government and Politics of Ontario*. 2nd ed. Toronto: Van Nostrand Reinhold, 1980, pp. 17-47.

Loreto, Richard, and Graham White. "The Premier and Cabinet." In Graham White, ed., *The Government and Politics of Ontario*. 4th ed. Scarborough, Ont.: Nelson, 1990.

Matheson, William. A. "The Cabinet and the Canadian Bureaucracy." In Kenneth Kernaghan, ed., *Public Administration in Canada: Selected Readings*. 5th ed. Toronto: Methuen, 1985, pp. 266-80.

Matheson, W. A. *The Prime Minister and the Cabinet*. Toronto: Methuen, 1976.

Nossal, Kim Richard. "Allison through the (Ottawa) Looking Glass: Bureaucratic Politics and Foreign Policy in a Parliamentary System." *Canadian Public Administration* 22 (Winter 1979): 610-26.

Plumptre, Timothy. "New Perspectives on the Role of the Deputy Minister." *Canadian Public Administration* 30 (Fall 1987): 376-98.

Robertson, Gordon. "The Changing Role of the Privy Council Office." *Canadian Public Administration* 14 (Spring 1971): 487-508.

Schultz, Richard. *Federalism, Bureaucracy and Public Policy.* Montreal: McGill-Queen's University Press, 1980.

Smith, Denis. "President and Parliament: The Transformation of Parliamentary Government in Canada." In Thomas A. Hockin, ed., *Apex of Power.* 2nd ed. Scarborough, Ont.: Prentice-Hall, 1977, pp. 308-25.

Van Loon, R. "The Policy and Expenditure Management System in the Federal Government: The First Three Years." *Canadian Public Administration* 26 (Summer 1983): 255-84.

Zussman, David. "Walking the Tightrope: The Mulroney Government and the Public Service." In Michael J. Prince, ed., *How Ottawa Spends: 1986-87: Tracking the Tories.* Toronto: Methuen, 1986, pp. 250-82.

CASES

In *Case Program in Canadian Public Administration* (Toronto: Institute of Public Administration of Canada):

The Draft Memorandum to Cabinet. By Douglas G. Hartle
Political Briefing Notes. By Michael J. Kirby and Sandford F. Borins

16

Interdepartmental and Intradepartmental Relations

DEPARTMENTAL AND AGENCY INTERACTION

It is difficult to separate an analysis of interdepartmental relations from a consideration of the impact of central agencies on these relations. In our discussion of the Cabinet decision-making system in the previous chapter, we described the various means by which central agencies assist the Cabinet and its committees to control and coordinate the activities of departmental ministers and officials. It is clear that under this system a great deal of consultation between departments and central agencies is required. It makes little sense for a minister to bring forward Cabinet memoranda or Treasury Board submissions without ensuring that account has been taken of the views of central agencies that are in a position to advise Cabinet and Cabinet committees on the desirability of departmental proposals.

Interdepartmental Committees

Consultation between and among departments is, of course, essential in the development of policy and program proposals. Over the decade before the Turner government of 1984, sectoral deputy minister committees, often called "mirror committees," were established to facilitate interdepartmental consultation on matters that were to be considered by the policy committees of ministers. PCO officials promoted interdepartmental coordination by participating in the meetings of these committees. As part of an effort to shift some power in the direction of the departments, these committees were abolished by Prime Minister Turner. There was still a need, however, to ensure appropriate interdepartmental consultation. Therefore, the Mulroney government decided that the sponsoring department should be responsible for ensuring that issues coming to Cabinet have been subject to adequate interdepartmental consultation.[1] For example, departments are expected to consult the Department of External Affairs when Canada's international relations might be affected and the Federal-Provincial Relations Office when federal-provincial relations are involved. The Mulroney government further required that Cabinet memoranda explain the consultations that have been undertaken by departments and highlight any interdepartmental disagreements that still remain. The Privy Council Office and, where relevant, other central agencies were advised to continue to call meetings of deputy ministers for the purposes of coordination and exchange of information.

A valuable coordinating role continues to be played by the Coordinating Committee of Deputy Ministers, which is chaired by the Secretary to the Cabinet and whose membership includes the deputy ministers from Finance, TBS, External Affairs, Justice, and the Federal-Provincial Relations Office. This committee provides an opportunity for an exchange of views between the Secretary to the Cabinet and the administrative heads of central agencies on matters of general concern to the government. Other meetings, including a monthly deputy ministers' luncheon and a weekly deputy ministers' breakfast, are called by the Secretary to the Cabinet for the purpose of informal discussion of matters of general interest. Still other interdepartmental committees at the deputy minister level (e.g., the Committee of Senior Officials on Executive Personnel) and at the assistant deputy minister level (e.g., the Interdepartmental Panel on Energy Research) serve a variety of purposes. Below these very senior levels, there are a large number of other committees involving public servants from two or more departments.

Types of Interdepartmental Committees

Audrey Doerr has provided a very useful classification of interdepartmental committees according to their major function.[2] *Committees to initiate* are created to mobilize departmental interest and support early on in the policy process. One of these committees might, for example, be created to review a Royal Commission report and make recommendations on the appropriate governmental response to its proposals. Either a department or a central agency could chair and lead the committee in its work.

Committees to negotiate or arbitrate are concerned with sorting out and reaching compromises on the appropriate allocation of roles and responsibilities for a particular matter. For example, the Interdepartmental Committee on Oceans coordinates the activities of departments and agencies in this area.

Committees to advise are concerned with providing advice to senior departmental officials and ministers with respect to the substance of policy or the coordination of policy development. An example is the 1988 Advisory Committee of Deputy Ministers, which was set up to advise and assist the Task Force on Barriers to Women in the Public Service.

Committees to evaluate are often created to assess policies or programs and to make appropriate recommendations for action. An example is the Committee of Senior Officials on Executive Personnel, chaired by the Secretary to the Cabinet, which, among other things, evaluates the performance of senior officials.

Committees to monitor "maintain a 'watching brief' on departmental activities in a particular policy or program area."[3] For example, the 1988 Interdepartmental Committee on Climate Change was one of several committees established to monitor activities in the environmental area.

Finally, *interdepartmental task forces* are usually temporary bodies composed of public servants who are loaned by departments and agencies for a particular task. For example, ten task forces, composed of more than ninety deputy ministers, assistant deputy ministers, and regional officials, were set up under the Public Service 2000 initiative.

The Effectiveness of Interdepartmental Committees

It is important to keep in mind that most of these interdepartmental bodies, whatever their primary function, are composed of representatives of both departments and central agencies. They can, therefore, not only help to coordinate policy development and implementation among departments, but they can also assist central agencies in their support of Cabinet and Cabinet committees.

Interdepartmental committees have been described as "the principal means of communication and deliberation in the federal bureaucratic establishment."[4] Attention has also been drawn to their value as "important means for central agencies to initiate or coordinate new undertakings. They support departmental policy-making by bringing together a number of interested parties and resolving conflicts before recommendations are made to ministers. In each instance, consensus and support are sought through coordination."[5] Other observers have cautioned against expecting much effective coordination through interdepartmental committees. In addition, "some participants have dubbed the interdepartmental committee system 'institutionalized discord'— the coordinate mechanism, in other words, has simply become in several respects one of the battlegrounds where interdepartmental combat occurs."[6] Richard Schultz has noted the enormous growth of what he calls "interdepartmentalism" that has resulted in more and more public servants being required "to negotiate . . . with officials in other departments. This negotiation process, bureaucratic politics, can only reinforce both the political role of members of the public service and correspondingly their influence in the system."[7] Similarly, H. L. Laframboise contends that "the blurring of departmental boundaries," together with such things as "the spread of collegial decision-making" and "the proliferation of watchdog agencies," has resulted in "an emphasis on interdepartmental negotiations, and this emphasis has been translated into a corps of interdepartmental diplomats of considerable dimensions."[8]

The effectiveness of interdepartmental committees varies from one committee to another, but in general they appear to serve a useful purpose in assisting Cabinet and central agencies to coordinate government activities.

Departments and Central Agencies

Central Agencies versus Departments

It is widely held that the expansion in the size and power of central agencies that occurred in the late 1960s and early 1970s reduced the power of both the ministers and senior officials of operating departments. The control and influence exercised by central agencies in the coordination of policy development, and in the allocation of human and financial resources for departmental programs, led to considerable tension in the relations between the agencies and line departments. The filtering of departmental policy and program proposals through Cabinet committees and central agencies helped to ensure that ministers and their senior officials understood the implications of their proposals for other departments and for the government as a whole. However, ministers and their officials spent a great deal of time and effort lobbying and bargaining with ministers and officials in other departments and in the central agencies. It was an extremely time-consuming process for ministers, and it tended to reduce their individual authority and influence in the Cabinet decision-making system. Richard French concluded that Prime Minister Trudeau's reforms of the Cabinet committee system "are generally understood to have instituted much needed structure and control after the helter-skelter confusion of the Pearson years."[9] However, he notes that "the sophisticated analytical demands and cumbersome procedures were seen as serious barriers to decisive action, resulting in the constant delay of 'analysis paralysis.' "[10] Similarly, "the advent of collegiality, the insistence on collective decision-making within the committee system, is believed to have frustrated some capable ministers, and the allegedly dominant role of certain senior PCO officials to have disheartened, even driven into early retirement, talented departmental officials."[11]

Richard Schultz, among others, has suggested that the role of central agencies in the decision-making process has been somewhat exaggerated. He contends that the line departments continue to possess powerful resources in any competition with central agencies. He notes that central agencies do not have the human resources or the expertise available to operating departments, that policy initiatives and policy implementation are primarily the responsibility of departments, that departments control the timing of their proposals and the information supporting them, and that departments may at times resist the coordinating efforts of central agencies.[12]

The power of central agencies vis-à-vis departments may indeed be overstated. Nevertheless, the Turner and Mulroney governments, during 1984 and 1985, decided that the number and influence of central agencies, combined with the complexities of the Cabinet committee system and PEMS, made the decision-making system too complicated. Too much emphasis was being placed on the process of policy formulation as compared to policy content. Several reforms, some of which have already been mentioned, were introduced to bring about a simpler, more hierarchical model of Cabinet government. These reforms included the abolition of two central agencies (MSERD and MSSD), a reduction in the number of Cabinet committees, the abolition of the sectoral deputy ministers' committees, the strengthening of staff support to ministers, and the simplification of the processes and procedures of Cabinet and its committees. These reforms were designed in large part to restore a greater measure of power in the decision-making process to the ministers of line departments.

Central Agencies

Despite the reforms in the decision-making system described above, the traditional central agencies, that is, the PCO, the FPRO, the TBS, and the Department of Finance, continue to exercise considerable power in policy development and implementation. Over time, however, there have been shifts in the relative power exercised by these agencies, both in their relations with departments and their relations with each other. Indeed, competition among the central agencies themselves helps to prevent the dominance of any one agency and, on occasion, helps departments to get their way by setting one agency against another.

The Treasury Board, which is a statutory Cabinet committee, was, until 1967, chaired by the Minister of Finance and received its staff support from the Department of Finance. In 1967 the Treasury Board became a separate department of government under a Cabinet minister known as the President of the Treasury Board. He took over the chair of the board from the Minister of Finance, who became an ex officio member of the committee. As noted in Chapter 8, the Treasury Board, with the assistance of its secretariat, carries out a very broad range of functions in the areas of expenditure management, human resource management, and government organization. There is an obvious need for cooperation and consultation between the TBS on the one hand, and the Department of Finance and the PCO on the other.

The Department of Finance lost some authority during the 1960s and 1970s not only to the Treasury Board but also to the Privy Council Office and to other central agencies. For example, the department had to share its advisory role on economic policy with the Board of Economic Development Ministers, which was established in 1978 and which evolved into the Cabinet Committee on Economic and Regional Development with MSERD as its secretariat. The PCO strengthened its capability to advise on economic policy by recruiting its own economists, and the PCO and PMO together organized informal groups of economists from the universities and the private sector to advise the Prime Minister.

Despite competing sources of advice and the adverse economic conditions of the 1970s, the Department of Finance continued to exercise strong influence on economic policy. Moreover, with the arrival of PEMS in 1979, the department's influence in the budgetary process was reaffirmed through its influence on the size of the overall budget and the level of the expenditure ceilings in the individual envelopes. While the PCO shared its role in economic and social policy with MSSD and MSERD, it continued to play a central role in the determination of government priorities and in the management of PEMS. The TBS lost some of its former influence on policy proposals to the sectoral policy committees of Cabinet and to MSSD and MSERD.

Then, the reforms in policy-making structures and processes made by Prime Ministers Turner and Mulroney again altered the power relationships among the central agencies.[13] The elimination of MSSD and MSERD gave the Department of Finance greater responsibility for assessing the economic effectiveness of proposed policies and programs. The PCO took on those secretariat responsibilities for the policy committees that were previously performed by MSSD and MSERD, and the PMO played a more active policy role. The 1989 reform of the Cabinet committee system described in the previous chapter also affected the powers of the central agencies. In particular, the influence of the Department of Finance was enhanced by its role as advisor both to the newly created Expenditure Review Committee with regard to expenditure control and deficit reduction, and to the Planning and Priorities Committee with regard to major expenditure allocations.

Increased Ministerial Authority and Accountability (IMAA)

In 1986, the Mulroney government initiated a new managerial process affecting relations between individual departments and one of the central agencies, namely Treasury Board Secretariat. This process is called Increased Ministerial Authority and Accountability (IMAA). The two primary objectives of IMAA are:

1. to provide ministers and senior managers with greater authority and flexibility so that they can cope with changing conditions and manage successfully with limited resources;
2. to increase the accountability of ministers and senior managers for achieving results, both in delivering programs and implementing Treasury Board policies.[14]

The Treasury Board Secretariat has explained the rationale for IMAA as follows:

> IMAA is an ongoing process of change in the management philosophy and culture of the public service of Canada. It involves the application of a variety of specific measures to foster a shift to managing for results, living within budget, increased delegations of authority and enhanced accountability.

> This shift . . . means that Ministers and departmental managers will increasingly be held accountable for the achievement of expected results for government programs. Appropriate accountability can best be measured when results can be satisfactorily stated and measured. . . . This would provide a meaningful basis for judging the effectiveness, efficiency and economy of government programs and their operations.[15]

There are two central dimensions to the implementation of IMAA. The first is a general review of Treasury Board policies to bring about a greater measure of delegation and deregulation, to simplify and reduce reporting requirements, and to shift the emphasis from compliance with rules to performance. This effort has already led to significant changes. For example, there has been a substantial decline in the number of annual departmental submissions to Treasury Board, and departments have received increased authority to reallocate resources within approved funding levels and to make purchases and contracts.

The second dimension involves the negotiation of Memoranda of Understanding (MOUs) between Treasury Board and individual departments. Departments are invited to present proposals for altering Treasury Board policies and to request delegated authority and diminished reporting requirements, leading to more productive management. Each MOU incorporates agreements on these matters and sets out an accountability framework within which the department's performance can be assessed. In addition, each MOU sets performance targets for a three-year period, at which time there is a major review of the agreement. However, the deputy minister reports each year to Treasury Board on the department's performance. This bilateral approach, between the board and individual departments, replaces government-wide regulation.

A significant advantage of MOUs is that they are tailored to the particular needs of individual departments, which can thereby escape from certain Treasury Board rules that are binding on all departments. To date, only a small number of departments have concluded MOUs with the board. It is, therefore, too early to assess the long-term impact of the IMAA process. It does constitute, however, a major effort to improve relations between departments and the government's central management agency.[16]

We turn now to an examination of the relations *within* departments between ministers and public servants and among the public servants themselves.

INTRADEPARTMENTAL RELATIONS

The internal structure of administrative organizations varies from one category of organization to another (e.g., from departments to Crown agencies to central agencies); it also varies from one organization to another within each category. In general, however, departments and those central agencies with departmental form are organized in a broadly uniform manner. They are structured in a pyramidal fashion, with a minister as the political head and a deputy minister as the administrative head of a formal organization, with layers of interlocking superior-subordinate relationships descending to the base of the pyramid.

The Deputy Minister

The Deputy and the Minister

The individual responsibility of ministers as political heads of departments links the Cabinet to the bureaucracy, and it establishes the minister as the locus of formal authority in the departmental hierarchy for both policy formulation and execution. Ministers not only make the final decisions on policy questions; they also bear constitutional, legal, and political responsibility for the proper administration of their departments. In practice, of course, ministers look for assistance to their senior departmental officials, especially to their deputy minister who is the administrative head of the department.

The deputy minister occupies a pivotal position at the border between the political and bureaucratic spheres of government. Although the Prime Minister has the power to appoint, transfer, and remove deputy ministers, their first loyalty is to their minister. This seemingly illogical arrangement reflects the fact that ministers have both individual and collective responsibilities and that deputies are expected to serve their ministers in both capacities. Deputies not only serve their own ministers, but, through their support of the ministers' collective responsibilities, they also serve the government as a whole. Moreover, deputies perform certain functions according to statute or on the authority of the Cabinet rather than of their minister. The Prime Minister's power to select deputies helps to ensure continuity in departmental administration despite a change of ministers, reminds deputies "of their need for a perspective encompassing the whole range of government," and "emphasizes the collective interest of ministers, and the special interest of the prime minister in the effectiveness of management in the public service."[17] The fact that the Prime Minister chooses both ministers and deputy ministers enables him or her to seek a compatible team in each department—both in terms of policy and management skills and in terms of "personal chemistry." The Prime Minister is in a position to arbitrate the occasional disputes that arise between deputies and their ministers, and can even refuse to shift deputies who are unacceptable to their ministers. For example, Joe Clark is reported to have granted a few ministers their request for a new deputy, but to have refused the request of the Minister of External Affairs that her deputy be dismissed or transferred.[18]

The Deputy's Control and Influence

The authority of the deputy minister is based on both statutes and conventions. Many of the deputy's administrative responsibilities are spelled out in departmental Acts, the Interpretation Act, the Financial Administration Act, the Public Service Employment Act, and the Official Languages Act. Departmental Acts usually provide for the appointment by the Governor in Council of a deputy minister who is to hold office at pleasure (that is, he or she may be replaced by the Prime Minister at any time). Some Acts actually delegate authority to the deputy for certain specified matters. The Interpretation Act is especially important, however, because it provides in section 23(a) that "words . . . empowering a Minister . . . to do an act or thing, . . . include . . . his . . . deputy." Thus, the minister can delegate a wide range of authority to the deputy. The Act states specifically, however, that the deputy cannot substitute for the minister in the making of regulations. Moreover, the deputy cannot answer to Parliament on behalf of the minister or sign Cabinet memoranda. The other Acts noted above delegate authority directly to the deputy or provide for delegation to the deputy by the Treasury Board or the Public Service Commission. In contrast to the deputy's administrative responsibilities, his or her responsibilities to provide policy advice to the minister and to the government as a whole are based more on traditions and practices than on statutes.

In the realm of policy *development*, A.W. Johnson contends that the deputy minister's role as policy advisor entails the initiation of policy recommendations and policy studies, without usurping the minister's initiative in these matters. He notes that "the cynics may suggest that this is power without responsibility; I suggest that it is more akin to responsibility without power."[19] The fact is that deputy ministers often do exercise power—in the form of influence—through policy initiatives in which their minister has had little involvement. In this connection, Mitchell Sharp has observed that

> the typical senior civil servant seems to be thought of as a quite intelligent but passive agent of government, waiting to be set in motion by his Minister and producing in time a memorandum of well-balanced pros and cons. There are occasions, of course, when the senior adviser has to perform exactly that function. But when I think back over my experience, I remember more occasions when civil servants by fruitful initiatives led the Government to adopt lines of policy which would have never occurred to them otherwise.[20]

The challenge, then, is to ensure that the deputy's role in policy formation combines power with responsibility. We shall see that deputies are either accountable to, or feel a sense of personal responsibility to, a wide variety of participants in the political system.

In the realm of policy *implementation*, Cabinet ministers may become involved in virtually any matter within the ambit of their departmental portfolio, including the organization and management of the department. While ministers are responsible for the administration of their department, their burdensome duties oblige them to leave most of the departmental administration to their deputy and other senior officials. Moreover, deputies tend to be jealous of their managerial responsibilities. They do not wish, or expect, ministers to intervene in administrative matters without their knowledge and consent. Ministers do on occasion become involved in administrative matters, and senior officials are obliged to accommodate them and obey their directions. Indeed, A.W. Johnson has asserted that one of the important jobs of the deputy head is "to try to interpret to his staff the rationale for ministerial forays into the day-to-day work of the civil service."[21]

The extent to which ministers become involved in administration (and public servants in policy formation) depends on individual personalities and capacities, as well as on situational and time factors related to a department's particular activities. Some ministers will, by virtue of past experience and personal predisposition, be very interested in administrative questions; others will prefer to leave departmental administration almost solely in the hands of the public servants. There appears to be no strong correlation between a minister's interest in administrative matters and his or her status as a strong or weak minister. The effective minister appears to be the one who will intervene forcefully on important or urgent matters of administration. Senior public servants may head off ministerial excursions into the administrative hierarchy not only by responding quickly to ministerial requests, but by anticipating requests and providing suggestions to deal with emerging problems that have not yet become a matter of ministerial concern.

Policy Advice or Management?

For reasons of partisan politics and personal advancement, both the Prime Minister and departmental ministers are primarily concerned with the formulation, rather than the implementation, of policy. It is not surprising, therefore, that many deputies perceive that their own careers will prosper if they focus on policy advice rather than on departmental management. It is notable also that deputies are obliged to compete with other sources of advice for their minister's attention on policy matters, whereas they have little competition in the sphere of departmental administration. Although deputies reported to the Lambert Commission that, on average, they spent two-thirds of their time on management, a majority of them ranked the tasks of "supporting my minister" and "ensuring that my department is responsive to the policy thrusts of government" as more important than management responsibilities.[22] This is a natural outcome of both a political system where ministers cannot be expected to be policy experts and a reward system that often seems to value policy contributions above sound management.

Deputy ministers can, and do, become overloaded by the combined burden of their policy and managerial duties. What has long been said about ministers can now be said about many deputy ministers—that is, they have too much to do and they do too much. A persuasive argument could be made that deputies should be viewed more as experts in the machinery and process of government than as experts in the substance of public policy. The tendency to rotate deputies quickly among departments means that they cannot gain sufficient knowledge about the content and implications of departmental policy. They must, there-fore, rely more heavily on the advice of their departmental specialists. The deputies' effective performance of their managerial duties is essential to their policy advisory responsibilities. The Lambert Commission observed that "dep-uty heads must be actively involved in the administration and operation of their departments if they are to be effective in offering policy advice and in develop-ing programs that can be designed and carried out with value for money in mind."[23]

The Accountability of the Deputy Minister[24]

The deputies' job is complicated by the many authorities to whom they are accountable. Deputies are *directly* accountable only to political and administra-tive superiors, to the courts, and to any internal governmental authorities (e.g., central agencies) to which accountability is required by law or the administrative hierarchy. They are not directly accountable to the legislature, pressure groups, the news media, or the public. While it is agreed that, in general, deputies are accountable first of all to their minister, in practice they receive directions, rewards, and penalties from a variety of sources. As shown in Figure 16.1, the sources of direct accountability include not only their minister but also the Prime Minister, the Public Service Commission, and Treasury Board. A former public servant, in a hypothetical letter from the Secretary of the Cabinet to the Prime Minister, wrote that "we have been remarkably successful in multiplying the number of authorities to which deputy ministers are accountable, and it would be difficult, even for a hostile observer, to find a gap in the web we have spun."[25]

Figure 16.1
ACCOUNTABILITY OF THE DEPUTY MINISTER

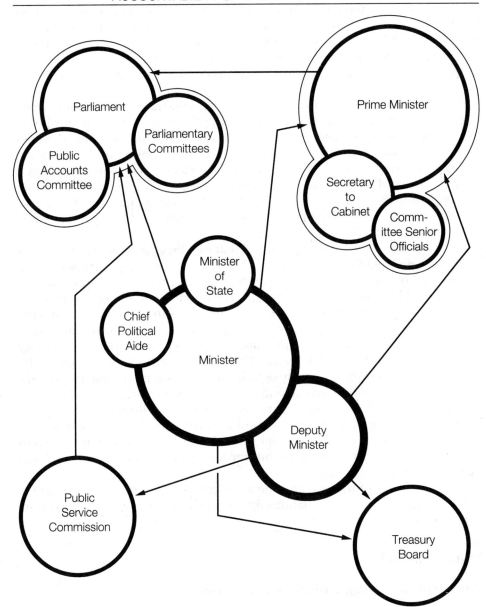

Source: Reproduced, with permission, from Gordon F. Osbaldeston, *Keeping Deputy Ministers Accountable* (Toronto: McGraw-Hill Ryerson, 1989), p. 8.

Despite the heavy burden of these existing accountability relationships, the Lambert Commission recommended that deputy ministers be required to account directly to the Public Accounts Committee of the House of Commons for the performance of specific or assigned duties, including those "relating to the probity and legality of expenditures, the economy and efficiency with which programs are run, and their effectiveness in achieving policy goals."[26] This proposal has been widely discussed in Canada's public administration community.

Critics of the proposal argue that the administrative matters for which deputies would be accountable cannot easily be separated from the policy matters for which ministers would be accountable; that holding deputies accountable for "their effectiveness in achieving policy goals" suggests, incorrectly, that ministers can usually provide clear policy objectives; that a formal, written division of responsibilities between a minister and his or her deputy is not in keeping with the traditional, informal pattern of relations between them; and that if public servants are held accountable to parliamentary committees their anonymity will suffer.

Supporters of the proposal contend that the direct accountability of deputies would stimulate them to pay greater heed to their management tasks, and to seek from those in authority over them clear statements of their responsibilities. Moreover, while at first glance, the proposal seems to threaten the doctrine and practice of ministerial responsibility, it is similar to the "accounting officer" mechanism in Britain whereby a senior departmental official, usually the equivalent of our deputy minister, accounts directly to the Public Accounts Committee for the expenditure of public funds. There has been no suggestion that this British practice encroaches to any significant extent on ministerial responsibility. It is argued further that deputies already appear before parliamentary committees to explain departmental policy and its administration; the responsibility for the defence of policy and administrative matters that are not delegated or assigned to deputies would remain with ministers. The anonymity of deputy ministers would decline somewhat, but the anonymity of their advice on policy matters would be preserved.

The outcome of this debate appears to be that no change will be made in the existing accountability relationships between deputies and parliamentary committees.

Ministerial Staff

The Expansion of Staff Assistance to Ministers

Relationships between ministers and deputy ministers are complicated further by the role of the minister's office staff. Ministerial assistants are appointed by the minister and are usually described as "exempt staff" because they are not subject to the provisions of the Public Service Employment Act. Since the tenure of ministerial assistants is tied directly to that of the minister, they are subject to the vicissitudes of partisan politics. A measure of employment protection is assured, however, by section 37(4) of the Public Service Employment Act, which provides that a person who has served at least three years as an executive assistant, a special assistant, or a private secretary to a minister is entitled to a position in the public service for which he or she is qualified at a level at least equivalent to that of private secretary to a deputy minister. Ministerial assistants frequently take advantage of this opportunity.

Since the early 1960s, the size of the minister's office staff has gradually increased; however, the influence of ministerial staff has not only waxed and waned over that period, but has also varied from one minister and one department to another. Until the Mulroney government of 1984, ministers were usually authorized under Treasury Board guidelines to hire an executive assistant, a policy advisor, as many special assistants as funds permitted, one private secretary, and support staff. Some ministers supplemented this staff by seconding departmental public servants and/or using departmental funds to hire people on a contract basis. When he came into office, Prime Minister Mulroney decided to upgrade the quality of ministerial staff by authorizing each minister to hire a chief of staff at a substantial salary. The chief of staff is intended to function, not as a senior policy advisor to the minister, but as the minister's chief political advisor and as the manager of the minister's office.[27] The PMO has been given a significant role in the selection of the chiefs of staff to ensure that they are sensitive to the Prime Minister's wishes and concerns.

The Functions of Ministerial Assistants

The role of the ministerial assistant is meant to be complementary to, rather than competitive with, the deputy head and other senior public servants. The functions of the minister's staff relate to the management of the minister's office and the enhancing of his or her political fortunes, rather than to the day-to-day administration of the department or to the development of substantive policy. Blair Williams has identified four major categories of work performed by ministerial assistants in support of their minister's onerous responsibilities.[28] The *planning, organization, and administration* function includes handling the minister's itinerary and managing his or her office. The *liaison* function involves facilitating effective relations between the minister on the one hand, and the department, other ministers, the party, Members of Parliament, and the minister's constituency on the other. It should be noted that ministerial staff increasingly deal with the concerns of pressure groups on behalf of their ministers. The *public relations* function requires interaction with the department's information services unit and the news media to advance the minister's political and policy objectives. The *research* function involves the collection of data and information to support the various other functions performed for the minister. Williams did not specifically mention the function of assisting the minister to control the bureaucracy, perhaps because ministers' offices do not have adequate staff to perform this function well. Donald Savoie has argued that the policy advisory capacity of the offices should be strengthened so that ministerial staff can assist ministers in giving policy directions to their departments and can evaluate the policy advice coming from the departments.[29]

Ministerial Staff and Departmental Officials

Harmonious relations between the minister's staff and departmental officials require a clear understanding of their respective spheres of action. Tension and conflict have resulted when ministerial assistants have tried to usurp the role of senior public servants by interfering in departmental administration or by impeding contacts between the minister and departmental officials.[30] Ministerial staff must be careful also not to use their proximity to the minister for personal or private reasons. In the mid-1960s, following public revelations of questionable activities by ministerial assistants, J. R. Mallory warned of the potential danger of interposing political officials between the minister and the career public service. He argued that "they lack the training and professional standards of the civil service." Moreover, "not only do these functionaries wield great power because they control access to the Minister and can speak in his name, but they may wield this power with ludicrous ineptitude and in ways that are clearly tainted with political motives."[31] No doubt as a result of the adverse publicity of the 1960s, ministerial assistants tended to keep a low profile after that time and they appear to have had little significant influence on the formulation of government policies and programs.[32] However, the influence of ministerial assistants is now on the rise as a result of the more active policy role being played by the chiefs of staff appointed under the Mulroney administration.

Departmental Management[33]

There is no doubt that efficient and effective management of government departments is primarily the responsibility of deputy ministers.

> It is the job of the deputy minister to harness the capabilities of the department and manage it on behalf of the minister. By managing, we mean the entire range of activities associated with directing a large and diverse organization within a complex environment. Depending on the department and circumstances, this normally includes some combination of activities such as budgeting, organizing and planning, and activities such as negotiating, motivating, communicating and influencing.... The value they (deputy ministers) should add to the minister's direction is threefold: knowledge of the department; familiarity with the requirements of collective management; and the objectivity of a non-partisan perspective.[34]

The incentive for deputy ministers to pay more attention to the quality of their policy advice than of their departmental management was explained above. The relative importance of policy advisory and management skills does, of course, vary from one department to another. Some departments (e.g., Finance) are mainly policy oriented whereas others (e.g., National Revenue) are mainly program oriented. In any event, sound departmental management is central to both the policy-advisory and policy-implementation responsibilities of the deputy minister. The quality of the deputy's performance depends greatly on the quality of the advice and assistance received from departmental subordinates. Thus, the success of the deputy, and indeed of the department and its minister, rests significantly on the extent to which the deputy is able to recruit, develop, and motivate competent departmental officials, especially senior managers.

In the federal public service, senior managers are members of the Management Category. The Public Service Commission has the authority to appoint public servants to this category, to promote them and move them from one department to another, and to appoint people to the category from outside the public service. However, the commission delegates to deputy ministers the authority to appoint or reassign members of the Management Category within their department, so long as there is no change in their occupational group or level. This arrangement gives deputy ministers some flexibility to deploy senior staff to meet their operational and career development needs.

In the management of their departments, deputies are constrained not only by the regulations and guidelines of the Public Service Commission but also by those of such central agencies as the PCO and the TBS. This chapter has already covered the diverse accountability mechanisms, including central agencies, to which deputy ministers are subject, and later chapters will examine the constraints on deputies and their departments in their management of human and financial resources. It is important to emphasize here that deputies are required to manage their departments in a political, legal, and bureaucratic environment that considerably restricts their freedom of action. This is one of the points of contrast between public and private sector management. The Cabinet, usually acting through central agencies, imposes various service-wide requirements on government departments with a view to achieving such objectives as efficiency and effectiveness, integrity, and representativeness. For example, the Planning Programming Budgeting System (PPBS), the Operational Performance Measurement System (OPMS), and program evaluation were introduced to promote efficiency and effectiveness;[35] conflict of interest guidelines were formulated to stimulate a high level of integrity; and an employment equity program was adopted to bring about a more representative public service. But, as explained above, Treasury Board's IMAA process is designed, in part, to reduce service-wide constraints on departments. The job of deputy ministers and their senior managers is to fulfill their responsibilities to the best of their abilities within the various constraints imposed by political executives and central agencies.

Deputy ministers play a critical role in pursuing not only interdepartmental coordination but intradepartmental coordination as well. Most government departments are so large that deputies can pursue coordination through regular, personal contacts with only the most senior departmental officials. Deputies are required, therefore, to delegate authority for coordinating departmental activities to their subordinates and to create formal coordinating mechanisms. Many departments have a management committee or an executive committee composed of the deputy and his or her immediate subordinates. This committee determines the overall objectives and priorities of the department and deals with major managerial issues. Deputies, in concert with these senior managers, devise structures and processes to facilitate the coordination of policies and programs at all levels of the department. Formal mechanisms such as committees are supplemented by a broad range of informal means of seeking coordination (personal contacts, telephone calls, etc.).

Provincial governments, like the federal government, seek coordination through Cabinet committees and central agencies and through both interdepartmental and departmental committees. They have, as a result, experienced some of the same tensions as those between central agencies and line departments. In discussing problems associated with New Brunswick's Cabinet decision-making system compared to a highly centralized decision-making system, Paul Leger asks what authority and responsibility remain for the minister and deputy minister of a department "when almost every policy issue has interdepartmental implications." Moreover, "how can anyone be held accountable for policy, when everyone is? . . . the possibility always exists that creative and constructive departmental initiatives can be lost in the search for the 'common good.'"[36] It is notable that, in mid-1988, the New Brunswick government reduced the number of Cabinet committees and made structural changes in the central agencies "to streamline the government's decision-making apparatus" and to strengthen government departments.[37]

CONCLUDING OBSERVATIONS

The story of interaction among the major players in the executive-bureaucratic arena is clearly a complicated one, but in essence it is a tale of swings in the pendulum of power between political executives and bureaucrats, and between departments and central agencies. Bureaucrats exercise a great deal of control and influence in the policy process, and political executives are not always successful in holding bureaucrats accountable for the exercise of this power. No matter what changes are made in the decision-making system, bureaucrats continue to play a pervasive and significant role. Control over the bureaucracy by the Prime Minister (or Premier) and the Cabinet is, however, only one means of holding bureaucrats accountable and responsible for their actions and decisions. The bureaucracy is far from a monolithic entity. We have seen in this chapter that bureaucrats compete with, and are constrained by, other bureaucrats. Subsequent chapters will show that other actors in the political system, namely legislators, judges, pressure groups, and the public, also check bureaucratic power.

NOTES

1. Ian D. Clark, "Recent Changes in the Cabinet Decision-Making System in Ottawa," *Canadian Public Administration* 28 (Summer 1985): 195.
2. Audrey Doerr, *The Machinery of Government in Canada* (Toronto: Methuen, 1981), pp. 138-142.
3. Ibid., p.141.

4. Colin Campbell and George Szablowski, *The Superbureaucrats: Structure and Behaviour in Central Agencies* (Toronto: Macmillan, 1979), p. 24.
5. Doerr, *The Machinery of Government in Canada* , pp. 138-39.
6. R.J. Van Loon and M.S. Whittington, *The Canadian Political System*, 4th ed. (Toronto: McGraw Hill Ryerson, 1987), p. 563.
7. Richard J. Schultz, *Federalism, Bureaucracy and Public Policy: The Politics of Highway Regulation* (Montreal: McGill-Queen's University Press, 1980), p. 188.
8. H.L. Laframboise, "The Future of Public Administration in Canada," *Canadian Public Administration* 24 (Winter 1982): 513.
9. Richard French, *How Ottawa Decides: Planning and Industrial Policy Making, 1968-1984*, 2nd ed. (Toronto: James Lorimer, 1984), p. 8.
10. Ibid.
11. Ibid.
12. Schultz, *Federalism, Bureaucracy and Public Policy*, pp. 182-89.
13. See Peter Aucoin, "Organizational Change in the Machinery of Canadian Government: From Rational Management to Brokerage Politics," *Canadian Journal of Political Science* 19 (March 1986): esp. 17-27.
14. Treasury Board, *The IMAA Handbook: A Guide to Development and Implementation*, Draft, (Ottawa: Treasury Board Secretariat, April 1, 1988), p. 4.
15. Ibid., p. 5.
16. See Barry Lacombe, "IMAA and the Operational Plan Framework," *Optimum* 19 (1988-1989): 70-89; Guy Leclerc, "IMAA and Management Representations—Meeting Accountability Requirements," *Optimum* 19 (1988-1989): 90-97; and Donald Roy, "Making IMAA Work—A Look at Five Key Issues," *Optimum* 20 (1989-1990): 56-64.
17. Royal Commission on Government Organization, *Report*, vol. 1 (Ottawa: Queen's Printer, 1965, p. 60.
18. J. Simpson, *The Discipline of Power* (Toronto: Personal Library, 1980), p. 132.
19. J. Johnson, "The Role of the Deputy Minister," in Kenneth Kernaghan, ed., *Public Administration in Canada: Selected Readings*, 5th ed. (Toronto: Methuen, 1985), p. 295.
20. Mitchell Sharp, "The Bureaucratic Elite and Policy Formation," in Kenneth Kernaghan, ed., *Bureaucracy in Canadian Government*, 2nd ed. (Toronto: Methuen, 1973), p. 73.
21. Johnson, "The Role of the Deputy Minister," p. 292.
22. Royal Commission on Financial Management and Accountability, *Final Report* (Ottawa: Supply and Services 1979), p. 452.
23. Ibid., p. 179.
24. For an excellent examination of the role of the deputy minister in the Canadian political system, see Gordon F. Osbaldeston, *Keeping Deputy Ministers Accountable* (Scarborough, Ont.: McGraw-Hill Ryerson, 1989). See also the discussion of the concept of *accountability* in Chapter 14.
25. H.L. Laframboise, "A Note on Accountability," *Optimum* 13-14 (1982): 84.
26. Royal Commission on Financial Management and Accountability, pp. 374-75.
27. David Zussman, "Walking the Tightrope: The Mulroney Government and the Public Service," in Michael J. Prince, ed., *How Ottawa Spends: 1986-87: Tracking the Tories* (Toronto: Methuen, 1986), p. 265.
28. Blair Williams, "The Para-political Bureaucracy in Ottawa," in H. D. Clarke et al., *Parliament, Policy and Representation* (Toronto: Methuen, 1980), pp. 222-23.
29. Donald J. Savoie, "The Minister's Staff: The Need for Reform," *Canadian Public Administration* 26 (Winter 1983): 509-24.

30. For an examination of relations between chiefs of staff and senior public servants in Quebec, see Andrew F. Johnson and Jean Daigneault, "Liberal 'chefs de cabinets ministériels' in Quebec: Keeping Politics in Policy Making," *Canadian Public Administration* 31 (Winter 1988): 501-517.

31. J.R. Mallory, "The Minister's Office Staff: An Unreformed Part of the Public Service," *Canadian Public Administration* 10 (March 1967): 27.

32. Savoie, "The Minister's Staff," p. 518.

33. For an examination of the management of government programs, see Chapter 22.

34. Osbaldeston, *Keeping Deputy Ministers Accountable*, p. 107.

35. See the discussion of these matters in Chapters 26 and 27.

36. Paul Leger, "The Cabinet Committee System of Policy-Making and Resource Allocation in the Government of New Brunswick," *Canadian Public Administration* 26 (Spring 1983): 33.

37. Government of New Brunswick, Press Release, June 29, 1988.

BIBLIOGRAPHY

Most of the items listed in the bibliography for Chapter 15 are also relevant to this chapter. See in addition the following items:

Canada. Royal Commission on Financial Management and Accountability. *Final Report.* Ottawa, Supply and Services, 1979, chs. 9-14.

Dobell, W. M. "Interdepartmental Management in External Affairs." *Canadian Public Administration* 21 (Spring 1978): 83-102.

Doern, G. Bruce. "The Cabinet and Central Agencies." In G. Bruce Doern and Peter Aucoin, eds., *Public Policy in Canada.* Toronto: Macmillan, 1979.

Doerr, Audrey. *The Machinery of Government in Canada.* Toronto: Methuen, 1981, chs. 4, 6.

Mallory, J. R. "The Minister's Office Staff: An Unreformed Part of the Public Service." *Canadian Public Administration* 10 (March 1967): 25-34.

Prince, Michael J., and John Chenier. "The Rise and Fall of Policy Planning and Research Units: An Organizational Perspective." *Canadian Public Administration* 23 (Winter 1980): 519-41.

Savoie, Donald J. "The Minister's Staff: The Need for Reform." *Canadian Public Administration* 26 (Winter 1983): 509-24.

Schultz, Richard J. "Prime Ministerial Government, Central Agencies and Operating Departments: Towards a More Realistic Analysis." In Thomas A. Hockin, ed., *Apex of Power.* 2nd ed. Scarborough, Ont.: Prentice-Hall, 1977.

Sharp, Mitchell. "The Bureaucratic Elite and Policy Formation." In Kenneth Kernaghan, ed., *Bureaucracy in Canadian Government.* 2nd ed. Toronto: Methuen, 1973, pp. 69-73.

Williams, Blair. "The Para-political Bureaucracy in Ottawa." In H. D. Clarke et al., eds. *Parliament, Policy and Representation.* Toronto: Methuen, 1980, pp. 215-30.

CASES

In *Case Program in Canadian Public Administration* (Toronto: Institute of Public Administration of Canada):

   The Draft Memorandum to Cabinet. By Douglas G. Hartle
   The Toronto Airport(s). By Sandford F. Borins
   Bureaucratie. By Guy Demers

Policy Analysis: A Case Study. By David Zussman

All Things to All People: Government and Its Client Groups. By Sharon Bider and Peter McNaughton

The Deputy Minister—A Fictional Sketch. By J.D. Love

Cases developed by the Canadian Centre for Management Development and distributed by the Case Program in Canadian Public Administration:

Refugee Claimants and the Law. By John William Pullen

17

The Legislature and the Bureaucracy

The conventional wisdom among students of Canadian government and politics is that during this century there has been a decline in the power of the federal Parliament and the provincial legislatures, and a rise in the power of the public service. The growth in the power of the public service, especially since the beginning of World War II, is generally acknowledged. Whether the overall power of the legislatures has actually declined is a debatable and complex issue. Nevertheless, it is widely recognized that, at present, the legislatures do not exercise effective power, in the sense of control and influence, over the executive in general and the public service in particular. The Royal Commission on Financial Management and Accountability argued:

> Under our system, Parliament must be the beginning and the end of the governmental process. It must scrutinize and approve all legislation and all proposals for the raising of revenues and the expenditure of funds, and must watch over the Government's implementation of the proposals to which it has assented. We think that Members of Parliament have not been adequately fulfilling their duty of forcing the Government to account for its administration.[1]

Neither the evolution nor the contemporary state of interaction between the legislatures and the public service has received much attention in the literature of Canadian political science and public administration.[2] Yet relations between the legislatures and the public service significantly affect the exercise of power in the Canadian political system, especially by Cabinet ministers, legislators, and public servants.

The power of the legislature over the public service is wielded primarily in an indirect fashion, through questioning and criticism of ministers responsible to the legislature for the administration of their departments. Since ministers are the formal constitutional intermediaries between legislators and public servants, the legislature's ability to affect the recommendations and decisions of public servants rests heavily on the interpretation and application of the constitutional convention of *ministerial responsibility*. Ministerial responsibility is in turn tightly bound with the conventions of *political neutrality* and *public service anonymity*. The definition and usage of these three constitutional conventions (often referred to as principles or doctrines) shape, to a large extent, the pattern of interaction between public servants on the one hand, and legislators and ministers on the other. For convenience, public service anonymity is included here under the broad heading of political neutrality.

MINISTERIAL RESPONSIBILITY AND POLITICAL NEUTRALITY

The meaning and relevance of ministerial responsibility have been subjects of continuing controversy in Canada in recent years. Some politicians, journalists, and academic scholars contend that the convention is a myth or that it is dead. But other commentators, who acknowledge the deficiencies of the traditional interpretation of ministerial responsibility, continue to treat it as a central feature of constitutional theory and practice. The Royal Commission on Financial Management and Accountability stated that the doctrine of ministerial responsibility is "a cornerstone" of the Canadian constitution in that "it identifies who has the final responsibility for decisions taken—the minister, and provides a forum in which he is publicly accountable—Parliament"[3] (or, in the provinces, the legislature).

It is important to clarify the meaning of ministerial responsibility, and its relation to the political neutrality of public servants, as a foundation for informed discussion of its effects on the exercise of legislative and bureaucratic power. The following analysis focusses on the federal Parliament, but the experience in the provincial legislatures is very similar.

As explained in Chapter 15, collective and individual ministerial responsibility are separate, but interrelated, conventions. *Collective responsibility*, in its application to the government as a whole, prescribes that the Prime Minister and the Cabinet must resign or ask the Governor General for a dissolution of Parliament if the House of Commons passes a vote of no confidence in the government. In its application to individual ministers, collective responsibility prescribes that a minister must support government decisions in public, or at least suppress any public criticism of them. If ministers find a particular decision unacceptable, they must either stifle their objections or submit their resignation.

This chapter centres primarily on *individual*, rather than collective, responsibility. In the academic literature, several meanings and implications are given to **individual ministerial responsibility**, but there is widespread agreement that it has two major components.[4] The first is that the minister is answerable to Parliament for all the administrative errors of his or her departmental subordinates, in the sense that he or she must resign in the event of a serious error by these subordinates. This component of ministerial responsibility is often described as a myth. The second component of the convention is that the minister is answerable to Parliament in that he or she must explain and defend the actions of his or her department before Parliament. The importance of this component is ignored or minimized by some commentators on ministerial responsibility in Canada.

The convention of political neutrality, like that of ministerial responsibility, merits analysis in terms of the extent to which it reflects contemporary political and administrative practice.[5] Interpreted broadly and including the convention of public service anonymity, political neutrality entails the separation of administration from politics and policy; the selection and promotion of public servants on the basis of merit rather than partisanship; the avoidance by public servants of partisan political activity, and of the public expression of personal views on government actions; the provision by public servants of confidential advice to their ministers; ministerial protection of public service anonymity; and the loyal implementation of government decisions by public servants, regardless of their personal views.

The Resignation of Ministers

The first component of ministerial responsibility requires that a minister must resign if a serious administrative error committed by his or her department is exposed. Despite frequent calls by Opposition parties for ministerial resignations on the grounds of actual or alleged departmental mismanagement, in practice ministers do not resign as penance for administrative bungling in their department. It is now almost universally accepted that it is unreasonable to hold ministers personally responsible, in the form of resignation, for the administrative failings of their subordinates. Ministers cannot hope to have personal knowledge of more than a small percentage of the administrative actions taken by their officials. Moreover, they must restrict their attention to those administrative matters that are especially important or politically sensitive. Former Prime Minister Trudeau stated that a minister "can't possibly know everything which is done in the Department by every last Civil Servant and therefore it would be folly to try and pretend that the Minister will be held accountable and must resign when somewhere down the line at the end of a corridor the ten thousandth person committed something illegal or contrary to Government standards or norms."[6]

These factors of size and complexity, together with the burden of the ministers' political obligations, compel them to rely on their senior officials for advice on the administrative, technical, and political implications of policy proposals and decisions. The power of public servants to make discretionary decisions in the implementation of policies further enhances their policy role, in that the implementation process has a substantial impact on the success of policy decisions and on the content of future policies. Thus, public servants are actively involved in politics in the sense of determining or influencing the allocation of public resources among competing forces. It is clear that the first element of the doctrine of political neutrality outlined earlier, namely that administration is separated from politics and policy, is a fiction. In a formal sense, ministers do make decisions and public servants execute those decisions, but public servants exercise enormous influence on both policy development and implementation. It is, therefore, unrealistic to expect ministers to accept personal responsibility for all the acts of their departmental officials. Why should ministers "carry the can" when they have little or no knowledge of its contents?

Thus, the vicarious responsibility of ministers for departmental actions is limited, and tied to the particular circumstances of the case at hand. This view has been supported by a committee of senior public servants who asserted that

> a Minister is subject to various degrees of responsibility. He must certainly accept full responsibility for matters done properly under his instructions or in accordance with his policy. However, in the case of a problem not affecting an important question of policy, he is generally thought to have met his responsibility if he takes the matter in hand. Where the matter is essentially between a complainant and a particular official, the Minister can hardly be expected to have had prior knowledge of the case or to have had an opportunity to influence it personally. He cannot be acquainted with, or personally criticized for, every detail of administration in his department.[7]

This statement implicitly raises the often ignored issue of distinguishing the minister's personal mistakes from those of his or her officials. It is usually a formidable task for Parliament and the public to discover whether specific administrative acts were "done properly under his [the minister's] instructions or in accordance with his policy." Ministers are understandably reluctant even to admit that an administrative error has been made by their department. And when confronted with proof of error, they will usually deny personal knowledge of, or involvement in, the events in question. On this basis, they then contend that they should not have to accept full responsibility in the form of resignation or, indeed, to assume any personal blame. If departmental failures are admitted or apparent, ministers are inclined to blame their officials rather than to accept personal or vicarious responsibility. The usual practice is that ministers inform Parliament that the fault lies with departmental officials and promise that the offenders will be disciplined and their mistakes corrected.

Cases do arise where the personal culpability of a minister is evident or where the magnitude of the error causes the government considerable embarrassment. Even if the minister "accepts full responsibility" in such situations, the practical effects on his or her career depend largely on personal, partisan, and situational factors. If the minister under attack is an unpopular member of Cabinet, if the electorate is unusually outraged, or if the government is in a minority position in Parliament, the Prime Minister might be tempted to seek or accept the minister's resignation. The long-standing practice in Canada, however, is to enfold the offending minister in the Cabinet's protective cloak, so that a matter of individual ministerial responsibility becomes one of collective responsibility. Nevertheless, a minister's reputation suffers from the unfavourable publicity that accompanies demands for his or her resignation so that after the next Cabinet shuffle or the next election, he or she may be heading a less prestigious department or sitting on a government backbench.

Two other aspects of ministerial resignation deserve brief mention. First, a number of recent cases in Canada show that ministers will almost invariably be compelled to resign if personal misconduct in the form of unethical, immoral, or illegal activities is revealed. For example, a federal minister resigned when it was revealed that he had forged the signature of his friend's husband so that she could obtain an abortion, and a provincial minister resigned when he was charged with having arranged the murder of his wife. Secondly, incumbent ministers cannot be held responsible, especially by way of resignation, for administrative sins allegedly committed within their departments during the tenure of their predecessors.

It is clear that, in practice, ministers do not resign to atone for either serious mismanagement by their officials or personal administrative mistakes. Indeed, if ministerial protestations of innocence are accepted at face value, ministers rarely make mistakes. Thus, the demand for ministerial resignations on the grounds of maladministration may appear to be a feeble weapon in the parliamentary arsenal of Opposition parties. Yet this component of ministerial responsibility has important consequences for both ministers and public servants. Parliamentary and public calls for one's resignation, like the probability of being hanged the next morning, effectively concentrate one's attention. A minister's efforts to refute or defuse the allegations are vigorously supported by his or her senior officials, whose duty it is to keep their minister out of trouble. The reputation and career prospects of public servants tend to prosper or suffer along with those of their minister.

In the event of maladministration by departmental officials, the conventions of both ministerial responsibility and political neutrality require that ministers protect the anonymity of the wrongdoers by declining to identify them publicly. Since public servants are expected to serve their minister loyally by supporting departmental policy in public even if they oppose it vigorously within the confines of the department, ministers are expected to shield them from public criticism. However, there have been some notable departures from conventional practice by ministers who have named, and blamed, officials in public. For example, in 1978, Jean-Pierre Goyer, then the federal Minister of Supply and Services, was sued for libel by a public servant whom he had criticized both inside and outside the House of Commons. Mr. Justice Lieff of the Ontario High Court, who awarded damages to the official for Mr. Goyer's statement outside the House, observed:

> It is a long standing convention of parliamentary democracy and the doctrine of ministerial responsibility which it encompasses that civil servants are to remain faceless to the public. Civil servants are responsible to their ministers. Ministers, as elected officials, are responsible to the public.... Furthermore,... no matter how advanced the state of erosion of public service anonymity... a minister should not be able to blame or castigate personally a civil servant of a department under his control in public and then fall back on the legal defence of qualified privilege. If that were the case and the civil servant were defamed he would be in the peculiar position of being prevented from obtaining vindication for spurious allegations by the minister.[8]

Although the instances in which ministers have publicly criticized their officials are exceptional, officials cannot invariably rely on their ministers to protect their anonymity. Moreover, in return for ministerial protection, public servants must not abandon the shelter of ministerial responsibility by engaging in unapproved forms of partisan political activity or in public criticism of government policies. Also, public servants must moderate their public praise of government actions and avoid public identification with specific policies, decisions, or views so that they may retain their office in the event of a change in the governing party. Ministers have a corresponding responsibility not to praise public servants in a manner that identifies them publicly with specific policy initiatives. Yet, at a press conference on December 22, 1969, Prime Minister Trudeau announced the move of a deputy minister from one department to another and observed that when the official was Deputy Minister of Indian Affairs and Northern Development, "he did a first-class job in developing the north ... one of his brain children, I suppose, was the Pan-Arctic which he developed with Mr. Laing, who was minister there ... and the whole Indian policy, I think, was largely the result of [the deputy] and his team."[9]

All these considerations point to the strong links between political neutrality and ministerial responsibility. It is notable, however, that some advocates of legislative reform believe that a weakening of these conventions is justifiable to achieve the greater good of increased administrative accountability. For example, the Special Committee on Reform of the House of Commons concluded that "the doctrine of ministerial accountability undermines the potential for genuine accountability on the part of the person that ought to be accountable— the senior officer of the department [the deputy minister]."[10]

The Answerability of Ministers

The second component of ministerial responsibility corresponds closely to its current practice. Ministers do explain and defend their department's policies and administration before Parliament, especially during question period. Opposition members and, on occasion, government backbenchers utilize a variety of other opportunities (for example, motions, opposition days) to seek information and explanations from ministers. But an inordinate amount of parliamentary, media, and public attention centres on the daily oral question period. It is notable that ministers almost always respond to questions in their sphere of responsibility, despite the fact that they can neither be obliged to answer nor to give reasons for refusing to answer.[11] A strong impetus to answer to Parliament is that a minister may suffer adverse political consequences for declining to answer. The Speaker of the House of Commons has observed that he "is not in a position to compel an answer—it is public opinion which compels an answer."[12] Certainly, a minister who refuses to answer questions on an important issue, especially if he does not provide a reasonable explanation for his position, receives severe criticism from Opposition members and the media. There is, therefore, both constitutional and political pressure on ministers to justify their department's actions to Parliament.

The willingness of ministers to answer questions in the legislature does not ensure that all their replies are informative, plausible, or even comprehensible. Experienced ministers tend to be artful dodgers who often bob and weave to avoid direct hits from Opposition inquiries and allegations. Brian Chapman admits that ministerial responsibility "may be a useful tag for harrying ministers in Parliament," but he notes that "even then it smacks rather of a verbal game of cowboys and Indians."[13] Nevertheless, on the premise that ministerial evasion and circumlocution on a serious matter may be motivated by a desire to conceal politically embarrassing information, not only Opposition members but also journalists may be prompted to investigate the matter more vigorously.

The fact that a single identifiable minister is answerable for the activities of a specific department assists backbench members of the legislature in their handling of constituents' inquiries or complaints about government administration. A question in the legislature is sometimes the last recourse of a member who has been unable to obtain a satisfactory answer through private correspondence with a minister.

Although, as noted earlier, ministers are not expected to resign for departmental errors made during the term of office of their predecessors, they must answer to Parliament for those errors. This rule ensures a focus of continuing responsibility for government administration, despite changes in the political heads of departments or in the governing party itself. Parliament's capacity to control and influence public servants is enhanced because one minister is required to answer for administrative actions, no matter when these actions took place. Incumbent ministers will usually be obliged to rely heavily on their departmental officials for knowledge of what occurred during the tenure of their predecessors. In such situations, the ability of ministers to answer to Parliament for their department rests largely on the continuity of administration provided by their permanent public servants. Thus, the operation of ministerial responsibility is closely tied to the permanency in office of public servants. Permanency, in turn, depends on the preservation of several of the other elements of political neutrality described earlier.

An important corollary of the answerability of ministers for the administration of their departments is that public servants do not answer directly to Parliament for their decisions and recommendations. In the words of S. E. Finer, "the minister alone speaks for his Civil Servants to the House and to his Civil Servants for the House."[14] The application of this principle protects the anonymity of public servants, since it provides that the minister, and only the minister, is answerable to Parliament. The willingness of a few ministers occasionally to name and blame their officials has had no significant effect on the status of official anonymity. The impact of allegations made against public servants by members of Parliament has, in general, also been minimal.

Nevertheless, a combination of factors related to the growth of bureaucratic power is bringing about a gradual decline in public service anonymity. These factors are:

- the heightened visibility arising from the increasing extent to which officials are required to explain government policies in public forums;
- the expanded coverage by journalists of the activities and identities of specific officials; and

- the more frequent appearances of public servants before legislative committees.

The traditional interpretation of ministerial responsibility not only precludes public servants from answering directly to Parliament; it also prevents them from responding publicly to parliamentary criticism of their administrative actions. The minister replies to public accusations against his or her officials. In the face of allegations of serious administrative error, however, public servants, with the permission of their minister, have appeared before parliamentary committees to explain and defend their actions. The practice of official reticence and ministerial defence that normally prevails extends to attacks on public servants by persons outside Parliament, notably journalists. As a result, responsibility for departmental administration is focussed on the minister, and public servants try to preserve official anonymity by avoiding involvement in public or political controversy.

The preceding analysis indicates that the resignation component of the convention of ministerial responsibility may be restated as follows: a minister is not answerable to Parliament for all the administrative errors of his or her department in the sense that he or she must resign in the event of a serious error by the department. The second component of the convention, namely that the minister is answerable to Parliament in that he or she must explain and defend the actions of the department before Parliament, is unchanged.

Reports of the death of individual ministerial responsibility are greatly exaggerated. If the life of the convention depended on ministerial resignations for the misdeeds of departmental subordinates, it would be mortally wounded. But because of the vitality of its answerability component, ministerial responsibility remains a central, operative convention of the Canadian constitution. Indeed, parliamentary debate on ministerial responsibility has centred on its interpretation and application, not on its existence. The concept of ministerial responsibility helps to define and determine how power is, and should be, exercised in the Canadian political system, and who is, or should be, held responsible for the exercise of that power. It provides a major frame of reference for the allocation of power and responsibility among ministers, legislators, and public servants. The fact that the practice of ministerial responsibility does not correspond in full to its theory does not justify denial of the existence or importance of the convention, especially in the absence of a viable alternative. V. Seymour Wilson, in his insightful analysis of ministerial responsibility and bureaucratic accountability, concludes that "Canadian discourse on administrative power continues to be dominated by the doctrine of ministerial responsibility,"[15] and that "ministerial responsibility and all its trappings will continue to be around for a long time."[16]

LEGISLATIVE CONTROL AND INFLUENCE

An essential condition for a complete and comprehensible system of responsibility in government is that elected or appointed officials, or both, bear responsibility for all government actions. In a parliamentary democracy, if officials waste public funds, break the law, or violate citizens' rights, the public expects that someone will be held accountable for these misdeeds. If ministers do not accept responsibility for departmental transgressions, the focus of blame shifts to public servants. But the conventions of ministerial responsibility and political neutrality still protect the anonymity of public servants and restrict their answerability to Parliament. As a result, some commentators claim that these conventions permit public servants to exercise power without publicity or responsibility.[17] On those exceptional occasions when blame is publicly attributed to specific officials, disciplinary action is handled as an internal administrative matter with the result that the public rarely learns what penalties, if any, are imposed. Consequently, it appears to the public that on some occasions neither ministers nor public servants are held accountable for maladministration.

Can the federal and provincial legislatures help to ensure responsibility in government by controlling or influencing bureaucratic action?[18] There are three major means by which this can be done. These are:

1. debates, questions, and other procedures in the legislature;
2. reliance on certain "watchdog" agencies that report directly or indirectly to the legislature; and
3. the use of legislative committees.

The first means, which involves influencing the bureaucracy indirectly by influencing ministers, has been discussed at length above.

Watchdog Agencies

The second means involves the use of such agencies as ombudsmen and auditors to assist legislators to affect bureaucratic behaviour. The office of the ombudsman, which is an extremely important watchdog agency in the provincial sphere of government, does not exist in the federal government. There are, however, a number of important federal agencies that are often described as "specialized ombudsmen" or "mini-ombudsmen." These are the offices of the Correctional Investigator, the Official Languages Commissioner, the Canadian Human Rights Commissioner, the Privacy Commissioner, and the Information Commissioner. The most prominent watchdog agencies in the federal sphere of government are the Public Service Commission and the Office of the Auditor General.

The Ombudsman

Among the most popular of the various institutional and procedural safeguards designed to check bureaucratic power is the **ombudsman**. The office of the ombudsman originated in Sweden in 1809 and was adopted by Finland in 1919. No other countries appointed an ombudsman until after the Second World War. Then a large number of countries around the world adopted the institution to help deal with the problem of ensuring that citizens' rights were protected in the face of rapidly growing bureaucracies in virtually every governmental jurisdiction.[19] An ombudsman has now been appointed in every Canadian province except Prince Edward Island, which because of its small size has less need for the institution. The first Office of the Ombudsman in Canada, indeed the first in North America, was established in Alberta in September 1967. The office of the ombudsman has also been widely adapted for use in non-governmental organizations, notably in universities.

The major function of an ombudsman is to investigate citizens' complaints about improper, unfair, or discriminatory administrative treatment. An ombudsman is usually authorized by statute to obtain access to the government documents and to call the witnesses necessary to investigate these complaints. If he or she believes that certain complaints are justified, the public servants involved will be requested to remedy the mistakes. The ombudsman is responsible to the legislature and presents an annual report to that body, describing the cases that have been dealt with by his or her office and the progress that has been made in redressing any administrative injustices. It is important to emphasize that

> ombudsmen possess influence rather than control. They cannot alter administrative decisions. But they are well placed to cause those who have this power to review and change decisions which, after careful examination, appear to be unreasonable, oppressive or simply wrong in the circumstances. This influence, like that of auditors general, derives from their authority to investigate matters in depth and, as a last resort, to report their findings publicly to the legislature.[20]

There are, of course, other means of recourse available to citizens who believe they have suffered injustice at the hands of the bureaucracy. These include direct appeals to the public servant responsible for the action at issue and/or to the public servant's superiors, to members of Parliament, to administrative tribunals such as the Tax Review Board, and to the courts. However, the hearing of appeals by officials in the same department or agency responsible for the original decision may not result in the fact or the appearance of impartiality; members of Parliament have neither time nor resources equivalent to those of an ombudsman; the jurisdiction of appeal tribunals is limited; and court action can be both costly and time-consuming. Citizens are usually required to exhaust all the legal remedies available to them before complaining to the ombudsman. Thus, ombudsmen deal with complaints about unfair, rather than illegal, administrative action. The simple and inexpensive process of bringing grievances to an ombudsman has great appeal for the average citizen.

A study by a group of federal senior public servants noted that a federal ombudsman "would increase the awareness of ministers and officials of the need to deal promptly and equitably with individuals who perceive that they are victims of an administrative injustice," and concluded that an ombudsman "would be a desirable adjunct to the existing system of complaint handling in the departments and agencies of the federal government."[21] Despite considerable discussion over the years of the desirability of creating a federal ombudsman,[22] including the introduction of a bill for that purpose,[23] there is little current interest in the proposal.

Mini-ombudsmen

Part of the explanation for the absence of a federal ombudsman is that the federal government has several "specialized ombudsmen" who serve a purpose similar to, but considerably narrower than, that of a general-purpose ombudsman. These include:

1. the Office of the Correctional Investigator, established in 1973 to investigate complaints made against prison authorities by, or on behalf of, inmates;
2. the Office of the Official Languages Commissioner, which was created in 1970 to administer the Official Languages Act by protecting the language rights of individuals, monitoring all federal agencies to ensure proper application of the Act, and making recommendations for improved adherence to the spirit and the letter of the Act;
3. the Canadian Human Rights Commission, which was established to implement the Canadian Human Rights Act (1976-77) and is responsible for investigating complaints of discrimination, trying to resolve or settle these complaints, and using research and public education to reduce discriminatory attitudes and behaviour;
4. the Office of the Information Commissioner, set up in 1983 to administer the Access to Information Act by investigating complaints against denial of access to government information;
5. the Office of the Privacy Commissioner, established in 1983 to implement the Privacy Act and, specifically, to inquire into complaints from persons who believe that their privacy rights have been abridged.[24]

The Correctional Investigator reports to Parliament through the Solicitor General, whereas the Human Rights, Information, and Privacy Commissioners report to Parliament through the Department of Justice. The Office of the Official Languages Commissioner is more independent of the executive in that its reports go directly to Parliament, where its work is scrutinized by the Joint Committee of the House and the Senate on Official Languages Policy and Programs.

The Public Service Commission

The federal **Public Service Commission** is an independent agency that serves Parliament as the guardian of the merit principle in human resource management.[25] The promotion of merit through the elimination of patronage has traditionally been a dominant concern of the commission. In this regard, J.E. Hodgetts has observed that the commission, "from its neutral vantage point, represents the institutionalized conscience of legislators, warding off the demon patronage rather like Alcoholics Anonymous wards off the demon rum on behalf of its membership."[26] The commission's annual report is tabled in Parliament by the Secretary of State for consideration by the Miscellaneous Estimates Committee.

The Auditor General

Aside from the Official Languages Commissioner, the only federal watchdog agency that reports to Parliament directly rather than through a minister is the Office of the Auditor General, which is discussed at length in Chapter 27. The Auditor General reports annually to Parliament on whether departments have kept proper financial records and whether public funds have been spent as appropriated by Parliament. Moreover, the Auditor General is authorized to report cases where "money has been expended without due regard for economy and efficiency; or... satisfactory procedures have not been established to measure and report the effectiveness of programs."[27]

The Auditor General enjoys considerable autonomy from executive control and can, therefore, significantly influence relations between Parliament and the executive. Ministers and public servants are fearful that the annual report of the Auditor General will single out their department or programs for criticism. Traditionally, the annual reports have provided powerful ammunition for the guns of the parliamentary Opposition by describing instances of inappropriate, questionable, and illegal government spending that are widely publicized in the media. Provincial auditors play a role similar to, but less publicized than, that of the Auditor General.[28]

Legislative Committees

Legislative committees are the third major means by which the legislature can exercise control or influence over the bureaucracy. The House of Commons has three types of committees: standing committees, special committees, and legislative committees. Most of the standing committees (e.g., Agriculture, Communications and Culture, Environment and Forestry) focus on a substantive sphere of government policy. Each committee covers one or more departments and agencies. For example, the Committee on Agriculture deals with the Department of Agriculture, the Canadian Dairy Commission, the Canadian Livestock Feed Board, the Farm Credit Corporation, and the National Farm Products Marketing Council. The other standing committees are called specialist standing committees; they include such committees as the Public Accounts Committee and the committees on Multiculturalism and on Elections, Privileges, and Procedures. There are also a few joint standing committees of the Senate and the House of Commons (e.g., the Joint Committee on Regulatory Scrutiny). There are about twenty-five standing committees.

In addition to the standing committees, special committees are set up as required to examine such specific issues as acid rain and child care, and legislative committees are established to examine specific government bills after these bills have passed second reading in the House of Commons. One advantage of the legislative committees is that the expertise, experience, and interests of the legislators can be matched to the subject matter of the legislation.

The functions of parliamentary committees may be divided into policy development (primarily involving evaluation of the purpose and content of proposed legislation), review of existing policies, and scrutiny of departmental administration (especially through examination of the estimates). In practice, these functions often overlap and committee members vary in the emphasis they place on each function. Kornberg and Mishler estimate that standing committees as a whole "spend about 50% of their time considering the estimates of the departments and divide the remainder of their time between scrutinizing current legislation and conducting investigations, collecting information on particular problems and preparing reports for the consideration of the House."[29]

The Public Accounts Committee and the Standing Joint Committee (i.e., of the Senate and the House of Commons) on Regulatory Scrutiny deserve special attention. They enjoy a greater measure of independence from Cabinet control because, unlike other committees, they are chaired by a member of the Opposition. In a majority government situation, however, the majority of the committees' members are from the government party.

The Public Accounts Committee examines both the *Public Accounts* (i.e., the government's year-end financial statements) and the Auditor General's Report as a basis for making recommendations to the House of Commons.[30] With the assistance of the Auditor General, the committee has uncovered, investigated, and reported on several scandals involving the expenditure of public funds, and has recommended corrective action in many other instances where public money has been improperly spent.

The Standing Joint Committee on Regulations and Other Statutory Instruments (now the Standing Joint Committee on Regulatory Scrutiny) was established by the Statutory Instruments Act, which came into force in January 1972.[31] The primary function of the committee is to scrutinize the use of delegated legislative authority by Cabinet, ministers, and public servants. The term **statutory instruments** refers to the rules, regulations, orders, etc., made by the executive, under delegated legislative authority. As noted in Chapter 13, the contemporary power of the bureaucracy rests, in part, on authority delegated to the executive by Parliament, whose members do not have the time or the expertise to provide in legislation for every contingency. The committee examines statutory instruments in the light of fifteen criteria, including, for example, whether a regulation "trespasses unduly on the rights and liberties of the subject" or "appears for any reason to infringe the rule of law or the rules of natural justice." It has requested, but has not yet received, permission to expand its terms of reference to include the review of draft bills for potential conflicts with the Canadian Charter of Rights and Freedoms.

The committee has severely criticized the government for lack of cooperation and inadequate responses to the committee's recommendations. In 1980, for example, the committee noted:

> There are also traditions in the Public Service, most notably in the drafting of statutes and subordinate legislation, which are more in keeping with administrative

ease than accountability to Parliament and observance of the law. The absence of a clearly articulated philosophy of respect for liberty and propriety in the activities of the executive government of Canada is a serious problem.[32]

Eric Hehner has suggested that, if ministers and government departments have no respect for this parliamentary committee, nobody else can be expected to take it seriously. Moreover, he worries that, unless members of Parliament provide an effective mechanism for reviewing the exercise of delegated legislation, "Parliament as we have known it will become relatively impotent."[33] The committee's warnings that the executive often does not exercise delegated authority in keeping with the intent of Parliament have received surprisingly little media attention.

Among the most common proposals for parliamentary reform are measures that will enhance the effectiveness of committees in evaluating the policies and scrutinizing the administrative actions of the executive. Public servants already answer to parliamentary committees by explaining the administrative and technical implications of existing and proposed policies. An increase in the investigative work, specialization, and expertise of committee members would enable them to engage in better informed, and more penetrating, questioning of officials. This would encourage public servants to perform their administrative tasks more economically, efficiently, and effectively, especially if committee members focussed their attention on the scrutiny of departmental administration. If members devoted a substantial portion of their efforts to policy development and policy review, officials would continue to refer to their minister those inquiries involving policy matters. But the enhanced competence of committee members, combined with the difficulty of separating policy and administrative considerations, would cause public servants to reveal more frequently and clearly their influence on policy formation. The effect on ministerial responsibility would be negligible because ministers would continue to deal with questions on the substance and direction of government policy.

The reinforcement and extension of the activities and expertise of parliamentary committees would improve Parliament's capacity to hold public servants accountable for the *administration*—but not for the *content*—of government policies. Thus, these reforms would not satisfy those who contend that the responsibility of public servants should be commensurate with their power in the political process. They claim that, in order for Parliament to play a significantly greater role in promoting administrative responsibility, there must be some shift in answerability for *policy* from ministers to public servants. The implementation of this proposal would have very important implications for Canada's parliamentary institutions and practices in both the federal and provincial spheres of government.

Relations between ministers and public servants would be complicated by the difficulty of distinguishing their respective contributions to the development of specific policies. The answerability of public servants to Parliament would compete with their accountability and loyalty to their minister. The remaining healthy component of ministerial responsibility—the answerability of ministers—would be severely weakened. Even the convenient fiction of a separation between policy and administration would be extremely difficult to maintain. There would be a dramatic decline in public service anonymity, and the senior echelons of the service would be politicized. Public servants would be compelled to defend their policy recommendations before parliamentary committees and the public. Officials would become personally associated with particular policies and would, therefore, become involved in political controversy. Security of tenure for senior officials would be replaced by a system of political appointments and a consequent turnover of public servants with a change of government.

This hypothetical pattern of relations between politicians and public servants indicates that public servants cannot be held answerable to Parliament for *policy* matters without major modifications in the present practice of ministerial responsibility and political neutrality. It also demonstrates the comparatively small extent to which the conventions have evolved from their traditional interpretation toward this pattern of behaviour. Current trends suggest that the conventions will continue to evolve, or will be altered, in the direction of greater administrative answerability to Parliament, but that ministers will retain formal responsibility for the defence of government policy. Thus, Parliament has the potential to increase its power over the public service, especially in the sphere of overseeing administration, without breaching those constitutional conventions most directly affecting the conduct of the public service.

The power of Parliament over the public service rests largely on its ability and inclination to control and influence the executive as a whole. But Parliament's success in checking the executive hinges on such factors as the devotion of committee members to their work, the creation of a non-partisan atmosphere in committee deliberations, the government's willingness to take committee reports seriously, and improved access to much government information now treated as confidential. Reforms in the structures and processes of Parliament would help to augment Parliament's power over both ministers and public servants. In particular, several measures could be adopted to increase the answerability of public servants for departmental administration. The Royal Commission on Financial Management and Accountability (the Lambert Commission)[34] made several useful recommendations for reforms to enhance the accountability of both ministers and senior bureaucrats to Parliament.[35]

The commission's recommendations involve a much more active role for parliamentary committees. The commissioners suggested that the deputy minister be designated the chief administrative officer of the department and be held directly accountable to Parliament through the Public Accounts Committee for specified administrative duties.[36] Ministers would remain accountable for policy objectives and decisions. Several years later, the Special Parliamentary Committee on Reform of the House of Commons (known as the McGrath Committee after its chairperson) discussed the possibility of an even broader measure of deputy ministerial responsibility:

We have heard many arguments that a new doctrine of deputy ministerial responsibility relating exclusively to matters of administration should be established.... Such a doctrine would set out the obligations of senior public servants and include the obligation to testify before parliamentary committees on matters of administration. Under this system, the testimony of deputy ministers before committees would be an everyday occurrence. Furthermore, regular open contact between the senior public service and Members of Parliament should lead to a more realistic understanding of administrative practices and more precise pinpointing of accountability.[37]

The Lambert commissioners also proposed that the number and size of standing committees in the House of Commons be reduced, and that these committees be allowed to recommend the partial reduction of proposed government expenditures and to submit substantive reports on the estimates to the House. In addition, each committee would have a chairperson elected for the life of a Parliament and a budget to hire staff.

The commissioners did not believe that their proposed reforms would erode the doctrine of ministerial responsibility. Indeed, they argued that "the concept of direct accountability of officials before Parliament through one of its committees would reinforce the minister's and the Cabinet's ability to be responsible for the conduct of the affairs of government."[38] The commissioners do acknowledge, however, that the success of efforts to increase government's accountability to Parliament on administrative matters depends largely on the determination of ministers and parliamentarians to achieve this end. J.R. Mallory notes that, in trying to improve the operations of the House of Commons, we must remember that "it is a political body made up of political parties whose *raison d'être* is to win the electoral battle and become the government. No activity, no matter how worthy, which does not accord with this primary objective is likely to be embraced by the House."[39]

The Report of the Special Parliamentary Committee on Reform of the House of Commons (the McGrath Report) contained many of the same proposed reforms as the Lambert Report mentioned above. The Mulroney government implemented some of the committee's recommendations, including those that reduced the size of parliamentary committees, ensured continuity in committee membership so as to encourage the development of special expertise among their members, provided committees with their own budgets for research staff and legal counsel, and permitted a parliamentary committee to review senior bureaucratic appointments, including those of deputy ministers and heads of Crown agencies. The committee also proposed that

each standing committee have before it the full departmental policy array to review and to report on, including, but not restricted to the following: the reasons for a department's statutes; the statutes themselves; a department's objectives in relation to its statutory mandate; the activities carried out in pursuit of these objectives; a department's immediate and long-term expenditure plans for these activities; and the achievements of the department measured against its objectives.[40]

This proposal, which was designed to enable members of Parliament to scrutinize government departments more effectively, was also accepted by the government.

As a result of these changes, there has been a modest move in the direction of more effective parliamentary control and influence over the executive in general and the bureaucracy in particular. Franks contends that "committees are now stronger and more influential than they ever have been in the past," but he notes also that "they can fill only a secondary place in parliament and the concerns of MPs. The responsibility still remains with the government to devise policies and administer the executive branch."[41] This judgment is confirmed by Sutherland who concludes that "the reforms to the standing committee system have not realized the aim of the McGrath Committee members to force a truly routine diminution of the government's monopoly over planning, spending and making policy."[42]

In addition to the three major forms of interaction between legislators and public servants described above, senior bureaucrats, with the consent of the minister concerned, provide occasional briefings to parliamentary caucuses on such matters as departmental structures and functions, and the operation and content of new programs. "The briefings are to provide factual and background material necessary to allow informed discussion of the subject under discussion, consistent with preserving the necessary confidences of government and with maintaining the traditional impartiality of public servants."[43] Finally, there are various informal contacts between legislators and public servants at social events and through oral or written requests for information about such matters as programs, budgets, and constituents' complaints.

A number of provincial governments have also taken some modest measures to enhance the accountability of ministers and public servants to the legislature, especially for financial administration. For example, in Ontario,[44] the Public Accounts Committee has been chaired by an Opposition member since 1968, and in 1977 the Provincial Auditor was authorized to report not only on the economy and efficiency of government operations, but also to verify that departments have appropriate procedures to enable them to report on the effectiveness of these operations.

Many students of the federal Parliament and provincial legislatures are pessimistic that the changes in government machinery and attitudes needed for a significant increase in legislative power over the bureaucracy will be made. Senior public servants do not view Parliament and its committees as a major focus of their accountability and, for the middle and lower ranks of the public service, "parliament is a distant and unimportant control."[45] Nevertheless, as noted above, some important reforms have recently been made. It was explained in Part III that the difficulty that legislatures have in exercising control and influence over departments is compounded with respect to Crown corporations and regulatory agencies, which enjoy a greater measure of autonomy than departments from executive, as well as legislative, control. In any event, even a more powerful legislature would be an insufficient instrument to ensure responsible public bureaucracy. The role of the legislature must be supplemented by controls and influences exercised by other actors in the political system, including the judiciary, which is discussed in the next chapter.

NOTES

1. Royal Commission on Financial Management and Accountability, *Final Report* (Ottawa: Supply and Services, 1979), pp. 52-53.
2. See, however, S. L. Sutherland and V. Baltacioglu, *Parliamentary Reform and the Federal Public Service* (London: National Centre for Management Research and Development, 1988).
3. Royal Commission, *Final Report*, p.371.
4. See, for example, S. E. Finer, "The Individual Responsibility of Ministers," *Public Administration* 34 (1956): 379; A. H. Birch, *Representative and Responsible Government* (London: George Allen and Unwin, 1964), pp. 139-40; R. M. Punnett, *British Government and Politics* (New York: Norton, 1968), p. 182; Jeffrey Stanyer and Brian Smith, *Administering Britain* (Glasgow: Fontana/Collins, 1976), pp. 180-81; Geoffrey Marshall and Graeme C. Moodie, *Some Problems of the Constitution*, 4th ed. (London: Hutchinson, 1967), pp. 67-74.
5. For an analysis of the evolution and present status of the convention of political neutrality, see Chapter 13.
6. Office of the Prime Minister, Transcript of Press Conference, November 18, 1977.
7. Government of Canada, *Report of the Committee on the Concept of the Ombudsman*, Ottawa, July 1977, p. 16.
8. *Stopforth v. Goyer*, 20 *Ontario Reports* (2d) 1978, p. 273. This decision was overturned in the Ontario Court of Appeal on the grounds that the occasion of Goyer's comments outside Parliament "was one of qualified privilege." 23 *Ontario Reports* (2d) 1979: 700.
9. Office of the Prime Minister, Transcript of Press Conference, December 22, 1969.
10. House of Commons, Special Committee on Reform of the House of Commons, *3rd Report*, June 1985.
11. Arthur Beauchesne, *Rules and Forms of the House of Commons of Canada*, 4th ed. (Toronto: Carswell, 1958), sec. 181 (3), p. 153.
12. House of Commons, *Debates*, February 6, 1978, p. 567.
13. Brian Chapman, *British Government Observed* (London: George Allen and Unwin, 1963), p. 38.
14. Finer, "The Individual Responsibility of Ministers," p. 394.
15. *Canadian Public Policy and Administration* (Toronto: McGraw-Hill Ryerson, 1981), p. 197.
16. Ibid., p. 220.
17. See, for example, J. R. Mallory, "Responsive and Responsible Government," Presidential Address, section II, *Transactions of the Royal Society of Canada*, series IV, 12 (1974), p. 221.
18. For a general discussion of bureaucratic power and administrative responsibility respectively, see Chapters 13 and 14.
19. For an account of the evolution of the Office of the Ombudsman—both in Canada and other countries—see Donald C. Rowat, *The Ombudsman Plan: The Worldwide Spread of an Idea*, 2nd ed. (Lanham, Md.: University Press of America, 1986.
20. Committee on the Concept of the Ombudsman, "The Ombudsman," in Kenneth

Kernaghan, ed., *Public Administration in Canada: Selected Readings*, 5th ed. (Toronto: Methuen, 1985), pp. 374-75.

21. Ibid., p. 379.

22. See Henry J. Llambias, "Canada: Introduction," in Gerald E. Caiden, ed., *International Handbook of the Ombudsman: Country Surveys* (Westport, Conn.: Greenwood Press, 1983), pp. 27-28, 34, and Rowat, *The Ombudsman Plan*, ch. 13.

23. In April 1978, the Liberal Government introduced Bill C-43, entitled the Ombudsman Act. For a critical analysis of the bill, see K. A. Friedmann and A. G. Milne, "The Federal Ombudsman Legislation: A Critique of Bill C-43," *Canadian Public Policy* 6 (Winter 1980): 63-67.

24. For additional information on the Offices of the Information Commissioner and the Privacy Commissioner, see Chapter 21.

25. For elaboration on the commission's functions and its relationship with the Treasury Board Secretariat, see Chapter 22.

26. J. E. Hodgetts, *The Canadian Public Service* (Toronto: University of Toronto Press, 1973), p. 264.

27. The Auditor General Act, Canada, *Statutes*, 1977, c. 34, s. 7 (2).

28. See Simon McInnes, "Improving Legislative Surveillance of Provincial Public Expenditures: The Performance of the Public Accounts Committees and Auditors General," *Canadian Public Administration* 20 (Spring 1977): 36-86.

29. Kornberg and Mishler, *Influence in Parliament: Canada*, p. 33.

30. See Sutherland and Baltaciolglu, *Parliamentary Reform*, ch. 3.

31. See Denys C. Holland and John P. McGowan, *Delegated Legislation in Canada* (Toronto: Carswell, 1989), ch. 5, and Gary Levy, "Delegated Legislation and the Standing Joint Committee on Regulations and Other Statutory Instruments," *Canadian Public Administration* 22 (Fall 1979): 349-65.

32. Standing Joint Committee on Regulations and Other Statutory Instruments (now the Standing Joint Committee on Regulatory Scrutiny), *Fourth Report*, July 1980.

33. Ibid., pp. 349, 350. See also J. R. Mallory, "Curtailing 'Divine Right': The Control of Delegated Legislation in Canada," in O. P. Dwivedi, ed., *The Administrative State in Canada* (Toronto: University of Toronto Press, 1982), pp. 131-49.

34. *Final Report*, chs. 21 and 22.

35. See also Special Committee on Reform of the House of Commons, *3rd Report*, June 1985, and the recommendations in Thomas D'Aquino, G. Bruce Doern, and Cassandra Blair, *Parliamentary Democracy in Canada: Issues for Reform* (Toronto: Methuen, 1983).

36. See the discussion of this proposal in Chapter 14.

37. Special Committee on Reform of the House of Commons, *3rd Report*, p. 21.

38. Ibid., p. 375.

39. J. R. Mallory, "Parliament in the Eighties," in R. Carty and W. Ward, eds., *Entering the Eighties: Canada in Crisis* (Toronto: Oxford University Press, 1980), p. 132.

40. Report of the Special Committee on Reform of the House of Commons, *3rd Report*, pp. 16-17.

41. C.E.S. Franks, *The Parliament of Canada* (Toronto: University of Toronto Press, 1987), p. 185.

42. Sutherland and Baltacioglu, *Parliamentary Reform*, p. 47.

43. Office of the Prime Minister, *Cabinet Procedures and Ministerial Guidelines*, September 18, 1984, Annex A—Briefings by Officials to Parliamentary Caucuses, dated June 1981.

44. See Graham White, *The Ontario Legislature* (Toronto: University of Toronto Press, 1989), ch. 8.
45. Franks, *The Parliament of Canada*, p. 233.

BIBLIOGRAPHY

Atkinson, Michael M. "Parliamentary Government in Canada." In Michael S. Whittington and Glen Williams, eds., *Canadian Politics in the 1980s*. 2nd ed. Toronto: Methuen, 1984, pp. 331-50.

Canada. House of Commons. Special Committee on Reform of the House of Commons. *3rd Report*. Ottawa: June 1985.

Canada. Royal Commission on Financial Management and Accountability. *Final Report*. Ottawa: Supply and Services, 1979, chs. 21-22.

Clarke, Harold D., Colin Campbell, F. Q. Quo, and Arthur Goddard, eds. *Parliament, Policy and Representation*. Toronto: Methuen, 1980.

Committee on the Concept of the Ombudsman, "The Ombudsman." In Kenneth Kernaghan, ed., *Public Administration in Canada: Selected Readings*. 5th ed. Toronto: Methuen, 1985, pp. 374-79.

Denton, T. M. "Ministerial Responsibility: A Contemporary Perspective." In R. Schultz et al., eds., *The Canadian Political Process*. Toronto: Holt, Rinehart and Winston, 1979, pp. 344-62.

Doerr, Audrey. "Parliamentary Accountability and Legislative Potential." In Harold D. Clarke et al., eds., *Parliament, Policy and Representation*. Toronto: Methuen 1980, pp. 144-59.

Gélinas, André. *Les parlementaires et l'administration au Québec*. Québec: Les Presses de l'Université Laval, 1969.

Jackson, Robert J., and Michael M. Atkinson. *The Canadian Legislative System*. 2nd ed. Toronto: Macmillan, 1980.

Holland, Denys C., and John P. McGowan. *Delegated Legislation in Canada*. (Toronto: Carswell, 1989).

Kersell, J. E. *Parliamentary Supervision of Delegated Legislation: The United Kingdom, Australia, New Zealand and Canada*. London: Stevens, 1960.

Kersell, J. E. "Statutory and Judicial Control of Administrative Behavior." *Canadian Public Administration* 19 (Summer 1976): 295-307.

Kornberg, Allan. *Canadian Legislative Behaviour*. Toronto: Holt, Rinehart and Winston, 1967.

Mallory, J. R. "Curtailing 'Divine Right': The Control of Delegated Legislation in Canada." In O. P. Dwivedi, ed., *The Administrative State in Canada*. Toronto: University of Toronto Press, 1982, pp. 131-50.

Rowat, Donald C. *The Ombudsman*. 2nd ed. Toronto: University of Toronto Press, 1968.

Rowat, Donald C. *The Ombudsman Plan*. Toronto: McClelland and Stewart, 1973.

Slatter, Frans F. *Parliament and Administrative Agencies*. Study paper for the Law Reform Commission of Canada. Ottawa: Supply and Services, 1982.

Stewart, John B. *The Canadian House of Commons: Procedure and Reform*. Montreal: McGill-Queen's University Press, 1977.

Vandervort, Lucinda. *Political Control of Independent Administrative Agencies*. Study paper for the Law Reform Commission of Canada. Ottawa: Supply and Services, 1979.

18

The Judiciary and the Bureaucracy

The last three chapters have examined the bureaucracy's relations with the executive and legislative branches of government. This chapter is concerned with the impact on the bureaucracy of the third branch of government—the judiciary. More specifically, it is concerned with the major concepts, issues, and developments in the sphere of judicial review of administrative action. It describes the grounds for judicial review, the remedies or forms of relief available, the use of privative clauses, and the utility of judicial review. The main focus of the chapter is the federal sphere of government and the Federal Court of Canada in particular, but attention is paid also to noteworthy developments in the provinces. The chapter begins by explaining briefly the judicial system, within which judicial review of administrative action takes place.

THE CANADIAN JUDICIARY

Unlike the executive and legislative branches of government, which are integrally linked to one another, the judiciary is independent from the other branches of government. The independence of judges is considered crucial to the impartial administration of justice and is guaranteed by various measures, including tenure in office for judges during good behaviour.

The structure of the courts in Canada is shown in Figure 18.1. This structure is determined by the Constitution Act of 1867, which provides for separate federal and provincial courts, but permits cases to be appealed from provincial to federal courts, including the Supreme Court of Canada, which stands at the apex of the judicial hierarchy. Section 101 of the Act authorizes Parliament to establish a court of appeal for Canada and any other courts required for "the better administration" of federal laws. Section 92 (14) grants to the provinces exclusive jurisdiction over the administration of justice in the provinces, "including the Constitution, Maintenance, and Organization of Provincial Courts, both of Civil and Criminal Jurisdiction, and including procedure in Civil Matters in those Courts." However, section 91(27) confers on the federal Parliament exclusive jurisdiction over criminal procedure, and sections 96, 99, and 100 give the federal government power over the appointment, salaries, and removal of all superior, county, and district judges in the provinces. Since the

Figure 18.1
THE HIERARCHY OF CANADIAN COURTS

1. Federal Courts—established by *federal* statutes with judges appointed by the *federal* government.

Supreme Court of Canada

Federal Court of Canada	
Trial Division	Court of Appeal

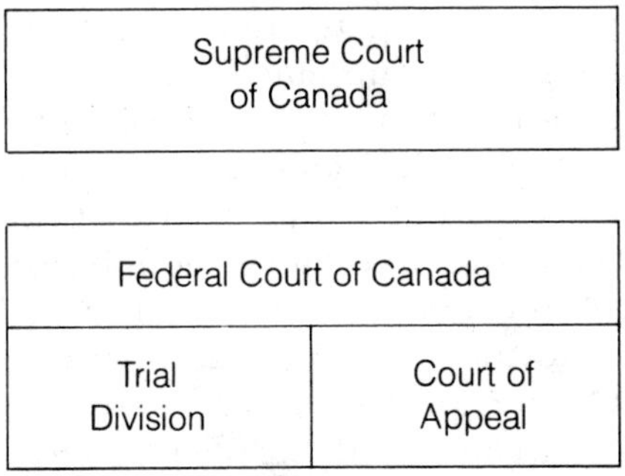

2. Provincial Courts—established by *provincial* statutes with judges appointed by the *federal* government.

Supreme Court or Superior Court of a Province	
Trial Division	Appellate Division

County or District Courts

Surrogate Courts

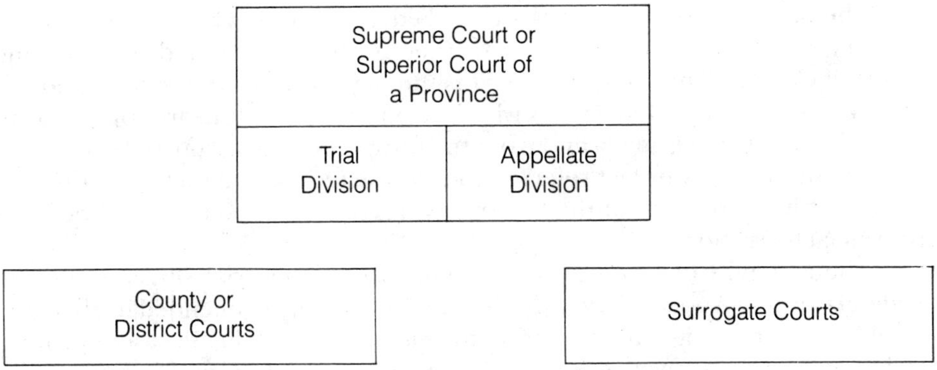

3. Provincial Courts—established by *provincial* statutes with judges appointed by *provincial* governments.

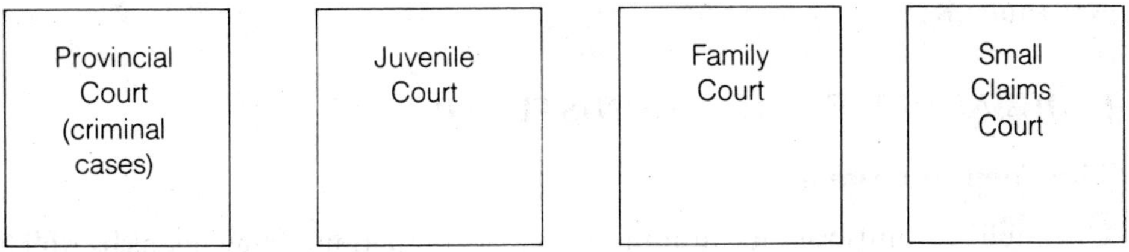

Provincial Court (criminal cases)	Juvenile Court	Family Court	Small Claims Court

provinces are authorized to create and operate certain courts for which the federal government is authorized to appoint and pay the judges, federal and provincial governments are required to cooperate in the administration of justice.[1]

The structure and the names of courts in the provinces vary from one province to another, but there are some broad similarities.[2] At the top of the court system in each province is a superior court that, depending on the province, bears such names as the Supreme Court, the Superior Court, or the High Court. These superior courts have jurisdiction in both criminal and civil cases, and they hear appeals from decisions of the lower courts.

The level below is composed of county or district courts that traditionally have had original jurisdiction over a certain geographical area in criminal cases and in civil cases in which the amount of money at stake is less than a certain amount. However, most provinces have merged their county or district courts with their superior courts. Thus, an intermediate level of courts whose judges are federally appointed is being eliminated. Surrogate courts responsible for such matters as the settlement of estates are also at this level.

Below the county, or district courts, and the surrogate courts are the provincial courts, which deal with criminal acts, juvenile offences, family problems, and small claims. The judges of these courts are appointed and paid by the provincial government.

The two major federal courts are the Federal Court of Canada, which is the primary court with which we are concerned in this chapter, and the Supreme Court of Canada. The Supreme Court is the highest court in the land and is a general court of appeal for both civil and criminal cases. It hears appeals from the Federal Court of Canada and from the provincial appeal courts. It also deals with questions of law or fact referred to it by the federal Cabinet (e.g., on such matters as interpretation of the Constitution Acts and the validity of federal or provincial legislation).

The Federal Court of Canada is composed of the Trial Division and the Federal Court of Appeal. Under the Federal Court Act,[3] as amended in 1990, the Trial Division has original jurisdiction to hear and grant relief in cases involving claims against the Crown, and exclusive jurisdiction to hear and grant relief in cases involving appeals against the decisions of most federal boards, commissions and other tribunals.[4] The Federal Court of Appeal has original jurisdiction to review the decisions of ten federal tribunals, which are described as "courts of record." The judicial review jurisdiction conferred on the Federal Court has been interpreted to embrace a broad range of decision-makers in the federal government.[5]

JUDICIAL REVIEW OF ADMINISTRATIVE ACTION

The Focus on Agencies

The public administration community, in its examination of the means by which responsible administrative behaviour may be pursued in Canada, has devoted relatively little attention to the utility of administrative law in general and judicial review of administrative action in particular. **Administrative law** is that branch of public law that

> deals with the legal limitations on the actions of governmental officials, and on the remedies which are available to anyone affected by a transgression of these limits. The subject invariably involves the question of lawful authority of an official to do a particular act which, in the absence of such authority, might well be illegal . . . and give rise to actionable wrong.[6]

Despite the neglect of administrative law in the field of public administration, since the early 1970s a substantial volume of publications has resulted from increased interest in the subject by the legal community. This development was partly a recognition of the extensive regulatory and adjudicative powers now exercised by administrative officials, especially those in semi-independent agencies. But the major stimulant was the creation in 1970 of the Federal Court of Canada and the court's subsequent review of the decisions of public authorities.

Like Britain, Canada has a large number of conventional government departments organized in hierarchical form and headed by ministers. But unlike Britain and like the United States, many government activities in Canada are conducted by agencies enjoying a measure of independence from government. John Willis has noted that, in the field of administrative law, Canadians "have inherited from England the principle of ministerial responsibility and the common law of judicial review, but have borrowed the institution of the 'independent regulatory commission' and many of the matters regulated from the United States and have modified them to suit our own peculiar conditions."[7] In particular, regulatory agencies in Canada are not as "independent" of the political executive as the independent regulatory commissions in the United States.

Nevertheless, as explained in Chapter 10, Crown agencies in Canada are less accountable than conventional departments to Cabinet, ministers, and Parliament. Thus, in the search for responsible administrative behaviour, judicial control is relatively more important with respect to agencies (boards, commissions, and tribunals) than to regular departments. Indeed, the primary focus of scholarly writings is on judicial review of decisions of federal and provincial agencies; comparatively little attention has been paid to judicial control of the decisions and actions of conventional departments.

From among the confusing assortment of Crown agencies, a category of agencies described as "independent deciding and advisory bodies" can be singled out on the grounds that these agencies possess regulatory, adjudicative, and/or advisory powers.[8] Within this category, two subcategories are of special relevance to the subject of this chapter. The first subcategory, composed of fourteen agencies, is that of *regulatory agencies*, "whose primary functions are licensing, making rules and orders, and supervising activities in a particular industry or sector of the economy, all of which have profound impact on, and control over, the behaviour of individuals and corporations."[9] This category contains such centrally important and politically sensitive agencies as the

National Energy Board, the Atomic Energy Control Board, and the Canadian Radio-television and Telecommunications Commission. The second sub-category, composed of six agencies, is that of *deciding tribunals,* which "perform a specialized adjudicative function affecting individual rights."[10] Agencies in this group include the Immigration Appeal Board and the Pension Appeal Board.

The reason for drawing attention to these regulatory agencies and deciding tribunals is not to suggest that conventional government departments and other Crown agencies do not exercise important discretionary powers that may be reviewed by the courts; rather the purpose is to highlight those bodies that are most visible to the public, that have a significant measure of independence from political direction and control, and that exercise administrative and quasi-judicial functions.

Discretionary Powers

The importance of judicial review and of other means of control over adminis-trative action arises in large part from the exercise of discretionary powers by public officials. Discretionary powers "are those which involve an element of judgment or choice by the person exercising them and comprise all government functions from fact finding to setting standards."[11] As noted in Chapters 13 and 17, bureaucrats exercise a striking number and variety of discretionary powers under delegated legislative authority. In 1977, the Law Reform Commission of Canada depicted a catalogue of almost 15,000 discretionary powers as "only the tip of the iceberg."[12] Most of these discretionary powers are delegated to the Governor in Council (i.e., the Cabinet), but they are also conferred on ministers and individual officials and on agencies, boards, commissions, and tribunals. (Unless otherwise specified, throughout the rest of this chapter, the term "tribunal" will be used to encompass all of these individual officials or groups of officials.)

Some statutes delegate discretionary powers to more than one authority. For example, under the Clean Air Act[13] much is left to be "prescribed" by the Cabinet; authority to determine standards and to determine who should be required to conform to them is delegated to the minister; and inspectors are given powers of enforcement to be applied in accordance with what the inspec-tor "reasonably believes" to be the facts or with what he or she "deems necessary." Rules made under delegated legislative authority are described by a variety of names, including regulations, statutory instruments, and orders in council. These rules constitute "subordinate" or "delegated" legislation. Although the courts do review the exercise of legislative functions, notably to determine whether the exercise is *ultra vires* (beyond the powers of) the organization exercising them, the major concern of the courts, and thus of this chapter, is the review of judicial and quasi-judicial functions.

Neither the Cabinet nor individual ministers can be expected to exercise their delegated powers solely on their own. For example, a minister could not find time to decide upon every application for a license. Thus, statutes often permit the Cabinet and ministers, either expressly or by "necessary intendment," to subdelegate authority. David Mullan states that there is a rule that ministers "are generally entitled to exercise their statutory powers through responsible persons in their departments and that in such circumstances ministerial decisions cannot be questioned on the basis that they were not made by the Minister personally."[14] He notes further that "this rule is founded on the doctrine of ministerial responsibility. The Minister is accountable to the Legislature but not to the courts for actions of his subordinates."[15] The subdelegation of discretionary powers has led to a condition of what has been described as "dispersed discretions" and a consequent decline in the accountability of public authorities to the legislature and, through the legislature, to the public. It is notable also that bureaucrats, on the basis of their experience and expertise, influence ministers by advising them as to the appropriate exercise of powers within ministerial discretion.

Appeal and Review

Judicial control over the decisions of tribunals may be founded on:

1. statutory provisions for appeal;
2. statutory provisions for review (known as statutory or direct remedies); or
3. on the courts' inherent supervisory jurisdiction over inferior tribunals.

No right of appeal against a tribunal's decision exists unless that right is expressly conferred by statute. Statutory provision may be made for appeals to the courts, to the Cabinet, to ministers, to deputy ministers, or to an administrative body either within a government department (e.g., the Determinations and Appeals Section of the Source Deductions Division, Department of National Revenue [Taxation]), or outside of it (e.g., the Immigration Appeal Board). The legislature often provides for statutory *review* as well as statutory appeal, but when neither is provided the courts may exercise their inherent supervisory authority to *review* the decisions of inferior tribunals.

Classification of Function

A central issue with respect to judicial review of administrative discretion is the *classification* of the function (i.e., administrative, judicial, quasi-judicial) performed by the tribunal. The nature of the function being exercised may well determine whether, and on what grounds, the courts will grant relief. The courts usually review the exercise of a judicial or quasi-judicial function, but not of an administrative function. It is painfully evident from a study of administrative law that the courts have had great difficulty in distinguishing precisely and consistently between these various functions.

René Dussault notes that

the main distinction between judicial and quasi-judicial functions is based on the complete absence of discretion in the former as contrasted with the existence of some discretion in the latter. When an administrative officer exercises judicial functions he is governed by a statutory direction to apply the law; his decision must be inferred from the law. But when he exercises quasi-judicial functions he has a statutory permission to use his own discretion and to be guided by considerations of public policy.[16]

Despite this distinction, in administrative law the courts normally use the terms judicial and quasi-judicial interchangeably.

An equally elusive, but much more important, distinction is that between an administrative function and a quasi-judicial function. Reid and Hillel note that, in classifying functions, courts consider whether the exercise of the power will affect existing rights; "if it has an effect, the classification will be quasi-judicial; if none it will be administrative. If the decision is based on policy, not law, or made in pursuance of an unfettered discretion, the classification will be 'administrative.' On the other hand, if law, or objective standards, limit the exercise of discretion, it will be classified as quasi-judicial."[17] They also assert that their general impression is that "classifying functions is less a logical system than a method by which the courts signal their intention to supervise tribunals or to abstain. Thus, a classification as quasi-judicial will signal an intention to exert a close supervision, whereas a classification as administrative will indicate an intention to supervise slightly, if at all."[18] In the area of licensing, for example, the functions of licensing authorities are usually classified as quasi-judicial,[19] but the functions of several authorities have been held to be administrative.[20]

Grounds for Review

The courts, unless otherwise instructed by statute, may review the exercise of administrative discretion if a tribunal has:

1. breached the rules of "natural justice";
2. violated the doctrine of *ultra vires*, that is, acted outside the jurisdiction conferred on it by statute by exceeding its powers, abusing its powers or committing errors of procedure; or
3. made errors of law.

Each of these grounds for judicial review will be examined briefly in turn.[21]

Natural Justice

The two fundamental principles of natural justice are *audi alteram partem* (hear the other side) and *nemo judex in sua causa debet esse* (no one should be a judge in his or her own cause.) The *audi alteram partem* principle encompasses the notions that a party whose rights might be affected should have:

1. adequate notice of the allegations against him or her and of the tribunal's intention to make a decision;
2. the right to be heard, specifically to present proofs and arguments;
3. the right to cross-examine witnesses and sometimes the right to legal representation; and

4. the right to an adjournment for a reasonable period of time to allow for preparation of his or her case.

In the case of *Blais v. Basford*,[22] the Minister of Consumer and Corporate Affairs terminated Blais's business license on the basis of a report by the superintendent of bankruptcy. The Federal Court ordered the reinstatement of the license on the grounds that "the Minister must act fairly and impartially and in this case should have offered Blais an opportunity to answer material in the report of the Superintendent." However, the application of the *audi alteram partem* principle depends on the circumstances of the case. Mr. Justice Mahoney of the Federal Court has observed that

> what is reasonable in a particular case may run the gamut from merely giving the person to be affected written notice of the bold facts upon which it is proposed to act and inviting his written comments to a full dress oral hearing with witnesses and cross-examination all around. Those seeking certainty from precedents in this area will be disappointed."[23]

According to the *nemo judex in sua causa* principle, all forms of bias should be excluded from the proceedings and decisions of tribunals. The courts may intervene in the event of either "actual" bias or "a real likelihood" or "reasonable apprehension" of bias. The latter form of bias includes such factors as kinship, friendship, or business relations with a party to the proceedings, hearing appeals from one's own decisions, or manifesting undue hostility toward one of the parties.

The two principles of natural justice explained above have traditionally applied only to tribunals exercising judicial or quasi-judicial functions, not to those exercising administrative functions. However, the Supreme Court of Canada has recently held that "even those exercising purely administrative or executive functions have a duty to act fairly and not arbitrarily and that, in certain instances, this will involve affording procedural protections to those affected by the decision."[24] This "duty to act fairly" requires that where the rights of an individual are affected, a procedure should be followed that not only meets the minimum standards imposed by the statute but also ensures that the case will be heard fairly.[25] A strong affirmation of this duty came in the landmark Nicholson case in which the Supreme Court overturned the dismissal of a probationary police constable because he was not given reasons for his dismissal or an opportunity to respond to those reasons.[26] The significance of this decision is that the legislation did not require that reasons and an opportunity to respond be given; the court simply felt that "fairness" required it.

Gerald Gall contends that the result of the Nicholson case and of the subsequent Martineau case[27] is that

> a court of superior jurisdiction may now review decisions of inferior tribunals on the ground that they were made in a manner that was procedurally unfair.... The doctrine of fairness is a part of the rules of natural justice. Indeed, it might be regarded as the core or central requirement of natural justice.[28]

It is especially notable that this doctrine of fairness applies to administrative tribunals exercising a purely administrative function, as well as to judicial or quasi-judicial tribunals.

The importance of procedural fairness in the decisions of administrative authorities can be demonstrated by reference to the case of Margaret Johnston,[29] the common-law widow of a war veteran. The Federal Department of Veterans Affairs had accused her of fraud and cut off her pension. The Federal Court of Appeal ordered the Department to reconsider the case on the grounds that the department had upheld its own decision in "blatantly unfair" hearings and described the case as a textbook example of why the courts must protect citizens from administrative abuse. The court said that it defies belief that a widow could be deprived of her means of support and accused of criminal activity "so quickly and so easily—without even giving the individual concerned prior notice of the case that appears to be existing against him or her and letting him or her have an opportunity to meet it."[30]

Ultra Vires

The courts will generally intervene and grant relief where a tribunal has acted outside the scope of authority bestowed on it by its governing statute. Where there has been an excess of powers, the courts have found all types of decisions *ultra vires*, whether judicial, quasi-judicial, or administrative. Indeed, excess of powers is the primary ground for judicial review. To take a hypothetical and extreme example, the action of an immigration tribunal in granting a license to drive would be declared *ultra vires*. The determination as to whether there has been an excess of powers obliges the courts to examine the enabling statute very carefully to see if Parliament has empowered the tribunal to act in a certain situation. It is the authority of the tribunal to make a decision, not the merits of the decision itself, which is at issue.

Another ground for review, that of *errors of procedure*, also requires that the courts look to the enabling statue. Parliament may specify that a tribunal exercise its powers according to specific procedures. We have already seen that on grounds of natural justice the courts may require tribunals performing judicial or quasi-judicial functions to follow certain rules of procedure. Regardless of natural justice principles, however, the courts will insist that tribunals follow the procedural rules set out in the statute; otherwise the decision stemming from errors of procedure will be declared *ultra vires*.

An *abuse of power* occurs when a tribunal uses its power for a purpose not authorized by Parliament under the enabling statute. Thus, in considering whether there has been an abuse of power, and consequently whether a decision is *ultra vires*, the courts tend to look beyond the enabling statute to examine Parliament's intention. Abuse of power is usually expressed in terms of discretion exercised by a tribunal for improper purposes, in bad faith, or on irrelevant grounds.

In the celebrated Canadian case of *Roncarelli v. Duplessis*, the Supreme Court found abuse of power when the Attorney General (who was also the Premier) of the Province of Quebec directed a licensing commission to cancel the liquor permit held by a tavern owner because he had acted as bondsman for persons accused of distributing allegedly seditious literature. The commission's decision was declared to be beyond its powers, and Justice Rand stated:

> In public regulation of this sort there is no such thing as untrammelled "discretion," that is, that action can be taken on any ground or for any reason that can be suggested to the mind of the administrator; no legislative act can, without express language, be taken to contemplate an unlimited arbitrary power exercisable for any person, however capricious or irrelevant, regardless of the nature or purpose of the statute . . . . "Discretion" necessarily implies good faith in discharging public duty; there is always a perspective within which a statute is intended to operate; any clear departure from its line or objects is just as objectionable as fraud or corruption.[31]

Errors of Law

The courts may review the decisions of tribunals for *errors of law on the face of the record.* The "record" for this purpose includes not only the formal decision but also the reasons for the decision, documents initiating the proceedings, documents on which the decision is based, and documents cited in the reasons for decision. The words "on the face of the record" indicate that the courts will not review a decision unless the error is apparent.[32]

The Federal Court Act's specification of the common law grounds for review cover all the grounds noted above. The court may review decisions on the grounds that a tribunal:

1. acted without jurisdiction, acted beyond its jurisdiction or refused to exercise its jurisdiction;
2. failed to observe a principle of natural justice, procedural fairness or other procedure that it was required by law to observe;
3. erred in law in making a decision or an order, whether or not the error appears on the face of the record;
4. based its decision or order on an erroneous finding of fact that it made in a perverse or capricious manner or without regard for the material before it;
5. acted, or failed to act, by reason of fraud or perjured evidence; or
6. acted in any other way that was contrary to law.

Forms of Relief

We turn now to a consideration of the common-law or ancillary remedies that the courts may use after the grounds for judicial review have been established. Statutory or direct remedies, namely appeal and review procedures provided by statute, were discussed above. The common-law remedies are employed when no other form of relief is available, convenient, or effective. They include the prerogative remedies, namely *certiorari*, prohibition, *mandamus, habeas corpus,* and *quo warranto,* as well as the remedies of injunction, declaration, and damages.

The most frequently used writs in Canada are *certiorari* and prohibition. *Certiorari* is a writ issued by a superior court to quash a decision already taken by an inferior tribunal, whereas prohibition is a writ to restrain a tribunal from taking a certain action. Both writs are generally used against tribunals exercising judicial or quasi-judicial functions. Moreover, the grounds on which these writs are available are breach of the rules of natural justice; absence, excess, or abuse of jurisdiction; and error of law on the face of the record. The Supreme Court held in the Martineau case, cited above, that a writ of *certiorari* will also be issued against tribunals exercising an administrative function if there is a violation of the doctrine of fairness.

Mandamus is a writ used to compel an inferior tribunal to exercise the authority conferred on it by statute. Unlike *certiorari* and prohibition, this writ is not restricted to tribunals exercising a judicial or quasi-judicial function. To obtain the writ of *mandamus*, an affected party must show that the tribunal is authorized or required to perform a certain duty, that the tribunal has been asked to perform that duty, and that refusal of the tribunal to perform the duty can be proved or implied.

An injunction is a remedy that requires an inferior tribunal to take a particular action or, more commonly, to refrain from taking some specified action beyond its powers. An injunction is generally available only if an equally effective alternative remedy is not available. It can be used against tribunals exercising administrative, as well as judicial or quasi-judicial, functions.

An action for declaration (or declaratory judgment) asks the court to declare and define whether some act taken or proposed by a tribunal is beyond its powers. Like an injunction, a declaration is available for administrative as well as judicial or quasi-judicial decisions. Actions for declaration are infrequent. Moreover, they are normally combined with requests for other forms of relief, notably injunctions.

Damages is a remedy that requires that a certain amount of money be paid to compensate for an injury or wrong done to an individual. Tribunals, like ordinary citizens, are liable to an action for damages. Obviously, the remedy of damages is most useful in situations where the tribunal has already taken some action or decision. A remedy like *certiorari* that simply quashes the original decision would be of little help once the harm has been done. The remedy of damages is available in respect to administrative as well as judicial and quasi-judicial functions. Damages were awarded against the Attorney General (and Premier) of Quebec in the case of *Roncarelli v. Duplessis* mentioned earlier.

Habeas corpus is a writ used to require that a person who has been detained be brought before a court for the purpose of determining whether or not the detention is legal. This writ is not used very much in the sphere of administrative law. It is normally restricted to immigration cases where it is often used to challenge orders for custody or deportation.

Quo warranto is a writ used to inquire into whether an appointment to a public office established by statute is legal. The use of this writ has in large measure been made unnecessary by statutory provisions relating to appointments to public office.

Privative Clauses

With a view to allowing administrative tribunals to operate efficiently and quickly, Parliament and the provincial legislatures frequently use **privative clauses**, that is, statutory provisions designed to prevent judicial review of administrative action. These clauses differ in the strength of their wording, but the standard privative clauses are typically worded as:

> No decision, order, direction, declaration or ruling of the tribunal shall be questioned or reviewed in any court and no order shall be made or proceedings taken in any court, whether by way of injunction, declaratory judgment, certiorari, mandamus, prohibition, quo warranto, or otherwise to question, review, prohibit or restrain the tribunal or any of its proceedings.

Despite the clear intention of the legislators to exclude judicial review through the use of privative clauses, Canadian courts have generally given little or no effect to these clauses. A major reason for the courts' dislike of privative clauses is that these clauses aim to interfere with the court's inherent supervisory jurisdiction over inferior tribunals and thereby free the tribunals from the traditional restraint of judicial review. Moreover, the courts presume that Parliament and the provincial legislatures did not intend, through the use of privative clauses, to permit tribunals to do anything they wish. There is, at present, a division of opinion among legal scholars as to the likely outcome of this dispute between the legislatures and the courts; however, the emerging doctrine of "a duty to act fairly," as well as certain provisions of the Canadian Charter of Rights and Freedoms, will likely reduce the impact of privative clauses.

Innovations in the Provinces

A Judicial Review Procedure Act was enacted by Ontario[33] in 1971, and by British Columbia[34] in 1976. The Ontario Act introduced an Application for Judicial Review, which was a new means of applying for judicial review of administrative action. This new remedy was one of the reforms proposed by the Royal Commission of Inquiry on Civil Rights in Ontario (the McRuer Commission), which explained the purpose of the remedy as follows:

> Instead of a multiplicity of forms of applications to compel, prohibit or set aside the exercise of statutory powers, there should be a single application to the court in which all the relief obtainable under any of the existing remedies would be available without the technical complexities, provoking much legalistic debate, which often obstruct, delay and sometimes defeat a decision on its merits.[35]

Among other things, the Act authorizes the court to treat applications for *certiorari*, prohibition, and *mandamus* as if they were applications for judicial review.

The British Columbia Judicial Review Procedure Act is very similar to the Ontario Act, but there are some important differences. For example, in British Columbia, the Act was not accompanied by the establishment of a new division of the Supreme Court; as a result, a single judge of the Supreme Court hears applications for judicial review.

In Ontario, the Judicial Review Procedure Act of 1971 was accompanied by the enactment of the Statutory Powers Procedure Act,[36] which set forth minimum rules for the proceedings of certain tribunals exercising statutory powers of decision. Among the procedures imposed on the tribunals are reasonable notice of hearing to the parties involved; hearings open to the public except under specified conditions; the right to representation by counsel; and the right to cross-examination. The Province of Alberta has a similar statute entitled the Administrative Procedures Act.[37]

THE UTILITY OF JUDICIAL REVIEW

There is a division of opinion, primarily between academic legal scholars and lawyers, over the desirability of the current trend toward the expansion of judicial review of administrative action. Several academic authors have regretted the increased willingness of the courts to question the exercise of administrative discretion.[38] These writers are in general agreement that judicial review is not intrinsically a good thing.

Indeed, judicial review has in practice a number of deficiencies as a means of preventing and remedying abuses of bureaucratic power and thereby helping to promote responsible administrative behaviour.[39] The courts review only a miniscule number of the millions of decisions made annually by administrative authorities. Thus, "although the spectre of judicial intervention may be an inhibiting factor for administrative agencies,... [i]t is a remote possibility in reality."[40] The success rate of litigants in respect to both judicial review and reconsideration by inferior tribunals is not high. Judicial review is uneconomic in that usually neither the amount of money nor the issue involved is significant enough to justify the high cost of the proceedings. Indeed, in a substantial proportion of cases, the litigants clearly have the financial resources to bear the cost; moreover, there are few cases of the social welfare type where the cost would tend to discourage aggrieved persons from seeking judicial review. Finally, judicial review tends to focus on certain areas of public administration (labour relations, tax assessment, and licensing) so that many areas of administrative action are relatively untouched by judicial review.

Those academic scholars favouring a narrow scope for judicial review point to the benefits of having decisions made by tribunals possessing expertise and experience in various areas of administrative activity and providing more expeditious and inexpensive proceedings than the courts. They acknowledge, however, that judicial review is the best form of control when values fundamental to the legal order as a whole (e.g., civil liberties values and constitutional issues) are in question. In Professor Hogg's words, "judicial review is rarely needed, but when it is needed nothing else will do."[41]

THE CANADIAN CHARTER OF RIGHTS AND FREEDOMS

The Charter is likely to have a very significant effect on administrative law in general and judicial review of administrative action in particular.[42] It came into full force only in 1985, and there have not yet been enough judicial decisions to provide an adequate basis for predicting its long-run impact on administrative law. However, one legal scholar has noted that "the imposition of the *Charter* as the supreme law of the land does mean that the sources of Canadian administrative law have been substantially increased. The legality of bureaucratic conduct is now decided not only in accordance with fidelity to legislation, but also by the normative concepts contained in the *Charter*."[43] Moreover,

> [t]he Charter must be taken seriously by administrators who, to date, may have had little if any experience with the judicial process. It must be regarded as a limitation upon every administrative action and every statutory instrument. It has 'constitutionalized' administrative law, procedure and practice.
>
> There is no point being irritated about it because it reduces administrative efficiency: that was precisely what it was intended to do. If the administration thinks that something is "reasonably justified," it must be prepared not merely to assert it, but to prove it. Gone are the days when one can simply say, "Trust us, we are the public service."[44]

The Charter has already had a considerable impact on the working lives of public servants at all levels of government. Many statutes and regulations have been amended to bring them into harmony with the Charter before they are challenged in the courts. And many decisions, especially in the lower courts, have had a major impact on public servants' day-to-day work. Indeed,

> most Charter cases involve decisions initially made by appointed officials in the executive branch of government. That is especially true of the criminal justice system, from which most Charter litigation has sprung, challenging the actions of a host of police officers, prosecutors, lower court judges, probation officers, and parole officers in the administration of our common law. In the labour field, too, a number of cases have arisen involving the practices and doctrines of appointed labour boards.[45]

It appears that the courts will use the Charter to assert strongly the rights of individuals. Sections 7 and 15 will have an especially important effect on administrative law and, therefore, on the conduct of public administration. Section 7, on legal rights, provides in part, "Everyone has the right to life, liberty and security of the person and the right not to be deprived thereof except in accordance with the principles of fundamental justice." In the *Singh* case,[46] for example, the Supreme Court held that it was a breach of "the principles of fundamental justice" not to provide an oral hearing to refugee claimants. Legal scholars have observed that the wording of section 7 "constitutionalizes" the procedural aspects of natural justice (or the duty to be fair), and that the reference to *principles of natural justice* "may ripen into a substantive (as opposed to a procedural) limitation on . . . the content of parent legislation which can be enacted [and]...provide a method to scrutinize the merits of a delegate's decision."[47]

Section 15 provides in part, "Every individual is equal before the law and has the right to the equal protection of the law without discrimination and, in particular, without discrimination based on race, national or ethnic origin, colour, religion, sex, age, or mental or physical disability." This section, which deals with equality rights, did not come into effect until 1985, but it has already spawned a large number of cases in the lower courts. The federal Department of Justice has predicted that section 15 will provide much better protection against discrimination than that provided by human rights laws and the Canadian Bill of Rights, because "section 15 is part of the Constitution. It can be used to strike down laws that offend its principles."[48]

As a result of section 15, governments have to ensure that their hiring and promotion requirements do not discriminate against such disadvantaged groups as women and disabled persons. Thus, this section is especially important to government efforts to promote employment equity. In the case of *Action travail des femmes*,[49] the Supreme Court imposed an employment equity program on Canadian National Railways, which was obliged to hire women for a specific percentage of jobs traditionally held by men.

The enormous potential for the courts to use the Charter to protect individual rights against government action is demonstrated in the case of Mario Duarte.[50] The issue in the case was whether, under the Charter, the police could legally have an informer record, surreptitiously and without a judicial warrant, his conversation with a suspected drug dealer. The Supreme Court had asserted in previous cases that the primary value served by section 8 of the Charter is privacy. And, in the Duarte case, the court came to the defence of personal privacy in the face of increasingly sophisticated surveillance technology. Justice La Forest stated:

> The very efficacy of electronic surveillance is such that it has the potential, if left unregulated, to annihilate any expectation that our communications will remain private. A society which exposed us, at the whim of the state, to the risk of having a permanent electronic recording made every time we opened our mouths might be superbly equipped to fight crime, but it would be one in which privacy no longer had any meaning.[51]

The Charter has already been used to advance the individual rights of public servants themselves. As explained in Chapter 13, restrictions on the political rights of public servants have been challenged under the Charter. As a result, there has been modest movement toward the extension of the political rights of public servants, especially in the sphere of partisan political activity.

The trend toward greater judicial activism in the review of administrative discretion that existed before the Charter came into force is highly likely to continue. But even if the importance of judicial review increases substantially, judicial control will remain as only one weapon in the arsenal of controls and influences available to preserve and stimulate responsible administrative behaviour. While there are occasions when only judicial review will do, administrative responsibility may usually be pursued by other means.

NOTES

1. Perry S. Millar and Carl Baar, *Judicial Administration in Canada* (Kingston and Montreal: McGill-Queen's University Press, 1981), ch. 4.
2. Note that Ontario has undertaken a major reform of its court system. For a brief explanation of the reforms, see Gerald L. Gall, *The Canadian Legal System*, 3rd ed. (Toronto: Carswell, 1990), pp. 157-58.
3. *Revised Statutes of Canada*, 1970, 2nd Supp., ch. 10, as amended by Canada, *Statutes*, 1990, c. 8.
4. Included among these tribunals are the Tax Court of Canada, the Canadian Radio-television and Telecommunications Commission, the Pension Appeals Board, the National Energy Board, and the Competition Tribunal.
5. Among the bodies held to be "federal boards, commissions or other tribunals" are the Tariff Board; the Hamilton Harbour Commissioners; the Minister of Consumer and Corporate Affairs, acting under the Bankruptcy Act; the Canadian Radio and Television Commission; the National Parole Board; the Commissioner of Penitentiaries; the Commissioner of Patents; and the chairman of a board of referees constituted under the Unemployment Insurance Act. Among the bodies held *not* to fall within the phrase are the Crown; the Liquor Control Board of the Northwest Territories; a District Supervisor under the Indian Act; and the Canadian Broadcasting Corporation. Robert F. Reid and David Hillel, *Administrative Law and Practice*, 2nd ed. (Toronto: Butterworths, 1978), pp. 474-75.
6. David Phillip Jones and Anne S. de Villars, *Principles of Administrative Law* (Toronto: Carswell, 1985), p. 1. The other two branches of public law are constitutional law and criminal law.
7. "Administrative Law in Canada," *Canadian Bar Review* 39 (1961): 254.
8. Royal Commission on Financial Management and Accountability, *Final Report* (Ottawa: Supply and Services, 1979), pp. 309-25 and 435-37.
9. Ibid., p. 309.
10. Ibid., p. 310.
11. Law Reform Commission of Canada, *A Catalogue of Discretionary Powers in the Revised Statutes of Canada* (Ottawa: Information Canada, 1975), p. 2.
12. Ibid., p. 23.
13. *Statutes of Canada*, 1970-72, ch. 47.
14. David J. Mullan, *Administrative Law* (Toronto: Carswell, 1973), pp. 3-49.
15. Ibid.
16. René Dussault, "Relationship between the Nature of the Acts of the Administration and Judicial Review: Quebec and Canada," *Canadian Public Administration* 10 (September 1967): 316.
17. Reid and Hillel, *Administrative Law and Practice*, p. 153.
18. Ibid., p. 119.
19. The following decisions have been classed as quasi-judicial: a public accountants council refusing to grant a license; a highway traffic board revoking a license because of a conviction for impaired driving; a superintendent of motor vehicles suspending

an owner's license; and the National Energy Board, in determining whether to issue a certificate for a pipeline. Ibid., p. 148.

20. Decisions held to be administrative include a public utilities commission quashing a license to operate a bus service; a motor carrier board considering an application for a license to operate a public service vehicle; the (former) Board of Broadcast Governors hearing an application for a broadcasting license; and the revocation of a driver's license. Ibid., pp. 137-38.

21. Many authorities in both Canada and Britain contend that infringements of "natural justice" and other justifications for judicial review may all be considered as "specialized applications of the *ultra vires* doctrine." J. F. Garner, *Administrative Law*, 4th ed. (London: Butterworths, 1974), p. 113. The Ontario Royal Commission of Inquiry into Civil Rights asserted that the principle of *ultra vires* comprehends "all powers of judicial review, except for review for error of law on the face of the record." *Report*, vol. 1, no. 1 (Toronto: Queen's Printer, 1968), p. 247.

22. (1972) F.C. 151 (C.A.).

23. "Hearings and Decisions: A Judge's Perspective," *Speakers' Remarks*, Seminar for Members of Federal Administrative Tribunals, April 5-7, 1978, Law Reform Commission of Canada, p. 105.

24. David J. Mullan, *Administrative Law*, 2nd ed.(Toronto: Carswell, 1979), p. 3-98.

25. Ibid.

26. *Nicholson v. Haldimand-Norfolk Police Commrs. Bd.* (1979), 1 S.C.R. 311.

27. *Martineau v. Matsqui Inst. Disciplinary Bd.*, No. 2 (1980), 1 S.C.R. 602.

28. Gall, *The Canadian Legal System*, pp. 361-62.

29. *The Globe and Mail*, April 12, 1990, p. A11.

30. Ibid.

31. (1959) S.C.R. 121 at 140.

32. Errors of law that have led to the quashing of the decisions of tribunals include an error in the interpretation of a statute; the censuring of a manger of a pharmacy when only the pharmacy was charged; failure to make the necessary inquiry; and failure to observe a statutory condition. Reid and Hillel, *Administrative Law and Practice*, pp. 382-83.

33. *Revised Statutes of Ontario*, 1980, c. 484.

34. *Revised Statutes of British Columbia*, 1979, c. 209.

35. *Report*, vol. 1, p. 325.

36. *Revised Statutes of Ontario*, 1980, c. 484.

37. *Revised Statutes of Alberta*, 1980, c. A-2.

38. See, for example, P. H. Hogg, "Judicial Review: How Much Do We Need?" *McGill Law Journal* 20 (1974): 157-76; Angus, "Judicial Review: Do We Need It?" in Daniel J. Baum, ed., *The Individual and the Bureaucracy*. (Toronto: Carswell, 1975), pp. 101-35; and Paul Weiler, *In the Last Resort: A Critical Study of the Supreme Court of Canada* (Agincourt: Carswell, 1974), pp. 131-54.

39. See especially Angus, "Judicial Review," pp. 101-14.

40. Ibid., p. 105.

41. Hogg, "Judicial Review," p. 99.

42. See G. J. Smith, *Charter of Rights and Administrative Law* (Toronto: Carswell, 1983).

43. Andrew J. Roman, "The Possible Impact of the Canadian Charter of Rights and Freedoms on Administrative Law," *Les Cahiers de Droit* 26 (June 1985): 341.

44. Ibid., p. 358.

45. Paul C. Weiler, "The Charter at Work: Reflections on the Constitutionalizing of Labour and Employment Law," *University of Toronto Law Journal* 40 (1990): 163. (Emphasis added.)
46. *Singh v. Minister of Employment and Immigration* (1985), 17 D.L.R. (4th), 422.
47. Jones and de Villars, pp. 39-40.
48. Canada, Department of Justice, *Equality Issues in Federal Law: A Discussion Paper* (Ottawa: Department of Justice, 1985), p. 6.
49. (1987) 1 S.C.R. 1114.
50. *Mario Duarte v. Her Majesty The Queen*, (1990), 1 S.C.R. 30.
51. Ibid., p. 44.

BIBLIOGRAPHY

Angus, W.H. "Judicial Review: Do We Need It?" *McGill Law Journal* 20 (1974): 177-212. Also printed in Daniel J. Baum, ed., *The Individual and the Bureaucracy*. Toronto: Carswell, 1975, pp. 101-35.

Canada. Law Reform Commission. *Federal Court–Judicial Review*. Working Paper 18. Ottawa: Supply and Services, 1977.

Canada. Law Reform Commission. *Judicial Review and the Federal Court*. Report no. 14. Ottawa: Supply and Services, 1980.

Canada. Law Reform Commission. *Toward a Modern Federal Administrative Law*. Ottawa: Law Reform Commission of Canada, 1987.

de Smith, S. A. *Judicial Review of Administrative Action*. London: Stevens and Sons, 1959.

Dussault, René. "Relationship between the Nature of the Acts of the Administration and Judicial Review: Quebec and Canada." *Canadian Public Administration* 10 (September 1967): 298-322.

Dussault, René, and Louis Borgeat. *Administrative Law: A Treatise*. 2nd ed. Toronto: Carswell, 3 vols.—1986, 1988, and 1989.

Finkelstein, Neil R. *Recent Developments in Administrative Law*. Toronto: Carswell, 1987.

Gall, Gerald. *The Canadian Legal System*. 3rd ed. Toronto: Carswell, 1990.

Hogg, Peter. "Judicial Review: How Much Do We Need?" *McGill Law Journal* 20 (1974): 157-76.

Kersell, J.E. "Statutory and Judicial Control of Administrative Behaviour." *Canadian Public Administration* 19 (Summer 1976): 295-307.

Millar, Perry S., and Carl Baar. *Judicial Administration in Canada*. Kingston and Montreal: McGill-Queen's University Press, 1981.

Mullan, David J. *Administrative Law*. 2nd ed. Toronto: Carswell, 1979.

Mullan, David J. *The Federal Court Act: Administrative Law Jurisdiction*. Prepared for the Law Reform Commission of Canada. Ottawa: Supply and Services, 1977.

Morton, F.L., and Leslie A. Pal. "The Impact of the Charter of Rights on Public Administration: A Case Study of Sex Discrimination in the Unemployment Insurance Act." *Canadian Public Administration* 28 (Summer 1985): 221-44.

Jones, David Phillip, and Anne S. de Villars. *Principles of Administrative Law*. Toronto: Carswell, 1985.

Reid, Robert F., and David Hillel. *Administrative Law and Practice*. 2nd. ed. Toronto: Butterworths, 1978.

Roman, Andrew J. "Regulatory Law and Procedure." In G. Bruce Doern, ed., *The Regulatory Process in Canada*. Toronto: Macmillan, 1978, pp. 68-93.

Roman, Andrew J. "The Possible Impact of the Canadian Charter of Rights and Freedoms on Administrative Law." *Les Cahiers de Droit* 26 (June 1985): 339-59.

Russell, Peter. *The Judiciary in Canada.* 3rd ed. Toronto: McGraw-Hill Ryerson, 1987.

Smith, G. J. *Charter of Rights and Administrative Law.* Toronto: Carswell, 1983.

CASES

Case Program in Canadian Public Administration (Toronto: Institute of Public Administration of Canada):

The Ben Fisher Case. By Nancy LePitre, Salim Mansur, and Wilbur Grasham

19

Intergovernmental Administrative Relations

Intergovernmental relations are critically important in the Canadian political system. Discussion of the processes and outcomes of interaction among federal, provincial, and municipal governments pervades both scholarly and popular writings on Canadian politics. One author has observed that Canada may be "the only country where you can buy a book about federal-provincial relations at an airport."[1] Intergovernmental relations affect virtually every policy field and have significant political, economic, social, and cultural consequences; they affect the day-to-day lives of Canadians by helping to determine such things as the cost of gasoline and oil, the quality of hospital care, and the availability of television programs.

This chapter contains basic information on the political, constitutional, and financial aspects of intergovernmental relations, but is primarily concerned with the administrative dimension of these relations. The focus is on the role of intergovernmental officials and their interaction with each other and with Cabinet ministers and legislators. This chapter examines:

1. the meaning and evolution of federalism and intergovernmental relations;
2. the striking growth since the early 1960s in the machinery for intergovernmental liaison;
3. models of intergovernmental relations that help to explain the functions of intergovernmental officials; and
4. the power and responsibility of these officials.

The impact of intergovernmental relations on government regulation was examined in Chapter 10.

FEDERALISM AND INTERGOVERNMENTAL RELATIONS

Meaning and Evolution

Federalism may be defined as a political system in which the powers of the state are formally divided between central and regional governments by a written constitution, but in which these governments are linked in an interdependent political relationship.[2] In the Canadian context, this definition captures the enduring legal and constitutional elements of Canadian federalism, the politics that pervade the federal system, and the necessity for intergovernmental interaction. Federalism and intergovernmental relations are not the same thing; rather, federalism provides the structural framework within which the process of intergovernmental relations takes place. The federal form of government ensures that there are at least two orders (or levels) of government (e.g., federal and provincial governments in Canada). In modern federal states, these orders of government tend to be highly interdependent and interactive. Broadly interpreted, the term **intergovernmental relations** embraces not only federal-provincial relations but also interprovincial, federal-municipal, and provincial-municipal relations. The main emphasis in this chapter is on federal-provincial liaison, but specific reference is made also to the activities of officials involved in interprovincial relations.

A recent book provided a dictionary of almost five hundred words and phrases that have been used to describe and explain concepts of federalism.[3] While several of Canada's many contributions to concepts of federalism were not acknowledged, Canada was mentioned in more than twenty entries on the list. In Canada, as elsewhere, both the meaning and evolution of federalism have frequently been explained by adding adjectives to the word federalism. For example, James R. Mallory[4] and Edwin R. Black[5] have each used five different labels to classify and explain concepts of Canadian federalism.

In Mallory's classification, **quasi-federalism** characterized the early decades of the Canadian federation during which the federal government dominated the provincial governments, in part by making frequent use of the federal constitutional powers to disallow and reserve provincial legislation. The next stage was **classical federalism**, which approached K.C. Wheare's celebrated "federal principle." This principle held that the powers of government are divided "so that the general and regional governments are each, within a sphere, co-ordinate and independent."[6] Between the late 1800s and 1930, except for the First World War, provincial powers increased as a result of strong political leadership in certain provinces and judicial decisions favouring the provinces in constitutional disputes with the federal government. Both the federal and provincial governments enjoyed exclusive jurisdiction in certain policy fields, and jurisdictional conflicts were resolved by the courts. Increased federal-provincial consultation was formally recognized by the first federal-provincial conference of First Ministers (the Prime Minister of Canada and the provincial Premiers) held in 1906, and federal assistance for the financing of provincial responsibilities began in such areas as transportation and agriculture. The growing importance and expense of the province's responsibilities for health, education, and welfare required not only federal subsidies but also a provincial search for new revenues through the use of such forms of taxation as personal and corporate income taxes.

This period of classical federalism was interrupted by the first phase of **emergency federalism**—the First World War—and was ended by the second phase—the Depression and the Second World War. During both wars, the courts supported the federal government's exercise of broad powers over the economy and over matters of property and civil rights, which, in peacetime, were clearly within provincial jurisdiction. During the Depression, the federal government provided financial assistance to the provinces through a variety of intergovernmental arrangements and, during the Second World War, the provinces withdrew from the fields of personal and corporate income tax in return for "rental" payments from the federal government.

It is difficult to pinpoint the precise date when **cooperative federalism** emerged, but Donald Smiley noted in the early 1960s that the development of Canadian federalism since 1945 had been "a process of continuous and piecemeal adjustment between the two levels of government," and that these adjustments had overwhelmingly been made through "interaction between federal and provincial executives" rather than through formal constitutional amendment or judicial interpretation.[7] Under cooperative federalism, the constitutional division of powers was preserved but federal and provincial ministers and public servants engaged in consultation and coordination to reach joint decisions on policies and programs of mutual concern.

During the late 1940s and the 1950s, the federal government dominated federal-provincial relations, but in the 1960s provincial governments gradually acquired the expertise and influence to deal with the federal government from a stronger position. Gradually also, **executive federalism**, a term first used by Donald Smiley, began to be applied more often than cooperative federalism to describe the nature of federal-provincial relations. Garth Stevenson has explained that the main features of cooperative federalism were "the fragmentation of authority within each level of government, the absence of linkages between different issues and functional domains, the forging of specific intergovernmental links by different groups of specialized officials, and the lack of publicity or public awareness of what was happening." Executive federalism, by way of contrast, involved "the concentration and centralization of authority at the top of each participating government, the control and supervision of intergovernmental relations by politicians and officials with a wide range of functional interests, and the highly formalized and well-publicized proceedings of federal-provincial conference diplomacy."[8]

By the latter half of the 1960s, the term cooperative federalism had become a misnomer because intergovernmental relations were characterized by a great deal of conflict and confrontation as well as consultation and collaboration. It is notable also that both cooperative federalism and executive federalism have coexisted with another centrally important variant of federalism described by Mallory as **double-image federalism**; this form combines interaction between the central government and the provinces with a special relationship between French- and English-speaking Canadians. Certainly, French-English relations have been a critical and persistent factor in intergovernmental relations, especially since the early 1960s.

Garth Stevenson contends that there are basically two concepts of Canadian federalism, and that they can be depicted as opposite ends of a continuum, with unity (centripetal federalism) at one pole and diversity (centrifugal federalism) at the other. "Centripetal federalists prefer to strengthen the federal government's power at the expense of the provincial governments; centrifugal federalists prefer to do the reverse."[9] Perhaps the most popular image in discussions of federal-provincial relations, however, is that of a pendulum swinging between the centralization of powers in federal hands and the decentralization of powers to the provinces.

Regionalism and Federalism

Regionalism refers to the territorial dimension of the Canadian community according to which particular areas or regions of the country are distinguished from others by political, economic, historical, cultural, and linguistic characteristics. Since the early 1960s, there has been a substantial increase in conflict between the federal government and the several regions of the country. There has also been much friction between and among the regions themselves. The term region is commonly interpreted in two ways; first, it is used interchangeably with the term province and, second, it is used to refer to one of five major areas in the country, namely, the Atlantic provinces, Quebec, Ontario, the prairie provinces, and British Columbia.

This regional dimension of Canadian federalism continues to have an enormous impact on both the politics and management of intergovernmental relations. It affects not only the content of government policies and programs, but also the structures and processes of individual governments and of intergovernmental relations. This can be easily demonstrated by reference to federal economic development policy and to the political and administrative mechanisms devised to formulate and administer this policy.[10]

This concern about regional considerations has led to greater emphasis since the late 1970s on the intrastate dimension of Canadian federalism as opposed to the traditional interstate dimension. **Interstate federalism** refers to "the distribution of powers and financial resources between the federal and provincial governments as well as the relations between those two orders of government," whereas **intrastate federalism** refers to "arrangements whereby the interests of regional units—the interests either of the government or of the residents of these units—are channelled through and protected by the structures and operations of the central government."[11] These arrangements could include reform of the electoral system to make each party in the House of Commons more representative of the various regions of the country; reform of the Supreme Court to make its members more sensitive to regional and provincial concerns, and reform or replacement of the Senate to provide more effective representation in Parliament of regional and provincial interests. In several western and Atlantic provinces, the creation of a "Triple E" Senate, that is an elected, equal, and effective Senate, is currently a major priority of constitutional reform. Among the proposed arrangements affecting the public service specifically are a bureaucracy that is more representative in its composition of the regions of the country, and formal representation of provincial governments in federal agencies, boards, and commissions.

Alan Cairns has distinguished between *centralist* and *provincial* intrastate federalism. The centralist version "is an attempt to weaken provincial governments by increasing the attractiveness of Ottawa to that complex regional/provincial network of interests, values, identities, and socio-economic power whose support is a crucial resource in intergovernmental competition." The provincial version is an attempt to provide direct representation of the provincial governments in the institutions and decision-making processes of the federal government.[12]

Much of the discussion of the instrastate perspective has centred on the federal Cabinet, the Senate, the Supreme Court, and the electoral system rather than on bureaucratic institutions and processes.[13] However, it has been suggested that the federal bureaucracy would be more sensitive to regional needs and aspirations if its composition was more representative of the regions (e.g., more senior public servants in Ottawa who were born in the Atlantic provinces), and if it was restructured with more emphasis on regional considerations (e.g., decentralization of power to federal field units in the regions).[14]

FEDERAL-PROVINCIAL FISCAL RELATIONS

While federal financial assistance to provincial governments dates to Confederation and was especially important during the Depression, federal-provincial fiscal relations have been an especially prominent theme in Canadian federalism since the Second World War. The subject is extremely complex and has been examined at length elsewhere.[15] However, a brief explanation of its development and characteristics is essential to understanding contemporary intergovernmental relations.

The federal-provincial financial relationship is based on four elements: conditional grants or shared-cost programs, tax collection agreements, established programs financing, and equalization. Each of these will be considered in turn.[16]

Conditional grants or shared-cost programs involve payments by the federal government to provincial governments choosing to undertake programs according to conditions specified by the federal government. The largest such program is the Canada Assistance Plan. The general thrust of this plan is that the federal government will pay one-half of the cost of provincial social assistance programs. In turn, the provincial programs must meet certain conditions, e.g., no discrimination against applicants from another province.[17]

The *tax collection agreement* is an agreement between the federal government and nine provinces that allows the federal government to collect both federal and provincial personal taxes (except for Quebec) and corporate taxes (except for Alberta, Ontario, and Quebec), and to remit the provincial portion of the taxes to the provinces. The purpose of this agreement is to provide an administrative convenience to provincial governments, and to limit tax competition between provinces by establishing some uniformity in the method of calculation.

Established Programs Financing (EPF) is a transfer payment program begun in 1977.[18] In that year, the federal government terminated three very large conditional grants to the provinces—for medicare, hospital care, and post-secondary education—and replaced them with a combination of cash payments and tax room. *Tax room* means that the federal government agrees to reduce its income tax rate by a certain number of "tax points" so that provincial governments can increase their tax rates accordingly. Because of the tax collection agreement discussed above, this type of shift is not evident to the taxpayer.

One of the characteristics of EPF is that the provincial governments are not obliged to spend the money on medical or hospital care or post-secondary education; they can use the funds generated for purposes of their own choosing. However, there are still some conditions attached to the receipt of the cash payments. For example, this is the mechanism that the federal government used to pass the Canada Health Act, which reduces the cash payments to any province that allows physicians to "extra-bill."

Equalization is a program through which the federal government makes unconditional grants to provinces that have a weak tax base.[19] An **unconditional grant** is a payment that can be used for any purpose the province desires; the federal government requires no accounting for how the money is spent. The purpose of the equalization program is to allow the so-called "have-not" provinces to provide adequate public services to their citizens without imposing excessively high taxes.

The current complex system of transfer payments could well weaken the accountability of the provincial governments for the expenditure of public funds. A strict concept of accountability would suggest that the government that gets the credit for spending funds should be the same government that must take the blame for raising taxes. The ability to spend someone else's money does little to encourage thrift or accountability. However, there are a number of valid reasons for transfer payments, including the need to redistribute wealth between provinces and the desire to have national programs with uniform national standards.[20]

One of the major controversies surrounding intergovernmental fiscal relations in recent years has been the use of conditional versus unconditional grants. The government providing the grant frequently favours conditional grants because they can be directed to specific purposes and accountability can be ensured through the use of specific regulations or audits. On the negative side, recipient governments sometimes feel that the conditions attached to grants are insensitive to local conditions and that the record-keeping and other administrative requirements imposed are excessive. Therefore, recipient governments tend to favour unconditional grants because this type of grant maximizes their freedom. Governments providing grants are concerned about unconditional grants because they could be used in ways that were deemed inappropriate by the providing government and because the government ultimately supplying the funds frequently does not receive the credit when the money is spent. This has brought about the federal government's recent concern about the inadequate "visibility" it has received for services paid for by federal funds, but provided by provincial governments.

In the 1950s and 1960s, the federal government introduced a number of shared-cost programs that encouraged provincial governments to embark on new programs. However, in the 1980s, faced with a weak economy and rising deficits, the federal government took unilateral action to reduce its transfer payments to provinces. This has incited the ire of provinces, which feel that the federal government pushed them into beginning these programs and is now leaving them "holding the bag." The federal government's tough stance on fiscal relations coincided with its tough stance on constitutional issues.

FEDERAL-PROVINCIAL CONSTITUTIONAL RELATIONS

The impact of federal-provincial relations on the evolution of Canada's constitution is a long and intricate story in which many of the constitutional issues have been primarily financial ones as well. There have, however, been a number of constitutional developments with special relevance for contemporary federal-provincial relations and, consequently, for the officials involved in these relations. As noted above, quasi-federalism and classical federalism gave way to cooperative, executive, and double-image federalism. Dissatisfaction with judicial interpretation of the division of powers contained in the British North America Act, the lack of a formula for amending the Act without the consent of the British Parliament, and the expansion in the scope and cost of government activities led to increasing use of extra-constitutional arrangements negotiated by the two orders of government.

A series of federal-provincial conferences that began in 1968 sought agreement on constitutional reform. These efforts were given enormous impetus by the election of the separatist Parti Québécois government in Quebec in 1976 and the 1980 referendum campaign on "sovereignty-association," at which time the federal government promised constitutional change. Also, during the 1970s and early 1980s, intergovernmental tensions were severely exacerbated by sharp disagreements over the ownership of natural resources, especially petroleum, and over the allocation of the revenues flowing from the exploitation of these resources. The dispute raged not only between the federal government and the energy-producing provinces (especially Alberta), but also between these provinces and the energy-consuming provinces (especially Ontario).

For the 1980-1981 constitutional meetings, the First Ministers agreed upon an agenda containing twelve contentious items—a statement of principles as a preamble to the constitution; a charter of human rights (including language rights); equalization; the nature of the economic union; a formula for amending the constitution in Canada (referred to as patriation of the constitution); a reformed upper house with regional representation; reform of the Supreme Court; the ownership of natural resources and related issues of trade and taxation; offshore resources; fisheries; communications (including broadcasting); and family law. Following the failure of the September 1980 meeting of

First Ministers, however, the federal government decided to proceed unilaterally to resolve the issue of constitutional amendment. After lengthy debate in the federal Parliament, the provinces were presented in November 1981 with a federal proposal for constitutional change, which all provinces, except Quebec, finally accepted. Agreements were reached on only a few of the agenda items, and these agreements were enshrined in the Constitution Act of 1982, which was approved formally by the British Parliament. This Act provided, among other things, an amending formula ensuring that all changes to the constitution would henceforth be made in Canada; a charter of rights and freedoms; a commitment to the principle of equalization; confirmation of provincial ownership of resources; and affirmation of the existing rights of aboriginal peoples.

Federal action during this period supported Prime Minister Trudeau's assertion in 1982 that cooperative federalism was dead. Moreover, there was little evidence of executive federalism at work in that federal-provincial conference diplomacy was replaced by unilateral federal decision-making. It is significant that in 1985 Prime Minister Mulroney found it desirable to announce the rebirth of cooperative federalism as a signal of a renewed federal commitment to consultation and collaboration with the provinces. Nevertheless, federal-provincial disagreements continue to fester.

During the late 1980s and the early 1990s, the major focus of attention in intergovernmental relations has been on the Meech Lake Accord and the Free Trade Agreement with the United States. The Meech Lake Accord, formally referred to as the Constitution Amendment, 1987, was negotiated by the First Ministers, with the assistance of their public service advisors, and was signed on June 3, 1987. The Accord consisted of a number of proposals for constitutional amendment, including recognition of Quebec as a distinct society, provision for provinces to opt out of any new federal spending programs within provincial constitutional jurisdiction, an amending formula, and arrangements for provincial participation in the selection of members of the Supreme Court and the Senate. From the perspective of the federal and Quebec governments, the primary purpose of the Accord was "to bring Quebec back into the constitutional family" after Quebec's refusal to accept the Constitution Act of 1982.

The Accord was to come into effect when it was ratified by the legislatures of all eleven governments. Under the terms of the Constitution Act, that ratification had to occur within three years, i.e., by June 23, 1990. During the three-year period, federal and provincial public servants played a very significant advisory role in the protracted negotiations over the ratification of the Accord; these negotiations culminated in a highly publicized and acrimonious First Ministers' Conference in mid-June, 1990. The conference appeared to have reached agreement on ratification of the Accord, but two provinces (Newfoundland and Manitoba) failed to obtain ratification before the June 23 deadline. Among the major objections to the Accord were its recognition of Quebec as a distinct society, its decentralization of power from the federal government to the provinces, its requirement of unanimous consent for Senate reform, and its lack of recognition of the rights of aboriginal peoples.

Intergovernmental tensions were greatly exacerbated by the unwillingness of some provinces to ratify the Accord, and by the unwillingness of the federal and Quebec governments to agree to major modifications of it. Following the death of the Accord, the province of Quebec announced its unwillingness to participate in any constitutional conferences for the foreseeable future and began formal consideration of its future association with the rest of Canada.

Unlike the Accord, the Canada-U.S. Free Trade Agreement, which came into effect in January 1989, involved no constitutional change. Like the Accord, however, the Agreement greatly strained intergovernmental relations because of strong differences of opinion among Canada's First Ministers as to its desirability. The Agreement, which was negotiated primarily by public servants, will have an enormous impact on public policy and intergovernmental relations. Its effective implementation will also require the advice and assistance of public servants in both the federal and provincial spheres of government.

Intergovernmental officials were major players in the extensive bargaining leading up to the major agreements noted above and are centrally involved in their implementation. The active participation of these officials in intergovernmental relations has, especially over the last three decades, resulted in an impressive array of intergovernmental administrative structures.

MACHINERY FOR INTERGOVERNMENTAL RELATIONS

The network of intergovernmental structures includes separate departments or other administrative units within governments,[21] administrative units within individual departments, intergovernmental secretariats, and a large number of intergovernmental committees. The creation of these structures has both resulted from, and stimulated the proliferation of, intergovernmental conferences and meetings. The major reasons for the development of this complicated web of intergovernmental contacts, especially between federal and provincial governments, are the expansion of the activities of all governments, the increased interdependence of federal and provincial responsibilities, and the consequent need to design and operate machinery to manage these contacts.

As early as 1972, there were 482 federal-provincial liaison bodies, ranging in scope and importance from the First Ministers' Conference to such specialized federal-provincial committees as those on meteorites and pest control.[22] There are now more than 1,000 federal-provincial *committees* of varying degrees of importance. Some of these committees meet more than once and some do not meet at all during a particular year. The number of federal-provincial *meetings* more than doubled between 1967 and 1977, and continued to increase until the early 1980s when fewer meetings were held because of the economic recession and the reduced importance of constitutional matters.[23] The number of federal-provincial meetings increased again following the election in September 1984 of the Mulroney government with its emphasis on the renewal of cooperative federalism. Among the many federal-provincial meetings are meetings of First

Ministers (the Prime Minister and the provincial Premiers), ministers, deputy ministers, and public servants below the deputy level.

The number of officials attending intergovernmental meetings varies greatly from one meeting to another, but it is notable that one of the largest gatherings, namely the First Ministers' Conference, attracts well over two hundred First Ministers, Cabinet ministers, and public servants. The number of intergovernmental officials attending such meetings does not, however, take account of the large number of officials who do not attend the meetings, but who are actively engaged in preparation for the participation of ministers and other officials.

It is difficult to distinguish precisely between *intergovernmental officials* and other public servants. The term is normally used to refer only to so-called intergovernmental affairs specialists. These are senior administrative officials who are engaged solely or primarily in intergovernmental business. They are usually housed in central agencies and are responsible for the coordination of intergovernmental matters both within their own government and with other governments. But, in varying degrees, many other officials are involved in intergovernmental relations. Thus, the term intergovernmental officials also refers to those officials whose formally designated responsibilities require them to spend the majority of their working hours on intergovernmental matters, but who are not normally described as intergovernmental affairs specialists. The most prominent among these officials are senior public servants in operating departments who look after intergovernmental issues affecting their department. In addition, there are officials, notably in senior positions, who devote relatively little time to intergovernmental issues, but whose occasional involvement has a major influence on the outcome of intergovernmental negotiations. It is evident that a large number of public servants are engaged in intergovernmental activities. The major focus of this chapter, however, is on the intergovernmental affairs specialists.

The critical importance of intergovernmental relations can be seen in the financial and human resources devoted to the conduct of these relations. Since the 1960s, the expansion in intergovernmental machinery and in the number and quality of the officials operating this machinery has been striking. The development of administrative structures geared specifically to the management of intergovernmental relations was a response to the growing number of meetings and the desire of governments to coordinate and rationalize the efforts of their departments in various policy fields. There is virtually no policy field in which federal and provincial governments are not engaged in consultation and negotiation. In 1961, the province of Quebec established a Department of Federal-Provincial Relations,[24] and gradually the federal government and other provincial governments have developed increasingly sophisticated mechanisms for handling intergovernmental business. In the federal government, the Federal-Provincial Relations Secretariat, which was established in the Privy Council Office in 1968, had by 1975 become the Federal-Provincial Relations Office (FPRO) with responsibility for coordinating federal-provincial relations both within the federal government and between the federal and provincial governments. The FPRO is headed by the Secretary to the Cabinet for Federal-Provincial Relations, who reports to the Prime Minister. In addition, many federal departments have formal federal-provincial units. All ten provincial governments established intergovernmental units either as separate departments or as part of the Premier's Office or the Cabinet Secretariat.

Intergovernmental secretariats have also been established to provide support services for the meetings of the many liaison bodies. The major secretariat is the Canadian Intergovernmental Conference Secretariat, which was established in 1973 to serve the conferences of First Ministers and all other intergovernmental bodies requesting its assistance.[25] It is jointly funded by the federal and provincial governments, and provides such services as looking after conference arrangements and agendas, preparing conference transcripts and summary statements, and distributing documents. Some federal-provincial bodies (e.g., the Canadian Council of Resource and Environment Ministers) have established their own secretariat.

Intergovernmental affairs specialists play a central role in government both in the organizational sense and in the development and implementation of policy. They must be adept in *intra*governmental as well as *inter*governmental bargaining. Their influence is based to a large extent on their ability to wend their way skilfully through the labyrinth of intergovernmental affairs in search of agreement with officials in their own government and in other governments. An important element of their expertise is in the *process* of intergovernmental relations. They must also be knowledgeable in a general way about the *substance* of a broad range of policy fields. Richard Schultz notes, however, that "central agencies are staffed by individuals who, while they may be specialists in the 'machinery of government' or in intergovernmental relations, are essentially amateurs and generalists when specific policy issues are discussed."[26]

A primary aim of intergovernmental affairs specialists is to ensure that operating departments in their own government will not weaken that government through the intergovernmental interactions in which they engage.[27] The extent to which these specialists perform primarily either a controlling or an advisory function to achieve this end varies from one government to another. There is a risk that *intra*governmental conflict between the specialists on the one hand, and officials in operating departments on the other, will result from "over-coordination" of intergovernmental relations within a single government. Some intergovernmental units (e.g., Alberta's Department of Federal and Intergovernmental Affairs) have greater legal authority and more resources than other units to promote coordination of the intergovernmental activities of operating departments. Moreover, intergovernmental units, like other central agencies, play a staff role and are, therefore, subject to the normal line-staff problems that arise in large organizations.

A critical element in the intergovernmental policy process is the multitude of informal contacts, especially by telephone, that supplement the formal meetings of officials. The respect and trust among officials developed during formal contacts pave the way for frank and productive discussions outside of, and between, formal meetings. During these discussions, officials exchange a great deal of information about their government's position on matters of continuing concern and negotiation. An essential attribute of intergovernmental officials is their ability to obtain current information about the perceptions and positions of other governments. This information is crucial in determining the officials' advice to their political and administrative superiors. The ability of officials to gather such information enables them to exercise more influence in the policy process.

In the 1950s and early 1960s, the undeveloped state of formal machinery for intergovernmental liaison meant that informal contacts among officials were essential to the effective conduct of federal-provincial relations. Despite the sophisticated infrastructure that has been built since that time, the increased magnitude and complexity of intergovernmental relations has meant that informal communications are still important to the smooth operation of the formal machinery. Indeed, this informal interaction has increased substantially since the mid-1960s.[28]

INTERPROVINCIAL ADMINISTRATIVE RELATIONS

Interprovincial relations are broadly similar to federal-provincial relations in their organization and participants. Interprovincial interactions occur on both a formal and informal basis; they involve both political executives (Premiers and ministers) and public servants, and they cover virtually all provincial policy fields. Most of the intergovernmental bodies created during the formalization of federal-provincial relations are also used to coordinate interprovincial relations.

Provincial political leaders and bureaucrats meet to discuss problems of mutual concern and, when appropriate, to work out joint or common solutions to these problems. Among the formal interprovincial mechanisms for collaboration is the Conference of Premiers, which is the provincial version of the First Ministers' Conference. The Premiers' Conference is held annually and is attended by all ten provincial Premiers and their senior advisors.

Below the level of the Premiers, ministers of most provincial departments meet regularly with their counterparts in other provinces not only to exchange information and ideas but also to seek interprovincial coordination. For example, the Canadian Council of Resource and Environment Ministers aims to bring about integrated comprehensive resource-use planning for social and economic development. Probably the most effective interprovincial interactions for seeking coordination are the meetings of public servants from both the senior administrative and the professional/technical levels of various departments. Aside from the interprovincial meetings, the many federal-provincial meetings provide opportunities for provincial officials to get together informally outside the meeting rooms. Moreover, many of the same political and bureaucratic officials participate in both types of meeting. These personal contacts are subsequently utilized, via telephone, fax, and letter, to seek interprovincial policy coordination.

There are also important interprovincial meetings organized on a regional basis; notably meetings of the Western Premiers' Conference and of the Council of Maritime Premiers. The latter body is composed of the Premiers of New Brunswick, Nova Scotia, and Prince Edward Island, and is served by a permanent secretariat. The council was established in 1971 "to promote unity of purpose, ensure maximum coordination of activities and establish the framework for joint actions and undertakings among the three governments."[29]

It is clear that the participation of officials in formal federal-provincial and interprovincial meetings is only the tip of a sizable iceberg. Below the "water-line" is a complex network of formal and informal interactions that significantly affect the outcome of intergovernmental negotiations. This network includes interaction between officials and other political actors; among officials in a single department or agency; between officials in different departments and agencies; and among officials in different orders of government.

MODELS OF INTERGOVERNMENTAL ADMINISTRATIVE INTERACTION

Three distinct, but complementary, models can be used to explain the role and the power of officials in the processes and outcomes of intergovernmental relations in Canada. These are the *cooperation, bargaining,* and *bureaucratic politics* models.

The *cooperation* model refers to intergovernmental relations involving, to a very large extent, program specialists from each order of government. Harmonious and productive interaction is facilitated because these program specialists share a body of knowledge and skills, and possess a common set of professional attitudes and values relating to their particular policy fields (e.g., welfare officials, foresters).[30] In this model, program specialists are permitted to exercise a large measure of autonomy from control by political and administrative superiors, especially those in intergovernmental relations units, treasury boards, and finance departments. The value of this model for explaining policy development and implementation in certain areas of federal-provincial relations has been demonstrated well in respect to the Canada Assistance Plan.[31]

This type of interaction was characteristic of the cooperative federalism period and was more prevalent in the post-war years until the early 1960s than it is now. Gradually during the 1960s and increasingly during the 1970s, the influence of program specialists suffered a relative decline as a result of the growing ascendancy in intergovernmental relations of central agency officials who pursued broader public policy goals than officials from program departments.[32] Donald Smiley anticipated that these central agencies would not develop "the kind of allegiance to common procedures and values which so much facilitates intergovernmental relations among program specialists" because "the concerns of the former relate to fundamental political choices about which consensus is more difficult to establish than in respect to more technical matters."[33]

The reduction in the importance of horizontal relations among program specialists, resulting from the increased influence of central agencies, was accompanied by the creation and growth of new structures and arrangements for the coordination of intergovernmental relations within each government. As a consequence of the institutional centralization of intergovernmental relations under what has been called executive federalism, fewer matters were handled at the lower levels of the governmental pyramid; rather, intergovernmental conflicts gravitated toward the political and senior administrative levels. Since ministers and senior administrators tended not to share values, attitudes, and skills to the same extent that program specialists did, the level of intergovernmental conflict increased. In this milieu, the *bargaining* model explains the processes and outcomes of intergovernmental relations better than the co-operation model.[34]

The bargaining model refers to intergovernmental relations involving primarily ministers and senior administrators from each order of government. Interaction takes the form of a bargaining process in which these ministers and officials present and defend their government's position on specific public policy issues. The focus of attention is on the political resources, strategies, and tactics used by participants in the process. Richard Simeon, on the basis of his study of federal-provincial negotiation over three broad policy issues, concluded that the participants in federal-provincial relations "are not scattered throughout the system in the form of federal cabinet members, members of Parliament, bureaucrats and party leaders; rather they are concentrated and limited largely to provincial Premiers, senior cabinet members, and senior officials on the one hand, and their federal counterparts on the other."[35]

A third model, which complements both the cooperation and bargaining models, is the *bureaucratic politics* model. This model, which has been used most often to study foreign policy, has also been recently applied to the study of intergovernmental relations in Canada.[36] The model refers to the bargaining over intergovernmental matters among ministers and officials in departments and agencies *within* each order of government. It is *intra*governmental rather than intergovernmental bargaining that is involved. Despite use of the term *bureaucratic* politics, the model is concerned with interaction among both ministers and officials.

Richard Schultz and Simon McInnes, in their case studies of federal-provincial negotiations, focus on the impact of *intra*governmental bargaining on *inter*governmental bargaining. Schultz contends that

> the bureaucratic politics model ... attempts to answer questions such as why the negotiators adopted the objectives, strategies and tactics they did .... Interactions between governments may not ... explain, by themselves, the outcomes of intergovernmental negotiations. From the bureaucratic politics perspective, the complex intergovernmental process cannot be separated from the direct relations between governments.[37]

Schultz also offers the bureaucratic politics model as a complement to what he describes as Simeon's "government-as-unitary-actor" model. Simeon states that the "perceptions, attitudes and behaviour" of political leaders and officials are his main concern, but that in his book "Canada's eleven governments are the actors" and that "for most purposes each will be considered as a single unit."[38]

The bureaucratic politics approach suggests that it might be more productive to consider *each* government as a loose coalition of organizations and the negotiating positions of the governments as *outcomes* of an internal negotiating process.

In the field of intergovernmental relations, governments are often treated as single actors because they normally present a united front in negotiations with other governments. This united front may, however, be a mask that conceals conflict among ministers and officials *within* governments. Neither departments and agencies nor whole governments are homogeneous entities. The process of intragovernmental bargaining, which is intertwined with that of intergovernmental bargaining, has been ignored or unduly minimized by many students of Canadian federalism. Intragovernmental bargaining over intergovernmental matters involves both elected and appointed officials, but much of this bargaining takes the form of internal administrative politics. Intragovernmental bargaining occurs not only over the substance of intergovernmental policy but also over the distribution of resources between intergovernmental programs and other government activities. Thus, officials who are not significantly engaged in intergovernmental relations indirectly affect the success of these relations by influencing the resources devoted to intergovernmental activities, both in the government as a whole and in individual departments and agencies.

THE POWER AND RESPONSIBILITY OF INTERGOVERNMENTAL OFFICIALS

The Power of Intergovernmental Officials

It has been suggested that there has been a politicization of intergovernmental affairs specialists. Politicization refers here to the process by which officials become increasingly involved in politics, either in the partisan sense or in the broader sense of the authoritative allocation of values for society. As explained in Chapter 13, public servants in general have become more politicized as a result of departures from some aspects of the traditional doctrine of political neutrality. Have intergovernmental officials become politicized and, if so, has this politicization taken different forms and emphases from that of other officials?

The overriding objective of intergovernmental relations is the determination of policy. Like other public servants, intergovernmental officials use their knowledge, experience, and discretionary authority to exercise power in the formation and administration of public policy; they engage in consultation and bargaining with other political actors; and their ministers rely heavily on them for advice on complex issues. Thus, in the intergovernmental field, as in other areas of government, the line between the policy contributions of ministers and officials is blurred.

However, the role of intergovernmental officials in the policy process can be distinguished from that of other officials in two significant ways. First, intergovernmental officials cannot exercise control, in the sense of authority, over their counterparts in other governments; rather, they must exercise influence through a process of bargaining. Compared to bargaining with pressure groups, for example, where government officials retain ultimate authority to decide or recommend a course of action, bargaining between governments requires give-and-take among negotiators of roughly equal status.

Second, intergovernmental officials, especially those who participate in formal meetings, enjoy more discretionary power in the bargaining process than most other officials. They are, therefore, more involved in politics in the broad sense than many of their colleagues. In the intergovernmental policy process, usually several governments, and often all eleven governments, are involved in a complicated bargaining process. The outcome of negotiations is frequently a tentative agreement representing a delicate balancing and accommodation of numerous and diverse interests. An excellent example is the Meech Lake Accord. The federal and provincial Cabinets, individual ministers, and even legislatures are sometimes reluctant to force a renewal of these intricate negotiations unless their objection to the agreement worked out by their officials is substantial.

Donald Smiley claims that the federal-provincial relations specialist, "in his stance toward other governments . . . has a single-minded devotion to the power of his jurisdiction. And because his counterparts in other governments have the same motivations, conflict is inevitable."[39] But the extent of concern over jurisdiction varies from government to government and from official to official.[40] Some governments, such as Quebec, and some officials, such as Alberta's officials during the energy negotiations, have been primarily disposed toward protection of jurisdiction. Other governments have sought to minimize future intergovernmental conflict by seeking to rationalize the distribution of powers through disentanglement and the clarification of accountability. Resistance to such rationalization, insofar as it involves the movement of power to another order of government, has often come from the department currently exercising that power rather than from intergovernmental affairs specialists.

Both scholars and practitioners of intergovernmental relations have perceived a tendency among intergovernmental officials to become somewhat more politicized than other bureaucrats. A distinguishing feature of the doctrine of political neutrality is that public servants explain policy and ministers defend it. But in the course of intergovernmental negotiations, the line between explanation and defence of policy becomes blurred. As a result, intergovernmental officials tend to be more involved in "politics" in the broad sense of that term.

Moreover, some intergovernmental officials occasionally develop an especially intense commitment to the objectives of their own government or their own minister that goes somewhat beyond the loyalty expected from public servants. This strong sense of loyalty appears primarily among senior intergovernmental specialists whose working environment is often highly political in the partisan sense, and whose duties require the management of conflict with other governments. They may be motivated both by pressure "not to let the minister down" and by personal commitment to government policies. It is natural for such loyalty and commitment to result from the obligation to continually explain and defend those policies. Vigorous defence by intergovernmental officials of the policies of the government of the day is not usually prompted by partisan support for the governing party, but it does on occasion have that appearance.

The Responsibility of Intergovernmental Officials

In the sphere of intergovernmental relations, pinpointing those who are actually, rather than formally, responsible for government decisions is difficult because an important locus of decision-making is an intergovernmental body of ministers or officials. There is not space here to examine the broad range of controls and influences that may promote responsible behaviour by intergovernmental officials. Attention will, therefore, focus on relations between intergovernmental officials in different jurisdictions, and between these officials and Cabinet members and legislators.

The increased influence of the provinces in federal-provincial relations rests on several factors, including the constitutional distribution of responsibilities, the relative wealth of a province, and the electoral success of its political leaders. However, a major reason for the growth of provincial power has been the heightened expertise of provincial intergovernmental officials. The expertise of federal officials, which explained to a large extent the federal government's dominant influence in intergovernmental relations during the 1950s and early 1960s, is now more closely matched by the expertise of provincial officials.

In the intergovernmental policy process, officials exercise significant power, in the sense of influence, over Cabinet members and legislators. Gordon Robertson, former secretary to the Cabinet for Federal-Provincial Relations, has asserted that "intergovernmental business in Canada . . . is conducted by Cabinet members, notably by First Ministers . . . Interministerial conferences are thus an adjunct to executive power, a demonstration of where power actually resides, and the centrepiece of what Donald Smiley has called 'executive federalism.' "[41] This assertion does not take adequate account of the fact that executive federalism involves relations between both ministers *and officials* and that officials exercise significant influence over policy development before, during, and after interministerial conferences. Moreover, as noted earlier, officials exert much policy influence in connection with the very large number of intergovernmental meetings below the ministerial level. The influence of intergovernmental officials arises not only from their expertise but also from the formal and informal bargaining, often on a multilateral basis, in which they engage on behalf of their ministers.

But the influence of intergovernmental officials in relation to ministers should not be exaggerated. Cabinet members, both individually and collectively, possess ultimate control over the government's stance on all intergovernmental matters. Officials must be highly sensitive to the desires of the Cabinet as a whole, and of individual ministers in regard to both the substance and strategy of negotiations. Moreover, Cabinet members are the central actors in making decisions on major and politically sensitive intergovernmental issues, and in much of the negotiation leading to those decisions.

Compared to Cabinet members, legislators have little control or influence over intergovernmental activities. Indeed, legislators do not exercise much power over the executive in general or officials in particular in any area of government activity.[42] There is general agreement with the observation that intergovernmental business in Canada "is conducted by governments . . . not by legislatures" and that "this works because a Cabinet in our parliamentary system can normally 'deliver' legislative support on virtually any matter, save possibly in minority situations."[43]

According to the principle of collective ministerial responsibility, the Cabinet is responsible to the legislature. Yet there is normally much more discussion of intergovernmental matters in conferences than in the federal Parliament or provincial legislatures. There are few opportunities for legislators to examine intergovernmental policy issues before legislation incorporating agreements reached at conferences is presented to the legislature. Since this legislation is often the outcome of complicated and protracted negotiations among governments, ministers are understandably reluctant to make changes at the legislative stage with which other governments may disagree. Robert Stanfield, former leader of the federal Progressive Conservative Party, has noted that "the frustrations of Members of Parliament are increased by federal-provincial deals, agreements and resulting legislation which confront Parliament as *faits accomplis*."[44] In a comment on Mr. Stanfield's remarks, Gordon Gibson, former leader of the Liberal Party in British Columbia, said that "federal-provincial agreements are so cast in stone from the time of the agreement that even if the opposition were able to convince the government that amendments should be made it would be too late to change things in any significant respect."[45] It is notable also that the federal Parliament and the provincial legislatures have not developed intergovernmental machinery, e.g., standing committees, to parallel the sophisticated mechanisms established by the executive.

Despite the claims of some journalists and politicians to the contrary, informed observers of the Canadian federal system deny that federal-provincial conferences constitute an additional order of government. There are differences of opinion, however, about the effect of intergovernmental meetings on the accountability of governments to Parliament and the provincial legislatures. Gordon Robertson has stated that "federal-provincial conferences do not in fact reduce the accountability as such of governments to Parliament and to legislatures. Parliament is the locus of responsibility and accountability for our national government but, because of the nature of our system, it is not the public and apparent locus of regional argument and compromise."[46] In a formal sense, this statement is accurate, but the weight of opinion supports Donald Smiley's contention that "to the extent that the actual locus of decision-making in respect to an increasing number of public matters has shifted from individual governments to intergovernmental groupings, the effective accountability of executives both to their respective legislatures and to those whom they govern is weakened."[47]

The accountability of intergovernmental officials is a serious concern, but accountability is only one of several values associated with the broad concept of administrative responsibility. Responsible intergovernmental officials must also be concerned with such values as responsiveness and effectiveness. It is important to determine not only whether these officials are accountable to ministers and legislators, but also whether they are sensitive to the needs and desires of other political actors and whether they are successful in achieving their government's objectives. Thus, in addition to intergovernmental and intragovernmental conflicts, officials face conflicts between administrative values (e.g., accountability vs. responsiveness, or responsiveness vs. effectiveness).

Intergovernmental management involves, to a very large extent, the management of conflict and complexity. Alan Cairns has observed that "contemporary intergovernmental coordination is not a simple matter of agreement between a handful of political leaders and their staff advisers. It requires ... the containment of ineradicable tendencies to conflict between the federal vision of a society and economy, and ten competing provincial visions."[48] The key role of intergovernmental officials in seeking to harmonize these diverse perspectives ensures that the management of intergovernmental relations will remain a dominant concern of students and practitioners of Canadian public administration.

NOTES

1. Peter C. Newman, *Maclean's Magazine*, October 1, 1979, p. 3.
2. Adapted from M.J.C. Vile, *The Structure of American Federalism* (London: Oxford University Press, 1961), p. 199.
3. William H. Stewart, *Concepts of Federalism* (Lanham: University Press of America, 1984).
4. James R. Mallory, "The Five Faces of Federalism," in P.-A. Crépeau and C.B. MacPherson, eds., *The Future of Canadian Federalism* (Toronto: University of Toronto Press, 1965), pp. 3-15.
5. Edwin R. Black, *Divided Loyalties: Canadian Concepts of Federalism* (Montreal: McGill-Queen's University Press, 1975).
6. K.C. Wheare, *Federal Government*, 4th ed. (London: Oxford University Press, 1963), p. 10.
7. Donald V. Smiley, "The Rowell-Sirois Report, Provincial Autonomy, and Post-War Canadian Federalism," *Canadian Journal of Economics and Political Science* 28 (February 1962): 54.
8. Garth Stevenson, *Unfulfilled Union*, 3rd ed. (Toronto: Gage,1989), p. 224.
9. Garth Stevenson, *Unfulfilled Union*, 2nd ed. (Toronto: Gage, 1982), pp. 41-42.
10. See, for example, Peter Aucoin and Herman Bakvis, "Regional Responsiveness and Government Organization," in Peter Aucoin, ed., *Regional Responsiveness and the National Administrative State, Research Study for the Royal Commission on the Economic Union and Development Prospects for Canada*, vol. 37 (Toronto: University of Toronto Press, 1985).
11. Donald V. Smiley and Ronald L. Watts, *Intrastate Federalism in Canada, Research Study for the Royal Commission on the Economic Union and Development Prospects for Canada*, vol. 39 (Toronto: University of Toronto Press, 1985), p. 4. Reprinted by permission of the University of Toronto Press in cooperation with the Royal Commission on the

Economic Union and Development Prospects for Canada and the Canadian Publishing Centre, Supply and Services Canada.

12. Alan C. Cairns, *From Interstate to Intrastate Federalism in Canada* (Kingston: Queen's University, Institute of Intergovernmental Relations, 1979), pp. 11-12.

13. See Smiley and Watts, *Intrastate Federalism.*

14. For an examination of the value of these suggestions, see Kenneth Kernaghan, "Representative and Responsive Bureaucracy: Implications for Canadian Regionalism," in Aucoin, ed., *Regional Responsiveness and the National Administrative State.*

15. See A. Milton Moore, J. Harvey Perry, and Donald I. Beach, *The Financing of Canadian Federation: The First Hundred Years* (Toronto: Canadian Tax Foundation, 1966) and D.V. Smiley, *Canada In Question: Federalism in the Eighties*, 3rd ed.(Toronto: McGraw-Hill Ryerson, 1980), ch. 6.

16. A good overview of the history and current state of the federal-provincial fiscal relationship is provided in Richard M. Bird, *Financing Canadian Government: A Quantitative Overview* (Toronto: Canadian Tax Foundation, 1979), ch. 5, and Canada, House of Commons, Parliamentary Task Force on Federal-Provincial Fiscal Arrangements, *Fiscal Federalism in Canada* (Ottawa: Supply and Services Canada, 1981).

17. A good summary of the provisions of most federal-provincial transfer payment programs is found in Canadian Tax Foundation, *The National Finances* (annual publication of the Canadian Tax Foundation, Toronto).

18. Thomas J. Courchene, *Refinancing the Canadian Federation: A Survey of the 1977 Fiscal Arrangements Act* (Montreal: C.D. Howe Research Institute, 1979).

19. The details of the current equalization formula are given in Canadian Tax Foundation, *The National Finances: 1988-1989* (Toronto: Canadian Tax Foundation, 1990), ch. 16. See also Thomas J. Courchene, *Equalization Payments: Past, Present and Future* (Toronto: Economic Council of Canada, 1984), ch. 2.

20. A general discussion of the rationale for intergovernmental transfers is provided in Robin W. Boadway, *Intergovernmental Transfers in Canada* (Toronto: Canadian Tax Foundation, 1980), ch. 3.

21. For an examination of the evolution of these intergovernmental bodies, see Timothy B. Woolstencroft, *Organizing Intergovernmental Relations* (Kingston, Ont.: Institute of Intergovernmental Relations, Queen's University, 1982); Bruce G. Pollard, *Managing the Interface: Intergovernmental Affairs Agencies in Canada* (Kingston, Ont.: Institute of Intergovernmental Relations, Queen's University, 1986); and John Warhurst, "Canada's Intergovernmental Relations Specialists," *Australian Journal of Public Administration* 42 (Winter 1983): 459-85.

22. Gerard Veilleux, "L'évolution des mécanismes de liaison intergouvernmental," in Richard Simeon, ed., *Confrontation and Collaboration: Intergovernmental Relations in Canada Today* (Toronto: Institute of Public Administration of Canada, 1979), pp. 44-45.

23. Bruce G. Pollard, *Managing the Interface: Intergovernmental Affairs Agencies in Canada,* pp. 70-71.

24. In 1967 this department was renamed the Department of Intergovernmental Affairs. It is notable that for a brief period in 1961, at the end of the Frost era, Ontario had a Department of Economics and Intergovernmental Relations.

25. This organization is the successor to the Constitutional Conference Secretariat established in 1968.

26. Richard Schultz, "Prime Ministerial Government, Central Agencies, and Operating Departments: Towards a More Realistic Analysis," in Thomas A. Hockin, ed., *Apex of Power*, 2nd ed. (Scarborough: Prentice-Hall, 1977), p. 232.

Government of Canada   Gouvernement du Canada

ORGANIZATION OF THE GOVERNMENT OF CANADA
APRIL 1,1990

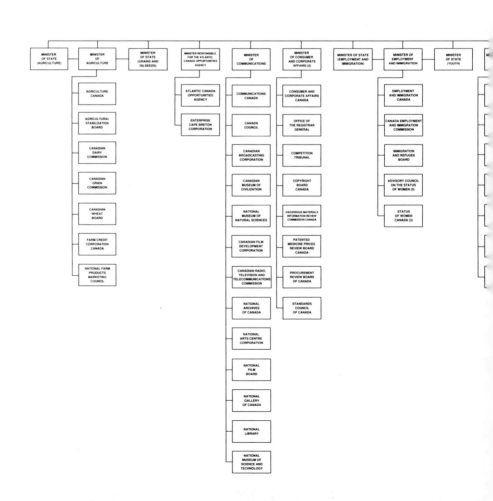

MINISTER OF STATE (AGRICULTURE)	MINISTER OF AGRICULTURE	MINISTER OF STATE (GRAINS AND OILSEEDS)	MINISTER RESPONSIBLE FOR THE ATLANTIC CANADA OPPORTUNITIES AGENCY	MINISTER OF COMMUNICATIONS	MINISTER OF CONSUMER AND CORPORATE AFFAIRS (2)	MINISTER OF STATE (EMPLOYMENT AND IMMIGRATION)	MINISTER OF EMPLOYMENT AND IMMIGRATION	MINISTER OF STATE (YOUTH)
	AGRICULTURE CANADA		ATLANTIC CANADA OPPORTUNITIES AGENCY	COMMUNICATIONS CANADA	CONSUMER AND CORPORATE AFFAIRS CANADA		EMPLOYMENT AND IMMIGRATION CANADA	
	AGRICULTURAL STABILIZATION BOARD		ENTERPRISE CAPE BRETON CORPORATION	CANADA COUNCIL	OFFICE OF THE REGISTRAR GENERAL		CANADA EMPLOYMENT AND IMMIGRATION COMMISSION	
	CANADIAN DAIRY COMMISSION			CANADIAN BROADCASTING CORPORATION	COMPETITION TRIBUNAL		IMMIGRATION AND REFUGEE BOARD	
	CANADIAN GRAIN COMMISSION			CANADIAN MUSEUM OF CIVILIZATION	COPYRIGHT BOARD CANADA		ADVISORY COUNCIL ON THE STATUS OF WOMEN (3)	
	CANADIAN WHEAT BOARD			NATIONAL MUSEUM OF NATURAL SCIENCES	HAZARDOUS MATERIALS INFORMATION REVIEW COMMISSION CANADA		STATUS OF WOMEN CANADA (3)	
	FARM CREDIT CORPORATION CANADA			CANADIAN FILM DEVELOPMENT CORPORATION	PATENTED MEDICINE PRICES REVIEW BOARD CANADA			
	NATIONAL FARM PRODUCTS MARKETING COUNCIL			CANADIAN RADIO, TELEVISION AND TELECOMMUNICATIONS COMMISSION	PROCUREMENT REVIEW BOARD OF CANADA			
				NATIONAL ARCHIVES OF CANADA	STANDARDS COUNCIL OF CANADA			
				NATIONAL ARTS CENTRE CORPORATION				
				NATIONAL FILM BOARD				
				NATIONAL GALLERY OF CANADA				
				NATIONAL LIBRARY				
				NATIONAL MUSEUM OF SCIENCE AND TECHNOLOGY				

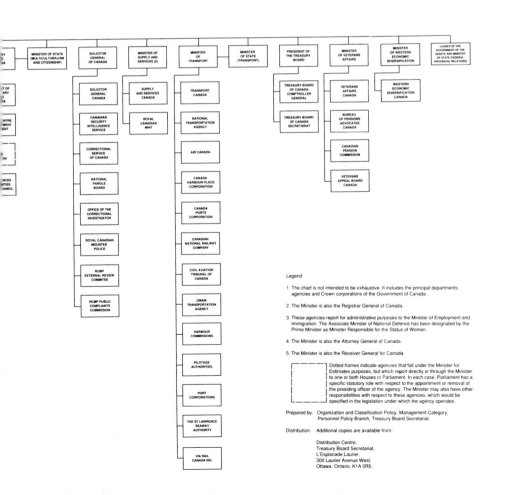

MINISTER OF STATE (MULTICULTURALISM AND CITIZENSHIP)

SOLICITOR GENERAL OF CANADA
- SOLICITOR GENERAL CANADA
- CANADIAN SECURITY INTELLIGENCE SERVICE
- CORRECTIONAL SERVICE OF CANADA
- NATIONAL PAROLE BOARD
- OFFICE OF THE CORRECTIONAL INVESTIGATOR
- ROYAL CANADIAN MOUNTED POLICE
- RCMP EXTERNAL REVIEW COMMITTEE
- RCMP PUBLIC COMPLAINTS COMMISSION

MINISTER OF SUPPLY AND SERVICES (5)
- SUPPLY AND SERVICES CANADA
- ROYAL CANADIAN MINT

MINISTER OF TRANSPORT
- TRANSPORT CANADA
- NATIONAL TRANSPORTATION AGENCY
- AIR CANADA
- CANADA HARBOUR PLACE CORPORATION
- CANADA PORTS CORPORATION
- CANADIAN NATIONAL RAILWAY COMPANY
- CIVIL AVIATION TRIBUNAL OF CANADA
- GRAIN TRANSPORTATION AGENCY
- HARBOUR COMMISSIONS
- PILOTAGE AUTHORITIES
- PORT CORPORATIONS
- THE ST LAWRENCE SEAWAY AUTHORITY
- VIA RAIL CANADA INC.

MINISTER OF STATE (TRANSPORT)

PRESIDENT OF THE TREASURY BOARD
- TREASURY BOARD OF CANADA COMPTROLLER GENERAL
- TREASURY BOARD OF CANADA SECRETARIAT

MINISTER OF VETERANS AFFAIRS
- VETERANS AFFAIRS CANADA
- BUREAU OF PENSIONS ADVOCATES CANADA
- CANADIAN PENSION COMMISSION
- VETERANS APPEAL BOARD CANADA

MINISTER OF WESTERN ECONOMIC DIVERSIFICATION
- WESTERN ECONOMIC DIVERSIFICATION CANADA

LEADER OF THE GOVERNMENT OF THE SENATE AND MINISTER OF STATE (FEDERAL-PROVINCIAL RELATIONS)

Legend

1. The chart is not intended to be exhaustive. It includes the principal departments, agencies and Crown corporations of the Government of Canada.

2. The Minister is also the Registrar General of Canada.

3. These agencies report for administrative purposes to the Minister of Employment and Immigration. The Associate Minister of National Defence has been designated by the Prime Minister as Minister Responsible for the Status of Women.

4. The Minister is also the Attorney General of Canada.

5. The Minister is also the Receiver General for Canada.

Dotted frames indicate agencies that fall under the Minister for Estimates purposes, but which report directly or through the Minister to one or both Houses of Parliament. In each case, Parliament has a specific statutory role with respect to the appointment or removal of the presiding officer of the agency. The Minister may also have other responsibilities with respect to these agencies, which would be specified in the legislation under which the agency operates.

Prepared by: Organization and Classification Policy, Management Category, Personnel Policy Branch, Treasury Board Secretariat.

Distribution: Additional copies are available from:

Distribution Centre,
Treasury Board Secretariat,
L'Esplanade Laurier,
300 Laurier Avenue West,
Ottawa, Ontario, K1A 0R5.

27. Donald V. Smiley, "An Outsider's Observations of Federal-Provincial Relations Among Consenting Adults," in Simeon, *Confrontation and Collaboration*, p. 110.
28. Veilliex, "*L'évolution*," p. 36.
29. Council of Maritime Premiers, *Annual Report*, 1984-85 (Halifax: Council of Maritime Premiers, 1985), p. 6.
30. This model is elaborated in Donald V. Smiley, "Public Administration and Canadian Federalism," *Canadian Public Administration* 7 (September 1964): 371-88, and *Constitutional Adaptation and Canadian Federalism Since 1945* (Ottawa: Information Canada, 1970), ch. 7.
31. Rand Dyck, "The Canada Assistance Plan: The Ultimate in Cooperative Federalism," *Canadian Public Administration* 19 (Winter 1976): 587-602. Professor Dyck acknowledges some limited relevance for the bargaining model, but notes that "the policy development involved in the Canada Assistance Plan can best be understood in terms of Smiley's discussion of shared norms among program administrators" (p. 598).
32. See Simon McInnes, *Federal-Provincial Negotiation: Family Allowances, 1970-1976* (Ph.D. diss., Carlton University, April 1978).
33. Smiley, "Public Administration and Canadian Federalism," p. 387.
34. For an explanation and application of what we call the bargaining model, see Richard Simeon, *Federal-Provincial Diplomacy: The Making of Recent Policy in Canada* (Toronto: University of Toronto Press, 1972), esp. chs. 2 and 13.
35. Ibid.
36. See Richard Schultz, *Federalism, Bureaucracy and Public Policy* (Montreal: McGill-Queen's University Press, 1980); McInnes, *Federal-Provincial Negotiation: Family Allowances 1970-1976*; and Kim Richard Nossal, "Bureaucratic Politics in Canadian Government," *Canadian Public Administration* 22 (Winter 1979): 298.
37. Schultz, *Federalism, Bureaucracy and Public Policy*, pp. 434-35.
38. Simeon, *Federal-Provincial Diplomacy*, p. 13.
39. Smiley, "An Outsider's Observations," p. 110. See also Veilleux, "*L'évolution*," p.45, and Roy E. Lloyd, "The Effects of the Changing Nature of Federal-Provincial Relations on the Role of the Bureaucracy" (Paper presented to the Annual Conference of the Institute of Public Administration of Canada, Victoria, September 1977), p. 9.
40. See Howard Leeson, "The Intergovernmental Affairs Function in Saskatchewan, 1960-1983," *Canadian Public Administration* 30 (Fall 1987): 399-420.
41. Gordon Robertson, "The Role of Interministerial Conferences in the Decision-Making Process," in Simeon, *Confrontation and Collaboration*, p. 80.
42. See Kenneth Kernaghan, "Power, Parliament and Public Servants: Ministerial Responsibility Reexamined," *Canadian Public Policy* 5 (Summer 1979): 383-96.
43. Robertson, "Role of Interministerial Conferences," p. 80.
44. "The Present State of the Legislative Process in Canada: Myths and Realities," in W.A.W. Neilson and J.C. MacPherson, eds., *The Legislative Process in Canada: The Need for Reform* (Toronto: Institute for Research on Public Policy; distributed by Butterworths, 1978), p. 44.
45. Ibid., p. 52.
46. Robertson, "Role of Interministerial Conferences," p. 83.
47. Smiley, "An Outsider's Observations," p. 107.
48. Alan Cairns, "The Governments and Societies of Canadian Federalism," *Canadian Journal of Political Science* 10 (December 1977): 722.

BIBLIOGRAPHY

Aucoin, Peter, and Herman Bakvis. "Regional Responsiveness and Government Organization: The Case of Regional Economic Policy in Canada." In Peter Aucoin, ed., *Regional Responsiveness and the National Administrative State*. Research study for the Royal Commission on the Economic Union and Development Prospects for Canada, vol. 37. Toronto: University of Toronto Press, 1985, pp. 51-118.

Black, E. R. *Divided Loyalties: Canadian Concepts of Federalism*. Montreal: McGill-Queen's University Press, 1975.

Cairns, Alan. "The Governments and Societies of Canadian Federalism." *Canadian Journal of Political Science* 10 (December 1977): 695-725.

Cairns, Alan. "The Other Crisis of Canadian Federalism." *Canadian Public Administration* 22 (Summer 1979): 175-95.

Careless, Anthony G.S. *Initiative and Response: The Adaptation of Canadian Federalism to Regional Development*. Montreal: McGill-Queen's University Press, 1977.

Doerr, Audrey. "Public Administration: Federalism and Intergovernmental Relations." *Canadian Public Administration* 25 (Winter 1982): 564-79.

Dyck, R. "The Canada Assistance Plan: The Ultimate in Cooperative Federalism." *Canadian Public Administration* 19 (Winter 1976): 587-602.

Dupré, J. Stefan, et al. *Federalism and Policy Development: The Case of Adult Occupational Training in Ontario*. Toronto: University of Toronto Press, 1973.

Kernaghan, Kenneth. "Representative and Responsive Bureaucracy: Implications for Canadian Regionalism." In Peter Aucoin, ed., *Regional Responsiveness and the National Administrative State*. Research study for the Royal Commission on the Economic Union and Development Prospects for Canada, vol. 37. Toronto: University of Toronto Press, 1985, pp. 1-50.

Robertson, Gordon. "The Role of Interministerial Conferences in the Decision-Making Process." In Richard Simeon, ed., *Confrontation and Collaboration—Intergovernmental Relations in Canada Today*. Toronto: Institute of Public Administration of Canada, 1979, pp. 77-88.

Savoie, Donald J. *Federal-Provincial Collaboration*. Montreal: McGill-Queen's University Press, 1972.

Schultz, Richard J. *Federalism, Bureaucracy and Public Policy: The Politics of Highway Transport Regulation*. Montreal: McGill-Queen's University Press, 1980.

Schultz, Richard J. *Federalism and the Regulatory Process*. Montreal: Institute for Research on Public Policy, 1980.

Simeon, Richard, ed. *Confrontation and Collaboration: Intergovermental Relations in Canada Today*. Toronto: Institute of Public Administration of Canada, 1979.

Simeon, Richard, ed. *Intergovernmental Relations*. Research studies for the Royal Commission on the Economic Union and Development Prospects for Canada, vol. 63. Toronto: University of Toronto Press, 1985.

Simeon, Richard. "Intergovernmental Relations and the Challenges to Canadian Federalism." *Canadian Public Administration* 23 (Spring 1980): 14-32.

Smiley, D. V. *Canada In Question: Federalism in the Eighties*. 3rd ed. Toronto: McGraw-Hill Ryerson, 1980.

Smiley, D. V. *Constitutional Adaptation and Canadian Federalism Since 1945*. Ottawa: Information Canada, 1970.

Smiley, Donald V., and Ronald L. Watts. *Intrastate Federalism in Canada*. Research study for the Royal Commission on the Economic Union and Development Prospects for Canada, vol. 39. Toronto: University of Toronto Press, 1985.

Stevenson, Don. "The Role of Intergovernmental Conferences in the Decision-Making Process." In Richard Simeon, ed., *Confrontation and Collaboration–Intergovernmental Relations in Canada Today*. Toronto: Institute of Public Administration of Canada, 1979.

Veilleux, Gerard. "Intergovernmental Canada: Government by Conference? A Fiscal and Economic Perspective." *Canadian Public Administration* 23 (Spring 1980): 33-53.

Wilson, V. Seymour. "Federal-Provincial Relations and Federal Policy Processes." In G. Bruce Doern and Peter Aucoin eds., *Public Policy in Canada*. Toronto: Macmillan, 1979, pp. 190-214.

Woolstencroft, Timothy B. *Organizing Intergovernmental Relations*. Kingston Ont.: Institute of Intergovernmental Relations, Queen's University, 1982.

CASES

Case Program in Canadian Public Administration (Toronto: Institute of Public Administration of Canada):

L'Affaire "Caloil." By Michel Paquin

Federal-Provincial Diplomacy: Re-Negotiating EPF. By David Siegel

Oil Spill in the Bay of Fundy: A Case Study in Crisis Management. By J. W. F. Pullen

The Allocation of a National Housing Budget. By Barbara Carroll

Cases developed by the Canadian Centre for Management Development and distributed by the Case Program in Canadian Public Administration:

A Crisis in the Fish Processing Industry. By Louise A. Dupuis

20

Pressure Groups, Political Parties, and the Bureaucracy

The political actors who influence public servants from outside government include not only other governments but also a number of non-governmental actors. The most prominent of these are pressure groups, political parties, the general public, and the news media. This chapter discusses the interaction of pressure groups and political parties with the bureaucracy; the next chapter discusses the bureaucracy's relations with the public and the media, and includes an examination of the issues of freedom of information and individual privacy.

PRESSURE GROUPS

Definition and Classification

Pressure groups (or interest groups)[1] are organizations composed of persons who have joined together to further their mutual interest by influencing public policy. These groups do not have hierarchical or legal authority over government officials. They do, however, exercise *influence* over both the development and implementation of public policy. Their efforts are commonly described as lobbying. To many Canadians, the term lobbying has unsavoury connotations of illegal, immoral, or inappropriate means of influencing government decision-makers.[2] This perception has its origins in the practice of lobbying in the United States during much of the nineteenth century, when "lobbyists" would frequent the lobbies and corridors of legislative buildings to influence legislators, sometimes with offers of bribes. **Lobbying** refers here simply to a legitimate means of influencing government decisions through individual or collective action.

Every policy field and every policy issue attracts the attention of one or more pressure groups. These groups are, therefore, extremely numerous and pervasive in the Canadian political system. They represent to government the interests of business, labour, agricultural, professional, social, welfare, religious, and public interest organizations. Examples of each of these types of organization are the Canadian Manufacturers' Association, the Canadian Labour Con-

440

gress, the Canadian Federation of Agriculture, the Canadian Bar Association, the Canadian Council on Social Development, the Canadian Welfare Council, the Presbyterian Church in Canada, and the Canadian Arctic Resources Committee. Some pressure groups have been established solely for the purpose of lobbying government, whereas for other groups lobbying is a very small, incidental part of their activities. Few groups have been organized solely to lobby government; most groups perform such other functions as exchanging information among their members and representing their members to the public.

The number of lobbyists and the extent of lobbying activity in Ottawa and the provincial capitals are difficult to measure with any precision. Lobbying is carried on not just by pressure group executives but also by professional lobbyists, lawyers, legislators (notably senators), and individual citizens. Lobbying by business people involves the public affairs departments of business firms, permanent staff members located in Ottawa, trade associations, public affairs consulting companies (which publish newsletters and assist clients to approach the appropriate government officials), and one-on-one contacts between senior business executives and public officials.[3]

It is estimated that the Lobbyists Registration Act of 1989 affects fifteen thousand lobbyists. This Act requires the registration of all persons who communicate with politicians and public servants in an effort to influence policies, legislation, regulations, grants, or contracts. The purpose of the legislation is not to regulate lobbyists, but to make the lobbying process better understood by identifying the lobbyists and the issues on which they are lobbying. The Act divides lobbyists into two groups. The first group includes about five thousand professional lobbyists who work for third parties on a fee-for-service basis. For each attempt to lobby, these lobbyists have to file a separate registration providing the name of the client and the subject matter of the lobbying. The second group is composed of about ten thousand people, each of whom lobbies for one organization as part of his or her duties as an employee of that organization. All that is required of these people is that they register once a year.

Pressure groups have been classified into a variety of types according to such criteria as their objectives, activities, and structure. But a broad and useful distinction can be made between *institutional* groups and *issue-oriented* groups.[4]

Institutional groups are characterized by organizational continuity and cohesion. They are highly knowledgeable about the policy-making process and about how to get access to public officials, in part because they usually employ a professional staff; their membership is stable; they have concrete and immediate operational objectives, but their ultimate aims are sufficiently broad that they can bargain with government over achieving particular concessions; and their long-term credibility with government decision-makers is more important than any single issue or objective. Examples of institutional groups are the Canadian Medical Association and the Canadian Chamber of Commerce.

Issue-oriented groups, however, tend to be poorly organized. They have little knowledge of government and of how to contact public officials; there is a constant turnover in their membership; they normally focus on only one or two issues; and they are not usually concerned about their long-term credibility with public officials. Examples of issue-oriented groups are those concerned about a particular threat to the environment and those opposed to specific projects of developers.

In reality, virtually all pressure groups fall on a continuum between these two extreme types and can be discussed in terms of the extent to which they possess the characteristics of primarily one type. Most groups can be described as either mature or fledgling groups depending on the extent to which their characteristics conform to the institutional or issue-oriented ends of the continuum.[5] A good example of a group that has gradually moved along this continuum is Greenpeace.

Another distinction is often made between *special interest* groups and *public interest* groups. The vast majority of pressure groups fall into the special interest category on the grounds that they are primarily motivated by particular interests that affect their members directly (e.g., the British Columbia Home Owners' Association or the Canadian Council of Furniture Manufacturers). **Public interest groups**, by way of contrast, are said to be concerned with the broader, more general interests of the public (e.g., the Consumers Association of Canada, the Canadian Arctic Resources Committee). As in the case of institutional and issue-oriented groups, special interest and public interest groups can best be depicted on a continuum because most groups are motivated by a mixture of self-interest and public interest. For tactical reasons, all groups tend to emphasize the extent to which their activities serve the public interest.

Functions of Pressure Groups

Communication

Given that the overriding objective of pressure groups is to influence the development and execution of public policies, it is not surprising that their main function is two-way communication between their members and public officials. The *content* of this communication ranges from detailed, technical data on existing or proposed policies, programs, and regulations to irate demands for government action on particular issues (e.g, environmental pollution). The *form* of the communication depends to some extent on its content, but it is determined also by the *type* of pressure group. Institutional groups tend to benefit more than issue-oriented groups from the fact that government-pressure group relations involve a two-way flow of communication and influence. Public officials rely, sometimes very heavily, on the expertise and experience of pressure groups for information on the efficacy of existing policies and on the implications of new proposals. Institutional-type groups, in large part because of the information they are able to provide to governments, have greater access to government officials, especially to Cabinet ministers and senior bureaucrats.

Bureaucrats and, to a lesser extent, Cabinet ministers also utilize pressure group contacts to communicate with the groups' members. Many pressure groups regularly pass along to their members, through newsletters and other internal means of communication, information about government policies and programs. This practice is mutually beneficial in that the group provides a service to its members and the bureaucrats get their message to the group's membership.

Legitimation

The communication function of pressure groups is closely related to another important function that groups perform in the political system—legitimation. Through consultation with pressure groups whose members will be affected by proposed policies, government officials can assess the probable effects of adopting these policies and can seek support for them. Such consultation gives these policies a measure of legitimacy in that those groups representing persons likely to be affected by the policies have had their views heard and ostensibly taken into account by government decision-makers. Certainly, government officials are well advised to consult any group whose opposition to policies could weaken the legitimacy of the policies in the eyes of the public.

Thus, bureaucrats routinely consult certain pressure groups in the development and implementation of policies. Indeed, in a major survey of pressure group behaviour, Robert Presthus found that 50 percent of federal bureaucrats and 68 percent of provincial bureaucrats in Canada described their departments' relations with lobbyists as either "almost an integral part of our day-to-day activity" or "usually taken into account during policy making."[6] The importance of the legitimation function is evident in the efforts of bureaucrats to promote the creation and maintenance of particular pressure groups. Presthus reported that 45 percent of federal bureaucrats and 50 percent of provincial bureaucrats answered yes to the question: "Has your own or any other Department ever created an interest group in order to facilitate the implementation of a policy or program?"[7] This activity not only ensures a complementary source of outside knowledge and experience; it also serves the legitimation function by ensuring outside support for the government's policies, facilitating group input into the policy process that might not otherwise take place, and promoting the representation of disadvantaged groups. For example, a former senior bureaucrat has acknowledged bureaucratic initiatives in "presenting for ministerial approval measures designed to assist members of disadvantaged sectors of society in forming groups and organizations and otherwise gaining some power in matters affecting their social and economic needs."[8]

Targets of Pressure Group Activity

It is critically important to the success of pressure groups that, in their interactions with government, they identify and aim at the right targets. They must decide first whether to direct their efforts to the federal, provincial, or local spheres of government—or to all of them.[9] The federal nature of Canada has important effects on the organization and operations of pressure groups. Many Canadian pressure groups are federations; that is, they are composed of provincial bodies that lobby the provincial governments and a national organization

Table 20.1
PROPORTION OF INTEREST GROUPS RANKING EACH TARGET FIRST

Target	Canada	United States
	%	%
Bureaucracy	40	21
Legislators	20	41
Cabinet	19	4
Legislative Committees	7	19
Executive Assistants	5	3
Judiciary	3	3
Others	6	9
	(393)	(604)

Source: Adapted from Robert Presthus, *Elites in the Policy Process* (London: Cambridge University Press, 1974), p. 255.

that focusses its efforts on Ottawa. Many other groups are not large enough to have provincial components or affiliates of a national organization and are obliged, therefore, to channel their limited resources to those governments where they will do the most good. Another impact of federalism on pressure group activity is that, to be effective on issues that involve more than one level of government, groups may be required to lobby federal, provincial, and local governments simultaneously.

Whether pressure groups are lobbying federal or provincial governments, the usual targets of their activity are Cabinet ministers, bureaucrats, and legislators, all of whom play important roles in the public policy process. This process may be divided into pre-legislative, legislative, and post-legislative stages. Bureaucrats are especially powerful in the post-legislative stage through their implementation of policy decisions.

As a result of their policy advisory responsibilities and the sheer volume of decisions they make, bureaucrats are the most frequent targets of pressure group activity. Table 20.1 shows that Canadian bureaucrats are a more common focus of attention by pressure group leaders than either Cabinet ministers and legislators in Canada or bureaucrats in the United States. Moreover, close observers of the Canadian political scene have attested to the prominent role of bureaucrats in government-pressure group interaction:

... the greatest leverage lies not with the politicians but with the bureaucrats.[10]

... civil servants are obviously of key importance and they are a target group that most successful interest groups understand has to be dealt with.[11]

Any lobbyist... will tell you that the real levers of power lie with the bureaucracy, among the mandarins whose own concerns and perceptions are the main source of policy.[12]

Most policy initiatives originate in the bureaucracy. One Ottawa lobbyist has noted that most new ideas begin deep in the civil service machine. The man in charge of some special office ... writes a memo suggesting a new policy on this or that. It works its way slowly up and up. At that stage civil servants are delighted ... to talk quietly to people like us, people representing this or that corporation or industry directly involved. This is the time to slip in good ideas.[13]

It is especially important for pressure groups to influence a policy before it becomes enshrined in a Cabinet memorandum, which is very difficult to change. It makes sense for pressure groups to lobby at the level or levels of the bureaucracy where a decision or recommendation affecting their interests can be made. Thus, lobbying will often be aimed at professional and technical personnel rather than at senior executives and managers.

Lobbyists are frequently advised to "leave no stone unturned" in their efforts to influence those government officials who can help them to achieve their objectives. An Ottawa lobbyist has advised that "the effective lobbyist will maintain contact with the project as it goes up through the department, making sure he talks to every rung on the ladder. If you forget to talk to someone, he or she may be offended, and may influence the policy to your detriment."[14] Pressure groups must, however, choose their targets very carefully so as not to spread their limited resources too thinly and end up having little influence anywhere.

The power of bureaucrats does not, of course, give them the final say on major public policy issues; that authority belongs to Cabinet ministers. Pressure groups are frequently obliged, therefore, to lobby ministers to influence not only the decisions of individual departments but also those of Cabinet as a whole and Cabinet committees. Moreover, ministers are often the ultimate target of lobbying aimed at bureaucrats and legislators by pressure groups that are striving to influence those who can influence ministers. Cabinet ministers have enormous power in all three stages of the policy process—if they decide to exercise that power. In practice, they have neither the time nor the inclination to participate actively in the post-legislative stage; rather, they tend to leave policy implementation to the bureaucrats.

Thus, it is tempting for group representatives to aim their *initial* lobbying efforts at Cabinet ministers. But, since ministers are busy people, it is usually inadvisable to approach them before other appropriate avenues of influence have been exhausted. There is little to be gained and something to be lost by expending a minister's time and goodwill when a bureaucrat or a legislator will serve just as well or even better. Admittedly, if a group gets Cabinet approval for a proposal, it has won its case. However, if a group loses at Cabinet level, there is no higher body with which it can lodge an appeal. Moreover, access to ministers is generally harder to obtain than to bureaucrats and legislators. For reasons outlined earlier, institutional-type pressure groups tend to receive readier access to ministers than do other pressure groups. Ministers, like bureaucrats, need contacts with experienced, knowledgeable, and influential groups not only to assess better the merits and costs of policy proposals but also to increase political support for the government as a whole or for their own departments. They also use pressure groups as an alternative source of information and advice to that provided by the bureaucracy. A former Cabinet minister has asserted that "deputy ministers and their supporting policy advisors have no particular monopoly on wisdom and they can as easily become victims of myopia or tunnel vision as anyone else."[15]

It has already been noted that, compared to Cabinet ministers and bureaucrats, legislators and legislative committees are a secondary target of pressure group activity. Nevertheless, legislative support for pressure groups can be extremely important, especially on issues of widespread public concern, and can complement a group's efforts to influence officials in the executive-bureaucratic arena. Government backbenchers have opportunities to influence government decisions in party caucus meetings and in formal and informal meetings with ministers and bureaucrats. Opposition members are anxious to receive representations from pressure groups so as to understand better the groups' problems and to obtain ammunition to be used against the government. If individual legislators and legislative committees had more influence on the formulation and implementation of public policy, pressure groups could usefully spend more time and effort lobbying the legislature. At present, it is understandable that knowledgeable pressure groups will spend comparatively little time trying to influence public policy during the legislative stage of the policy process.

After identifying and selecting their targets from among ministers, bureaucrats, and legislators, pressure groups have to focus on more specific targets, that is, on the most appropriate minister(s), department(s), legislator(s), and legislative committee(s). Pressure groups must know not only whom to lobby but, as we shall see, what tactics will best ensure success. Above all, groups need to get access to government decision-makers; otherwise they are obliged to influence public policy indirectly by influencing the news media and public opinion. This latter method of persuasion can be effective, but in general it is less successful, especially over time.

Recognition of Pressure Groups

Pressure group access to public officials, particularly to bureaucrats, depends largely on the extent to which the group has earned official recognition, that is, on the extent to which officials perceive the group as useful, credible, and legitimate. Professor David Kwavnick has noted:

> One of the major prizes in the struggle between competing interest groups . . . is tangible *recognition* by government of the status and representative capacity claimed by interest group leaders for their respective organizations. Such recognition is conferred when government canvasses interest group leaders for nomination to official bodies and when government calls a group's leader into consultation on legislative or administrative matters.[16]

Clearly, recognition facilitates both access and influence for pressure groups. Those groups that are regularly consulted by government have an early-warning system that alerts them to governmental initiatives affecting their interests. They are in a better position than other groups, therefore, to anticipate or react to these initiatives. Once groups have achieved this level of recognition, they are wise to ensure that they preserve it by cultivating their contacts in government and continuing to do whatever brought them recognition in the first place.

What are the bases of recognition? The first basis is the *expertise* and *experience* that pressure groups are able to provide to government officials. Bureaucrats naturally tend to consult and to grant readier access to those groups on whom they can rely for accurate data required for informed policy-making. A former Cabinet minister has attributed the success of an especially effective pressure group to the fact that "their information is as good as the government's.... They do not appear before the executive or... agencies of government with half-baked information."[17]

Certain pressure groups gain and maintain recognition more easily than other groups because they constitute the *sole clientele*, or a large part of the clientele, of a specific department (e.g., farmers' organizations vis-à-vis the Department of Agriculture or labour organizations vis-à-vis the Department of Labour). This clientele relationship involves reciprocal costs and benefits. A department can rely on a clientele group as a source of information and as a channel of communication to the group's members. It can also use the group to get support for its policies from other departments and, indeed, from the general public by claiming to speak for the interest of the major group affected by the department's policies. To do this, the department must maintain good relations with the group and take special pains to avoid open conflict with it. Similarly, the group can benefit in the way of access and influence by receiving such departmental recognition. But if a group is tied too closely to a single department, it may have nowhere else to go, with the result that the department may be able to influence its activities unduly. So far as possible, therefore, a group will normally cultivate support in other departments so that not all of its lobbying "eggs" are in a single basket.

Another important basis of pressure group recognition is the group's *political clout*. Not only ministers and legislators but also bureaucrats are interested in the political impact pressure group activity can have on the next election. While bureaucrats are expected to be nonpartisan, they are at the same time expected to be politically sensitive. They should be able to advise the minister as to the likely effects of proposed policies on various segments of society, including those segments represented by influential pressure groups. Thus, bureaucrats should strive to be aware of the possible effects of government decisions on the voting behaviour of a pressure group's membership. Moreover, bureaucrats need to know what the likely implications of policy proposals will be on the bureaucratic or organizational politics within the government itself. A former Cabinet minister has stated that "most civil servants are professionally disposed to push or recommend policy that is likely to achieve political support both at the cabinet level and within the public service."[18] Thus, bureaucrats are more likely to grant official recognition to groups that have the resources to influence the political fortunes of their minister or of the government as a whole. Moreover, they will be more favourably disposed toward groups that can help them to help the minister.

A final notable source of recognition is the use by pressure groups of lobbying tactics that are approved by, or at least acceptable to, government decision-makers.

Pressure Group Tactics

Before deciding on the tactics to be employed, effective pressure groups take special pains to identify the appropriate targets of their lobbying activities (e.g., federal, provincial, and local governments; ministers, bureaucrats, and legislators). They then progressively focus in on the organizations and individuals within government most likely to be of assistance to them. It is evident that groups require up-to-date and accurate knowledge of the machinery of government to find their way through the labyrinth of government to the correct targets. Once this has been done, lobbying tactics can be geared to the needs and biases of these targets.

Ideally, an excellent tactic for pressure groups is to lobby all those government officials who can influence or actually make a decision affecting their interests. Realistically, however, most groups are obliged to utilize their limited financial and staff resources to lobby carefully selected officials. It is important, therefore, that groups lobby at the most appropriate level of the governmental hierarchy. Effective lobbying, both in the short and the long run, requires groups to provide officials with well-researched and relevant data. Thus, once access has been granted, pressure groups must ensure that their arguments are based on very thorough homework so as to enhance their success in influencing a specific policy, as well as increasing their long-run credibility and legitimacy.

Groups are also well advised to attempt to influence policy at the earliest possible stage of its development, and to follow the progress of that policy all the way through the policy-making process, including the post-legislative or implementation stage. "Any organization seeking to influence public policy must be prepared to come back again and again at whatever level of government is dealing with an issue. In other words, the group must have tenacity."[19] Groups will be able to perform this task more successfully if their contacts with government officials are sufficiently cordial and continuous to allow them to anticipate or learn quickly about policy initiatives. Thus, once again, a group's tactics are determined significantly by the extent of its recognition.

In general, pressure groups seek to influence public officials, especially bureaucrats, through quiet, behind-the-scenes consultations, rather than through media campaigns and public demonstrations that are designed to influence decision-makers indirectly. Institutional-type pressure groups are more likely to use the former tactic because they are interested in influencing government decisions on a number of issues over a period of time, whereas issue-oriented groups tend to focus on a single problem or have fewer of the resources that encourage government officials to grant them recognition and access. In the face of limited opportunities to make their case directly to public officials, they hope to influence public policy indirectly by mobilizing public support for their cause through the news media and even public demonstrations. Institutional groups are more likely to absorb defeat on a particular issue without "going public" because they know that there are other battles to be fought and that mounting public and media campaigns to win their point are unlikely to be to their long-run advantage. They are inclined to minimize publicity and confrontation and to avoid the adversarial approach. The head of the Grocery Products Manufacturers Association has stated that "we're not prepared to go on Parliament Hill and slaughter a pig to have our representations heard— unless we're absolutely forced to."[20] And the president of the Retail Council of Canada has observed that "the marshalling of public support through the media is sometimes the right recipe for tackling a particular issue, but not often. Only the most simplistic of issues is likely to be well understood by the public."[21] Pressure groups need to remember that official recognition is hard to win but relatively easy to lose. This consideration significantly determines the tactics used by many groups.

The discreet approach to lobbying is more acceptable to bureaucrats because they want to keep their minister out of trouble and keep themselves out of the public spotlight. Neither they nor the department as a whole wish to be the object of public attack as this is likely to affect detrimentally their own, and possibly their minister's, career prospects. Moreover, when government officials and group representatives meet in private and in confidence, where they are removed from the immediate pressure of public and media opinion, it is easier for them to work out an accommodation of their differences.

Certainly, some pressure groups, especially those of the issue-oriented variety, have had great impact on specific policy decisions by mobilizing public opinion on their side. It is also possible for groups to influence decisions without enjoying much in the way of access based on official recognition and without going to the media or the public. This usually will require the pushing of several pressure points at the same time (i.e., ministers, bureaucrats, and legislators). On some occasions, even institutional groups resort to media campaigns or join with issue groups to pressure the government. These are exceptional situations, however, and the aim of most groups, including those concerned about a single issue of lasting importance, is to use those tactics most likely to achieve their objectives while preserving or enhancing their official recognition.

Representatives of well-recognized pressure groups are more likely to be invited to become members of one or more of the many advisory councils or committees established by the government or by individual departments to advise ministers or bureaucrats on policy. Appointment to such bodies as the Economic Council of Canada, the National Advisory Council on Aging, and the Canadian Advisory Council on the Status of Women gives group members an opportunity to advance the interests of the groups or clientele they were appointed to represent.

Well-recognized groups tend to adhere to the "rules of the game" for government-pressure group relations. These rules are not spelled out in any document; rather, they are composed of understandings based on experience as to what kind of behaviour is expected on both sides. With respect to bureau-cracy-group relations, perhaps the most important of these informal rules is that private exchanges of information and opinion are to be kept confidential. Bureaucrats do not expect that the content of their private discussions with group representatives will be reported publicly or used as a basis for criticism of themselves or their department in other parts of the government. Similarly, pressure groups do not expect that the substance of their submissions to government will be shared with competing pressure groups or, without their consent, with other interested parties in the policy process.

Both common sense and the present nature of the policy process suggest that pressure group representations to government should, where feasible, be framed in terms of the public interest. The requests of pressure groups are more likely to be met if they are attuned to the priorities and plans of the government than if they amount to blatant, self-interested special pleading. For example, in a time of high inflation and high unemployment, officials are likely to look favourably on proposals that may reduce inflation and unemployment. Similarly, proposals that require the expenditure of substantial public funds during a time of severe economic restraint are unlikely to receive a sympathetic hearing. In short, pressure groups can advance their own interests by demonstrating that these interests enhance, or at least complement, the broader public interest. One lobbyist has observed that lobbying

> has evolved into a straightforward process of doing your homework. And the more you know, the more professional your approach to government, the more balanced your presentation, the more willing you are to look beyond your own interests and take the good of the country into account . . . , the more open government becomes to what you have to say—and the more often it solicits direct input when formulating new policy or making changes to current legislation.[22]

One effective and frequently used tactic to demonstrate the public interest—or at least a broad interest—in a group's submission is to engage in cooperative lobbying. This requires that groups create formal or informal alliances with other groups who share their views on a particular policy issue. Cooperative lobbying enables several groups to present a united front to government as an indication of widespread concern. At the same time, the groups profit from this cooperative arrangement by sharing information and contacts. Even competing pressure groups may benefit from consultation with one another, because they can learn the content and strength of their opponents' arguments, even if they cannot work out a common position to present to government. But the lobbyists "will be better received if they have reached an accommodation with the other interested protagonists—be they labour, other industries, consumers, etc."[23]

Effects of Changes in the Policy Process

As noted earlier, pressure groups need to be knowledgeable about the policy process in general, and about the organization and operations of the specific departments and agencies they wish to influence. Groups must be especially vigilant to keep up to date on changes in structures and procedures in both the executive-bureaucratic and the legislative spheres of government.[24] Such changes often signal shifts in the distribution of power within government, and can therefore significantly affect the appropriate targets and tactics of pressure group activity.

Among the most important changes are those that affect the relative power of ministers and bureaucrats, departments and central agencies, and ministers and backbenchers. For example, during the Trudeau years, it was widely argued that the expansion of the Cabinet committee system and the growth in the size and responsibilities of the Prime Minister's Office and the Privy Council Office resulted in a greater concentration of power in the hands of ministers and central agency officials relative to departmental officials. The priorities set by ministers with the advice of central agency officials provided the policy framework within which government decisions were made. It became important, therefore, that pressure groups influence not only the policy and program decisions of individual departments and agencies but also the general priorities of government. They were encouraged to frame their proposals so as to take account of the broader public interest rather than simply appealing to the narrower interests of individual departments. They also had to be sensitive to the central agencies' concern for coordination among the policies and programs of various departments. As a result of these changes, pressure groups often had to seek greater access to ministers and central agency officials. This proved to be a difficult task because ministers were busy and central agency officials tended to minimize contacts with pressure groups on the grounds that central agencies had much less influence on public policy than was generally perceived.

Changes in the budgetary process are especially important for pressure group activity. Groups need to be familiar with the major actors and stages in the budgetary process so that they know when and where to exert influence if their proposals require the expenditure of public funds.

An additional challenge for pressure groups arises from their need to detect actual, as opposed to apparent, shifts in power. For example, it it generally agreed in retrospect that during the 1970s the power of the central agencies vis-à-vis operating departments was somewhat exaggerated and that departments still had considerable expertise enabling them to influence the decisions of ministers and central agency officials.

Legislative changes can also have substantial impact on the targets and tactics of pressure groups. The standing committee system of the federal Parliament gives that body a significant role in the examination of policy proposals and in the scrutiny of government administration. Parliamentary committee meetings provide a formal opportunity for pressure groups to present their views on the content and implementation of policies and programs. As a result, pressure groups now spend more time lobbying individual legislators and making formal submissions to committees. Groups cannot realistically expect these lobbying efforts to result in changes to the general thrust of legislation introduced into Parliament by Cabinet ministers. Pressure groups can, however, educate legislators on their purposes and problems, in the hope of bringing about minor changes in legislation and promoting their interests in party caucus and in parliamentary discussions. If legislative reform results in greater clout for legislative committees in the development and oversight of policy, pressure groups will have a much greater incentive to lobby legislators.

The impact of changes in policy-making structures and procedures will vary according to the type of pressure group. Institutional groups are likely to be able to adapt more quickly and effectively to changes affecting the channels of access and influence in the executive-bureaucratic arena. But legislative reforms that give more control or influence to committees will tend to force institutional groups more into the open so that they will be obliged to compete on a more equal footing with issue-oriented groups, which are more visible and tend to make more use of the media and of public opinion campaigns.

POLITICAL PARTIES AND IDEOLOGIES

Public administration scholars have paid very little attention to interaction between political parties and the bureaucracy. The functions of political parties are usually described as interest aggregation and articulation, the recruitment and training of political leaders, and the education and socialization of the public on political matters; control or influence over the bureaucracy is rarely mentioned. In brief, **political parties** are organizations that seek to get their members elected to political office and to gain and maintain control of the government. They pursue this objective both inside and outside the govern-ment. The internal and external components of a political party are often referred to as the parliamentary and the extra-parliamentary party. Earlier chapters discussed relations between the bureaucracy and the parliamentary party, that is, the parties' elected members in the legislature and in party caucus. The brief treatment of political parties provided here is concerned with the impact on the bureaucracy of the extra-parliamentary parties, that is, the parties' national and provincial executives and offices, and the constituency associa-tions.

Political parties, whether acting through an executive elected by party members or through party meetings and conventions, are generally perceived to be quite remote from the operations of the bureaucracy. The influence of political parties on bureaucratic decisions and recommendations tends to be indirect and often intangible. This influence is, however, greater than is popu-larly perceived.

There are two general types of interaction between political parties and bureaucrats. The first involves the bureaucrat as citizen; the second involves the bureaucrat as government employee.

The most direct contacts between bureaucrats and political parties take the form of participation by public servants in the activities of political parties. As noted in Chapter 13, significant restrictions have been placed on the partisan political activities of public servants so as to preserve political neutrality. Within the bounds of these restrictions, public servants do seek nomination and election to public office and provide various forms of support for individual candidates and political parties. The right of public servants to participate in partisan political activities has gradually been extended over the past twenty years and there are strong pressures for further relaxation of the constraints on such activities. Through the limited opportunities to contribute directly to political parties, bureaucrats can have some direct influence on the policy positions adopted by political parties, but their participation usually has to be very circumspect. The most senior public servants and those in sensitive positions are usually excluded from any kind of partisan political activity. As noted in Chapter 13, however, some senior public servants are political appointees, that is, their appointment by the governing party is based on the fact that they have been involved in partisan politics.

The influence of the extra-parliamentary wing of political parties on the bureaucrat as government employee is indirect and difficult to assess. This influence is exercised in the the form of policies, proposals, and promises that have implications for the bureaucracy as a whole or particular parts of it, and that are made during party meetings, leadership conventions, and election campaigns. Political candidates and political parties, especially if they are in Opposition, frequently join in the bureaucrat bashing that generally falls on such fertile ground among the electorate. Charges of inefficient, ineffective, and unresponsive bureaucratic behaviour are usually accompanied by promises of cutbacks in the number of public servants and in the amount of money they spend. It is understandable that political parties that have been in Opposition for a long time, e.g., the Conservatives in Ottawa, should become antagonistic toward the bureaucracy and view some bureaucrats as being too close to the governing party. This leads to threats that many senior bureaucrats will be turfed out with a change in government, and to unhappiness among many of the party faithful when these threats are not carried out.

Aside from attacks on the general performance of the bureaucracy, political parties and their leaders adopt party platforms which have implications for public servants working in particular policy fields, and which can range from broad promises to reduce expenditure on social policy to specific promises to abolish certain programs or agencies. While experience has shown that once in office political leaders often substantially deviate from their party's platform, policies set by political parties can be very influential, especially through the publicity received in the news media.

There are often significant differences among political parties in the way they view the bureaucracy. For example, in the federal sphere, the argument is often made that the two major political parties are simply two sides of the same coin. Nevertheless, the Progressive Conservative Party tends to be more inclined than the Liberal Party to lament the size and expenditures of government and to propose such solutions as privatization of Crown corporations and deregulation. The New Democratic Party, which favours policies likely to require a larger governmental apparatus and which is affiliated with the trade union movement, generally avoids broad attacks on the bureaucracy and vigorously supports collective bargaining in the public sector.

It is difficult for bureaucrats to separate completely their role as citizen or voter from that of government employee and it is, therefore, reasonable to assume that, on occasion, sympathy for a political party will carry over into decisions or recommendations on the job. Equally problematic is assessing the effect of the ideological commitments of bureaucrats. These commitments do not have to be manifested by a formal or emotional attachment to a particular political party; the bureaucrat who is politically neutral in the partisan sense still has many opportunities to inject personal ideological preferences into the policy-making process. These preferences will obviously affect the bureaucrat's views on major policy issues involving such social values as the redistribution of income and the protection of human rights.

There are well-documented cases in Canada where the ideological preferences of bureaucrats appear to have had a significant influence on policy development. There was substantial and successful resistance by senior bureaucrats to the social values and goals of the CCF government that defeated the Liberals in Saskatchewan in 1944.[25] Another example is provided by Richard Splane, who has described the important influence of the federal bureaucrats, notably social workers in the Department of National Health and Welfare, on the reform of social policy in Canada.[26] Within the framework of support for such reform by successive ministers, the credo of these bureaucrats "consisted almost wholly of a belief that in the interests of all Canadians, and particularly of those least-advantaged, a high priority should be given to the development of a comprehensive nation-wide social security system."[27]

CONCLUDING OBSERVATIONS

The growth in the number and apparent influence of pressure groups has raised concern that they rival, and even threaten to supplant, political parties as the primary channel of communication between citizens and their governments. Unlike political parties, however, pressure groups do not seek, through the electoral process, overall control of government and thereby of policy-making and implementation; rather, pressure groups attempt to affect particular government decisions. Moreover, political parties aggregate the needs and wishes of a vast number of interests in society, whereas pressure groups aggregate the views of a much narrower range of interests. While such large pressure groups as the Canadian Labour Congress and the Canadian Manufacturers' Association are concerned about a wide range of policy issues, at the other extreme there are pressure groups with a very small membership who are concerned about a single issue (e.g., a group of people opposed to a halfway house in their neighborhood).

Collectively, pressure groups have, in fact, diminished to some extent the role of political parties as intermediaries between the citizen and the state. But the increasing attraction of pressure group activity is, in large part, a response to the decline of political parties in the political system for reasons other than the proliferation and influence of pressure groups. Members of political parties who become backbench members of the legislature exercise little power in the political system compared to Cabinet ministers and senior bureaucrats. Further-more, lobbyists are usually better able than individual legislators to deal with technical matters. "If a plant manufacturing railway box cars is threatened with closure and the loss of two thousand jobs, that would be an appropriate area of concern for the local Member of Parliament. [However], if... that same plant had a problem with the Department of Transport on the safety aspects of the design of a journal box, that would be more appropriate for solution by that company's management or the industry's trade association."[28] It is natural that citizens should pursue their self-interest by using whatever channel of communication best enables them to influence public policy.

The bureaucracy is influenced not only by pressure groups and political parties but also, as explained in the next chapter, by the news media and the public.

NOTES

1. For our purposes, these two terms can be used interchangeably. It is notable, however, that often the term interest group is used when the broad range of functions performed by these groups is under consideration, whereas the term pressure group is used when the focus of discussion is primarily on the exercise of political pressure.

2. Professor William Stanbury has observed that "our attitude toward lobbying can be likened to that toward sex. At one and the same time they are perceived as healthy and natural acts, but they are also seen as embarrassing, slightly taboo, even 'dirty' activities to be removed from polite conversation." "Lobbying and Interest Group Representation in the Legislative Process," in W. A. W. Neilson and James C. MacPherson, eds., *The Legislative Process in Canada* (Montreal: Institute for Research on Public Policy, 1978), p. 175.

3. James Gillies, *Where Business Fails* (Montreal: Institute for Research on Public Policy, 1981), pp. 60-76.

4. See A. Paul Pross, "Pressure Groups: Adaptive Instruments of Political Communication," in A. Paul Pross, ed., *Pressure Group Behaviour in Canadian Politics* (Toronto: McGraw-Hill Ryerson, 1975), pp. 10-18.

5. William D. Coleman distinguishes between the "policy advocacy" (lobbying) role of pressure groups and their growing "policy participation" role (their active participation in the formulation or implementation of public policy, or both). "Analyzing the Associative Action of Business: Policy Advocacy and Policy Participation," *Canadian Public Administration* 28 (Fall 1985): 413-33.

6. Robert Presthus and William Monopoli, "Bureaucracy in the United States and Canada: Social, Attitudinal and Behavioral Variables," *International Journal of Comparative Sociology* 18 (March/June 1977): 186.

7. Ibid., 187.

8. Richard Splane, "Social Policy-Making in the Government of Canada: Reflections of a Reformist Bureaucrat," in S. A. Yelaja, ed., *Canadian Social Policy* (Waterloo: Wilfrid Laurier University Press, 1978), p. 215.

9. For a discussion of the impact of federalism on pressure group activity in Canada, see Helen Jones Dawson, "National Pressure Groups and the Federal Government," in Pross, ed., *Pressure Group Behaviour*, pp. 30-35.

10. Jim Bennett of the Canadian Federation of Independent Business, quoted in *The Globe and Mail*, 25 October 1980, p. A11.
11. Hugh Faulkner, "Pressuring the Executive," *Canadian Public Administration* 25 (Summer 1982): 244.
12. John Gray, "Insiders Go to Mandarins before Ministers," *The Globe and Mail*, October 27, 1980, p. 1.
13. Quoted in Clive Baxter, "Familiars in the Corridors of Power," *The Financial Post*, July 12, 1975, p. 6.
14. Andrew Roman, "Comments on Lobbying," in Neilson and MacPherson, eds., *The Legislative Process in Canada*, pp. 214-15.
15. Faulkner, "Pressuring the Executive," p. 241.
16. David Kwavnick, "Pressure Group Demands and the Struggle for Organizational Status: The Case of Organized Labour in Canada," *Canadian Journal of Political Science* 3 (March 1970): 58. (Emphasis added.)
17. Faulkner, "Pressuring the Executive," 246.
18. Ibid., 242.
19. Ibid., 247.
20. David Morley, quoted in Julianne Labreche, "The Quiet Persuaders of Parliament Hill," *Financial Post*, November 29, 1980, p. 34.
21. Alasdair J. McKichan, "Comments on Lobbying," in Neilson and MacPherson, eds., *The Legislative Process in Canada*, p. 223.
22. Quoted in Mary Ann Smythe, "Once -a-Year Meetings, Limited Access and Cronyism are No Longer Enough," *The Globe and Mail*, June 5, 1989, p. B28.
23. McKichan, "Comments on Lobbying," in Neilson and MacPherson, eds., *The Legislative Process in Canada*, p. 220.
24. See Peter Aucoin, "Pressure Groups and Recent Changes in the Policy-Making Process," in Pross, ed., *Pressure Group Behaviour in Canadian Politics*, pp. 174-92.
25. S.M. Lipset, *Agrarian Socialism: The Cooperative Commonwealth Federation in Saskatchewan* (Berkeley: University of California Press, 1959), ch. 12.
26. "Social Policy-Making in the Government of Canada: Reflections of a Reformist Bureaucrat," in S.A. Yelaja, ed., *Canadian Social Policy* (Waterloo: Wilfrid Laurier University Press, 1978), pp. 209-26.
27. Ibid., p. 211.
28. McKichan, "Comments on Lobbying," in Neilson and MacPherson, eds., *The Legislative Process in Canada*, p. 221.

BIBLIOGRAPHY

Aucoin, Peter. "Pressure Groups and Recent Changes in the Policy-Making Process." In A. Paul Pross, ed., *Pressure Group Behaviour in Canadian Politics*. Toronto: McGraw-Hill Ryerson, 1975, pp. 174-191.

Coleman, William D. "Analyzing the Associative Action of Business: Policy Advocacy and Policy Participation." *Canadian Public Administration* 28 (Fall 1985): 413-33.

Dawson, Helen Jones. "Consumers Association of Canada." *Canadian Public Administration* 6 (March 1963): 92-118.

Dawson, Helen Jones. "Interest Group: The Canadian Federation of Agriculture." *Canadian Public Administration* 3 (June 1960): 134-49.

Dawson, Helen Jones. "National Pressure Groups and the Federal Government." In A.

Paul Pross, ed., *Pressure Group Behaviour in Canadian Government.* Toronto: McGraw-Hill Ryerson, 1975, pp. 30-35.

Dawson, Helen Jones. "Relations between Farm Organizations and the Civil Service in Canada and Great Britain." *Canadian Public Administration* 10 (December 1967): 450-70.

Faulkner, J. Hugh. "Pressuring the Executive." *Canadian Public Administration* 25 (Summer 1982): 240-53.

Gillies, James, and Jean Piggott. "Participation in the Legislative Process." *Canadian Public Administration* 25 (Summer 1982): 254-64.

Kwavnik, D. *Organized Labour and Pressure Politics: The Canadian Labour Congress, 1956-1968.* Montreal: McGill-Queen's University Press, 1972.

Lipset, S. M. *Agrarian Socialism: The Cooperative Commonwealth Federation in Saskatchewan.* Berkeley: University of California Press, 1959.

Paltiel, Khayyam Z. "The Changing Environment and Role of Special Interest Groups." *Canadian Public Administration* 25 (Summer 1982): 198-210.

Presthus, R. *Elite Accommodation in Canadian Politics.* Toronto: Macmillan, 1973.

Presthus, R. *Elites in the Policy Process.* Cambridge: Cambridge University Press, 1974.

Pross, A. Paul. *Group Politics and Public Policy.* Toronto: Oxford University Press, 1985.

Pross, A. Paul. "Input Versus Withinput: Pressure Group Demands and Administrative Survival." In A. Paul Pross, ed., *Pressure Group Behaviour in Canadian Politics.* Toronto: McGraw-Hill Ryerson, 1975, pp. 149-171.

Pross, A. Paul, ed. *Pressure Group Behaviour in Canadian Politics.* Toronto: McGraw-Hill Ryerson, 1975.

Pross, A. Paul. "Pressure Groups: Talking Chameleons." In Michael S. Whittington and Glen Williams, eds., *Canadian Politics in the 1980s.* 2nd ed. Toronto: Methuen, 1984, pp. 287-311.

Stanbury, W. T. *Business Interests and the Reform of Canadian Competition Policy.* Toronto: Methuen, 1977.

Stanbury, W. T. "Lobbying and Interest Group Representation in the Legislative Process." In W. A. W. Neilson and J. C. MacPherson, eds., *The Legislative Process in Canada.* Montreal: The Institute for Research on Public Policy, 1978, pp.167-207.

Taylor, Malcom G. "The Role of the Medical Profession in the Formulation and Execution of Public Policy." *Canadian Public Administration* 3 (Fall 1970): 233-55.

Thorburn, Hugh G. *Interest Groups in the Canadian Federal System.* Special Study for the Royal Commission on the Economic Union and Development Prospects for Canada. Vol. 69. Toronto: University of Toronto Press, 1985.

Thorburn, Hugh G., ed. *Party Politics in Canada.* 5th ed. Scarborough, Ont.: Prentice-Hall, 1979.

Winn, C., and J. McMenemy. *Political Parties in Canada.* Toronto: McGraw-Hill, 1976.

CASES

Case Program in Canadian Public Administration (Toronto: Institute of Public Administration of Canada):

Closing the Baldwin Hospital. By Harold B. Wodinsky, Marsha Barnes, and Raisa B. Deber

Screening the Boat People? Case Studies in Health Policies. By Peter Owen, Peggy Purvis, and Raisa B. Deber

All Things to All People: Government and Its Client Groups. By Sharon Bider and Peter McNaughton

La politique du transport urbain dans la région de Québec. By Louise Quenel-Ouellet and Gilles Bouchard

L'Affaire "Caloil." By Michel Paquin

The Grain Dust Case: Public Policy Analysis and Regulation. By G. B. Doern and John Kowlaski

Suncor Inc. By J. R. D'Cruz

We'll Take You On, Mr. Toyota: A Case on Japanese Imports and the Future of the Canadian Automobile Industry. By Sandford F. Borins, John M. Curtis, R. Moroz, and Tony R. Washington

Regulatory Decision: Airlines. By Peter Clancy

Cases developed by the Canadian Centre for Management Development and distributed By the Case Program in Canadian Public Administration:

Negotiating the Native Friendship Centre Program: A Case Study in Federal-Provincial and Interest Group Relations. By G.T. Rayner

In Mark C. Baetz and Donald H. Thain, *Canadian Cases in Government–Business Relations* (Toronto: Methuen, 1985):

#17–The Canadian Federation of Independent Business and the MacEachen Budget

#18–Imperial Oil and the "Bertrand Report"

21

The Public, the Media,
and the Bureaucracy

It is widely acknowledged that "Canada combines the British tradition of a strong executive and centralized leadership with a *relative* freedom from mass pressure and popular constraint."[1] Nevertheless, Canadian politicians pay much lip-service to the importance of public input into the policy-making process, and in a democratic society a persuasive argument can be made for encouraging such input.

The discussion in the previous two chapters of relations between the bureaucracy and non-governmental actors is supplemented in this chapter by an examination of bureaucratic interaction with the public and the media. The nature of this interaction is significantly influenced by the pressures for freedom of information and individual privacy, which are examined in the latter half of this chapter.

THE PUBLIC AND PUBLIC OPINION

In practice, politicians and bureaucrats face formidable obstacles in eliciting and assessing public input. It is difficult even to define the *public* and so to discern the public's *opinion* on political and administrative issues. The term public is variously defined as the total population, the total adult population, the electorate, an aggregation of pressure groups, the most influential organized interest, and so on. A useful distinction is often made between the public as a whole and the multiple *publics* or segments of the public that make up the total population. The public is clearly not a homogeneous entity whose collective view can easily be obtained; rather, it is fragmented into a large variety of organized and unorganized groups and individuals whose opinions on many issues conflict. Public opinion, then, is an aggregate of individual and group opinions.

The public and public servants have strong incentives to interact. Public servants actively seek the public's views as at least a partial basis for making both recommendations and decisions. They not only want to inform the public about government activities and to seek the public's reaction to existing and proposed policies and programs; they also want to stimulate widespread support among the population for their departments' undertakings. For the public, the extent of the bureaucracy's power provides good reason for efforts to enhance public influence on government decision-making. J. A. Corry has observed that "the clamour for citizen involvement" arises, in part, from the suspicion among citizens "that decisions that impinge solely on them are actually being made, not by their representatives in the legislatures or by ministers directly responsible to their representatives," but rather "on high by persons nameless and faceless to them."[2] Certainly, members of the public, in their capacity as voters, are far removed from the most important official decision-makers—Cabinet ministers and senior bureaucrats.

The traditional mechanisms for interaction between government and society, namely the electoral system, political parties, legislators, pressure groups, and the mass media, permit the public to exercise little direct influence over politicians and bureaucrats. The electorate obviously constitutes an extremely large and important segment of the public, but election results are a very inexact measure of public attitudes on any specific public policy issue. Similarly, political parties in Canada reflect a wide range of opinion on policy issues. Neither the electoral system nor political parties are an effective means by which the public can influence bureaucratic decisions. Furthermore, legislators have insufficient capacity and inclination to hold ministers responsible for their administration of departments and agencies. Yet bureaucrats, to whom ministers delegate substantial powers, are even further removed from legislative control and influence. Thus, the public, acting through its elected representatives, has relatively little influence over the bureaucracy.

Pressure groups are another extremely important segment of the public, but despite their professed concern for the broad public interest, their primary concern is usually their self-interest. Moreover, these groups are often in conflict with one another. Even so-called public interest groups (e.g., the Consumers' Association of Canada) can legitimately claim to speak for only a portion of the public. The mass media provide other channels of communication between the public and the bureaucracy by reflecting and, to some extent, shaping public opinion. But, like pressure groups, various media organizations disagree on public policy issues and therefore send conflicting signals to government officials as to the content of public opinion.

PUBLIC PARTICIPATION

During the 1960s, there was an upsurge of public concern that these traditional mechanisms provided inadequate opportunities for public input into the policy process. The institutions and processes of representative democracy were complemented by a vigorous emphasis on what was popularly described in Canada and elsewhere as participatory democracy. During the 1968 federal election campaign, Pierre Elliott Trudeau frequently used this term to sum up his commitment "to make government more accessible to people, to give citizens a sense of full participation in the affairs of government, and full control over their representatives."[3] To achieve these ends, demands were made both for improvements in the representative system (i.e., public input through popularly elected representatives and political parties) and for instruments to permit more *direct* public participation in the policy process (e.g., task forces and advisory bodies).

Public participation is a broader concept than citizen participation, although the two terms are often used interchangeably. **Public participation** refers to a broad range of direct and indirect forms of participation, including citizen participation. **Citizen participation** connotes direct participation of individual citizens and citizen' groups in government decision-making. It is notable that the purpose of citizen participation is more to stimulate decision-makers to take account of a wider range of considerations at an earlier stage in the policy process than to enable citizens to scrutinize the administration of government programs.

Sherry Arnstein has provided a helpful means of conceptualizing the gradations of citizen participation by identifying eight rungs on "a ladder to citizen participation."[4] The ascending rungs on the ladder depict a progression of citizen involvement from forms of "non-participation" to participation involving the actual exercise of citizen power. The eight rungs make up three major levels. The first and lowest level is labelled *non-participation* and includes:

1. manipulation by the power structure; and
2. therapy for the organization.

The second level is described as *token participation* and includes:

3. communication with the groups;
4. consultation with the groups; and
5. placation of the groups.

The third and highest level, that of *real citizen power*, contains the rungs of:

6. partnership;
7. delegated power; and
8. citizen control.

We shall see that much of what passes for citizen participation in Canada is, in Arnstein's terms, a form of tokenism.

Virtues and Limitations of Public Participation

Advocates of increased public participation in general and citizen participation in particular contend that participation benefits both members of the public and government officials. It is argued that the overriding benefit to the public is greater *responsiveness* of government decisions, programs, and services to the public's needs and desires. Participation facilitates a valuable exchange of information between the government and citizens who are directly—and often acutely—affected by government activities. Politicians and public servants thereby become more knowledgeable about the impact of their decisions, especially on individuals and groups whose views and concerns might otherwise be overlooked. Easier and more equal access to official decision-makers stimulates participation by individual citizens and by such groups as the poor and aboriginal peoples; it thereby helps to reduce the influence of well-organized and well-connected interests that usually enjoy good access to government officials.

In addition, individual participants can receive substantial educational and social returns from participation. Exposure to new ideas and to people with different values develops greater tolerance and sensitivity toward the views of others. Moreover, working with other people for common objectives promotes a sense of belonging and can enhance one's self-image. It is notable that these benefits can accrue to participants even when the government's commitment to meaningful participation is not genuine.

For government officials, public participation not only helps to ensure that their decisions will be more responsive to public wants and needs; it also enhances the legitimacy of these decisions in the eyes of those who have made a direct or indirect input into the policy process. Participating individuals and groups are more likely to accept decisions when they see—or perceive—that their views have been heard and taken into account. The argument is frequently made that public participation enhances the *effectiveness* as well as the responsiveness of public decisions by sensitizing government officials to the likely consequences of their decisions.

Critics of increased participation express, with varying degrees of intensity, one or more of the following concerns. Improving opportunities for indirect public input into the policy process through legislatures and political parties is praiseworthy, but Canadians in general are not inclined to participate actively and directly in the policy process. Thus, the creation or reform of institutions and procedures to promote direct citizen interaction with government officials is not worth the effort. Moreover, the benefits that may result from the heightened responsiveness of public officials and especially of bureaucrats, who make the bulk of government decisions, have offsetting disadvantages. Consultation with citizens, citizens' groups, and advisory bodies can be extremely time-consuming and, therefore, an inefficient use of the time and energy of public officials. Such consultation can also lead to less efficient and effective government by causing delays in the making of decisions and the delivery of programs. Efficiency and effectiveness can be further reduced if "expert" public servants are obliged to take undue account of the views of "amateur" citizens. Alan Altshuler has asserted that "groups of laymen—and especially groups of poorly educated laymen with little or no administrative experience—have particular handicaps as decision-makers. They have little time to devote to consideration of the issues; their concerns are selfish and immediate; they lack technical competence."[5]

Another concern about the development of participative mechanisms is that they may create a mere facade of increased involvement by traditionally underrepresented groups. For example, the poor and the uneducated may participate more actively but, on balance, enjoy no greater influence than they had before. Organized interests that are already influential often use participative mechanisms to obtain even better access to government officials and thereby to exercise even greater influence on government decisions—sometimes at the expense of less well-organized but more deserving citizens. Public servants can also use citizen participation to their advantage. They can blur the lines of accountability by delegating decision-making powers to citizens' groups or by sharing these powers. They can encourage participation so as to co-opt or pacify citizens who might otherwise publicly criticize government policies and programs. Finally, public servants can build support for—or reduce opposition to—their activities by involving affected interests in the decision-making process.

Mechanisms for Public Participation

Despite these concerns, efforts to facilitate public participation have, since the 1960s, been undertaken by all levels of government in Canada.

Both political parties and pressure groups have been affected by the trend toward greater public participation. The inner workings of Canada's major political parties have been democratized to allow increased participation by their members in shaping the parties' stance on policy issues. New pressure groups have sprung up to exert influence on behalf of previously unrepresented or underrepresented segments of the population. Government officials have encouraged the participation of groups representing such interests as consumers, environmentalists, and the poor by assisting them with public funds. Citizens groups' (e.g., residents' and ratepayers' associations) concerned with such issues as housing, zoning, and transportation have been especially active in the sphere of local government.

The parliamentary system has been reformed to provide more opportunities for testimony on policy issues by members of the public, including individual citizens, and more appearances by public servants before legislative committees to explain government policies and programs. Parliamentary committees have travelled to various parts of the country to consult individuals and groups on policy questions, and effective use has recently been made of parliamentary task forces, now described as special committees. These are composed of backbench members of all political parties who, acting largely on a non-partisan basis, consult members of the public and make recommendations to government on such policy matters as regulatory reform, North-South relations, and federal-provincial fiscal arrangements.

Legislative committees have also enhanced public participation by holding hearings to examine the *coloured papers*,[6] especially white papers and green papers, issued by government. The publication of these papers provides the public with information about existing and proposed policies (e.g., in the areas of tax reform, immigration, public access to information) as well as an invitation to comment on these policies. The extent and impact of public participation resulting from the issuing of these papers vary greatly, depending on both citizen and legislative interest in the subject matter. The number of submissions from the public can be impressive. For example, the House of Commons committee examining the White Paper on Tax Reform (1969) received 524 briefs and 1,093 letters and other submissions from groups and individuals.[7] However, the federal government has not yet developed systematic mechanisms to provide for parliamentary and public participation in the consideration of coloured papers.

Even Royal commissions—a traditional source of policy advice to the executive—responded to the public participation movement by seeking the public's views more frequently and systematically (e.g., the federal Royal Commission on Bilingualism and Biculturalism, the Ontario Royal Commission on Electric Power Planning). But task forces of various kinds have been used much more often than Royal commissions to obtain information and ideas from the public and to assess public opinion (e.g., the 1966 Task Force on Housing, the 1977 Task Force on National Unity, and the many departmental task forces on a broad range of topics).

Both Royal commissions and task forces use public opinion surveys (often called social surveys) to assess the public's views on current and proposed government activities. The extensive use of such surveys by Cabinets, political parties, and individual politicians is well known. The public is less knowledgeable, however, about the existence and the results of the many public opinion surveys, of varying degrees of sophistication and reliability, that are conducted by or for government departments. The results of these surveys are not routinely disclosed to the public, but many are now available under the Access to Information Act. In general, the data from social surveys are a useful input for the government's assessment of public opinion. An advantage of these surveys is that they can provide information on the needs and desires of all segments of the public, including those who are disadvantaged, unorganized, or uneducated. A survey carried out for the 1969 Task Force on Government Information showed that a very large number of Canadians could not participate effectively because they knew so little about government and the services it provides.[8]

Another means by which public participation can be pursued is through the use of advisory bodies to government. The creation of advisory boards and councils is in keeping with the desire for more *direct* citizen participation in government decision-making. Unlike most of the mechanisms discussed above, advisory bodies can be used for direct interaction between citizens and public officials, especially bureaucrats. A large number of advisory bodies have been established at all levels of Canadian government to provide advice to politicians and bureaucrats (e.g., the Economic Council of Canada advises the federal Cabinet; various provincial councils on the status of women, the elderly, the handicapped, etc., advise the relevant government departments). Many advisory bodies containing representatives of citizens' groups have been established as non-governmental organizations supported by public funds.[9] It is very difficult to find genuine cases of an actual delegation of authority over decision-making, program administration, and/or the expenditure of public funds to groups of citizens at the community level.

A more controversial response to the public participation movement has been the provision of government funding for groups that otherwise would be unable to afford to participate effectively in the policy process. Some observers of the political scene find it strange that a government would provide funds for groups that are likely to use those funds to make life more difficult for the government. There is no doubt, however, that such funding widens the range of groups that are able to participate effectively in government decision-making, and increases the range of viewpoints to which public officials are exposed. In the federal sphere of government, for example, consumers' and native peoples' groups have been the main beneficiaries of this kind of government funding. It is no easy task for government to decide which groups should be funded, how much money they should receive, and which departments or agencies should provide it. Despite the problems of administering government funding to such groups, the practice seems likely to expand.

Despite these advances in the level and means of public participation since the late 1960s, there remains a gap between promise and performance. Perceptions of the size of this gap vary according to individual views about the appropriate extent of participation. Few instances of public participation in Canada have been found above the "tokenism" rungs of Arnstein's ladder of citizen participation. Kenneth Bryden contends that public participation in Canada has been largely of an "instrumental" rather than a "consummative" nature. He notes that "participation as instrumental action is based on the idea of *taking part* in political life in order to protect and advance one's individual interests in a competitive situation." However, consummative participation refers to participation as an end in itself and "involves *sharing* in a community by cooperating for a common good, thereby fostering the participant's development and self-realization."[10]   To enhance public participation in general, Bryden recommends the establishment of an information network, devolution of authority in large organizations, and direct participation in decision-making in the neighbourhood and in the workplace.[11]

The fundamental mechanism for public participation in the Canadian political system is the process of nominating and electing public officials. But the mechanisms discussed above have provided a vital complementary means of involving members of the public in the policy process. In particular, they have stimulated a greater sense of responsiveness to the public among politicians and bureaucrats. Elected officials, notably Cabinet ministers, have neither the time nor the expertise to handle all the representations made by members of the public. Certainly, in the municipal sphere, the result of efforts to facilitate citizen participation has largely been to increase citizen interaction with public employees rather than with councillors. Thus, participation has affected bureaucrats not only indirectly through their political superiors but also directly, through increased interaction with individual citizens and citizens' groups.

THE MEDIA

Like pressure groups, the media of mass communication, commonly known as the mass media or the news media, act as intermediaries between the government and the public. The term mass media includes radio, television, newspapers, and magazines. Unlike pressure groups, the mass media transmit much information for the sake of transmitting information rather than for the purpose of influencing public policy. Moreover, compared to pressure groups, which tend to represent well-defined interests to carefully identified officials, the media's audience, both within government and among the public, tends to be broader and more diffuse.

The Media and the Government

A key function of the media is to provide information to the public. Similarly, a major responsibility of government in a democratic society is to inform the public about the institutions and processes of government, and about the programs and services offered by departments and agencies. In varying degrees, all government departments generate news and information. For some departments, like Statistics Canada, performing the service of gathering and disseminating information to the public is their main function. Other departments provide information of importance to the public (e.g., the Department of Energy, Mines and Resources on energy conservation), or to more specialized groups (e.g., the Department of National Health and Welfare on income security for the elderly, and several other departments on scientific and technological advances). In addition, as a basis for policy development and implementation, government officials require information on the needs and demands of the citizens they serve. In contrast to their relations with many pressure groups, government officials do not usually look to, or depend on, the media for information of a technical nature; rather, they are interested in media coverage of a political or policy nature bearing on the activities of other governments or the attitudes of the general public—or particular sections of the public.

In the sphere of government-media interaction, the major participants on the government side are ministers, Members of Parliament, and public servants, especially senior public servants and information officers in government departments and agencies. On the media side, the primary participants are journalists, editorial executives, and the owners of print and broadcast organizations. The media and the government pursue different objectives through their provision of information. In very general terms, government officials want to get their message to the public without stirring up the political waters. In some cases, this is useful to the media because it provides them with a ready source of up-to-date news at minimal cost; however, the media's objective of attracting a large audience can often be best achieved by rocking the boat. It is notable that the media are by no means a homogeneous entity; thus, the government can occasionally achieve its objectives in communicating with the public by taking advantage of competition and conflict between various media organizations.

The media play a critical role as two-way channels of communication between the governors and the governed. Newspapers, magazines, television, and radio carry information from the public to politicians and bureaucrats and from these officials to the public. The media not only serve as "filters" for this information; they aim also to influence the attitudes and behaviour of both government officials and members of the public. Thus, the media both reflect and influence public opinion.

Governments cannot and do not rely solely on the media to communicate with the public. Much information is exchanged through correspondence and telephone calls between officials and citizens and through government publications and direct mailings aimed at the general public or particular groups. But government information appears to be transmitted most effectively through the media. Indeed, a survey for the federal Task Force on Government Information found that Canadians learn about government programs primarily through the mass media. In order of priority, the reported sources of federal information were "television, newspapers and magazines, radio, friends and relatives, government publications, public servants and Members of Parliament, and associations and clubs."[12] It is noteworthy that a substantial portion of government information that is transmitted through the media takes the form of advertising paid for by public funds. This aspect of the relationship between government and the media could potentially compromise the integrity of the media.

A broad, and admittedly oversimplified, distinction can be made between two categories of government-media interaction. The first category involves the exchange of information, largely of a factual nature, on the content and administration of government programs. The main actors in this first category are public servants at various levels of the administrative hierarchy. The second category involves an exchange of news and views, primarily on political and policy issues. The most important actors in this second category are politicians and senior public servants.

The Media and Public Servants

Most government contacts with the media are handled by public servants who strive to utilize the media to support their political superiors, to publicize their department's activities, to obtain favourable comment on these activities, and to seek public reaction to proposed policies and programs (sometimes in the form of "trial balloons"). Public servants also attempt to keep secret from the media any information that would affect adversely their departments or themselves; and if damaging information is uncovered by the media, public servants usually work to minimize its negative impact. Moreover, the amount and type of information provided by public servants is significantly affected by rules and conventions on the confidentiality of government documents and on the bounds of permissible public comment. Public servants must be especially careful not to stray too far over the nebulous line between politics and administration by performing the minister's role of defending or speculating upon public policy.

The media do not perceive their primary function vis-à-vis government as publicizing government activities in a manner designed to please public officials. The media do transmit a great deal of factual material from government to the public, but they serve several other functions in their interactions with government. The media see themselves more as watchdogs of the public interest than as purveyors of government information. They help to set the public agenda by selecting from the enormous volume of available information those items to which they will give special prominence or continuing attention. They contribute to the development of public policy by subjecting events and personalities to critical analysis through such means as newspaper editorials and television documentaries. They stimulate reform in government by exposing mismanagement, corruption, and illegality. And they make judgments as to what government-provided information is publicity that merits dissemination and what appears to be propaganda to be disregarded.

Our earlier discussion of relations between politicians and bureaucrats suggested that media coverage of bureaucratic activities and personalities has somewhat diminished the anonymity of public servants. In addition to assessing the regular activities of public servants, the media have a strong incentive to break through the barriers of government secrecy to get a controversial, dramatic, or exciting story that may involve public servants. The media are, however, subject to such legal restraints on their activities as the Official Secrets Act, the laws of libel, and requirements regarding the revealing of sources of information. Moreover, in Canada, there is not much of a tradition or practice of investigative journalism, especially of the type whereby "crusading" journalists expose and publicize government scandals or mismanagement.

Given the intermediary role of the media between the government and the public, government officials are well-advised to develop and preserve cordial relations with both print and electronic media. They can accomplish this, in part, by providing material in an appropriate form and at the proper time. Similarly, media representatives can gain the trust and confidence of public officials by "responsible" use of government information. The development of informal relationships based on friendship and long association are also mutually beneficial to the exchange of information. Where political and policy issues are involved, the desire of politicians and bureaucrats to "tell the department's story" may well conflict with the media's desire to tell the whole story. Certain "friendly" journalists may receive preferential treatment in the form of advance notice of upcoming developments, access to public officials, or confidential information. They must be careful, however, that they are not thereby captured and manipulated by public servants.

Much of the impact of the media on public servants is, of course, indirect. Although, as noted earlier, the news media do on occasion focus on the activities of individual public servants, bureaucratic anonymity is still basically intact. Public servants can be greatly affected, however, by news stories dealing in a critical or erroneous way with their departments or with policies or programs for which they have some responsibility. Care should be taken not to exaggerate the overall influence of the media on the bureaucracy; but the potential influence of the media and its actual influence in particular circumstances help to constrain the exercise of bureaucratic power.

There are few research studies on which to base an assessment of the media's impact on the attitudes and decisions of public servants. The nature and importance of interaction with the media depend on such factors as the public servants' responsibilities, their level in the hierarchy, and their department.

Information officers seek to enhance the reputation of their departments through such public relations efforts as providing briefings for journalists and churning out press releases. Senior public servants are anxious to ensure that media coverage of departmental activities does not embarrass their political superiors. Thus, senior bureaucrats who brief ministers for questions in the legislature or from the media monitor news stories so as to anticipate questions that might be asked. For example, news stories in *The Globe and Mail, The Financial Post,* and *Le Devoir* are often the basis for questions to ministers in the House of Commons.

FREEDOM OF INFORMATION AND INDIVIDUAL PRIVACY[13]

Freedom of Information

It is widely argued that open access to government information enables the public and the media to make a more informed contribution to government decision-making. This issue of access to information is discussed separately not only because of its importance for relations between the bureaucracy and both the public and the media, but also because of its implications for ministerial responsibility and political neutrality.

The government of Canada has traditionally operated on the principle that all government information is secret unless the government decides to release it. Many proponents of freedom of information legislation contend that this principle should be reversed so that all government information will be released unless the government can make a good case for keeping it secret. Under this latter approach, the burden on the public of justifying requests for the disclosure of information is lifted and the burden of justifying non-disclosure of information is imposed on the government, specifically on ministers and public servants. The federal **Access to Information Act** (the ATI Act)[14] permits the government to keep a great deal of information confidential, but, in general, the Act follows the second approach. Its stated purpose is

> to provide a right of access to information in records under the control of a government in accordance with the principles that government information should be available to the public, that necessary exceptions to the right of access should be limited and specific and that decisions on the disclosure of government information should be reviewed independently of government.[15]

Ministerial Responsibility and Political Neutrality

Discussion of freedom of information legislation in both the federal and provincial spheres of government has centred on the issue of whether such legislation would unduly encroach on ministerial responsibility. Somewhat less concern has focussed on the possible reduction in the political neutrality and anonymity of public servants.

It is easy to understand why ministers and senior public servants do not share the enthusiasm of people outside government for freedom of information legislation and for access to material on the decision-making process in particular. The release of information revealing ministerial and public service contributions to, and debates over, policy has important consequences for both ministerial responsibility and political neutrality. Documents that expose disagreement among ministers or between ministers and public servants could be exploited by the government's opponents to the political disadvantage of the ministers. It is natural that ministers should not want to answer to the legislature and the public for the content of documents that are likely to be controversial and that could be kept secret. Ministers do not deliberately seek trouble.

Similarly, senior public servants generally resist the expansion of public access to official documents that disclose their personal views and values on policy issues. If public servants are drawn into public debate over their contributions to policy development, their anonymity will decline. Moreover, to the extent that the public servants' written advice is at odds with their minister's decision, both ministers and public servants may be publicly embarrassed. Ministers may strive to avoid such situations by surrounding themselves with political appointees or with "yes-men." This will threaten both the frankness and the completeness of departmental advice and also undermine the security of tenure associated with a career in the public service.

The impact of more open government on the doctrines of ministerial responsibility and political neutrality should not, however, be exaggerated. The evolution of these doctrines that has already occurred has been explained in Chapters 13 and 17. The implementation of freedom of information legislation requires further evolution of these doctrines, but it does not require their drastic alteration or abandonment. The importance of the doctrine of ministerial responsibility in particular will be evident in the following sections on exemptions and the review process. Exemptions refer to classes of information that may, or must be, kept secret; the review process refers to mechanisms for reconsidering and/or overruling decisions by ministers or public servants not to disclose information.

Exemptions

The subjects of exemptions and review mechanisms are closely related. Judgments on the number and nature of exemptions considered desirable depend to a large extent on the method adopted to review complaints about non-disclosure. If ministers have the final authority to determine whether a particular document falls into an exempted category, they will be inclined to approve legislation providing for a small number of specific exemptions. But if a person or body independent of ministers makes the final determination on exemptions, ministers will likely favour legislation that contains a large number of specific exemptions or a smaller number of very broad exemptions. Thus, decisions on the exemptions to be included in the legislation are usually taken in relation to the review mechanisms that will be adopted.

There is much agreement from one government to another that certain types of information should be kept secret, such as documents relating to national defence and security, personal information on individual citizens, financial or commercial information collected by government on a confidential basis, and records of criminal investigations. There is, however, considerable variation among governments in the comprehensiveness of the exclusions within the different classes of information.

In Canada, the exemptions (and exclusions) set out in the ATI Act are substantial. The Act provides, subject to a number of exemptions, that a Canadian citizen, a permanent resident, or a Canadian corporation "has a right to and shall, on request, be given access to any record under the control of a government institution" (section 4). However, records containing information obtained in confidence from a foreign government, an international organization or a provincial, municipal, or regional government in Canada are exempted from disclosure unless the government or the organization in question agrees to release or permit the release of the records (section 13).

The confidentiality of records may be retained if they "could reasonably be expected to be injurious to the conduct... of federal-provincial affairs, including information (a) on federal-provincial consultations or deliberations; or information (b) on strategy or tactics" of the Canadian government bearing on the conduct of federal-provincial affairs (section 14).

Very broad exemption is also provided for information that, if disclosed, "could reasonably be expected to be injurious to the conduct of international affairs, the defence of Canada or any state allied or associated with Canada or the detection, prevention or suppression of subversive or hostile activities" (section 15).

In addition, records may be exempted from disclosure if they contain information relating to law enforcement and investigation (section 16), or if their release might threaten the safety of individuals (section 17) or affect adversely the financial interests of Canada (section 18). Records are also exempted if they contain personal information (section 19) or if they contain trade secrets, financial, commercial, scientific, or technical information, which, if disclosed, could harm a third party (that is, firms and corporations) (section 20).

Some exemptions and some specific exclusions in the Act reflect the concern of ministers and public servants about the preservation of ministerial responsibility and public service anonymity. *Exemptions* include advice developed by or for a government institution or Cabinet minister; an account of consultations involving public servants and a Cabinet minister (or a Cabinet minister's staff); plans developed for negotiations conducted by the government; and plans bearing on personnel management or the administration of a government institution that have not yet been put into operation (section 21). *Exclusions* from disclosure relate to "confidences of the Queen's Privy Council for Canada" (i.e., the Cabinet). The excluded documents include Cabinet memoranda; discussion papers prepared for Cabinet; Cabinet agendas or records of Cabinet deliberations or decisions; records relating to consultation among ministers in respect to government decisions and policies; records used to brief ministers on these decisions and policies; and draft legislation (section

69). These exclusions do not apply to "confidences" more than twenty years old; discussion papers relating to decisions that have been made public; and all other discussion papers more that four years old (section 69).

The length and breadth of the exemptions and exclusions in the Act have been severely criticized by many segments of the Canadian public. Thus, the review mechanism established to make the final decision on the exemptions is a critically important component of the ATI Act. Before examining the review process, however, it is an enlightening experience to play the party game called "Airplane." This game was utilized by Canada's first Information Commissioner to explain to students that, although in the abstract they may strongly favour unlimited access to government information, they may in practice see some virtue in the Act's exemptions. The scenario for the game is as follows:

> An airplane skidded off the runway; the passengers were unhurt save for one who died, apparently from a heart attack. For some unknown reason the passengers were left incommunicado at the airport under police protection.

> Students are assigned to play the following roles: an arms dealer who holds a new patent on a weapon sought by many governments; a diplomat known to be engaged in high level peace negotiations; an aging actress and her lover, a well-known sex symbol; an RCMP officer who is escorting a prisoner-informer being taken to protective custody in another penitentiary; a student who was supposed to be at class; a Minister of Transport; a Solicitor General; a commissioner of the RCMP; the Information Commissioner; and a representative of the estate of the dead person. Finally, someone plays the journalist who is assigned to the story and must obtain the passenger list under the Access to Information Act.[16]

The Information Commissioner noted that "it is amazing how quickly [students] become protective of their characters" and that "it soon becomes clear that freedom of information invariably involves disclosure of information, collected by someone else, affecting yet another person's interests."[17] This game demonstrates well the need to balance the public's right to know with the individual's right to privacy. In addition to the provisions in the ATI Act exempting personal information from disclosure, individual privacy is protected by the Privacy Act discussed later in this chapter.

The Review Process

Initially, the task of applying the exemption provisions to requests for access to government documents is performed by public servants. However, instances arise where citizens wish to appeal to a higher authority against a public servant's decision to deny access to all or part of certain documents. Thus, freedom of information legislation must provide a review process that specifies the person or persons with authority to review the decisions of public servants.

Experience in Canada suggests that ministers and public servants tend to favour a review process in which ministers have ultimate authority to decide whether a particular document will be released. However, people outside government tend to prefer a review mechanism that allows ministerial decisions on access to be overruled. The system adopted for the ATI Act is a *two-tier* review mechanism involving an Information Commissioner *and* judicial review. Under the Act, the Information Commissioner is authorized to receive and investigate complaints when access to a record is refused; when unreasonable fees are imposed for searching for or producing a record; where a public official unreasonably extends the time limit for producing a record; when a record is not provided in the official language requested; and "in respect of any other matter relating to requesting or obtaining access to records" under the Act. The commissioner may also initiate a complaint on "reasonable grounds." After investigating a complaint, the commissioner recommends whether or not a record should be released; he or she cannot require that a record be disclosed. Following the commissioner's investigation, the complainant, or the commissioner with the complainant's consent, may apply to the Federal Court for review of any refusal to disclose a record. The court may then order the head of a government institution to disclose—or not to disclose—all or part of a record.

Implementation of the Access to Information Act

People seeking information under the Act must write to the appropriate department and must identify as precisely as possible the information they require. Assistance in this regard is available in the *Access Register*, which contains a description of the records held by each department. Copies of the register and of access request forms can be obtained in public libraries and government information offices in major population centres, as well as in about two thousand postal stations in rural areas. Each department has an access coordinator to assist applicants to identify the records required. The department has thirty days either to produce the information requested or to provide reasons why a request has been denied. If the request is for a large number of records or is complicated, the department can extend the time limit but must inform the applicant of the situation. The role of the Information Commissioner and the Federal Court in cases where access to information is denied was described earlier. An application fee of five dollars must accompany each request for information. Applicants must also pay for any time in excess of five hours spent in processing a request and for copying and computer-processing time.

During the 1988-1989 fiscal year, government institutions received 8,853 requests for information, an increase from 2,229 five years earlier. Ten institutions received 75 percent of the requests. The number of requests made to these institutions ranged from 2,381 for the Department of Supply and Services and 1,625 for Revenue Canada (Taxation) down to 199 for the RCMP and 176 for the Correctional Service. Of these requests, 51.8 percent came from business, 27.3 percent from individuals, and 6.9 percent from the media. In the cases where applicants received none or only part of the information they requested, by far the most frequent reasons for denying access were that the records contained third-party information, personal information, or information about government operations.[18]

During the same fiscal year, the Office of the Information Commissioner received 2,811 complaints.[19] More than half of the 642 complaints investigated during the year arose from a refusal to disclose all or some of the information requested. The commissioner found that about a third of these complaints were well-founded and resulted in remedial action by the government institution involved.[20] Over the six-year period from 1983 to 1989, 196 applications for review were lodged with the Federal Court; thirty-five of these were initiated by the commissioner herself.[21]

A widely held view among proponents of freedom of information legislation is that it will gradually change the attitude of ministers and public servants toward public access to official information. It has been suggested also that government officials will become more supportive of open government when they realize that it has more benefits and fewer disadvantages than they antici-pated. However, after the first seven years of experience with the federal Access to Information Act, the federal commissioner lamented both political and bureaucratic resistance to freedom of information and suggested that "the tendency to withhold government information should give way to attitudes favouring its disclosure."[22]

The Leaking of Confidential Information

The exemption or exclusion from disclosure of certain classes of information provides both opportunity and motivation for the unauthorized disclosure (commonly called "leaking") of confidential information. Such disclosure normally involves leaks of government documents, often enclosed in plain brown envelopes, to the media or to Opposition members of the legislature. Beginning in the early 1970s, there has been a seemingly unprecedented number of leaks, especially from the federal government. Since 1983, these leaks have, of course, been largely confined to material that remains confidential under the Access to Information Act. Confidential information is sometimes leaked by public servants who believe that they are acting in the public interest, but information is also leaked for reasons unrelated to a search for the public interest (e.g., vindictiveness, partisan politics). Moreover, some of this informa-tion is leaked not by bureaucrats but by Cabinet ministers trying to float trial balloons on policy issues.

The unauthorized disclosure of confidential information is constrained by a variety of statutes and regulations. The most severe instrument is the Official Secrets Act, which is intended to combat espionage by providing up to fourteen years in prison for persons who disclose secret information to foreign powers. Offences under this Act are rare and its penalties are too harsh for comparatively minor offences in the sphere of confidentiality. However, employees are required to take an oath of office and secrecy by which they swear (or affirm) that they will not, without proper authorization, make known any confidential matter that comes to their knowledge. In situations where the duties of a position involve the handling of classified material or access to it, a security clearance may be required for all candidates seeking that position.

Provincial public servants are also subject to the Official Secrets Act and are required to take an oath of office and secrecy. Moreover, certain departments in both orders of government are specifically required by statute to preserve the confidentiality of certain information. For example, provincial taxing and assessment statutes generally provide penalties for the disclosure of confidential information to people not legally entitled to receive it.

In practice, it is very difficult to pinpoint and discipline public servants who have surreptitiously disclosed confidential information and the practice is, therefore, an effective and usually risk-free method by which bureaucrats can oppose government policy or expose what they believe to be government abuse, negligence, or corruption. The penalty for those who are caught is uncertain, but it can be severe. For example in 1985, a senior employee of the federal Department of Indian Affairs and Northern Development, who allegedly leaked a confidential document describing the Conservative government's plans to cut costs on Indian programs, was dismissed and charged with breach of trust under the Criminal Code—an offence that carries a maximum sentence of five years imprisonment. The criminal charge was subsequently withdrawn, but the dismissal was not.[23]

Individual Privacy

Concern for individual privacy is the other side of the coin from concern about access to information. Indeed, the Privacy Act[24] and the Access to Information Act came into effect on the same day, July 1, 1983. The **Privacy Act** replaces, and expands on, the protection to individual privacy previously provided in the Canadian Human Rights Act. Individual privacy is protected by restricting access to personal information held by the federal government on Canadian citizens and permanent residents. The Act contains principles of fair information practices that direct government institutions to limit their collection of information to what is needed to do their work; if possible, to gather the information directly from the individuals concerned; to inform the individuals what use is to be made of the information; and to "take all reasonable steps" to ensure accuracy and completeness of the information. In addition, individuals have the right to see all information that the government has on them in its roughly 2,200 federal personal information banks. Copies of the Personal Information Index, which describes the activities of each department, what kind of information it collects, and whom to contact for access, are available in public libraries and post offices across Canada.

A Privacy Commissioner is appointed under the Act to initiate complaints on his or her own initiative and to investigate complaints from individuals who believe that their privacy rights have been denied. Grounds for complaint include denial of some or all of the information requested, denial of the right to correct or annotate some of the information on one's file, and use of information that contravenes the Act. The first commissioner described himself as both "a specialized ombudsman for privacy, the single voice in the federal government with a mandate to speak on behalf of privacy rights," and an auditor responsible for determining "whether personal information is collected, held by, and disposed of by federal government institutions" according to the Act.[25]

During the first seven years of the Act, government agencies received 300,000 applications regarding access to personal information.[26] During the 1988-1989 fiscal year alone, 59,631 requests were received. In 64.1 percent of these cases, all the information requested was disclosed, and in another 21.6 percent some of the information was disclosed. In the small number of cases (0.4 percent) where the information was exempted from disclosure, the major reason was that the information requested was about another individual. During the same twelve-month period, the Office of the Privacy Commissioner completed work on 1,028 complaints regarding the denial of privacy rights; 434 of the complaints were discovered to be well-founded.[27]

The commissioner's annual report makes fascinating reading. He noted in 1990 that the most frequently received question relates to when a social insurance number must be given, but other contacts include media requests for comment on matters with potential privacy implications; citizens' concerns about telephone gadgetry showing a caller's telephone number on a screen; an Auditor General's proposal for an anonymous fraud hotline; and a municipal council's proposal to circulate detailed profiles of released offenders. The Privacy Commissioner noted also that "privacy has moved from a peripheral social issue . . . into the mainstream of public consciousness."[28] He asked:

> What chance does privacy have when satellites can conduct surveillance from more than 300 kilometres in the sky? Audio eavesdropping no longer demands physical access to a building in order to plant listening devices. And, of course, most of us carry in our wallets or purses the key to vast amounts of highly sensitive personal information. Our ubiquitous bank and credit cards leave a trail of where we travel, eat, shop and sleep—perhaps by matching records—even with whom! George Orwell could not have imagined the new possibilities of Big Brother.[29]

Information and Privacy Legislation in the Provinces

Six provincial governments (Manitoba, New Brunswick, Newfoundland, Nova Scotia, Ontario, and Quebec) have enacted freedom of information legislation. The Government of Nova Scotia, with the enactment of its Freedom of Information Act in 1977, was the first government in the Commonwealth to make access to information a legal right. The New Brunswick Right to Information Act, which was adopted in 1978 and came into force in 1980, is especially notable for its review mechanism. An individual who has been denied access to information by a minister may appeal the minister's decision, either to the provincial ombudsman or to a judge of the Supreme Court. The ombudsman can only *recommend* to the minister that the information be released whereas the judge can *order* its release. Moreover, if an individual is not satisfied with the minister's response to the ombudsman's recommendation, he or she can still appeal the minister's decision to a Supreme Court judge.

The most comprehensive provincial statute in this area is the Quebec Act on Access to Documents held by Public Bodies and the Protection of Personal

Privacy,[30] which was enacted in 1982 and came into effect in stages between 1982 and 1984. An Access to Information Commission, headed by a chairperson and two other commissioners, was created to enforce the Act, and to serve as a court to settle disputes between the government and citizens on matters of access to information and individual privacy. The Act applies to more than 3,500 government administrative units, including departments, agencies, Crown corporations, municipalities, and private and public educational institutions.

Few provincial governments have enacted privacy legislation. In Ontario and Quebec, the freedom of information and privacy legislation is combined in a single Act. In Ontario, for example, the Freedom of Information and Protection of Privacy Act provides a right of access to citizens while at the same time protecting the privacy of individuals with respect to information held by the province's government institutions. The government publishes a Personal Information Index to assist the public in locating information, and, if an access request is denied, an appeal can be made to the Information and Privacy Commissioner.

CONCLUDING OBSERVATIONS

Although participative mechanisms are still at a rudimentary stage in Canada, advocates of public participation have grounds for optimism. The opportunities for participation incorporated into many of the formal mechanisms for government decision-making are unlikely to be withdrawn. There is, therefore, reasonable promise that participative mechanisms will be expanded and refined, and that public input into the policy process will be further enhanced.

In addition, the gradual movement toward greater openness at all levels of Canadian government through the enactment of freedom of information legislation helps to ensure that *public* participation is *informed* participation. At the same time, legislative measures are being taken to maintain the privacy of information held by the government on individual citizens. In the Canadian context, legislation on these two matters is very recent; we can, therefore, expect that this legislation will be modified and refined on the basis of experience with its implementation and new advances in information technology.

NOTES

1. Richard E.B. Simeon, "The 'Overload Thesis' and Canadian Government," *Canadian Public Policy* 2 (Autumn 1976): 550. (Emphasis in original.)
2. J.A. Corry, "Sovereign People or Sovereign Governments," in H.V. Kroeker, ed., *Sovereign People or Sovereign Governments* (Montreal: Institute for Research on Public Policy, 1981), p. 11.
3. Pierre Elliott Trudeau, *Campaign Speech: Ottawa* (Ottawa: The Liberal Party of Canada, 1968).
4. Sherry R. Arnstein, "A Ladder to Citizen Participation," *Journal of the American Institute of Planners* 35 (July 1969): 216-24.
5. Alan Altshuler, *Community Control* (Washington, D.C.: Urban Institute, 1970), p. 45.

6. For a more detailed discussion of coloured papers, Royal commissions, task forces, and advisory councils, see Chapter 11.
7. Audrey Doerr, "The Role of Coloured Papers," *Canadian Public Administration* 25 (Fall 1982): 372.
8. Government of Canada, *To Know and Be Known*, Report of the Task Force on Government Information (Ottawa: Queen's Printer, 1969), vol. 1, p. 3.
9. For an account and an evaluation of efforts to encourage citizen participation in Winnipeg, see Phil H. Wichern, *Evaluating Winnipeg's Unicity: Resident Advisory Groups, 1971-1984*, Research and Working Papers, no. 11 (Winnipeg: Institute of Urban Studies, University of Winnipeg, 1984).
10. Kenneth Bryden, "Public Input into Policy-Making and Administration," *Canadian Public Administration* 25 (Spring 1982): 94. (Emphasis in original.)
11. Ibid., 100-105.
12. *To Know and Be Known*, vol. 2, p. 50.
13. For an examination of these two matters in the Canadian context, see Kenneth Kernaghan and John Langford, *The Responsible Public Servant* (Toronto: Institute of Public Administration of Canada, and Halifax: Institute for Research on Public Policy, 1990), ch. 4.
14. Canada, *Statutes*, 1980-81-82-83, c. 111, Schedule I.
15. Ibid., p. 10.
16. See Office of the Information Commissioner, *Annual Report, 1983-1984* (Ottawa: Supply and Services, 1984), p. 3.
17. Ibid.
18. These data are taken from Treasury Board Secretariat, *Access to Information Act, Privacy Act: Second Consolidated Annual Report by the President of the Treasury Board, 1988-1989*, pp. 8-12.
19. Office of the Information Commissioner, *Annual Report, 1988-1989* (Ottawa: Supply and Services, 1989), p. 34.
20. Ibid., p. 38.
21. Ibid., p. 72.
22. Office of the Information Commissioner, *Annual Report, 1989-1990* (Ottawa: Supply and Services, 1990), p. 2.
23. See *The Globe and Mail*, September 7, 1985, p. A5.
24. Canada, *Statutes*, 1980-81-82-83, c. 111, Schedule II.
25. Office of the Privacy Commissioner, *Annual Report, 1983-1984* (Ottawa: Supply and Services, 1984), pp. 2, 7.
26. Office of the Privacy Commissioner, *Annual Report, 1989-1990* (Ottawa: Supply and Services, 1990), p. 3.
27. Ibid., p. 30.
28. Ibid., p. 2
29. Ibid., p. 3.
30. Quebec, *Statutes*, 1982, c. 30.

BIBLIOGRAPHY

Altshuler, Alan. *Community Control*. Washington, D.C.: Urban Institute, 1970.
Arnstein, Sherry R. "A Ladder to Citizen Participation." *Journal of the American Institute of Planners* 35 (July 1969): 216-24.

Black, E.R. *Politics and the News.* Toronto: Butterworths, 1982.

Bryden, Kenneth. "Public Input into Policy-Making and Administration." *Canadian Public Administration* 25 (Spring 1982): 81-107.

Canada. Hon. John Roberts, Secretary of State. *Legislation on Public Access to Government Documents.* Ottawa: Supply and Services, June 1977.

Canada. *To Know and Be Known.* Report of the Task Force on Government Information. Ottawa: Queen's Printer, 1969.

Doerr, Audrey. "The Role of Coloured Papers." *Canadian Public Administration* 25 (Fall 1982): 366-79.

Draper, James A., ed. *Citizen Participation: Canada.* Toronto: New Press, 1971.

Fletcher, Frederick J. *The Newspaper and Public Affairs.* Research Study no. 7 for the Royal Commission on Newspapers. Ottawa: 1981.

Fox, David. *Public Participation in the Administrative Process.* Study paper for the Law Reform Commission of Canada. Ottawa: Supply and Services, 1979.

Fox, Larry. *Freedom of Information and the Administrative Process.* Toronto: Ontario Royal Commission on Freedom of Information and Individual Privacy, Research Study no. 10, 1979.

Galnoor, I., ed. *Government Secrecy in Democracies.* New York: Harper & Row, 1977.

Government of Ontario. *Citizen Participation: A Working Paper.* Toronto: Committee on Government Productivity, 1971.

Kernaghan, Kenneth. *Freedom of Information and Ministerial Responsibility.* Toronto: Ontario Royal Commission on Freedom of Information and Individual Privacy, Research Study no. 2, 1978.

Knight, K. W. "Administrative Secrecy and Ministerial Responsibility." *Canadian Journal of Economics and Political Science* 32 (February 1966): 77-84.

Kroeker, H. V. *Sovereign People or Sovereign Governments.* Montreal: Institute for Research on Public Policy, 1981.

Lotz, Jim. "Citizen Participation: Myths and Realities." *Optimum* 5 (1974): 53-60.

Lotz, Jim. "Public Hearings–For Confrontation or Dialogue?" *Optimum* 9 (1978): 5-12.

McDonald, Virginia. "Participation in the Canadian Context." *Queen's Quarterly* 84 (1977): 457-75.

McNiven, J. D. "Bureaucratic Imperatives and Citizen Access: Some Theoretical Possibilities." *Optimum* 7 (1976): 22-32.

Meisel, John. "Citizen Demands and Government Response." *Canadian Public Policy* 11 (Autumn 1976): 564-76.

Mishler, William. *Political Participation in Canada.* Toronto: Macmillan, 1979.

Rankin, T. Murray. *Freedom of Information in Canada: Will the Doors Stay Shut?* Ottawa: Canadian Bar Association, 1979.

Robertson, Gordon. "Confidentiality in Government." *Archivaria* 6 (Summer 1978): 3-15.

Rowat, Donald C., ed. *Administrative Secrecy in Developed Countries.* New York: Columbia University Press, 1979.

Rowat, Donald C. "How Much Administrative Secrecy?" *Canadian Journal of Economics and Political Science* 31 (November 1965): 479-98.

Rowat, Donald C. "The Right of Public Access to Official Documents." In O. P. Dwivedi, ed., *The Administrative State in Canada.* Toronto: University of Toronto Press, 1982, pp. 177-92.

Siegel, Arthur. *Politics and the Mass Media in Canada.* Toronto: McGraw-Hill Ryerson, 1983.

Smiley, D. V. *The Freedom of Information Issue: A Political Analysis.* Toronto: Ontario Royal Commission on Freedom of Information and Individual Privacy, Research Study no. 1, 1978.

Sproule-Jones, Mark. "A Description and Explanation of Citizen Participation in a Canadian Municipality." *Public Choice* 17 (Spring 1974): 73-83.

Thayer, Frederick C. *Participation and Liberal Democratic Government.* Toronto: Committee on Government Productivity, 1971.

Wronski, W. "The Public Servant and Protest Groups." *Canadian Public Administration* 14 (Spring 1971): 65-72.

CASES

Case Program in Canadian Public Administration (Toronto: Institute of Public Administration of Canada):

Closing the Baldwin Hospital. By Harold B. Wodinsky, Marsha Barnes, and Raisa B. Deber

Screening the Boat People? Case Studies in Health Policies. By Peter Owen, Peggy Purvis, and Raisa B. Deber

All Things to All People: Government and Its Client Groups. By Sharon Bider and Peter McNaughton

La politique du transport urbain dans la région de Québec. By Louise Quenel-Ouellet and Gilles Bouchard

The Development Dilemma: The Case of Quinpool Road. By Katherine A. Graham in conjunction with E. Grant MacDonald and T.J. Plunkett

VI

THE MANAGEMENT OF ORGANIZATIONAL RESOURCES

22

The Management of Government Programs

This part of the book discusses the day-to-day management of government programs. It describes the issues with which managers must deal and the tools they use to deal with them. Chapters 23 to 25 concentrate on such issues of human resource management as staffing and classification, employment equity, and collective bargaining. Chapters 26 and 27 discuss budgeting and financial management. This chapter focusses on some of the broad management issues and techniques that transcend the management of human and financial resources.

The first concept presented will be one of the most comprehensive management techniques developed in recent years—strategic planning. This will be followed by an introduction to another recent innovation that is gaining importance—the use of computers and management information systems. After discussing these positive management tools, the next section will describe some constraints on good management in government organizations. The advantages and disadvantages of the increasing use of contracting out will be weighed. On a somewhat negative note, the chapter will conclude with a discussion of how governments have dealt with downsizing, cutbacks, and program terminations.

STRATEGIC PLANNING

In recent years, a number of new management practices with names like corporate management, corporate planning, and strategic planning have developed. In this chapter, the term strategic planning is used to cover all of these, but it is important to understand that practitioners and writers may define each of these terms in a slightly different manner.

This section discusses the general concept of strategic planning and describes in detail one method of implementing it. It then assesses the application of strategic planning in Canadian governments. This entire field is complex, and the literature on it has burgeoned in the past few years. Thus, this section is not intended to be comprehensive, but rather to provide a quick overview of the field. For those interested in more depth, a number of books are listed in the bibliography of this chapter.

The Concept of Strategic Planning

The first part of this book described the operation of standard bureaucratic organizations. It emphasized that these kinds of organizations are very good at accomplishing repetitive tasks, but that they do not manage change very well. All organizations change over time because their external environment changes, and because their internal culture changes. The only issue is whether the change will be planned, systematic change or rudder-less, free-form change. The purpose of strategic planning is to allow organizations to engage in planned, systematic change.

Strategic planning is also very important as a priority-setting exercise. Governments are being pressed to do many different things. Making choices about which programs to emphasize has been made more difficult by the resource constraints that all governments face. The easy course is to continue to do what has always been done. It is very difficult to introduce new ideas. Strategic planning searches for new problems and opportunities and ensures that they receive an appropriate position on the agenda.

John M. Bryson has defined strategic planning as

> a disciplined effort to produce fundamental decisions and actions that shape and guide what an organization (or other entity) is, what it does, and why it does it. At its best, strategic planning requires broad-scale information gathering, an exploration of alternatives, and an emphasis on the future implications of present decisions. It can facilitate communication and participation, accommodate divergent interests and values, and foster orderly decision making and successful implementation.[1]

Strategic planning involves the entire organization and is broader than any other kind of planning. In fact, strategic planning was developed because of a recognition that narrower forms of financial or human resource planning were too restricted to provide the broad picture of where the organization ought to be going.[2]

Bryson is a prolific writer and an experienced practitioner of strategic planning in the public sector. He suggests an eight-step process.[3]

Step 1. Initiating and Agreeing on a Strategic Planning Process. Everyone involved in the process, especially senior decision-makers, must understand the process and agree on it.

Step 2. Clarifying Organizational Mandates. Before embarking on change, every organization should understand the core activities that it *must* undertake and the outer boundaries of actions that it can and cannot perform.

Step 3. Clarifying Organizational Mission and Values. This is the key step in the process because it requires that an organization define what its main role will be. It is surprising that so many organizations exhibit confusion in this area, but it is a symptom of the random change that occurs over time in the absence of a planned change process.

The first part of this step is to perform a stakeholder analysis. Bryson defines a stakeholder as any person, group, or organization that can place a claim on an organization's attention, resources, or output, or is affected by that output. Examples of government's stakeholders are citizens, taxpayers, service recipients, the governing body, employees, unions, interest groups, political parties, the financial community, and other governments.[4]

A stakeholder analysis first identifies who the stakeholders are (not always an easy task), then determines what stakeholders want from the organization, and what the organization needs from stakeholders, e.g., money, political support.

Out of this process, a mission statement can be established. Figure 22.1 illustrates a portion of the mission statement of Brock University. Note how the mission statement speaks to all stakeholders. The purpose of the mission statement is to provide a short description of how the organization sees itself and what its goals are. It is a way of communicating with outsiders such as stakeholders, but it is also valuable as a way of focussing the attention of members of the organization.

In these first three steps, the organization has decided where it wants to go; now it is time to determine how to get there.

Step 4. Assessing the External Environment. Organizations must monitor the political, economic, social, and technological forces and trends (PESTs) facing them. It is important to understand that these PESTs contain both opportunities and threats. Organizations must take particular note of how changes in the PESTs are having an impact on their stakeholders.

Step 5. Assessing the Internal Environment. One way to identify internal strengths and weaknesses is to determine the efficiency with which inputs are converted to outputs. Problems in this conversion process will illustrate problems in the internal environment.

Another part of assessing the internal environment is comparing the output of the organization to the output desired by stakeholders—not the outputs desired by management. This process will determine the extent to which the internal environment is sensitive to external concerns.

At this point, the organization will have completed what Bryson refers to as a SWOT analysis (strengths, weaknesses, opportunities, and threats). This process helps to determine where the organization sits within its environment; the next steps are geared to developing an organizational strategy for coping with the environment.

Step 6. Identifying the Strategic Issues Facing an Organization. This step identifies the limited number of issues that will have a real impact on the future of the organization—in either a positive or negative direction. These must be issues over which the organization has some control, e.g., it would a waste of resources to decide how to prevent a meteorite from striking the organization's headquarters. These issues must be very important issues, posing either major threats or opportunities.

Figure 22.1
BROCK UNIVERSITY MISSION STATEMENT

Preface

Brock University, located on an attractive site in the Niagara Region of Ontario, was founded in 1964 as the direct result of local and provincial initiatives. Through Faculties of Business, Education, Humanities, Mathematics and Science, Physical Education and Recreation, and Social Sciences, Brock offers education in a wide range of undergraduate programs and in selected graduate programs. The University serves as a resource centre for the residents of the Niagara Peninsula, supports life-long learning, and contributes to the intellectual, cultural, social and physical life of the community. It is the aim of Brock University to enhance its stature as a centre of teaching, research and other creative society.

A. Academic Focus and Environment

It is the mission of Brock University:

1. to provide a broadly-based liberal undergraduate education in the arts and sciences and in professional and interdisciplinary programs and to offer graduate studies in selected disciplines.
2. to maintain excellence in teaching, scholarship and other creative activity as interconnected components of the University's responsibility...

B. Students

It is the mission of Brock University:

1. to prepare students for advanced study, professional success, community responsibility and a richer life by developing a passion for life-long learning and the abilities to think creatively and critically, to communicate clearly, to maintain high ethical standards, to exercise sound judgment, and to be involved in addressing societal and environmental issues.
2. to foster an environment for students which encourages not only intellectual growth but also physical and social well-being through a diversity of extra-curricular activities and experiences designed to enrich their lives, develop their talents and provide opportunities to discover and pursue new interests...

C. University Personnel

It is the mission of Brock University:

1. to support, encourage and nurture faculty and staff in their pursuit of personal growth and professional development, recognizing that male and female career patterns may differ.
2. to encourage wide-spread participation of faculty and staff in policy formulation...

D. The Community

It is the mission of Brock University:

1. to serve as a learning, cultural, artistic and recreational centre in the Niagara Region, and work cooperatively to address local and regional issues.
2. to welcome and support international students and faculty and to encourage exchange programs and collaboration with universities in other countries in order to promote international understanding and cooperation.

Step 7. Formulating Strategies to Manage the Issues. This involves developing alternative strategies for dealing with the issues, assessing the barriers to implementing each of the strategies, and deciding which alternative to pursue.

> An effective strategy must meet several criteria. It must be technically workable, politically acceptable to key stakeholders, and must accord with the organization's philosophy and core values. It should be ethical, moral, and legal. It must also deal with the strategic issue it was supposed to address.[5]

The last sentence ought to be self-evident, but Bryson contends that many planning exercises become so caught up in satisfying political and other needs that their ultimate aim is overlooked.

This step is not completed until both a long-term strategy (two to three years) and a detailed work plan (six to twelve months) have been established. At this point, the strategic plan acts as a macro-plan for the entire organization and, therefore, provides a framework for other operational plans within individual organizational units. For example, strategic planning in the federal government could be an important input for human resource planning.[6]

Step 8. Establishing an Effective Organizational Vision for the Future. This is the organization's vision of what it will look like if it successfully implements its strategies. This is usually not essential to a good strategic planning exercise, but it gives everyone involved in the process a sense of mission. It can act as a very powerful motivating force and help the organization and all of its employees focus their attention.

The Application of Strategic Planning in Canadian Governments

The literature on the application of strategic planning in Canadian governments indicates that there have been success stories.[7] However, there have been problems as well.

The basis of some problems rests in the difficulty of engaging in planning in a volatile political situation. Coldly rational planning is very difficult when governments are pressed to satisfy conflicting goals.

> [G]overnment is expected to set a standard in terms of efficiency, of fair treatment of workers and the public, of diligence, and of cost-effectiveness—a set of objectives which are clearly inconsistent, at least some of the time. But if any one of them is not met, there are political consequences.[8]

The difficulty of reconciling divergent goals was demonstrated in the Alberta Department of Energy and Natural Resources when a planning exercise actually heightened tensions between organizational units when it forced previously separate units to engage in an integrated planning exercise.[9] The tension between the units had quietly simmered for a long time, but this exercise forced it into the open.

There is also a problem of the differing perspective of politicians and public servants. Strategic planning is usually done on the basis of *programs*, because that is the way public servants operate. However, politicians are more concerned with *issues* that frequently span a number of programs and departments, and that change much more rapidly than programs.[10] Thus, it can be very difficult to obtain ministerial support for a planning process that does not satisfy a political need.

In sum, strategic planning can be a very good way of reconciling conflicting directions and focussing the attention of members of the organization. However, in some circumstances, it can be very difficult to implement and it can even heighten tensions.

COMPUTERS AND MANAGEMENT INFORMATION SYSTEMS

In the 1990s, it is common to view computers and management information systems as being very closely related, but the terms are not synonymous. A computer is a piece of hardware, which, when loaded with software, can provide management information, play video games, or diagnose a fault in a car engine.

Management Information Systems

A **management information system (MIS)** has been defined as

> an organized method of providing past, present and projection information relating to internal operations and external intelligence. It supports the planning, control, and operational functions of an organization by furnishing uniform information in the proper time-frame to assist the decision-making process.[11]

So an MIS can be located in a computer, but it can also be a card file or even a pocket notebook. While it is important to distinguish between an MIS and the computer that usually supports it, in the 1990s, an MIS is virtually always a computer-based system of some kind.

The first MISs were developed for accounting purposes, but now they are in use in all sorts of areas. When the cashier at Canadian Tire enters a long series of numbers into the cash register, he or she is making an entry into an MIS that records changes in inventory. At some universities, students can telephone an MIS from the comfort of their homes to register in courses. Many provinces now have an MIS that prevents people from renewing their automobile or driver's licences if they have unpaid traffic tickets.

An elaboration of Kennevan's definition makes it clear what MISs are and why they have become so important. An MIS provides information on a real-time basis so that managers can make immediate decisions. For example, an airline manager wanting to make a decision about how many seats on a particular flight to offer at a discount fare can obtain up-to-the-minute information about the number of seats already sold and the usual load factor on the flight.

The ideal MIS would provide information about external, as well as internal, events. For example, our airline manager might want to know whether there was heavy competition on the route under consideration and whether the load factor on the flight is likely to be influenced by some unusual situation such as a convention or a major sporting event.

An MIS ought to assist in all aspects of managing. In the airline example, the MIS should help in making fare decisions as well as scheduling crew members, scheduling aircraft, ordering meals, and, finally, providing an early indication of the company's profit picture.

The Evolution of Computer Technology

In earlier times, a computer was a huge machine (called a mainframe) kept in a climate-controlled environment and approached only by those with highly specialized training. Over the years, computers have become smaller and more "user-friendly" so that now many public servants have microcomputers on their desks. The user-friendly nature of these new machines means that people do not have to know anything about computers to use them, in the same way that a driver does not have to know anything about the mechanics of a car in order to drive one.

At first, these microcomputers were stand-alone devices located on a desk and unable to communicate with any other computers. However, over time the technology was developed to allow these computers to communicate with other nearby computers through the use of LANs (local area networks), and to communicate with a mainframe some distance away. A large number of people located great distances apart can now communicate with one another, and can use common application packages and databases resident in one central computer.

E-mail (electronic mail) is becoming a very common way to communicate. E-mail allows a person to send a message from his or her computer to someone else's computer anywhere in the world. Unlike telephone messages, the recipient does not have to be present to receive the message. It simply sits in his or her computer until the person accesses it.

E-mail also allows a message to be sent to everyone in an organization at the same time. This aspect of E-mail could revolutionize organizational communications because

> [i]nformation which previously was not shared because of the time pressures of other business can now be transmitted over new electronic message circuits. Some of these messages may appear trivial to an outsider, but their sharing may serve an important morale function for the group.[12]

Networking capability should vastly improve organizational communication, but it has also raised technical concerns about compatibility. When sophisticated word processors and microcomputers first became available, each user in an organization simply made his or her own decision about what was most useful and purchased it. This resulted in a broad range of different machines in the same office, which worked well in the early years, but when LANs and connections to the mainframe were introduced, it became important that all equipment purchased was compatible. This created tension when individuals could no longer make their own decisions and central agencies specified the type of equipment to be purchased. The tension heightened when those agencies sometimes took a great deal of time to make the decision.

Privacy and Security

Another serious concern has been the privacy and security of computer systems. Governments collect huge amounts of information about everyone. Government computers somewhere contain information about our health, income, marital status, level of education, and even the number of flush toilets in our homes. With modern telecommunications and database capabilities, it is *technically* very easy to match and cross-check all of this information, but, as Chapter 21 pointed out, the ethical questions are very difficult.[13] For example, should a government agency concerned with financial support for deserted spouses and children have access to income tax records to locate the delinquent spouse? Should public health authorities have access to an individual's health insurance records to locate people who have been treated for AIDS and other communicable diseases?

Governments have generally responded to concerns about privacy and security by passing legislation that requires that information be used only by the agency that collected it for the purpose for which it was collected. This effectively prohibits sharing and cross-matching of data. Unfortunately, one occasionally hears of isolated incidents where these laws are violated. And some citizens are uneasy at even the thought that so much sensitive information about them is transmitted on telecommunications lines and stored on mechanical devices.

This concern has been heightened with the proliferation of devices that can access the mainframe. In the early days, the mainframe was a stand-alone device kept in a secured area. Improvements in technology now allow computers to be connected to other computers and input and output devices. "What use then is the sophisticated security over the mainframe and its data bases when some of the same data are held on mere floppy disks?"[14] The large number of decentralized devices increases the possibility that an irresponsible person will use sensitive data for inappropriate purposes.

There is also the possibility of illegal access to records stored in MISs. It is now a practical necessity in most cases that computers be connected to telephone lines to facilitate movement of data. Systems managers are sensitive to the security problems this causes and attempt to protect their data from unlawful tampering. However, when a system is attached to outside communication lines, it is almost impossible to provide absolute security in the face of dedicated "hackers" or others who attempt to steal information from these systems.

All indications are that the public should not panic. Governments are sensitive to public concerns about privacy and security, and exercise great care to ensure that unauthorized access to data does not occur, but absolute security in this regard can never be guaranteed.

Computers and Jobs

Another concern about computer systems has been that they will result in the reduction of jobs. Paper-based systems tended to be labour-intensive. One person prepared the source documents; another person used the information to update a central database (actually, this could involve several people if more than one database had to be updated); and, finally, someone had to file the original paper document. In a computer system, all of these steps can be performed instantly by one person making one entry in a microcomputer or terminal.

The experience of B.C. Hydro is quite illuminating:

> Since 1981 employment levels in B.C. Hydro have dropped approximately 37 per cent while sales have continued to increase. Although technology is not the main cause of this decrease, it appeared that the technological innovations introduced throughout the company have enabled operations to continue with fewer employees.[15]

In practice, there have been few examples of large-scale layoffs as a direct result of computerization. Most reductions have been handled through retirements, transfers, and so forth. The standard argument is that mass layoffs ought to be avoided because workers will be more accepting of the new technology if they do not perceive that their jobs are threatened by it.

However, there is another line of thought that suggests that computers will actually increase job opportunities:

> I know some firms that brought computing devices into the accounting department, expecting that this would reduce the need for accountants and bookkeepers. But what happened is that with the computer they were able to get immediate answers to questions they'd never thought of asking before! As a result, they ended up with a larger staff in the accounting department, because with these new tools at their disposal they were able to increase market share and efficiency of production.[16]

The impact of computers on total employment levels seems unclear at this point, but it is clear that computerization will continue to have a definite effect on both the composition of the workforce and the manner in which work is organized.

Computers will likely reduce secretarial and clerical jobs and increase the need for people with the skills to design hardware and software and interpret the output of the sophisticated software packages. Since women are highly over-represented in secretarial and clerical positions, they will be hurt by these changes much more than men. "Canadian women are on a collision course between their continuing concentration in clerical occupations and industry's apparently diminishing requirements in that line of work."[17]

> The current generation of micro-computers makes typing a letter or even a lengthy report so simple that even a man can do it. They also reduce the total volume of work that needs to be done. Preparing successive drafts of a report is no longer a lengthy typing process for each new draft. One simply makes the necessary changes, enters

the print command, and goes to the coffee room to join the everlasting conversation about the high level of stress in the modern-day workplace.[18]

In the new workplace, the skills gulf between the word-processing machine operator and the analyst is such that mobility is difficult, if not impossible.[19] In the old workplace, it was quite possible for a woman to progress from clerk to senior clerk to supervisor to middle manager and so on. In the new workplace, middle-level employees need skills that can only be obtained in a college or university, so there is no reason for the word-processing machine operator to aspire beyond her current position. "Clerical workers generally have the fewest opportunities for educational leave and staff training, and women have particular problems upgrading their qualifications because of family and related considerations."[20]

Computers could not only change the size and composition of the workforce, but they could also have an impact on how work will be organized. People will now be able to work in their own homes and use telephone lines to transmit their work to a central computer. This is a positive development for many people, including parents of young children who will not have to struggle with daycare, and people with physical disabilities who find the journey to work difficult.

However, it will also have negative impacts. First, it will add another barrier to upward mobility within the workplace. Someone working at home does not develop the general background knowledge about the organization and its work that is necessary for promotion.

Second, most people enjoy the social nature of work that will be missing when more people work in the solitude of their own homes. Theoretically, people could work together for years by exchanging messages through E-mail and not recognize each other at the shopping centre.

Third, working at home could affect the allegiance that people feel to their work organization. It is difficult to develop loyalty to an organization when you hardly know the other people who work there, or even what the head office building looks like.

Fourth, employers who encourage this kind of work situation are probably aware that it will be very difficult for unions to organize people who work in their homes.

Mental and Physical Health Concerns

The increasing use of computers has brought concerns about both the mental and physical health of the people using them. The thoroughness and precision of computers allow supervisors to monitor exactly what employees are doing every minute of every workday. Goofing off when the boss is gone is an old tradition. Some might consider it laziness, but in monotonous or stressful jobs a certain amount of relaxation is necessary. The constant feeling that "Big Brother" is watching is very stressful.

The computer's silent monitoring of every action and its implicit pressure for greater output further depersonalizes the work-place. Women interviewed for this study complained that having a daily record of their number of keystrokes per hour (in data-entry work) or sales volumes (in cashier work), plus a detailed breakdown of their time away from the machine, acted as a source of anxiety to them.[21]

There have also been concerns about physical problems. There have been long-standing complaints about eye strain caused by looking at a monitor for eight hours a day. Manufacturers have made many changes in the colour projected on the screen to lessen this problem, but some users still experience difficulty.

A more serious concern has been registered about the effect that X-ray emissions from computers might have on the physical health of users. This is usually raised when a cluster of women who work together all experience miscarriages or have babies with birth defects. Studies in this area are at a very early stage. Of course, all manufacturers argue that their machines are safe, but not all unions and workers agree.[22]

CONSTRAINTS ON GOOD MANAGEMENT

There are frequent pleas for government to manage its affairs in a more "business-like" fashion. The usual implication in these pleas is that public sector managers are somehow less competent and/or less disciplined and/or less hard-working than their private sector counterparts. However, there might be certain characteristics of government that prevent public service managers from engaging in business-like behaviour.

When most people talk about business-like management, they are referring to profit-maximizing, cost-minimizing behaviour. However, government is a political organization established to fulfill political, not necessarily economic or business, objectives.

In 1983, the Auditor General of Canada undertook a major study of "Constraints to Productive Management in the Public Service."[23] Officials of the Office interviewed public and private sector managers to identify differences in the managerial environment in the two sectors. They concluded that

> [t]here seem to be characteristics in the public service environment that make it difficult for managers to focus on productive management; that is to say, to concentrate on economy, efficiency, and effectiveness and ensure that satisfactory results are achieved at reasonable cost.[24]

Specifically, they identified three broad constraints, each of which has a number of elements.

Political Priorities Have a Major Impact on Productive Management

Politicians are concerned, first and foremost, with winning public support. The public judges politicians by their public persona and policy initiatives, not by how well they manage their departments. Therefore, politicians are not interested in expending a great deal of effort in managing their departments well, and they are not very interested in rewarding public service managers who do. Politicians want public servants who provide good policy advice and who keep them out of trouble. Good management falls a distant third.

In an effort to gain political support, governments frequently make decisions that are not efficient in the narrow economic sense. Many governments are systematically decentralizing their operations by moving organizational units out of the capital city. This imposes a significant one-time cost and probably increases annual operating costs, but it also demonstrates the government's commitment to regional development.

This example illustrates that governments are not oriented toward a single goal such as profit-maximization; rather, they typically must satisfy several goals simultaneously, some of which can conflict with one another, and some of which cannot even be stated openly. In this complex environment, it should not be surprising that governments sometimes do things that would not stand the test of business-like principles.

Management Feels Unduly Constrained by Administrative Procedures and Conflicting Accountability Requirements

Public sector managers feel that they have responsibility to manage, but not the requisite authority. They are faced with so many constraints that there are few things they can do without requesting authority from some other organizations.

> Treasury Board determines how departments budget, classify positions and organize functions. The Public Service Commission prescribes how managers will hire and promote staff. The Comptroller General sets guidelines for internal audit and evaluation. The Department of Supply and Services establishes procedures for making purchases. Public Works has responsibility for the acquisition and maintenance of accommodation. Departmental staff groups tell the manager how to plan, deal with personnel, administer regulations, keep accounts, measure performance. Audit groups check for weaknesses and make recommendations for change. Each of these groups has some authority to prescribe how managers should act, yet assumes little or no responsibility for the results of managers' actions, should they turn out to be unsatisfactory because of conflicting demands.[25]

None of the agencies mentioned in the above quotation is concerned about productivity or quality of service delivery to the public. Instead, each is concerned about applying rules and regulations in one specific area. None is concerned about overall quality of management. Gordon F. Osbaldeston, a former senior civil servant and an experienced and astute observer of the Ottawa scene, has argued that this creates a "tendency to substitute rules for responsibility and management processes for performance and productivity."[26] The fear in this kind of environment is that managers are evaluated by their ability to follow the rules rather than their ability to motivate employees or deliver services.

The Auditor General's report contains a glaring example of the problem of responsibility without authority. The Department of Labour felt that it had to reclassify some of its positions in order to attract enough people with appropriate qualifications to carry out its program responsibilities. The amount of money involved was minimal, but Treasury Board refused to approve the reclassification because it was afraid of setting a precedent. After six years of negotiations, a compromise was finally achieved.[27]

There Are Few Incentives for Productive Management, but Many Disincentives

Because of the restrictions discussed in the previous section, there are few incentives that can be given to managers to reward a job well done. There is a merit element in the annual pay adjustment that can be withheld from poor performers; however, many managers give the merit element to everyone in order to avoid grievances. Concerns about equity and union-management relations restrict the provisions of other non-monetary incentives, e.g., educational leave, improved office accommodation.

By contrast, there are many disincentives to good management:

- If a manager introduces efficiencies that save money, the money saved goes back into the Consolidated Revenue Fund. The common Ottawa expression for this is money "going up the flue." In fact, a manager who consistently underspends his or her budget can be rewarded by being cut back further on the grounds that the funding is not needed.
- When budget cuts are made, they are frequently applied across the board; thus, cost-conscious managers suffer far more than managers who pad their budgets.
- It is so difficult to remove unsatisfactory staff members that it is easier to hire a second person to do the job of the recalcitrant employee and let the person get paid for doing nothing.

There is a general feeling that managers are rewarded more for providing good policy advice than for managing their department. This is reflective of the value system of politicians, because, as discussed earlier, they are more concerned with policy matters than good management.

The Auditor General might be guilty of overstating for effect, but the general thrust of the criticisms ring true to any student of government in the 1980s. The major question, then, is: What steps have been taken since 1983 to redress the situation?

Responses to "Constraints"

In the years since the Auditor General's "Constraints" report, a number of attempts have been made to improve management practices. This section will provide a short description and assessment of some of these changes.

Public Service 2000 (PS 2000) is an initiative launched by Prime Minister Mulroney in 1989.

> The overriding aim of Public Service 2000 is to ensure that public servants have the tools and the authority to perform effectively in an increasingly demanding national and international environment. Accomplishing this goal will require changes in the structure and operations of the public service and, more importantly, in the management culture of the organization.[28]

Ten task forces were established, each chaired by a very senior public servant, to examine how the federal government can meet the challenges of the 21st century. One theme that runs through several of the task forces' recommendations is the need to restructure the relationship between operating departments and central agencies in order to relieve some of the burdens that departments now feel. At the time of writing, it is too early to predict exactly what changes will be made in this area, but PS 2000 has raised the profile of this problem and many people seem to be committed to making changes.

Increased Ministerial Authority and Accountability (IMAA) is discussed more fully in other chapters. This is an attempt to relax some of the detailed regulations and allow departments more autonomy if they sign a Memorandum of Understanding (MOU) with Treasury Board. This is clearly a move in the right direction,[29] but it is such a significant departure from the status quo that it requires a great deal of preparation and consideration on the part of both sides to arrive at an MOU.

Program evaluation is discussed in more detail in Chapter 7. Like IMAA, this is a mixed success. The concept of evaluation sounds good, but not enough departments are taking it seriously as a management tool.[30]

Cost recovery and *fee-for-service* programs have been introduced in some departments to introduce more market-like discipline. The fact that departments are allowed to credit the funds received against their appropriation should change the incentive system facing managers to some extent, but it is difficult to emulate market conditions in areas such as passport issuance where governments have a monopoly.

In sum, the positive outcome of the Auditor General's "Constraints" article is that senior managers are now aware that there is a serious problem and they have begun devoting serious consideration to how it should be solved. The negative side is that the problems identified seem more intractable than first thought.

DEALING WITH FINANCIAL RESTRAINT

In the mid-1970s, governments ended a thirty-year growth period and shifted abruptly into a much more restrained mode of operation.[31] At first, it was expected that this was just a temporary phase like some of the short-term hiring freezes that occurred during the growth period, but this restraint has now persisted for fifteen years and shows no signs of abating. It is a reflection of a general slowing of growth in the economy.

These declining growth rates have forced Western governments to confront some politically sensitive tradeoffs that are inherent in mixed economic systems but are largely ignored during periods of rapid growth. These tradeoffs include (1) the choice between inflation or unsatisfied public demands for goods and services; (2) the choice between providing services through tax-supported bureaucracies or through market arrangements; (3) the choice between attempting to provide equal health, housing, and educational opportunities to all citizens or (in effect) rationing opportunities to those who can afford to pay for them; and (4) the choice between spending for national defense or spending to alleviate the hardship of the poor, the sick, and the underprivileged (i.e., the dilemma of "guns vs. butter").[32]

The challenge of government in this period is to provide the same or higher levels of public service with less funding and to maintain staff morale. Obviously, this is a very difficult task.

Causes of Financial Restraint

Many of the causes of financial restraint flow from the generally weakened nature of the economy. Not all of the causes discussed below have affected all governments equally, but these problems are fairly widespread.

Flattened tax revenues have affected some governments severely. There are a number of reasons why tax revenues have levelled off in recent years. In some geographic areas, business activity has been down with an attendant reduction in taxes generated. Provinces such as Alberta and Saskatchewan, whose economies rely extensively on one resource, are very much at the mercy of the world markets for that resource. This creates "boom-and-bust" cycles, which have been more "bust" than "boom" in recent years.

It has also been suggested that governments are the authors of their own misfortune because they have not used the tax system as fully as they should. In general, they have used the corporate tax system less in recent years and are relying more on the personal income tax. Isabella Bakker points to tax expenditures and tax deferrals that benefit businesses as two reasons why taxes have not kept pace with expenditure.[33]

Many jurisdictions have also suffered from *reductions in transfer payments from other governments*. Some provincial and local governments depend on transfer payments from other levels of government for more than half of their total income. As the federal government has felt the pinch, it has exercised tighter control over levels of transfers to provincial governments. Provincial governments, in turn, have felt that they must compensate for their reduced revenues from the federal government by reducing transfer payments to local governments.

In some jurisdictions, *surging expenditures* in the 1950s and 1960s simply could not be sustained over the longer term. During this period of buoyant revenue, governments launched many new programs without understanding the cumulative impact that all of these programs would have on total expenditures. In the 1960s and 1970s, when that cumulative impact began to be felt, governments quickly realized that they could not allow these programs to continue to grow in an unrestrained fashion.

Political ideology has also had a significant impact on restraint programs. It is likely that Canadians' views of government and, indeed, of all traditional large institutions are undergoing a fundamental change.

> All Canadian governments are now witnessing (1) a loss of faith in government that is not unlike an earlier loss of faith in private institutions, (2) a restructuring of the balance of interests that underlie our socio-economic order, and (3) a challenge to our structures of government that are perceived to be bureaucratic empires unresponsive to public opinion or political direction.[34]

The positive, activist view of government that prevailed in the post-World War II period has given way to an attitude that is much more suspicious of the increasing role of government. In recent years, politicians have found "bureaucrat-bashing" to be a very convenient way to win votes.

> Most taxpayers believe that government programs are wasteful. As inflation and recession cause them to experience increased personal financial stress, citizens are more inclined to demand that their taxes be lowered, that government productivity be improved, and that waste in government be eliminated.[35]

This has created an odd dichotomy in which outraged citizens have loudly proclaimed that government is evil and government programs should be eliminated, but have screamed equally loudly when programs affecting them were slated for cuts.

Some agencies lose *political or societal support* for their goals, which makes it very difficult for them to obtain adequate levels of funding. Sometimes this can come about through changes in political views held by societies. For example, if society begins to feel that those who must rely on social services are responsible for their own fates, then it is more difficult for politicians to provide funding to social service agencies. In other cases, organizations are the cause of their own difficulties as when an agency is the subject of a serious scandal or a public display of mismanagement.

Organizations have responded to financial constraints in a variety of ways. Some have recognized that the tightening of resources is a long-term trend and they would have to develop a long term strategy to deal with it, while others have simply muddled through.

Strategies for Managing Restraint

Two writers in the field of cutback management have defined the basic problem as "how to wind back bureaucratic spending and staff with the least damage to whatever is held dear (including one's hold on power)."[36]

The first strategy that an organization could use to deal with restraint is to *resist the imposition of restraint.*[37] Management could engage such a fight by building a coalition of important individuals and groups to make it clear to budget-cutters how important the organization is.

This coalition could involve a wide range of what might, under other circumstances, appear to be strange bedfellows. For example, management and union could combine forces in the common cause of protecting their jobs. Management could also employ client groups, outside interest groups, and professional associations to testify to the importance of the agency under fire. Large public meetings help clarify to both the media and political decision-makers how important an agency is in the eyes of the community.

However, there are dangers in these tactics. Fighting back will obviously irritate the decision-makers who are trying to impose the cuts. This might cause them to take punitive action against ringleaders who would otherwise have been spared. Alternatively, the budget-cutters might retreat temporarily but return in future years with an even more devastating and well-thought-out plan. Also, the support groups are a limited resource. They can be activated once or twice to support the cause, but interest usually wanes as the fight drags on. There is nothing more embarrassing than a public meeting with a sparse turnout; it makes it clear to politicians that support for the organization is very weak.

There are a number of strategies available to an organization that decides to accept restraints. These will be discussed in order from least to most radical.

Many organizations are now using *volunteers* to assist in the performance of some duties. There is a long tradition of volunteerism in firefighting and hospitals, but it is now expanding into such areas as recreation and social services. Sometimes a symbiotic relationship can develop between an educational institution wanting to give its students practical experience and a government needing volunteers. The obvious problem in relying on volunteers is obtaining adequate numbers of appropriately trained people.

Many governments have begun to employ *user fees* more extensively.[38] Some governments are now charging for services that were provided free at one point, and in other cases governments are increasing what were nominal fees to a point where the fee covers the actual cost of providing the service. There are two purposes behind the imposition of user fees. The most obvious is to provide revenue to the government, but the second is to restrict demand for the service.

There is always some controversy surrounding the initial imposition or increase of user fees. People are upset at the idea of being subjected to increasing levels of taxation and also having to pay sharply increased user fees. User fees can be seen as regressive forms of taxation. A charge to use a swimming pool that seems nominal to a wealthy family with one child might pose a significant burden to a poorer family with several children.

For these reasons, politicians have ambivalent feelings about the imposition of user fees. On the one hand, fees are a good source of revenue directed at those who use the service. On the other hand, they can be a political minefield if they irritate well-organized groups such as sports leagues.

Many governments are *contracting out* certain services to save money. Like some of the other responses to fiscal stress, this is not a new idea. Governments have been contracting out the provision of legal services, specialized computer services, and road construction and maintenance for a long time. What has changed recently is the range of services that governments have been contracting out and the innovativeness of the arrangements.[39]

It is expected that when governments contract for services instead of providing them internally, the services will be provided more cheaply. There are a number of reasons for this expectation.

Some governments are not large enough to benefit from the economies of scale and specialization that larger, more specialized organizations can generate. Many municipalities contract with a computer service bureau to do some of their accounting functions, particularly the preparation of tax bills. It is more efficient for one large service bureau to develop specialized software than for each municipality to write its own.

Another reason for contracting out is the expectation that the competition that the process generates would force organizations providing the service to be efficient, which would, in turn, drive down costs. When government bureaucracies deliver services in a monopoly operation, they can become rigid and complacent. Often governments are forced to operate in an inefficient manner because they must comply with the rules and regulations discussed earlier in this chapter. Smaller, more free-wheeling entrepreneurial organizations operate more efficiently because they are not bound by the same rules.

In addition to economic efficiency, contracting out provides governments with a significant amount of flexibility.[40] It allows governments to provide services without buying expensive equipment and hiring staff, which makes it difficult to abandon the service when public tastes change.

Contracting out does not imply that the contractor will always be a private sector firm. There are many cases of governments contracting with other governments. Eight provinces have contracted to have the Royal Canadian Mounted Police provide some police services within their province. The Regional Municipality of Hamilton-Wentworth provides certain land-use planning and engineering services to the City of Hamilton. There are also many cases in which governments contract with not-for-profit social agencies for the delivery of social services.

Contracting out has provided evidence that public bureaucracies are not inherently less efficient than their private sector counterparts. In fact, examples can be cited of public bureaucracies reorganizing to make themselves more effective in order to head off private sector competition.[41]

However, some caveats must be registered about contracting out. It works better for some services than for others. It has generally worked well where it is relatively easy to monitor the amount of work done and the quality of the work. Solid waste collection has been a popular candidate for contracting out,[42] but the contracting out of social services can be problematic.[43]

Apparent savings on the actual provision of the service can disappear if the costs of monitoring the quality of service delivered is expensive. Governments can be particularly vulnerable if they are dealing with a private sector firm that has an effective monopoly.[44]

Contracting out can also engender political conflicts. Recipients of the service are sometimes concerned that the quality of the service will change when the service providers change. Employees who are currently delivering the service usually oppose contracting out. This is particularly problematic when the workers are unionized. When the contractor is non-union, contracting out is seen as a form of "union-busting."

Some organizations prefer to use equal *across-the-board cuts* to implement restraint. One of the arguments for this approach is that it is fair because it forces everyone to bear a portion of the pain. It can also be the easiest alternative politically.

> Cutting back equally and across the board is much less risky than suggesting that certain social needs can be more urgent than others. Similarly, there is more political wisdom in pretending that all programs are equally efficient and effective than in trying to identify the real impact of some programs.[45]

However, the very fact that the burden is spread equally is sometimes seen as unfair. Some organizational units are more central to the mandate of the overall organization and, therefore, cuts to these organizations will weaken the overall organization more than cuts elsewhere. Other parts of the organization might have already suffered serious shocks, e.g., rapidly expanding client load, which make it difficult for them to bear their "fair" share.

Hiring freezes demonstrate some of the same problems as across-the-board cuts. There is no guarantee that hiring freezes will affect all units equally. They could lead to the devastation of some units with high turnover and not touch more stable units. Hiring freezes are not sensitive to changes in the demand for services and could result in serious cutbacks in areas of expanding demand and not touch declining areas.

Small, short-term financial restraint can probably be handled by across-the-board cuts and hiring freezes, but these are dangerous techniques for handling more serious, long-term restraint. Their continual imposition could slowly, but systematically, destroy the ability of *every* organizational unit to provide services. Obviously this would weaken the credibility of the entire organization.

Sometimes, selective *program termination* is the only solution. When it is clear that restraint will be serious and long term, it is necessary for managers to engage in strategic planning to decide how they want the organization to work after downsizing.[46] Radical restraint will produce not just a *quantitatively smaller* organization, but a *qualitatively different* organization. Thus, a decision might have to be made to eliminate certain programs or deliver some services in a completely different manner.

It can be very difficult to terminate a program because both managers and clients will probably resist. Robert D. Behn has prepared a series of tips to assist in this difficult process. A few of them are:[47]

- "Don't float trial balloons." This gives supporters of the program an opportunity to mobilize others. It is better to announce termination of the program and stand firm.

- "Focus attention on the policy's harm." All policies, regardless of their benefits, have some harmful side effects, even if it is only that they use resources which could be employed elsewhere.
- "Accept short-term cost increases." With severance pay to employees, payments to contractors to allow for early termination of contracts, etc., the one-time cost of terminating a program might be greater than the annual cost of operating it. Would-be program terminators will simply have to accept the short-term media and other criticism which this will generate and remember that there is a long-term benefit.
- "Buy off the beneficiaries." Offer the more vocal critics something else instead of this policy. Obviously, care must be taken to ensure that the cost of the sweetener (including all future costs) does not exceed the cost of the program terminated.

CONCLUSION

This chapter has covered some of the significant issues that government managers in the 1990s must face and some of the techniques that they are using to deal with them. The next five chapters will provide more detail on how public servants go about managing human and financial resources.

NOTES

1. *Strategic Planning for Public and Nonprofit Organizations* (San Francisco: Jossey-Bass Publishers, 1988), p. 5.
2. Jack Koteen, *Strategic Management in Public and Nonprofit Organizations* (New York: Praeger, 1989), p. 18.
3. Bryson, *Strategic Planning*, ch. 3.
4. Ibid., p. 52.
5. Ibid., p. 60.
6. Jennifer McQueen, "Integrating Human Resource Planning with Strategic Planning," *Canadian Public Administration* 27, no. 1 (Spring 1984): 1-13.
7. Gaétan Lussier, "Planning and Accountability in Employment and Immigration Canada," *Canadian Public Administration* 28, no. 1 (Spring 1985): 134-42; Robert Loo, "Strategic Planning for Mental Health Services in Canada's Federal Police Services," *Canadian Public Administration* 29, no. 3 (Fall 1986): 469-73.
8. Benjamin Levin, "Squaring the Circle: Strategic Planning in Government," *Canadian Public Administration* 28, no. 4 (Winter 1985): 601.
9. Ken Langhorn and Bob Hinings, "Integrated Planning and Organizational Conflict," *Canadian Public Administration* 30, no. 4 (Winter 1987): 550-65.
10. Levin, "Squaring the Circle," pp. 602-603.
11. Walter J. Kennevan, as quoted in Raymond McLeod, Jr., *Management Information Systems* (Chicago: Science Research Associates, 1979), p. 14.
12. Ted Grusec, "Office Automation Trials in the Federal Government: Lessons for Managers," *Canadian Public Administration* 29, no. 4 (Winter 1986): 559.
13. Kenneth Kernaghan and John Langford, *The Responsible Public Servant* (Halifax: The Institute for Research on Public Policy, and Toronto: The Institute of Public Administration of Canada, 1990), ch. 4.

14. Bruce A. Macdonald, "Information Management in the Public Service: Summary of Discussions," *Canadian Public Administration* 29, no. 1 (Spring 1986): 9.

15. Jill E. Davidson, "Tech Change: Boon or Bane for Professionals, Supervisors and Middle Managers," *Canadian Public Administration* 29, no. 4 (Winter 1986): 563.

16. Stuart L. Smith, *Technology and Work in Canada's Future* (Toronto: The Governing Council of the University of Toronto, 1986), p. 54.

17. Heather Menzies, *Women and the Chip* (Montreal: The Institute for Research on Public Policy, 1981), p. 75.

18. David Siegel, "The Changing Shape and Nature of Public Service Employment," *Canadian Public Administration* 31, no. 2 (Summer 1988): 187.

19. Eli Ginzberg, Thierry J. Novelle, and Thomas M. Stanback, Jr., *Technology and Employment: Concepts and Clarifications* (Boulder, Colo: Westview Press, 1986), chs. 3 and 4.

20. Menzies, *Women and the Chip*, p. 65.

21. Ibid., p. 63.

22. Ontario Public Service Employees Union, *The Hazards of VDTs* (Toronto: Ontario Public Service Employees Union, 1981).

23. *Report of the Auditor General of Canada to the House of Commons, Fiscal Year Ended March 31, 1983* (Ottawa: Auditor General of Canada, 1983), pp. 53-87.

24. Ibid., p. 53.

25. Ibid., p. 61.

26. *Keeping Deputy Ministers Accountable* (Scarborough, Ont.: McGraw-Hill Ryerson, 1989), p. 75.

27. *Report of the Auditor General, 1983*, p. 66.

28. Paul M. Tellier, "Public Service 2000: The Renewal of the Public Service," *Canadian Public Administration* 33, no. 2 (Summer 1990): 124.

29. C. Lloyd Brown-John, " 'If You're So Damned Smart Why Don't You Run Government Like a Business?' " in Katherine A. Graham, ed., *How Ottawa Spends: 1990-91: Tracking the Second Agenda* (Ottawa: Carleton University Press, 1990), pp. 227-29.

30. Ibid., p. 229.

31. These phases are well-chronicled in L. R. Jones and Jerry L. McCaffery, *Government Response to Financial Constraints: Budgetary Control in Canada* (New York: Greenwood Press, 1989).

32. Charles H. Levine, "The New Crisis in the Public Sector," in Charles H. Levine, ed., *Managing Fiscal Stress: The Crisis in the Public Sector* (Chatham, N.J.: Chatham House, 1980), p. 3.

33. "The Size and Scope of Government: Robin Hood Sent Packing," in Michael S. Whittington and Glen Williams, eds., *Canadian Politics in the 1990s*, 3rd ed. (Scarborough, Ont.: Nelson Canada, 1990), pp. 440-41.

34. Peter Aucoin, "The Politics and Management of Restraint in Government: An Overview," in Peter Aucoin, ed., *The Politics and Management of Restraint in Government* (Montreal: The Institute for Research in Public Policy, 1981), p. 3.

35. Levine, "The New Crisis in the Public Sector," p. 5.

36. Andrew Dunsire and Christopher Hood, *Cutback Management in Public Bureaucracies* (Cambridge: Cambridge University Press, 1989), p. 186.

37. Some examples of strategies are described in Cynthia Hardy, "Fighting Cutbacks: Some Issues for Public Sector Administrators," *Canadian Public Administration* 28, no. 4(Winter 1985): 531-49; Cynthia Hardy, *Strategies for Retrenchment and Turnaround: the Politics of Survival* (Berlin: Walter de Gruyter, 1990), ch. 13 and passim.

38. Neil B. Ridler, "Fiscal Constraints and the Growth of User Fees Among Canadian Municipalities," *Canadian Public Administration* 27, no. 3 (Fall 1984): 429-36.
39. A partial catalogue of both these things is found in Robert L. Bish, "Improving Productivity in the Government Sector: The Role of Contracting Out," in David Laidler (research coordinator), *Responses to Economic Change* (Toronto: University of Toronto Press, 1986), pp. 209-11.
40. John Johnston, "Public Servants and Private Contractors: Managing the Mixed Service Delivery System," *Canadian Public Administration* 29, no. 4 (Winter 1986): 549.
41. James C. McDavid and Gregory K. Schick, "Privatization Versus Union-Management Cooperation: The Effects of Competition on Service Efficiency in Municipalities," *Canadian Public Administration* 30, no. 3 (Fall 1987): 472-88.
42. E. E. Savas, "Policy Analysis for Local Government: Public vs. Private Refuse Collection," in Levine, ed., *Managing Fiscal Stress*, pp. 281-302.
43. Lorna F. Hurl, "Privatized Social Service Systems: Lessons from Ontario's Children's Services," *Canadian Public Policy* 10, no. 4 (December 1984): 395-405.
44. Lydia Manchester, "Alternative Service Delivery Approaches and City Service Planning," in Lawrence K. Finley, ed., *Public Sector Privatization: Alternative Approaches to Service Delivery* (New York: Quorum Books, 1989), p. 15.
45. Eli Teram and Pamela G. Hines, "The Case for Government Involvement in the Management of Cutbacks by Public Service Organizations," *Canadian Public Administration* 31, no. 1 (Fall 1988): 333.
46. Such an exercise is described in Ivan Robinson, "Managing Retrenchment in a Public Service Organization," *Canadian Public Administration* 28, no. 4 (Winter 1985): 513-30.
47. "How to Terminate a Public Policy: A Dozen Hints for the Would-Be Terminator," in Levine, ed., *Managing Fiscal Stress*, pp. 327-42.

BIBLIOGRAPHY

Aucoin, Peter, ed. *The Politics and Management of Restraint in Government.* Montreal: The Institute for Research in Public Policy, 1981.
Auditor General of Canada. *Report of the Auditor General of Canada to the House of Commons, Fiscal Year Ended March 31, 1983.* Ottawa: Auditor General of Canada, 1983.
Bakker, Isabella. "The Size and Scope of Government: Robin Hood Sent Packing." In Michael S. Whittington and Glen Williams, eds., *Canadian Politics in the 1990s,* 3rd ed. Scarborough, Ont.: Nelson Canada, 1990, pp. 423-47.
Bish, Robert L. "Improving Productivity in the Government Sector: The Role of Contracting Out." In David Laidler (research coordinator), *Responses to Economic Change.* Toronto: University of Toronto Press, 1986, pp. 203-37.
Brown-John, C. Lloyd, " 'If You're So Damned Smart Why Don't You Run Government Like a Business?' " In Katherine A. Graham, ed., *How Ottawa Spends: 1990-91: Tracking the Second Agenda.* Ottawa: Carleton University Press, 1990, pp. 219-45.
Bryson, John M. *Strategic Planning for Public and Nonprofit Organizations.* San Francisco: Jossey-Bass Publishers, 1988.
Davidson, Jill E. "Tech Change: Boon or Bane for Professionals, Supervisors and Middle Managers." *Canadian Public Administration* 29, no. 4 (Winter 1986): 562-66.
Dunsire, Andrew, and Christopher Hood. *Cutback Management in Public Bureaucracies.* Cambridge: Cambridge University Press, 1989.

Finley, Lawrence K., ed. *Public Sector Privatization: Alternative Approaches to Service Delivery.* New York: Quorum Books, 1989.

Ginzberg, Eli, Thierry J. Novelle, and Thomas M. Stanback, Jr. *Technology and Employment: Concepts and Clarifications.* Boulder, Colo.: Westview Press, 1986.

Grusec, Ted. "Office Automation Trials in the Federal Government: Lessons for Managers." *Canadian Public Administration* 29, no. 4 (Winter 1986): 556-62.

Hardy, Cynthia. "Fighting Cutbacks: Some Issues for Public Sector Administrators." *Canadian Public Administration* 28, no. 4 (Winter 1985): 531-49.

——. *Strategies for Retrenchment and Turnaround: The Politics of Survival.* Berlin: Walter de Gruyter, 1990.

Hurl, Lorna F. "Privatized Social Service Systems: Lessons from Ontario's Children's Services." *Canadian Public Policy* 10, no. 4 (December 1984): 395-405.

Johnston, John. "Public Servants and Private Contractors: Managing the Mixed Service Delivery System." *Canadian Public Administration* 29, no. 4 (Winter 1986): 549-53.

Jones, L. R., and Jerry L. McCaffery. *Government Response to Financial Constraints: Budgetary Control in Canada.* New York: Greenwood Press, 1989.

Kernaghan, Kenneth, and John Langford. *The Responsible Public Servant.* Halifax: The Institute for Research on Public Policy, and Toronto: The Institute of Public Administration of Canada, 1990.

Langhorn, Ken, and Bob Hinings. "Integrated Planning and Organizational Conflict." *Canadian Public Administration* 30, no. 4 (Winter 1987): 550-65.

Levin, Benjamin. "Squaring the Circle: Strategic Planning in Government." *Canadian Public Administration* 28, no. 4 (Winter 1985): 600-605.

Levine, Charles H., ed. *Managing Fiscal Stress: The Crisis in the Public Sector.* Chatham, N. J.: Chatham House, 1980.

Loo, Robert. "Strategic Planning for Mental Health Services in Canada's Federal Police Services." *Canadian Public Administration* 29, no. 3 (Fall 1986): 469-73.

Lussier, Gaétan. "Planning and Accountability in Employment and Immigration Canada." *Canadian Public Administration* 28, no. 1 (Spring 1985): 134-42.

MacDonald, Bruce A. "Information Management in the Public Service: Summary of Discussions." *Canadian Public Administration* 29, no. 1 (Spring 1986): 1-16.

McDavid, James C., and Gregory K. Schick. "Privatization Versus Union-Management Cooperation: The Effects of Competition on Service Efficiency in Municipalities." *Canadian Public Administration* 30, no. 3 (Fall 1987): 472-88.

McQueen, Jennifer. "Integrating Human Resource Planning with Strategic Planning." *Canadian Public Administration* 27, no. 1 (Spring 1984): 1-13.

Menzies, Heather. *Women and the Chip.* Montreal: The Institute for Research on Public Policy, 1981.

Northcott, Jim, Michael Fogarty, and Malcolm Trevor. *Chips and Jobs: Acceptance of New Technology at Work.* London: Policy Studies Institute, 1985.

Ontario Public Service Employees Union. *The Hazards of VDTs.* Toronto: Ontario Public Service Employees Union, 1981.

Osbaldeston, Gordon F. *Keeping Deputy Ministers Accountable.* Scarborough, Ont.: McGraw-Hill Ryerson, 1989.

Ridler, Neil B. "Fiscal Constraints and the Growth of User Fees Among Canadian Municipalities." *Canadian Public Administration* 27, no. 3 (Fall 1984): 429-36.

Robinson, Ivan. "Managing Retrenchment in a Public Service Organization." *Canadian Public Administration* 28, no. 4 (Winter 1985): 513-30.

Siegel, David. "The Changing Shape and Nature of Public Service Employment." *Canadian Public Administration* 31, no. 2 (Summer 1988): 159-93.

Smith, Stuart L. *Technology and Work in Canada's Future.* Toronto: The Governing Council of the University of Toronto, 1986.

Tellier, Paul M. "Public Service 2000: The Renewal of the Public Service." *Canadian Public Administration* 33, no. 2 (Summer 1990): 123-32.

Teram, Eli, and Pamela G. Hines. "The Case for Government Involvement in the Management of Cutbacks by Public Service Organizations." *Canadian Public Administration* 31, no. 1 (Fall 1988) 321-34.

CASES

In *Case Program in Canadian Public Administration* (Toronto: Institute of Public Administration of Canada):

The Role of the Manager in the Management of Change: An Exercise in Downsizing. By André LeBlond and David Zussman

Managing Change Under Restraint. By Benjamin Levin

Cases developed by the Canadian Centre for Management Development and distributed by the Case Program in Canadian Public Administration:

Workforce Adjustment. By Robert Stephens

Choices for the Manager. By John William Pullen and Richard Paton

Toxic Chemicals. By Richard Paton and John William Pullen

Saint John District. By Nancy Mitchell

How to Improve Productivity and Quality of Service to the Public with Less Resources. By Philippe Clément, Marcel Côté, and Jocelyne Pinsonneault

Management of an Organization During a Strike. By Seymour Hamilton

The New Central Region. By Nancy Mitchell

23

The Management of
Human Resources

While it is true in government as elsewhere in Canadian society that "money talks," a persuasive argument can be made that "the *management of personnel* in all its aspects is as important as, if not more important than, *financial management* in achieving effective overall management of government activities."[1] Certainly, the competence and performance of public employees are key determinants of successful policy formation and execution. This chapter examines the management of human resources in Canadian government by explaining the concept of merit, the evolution of human resource management, the legislative and organizational environment in which this management is set, and the major processes involved.[2]

THE CONCEPT OF MERIT

Merit is the most pervasive and enduring theme in human resource management. To understand the concept of merit, one must distinguish between the merit *principle* and the merit *system*. As explained in Chapter 13, the merit *principle* requires that:

1. Canadian citizens should have a reasonable opportunity to be considered for employment in the public service; and
2. Selections must be based exclusively on merit...."[3]

The courts have consistently defined merit as "best qualified." The *merit system* "is the mechanism in use at any time by which these goals are achieved...A merit system is an administrative device *which can and should be adapted to changing circumstances.*"[4] The need to balance the merit principle with other considerations is evident in the assertion of the federal Public Service Commission that

> [a]ppointments to the Public Service are based on merit, and public servants advance within [the service] in accordance with merit. This means that the knowledge, experience and abilities of candidates are evaluated against the requirements for the position, that the best qualified person is selected, and that the treatment of public servants and those seeking employment in the Public Service is fair and equitable. The Public Service must be highly competent, totally professional and politically neutral in providing advice to the government and quality services to the

Canadian public. It also must be representative of the population it serves. Its staffing system must be easy to manage, economical to operate and sufficiently flexible to meet changing operational needs.[5]

Despite the advances in organizational theory during this century, organizational practice in public sector human resource management continues to be based to a large extent on the scientific management school of thought that emerged in the early decades of the century. But "current organizational theory, which views organizations more in terms of social systems, suggests that individuals should know the results expected of them [and] have some influence over the work they perform and over the possible application and development of their own abilities to varying tasks in support of those results."[6] In brief, it is argued that a less rigid interpretation of merit should be complemented by enhanced concern about some of the influences on motivation considered in Chapters 4 and 5.

The human resource policies of our public services do not always reflect what we have learned from organizational theorists about the behaviour of people in organizations. The objective of human resource management should be to supply a sufficient number of well-qualified and well-motivated persons at the appropriate time to ensure successful development and implementation of government policies and programs. Greater emphasis has traditionally been placed on providing well-qualified, rather than well-motivated, public employees. Given the evolution of human resource management in the unique Canadian environment and the recency of important insights into organizational behaviour, this emphasis is understandable. The long-standing concern about the quality of employees' preparation and performance can now, however, be combined with increased attention to the quality of their working life and its effects on their performance.

There have been few significant events, developments, or reforms in the public service that have not affected human resource management in general and merit in particular. Merit has been pursued within the broader context of the administrative values discussed in Chapter 12. The priority that public servants assign to each of these values at any given time is a reflection of the desires and expectations of the various actors in the political system who control or influence public servants. Among the most important of these actors are political superiors. The uniqueness of human resource management in the public, as opposed to the private, sector can be explained in large part by the political environment within which public servants work. Evidence of the importance of the politics of human resource management has been provided in earlier discussion of such matters as political appointments, political partisanship, public comment, anonymity, permanency in office, ministerial responsibility, and representative bureaucracy. Additional evidence is set forth in this chapter.

EVOLUTION OF HUMAN RESOURCE MANAGEMENT

The development of human resource management in Canada may fruitfully be viewed in terms of the effect on merit, and to a lesser degree on motivation, of the shifting importance of the dominant administrative values. In the federal sphere of government, this evolution may for analytical purposes be divided chronologically into five periods—pre-1918, 1918-1945, 1946-1966, 1967-1978, and 1979 to the present. In each of these periods, human resource management has been affected by a different mix of administrative values as the priority of the various values has risen and declined.

The Patronage Era

The pre-1918 period was dominated by efforts to promote political neutrality by eliminating, or at least minimizing, political patronage in the appointment of public servants.[7] Indeed, between 1867 and 1918, as many as five Royal commissions and a judicial inquiry on the federal public service devoted considerable attention to the evils of patronage. The first major step toward the abolition of patronage was the Civil Service Amendment Act of 1908, which established the Civil Service Commission. The Act also provided for appointment on the basis of merit and for heavy penalties for partisan political activities by public servants. However, the Act applied only to the "inside service," that is, those public servants working in Ottawa.

From Patronage to Merit

The second period (1918-1945) began with the passage of the Civil Service Act in 1918. The search for political neutrality was supplemented by concern for efficiency. The major objective of the Act was the "promotion of economy and efficiency in the non-political public service." Merit was to be achieved through "selection and appointment without regard to politics, religion or influence," and through "the application of methods of scientific employment to maintain the efficiency of these selected employees after they enter the service." The Act applied to both the "inside" and "outside" services. Severe restrictions in this Act on partisan political activities remained virtually unchanged until 1967.

Continued pursuit of political neutrality and efficiency had important effects on human resource management. The emphasis during the 1920s on eradicating patronage rather than on improving efficiency led to a very significant decline in patronage appointments and partisan political activities by 1930. In the 1930s, the Civil Service Commission, with its persistent focus on merit in terms of selection of the best qualified candidates, lost ground to the Treasury Board, which emphasized economy and efficiency, not only in the human resource area but throughout government. This emphasis continued during the war years.

The Roots of Reform

The post-war period (1945-1966) provided a strikingly different environment for human resource management. The rapid expansion of government activities in an increasingly complex and technological society required not only a much larger number of employees but also a greater proportion of employees with professional, technical, and managerial skills. By the end of this period, public service unions had won the right to bargain collectively and to strike. Efficiency remained the paramount administrative value as the Royal Commission on Government Organization (the Glassco Commission)[8] examined human resource management as part of its task to recommend changes to "promote efficiency, economy and improved service in the dispatch of public business." Political neutrality was a continuing, but secondary, concern. As will be explained in Chapter 24, representativeness emerged as a primary administrative value, specifically in regard to remedying the long-standing discrimination in the public service against French-speaking Canadians.

The Fruits of Reform

The 1967-1978 period was an especially momentous one in the evolution of human resource management. Public service managers in general and personnel managers in particular felt the full effects of reforms generated in the previous period. Among the most important reforms were collective bargaining, language training, new management techniques, and departmental reorganizations.

A larger number of administrative values contended for precedence during the 1967-1978 period. The former emphasis on economy and efficiency was supplemented by vigorous concern for effectiveness. Disclosures of mismanagement and of inefficient and ineffective use of public funds led to widespread anxiety about the accountability of public servants. Revelations of numerous ethical offences involving government officials aroused unprecedented concern about the integrity of these officials. The representativeness of the public service became a major issue as the claims of women, aboriginal peoples, and the handicapped were added to those of French-speaking Canadians. The Trudeau government's promises of participatory democracy gave responsiveness a higher place among the bureaucrats' value priorities. Finally, the importance of political neutrality was renewed with the increased recognition of the changing role of bureaucrats in the political system.

The Present Discontents

In 1979, the Special Committee on Personnel Management and the Merit Principle[9] (the D'Avignon Committee) reported that the basic human resource problems were a lack of leadership, excessive and inflexible regulation, managers who were ill-equipped for managing, and an absence of accountability for the proper management of human resources. As explained below, the government has taken several initiatives during the past decade to seek remedies to these problems. It was evident by the end of the 1970s that the traditional concept of merit would have to be re-evaluated and reinterpreted to take account of other governmental concerns and objectives affecting human resource management. Indeed, in recent years, the Public Service Commission has repeatedly proposed, and the Treasury Board has agreed, that the principles of the merit system noted near the beginning of this chapter should govern all aspects of human resource management. These principles significantly overlap with the primary administrative values discussed in earlier chapters. We shall see that during the 1980s and early 1990s the values of efficiency, accountability, and representativeness have had an especially important impact on human resource management.

In December 1989, the federal government announced the creation of Public Service 2000. This initiative consisted of the creation of a number of task forces composed of senior public servants and dealing with such matters as occupational classification, compensation and benefits, staffing, training and development, staff relations, budget controls, and service to the public. The overall purpose of Public Service 2000 was to recommend measures "to enable the Public Service to provide the best possible service to Canadians into the 21st century."[10] The specific objectives were to bring about a public service that:

- is professional, highly qualified, non-partisan and imbued with a mission of service to the public;
- recognizes its employees as assets to be valued and developed;
- places as much authority as possible in the hands of front line employees and managers; and
- provides scope for different organizational forms to meet differing needs, but in the context of a single Public Service.[11]

Some of the actual and proposed reforms of the human resource management system that emerged from the deliberations of the Public Service 2000 task forces are examined at various points in this chapter.[12]

THE LEGISLATIVE AND ORGANIZATIONAL FRAMEWORK

The function of human resource management pervades government, but the development and administration of human resource policy in the federal government are determined largely by a few key statutes and organizations. The scope and objectives of human resource activities and their allocation among these organizations are set out in three major statutes. The Financial Administration Act (FAA) of 1951 states that the Treasury Board is charged, among other things, with broad responsibility for "personnel management in the public service, including the determination of terms and conditions of employment of persons therein." The Public Service Employment Act (PSEA) of 1967 grants the Public Service Commission (PSC) exclusive authority to appoint persons to and within the public service according to merit, and to manage such matters as appeals, layoffs and dismissals, and political partisanship. The Public Service

Staff Relations Act, also passed in 1967, sets out the responsibilities of the Public Service Staff Relations Board and provides for the structure and operation of the collective bargaining process and for the resolution of disputes and grievances.

Other notable statutes affecting human resource management are the Official Languages Act of 1969, which designates French and English as Canada's official languages, provides for their use in the federal government, and authorizes an Official Languages Commissioner to report on this usage; the Canadian Human Rights Act (1977), which covers such matters as discriminatory employment practices and the privacy of personal information; and the Public Service Superannuation Act (1975), which is concerned with pension and death benefits.

The major authority for the formulation and implementation of human resource policy is vested in the Treasury Board[13] and the Public Service Commission. The Treasury Board is a Cabinet committee composed of six ministers, including the President of the Treasury Board as chairperson. It is supported by the Treasury Board Secretariat, which is headed by a secretary with the rank of deputy minister and is, in effect, the central management agency of government. Its very broad responsibilities in the human resource field include the development and interpretation of policies, programs, and procedures in regard to the organization of the public service; positions; compensation; training and development; official languages; discipline; working conditions; human resource needs and their utilization; classification of employees and employee benefits; and other terms and conditions of employment necessary for effective human resource management. In addition, the secretariat represents the government as employer in the collective bargaining process. Although most of the secretariat's several branches are involved, to some extent, in human resource management, the leading role is played by the Personnel Policy Branch headed by a deputy secretary.

The Public Service Commission's overriding objective is "to ensure that appointments to and within the Public Service are based on merit; that they meet the needs of the Public Service; and that they are free from discrimination on the basis of sex, race, national origin, religion, colour, marital status or age."[14] To pursue this objective, the commission has authority to recruit, select, promote, transfer, demote, and dismiss public servants; to provide staff development and training, including language training, within the framework of Treasury Board policies; to hear and decide appeals relating to appointments or to demotions and dismissals for incompetence or incapacity; to investigate allegations of discrimination in public service employment practices; and to administer regulations on political activities by public servants, including decisions on requests for leave of absence to seek political office. The commission, unlike the Treasury Board, does not report to a Cabinet minister; rather, under the Public Service Employment Act, the commission is a politically independent agency that is accountable to Parliament for the administration of the Act. The commission is headed by a chairperson of deputy minister rank and two commissioners.

Both the board and the commission delegate much of their operational authority for various human resource activities to departments under the direction of deputy ministers, and have created mechanisms and procedures to help ensure that deputy ministers and other departmental officials are accountable for their exercise of that delegated authority. These mechanisms include general statements of procedures to be followed and after-the-fact monitoring mechanisms to ensure that they have been followed.

In addition to the board and the commission, federal organizations with important roles in human resource management are the Public Service Staff Relations Board (PSSRB) (discussed under collective bargaining in the next chapter), the Privy Council Office (PCO), the Committee of Senior Officers on Executive Personnel (COSO), and the Advisory Committee on Executive Compensation.

The PCO's human resource functions are limited in their scope but critical in their impact because the PCO exercises the major influence on human resource policy and appointments for the most senior ranks of the public service. It is the Prime Minister's prerogative to make a large number of order in council appointments, including deputy ministers, heads of Crown agencies, and federal judges. The Clerk of the Privy Council , who is also Secretary to the Cabinet, advises the Prime Minister on the qualifications of existing and prospective order in council appointees. In this capacity as advisor on senior appointments, the clerk is assisted by the Senior Personnel Secretariat in the PCO, which, in turn, provides advice on career-planning and on senior personnel policy. In addition, this secretariat provides staff support to the Committee of Senior Officials (COSO), established in 1968, and to the Advisory Group on Executive Compensation, also established in 1968. COSO undertakes an annual evaluation of the performance of order in council appointees and makes salary recommendations for them to the government. It is composed of three permanent members (the Clerk of the Privy Council and Secretary to the Cabinet as chairperson, the secretary of the Treasury Board, and the chairperson of the Public Service Commission) and four other senior deputy ministers appointed on a rotating basis. The Advisory Group on Executive Compensation is composed of leading private sector executives, who make recommendations to the government on rates of pay and conditions of employment for public service managers.

THE MAJOR HUMAN RESOURCE PROCESSES

In practice, the distribution of responsibilities for human resource management among the key organizations discussed above and the many other administrative bodies within government is very complex. A comprehensive examination of the entire field of human resource management in Canadian government cannot be provided here, but we have set out below an explanation of the major human resource processes, namely, classification, human resource planning, staffing, training and development, and performance evaluation. The issue of political neutrality, which has important implications for human resource management, was discussed in Chapter 13.

Job Classification

Job classification is the process by which jobs are assigned to an occupational group within an occupational category and to a level within that group.[15] Both logically and chronologically, classification normally precedes the other main human resource processes. It supplies an essential basis for effective human resource management in general and appropriate wage and salary administration in particular.

An **occupational category** includes a broad range of occupations of the same type, distinguished by the nature of the duties performed and the education required. The six occupational categories in the federal public service and the approximate number of employees in each category at the end of 1989 were:[16] Management (4,632), Scientific and Professional (23,080), Administrative and Foreign Service (58,812), Technical (26,058), Administrative Support (65,112), and Operational (36,402). An occupational *group* within a category includes occupations that require similar types of work involving similar skills (e.g., the actuarial science group within the Scientific and Professional Category) and that are often related to the labour market outside the public service. There are seventy-two occupational groups and 106 subgroups in the federal public service.

It is generally agreed that having such a large number of groups and subgroups creates a complex and cumbersome system that leads to such problems as artificial barriers to mobility and difficulties in implementing pay equity. Thus, the Public Service 2000 Task Force on Classification and Occupational Group Structures recommended that the six occupational categories be abolished and the existing groups and subgroups be combined into twenty-three distinct occupational groups and eight subgroups.[17]

The primary task in classification is **job evaluation**, which consists of:

1. the analysis of a job in terms of its duties and responsibilities, its physical and mental demands, the knowledge and skills it requires, and the conditions under which it is performed;
2. the writing of a job description which explains the duties, working conditions, and other aspects of the job; and
3. the assessment of these job characteristics against the classification standard established for the relevant occupational group.

Each group has a **classification standard**, which contains a definition of the category within which the group falls, the groups within each category, the job evaluation plan, and the descriptions of benchmark positions[18] to be used as guides for assessing jobs and rating them according to their level in the group. Jobs at the same level are assigned the same salary range. Since classification is essentially a matter of judgment, it is common practice to obtain more than one person's judgment by having jobs evaluated and rated by committees who advise the official responsible for the final decision. This work is usually done within departments, but is subject to review by Treasury Board.

The Management Category

An extremely important reform in human resource management in the early 1980s placed virtually all of the federal government's top executives and managers in a newly created **Management Category,** which contains over 4,600 employees. Previously, the only distinct management group was the Senior Executive Category, which consisted of almost 1,400 executives. The other managers were spread over fifty-five different occupational groups. The Management Category consists of the Executive (EX) and Senior Management (SM) groups. The category includes senior public servants who have responsibility for policy development; program formulation and delivery; the design and operation of management machinery; and the management of human resources, finances, and public affairs. The EX Group is composed of five levels up to and including most assistant deputy ministers, and the SM Group is made up of a single level immediately below the EX Group.

The primary objectives of the formation of the category were:

1. to establish a single classification system for all senior managerial personnel;
2. to establish a simplified staffing system designed to attract, develop, and retain management talent;
3. to increase the flexibility of deputy ministers to redeploy senior managers in response to changing needs;
4. to increase the accountability of managers by specifying accountabilities in job descriptions;
5. to provide training and development programs to give managers the knowledge and skills required to manage in a context of increased accountability;
6. to establish a new compensation system that will ensure fair and equitable compensation both within the public service and in relation to the private sector; and
7. to set up a pay system clearly linked to performance, including rewards for outstanding achievement.

A review by the Public Service 2000 Task Force on The Management Category identified several interrelated problems with the category. These included

> the multiplicity of layers within the executive cadre which slows decision-making and blurs lines of accountability; the lack of clearly articulated and shared values to guide behaviour; the lack of cohesiveness within the management cadre and falling levels of morale and job satisfaction as one goes down the management hierarchy; inadequate delegation to employees of the powers they need to achieve the results for which they are being held responsible; the increasing difficulty of attracting and retaining high achievers in the executive ranks; the lack of representation of certain groups within the Canadian population; and the welter of rules and regulations governing how we recruit, select, develop, promote, reward and discipline managers which impose a heavy administrative cost and inhibit creativity and initiative.[19]

The task force proposed reforms to deal with each of these deficiencies.[20]

Human Resource Planning

Human resource planning is the process through which a government strives to ensure that it has—and will continue to have—the appropriate quantity and quality of employees to carry out its responsibilities. This process aims to eliminate the gap between the existing supply of qualified employees and the current and anticipated demand for them. There is a close relationship between this planning and virtually all other areas of human resource management. In the government of Ontario, for example, the process of human resource planning is considered to be composed of supply and demand forecasting, career planning, employee appraisal and assessment, training and development, and recruitment.[21]

In the areas of staffing and of training and development in particular, human resource planning requires that an appropriate balance be struck between the government's desire for human resources of specific kinds and the career aspirations of individual employees. Human resource planning would be a much simpler task if governments could treat current and future employees as automatons. Individuals could then be inserted in the appropriate slots in the administrative hierarchy as they completed prescribed forms of management experience and training. However, career development does not always conform to organizational needs. Individuals have career goals, job preferences, and personal idiosyncrasies that often run counter to the government's need for employees with particular qualifications. Individuals may not want to accept positions for which they have the required skills and experience, or they may not wish to engage in training, or in particular forms of it.

It is useful to distinguish between human resource planning *by* managers and *for* managers. Planning *by* managers "must include consideration of the number and kinds of people who will be needed to carry out departmental programs; when, where and how they will be obtained; what training or development they will need; how much they will cost; and the implications for program plans of inability to obtain the people required."[22] Thus, human resource planning is an essential part of both financial and program planning. Indeed, departments submit Multi-Year Human Resource Plans (MYHRP) to Treasury Board and the Public Service Commission. These MYHRPs are an essential part of the expenditure budget process and support the departments' Multi-Year Operational Plans. The MYHRPs provide the board and the commission with information on the departments' human resource needs and on departmental concerns that require action by central agencies. Treasury Board uses these plans as a basis for policies and programs dealing with such matters as management training and employment equity.

Human resource planning *for* managers takes place within the context of managing the Management Category described above. Indeed, a major reason for creating the category was to facilitate planning for human resource needs that would produce highly qualified executives and senior managers. These senior public servants now receive formal management training to enable them to conduct appropriate human resource planning for the rest of the public service.

Staffing

The integral link between attracting capable employees and attaining program objectives suggests that staffing may well be the key element of human resource management. We have already seen that determining staffing needs and the means of meeting these needs is a central feature of human resource planning. At the beginning of this chapter, we also saw the importance in the staffing system of balancing the merit principle with other principles. The Public Service 2000 Task Force on Staffing set out the following guiding principles to which the entire staffing system should conform:

- It has sufficient flexibility to respond to the human resource needs of departments to support them in fulfilling their responsibilities to the Canadian public and the government of the day.
- It contributes to a highly competent public service.
- It presents no systemic barriers to a representative public service and it can respond to policies regarding the correction of representation imbalances.
- It meets the requirements of fairness and administrative due process.
- It requires that the recruitment and promotion of public servants be free from political, bureaucratic or personal patronage.
- It is simple and efficient to operate.[23]

Staffing is a complex process, especially in government where account must be taken of policy and procedural considerations that are absent in most private sector organizations (e.g., language requirements). However, the staffing process in Canadian governments is normally characterized, and to some extent simplified, by a number of policy and program components (e.g., delegation of staffing authority, open and closed competitions) and of sequential and interrelated steps (e.g., written tests, interviews). Moreover, these policies, programs, and procedures are usually spelled out in considerable detail in a human resource management manual.

The central activities in staffing are recruitment, promotion, and deployment. **Recruitment** involves identifying candidates for public service positions from outside the public service by such methods as inviting job applications from within and from outside the public service and using a human resource inventory system. *Promotion* involves the appointment of an employee from within the public service to a position for which the maximum rate of pay is greater than that of the employee's former position. *Deployment* involves the appointment of an employee to another position at the same level as his or her existing position, or to a higher or lower level, provided that there is no change in the employee's personnel classification. In turn, all of these activities involve **selection**, that is, the screening of candidates through such means as application

forms, written examinations, interviews, and a review of the candidate's creden-
tials and past performance. The activities of recruitment and selection are
followed by appointment to a specific position or level in the public service.

The Public Service Commission has statutory authority over staffing. It
establishes and enforces selection standards, and it appoints the more than four
thousand members of the Executive (EX) and Senior Management (SM) groups
within the Management Category. Most other appointments are made by individual departments under authority delegated by the commission.

It is difficult to design and operate a staffing system that will fully satisfy all
the parties affected by it. The D'Avignon Committee noted that the staffing
system in the federal government was "viewed by managers as slow, inflexible
and inefficient; by bargaining agents as misguided and inequitable; and by
employees as frequently failing to ensure that their qualifications are fairly and
objectively assessed."[24]

More than a decade later, the Public Service 2000 Task Force on Staffing
concluded that these problems still existed and that the staffing system failed on
two counts. First, its users do not understand it and use it to attain their objectives
and, second, employees do not believe that it is administered with integrity.
"Because managers see the system as a maze of red tape to be circumvented,
employees, who see the system being circumvented, have become suspicious of
its capacity to ensure fairness and suspicious of the good faith of managers."[25]
The task force noted that the individual components of the system worked
reasonably well. The major source of the problem

> is the management philosophy that underlies the current staffing system—a philos-
> ophy that favours the exercise of external control rather than the exercise of
> individual responsibility, a philosophy that favours error prevention rather than
> accountability, a philosophy that relies on rules rather than judgment.... There
> must be a major shift in the administrative culture in which the staffing system is
> imbedded."[26]

The obstacles to achieving a satisfactory staffing system can be easily demonstrated by reference to specific problem areas. Consider first the area of delegated staffing authority. By 1967, the Public Service Commission had not
formally delegated any staffing authority to federal departments, but by 1985
delegated staffing authority covered about 98 percent of public service appointments. The stated aim of the Public Service Commission in this area is to protect
employees' rights while providing managers with the flexibility they need "to be
accountable for their actions and to provide effective and efficient management."[27] To this end, the commission establishes basic staffing policies and
guidelines and then audits departmental compliance with them. Among the
staffing deficiencies revealed by the audits have been insufficient or non-existent
documentation with respect to statements of qualifications, lists of interview
questions, rating guides, and selection board reports; inadequate training of
managers in staffing; imprecise allocation of staffing responsibilities between
managers and staffing officers; and departures from established rules and
regulations in making acting appointments.

The delegation of staffing authority was a partial response to a second staffing problem, namely long delays and procedural rigidities in recruitment and selection. A 1981 study showed that, compared to three large Canadian corporations, the federal government's selection processes "generally took 34 working days longer to complete a promotional competition, largely because of statutory notice requirements (20 days) and subsequent rights of appeal (a further 14 days)."[28]

A third problem in the staffing area is the perception of many employees that selection board procedures do not necessarily result in the choice of the most meritorious candidate. There is unhappiness about the relative weighting given to the factors of knowledge, abilities, sensitivity, potential for advancement, and seniority. There is also concern about the inadequate training of board members in selection techniques; about the inadequacy of the interview technique for predicting probable success and assessing the relative merits of candidates with roughly the same qualifications; and about bureaucratic patronage resulting from the bias of board members toward certain candidates. A former public service commissioner has stated that despite efforts to adhere to the merit principle

> we know... managers are understandably inclined to favour their immediate staff, whose work they have already seen, over other candidates; managers tend to select in their own image; interviews, even if structured, are an imperfect predictor of success in a job; written examinations, while undoubtedly more objective, may in fact be no more reliable a predictor; and the criteria for certain jobs tend to be overblown or to be of questionable relevance to successful job performance.[29]

A final problem in the staffing area is reconciling the merit principle with the desire for a *representative* public service. This matter is discussed at length in the next chapter.

Training and Development[30]

In some governments, the terms *training* and *development* are used interchangeably, whereas in other governments a distinction is made between training, which prepares people to perform their present jobs, and development, which prepares them for future jobs. Still other governments include development as part of training. For example, the federal government defines training as "any learning activity that contributes to the acquisition by employees of knowledge, skills and experience that helps them to do their present jobs efficiently or prepares them to assume other responsibilities."[31] This latter definition will be used here. In the federal government, while Treasury Board is responsible for overall policy direction, the Public Service Commission conducts central training courses and programs, and provides advice and assistance to departments; in addition, individual departments provide programs to meet their own needs.

A great variety of objectives and approaches are involved in the training of government employees. Among the objectives are making sure that employees can perform their current responsibilities adequately, retraining employees who have become surplus, orienting employees who have taken on a new job, and ensuring through developmental training that qualified employees will be available to meet future needs. The three main approaches to the process are:

1. formal classroom training within government;
2. formal classroom training by universities, colleges, or consulting firms; and
3. on-the-job training and experience.

The programs available range from intensive one-day or weekend sessions through residential sessions lasting several days or as long as two months, to funded educational leave for as long as a year for senior managers.

Despite the large investment of time and money that some governments make to train their employees, it is widely acknowledged that virtually every government needs to do more. It is also generally recognized that there are formidable obstacles to substantially increasing the current level of investment.

First, elected politicians in general are not very sympathetic to calls for more training. Many politicians are reluctant to allocate resources for this purpose because the benefits are not immediately evident or easily evaluated, and/or the political payoff is not apparent. Second, even among some senior appointed officials, there is insufficient recognition of the necessity for adequate training. In some governments, especially at the municipal level, there appears to be little concern about the adequacy of personnel to meet the demands of existing positions, much less about planning for those employees required in the 1990s and beyond. The "hope and a prayer" approach to training, according to which governments trust that qualified personnel will somehow emerge when needed, is woefully inadequate.

The scarcity of financial resources is another major obstacle to developing and preserving a body of highly skilled and knowledgeable employees, even among those governments where the importance of training and development is readily acknowledged. Training and development programs are costly, not only in terms of the infrastructure required to make opportunities available but also in terms of the time lost from substantive work while employees are taking courses. Financial support for training and development is also related to what is sometimes described as "the great training robbery." It is often difficult to show that those who have completed certain programs are better able to perform their present duties or to take on new and more challenging tasks. It is reasonable for politicians to ask whether a good case can be made for investing in this area. More attention needs to be paid, therefore, to evaluating the wide assortment of available programs.

The Public Service 2000 Task Force on Training and Development proposed several guiding principles as a basis for future policies and priorities in training and development. Among these principles:

- Training and development is an investment in better government and better service to the public.
- Good human resource management and development policies will be

necessary to attract and retain good people in the public service in the future.

- Training and development of staff is an integral part of management at all levels, embracing a broad range of activities and priorities of which classroom training is but one.
- Equity in training and development means responding adequately to needs of the individual, as well as corporate needs, including the need to redress previous inequities.[32]

Governments have recently placed greater emphasis on the training of managers who are, in turn, encouraged to ensure that their subordinates are adequately trained. This emphasis is reflected in the importance attributed to the training of the federal Management Category and its counterpart in other governments. In 1988, the federal government announced the establishment of the Canadian Centre for Management Development as an institution dedicated to excellence in teaching and research in public sector management. The centre aims to provide senior managers with the skills, research, and practical solutions needed to make government operations as efficient and effective as possible. In addition, the Centre strives

> to encourage pride and excellence in the management of the Public Service and to foster among Public Service managers a sense of the purposes, values and traditions of the Public Service; . . . to attract through its programs and studies persons of high calibre to the Public Service and to support their growth and development as public sector managers committed to the service of Canada; . . . and to encourage a greater awareness in Canada of issues related to public sector management . . . [33]

Performance Evaluation

Performance evaluation (often called employee appraisal) is a process involving the systematic collection and analysis of information about the performance of employees over time. It is integrally linked to the other human resource processes discussed above. Employees must not only be recruited, selected, trained, and paid; they must also be evaluated in terms of their overall performance. Effective employee appraisal must be preceded by the process of *performance review*, which is "a continuous process in which a supervisor and an employee consider the duties to be performed by the employee, the achievements expected, the evaluation criteria and the results actually achieved."[34] *Employee appraisal*, which is based on this performance review, "identifies an employee's various qualifications, estimates potential, identifies and proposes responses to training and development needs, and indicates future assignments."[35] This employee appraisal is contained in a formal written report that often includes a summary of the performance review.

The overriding purpose of performance evaluation is to improve the contribution and motivation of each employee. More specifically, it provides a means of assessing the advisability of pay increases and promotion, the strengths and weaknesses of an employee's present performance, and his or her potential for advancement and need for training and development. In addition, performance evaluation gives supervisors a regular opportunity to communicate with and motivate their employees and to check the effectiveness of such other human resource processes as selection and training.

A formal appraisal report is typically prepared once each year for permanent employees and more frequently, usually quarterly, for probationary employees. To facilitate comparison of employees within a single department and with employees in other departments, a common set of evaluation categories is normally used across the government as a whole. For example, the federal government uses the five categories of outstanding, superior, fully satisfactory, satisfactory, and unsatisfactory. It is notable that the supervisor's own evaluation is affected by his or her effectiveness in evaluating subordinates.

Performance evaluation, like job classification, is a difficult undertaking because it involves a substantial measure of personal judgment. It is widely recognized that the objectivity, validity, and reliability of rating systems are often questionable. The fact that one supervisor's "superior" is another supervisor's "satisfactory" raises questions about the justice of the process.

Performance evaluation, which is supposed to help employees to enhance their contribution and motivation, can often have the opposite effect. Employees are aware of the impact of performance evaluations on their compensation and career prospects; thus, they frequently view evaluations with trepidation. If the process and the outcome of evaluation are not seen as fair, they may actually reduce the employees' motivation to perform at their current level. The matter of fairness is complicated by the fact that many employees have an inflated perception of their performance and may well resent even a "satisfactory" rating. Supervisors, in turn, are sensitive to these high expectations and to the career impact of evaluation decisions; they are, therefore, reluctant to assign low ratings that they then have to explain and defend in face-to-face meetings with employees. Supervisors are especially reluctant to assign ratings that may get them involved in the time-consuming process of grievances and appeals. Consequently, supervisors are understandably tempted to rate each employee as at least satisfactory. The annual employee appraisal tends to be easier when supervisors provide employees with an informal, ongoing assessment of their performance rather than storing up the good and bad points of an employee's performance for discussion at a single time during the year.

CONCLUSIONS

The management of human resources is a centrally important function of government that is closely related to several of the subjects examined in earlier chapters. Many of the issues discussed in this chapter are of an enduring nature; despite continuing efforts, they have not yet been resolved to the satisfaction of the government or its employees. Two additional issues, namely employment equity and collective bargaining, have emerged more recently. These two issues are likely to have a significant continuing impact on public administration in all spheres of Canadian government; they are, therefore, discussed separately in the next two chapters.

NOTES

1. Canada, Royal Commission on Financial Management and Accountability, *Final Report* (Ottawa: Supply and Services, 1979), p. 25. (Emphasis added.)
2. For an examination of the evolution and issues of personnel management in the provinces, see J.E. Hodgetts and O.P. Dwivedi, *Provincial Governments as Employers* (Montreal: McGill-Queen's University Press, 1974). See also, by the same authors, "Administration and Personnel," in David J. Bellamy, Jon H. Pammett, and Donald C. Rowat, eds., *The Provincial Political Systems: Comparative Essays* (Toronto: Methuen 1976), pp. 341-56.
3. R. H. Dowdell, "Public Personnel Administration," in Kenneth Kernaghan, ed., *Public Administration in Canada*, 4th ed. (Toronto: Methuen, 1982), p. 196.
4. Ibid. (Emphasis added.)
5. Treasury Board of Canada, *The Manager's Deskbook* (Ottawa: Supply and Services, 1989), p. 3.1-1.
6. Ibid.
7. Valuable information and analysis on the nature and extent of patronage from the pre-confederation period to the mid-1930s are provided by R. McGregor Dawson in *The Principle of Official Independence* (London: P. S. King and Son, 1922), ch. 3; *The Civil Service of Canada* (Oxford: Oxford University Press, 1929); and "The Canadian Civil Service," *Canadian Journal of Economics and Political Science* 2 (August 1936). For a detailed treatment of the evolution of merit in the Canadian federal public service, see J. E. Hodgetts, William McCloskey, Reginald Whitaker, and V. Seymour Wilson, *The Biography of an Institution: The Civil Service of Canada, 1908-1967* (Montreal: McGill-Queen's University Press, 1974).
8. *Report* (Ottawa: Queen's Printer), 1962-63, 5 vol.
9. *Report* (Ottawa: Supply and Services, 1979), p. 5.
10. Government of Canada, Office of the Prime Minister, *Public Service 2000*, Press Release, December 12, 1989.
11. Ibid.
12. While this book was in press, the federal government published a white paper entitled *Public Service 2000: The Renewal of the Public Service of Canada* (Ottawa: Supply and Services, 1990).
13. For an account of the functions of Treasury Board and its Secretariat, see Chapter 8.
14. Public Service Commission, *Strategy Document for 1982-1987*, p. 4.
15. See also the discussion of occupational categories and groups in the section of Chapter 25 on the structure of bargaining units.
16. Canada, Public Service Commission, *Annual Report 1989* (Ottawa: Supply and Services, 1990), pp. 86-87.
17. Treasury Board, *PS 2000, Report,* July 20, 1990, pp. 22 ff.
18. A benchmark description is "the description of illustrative work performed in a job which exemplifies the degrees of the factors and/or the classification levels in an evaluation plan." It is usually made up of "the identification of information, a summary of the duties stating the function and purpose of the job, a list of duties, the percentage of time devoted to each duty, and specifications written in terms of factors used in the rating plan." Government of Canada, Treasury Board Secretariat, *Personnel: A Manager's Handbook* (Ottawa: Supply and Services, 1982), p. 82.

19. *Report, Executive Summary*, August 7, 1990, p. i.
20. *Report*, August 7, 1990.
21. Management Board of Cabinet, *Human Resources Planning*, OPS Management Series Process 22-3, (Toronto: Queen's Printer, 1982), p. 7.
22. *Personnel: A Manager's Handbook*, p. 24.
23. *Report*, August 8, 1990, p. 9.
24. *Report*, p. 183.
25. Treasury Board, *Report*, August 8, 1990, p. 3.
26. Ibid., p. 4.
27. Public Service Commission, *Annual Report 1981*, p. 4.
28. Ibid., p. 13.
29. John Edwards, "Equal Opportunity in the Public Service," *Dialogue* 6 (February 1982): 4.
30. See the recommendations for reform in the the sphere of training and development contained in the *Public Service 2000 Task Force Report on Staff Training and Development*, July 23, 1990.
31. *Personnel: A Manager's Handbook*, p. 51.
32. Treasury Board, *Public Service 2000, Report of the Task Force on Training and Development*, Executive Summary, August 8, 1990, p. 2.
33. Canada, *Statutes* (Bill c-34, introduced June 27, 1989).
34. *Personnel*, p. 49.
35. Ibid.

BIBLIOGRAPHY

Baker, Walter. "Executive Manpower Requirements of the Canadian Public Services in the 1980s." In Kenneth Kernaghan, ed., *Executive Manpower in the Public Service: Make or Buy?* Toronto: Institute of Public Administration of Canada, 1975, pp. 39-62.

Bird, Richard M. *The Growth of Public Employment in Canada*. Toronto: Butterworths, 1979.

Borins, Sandford F. *The Language of the Skies: The Bilingual Air Traffic Control Conflict in Canada*. Montreal: McGill-Queen's University Press, 1983.

Campbell, Colin, and George Szablowski. *The Superbureaucrats: Structure and Behaviour in Central Agencies*. Toronto: Macmillan, 1979.

Canada. *Beneath the Veneer. Report of the Task Force on Barriers to Women in the Public Service*. Ottawa: Supply and Services, 1990, 4 vol.

Canada. Treasury Board, Public Service 2000. *PS 2000: Reports and Summaries of the Task Forces*, August 14, 1990.

Canada. Civil Service Commission. *Personnel Administration in the Public Service*. Ottawa: Queen's Printer, 1958.

Canada. *Public Service 2000. The Renewal of the Public Service of Canada*. Ottawa: Supply and Services, 1990.

Canada. *Report of the Special Committee on the Review of Personnel Management and the Merit Principle*. Ottawa: Supply and Services, 1979.

Canada. Royal Commission on Administrative Classification in the Public Service. *Report*. Ottawa: King's Printer, 1946.

Canada. Royal Commission on Financial Management and Accountability. *Final Report*. Ottawa: Supply and Services, 1979.

Canada. Royal Commission on Government Organization. *Report*. 5 vols. Ottawa: Queen's Printer, 1962.

Dowdell, R. H. "Public Personnel Administration." In Kenneth Kernaghan, ed., *Public Administration in Canada: Selected Readings*. 4th ed. Toronto: Methuen, 1982.

Hodgetts, J. E. *Pioneer Public Service: An Administrative History of the United Canadas*. Toronto: University of Toronto Press, 1955.

Hodgetts, J. E., and O. P. Dwivedi. *Provincial Governments as Employers*. Montreal: McGill-Queen's University Press, 1974.

Hodgetts, J. E., William McCloskey, Reginald Whitaker, and V. Seymour Wilson. *The Biography of an Institution: The Civil Service of Canada, 1908-1967*. Montreal: McGill-Queen's University Press, 1972.

Kuruvilla, P. K. "Public Service Recruitment in Canada: Some Perspectives and Problems." *Indian Journal of Public Administration* 26 (January-March 1980): 62-90.

Kuruvilla, P. K. "Training and Development in Public Service: The Canadian Experience." *Indian Journal of Public Administration* 26 (July-September 1980): 814-26.

Laframboise, H. L. "Administrative Reform in the Federal Public Service: Signs of a Saturation Psychosis." *Canadian Public Administration* 14 (Fall 1971): 303-25.

Love, J. D. "Personnel Organization in the Canadian Public Service: Some Observations on the Past." *Canadian Public Administration* 22 (Fall 1979): 402-14.

Love, J. D. "The Merit Principle in the Provincial Governments of Atlantic Canada." *Canadian Public Administration* 31 (Fall 1988): 335-51.

Manion, John. "New Challenges in Public Administration." *Canadian Public Administration* 31 (Summer 1988): 234-46.

Siegel, David. "The Changing Shape and Nature of Public Service Employment." *Canadian Public Administration* 31 (Summer 1988): 159-93.

Stahl, O. Glenn. *Public Personnel Administration*. 8th ed. New York: Harper & Row, 1983.

CASES

In *Case Program in Canadian Public Administration* (Toronto: Institute of Public Administration of Canada):

The Problem Program. By L.S. Wong

Implementing Bilingual Air Traffic Control in Quebec. By Sandford F. Borins

The Ben Fisher Case. By Nancy LePitre, Salim Mansur, and Wilbur Grasham

Trying to Fire the Medical Officer of Health: A Case Study. By Alison McGear, Ted Darby, and Raisa B. Deber

The Role of the Manager in the Management of Change: An Exercise in Downsizing. By André LeBlond and David Zussman

Flex Time At the Health Department. By Nancy Patterson

Cases developed by the Canadian Centre for Management Development and distributed by the Case Program in Canadian Public Administration:

Impasse: Team Building. By John Hunter

Reorganizing Human Resources at Statistics Canada. By Philippe Clément

Toxic Chemicals. By Richard Paton and John William Pullen

24

Representative Bureaucracy and Employment Equity

This chapter examines in turn two closely related issues in human resource management, namely representative bureaucracy and employment equity. The latter part of the chapter focusses on pay equity, which is one component of the employment equity issue.

REPRESENTATIVE BUREAUCRACY

Representative bureaucracy is a difficult concept that has been interpreted in a variety of ways.[1] A strict interpretation of **representative bureaucracy** would require that the public service be a microcosm of the total society in terms of a wide range of variables, including race, religion, language, education, social class, and region of origin. However, there is disagreement in scholarly writings as to what purposes representative bureaucracy serves, what degree of representativeness is desirable, and what variables should be included. Proponents of representative bureaucracy recommend its adoption on the following grounds:

1. Public servants exercise significant power in the political system.
2. External controls over public servants by the political executive, the legislature, and the courts are inadequate to check bureaucratic power and thereby to ensure bureaucratic responsibility.
3. A public service that is representative of the total population will be responsive to the needs and interests of the general public and will therefore be more responsible. This central proposition of the theory of representative bureaucracy is based on several subpropositions:
    (a) If the values of the public service as a whole are similar to those of the total population, then the public service will tend to make the kind of decisions that the public would make if it were involved in the decision-making.
    (b) The values of public servants are moulded by the pattern of socialization they experience before they enter the public service, that is, by such socializing forces as education, social class, occupational background, race, family, and group associations.
    (c) The values arising from this socialization will not be modified by prolonged exposure to bureaucratic values.

(d) The values arising from socialization will be reflected in the behaviour of public servants and therefore in their recommendations and decisions.

(e) Thus, the various groups in the population should be represented in the public service in approximate demographic proportion so that public servants will be responsive to the interests of these groups both in policy development and program delivery.

Critics of representative bureaucracy acknowledge the substantial power of public servants and the consequent need to provide controls to preserve and promote bureaucratic responsibility. They contend, however, that the assertion that external controls are inadequate to ensure responsible administrative conduct requires more investigation. These critics also point to the logical and empirical failings of the theory of representative bureaucracy.

They contend that in a representative public service the values of the public service as a whole will not be similar to those of the general population; rather, the values of individual public servants *may* be similar to the values of those groups in the population they are supposed to represent. Moreover, the public service as a whole does not make decisions; rather, decisions are made by individual public servants who, by acting on behalf of groups whom they represent, would serve the interests of particular segments of the public rather than the total population. Also, it is not sufficient for the public service as a whole to be broadly representative of the total population; for all interests to be represented in the decision-making process, each major administrative unit must be representative of the total population, especially at its senior levels where the most important recommendations and decisions are made.

Opponents of representative bureaucracy observe further that a public servant with certain social and educational origins will not necessarily share the values of persons outside the public service who have similar origins. The lifelong process of socialization continues after entry to the public service in the form of resocialization to the values of the service as a whole, or of particular administrative units. Moreover, representatives of a specific group in the population, particularly if they achieve high office in the public service, are likely to be upwardly mobile and may well share the socio-economic and other values of those with whom they work, rather than of the group from which they came. In this regard, Peta Sheriff regrets the lack of research on the strength of pre-occupational and post-occupational experience, and concludes that although "the very cornerstone of the representative bureaucracy thesis has no direct evidence to support it . . . the suspicion that pre-occupational socialization must have some influence is sufficient to maintain the thesis."[2] However, even if public servants continue to share the values of certain groups, despite organizational socialization, these values may not be significantly reflected in the public servants' behaviour.

Thus, it is logically possible to have a representative public service that is not responsive and a responsive public service that is not representative. Indeed, Meier and Nigro conclude that the most senior levels in the United States public service "are an unrepresentative demographic group holding quite representative attitudes."[3]

Canadian Writings

The major points of contention in a debate on representative bureaucracy in Canada[4] involve the extent to which the values of efficiency, effectiveness, neutrality, and responsiveness conflict with, or complement, that of representativeness. In this debate, Donald Rowat objects to John Porter's sacrifice of representativeness for the sake of efficiency and suggests that both values can be achieved. He argues that representativeness "is essential to the efficiency of the bureaucracy, in the sense of the latter's effectiveness in a democratic, pluralistic society."[5] Porter asserts that people of various social origins will be found in the bureaucracy in roughly the same proportion as in the population as a whole *if* government recruitment and promotion policies do not discriminate against particular groups, *if* educational facilities to qualify persons for public service appointments are equal as between these groups, and *if* these groups are equally motivated to join the public service. He contends that "in the theoretically ideal bureaucracy, the candidate for office neither gains nor loses as a result of ethnic, religious or regional origins."[6]

Rowat, who is more concerned with what can be realized in practice than with a search for a theoretically ideal bureaucracy, observes that Porter's conditions of equality do not exist and cannot be easily achieved. He contends that representativeness must be actively sought, even at the expense of technical efficiency and neutrality. Intelligent people with the potential to rise to higher levels in the service could be recruited and provided with the required in-service education and training. Moreover, competent members of underrepresented groups could be brought into the public service from outside. Porter opposes the recruitment of outsiders on the grounds that this practice threatens the neutrality of the service and the concept of the bureaucratic career. He states that "since the basis of power associations are frequently ethnic, regional or religious, the idea that these groups should be represented in the bureaucracy contradicts the notion of the official as the servant of the state."[7] Rowat does not agree that the appointment of "bureaucratic outsiders" would endanger political neutrality, and he argues that a public service that complemented career public servants with outsiders would be more responsive, since a career bureaucracy tends to "lose contact with and lack understanding of the changing feelings, needs and desires of the great variety of people and groups found in our dynamic, pluralistic society."[8]

Rowat does not suggest that underrepresented groups should be represented in precise proportion to their presence in the total population, and he rejects the use of quotas for recruitment and promotion as unworkable. He does suggest, however, that recruitment to the public service should be guided by the principle of representation.

Porter objects on several grounds to Rowat's plea for representativeness. He first poses the basic question as to which of the many groups in society should be represented in the public service. He then contends that Rowat's proposals for recruiting members of underrepresented groups and providing them with in-service training serve the principle of equal opportunity rather than representativeness. He states also that "in a society of classes, the upwardly mobile are seldom representative of the social interests from which they originated."[9] Finally, he notes the assumption in the theory of representative bureaucracy that political institutions are inadequate to cope with modern demands and questions the view that "ways can be found for governmental bureaucracy to make up for the deficiencies in our representative political institutions."[10]

Two decades after the Porter-Rowat debate, Wilson and Mullins expressed doubt that "members of a bureaucracy chosen from various relevant groups will be likely to act as agents or spokesmen for their groups and group interests."[11] Moreover, they concluded that support for representative bureaucracy "on the assumption that it would be politically representative in any meaningful sense is not only bogus, but also dangerous."[12] Like Rowat, Wilson and Mullins assert that technical efficiency should not be stressed at the expense of representativeness.

Another perspective on the issue of representative bureaucracy in Canada has been provided by Dennis Olsen, who updated to 1973 the study of the bureaucratic elite conducted by John Porter in 1953. On the basis of an examination of data on the social background, career, and education of federal and provincial bureaucrats, Olsen concluded that, compared with the 1953 bureaucratic elite, the 1973 group is "more open, more heterogeneous, and probably more meritocratic."[13] However, these changes have taken place very slowly, and he envisages that the overall future pattern will be characterized by a "marked persistence of both social class and ethnic preferences in recruitment."[14]

The Representativeness of the Canadian Bureaucracy

Data on several aspects of the current composition of the Canadian public service in relation to the total population are unavailable. The data that are available indicate that the service is not a microcosm of Canadian society. A number of important groups are underrepresented in the service, and both the senior and middle echelons are unrepresentative of the general population. The middle ranks are more representative than the senior level, however, and are representative of the total population on the criterion of region of origin. Beattie et al. concluded that, compared to the senior bureaucracy, the middle level was "quite open and heterogeneous." It drew "amply from a wide range of significant social categories in the Canadian mosaic—new and old-stock Canadians, the several regions of Canada, rural and urban areas, the various social class levels—all sectors, in fact, except the Francophone population of Canada."[15] By way of contrast, the senior level of the bureaucracy contained an overrepresentation of males, anglophones, the middle and upper classes, Ontarians, and the well-educated.

But Dennis Olsen, after comparing data from 1953 and 1973, concluded that the senior ranks have gradually become more representative of the general population. He asserts that "the new elite is drawn from a little lower in the class system, ethnic representation is a little more balanced, the new elite is more highly educated than the old, and . . . a greater proportion of the new elite is made up of *career* civil servants."[16] Nevertheless, the senior level is not very representative of the total population. For example, 92 percent of the bureaucratic elite had university degrees compared to 8 percent of the male labour force; only 3 percent were women; and persons of British ethnic origin were substantially overrepresented, persons of French origin were slightly underrepresented, and all other ethnic groups were heavily underrepresented.[17] In terms of social class, the bureaucratic elite was primarily of middle-class origin and "only 15% of the bureaucratic elite . . . could be described as *possibly* of working class origin."[18]

It is not the policy of the federal government to establish in the public service a microcosm of the Canadian mosaic by pursuing exact demographic representation of all groups in society; rather, the government's aim is to achieve a more proportionate representation of a limited number of politically significant, but underrepresented, groups. In this regard, the government has argued that the underrepresentation of such groups as francophones, women, and aboriginal peoples may diminish the sensitivity of the public service to the needs of certain segments of the population. Thus, a prime motivation underlying present efforts to represent these groups more adequately is to make the public service more responsive, both in the provision of policy advice and the delivery of services. As explained above, the assumption that representativeness will promote responsiveness is central to the theory of representative bureaucracy. The government also presumes that members of underrepresented groups who join the public service will remain sensitive to the needs and claims of these groups.

In view of the deficiencies of the theory of representative bureaucracy outlined earlier, the benefits of representation in terms of increased responsiveness are likely to be less than anticipated. However, we know very little about the extent to which the expanded representation of francophones, women, and aboriginal peoples has had a policy impact by advancing the substantive interests of these groups.

Increased representation has effects that are not covered by the theory of representative bureaucracy. Representation has a symbolic impact that helps to promote quiescence and stability in the Canadian political system and explains, in part, its appeal to government officials. The statutes, regulations, and administrative units designed to increase the representation of underrepresented groups evoke symbols of equality of opportunity and upward mobility for members of these groups. In the name of equal opportunity, the government has instituted programs to recruit and train group members who have not enjoyed equal access to the public service. Also, recruitment to senior posts from outside the service and post-entry training geared to promotion to the higher ranks of the service demonstrate the opportunities for group members to attain senior policy-making posts. Thus, group members who are appointed to, and promoted in, the public service can serve a very important role as models for other members to emulate.

Government actions to increase the representativeness of the public service serve a partisan political purpose in that they help to sustain or increase electoral support for the governing party. Evidence of partisan motivation can be seen in the fact that the groups for whom increased representation has been sought have mobilized for political action and are highly visible and vocal in their demands for greater participation in the political and administrative systems. The government's efforts on behalf of underrepresented groups have brought about a more representative public service. It is not practicable, however, to attempt to represent proportionately all the myriad groups that make up the Canadian mosaic. Experience to date suggests that future government measures toward a more representative public service will be directed primarily to under-represented groups that become politically influential.

EQUAL OPPORTUNITY AND EMPLOYMENT EQUITY

The issues of representative bureaucracy and equal opportunity are closely linked in that the attainment of a representative public service depends largely on the extent to which various groups in society have equal access to employment in the public service. The federal and provincial governments have adopted a wide range of programs to promote equal opportunity in the public service for segments of the population that have historically been under-represented there. As explained above, the federal government is committed to improving the representation of certain "target groups," namely women, members of visible minority groups, persons with disabilities, and aboriginal peoples. In the federal sphere, francophones are not treated as one of the target groups; rather, they are treated separately as part of the government's efforts to ensure equitable participation in the public service of Canada's two official language communities. Among the provinces, there is some variation as to the particular groups considered to be inadequately represented. The under-representation of women is an important concern in all provinces, whereas concern about the participation of such groups as francophones and aboriginal peoples is limited to provinces where these groups constitute a significant proportion of the population.

The term *equal opportunity* was largely displaced in the early 1980s by the term *affirmative action*, which was in turn soon displaced by the term **employment equity**. The terms affirmative action and employment equity are often used interchangeably; both can usefully be viewed as means to the end of equal opportunity. In June 1983, the government announced its continued commitment to a bureaucracy that is representative of and responsive to the people it serves,[19] and introduced an *affirmative action* program to accelerate the participation in the public service of the target groups. Affirmative action was defined as "a comprehensive systems-based approach to the identification and elimination of discrimination in employment. It makes use of detailed analyses to identify and systematically remove employment policies, practices and procedures which may exclude or place at a disadvantage the three target groups"[20] (women, aboriginal peoples, and disabled persons).

The government stressed that the merit principle would be preserved and that the numerical goals being set were not quotas, but rather "an estimate of what can be achieved when systemic barriers are eliminated and some temporary special measures are put in place to accelerate training and development experience."[21] The President of the Treasury Board announced that implementation of the affirmative action program would be viewed as a major consideration in the performance of deputy ministers. Thus, while this program does not establish quotas, it moves in that direction by using temporary special measures, numerical goals, and pressure on senior bureaucrats to achieve these goals.

The legal basis for affirmative action programs in the federal sphere of government was laid in 1977 by the Canadian Human Rights Act. This Act established the Canadian Human Rights Commission to investigate complaints about discrimination by federal departments, Crown corporations, and businesses under federal jurisdiction, to work out settlements in individual cases, and to promote the reduction of discriminatory practices through publicity and research. The wording of section 15(1) of the Act suggests that measures taken to redress historical imbalances in the participation of certain groups does not amount to "reverse discrimination."

More recently, the recommendations of the Royal Commission on Equality in Employment[22] (the Abella Commission) and the coming into force of section 15—the equality rights section—of the Canadian Charter of Rights and Freedoms have supported the federal government's affirmative action programs. The report of the commission argued that

> [s]ometimes equality means treating people the same, despite their differences, and sometimes it means treating them as equals by accommodating their differences.... We now know that to treat everyone the same may be to offend the notion of equality.... Equality means nothing if it does not mean that we are of equal worth regardless of differences in gender, race, ethnicity, or disability.... Ignoring differences and refusing to accommodate them is a denial of equal access and opportunity. It is discrimination.[23]

It is important to note that affirmative action programs are protected under the Charter. Section 15 guarantees "equal protection and equal benefit of the law without discrimination," and then goes on to say that this guarantee "does not preclude any law, program or activity that has as its object the amelioration of conditions of disadvantaged individuals or groups including those that are disadvantaged because of race, national or ethnic origin, colour, religion, sex, age or mental or physical disability." In other words, preferential treatment for groups that have historically suffered from discrimination does not constitute reverse discrimination.

As noted above, the term employment equity, which came into frequent use in 1985, is very similar in meaning to affirmative action. Employment equity is currently defined by the federal Public Service Commission as "employment practices designed to ensure that the regular staffing process is free of attitudinal and systemic barriers in order that the Public Service reflects all groups present in the Canadian labour force, and designed to ensure that corrective measures are applied to redress any historical disadvantage experienced by certain designated groups."[24] The term *systemic barriers* (or systemic discrimination) refers to an employment policy, practice, procedure, or system that excludes, or has a negative effect on, women or minority groups, whether or not that effect was intended, and that cannot be justified as being job-related. For example, if 15 percent of the geologists in Canada are women, but only 6 percent of the geologists in the Department of Energy, Mines and Resources are women, the burden is on the department to show that this is not the result of discrimination. The explanation could be that the department requires that all the geologists it hires have ten years of working experience and that relatively few female geologists have that experience. Consideration would be given to removing this requirement because its impact is to penalize women more than men, even though no discrimination was intended by the requirement.

In September 1985, the federal government announced special measures to promote employment equity in the federal public service for *members of visible minority groups.*[25] These initiatives were, in part, a response to the recommendations of the House of Commons Special Committee on Participation of Visible Minorities in Canadian Society.[26] A government survey showed that members of visible minority groups were underrepresented in the public service in that they made up about 1.7 percent of the service compared to more than 4 percent of the labour force. The new measures included revising employment application forms to allow members of visible minority groups to so identify themselves, providing estimates of the availability of qualified members of these groups in the labour market to help public service managers establish targets for hiring members of these groups, and incorporating a special section on visible minorities in training courses for public service managers. Then, in March 1986, the House of Commons passed the federal Employment Equity Act (Bill C-62), which requires employers who employ "one hundred or more employees on or in connection with a federal work, undertaking or business" to report annually to the government on the extent to which they have achieved results in promoting employment equity.

In the federal government, the Treasury Board Secretariat and the Public Service Commission have played the leading roles in developing, implementing, and monitoring employment equity programs. The two agencies devised programs for francophones and women in the 1960s that were strengthened and supplemented by programs for aboriginal peoples, visible minorities, and the disabled during the 1970s and 1980s.

These programs may be grouped into three categories, namely training and development, new or modified administrative units and practices, and vigorous recruitment. In the sphere of training and development, programs have included training opportunities to upgrade women in the Administrative Support category for promotion to management posts, and the Northern Careers Program for aboriginal peoples. Among the administrative structures established in the Public Service Commission are the Women's Career Counselling and Referral Bureau and the Office of Native Employment. Special efforts have been made through a variety of programs to recruit qualified persons from every target group. Departments and agencies are required to run employment equity programs to promote representativeness and fairness in the public service. Similar initiatives have been taken by provincial governments.

These programs to overcome artificial institutional barriers to public service employment are of limited use in overcoming attitudinal barriers, notably prejudice against the target groups, which exists not only in the public service but in Canadian society as a whole. There is, however, an ongoing effort in government to "sensitize" public service managers to the importance of removing obstacles to equal access to public service employment. To ensure that managers are sensitive to this effort, success in enhancing the participation of these groups is now deemed to be one element of the managers' performance evaluation. The Public Service Commission has observed that "an important positive re-enforcement to managerial sensitization is the evaluation of managers vis-à-vis their utilization of human resources ... specifically with respect to the participation of under-represented groups."[27]

There have been complaints from public servants and from their unions that equal opportunity programs violate the merit principle and discriminate against candidates outside the target groups for appointment and promotion. The commission has responded by explaining that merit is a dynamic principle; its application must be reconciled with such other values as responsiveness, representativeness, fairness, equity, and economy. Moreover, according to the commission, the equal opportunity programs do not amount to reverse discrimination because individual abilities, rather than group characteristics, are emphasized in appointments and promotions.

The former Secretary General of the federal Public Service Commission has explained that

> equal treatment is not necessarily equitable treatment and ... discrimination means practices or attitudes that have, by design or impact, the effect of limiting an individual's or group's right to the opportunities generally available to others. It also deprives the Public Service and other employers of valuable talent. ...
>
> We are learning that selection according to merit is not served if well qualified people are either prevented from entering the Public Service or from moving up in accordance with their experience and ability. We are also understanding and recognizing that it is because their competence was not recognized in the past that some groups are underrepresented today.[28]

Nevertheless, the commission has opposed the setting of *quotas* for the employment of underrepresented groups on the grounds that

1. it is very difficult to decide which groups or interests in society should be represented;
2. quotas clash with the merit principle by creating two classes of public servants—those who received their jobs because they were meritorious and

those who received them because they were members of an under-represented group.

The commission has supported the Treasury Board requirements that departments set realistic *targets* for increasing the representation of the target groups. The commission asserts that these targets are not quotas; rather, they are described as yardsticks by which the government's success in attracting qualified candidates from underrepresented groups can be measured. In 1988, Treasury Board announced that the government had met or exceeded its employment equity targets for the 1985-1988 period and stated new targets for the next three-year period.

To assess the extent to which the federal government's employment equity programs have been successful, it is useful to examine briefly the experience of three major groups that, historically, have been underrepresented in the public service, namely, francophones, women, and aboriginal peoples.

Francophone Representation

Barriers to equal opportunity for French-speaking people have existed both in the government and in the francophone community itself for most of this century. During the post-Confederation period before the 1918 Civil Service Act, francophones were numerically well-represented in the public service. They were not, however, as well represented as anglophones at the senior levels. Moreover, many of the francophone appointments rested on patronage, whereas the 1918 Act emphasized merit and efficiency. Especially after 1918, the public service was pervaded by an anglophone linguistic and cultural bias. Merit and efficiency were linked to formal education and technical qualifications. French-language or bilingual competence was not considered a component of merit or likely to enhance efficiency. Furthermore, written examinations and interviews for recruitment and promotion reflected anglophone values and the anglophone educational system, to the disadvantage of francophones. Finally, the view was widely held that the Quebec educational system was a significant barrier to francophone representation because it emphasized education for such occupations as law, medicine, and the priesthood, and did not therefore provide its graduates with the technical, scientific, and commercial skills required for appointment to the public service.

All these factors combined to reduce the motivation of francophones to seek or retain positions in the federal administration. The result was a decline in the proportion of francophones in the public service from 21.58 percent in 1918 to 12.25 percent in 1946, and a decline at the deputy minister level during the same period from 14.28 percent to zero.[29]

During the early 1960s, the so-called Quiet Revolution in Quebec focussed national attention on francophone grievances about their inadequate participation in the public service. And the Glassco Commission reported in 1963 that francophones were badly underrepresented in the service. The commissioners noted that public confidence in the public service will depend on "how representative it is of the public it serves," and that to achieve representativeness, "a career at the centre of government should be as attractive and congenial to French-speaking as to English-speaking Canadians."[30]

Then, in 1966, Prime Minister Pearson made his landmark statement on bilingualism in the public service, in which he promised that the "linguistic and cultural values of the English-speaking and French-speaking Canadians will be reflected through civil service recruitment and training."[31] The Royal Commission on Bilingualism and Biculturalism, which reported in 1967, gave enormous impetus to this objective. Prime Minister Trudeau, in accepting in principle the broad objectives proposed for the public service in the commission's report, stated that "the atmosphere of the public service should represent the linguistic and cultural duality of Canadian society, and . . . Canadians whose mother tongue is French should be adequately represented in the public service—both in terms of numbers and in levels of responsibility."[32] Then, in keeping with the aim of the Official Languages Act passed in 1969,[33] the Treasury Board established the Official Languages Program, with three major objectives—providing services to, and communicating with, the public in both official languages, enabling public servants to work in the official language of their choice, and achieving the full participation in the service of members of both the anglophone and francophone communities.

In a concerted effort since the late 1960s to increase francophone representation in the public service, the major strategies adopted by the government have included more active recruitment of francophones, the designation of language requirements for public service positions, and the development of an extensive language training system.[34] Individual public servants and public service unions severely attacked these measures on the grounds that the measures violate the merit principle and amount to reverse discrimination against anglophones. The government's response to these charges was that bilingual competence is an element of merit and that, by increasing the number of positions requiring bilingual competence, the opportunities for qualified francophones is also increased. As a result, the merit principle and the goal of a more representative public service are both achieved.

These remedial strategies have helped to reduce institutional barriers in the government to francophone representation. Attitudinal change is more difficult to measure, but there appears to be less overt resistance to government programs in this area than there was initially, and the public service milieu is now a much more bilingual one. In addition, a significant perceived barrier in the francophone community has been largely overcome in that, since 1960, the Quebec educational system has produced large numbers of university and college graduates with the requisite qualifications for public service appointments.

A tangible indicator of progress is the fact that francophones are now represented in the public service in almost exact proportion to their numbers in the total population—an increase from 12.25 percent of the service in 1946 to 28.6 percent in 1989.[35] However, only 22.4 percent of the Management Category is composed of francophones. In 1985, the Official Languages Commissioner reported that "in spite of general progress, the underlying problems are practically the same as those pointed out in every Annual Report since 1980: Anglophones are under-represented in Quebec and in the Administrative Support category; Francophones are under-represented in management generally..., in the Scientific and Professional category and in bilingual regions outside Quebec."[36]

Female Representation

The underrepresentation of women in Canada's public services, especially at the middle and senior levels, has existed from Confederation to the present day because of obstacles to equal opportunity, both in the government and in society generally.

By 1885, only 23 of 4,280 public servants were women and more than one-third of these were junior clerks in the Post Office Department. The proportion of women in the service rose gradually to 14 percent in 1928 and to 18.7 percent in 1937. It accelerated during the war years and reached 35 percent in 1943 but declined after the war and remained at about 27 percent during the 1960s.[37] Since, by 1970, women constituted about 30 percent of the total labour force, they were not badly underrepresented in the public service in relation to the private sector. However, they were—and remain—poorly represented at the senior levels of the service. In 1971, only 14.1 percent of officer positions in the service were held by women, whereas women made up 29.3 percent of the service as a whole.[38]

Before 1970, the government took little action to promote female representation in the public service. It was not until 1955 that the restriction against hiring married women for government employment was abolished. The Royal Commission on Government Organization (the Glassco Commission) noted in 1963 that the government had not fully implemented equality of treatment for women, and called upon the government to show "creative leadership in providing equal opportunities for women."[39] In the 1967 Public Service Employment Act, sex was included along with race, national origin, colour, and religion as a basis on which it was forbidden to discriminate. Then the Royal Commission on the Status of Women reported in 1970 that women do not enjoy equal opportunity to "enter and advance in Government Service, and that their skills and abilities are not being fully used there. Attitudes and practices seem to be at fault."[40] The commissioners made numerous recommendations to ensure equality of opportunity for women in the public service, and the government implemented most of these recommendations.

Barriers to equal opportunity for women have been similar in the public and private sectors of society. The under-utilization of women has generally been attributed to differences in formal education and work experience between men and women, and to low career expectations, high absenteeism, and high turnover among female employees. Studies on the role of women in the public service conclude that these factors are not sufficient to explain fully the lower salaries and subordinate positions received by women. The Task Force on

Barriers to Women in the Public Service reported in 1990 that the public service loses proportionally more women than men because of one or more of the following barriers:

- attitudes, which keep them away from advancement and development;
- a corporate culture, which seems suffocating, if not hostile;
- extreme difficulty in balancing work and family responsibilities.[41]

As with francophones, the government has used a variety of strategies to remove barriers to female representation, including new administrative structures, active recruitment, and training. To date, the success of these government strategies to increase female representation has been modest, but progress is being made. Between 1975 and 1989, the percentage of women in the public service rose from 35.6 percent to 43.6 percent. At the end of 1989, women made up 83.1 percent of the Administrative Support Category and 14.1 percent of the Management Category[42] (an increase from 5.9 percent of the Management Category in 1983).

The Representation of Aboriginal Peoples

The underrepresentation of aboriginal peoples[43] reflects the lack of effective aboriginal participation in the Canadian labour force as a whole, and results from a formidable array of institutional and attitudinal barriers to representation, both in the government and in the aboriginal community. Aboriginal peoples have been isolated culturally and geographically from the mainstream of Canadian society. Inadequate educational facilities and opportunities have made it difficult for them to obtain the academic qualifications required for entry into the public service, especially at the senior levels. As a result of the small number of aboriginal peoples in the public service, and of their concentration in the lower ranks, they are not sufficiently aware of career opportunities in the more senior echelons. There is no visible cadre of aboriginal public servants whose achievements they are motivated to emulate. Furthermore, the government's recruitment practices tend to emphasize formal academic qualifications rather than practical experience, and to stress competence in the French or English languages rather than in an aboriginal language. Discriminatory attitudes toward aboriginal peoples that are widespread in Canadian society are found also in the public service.[44]

These various governmental and societal factors have combined to discourage aboriginal peoples from seeking positions in the service, and to confine those who do enter primarily to lower-level positions. To overcome these obstacles, the federal government has adopted strategies similar to those used to increase the representation of francophones and women. New administrative units have engaged in active recruitment and training of aboriginal peoples.[45] According to the 1981 census, aboriginal peoples constitute 2 percent of the Canadian population and 1.3 percent of the labour force. By the end of 1988, largely as a result of the government's special efforts, aboriginal peoples made up 1.9 percent of the public service. However, they comprised only 0.8 percent of the Management Category.

Pay Equity

Pay equity—or equal pay for work of equal value—is an issue of considerable current importance in the management of human resources in both the public and private sectors of the economy. It is one component of the broader concept of employment equity discussed above.

Pay equity is a short-hand term for *equal pay for work of equal value.* This concept must be distinguished from that of *equal pay for equal work*, which requires that men and women be paid the same for doing the same job, or for a job that is very similar. The concept of equal pay for work of equal value permits comparisons to be made between different jobs performed for the same employer. For example, if one job classification, such as a public health nurse, is of equal value to another, such as a public health inspector, then employees in these two categories should receive the same base pay.

A primary purpose of pay equity programs is to ensure that women receive equal pay for doing work that has the same value as that done by men. Historically, women have been segregated into certain low-paying jobs (e.g., clerical, sales, and service jobs); these jobs have received lower rates of pay than jobs of equivalent value that are traditionally performed by men. Pay equity programs strive to devise a job evaluation method that removes sex bias from job classifications. If the requirements of a female-dominated job category, such as secretary, were found to be equivalent in terms of skill, effort, responsibility, and working conditions to those of a higher-paid job category in which males predominated, then a pay adjustment would be made for the female-dominated category.

The implementation of pay equity usually involves four steps.[46] The first step is the identification of jobs that are predominantly female; gender dominance can be defined, for example, as 70 percent or more of either sex. The second step is evaluation of jobs by a job evaluation procedure that is gender-neutral. Third is the comparison of jobs; this may take the form, for example, of formulating rules for comparing male jobs to female jobs. The final step is adjustment of the pay of undervalued female jobs to that of the male-dominated group with which they have been compared.

Among the concerns about pay equity programs is the argument that the value of dissimilar jobs cannot be easily compared. In particular, it is argued that, in addition to the usual components of job evaluation described in the previous chapter, account must be taken of such factors as market considerations, that is, the supply of and demand for people able to perform certain jobs, and the collective bargaining process. Despite these and other concerns about pay equity,[47] most governments in Canada are convinced that the benefits of pay equity outweigh the disadvantages. The provinces of Manitoba, New Brunswick, Nova Scotia, Ontario, and Prince Edward Island have enacted pay equity legislation for their employees based on a "proactive" system-wide approach that requires employers to implement pay equity regardless of whether a complaint has been made or whether there is solid evidence of wage discrimination. In March 1990, the Ontario government announced that it would pay out $96 million over a three-year period to remedy wage discrimination against provincial employees. The federal government and the Quebec government also have pay equity legislation, but they have adopted a "complaints-based," rather than a proactive, approach. In Newfoundland, pay equity is a formal part of the collective bargaining process.

In the federal government, and in most provincial governments, the battle for pay equity legislation has been won. The challenge now lies in implementing and enforcing the legislation effectively, and evaluating the extent to which the goals of pay equity are achieved in practice and the extent to which pay equity contributes to the broader objective of employment equity.

NOTES

1. For an examination of the theory of representative bureaucracy and its inadequacies, see V. Subramaniam, "Representative Bureaucracy: A Reassessment," *American Political Science Review* 61 (December, 1967): 1010-1019; Arthur D. Larson, "Representative Bureaucracy and Administrative Responsibility: A Reassessment," *Midwest Review of Public Administration* 7 (April 1973): 78-89; Kenneth John Meier, "Representative Bureaucracy: An Empirical Analysis," *American Political Science Review* 69 (June 1965): 526-42; and V. Seymour Wilson and Willard A. Mullins, "Representative Bureaucracy: Linguistic/Ethnic Aspects in Canadian Public Policy," *Canadian Public Administration* 21 (Winter 1978): 513-38.
2. Peta E. Sheriff, "Unrepresentative Bureaucracy, " *Sociology* 8 (1974): 449.
3. Kenneth John Meier and Lloyd C. Nigro, "Representative Bureaucracy and Policy Preferences: A Study in the Attitudes of Federal Executives," *Public Administration Review* 36 (July-August, 1976): 467.
4. John Porter, "Higher Public Servants and the Bureaucratic Elite in Canada," *Canadian Journal of Economics and Political Science* 24 (November 1958): 483-501; Donald C. Rowat, "On John Porter's Bureaucratic Elite in Canada," ibid., vol. 25 (May 1959): 204-207; and John Porter, "The Bureaucratic Elite: A Reply to Professor Rowat," ibid., vol. 25 (May 1959): 207-209.
5. Rowat, "On John Porter's Bureaucratic Elite," 204.
6. Porter, "Higher Public Servants," 490-91.
7. Ibid., 490.
8. Rowat, "On John Porter's Bureaucratic Elite," 207.
9. Porter, "The Bureaucratic Elite," 208.
10. Ibid., 209.
11. Wilson and Mullins, "Representative Bureaucracy," 533.
12. Ibid., 534.
13. *The State Elite* (Toronto: McClelland and Stewart, 1980).
14. Ibid., p. 82.
15. Christopher Beattie, Jacques Desy and, Stephen Longstaff, *Bureaucratic Careers: Anglophones and Francophones in the Canadian Public Service*, Research study no. 11 for

the Royal Commission on Bilingualism and Biculturalism (Ottawa: Information Canada, 1972), p. 87.

16. Olsen, *The State Elite*, p. 82. (Emphasis in original.)

17. Ibid., pp. 71-78.

18. Ibid., p. 79. (Emphasis in original.)

19. Treasury Board, *Affirmative Action in the Public Service*, News Release, June 27, 1983.

20. Ibid.

21. Ibid.

22. *Report* (Ottawa: Supply and Services, 1984).

23. Ibid., p. 3

24. Canada, Public Service Commission, *Annual Report 1988* (Ottawa: Supply and Services, 1989), p. 140.

25. Treasury Board, *Special Employment Measures for Members of Visible Minority Groups*, News Release, September 9, 1985. These measures were expanded in mid-1986. See Treasury Board, *Enhanced Employment Opportunities to Help Visible Minority Persons and Other Affirmative Action Target Groups*, News Release, June 26, 1986. Visible minority groups include, among others, Asians, Blacks, Chinese, Japanese, Koreans, and North Africans.

26. Canada, House of Commons, *Equality Now! Report of the Special Committee on Visible Minorities in Canadian Society*, Issue no. 4, March 8, 1984.

27. Public Service Commission, *Equality of Access: Equal Opportunity Programs and the Merit Principle* (Ottawa: Public Service Commission, 1982), p. 3.

28. Lise Pigeon, "Towards a Representative Public Service: The Experience of the Canadian Federal Government," Address to the Conference of the Institute of Public Administration of Canada (New Brunswick Region), Fredericton, N.B., March 13, 1989.

29. Wilson and Mullins, "Representative Bureaucracy," p. 520.

30. Royal Commission on Government Organization, *Report*, vol. 1 (Queen's Printer, 1963), pp. 27-29.

31. House of Commons, *Debates*, April 6, 1966, p. 3915.

32. Ibid., June 23, 1970, p. 8487. (Emphasis added.)

33. A new Official Languages Act was proclaimed in September 1988. Among other things, the new Act recognizes that the participation rates of anglophones and francophones may vary from one department to another, depending on such considerations as the department's mandate, clientele, and location.

34. For information on the implementation and effectiveness of these strategies, see the annual reports of the Commissioner of Official Languages. See also the first annual report of Treasury Board to Parliament entitled *Official Languages in Federal Institutions: Annual Report, 1988-1989* (Ottawa: Supply and Services, 1989). On the history of language-training programs and the Office of the Commissioner of Official Languages, see the 12-volume work by Gilles Bibeau, *Report of the Independent Study on the Language Training Programmes of the Public Service of Canada*, 1975.

35. Public Service Commission, *Annual Report 1989* (Ottawa: Supply and Services, 1990), p. 87.

36. Commissioner of Official Languages, *Annual Report 1985* (Ottawa: Supply and Services, 1986), p. 41.

37. Stanislaw Judek, *Women in the Public Service* (Ottawa: Queen's Printer, 1968), pp. 7-9 and Kathleen Archibald, *Sex and the Public Service* (Ottawa: Queen's Printer, 1970), p. 106.

38. Calculations based on Public Service Commission, *Annual Report 1971* (Ottawa: Information Canada, 1972), pp. 44-5.
39. Vol. 1, p. 275.
40. Royal Commission on the Status of Women, *Report* (Ottawa: Information Canada, 1970), p. 138.
41. *Beneath the Veneer: Report of the Task Force on Barriers to Women in the Public Service,* vol. 1 (Ottawa: Supply and Services, 1990), p. 116.
42. Public Service Commission, *Annual Report* 1989 (Ottawa: Supply and Services, 1990), pp. 86-87.
43. The term aboriginal peoples includes status Indians, non-status Indians, Inuit and Métis.
44. See *Native People and Employment in the Public Service of Canada,* a report prepared by Impact Research for the Public Service Commission, October 1976, pp. 40-44.
45. See Public Service Commission, *Annual Report 1985* (Ottawa: Supply and Services, 1986), pp. 27-28.
46. Morley Gunderson and Roberta Edgecombe Robb, "Legal and Institutional Issues Pertaining to Women's Wages in Canada," a paper prepared for the Conference on Women's Wages, "Stability and Change in Six Industrialized Countries," Chicago, March 1990, p. 4.
47. For an examination of the costs and benefits of pay equity, see Roberta Edgecombe Robb, "Equal Pay for Work of Equal Value: Issues and Policies," *Canadian Public Policy* 13 (1987): 445-61.

BIBLIOGRAPHY

Agocs, Carol. "Affirmative Action, Canadian Style: A Reconnaissance." *Canadian Public Policy* 12 (March 1986): 148-62.
Archibald, Kathleen. *Sex and the Public Service.* Ottawa: Queen's Printer, 1970.
Beattie, Christopher. *Minority Men in a Majority Setting.* Toronto: McClelland and Stewart, 1975.
Canada. Royal Commission on Bilingualism and Biculturalism. *Report.* Vol. 3. Ottawa: Queen's Printer, 1965.
Chartrand, P. J., and K. L. Pond. *A Study of Executive Career Paths in the Public Service of Canada.* Chicago: Public Personnel Association, 1970.
Cloutier, Sylvain. "Senior Public Servants in a Bicultural Society." *Canadian Public Administration* 11 (Winter 1968): 395-406.
Judek, Stanislaw. *Women in the Public Service.* Ottawa: Queen's Printer, 1968.
Kernaghan, Kenneth. "Representative Bureaucracy: The Canadian Experience." *Canadian Public Administration* 21 (Winter 1978): 489-512.
Kingsley, J. Donald. *Representative Bureaucracy: An Interpretation of the British Civil Service.* Yellow Springs, Ohio: Antioch Press, 1944.
Krantz, Harry. *The Participatory Bureaucracy.* Lexington: Lexington Books, 1976.
Krislov, Samuel. *Representative Bureaucracy.* Englewood Cliffs, N.J.: Prentice-Hall, 1974.
Kuruvilla, P. K. "Public Service Recruitment in Canada: Some Perspectives and Problems." *Indian Journal of Public Administration* 26 (January-March 1980): 62-90.
Larson, Arthur D. "Representative Bureaucracy and Administrative Responsibility: A Reassessment." *Midwest Review of Public Administration* 7 (April 1973): 79-89.
Olsen, Dennis. *The State Elite.* Toronto: McClelland and Stewart, 1980.

Porter, John. "Higher Public Servants and the Bureaucratic Elite in Canada." *Canadian Journal of Economics and Political Science* 24 (November 1958): 483-501.

Porter, John. "The Bureaucratic Elite: A Reply to Professor Rowat." *Canadian Journal of Economics and Political Science* 25 (May 1959): 207-209.

Rowat, Donald C. "On John Porter's Bureaucratic Elite in Canada." *Canadian Journal of Economics and Political Science* 25 (May 1959): 204-207.

Wilson, V. Seymour, and Willard A. Mullins. "Representative Bureaucracy: Linguistic/Ethnic Aspects in Canadian Public Policy." *Canadian Public Administration* 21 (Winter 1978): 513-38.

Winn, Conrad. "Affirmative Action and Visible Minorities: Eight Premises in Search of Evidence." *Canadian Public Policy* 11 (December 1985): 684-700.

Winn, Conrad. "Affirmative Action for Women: More Than a Case of Simple Justice." *Canadian Public Administration* 28 (Spring 1985): 24-46.

CASES

In *Case Program in Canadian Public Administration* (Toronto: Institute of Public Administration of Canada):

The Problem Program. By L.S. Wong

Implementing Bilingual Air Traffic Control in Quebec. By Sandford F. Borins

The Ben Fisher Case. By Nancy LePitre, Salim Mansur, and Wilbur Grasham

Trying to Fire the Medical Officer of Health: A Case Study. By Alison McGear, Ted Darby, and Raisa B. Deber

25

Collective Bargaining

Public sector collective bargaining is a continuing source of concern and controversy in Canadian society. Among the many important issues in public personnel management, the issue of collective bargaining has received the most attention from both scholars and the general public. A recent book begins by asserting that "in the past fifteen years, no change *in Canadian public administration* has had greater impact than the advent of collective bargaining for public sector employees."[1] Another recent book begins by stating that "among the leading developments *in Canadian industrial relations* since the mid-1960s have been the extension of collective bargaining rights, frequently including the right to strike, to employees of senior levels of government, and the rapid expansion of bargaining in this sector as well as in the parapublic sector, such as hospitals and schools."[2]

The primary reason for the focus on public sector collective bargaining in both the public administration and industrial relations communities is that its processes and outcomes have significant effects beyond our governments as well as within them. For example, public sector strikes disrupt the provision of such important government services as mail delivery, air traffic control, and police protection. Moreover, collective bargaining agreements in the public sector on wages, fringe benefits, and working conditions influence settlements in the private sector.

Compared to the private sector, the emergence of collective bargaining in the public sector is very recent. It was during the period from the early 1960s to the mid-1970s that the federal government and most provincial governments granted their employees the statutory right to bargain collectively. The growth of public service unionism over the past two decades has, however, been extremely rapid.[3] Public sector employees constitute slightly less than one quarter of the total labour force, but they make up almost one half of all union members. Moreover, the three largest unions in Canada are public service unions—the Canadian Union of Public Employees (mostly municipal government employees), the National Union of Provincial Government Employees, and the Public Service Alliance of Canada (federal government employees).

This chapter examines the evolution, the legal and administrative framework, and the operation of collective bargaining in the public sector. While this examination reflects the fact that most of the scholarly and public attention given to collective bargaining has centred on the federal sphere of government, reference is also made to developments in the provincial and municipal realms.

THE EVOLUTION OF PUBLIC SECTOR COLLECTIVE BARGAINING

Municipal government employees received the right to bargain collectively earlier than their federal and provincial counterparts. Collective bargaining in the municipal sphere of government has developed rapidly since the Second World War, so that now almost all municipal corporations with more than fifty employees and a population exceeding ten thousand bargain collectively with at least some of their employees.[4] Aside from police and firefighters, nearly all of whom are prohibited from taking strike action and for whom special legislation is usually provided, municipal employees have long had the same rights under provincial labour legislation as private sector employees. The majority of municipal employees who have the right to bargain collectively belong to the Canadian Union of Public Employees, which is affiliated with the Canadian Labour Congress. (The congress is a central union body with ninety national and international member unions, which, in turn, have more than two million individual members.)

Many other public sector employees, in both the federal and provincial spheres of government, have long enjoyed the right to bargain collectively under general labour legislation. Included in this group are employees of various government boards and agencies, e.g., the CBC and the CNR in the federal sphere, and hydro-electric commissions and liquor control boards in the provinces. In addition, in the health and education sectors many employees have, under general labour legislation, the right to bargain collectively, including the right to strike; for other employees in this sector, the right to strike is denied or restricted in some way.

For federal and provincial employees in regular government departments, the right to bargain collectively was slow in coming—except in the province of Saskatchewan. As early as 1944, the Co-operative Commonwealth Federation (CCF) government in that province included its employees under the general provincial labour legislation (the Trade Union Act). Other provincial governments, including Ontario in 1962, gradually gave their employees the right to bargain collectively, but it was not until 1965 that a second provincial government—the Government of Quebec—granted its employees the right to strike. The federal government granted collective bargaining with the right to strike in 1967, and several provincial governments (New Brunswick, British Columbia, and Newfoundland) did the same shortly thereafter. The other provinces have adopted collective bargaining for government employees, but have substituted third-party arbitration (to be explained later) for the right to strike.

The Evolution of the Federal System

The development of the federal regime for collective bargaining in the public service merits special attention because it is generally perceived to be a unique and imaginative approach to labour relations in the public sector, and because its operation has been the focus of so much controversy. Although public service staff associations did not receive legal recognition until the Civil Service Act of 1961, one of the first associations—the Civil Service Rifle Association—was created exactly a century earlier. Postal workers organized into staff associations as early as 1889 when the Railway Mail Clerks Association was established. This was followed by the Federated Association of Letter Carriers in 1891 and the Canadian Postal Employees Association in 1911. Other categories of employees organized into such associations as the Civil Service Association of Ottawa (1907), the Civil Service Federation (1909), the Professional Institute of the Public Service of Canada (1920), and the Amalgamated Civil Service of Canada (1920).[5]

The efforts of the staff associations to persuade the government to adopt some mechanism for consulting with them finally led, in 1944, to the creation of the National Joint Council of the Public Service of Canada, which was closely modelled on the National Whitley Council in the United Kingdom.[6] The National Joint Council was an *advisory* body with an official side composed of senior public servants and a staff side composed of people chosen from the staff associations, according to the size of their membership. According to the government, the purpose of the council was

> to provide machinery for regular and systematic consultation and discussion between the employer and employee sides of the public service in regard to grievances and conditions of employment, and thereby to promote increased efficiency and better morale in the public service.[7]

The duties of the council were to make recommendations to the Cabinet, the Treasury Board, and/or the Civil Service Commission on such matters as recruitment, training, hours of work, promotion, discipline, health, welfare, and seniority.

The council was successful in improving communication and general relations between the government and its employees, and in enhancing employee morale. However, by the early 1950s, the staff associations were sufficiently disillusioned with their ability to influence government policy through the consultative mechanism of the council that they began to agitate for the right to bargain collectively. The Civil Service Act of 1961 granted legal recognition to the staff associations for the first time, and gave them the right to be consulted on remuneration as well as on terms and conditions of employment. However, the consultative procedures proved unsatisfactory to the staff associations, who renewed their agitation for collective bargaining. Then, during the 1963 federal election campaign, the Liberal Party promised, if elected, to introduce collective bargaining. Following their return to office as a minority government, the Liberals, with the strong support of the New Democratic Party, appointed the Preparatory Committee on Collective Bargaining, which was composed entirely of senior public servants and chaired by A. D. P. Heeney. The committee's terms of reference were "to make preparations for the introduction into the Public Service of an appropriate form of collective bargaining and arbitration, and to examine the need for reforms in the systems of classification and pay applying to civil servants and prevailing rate employees."[8]

In addition to proposing the system of collective bargaining discussed below, the committee recommended that the National Joint Council be preserved "as a forum for the systematic study and discussion of problems that transcend those of particular bargaining units."[9] The government accepted this recommendation, and the council continues to exist as an effective mechanism for promoting the efficiency of the public service and the well-being of public servants by providing for consultation between the government and employee organizations.[10] The council deals with such matters as relocation policy, travel policy, and disability insurance. These are matters for which it is appropriate to have the same policy across the entire public service. These matters could not be easily and quickly negotiated separately by over eighty different bargaining units.

The resistance of the federal and provincial governments to public sector collective bargaining had been founded in part on the principle of *the sovereignty of the state*. The application of this principle to public sector labour relations meant that the government could not adopt a system, such as collective bargaining or compulsory arbitration, which required it to give up its final decision-making authority in order that terms and conditions of employment could be determined jointly. As late as 1964, Jean Lesage, the Premier of Quebec, proclaimed that "the Queen does not negotiate."[11] Governments were willing to downplay this argument somewhat when collective bargaining was established, but we shall see that some remnants of the principle of sovereignty remain in that the system of collective bargaining in federal and provincial governments is somewhat more restrictive than that found in the private sector.

THE LEGAL AND ADMINISTRATIVE FRAMEWORK OF THE FEDERAL SYSTEM

The Preparatory Committee's recommendations led to the enactment of a statutory framework for collective bargaining[12] made up of two new statutes— the Public Service Staff Relations Act[13] (PSSRA), the Public Service Employment Act[14] (PSEA)—and an amended statute, the Financial Administration Act[15] (FAA). The PSSRA, which is discussed at length below, sets out the structures and processes of the collective bargaining system. The PSEA replaced the Civil Service Act and, among other things, abolished the Civil Service Commission's function of making recommendations to the Treasury Board on managerial matters such as pay determination. Amendments to the FAA specified the Treasury Board as employer for most of the public service, and gave it the responsibility for negotiating collective agreements and determining other aspects of personnel policy.

The Public Service Staff Relations Act

This Act is administered by the Public Service Staff Relations Board, which is appointed by the federal Cabinet. The board is composed of a chairperson, a vice-chairperson, no fewer than three deputy chairpersons, and such other full-time and part-time members as the Cabinet deems necessary to fulfill the board's responsibilities. Subsequent discussion of the Act's provisions will show that the board plays an extremely important role in the collective bargaining system. It has responsibility for a broad range of matters, including the structure of bargaining units, the determination of exclusions from bargaining units, the settlement of interest disputes (i.e., disputes arising from the renegotiation of a collective agreement), and the settlement of rights disputes (i.e., disputes arising during the term of a collective agreement). In the collective bargaining process, the interests of the government as employer are represented by the Treasury Board, which is usually assisted by the relevant departmental representatives.

A Pay Research Bureau, which is administered by the PSSRB, prepares data on rates of pay, employee earnings, conditions of employment, and related practices prevailing both within and outside the public service. This information provides employers and bargaining agents with objective information and gives conciliators, conciliation boards, and arbitration boards access to material needed to fulfill their responsibilities.

The Structure of Bargaining Units

As explained in Chapter 23, all employees belong to one of the seventy-two occupational groups in the public service and these groups are classified into six occupational categories. The existing categories and some of the groups within them are shown in Table 25.1.

Employee organizations (e.g., the Public Service Alliance of Canada, the Professional Institute of the Public Service) wishing to bargain with the government must be certified as **bargaining agents**. These employee organizations act as bargaining agents for **bargaining units**. A bargaining unit is a group of two or more employees that is determined under the PSSRA to constitute a unit of employees appropriate for collective bargaining. The bargaining units for which employee organizations act as bargaining agents must be based on the occupational groups into which the public service is divided by the Public Service Commission under the PSEA. Public service unions can act as the bargaining agent for more than one bargaining unit.

Exclusions from Collective Bargaining

The PSSRA provides for the exclusion of certain persons from collective bargaining. Those excluded are persons in managerial and confidential positions, as well as persons appointed to statutory positions (e.g., officers of Parliament, deputy heads), those who are locally engaged outside Canada, and those holding casual or part-time positions. In some cases, a whole group of employees

Table 25.1
OCCUPATIONAL CATEGORIES AND GROUPS IN THE FEDERAL PUBLIC SERVICE

Occupational Category	Occupational Group
Management	Executive
	Senior Management
Scientific and Professional	Biological Sciences
	Law
	Scientific Regulation
Administrative and Foreign Service	Administrative Services
	Computer Systems
	Foreign Affairs
Technical	Aircraft Operations
	Electronics
	Primary Products Inspection
Administrative Support	Clerical and Regulatory
	Data Processing
	Office Equipment
Operational	Correctional
	Firefighters
	General Labour and Trades

is excluded (e.g., legal officers in the Department of Justice, personnel administrators). The rationale for the exclusion of most of these groups is that their membership in a bargaining unit would conflict with their responsibilities for negotiating or administering collective agreements.

The Scope of Bargaining

Under the PSSRA, certain subjects are excluded from collective bargaining. Subsection 56(2) states that no term or condition of employment may be included in a collective agreement if it requires legislative implementation (except for the appropriation of moneys), or if it is established under certain specified statutes. These statutes include the PSEA and the Public Service Superannuation Act.[16] This means that there can be no bargaining on matters falling within the jurisdiction of the Public Service Commission, namely, recruitment, promotions, transfers, layoffs, discharge for incompetence or incapacity, rejection during the probationary period following recruitment, promotion or transfer, and superannuation (pension). Moreover, section 7 confirms the authority of the employer to determine the organization of the public service, to assign duties to positions, and to classify positions. This means that there can be no bargaining over such matters as job evaluation, the distribution of work, and the determination of duties.

Some of these limitations are specifically confirmed by subsections 86(3) and 70(3), which declare that "standards, procedures or processes governing the appointment, appraisal, promotion, demotion, transfer, lay-off or release of employees" may not be included in a conciliation board report or an arbitral award (i.e., a decision by an arbitration board). Moreover, subsection 70(4) provides that an arbitral award may not deal with any term or condition of employment that was not a subject of negotiation between the parties during the period before arbitration was requested. However, subsection 70(1) specifically provides that an arbitral award *may* "deal with rates of pay, hours of work, leave entitlements, standards of discipline and other terms and conditions of employment directly related thereto."

The Resolution of Interest Disputes

Interest disputes involve a renegotiation of an existing collective agreement. The PSSRA provides an innovative approach to resolving such disputes. At the beginning of each round of talks for a new agreement, the bargaining agent must specify which of two possible methods of impasse resolution it wishes to have applied during the bargaining process:

1. the referral of a dispute to binding arbitration; or
2. the referral of a dispute to a conciliation board followed, if necessary, by strike action.

Thus, if the bargaining unit chooses the arbitration route, it has no right to strike. Once a choice has been made, it cannot be altered until the next round of negotiations.

No matter which option is chosen, if negotiations reach an impasse, either the bargaining agent or the employer may request that the chairperson of the PSSRB appoint a conciliator (also called a mediator) to help reach a settlement. The chairperson rarely refuses such a request. The conciliator must report to the chairperson, within fourteen days or a longer period specified by the chairperson, on the probability of success or failure in reaching a settlement. As of September 1, 1981, conciliators had been appointed in just over 28 percent of the sets of negotiations leading to the 871 collective agreements[17] reached under the PSSRA. If no agreement is reached as a result of conciliation, the next stage depends on whether the arbitration or conciliation-strike route has been chosen.

If the *arbitration route* of dispute resolution has been selected, the parties are expected to reach agreement on as many issues as possible before either party requests arbitration. If arbitration is requested with respect to the matters still in dispute, the PSSRB sets up a three-member body composed of one of its permanent members as an impartial presiding officer, and two other members. One of these two members is from a panel representing the employer's interests, and the other is from a panel representing the employees' interests.

Section 68 of the PSSRA sets out the following criteria upon which arbitral awards are to be made:

(a) the needs of the Public Service for qualified employees;
(b) the conditions of employment in similar occupations outside the

Public Service, including such geographic, industrial or other variations as the Board may consider relevant;

(c) the need to maintain appropriate relationships in the conditions of employment as between different grade levels within an occupation and as between occupations in the Public Service;

(d) the need to establish terms and conditions of employment that are fair and reasonable in relation to the qualifications required, the work performed, the responsibility assumed and the nature of the services rendered; and

(e) any other factor that to it appears to be relevant to the matter in dispute.

The arbitration board will listen to the arguments presented on both sides and then produce a decision. The document containing the decision looks like, and has the same status as, a collective agreement, but it is technically referred to as an arbitral award. The award is final and binding on both parties.

If the *conciliation-strike route* of dispute resolution has been selected and if the parties are unable to reach agreement on all or some of the matters on the bargaining table, either party may request that a conciliation board be established. Each party chooses one person for the conciliation board, and these two persons choose a third person to act as chairperson. The conciliation board is responsible for consulting the parties and reporting its findings and recommendations to the chairperson of the PSSRB within fourteen days or a longer period agreed upon by the parties or specified by the chairperson.

A very important precondition to the establishment of a conciliation board is a determination of *designated employees*. These are employees who are members of a bargaining unit but who are forbidden by subsection 79(1) of the PSSRA to take part in a lawful strike because their duties "consist in whole or in part of duties the performance of which at any particular time or after any specified period of time is or will be necessary in the interest of the safety or security of the public." The purpose of this provision is to ensure that the performance of certain essential services (e.g., by hospital workers, corrections officers) will not be disrupted by a public service strike. At the beginning of a round of bargaining, the employer provides a statement to the PSSRB and the relevant bargaining agent as to which employees or classes of employees are considered to be designated employees. If the bargaining agent files objections to the employer's statement, the determination as to designated employees is made by the PSSRB, subject to an appeal to the courts.

If the recommendations of the conciliation board are unacceptable either to the employer or the union, the union has *the right to strike* seven days after the report is submitted to the chairperson of the PSSRB. Aside from designated employees, the right to strike is forbidden to employees in a bargaining unit for which a bargaining agent has not been certified by the PSSRB, and to employees in a bargaining unit for which arbitration has been chosen as the process of dispute settlement. Moreover, employees in a bargaining unit for which the conciliation-strike route has been chosen may not strike during the time that a collective agreement applicable to their bargaining unit is in force. Employee organizations are forbidden to declare or authorize a strike that would involve employees in an unlawful strike.

The Resolution of Rights Disputes

Federal public servants have a very broad right under subsection 90(1) of the PSSRA to present grievances, not only in relation to the provisions of a collective agreement or an arbitral award but also in relation to "a provision of a statute, or of a regulation, by-law, direction or other instrument made or issued by the employer, dealing with terms and conditions of employment." Moreover, the right to present a grievance extends to employees in managerial or confidential positions who are not permitted to belong to a bargaining unit, and even, on some matters, to former employees.

Employees with a grievance are normally required to begin by using the three or four levels of the grievance procedure in their department. However, grievances in the areas of classification and discharge are heard first at the final level of the department's grievance procedure. Grievances relating to the interpretation or application of a collective agreement or arbitral award, and to disciplinary action leading to discharge, suspension, or a financial penalty may be referred to third-party **adjudication** when the grievor is not satisfied with the results of the departmental grievance procedure. In such cases, the PSSRB selects an adjudicator from among its members. Employees may request that their grievance be heard by a board of adjudication. If the employer has no objection to this request, the board will consist of a member of the PSSRB as chairperson and one person selected by each of the parties.

Aside from the right to present grievances under the PSSRA, employees have the right under the PSEA to present appeals to the Public Service Commission in relation to appointments, release for incompetence or incapacity, violations of the rules on political partisanship, and fraudulent practices during an examination conducted by the commission.

THE OPERATION OF THE FEDERAL SYSTEM

This section examines the areas of disagreement between the federal government and the public service unions on each of the subjects discussed in the previous section. Several bodies of inquiry have examined these problem areas and have recommended changes in the PSSRA to remedy them. Of particular importance are the reports by Jacob Finkelman,[18] the first chairperson of the PSSRB, by the parliamentary committee on employer-employee relations in the public service,[19] by the D'Avignon Committee,[20] and by Public Service 2000.[21] The recommendations in these reports have not yet led to significant changes in the PSSRA, but many of them are the subject of continuing discussions between the government and the public service unions. In general, the unions would prefer to have a collective bargaining system for the public sector that is based on the Canada Labour Code. Under the code, which regulates collective bargaining in the private sector, more matters are left to negotiation than under the PSSRA. The Treasury Board in 1987[22] and the Public Service 2000 Task Force on Staff Relations in 1990[23] proposed a number of changes to the PSSRA; several of these proposed changes are mentioned below.

The Structure of Bargaining Units

A large number of bargaining units have resulted from the requirement that the units must correspond to the occupational groups into which the public service is divided. There are, at present, seventy-two occupational groups and eighty-two bargaining units (ten of the groups are divided into supervisory and non-supervisory units). This means that bargaining is virtually a constant process for the larger public service unions, which represent several bargaining units, and for the Treasury Board. In 1989, the Public Service Alliance of Canada represented as many as thirty-seven separate bargaining units. It has been argued that a reduction in the number of bargaining units would benefit the unions, the employer, and the public in that it would do away with the need to negotiate similar or identical provisions for inclusion in separate agreements, and would reduce the number of interruptions of service to the public if negotiations break down. Finkelman and Goldenberg note some possible disadvantages from the consolidation of bargaining units,[24] but recommend that the PSSRB be given authority to bring about such consolidation where "it is shown in any particular case that it would be in the public interest to do so."[25] The Public Service 2000 Task Force on Classification and Occupational Group Structures recommended that the occupational categories be abolished and that the number of groups be reduced to twenty-three.[26]

Exclusions from Collective Bargaining

There has been a great deal of controversy between the government and public service unions over the exclusion from collective bargaining of persons employed "in a managerial or confidential capacity."[27] The unions have complained that some employees have been excluded, not because of the duties they perform, but because the government wants to keep a certain number of people on the job to run the operation in the event of a strike. In 1987, the Treasury Board proposed that the definition of managers in the PSSRA be significantly enlarged to apply to employees with responsibility for "development, implementation or administration of government policies or programs and/or for effective control of employees." The Public Service 2000 Task Force on Staff Relations recommended a reduction in the number of exclusions.

The Scope of Bargaining

Federal public service unions have been successful in achieving many of the terms and conditions of employment that are standard in private sector collective agreements. In addition, they are well ahead of the private sector in negotiating benefits in such areas as severance pay, maternity leave, and education leave. However, as noted earlier in this chapter, they are prohibited under the PSSRA from bargaining on such centrally important matters as classification, job security, staffing procedures, and superannuation. The unions continue to press strongly for a broadening of the scope of bargaining, especially in these areas.

The Resolution of Interest Disputes

The issue of the scope of bargaining is closely related to that of the settlement of interest disputes in that the scope of matters that are arbitrable under the PSSRA is narrower than that of matters that are bargainable. As a result, if the bargaining agent chooses the arbitration route of dispute settlement, the employer can withdraw from any agreement reached to that point on non-arbitrable issues. One of the Treasury Board's 1987 proposals was that the scope of both arbitration and negotiation be made identical so that all bargainable issues would be subject to arbitration as well. The Public Service 2000 Task Force on Staff Relations agreed.

Initially, the public service unions selected the arbitration route rather than the conciliation-strike route to the resolution of interest disputes. However, during subsequent negotiations there has been a gradual move in the other direction so that a majority of the bargaining units has now chosen the conciliation-strike option. Finkelman and Goldenberg note that some of the reasons for this development are that "wages have been eroded by inflation, fears for job security have increased and, probably most important, more militant groups seem to have achieved better settlements."[28] Thompson and Swimmer conclude, however, that this development "seems more the result of constraints placed on arbitrators under that Act [the PSSRA] than of any general increase in militancy of pro-strike sentiments among federal workers."[29]

The unions object to being required to select either the arbitration or conciliation-strike option before bargaining begins because the government can "manoeuvre by obliging unions to accept less in nonarbitrable areas to avoid going to arbitration in other areas. The employer can also force trade-offs in regard to nonarbitrable issues because, if nonarbitrable issues are in dispute, the unions have to accept trade-offs demanded by the employer or drop the issues entirely."[30] Thus, the unions would prefer that bargaining units be permitted to choose the dispute resolution mechanism at the time that an impasse arises in the bargaining process. Another approach would be to permit bargaining agents to change their choice from conciliation strike to arbitration at any time during the bargaining process. This latter approach would be especially valuable for bargaining units that discovered that the number of "designated employees" was so large as to destroy the units' capacity to conduct an effective strike. In 1987, the Treasury Board proposed that the PSSRA be amended so that if an impasse occurred under the conciliation-strike route, the PSSRB could appoint a conciliator or the parties could mutually agree to refer all outstanding issues to arbitration.

Despite considerable disagreement over the number of employees to be designated as performing essential services, the government and the bargaining agents had, by 1980, reached a generally acceptable working arrangement on the issue of designated employees. Then, in 1980, the Minister of Transport proposed to the PSSRB that, in the event of a strike in the air traffic control unit, all operational traffic controllers should be designated. The PSSRB decided that it should designate only the number of employees necessary to maintain a level of service that would ensure the safety or security of the public. However, the Federal Court of Appeal,[31] in a decision upheld by the Supreme Court of Canada in 1982,[32] ruled, among other things, that the PSSRB could not discriminate between employees performing similar duties by designating only a few of them. As a result, designation has become largely a management right. Between 1982 and 1987, the percentage of bargaining units whose members are designated as essential rose from roughly 15 percent to 40 percent and, for some units, as high as 100 percent.[33] Moreover, in 1987, the Treasury Board proposed that the PSSRA be amended to broaden the definition of a designated position beyond public safety and security to include public health, protection of federal public property, and long-term research and experiments.

The Public Service 2000 Task Force on Staff Relations recognized that in the past decade the designation of employees to provide essential services has "exceeded a reasonable definition of those required to provide the minimum level of services for the protection of the Public."[34] To remedy this problem, the task force, among other things, recommended that criteria be developed to define essential services, and that "a body be established to administer these criteria and to determine the numbers of employees designated to perform essential duties."[35]

Relations between the government and the unions were greatly aggravated by the enactment of the Public Sector Compensation Restraint Act (PSCRA), which was the cornerstone of the federal government's "6 and 5" program introduced in June 1982. This Act suspended, for federal employees, the right to bargain collectively on monetary matters and the right to strike for a period of two years. Compensation increases were limited to specified percentages. Most provincial governments followed the federal lead by introducing similar restraints on employee compensation. Following the expiry of the PSCRA, normal collective bargaining has been restored, but public service unions are concerned that Parliament and provincial legislatures will be more inclined in the future to take legislative action to reduce "excessive" wage settlements or to end "disruptive" strikes. During the two decades since the enactment of the PSSRA, there has been considerable public pressure to reduce the rights of public servants to engage in collective bargaining and especially to take strike action. Yet "by any measure, strikes in the public sector have not been numerous. The federal public service ... has, with the exception of the Post Office, been especially peaceful .... public sector strikes have occurred most frequently in

Quebec."[36] There have, however, been major public sector strikes in recent years in British Columbia, Saskatchewan, and Newfoundland.

The federal government's approach to the resolution of interest disputes has been described as the *choice of procedures* approach. There are several possible alternatives to this approach.[37] There is, first, the straightforward right to strike, which is prevalent in private sector collective bargaining. Second, there is *conventional interest arbitration*, which is the most common alternative to strike action. If the employer and the union cannot reach a settlement, they submit their differences to an arbitrator who assesses the merits of the arguments made by each side and then makes a decision, which is binding. The choice of procedures approach is a combination of these two approaches. A third approach is a *controlled strike*, which enables unions to take strike action, but requires that a number of designated employees from the bargaining unit stay on the job to provide essential services. The federal scheme also incorporates this approach.

A fourth approach is called *final-offer selection*. This approach differs from conventional interest arbitration in that the arbitrator is required to select, without proposing or making any change, either the position put forward by the employer or that put forward by the union. It is hoped that both sides will make reasonable concessions during the negotiations out of fear that an arbitrator might choose the other side's total position.

The Resolution of Rights Disputes

The issue of the resolution of rights disputes [38] (disputes arising during the term of a collective agreement), like that of interest disputes, is related to the issue of the scope of bargaining. The extension of the scope of bargaining along the lines discussed above would oblige the government to expand its capacity for grievance adjudication because employees would have many more opportunities to present grievances. Moreover, there is some overlap between the PSSRA and the PSEA on the reasons for termination of employees. This has led to confusion among mangers as to whether action for termination should be taken under the PSSRA provisions for discipline or under the PSEA provisions for incompetence or incapacity. To resolve this uncertainty, the PS 2000 Task Force on Staff Relations proposed that demotions and terminations, whether for discipline or for incompetence or incapacity, be handled under the PSSRA.[39] This solution is also favoured by the public service unions.

COLLECTIVE BARGAINING IN THE PROVINCES

The structure and operation of collective bargaining differ considerably from one province to another.[40] In the provinces, as in the federal sphere, it is the resolution of interest disputes that has attracted the most public and academic attention. This issue of interest dispute resolution is used here to illustrate the variety of approaches to the conduct of collective bargaining in the provinces.[41]

A helpful means of explaining briefly the different approaches to interest dispute resolution in provincial governments is to discuss each province under one of four models of public sector collective bargaining. These are the private sector model, the hybrid (essential services) model, the public-private model, and the formal public sector model.[42]

The *private sector model* applies to Saskatchewan and Manitoba, where public sector employees are covered by the same legislation as private sector employees. Certain groups of employees in some provinces (e.g., police and firefighters in Nova Scotia and New Brunswick) are subject to private sector collective bargaining legislation and have the right to strike, while the rest of the public service is covered by separate legislation.

The *hybrid (essential services) model* applies to British Columbia and Quebec, where public employees are covered by the same legislation as private sector employees, but where both public and private sector employees are covered also by essential services legislation. Thus, these provinces have characteristics of both the private sector model and the public-private model described below. Public sector employees have the statutory right to strike in these provinces, but there are exceptions (e.g., teachers in British Columbia and public safety employees in Quebec).

The *public-private model* applies to New Brunswick, Newfoundland, and to the federal regime, which has been examined above in detail. The labour relations regime in all three governments is similar to that for private sector employees, but the public and private sectors are covered by separate legislation. In New Brunswick and in the federal government, the public sector legislation is distinguished by its provisions for a choice of mechanisms for dispute resolution and for the designation of essential employees who are forbidden to participate in a strike. The legislation in Newfoundland is more restrictive with respect to such matters as the designation of employees and the availability of arbitration.

The *formal public sector model* applies to Alberta, Ontario, Prince Edward Island, and Nova Scotia, although the classes of employees covered by the legislation differ somewhat from one province to another. Among the important features of the legislation under this model are that the public sector is treated separately from the private sector, strikes are prohibited, and disputes are resolved through a conventional tripartite arbitration system.

CONCLUSIONS

In all spheres of Canadian government, collective bargaining for public employees is probably the single most important issue in human resource management. The introduction of public sector collective bargaining is very recent in the federal and provincial spheres, and a great deal of fine-tuning of the process remains to be done. The PSSRA, for example, does not provide a framework for employer-employee relations that is satisfactory to the government, the general public, or the public service unions. Yet the continuing disagreements over the interpretation and application of the Act and the existence of well-considered proposals for its reform have not led to significant changes in its provisions. The government's hesitation in implementing proposed reforms is due, in part, to differences of opinion among members of the public regarding the desirability of permitting government employees to bargain collectively and to take strike action. The most significant challenge for public service unions is "to convince the public at large and union members in the private and public sectors that their cause is just. Are public employees really overpaid, underworked and blessed with lifetime job security? Given the available evidence, it is possible to confront the stereotype head on and demonstrate it is mythology."[43]

It seems unlikely that the right to strike will be withdrawn in those jurisdictions where it has been granted. However, in several provincial governments, public service unions and their supporters are still waging a campaign for the right to strike. In virtually all jurisdictions, including the federal government, there are strong pressures for reform of the existing collective bargaining regime. Moreover, employer-employee relations have been severely aggravated in recent years by legislation involving restraints on compensation, restraints on collective agreements, changes to the "rules of the game," and direct legislative intervention[44] as well as layoffs, cutbacks, and the contracting out of services.

The future of public sector labour relations can be assessed in the light of two contrasting hypotheses.[45] According to the *doomsday* hypothesis, the public sector restraint programs described above were simply part of a series of temporary government measures designed to advance business interests behind a facade of protecting the public. These measures included the frequent use of back-to-work legislation, the jailing of union leaders, and reducing the right to strike by designating an increasing number of public sector workers as essential. Given such measures, combined with the fact that the right to strike was not included as a fundamental freedom in the Charter of Rights and Freedoms, "one can see the emergence of an era of relatively permanent restrictions on the rights of labour."[46] This scenario envisages that many of the rights that public sector employees won during the post-war period will be lost.

The *optimistic* hypothesis holds that the wage restraints of the early 1980s were imposed because of the severe economic problems of high inflation and high unemployment. Thus, when the economy improved, it was argued, normal collective bargaining would resume. Thompson and Swimmer provided substantial evidence to support the optimistic view. They warned, however, that if the doomsday hypothesis was realized, workers would become disillusioned with the collective bargaining process, and this would lead to increased militancy by public sector employees and a greater role for politicians, as opposed to public sector managers, in public sector labour relations. By 1988, Swimmer had concluded that experience during the last few years had supported the doomsday hypothesis. In particular, he noted that "the federal government has successfully devalued, if not removed, the right to strike via the designation process."[47] The tensions arising from disagreements over the designation issue and other matters will ensure that collective bargaining remains a dominant dimension of the study and practice of public administration.

NOTES

1. Mark Thompson and Gene Swimmer, eds., *Conflict or Compromise: The Future of Public Sector Industrial Relations* (Montreal: The Institute for Research on Public Policy, 1984), p. xviii. (Emphasis added.)

2. Jacob Finkleman and Shirley B. Goldenberg, *Collective Bargaining in the Public Service: The Federal Experience in Canada* (Montreal: Institute for Research on Public Policy, 1983), vol. 1, p. 1. (Emphasis added.) This two-volume work contains an excellent comprehensive examination of the evolution of the federal collective bargaining regime.

3. For a succinct account of the growth of public sector unionism in the federal, provincial, and municipal spheres of government, see Joseph B. Rose, *Growth Patterns of Public Sector Unions,"* in Thompson and Swimmer, *Conflict or Compromise,* pp. 97-108.

4. See T. J. Plunkett, "Municipal Collective Bargaining," in *Collective Bargaining in the Public Service* (Toronto: Institute of Public Administration of Canada, 1973), p. 4 and Shirley B. Goldenberg, "Public Sector Labour Relations in Canada," in *Public Sector Bargaining,* Industrial Relations Research Association Series (Washington: Bureau of National Affairs, 1979), p. 254.

5. See J. E. Hodgetts, *The Canadian Public Service* (Toronto: University of Toronto Press, 1973), pp. 323-25 and J. E. Hodgetts, William McCloskey, Reginald Whitaker, and V. Seymour Wilson, *Biography of an Institution: The Civil Service Commission of Canada, 1908-1967* (Montreal: McGill-Queen's University Press for the Institute of Public Administration of Canada, 1972).

6. For an account of the evolution of the council, see L.W.C.S. Barnes, *Consult and Advise: A History of the National Joint Council of the Public Service of Canada, 1944-1974.* (Kingston Ont.: Queen's University, Industrial Relations Centre, 1975).

7. J. L. Ilsley, Minister of Finance, as quoted by P. K. Kuruvilla in "Collective Bargaining in the Canadian Federal Public Service," in Kenneth Kernaghan, ed., *Public Administration in Canada: Selected Readings,* 5th ed. (Toronto: Methuen, 1985), p. 224.

8. The Preparatory Committee on Collective Bargaining in the Public Service, *Report* (Ottawa: Queen's Printer, 1965), p. 1.

9. Ibid., p. 40.

10. See Finkelman and Goldenberg, *Collective Bargaining in the Public Service,* vol. 1, ch. 5.

11. Shirley B. Goldenberg, "Collective Bargaining in the Provincial Public Services," in *Collective Bargaining in the Public Service* (Toronto: Institute of Public Administration of Canada, 1973), p. 11.

12. See Robert A. Vaison, "Collective Bargaining in the Federal Public Service: The Achievement of a Milestone in Personnel Relations," *Canadian Public Administration* 12 (Spring 1969): 108-122.

13. Canada, *Statutes,* 1966-67, c. 72.

14. Canada, *Statutes,* 1966-67, c. 71.

15. Canada, *Statutes,* 1966-67, c. 74.

16. The other statutes specified in the Act are the Government Employees [Workmen's] Compensation Act and the Government Vessels Discipline Act.

17. A collective agreement is "an agreement in writing entered into between the Employer on the one hand, and a bargaining agent, on the other hand, containing provisions respecting terms and conditions of employment and related matters." The Treasury Board Secretariat and the Public Service Commission, *Personnel—A Manager's Handbook* (Ottawa: Supply and Services, 1982), p. 66.

18. *Employer-Employee Relations in the Public Service of Canada: Proposals for Legislative Change,* The Finkelman Report (Ottawa: Information Canada, 1974), Part I, 301 pp. and Part II, 82 pp.

19. See Special Joint Committee of the House of Commons and the Senate on Employer-Employee Relations in the Public Service, *Report to Parliament,* Issue no. 47, February 26, 1976.

20. Special Committee on the Review of Personnel Management and the Merit Principle, *Report* (Ottawa: Supply and Services, 1979).

21. *PS 2000, Report of the Task Force on Staff Relations,* August 6, 1990 (Privy Council Office, Government of Canada).

22. See the detailed discussion of the Treasury Board proposals in Gene Swimmer, "Changes to Public Service Labour Relations Legislation: Revitalizing or Destroying Collective Bargaining?" in Michael J. Prince, ed., *How Ottawa Spends, 1987-88* (Toronto: Methuen, 1987), pp. 300-316.

23. *Report,* August 6, 1990.

24. Finkelman and Goldenberg, *Collective Bargaining in the Public Service,* vol. 1, p. 116.

25. Ibid., vol. 2, p. 697. In July 1986, the Treasury Board and the Professional Institute of the Public Service (PIPS) signed a memorandum of agreement to negotiate a master agreement covering a large number of bargaining units. According to a joint news release of the PIPS and Treasury Board on August 14, 1990, the third of these master agreements (signed on the day of the news release) covered nine thousand employees in eighteen bargaining units. In the event of an impasse at the master bargaining table, "either party can request a conciliation board with authority to render a binding decision on a broader range of issues than an arbitration board while eliminating the possibility of strike activities by the members of these 18 bargaining units."

26. *PS 2000, Report,* July 20, 1990, pp. 22 ff. (Privy Council Office, Government of Canada).

27. See Finkelman and Goldenberg, *Collective Bargaining in the Public Service,* vol. 1, pp. 31-45.

28. Ibid., vol. 2, p. 699.

29. Mark Thompson and Gene Swimmer, "The Future of Public Sector Industrial Relations," in Thompson and Swimmer, p. 462. See also in the same book Gene Swimmer, "Militancy in Public Sector Unions," pp. 147-95 and Douglas A. Smith, "Strikes in the Canadian Public Sector," pp. 197-228.

30. Kuruvilla, "Collective Bargaining," p. 228.

31. *Re the Queen in Right of Canada and Canadian Air Traffic Control Association No. 2* (1982) 128 D.L.R. (3d) 685.

32. (1982) 1 S.C.R. 696.

33. Gene Swimmer, "Changes to Public Service Labour Relations Legislation," in Prince, *How Ottawa Spends: 1987-1988,* pp. 296, 313-14.

34. *Public Service 2000—Report of the Task Force on Staff Relations,* August 6, 1990, p. 4. Reproduced with permission of the Minister of Supply and Services Canada, 1991.

35. Ibid., p. 1.

36. Thompson and Swimmer, "The Future of Public Sector Industrial Relations," in Thompson and Swimmer, *Conflict or Compromise,* p. 458.

37. See Allen Ponak and Mark Thompson, "Public Sector Collective Bargaining," in John Anderson, Morley Gunderson, and Allen Ponak, *Union-Management Relations in Canada,* 2nd ed. (Don Mills, Ont.: Addison-Wesley, 1989), pp. 394-98.

38. See Katherine Swinton, "Grievance Arbitration in the Public Sector," in Thompson and Swimmer, *Conflict or Compromise*, pp. 343-71.
39. *Report*, p. 7.
40. For an account of the evolution of collective bargaining in the provinces, see J.E. Hodgetts and O.P Dwivedi, *Provincial Governments as Employers* (Montreal: McGill-Queen's University Press, 1974), ch. 10.
41. For two very helpful summaries of dispute resolution processes in the federal, provincial, and municipal spheres of Canadian government, see Table 15.2 in Ponak and Thompson, "Public Sector Collective Bargaining," pp. 388-89, and Table 14.3 in Gene Swimmer, "Critical Issues in Public Sector Industrial Relations," in Sethi, Amarjit S., ed., *Collective Bargaining in Canada* (Scarborough, Ont.: Nelson Canada, 1989), pp. 408-409.
42. This classification is used in Kenneth P. Swan, "Differences Among Provinces in Public Sector Dispute Resolution," in David W. Conklin, Thomas C. Courchene, and William A. Jones, eds., *Public Sector Compensation* (Toronto: Ontario Economic Council, 1985), pp. 49-75; it is adapted from H. W. Arthurs, *Collective Bargaining by Public Employees in Canada: Five Models* (Ann Arbor, Mich.: Institute of Labour and Industrial Relations, University of Michigan, 1971).
43. Gene Swimmer, "Critical Issues in Public Sector Industrial Relations," in Sethi, *Collective Bargaining in Canada*, p. 419.
44. See Swan, "Differences Among Provinces," pp. 65-71.
45. Thompson and Swimmer, "The Future of Public Sector Industrial Relations," in Thompson and Swimmer, *Conflict or Compromise*, pp. 442-45 and 465-66.
46. L. V. Panitch and D. Swartz, "From Free Collective Bargaining to Permanent Exceptionalism: The Economic Crisis and the Transformation of Industrial Relations in Canada," in Thompson and Swimmer, *Conflict or Compromise*, pp. 407-35.
47. Swimmer, "Critical Issues," in Sethi, *Collective Bargaining in Canada*," p. 419.

BIBLIOGRAPHY

Arthurs, H. W. *Collective Bargaining by Public Employees in Canada: Five Models*. Ann Arbor, Mich.: Institute of Labor and Industrial Relations, University of Michigan, 1971.

Barnes, L. W. C. S. *Consult and Advise: A History of the National Joint Council of the Public Service of Canada, 1944-1974*. Kingston: Industrial Relations Centre, Queen's University, 1975.

Barnes, L. W. C. S., and Kelly, L. A. *Interest Arbitration in the Federal Public Service of Canada*. Kingston: Industrial Relations Centre, Queen's University, 1975.

Canada. Preparatory Committee on Collective Bargaining in the Public Service. *Report*. Ottawa: Queen's Printer, 1965.

Canada. Privy Council Office. Public Service 2000. *PS 2000, Report of the Task Force on Staff Relations*, August 6, 1990.

Canada. *Public Service 2000. The Renewal of the Public Service of Canada*. Ottawa: Supply and Services, 1990.

Canada. Special Committee on the Review of Personnel Management and the Merit Principle. *Report*. Ottawa: Supply and Services, 1979.

Christensen, Sandra. *Unions and the Public Interest*. Vancouver: The Fraser Institute, 1980.

Conklin, David W., Thomas C. Courchene, and William A. Jones, eds. *Public Sector Compensation*. Toronto: Ontario Economic Council, 1985.

Daniel, Mark J., and William E. A. Robinson. *Compensation in Canada: A Study of the Public and Private Sectors.* Ottawa: The Conference Board of Canada, 1980.

Finkelman, J. *Employer-Employee Relations in the Public Service of Canada: Proposals for Legislative Change.* Ottawa: Information Canada, 1974.

Finkelman, Jacob, and Shirley Goldenberg. *Collective Bargaining in the Public Service: The Federal Experience in Canada.* 2 vols. Montreal: Institute for Research on Public Policy, 1983.

Foot, David K., ed., *Public Employment and Compensation in Canada: Myths and Realities.* Toronto: Butterworths for the Institute for Research on Public Policy, 1978.

Hodgetts, J. E., and O. P. Dwivedi. *Provincial Governments as Employers.* Montreal: McGill-Queen's University Press, 1974.

Institute of Public Administration of Canada. *Collective Bargaining in the Public Service.* Toronto: Institute of Public Administration of Canada, 1973.

Kuruvilla, P. K. "Collective Bargaining in the Canadian Federal Public Service." In Kenneth Kernaghan, ed., *Public Administration in Canada: Selected Readings.* 5th ed. Toronto: Methuen, 1985, pp. 224-35.

Love, J. D. "Personnel Reorganization in the Canadian Public Service: Some Observations on the Past." *Canadian Public Administration* 22 (Fall 1979): 402-14.

Maslove, Allan, and Gene Swimmer. *Wage Controls in Canada, 1975-1978.* Montreal: Institute for Research on Public Policy, 1980.

Swettenham, John, and David Kealy. *Serving the State: A History of the Professional Institute of the Public Service of Canada, 1920-1970.* Ottawa: The Professional Institute of the Public Service of Canada, 1970.

Thompson, Mark, and Gene Swimmer, eds. *Conflict or Compromise: The Future of Public Sector Industrial Relations.* Montreal: Institute for Research on Public Policy, 1984.

Vaison, Robert A. "Collective Bargaining in the Federal Public Service: The Achievement of a Milestone in Personnel Relations." *Canadian Public Administration* 12 (Spring 1969): 108-22.

CASES

In *Case Program in Canadian Public Administration* (Toronto: Institute of Public Administration of Canada):

M.T.L. Simulation: Public Sector Collective Bargaining. By Gene R. Swimmer and Claude P. Parent

Autorité et syndicalisme à Radio-Québec. By Kenneth Cabatoff

The Northville Simulation. By Gene R. Swimmer and Allan M. Maslove

The Ben Fisher Case. By Nancy LePitre, Salim Mansur, and Wilbur Grasham

Students or Doctors? The Emergence of Collective Bargaining Among Interns and Residents in Ontario. By Harold Wodinsky, Richard Nurse, and Raisa B. Deber

The Borough of York Strike. By D. Wayne Taylor

A Conflict of Loyalties. By Kenneth Kernaghan

26

The Budgetary Process

The previous three chapters considered the management of human resources. This chapter will discuss the establishment of revenue and expenditure budgets. The next chapter will focus on financial operations during a fiscal year after the initial budget has been established. It is sometimes said that the budgetary process has three phases—preparation, adoption, and execution. This chapter will treat preparation; the next will deal with adoption and execution.

This chapter begins with a brief discussion of the preparation of the revenue budget, then proceeds to a discussion of various theories of the expenditure budget and a description of the preparation of the federal expenditure budget. The appendix at the end of the chapter explains the components of government financial statements in everyday language.

Establishing a budget is certainly one of the single most important acts that any government performs.

> Government and governing are about the use of power and resources to deliver public sector goods and services and to modify private sector behaviour in pursuit of societal objectives. Along the way, an imposing variety of conflicts and trade-offs must be resolved or, at least, addressed. How are the social objectives determined? Who plays a role in their articulation? What resources (and whose resources) are to be mobilized to fund the operations of government? How are these resources to be conscripted? What quantities of resources on the one hand, and public goods and services on the other, are optimal or appropriate? How does government operate to maintain its capacity to govern over extended periods of time?
>
> Budgeting, because it must address all these questions, is the quintessential act of governing.[1]

One of the great difficulties in preparing a government budget is that the budget typically has many objectives, not all of which are consistent with one another. In preparing a personal budget, one usually thinks in terms of the fairly uni-dimensional problem of adjusting expenditures to fit a relatively fixed income. The complicating factor in the preparation of government budgets is that they must address at least three objectives.

First is the *setting of macroeconomic policy* or at least that part of it that is influenced by fiscal instruments, i.e., levels of aggregate revenue, expenditure, and surplus or deficit. Governments set total revenue and expenditure targets so as to stimulate the economy or slow it down.

The second objective involves *influencing behaviour at a more micro level.* Governments frequently use tax provisions, not just to raise revenue, but rather to encourage people to do, or refrain from doing, certain things. For example, customs duties raise a sizable portion of government revenue, but their main objective is to protect domestic industry.

Another example of this use of the budget that has received increasing attention in recent years is tax expenditures. **Tax expenditures** are benefits enjoyed in the form of reduced taxes for individuals or corporations who do (or refrain from doing) certain things. For example, there have been programs that encouraged people to invest in scientific research or Canadian-made movies in exchange for a tax benefit. These tax expenditures were used in place of outright cash grants. Their attraction stemmed from the obviously mistaken notion that tax reductions did not really "cost" anything because they did not show up as expenses.[2] Thus, departments could adopt particular policies through a tax expenditure with no idea of, or concern for, its cost to the treasury.

The third objective of a budget is simply to *raise the resources needed to fund expenditures.* This involves estimating the amounts to be received from various tax and non-tax sources of revenue, and adjusting those under the control of the government so that adequate funds are raised. Thus, the mark of a good tax system is that it produces reasonably stable amounts of money from year to year, but, even more important, the amount ought to be predictable well in advance, so that the government knows where it will stand as the year progresses.[3]

The most difficult aspect of these three objectives is that not all point toward the same action at the same time. For example, in difficult economic times, government will need more revenue to fund unemployment insurance and social assistance plans. However, macroeconomic principles suggest that it is desirable to reduce taxes to stimulate spending in hard economic times. The continuing adjustment of these seemingly irreconcilable factors makes government budgeting a most difficult task.

THE REVENUE BUDGET

It is an important principle of responsible government that no tax can be imposed without the approval of the legislature. At least once each year, the federal Minister of Finance or provincial Treasurer prepares a revenue budget that contains, among many other things, a request to the legislature to impose or change certain taxes. Actually, the government uses the revenue budget to:

1. describe and interpret the major economic events of the recent past and the government's view of the economic outlook (frequently with the intent of altering private expectations);
2. congratulate itself for any past improvement in the state of the economy and shift the blame for any past deterioration;
3. announce changes (including no change) in fiscal policy (tax/expenditure/borrowing/lending) designed to stabilize the economy;
4. propose changes in the tax/tariff structure designed to
   (a) implement social (income/wealth redistribution) policy,

> (b) implement economic (resource allocation) policy,
> (c) eliminate "technical" flaws or difficulties with existing tax/tariff structures; and
>
> 5. deal with special measures such as incomes policy, federal-provincial fiscal relations, pensions, and special studies.[4]

The fiscal year of the federal and provincial governments begins on April 1 and ends the following March 31. There is a relatively short-lived tradition that the Minister of Finance presents the federal revenue budget close to the beginning of the fiscal year. Finance Minister Wilson has presented persuasive arguments that mid-January to mid-February is the ideal time.[5] There is no set rule for this timing; budgets are sometimes presented at other times of the year and more than one budget can be presented in the same year. These deviations stem from either political considerations, e.g., the desire to present an attractive budget on which to fight an election, or from volatile economic conditions such as changing international trade situations or energy prices.

The revenue budget is presented as a part of the minister's budget speech. There is no set format for this speech, but it usually contains most of the following elements:

> 1. a review of economic conditions and problems based on information from a White Paper tabled a few days earlier [or at the same time as the budget];
> 2. a statement of government revenues and expenditures over the past year and a comparison with the previous budget's estimation;
> 3. an estimation of government expenditures and revenues for the upcoming year and the surplus or deficit;
> 4. notice of any ways and means motions—that is, motions to introduce bills to amend various tax acts.[6]

The third and fourth items are usually given the greatest attention. In recent years, when government deficits have been the rule, the level of the deficit and the attendant government borrowing requirements provide important signals to money markets. The notice of ways and means motions holds the greatest interest for most taxpayers because this is the announcement of changes in tax structure or rates, which means that new taxes will be introduced, new items taxed, or tax loopholes opened or closed.

The minister's budget speech is given much more attention than other speeches in the legislature. Because it says so much about the government's financial situation, it can be regarded as a sort of "mini-throne Speech." The date and time are set several weeks in advance at an hour when stock markets are closed so that the contents of the speech will not affect stock prices precipitously. The media pay great attention to the event and it is usually broadcast live on radio and/or television, followed by analysis by learned economists, representatives of interest groups, and the inevitable homey interviews with the "average family." Several days of the legislature's time are set aside for what is euphemistically called debate on the budget speech. Actually it is a time for the Opposition parties to criticize the minister for past mistakes and anticipated future mistakes.

After this debate, there is a vote of confidence concerning the overall budget. Since it is a vote of confidence, if it does not carry, then the government must, by convention, resign. This is what happened to the Trudeau government in 1974 and to the short-lived Clark government in 1979.

Assuming that the government does survive the initial vote of confidence, the Minister of Finance will then introduce, over the next few months, a series of motions implementing the specific taxation measures presented in the budget. Votes on these motions can be matters of confidence if the specific measure is central to the total budget package, but they are not ordinarily considered to be matters of confidence. However, defeat of a major tax measure can pose a serious problem for a government, because alternative sources of revenue will have to be found.

Budget Preparation

A later section of this chapter contains a lengthy discussion of the process involved in the preparation of the expenditure budget. It is difficult to discuss the preparation of the revenue budget in the same manner, because it is very much the personal work of the Minister of Finance or provincial Treasurer and his or her senior public servants.[7] The secrecy of the revenue budget is considered very important because if some taxpayers had advance information about certain tax and other provisions of the budget, they could either profit unfairly or evade the intended effects of the provisions of the budget.

The minister is not totally isolated from public concerns in the preparation of the budget. While the budget is being prepared, the minister is kept constantly aware of the desires of other governments, business, labour, and other interest groups, and he or she usually consults in a general way with Cabinet colleagues and, shortly before public presentation of the budget, the minister will also consult with the Governor of the Bank of Canada.[8] Prime Minister Mulroney has been deeply involved in the preparation of the revenue budget, in contrast to previous Prime Ministers.[9] However, any breaches of secrecy that make information available to the general public are considered to be very serious.

The parliamentary tradition is that a Minister of Finance must resign if there is any leak of information about the budget. Resignations for this reason have occurred in Britain,[10] but there has never been a resignation in Canada. There have been several cases where Ministers of Finance or provincial Treasurers have suffered significant political embarrassment because of alleged violations of secrecy. In 1963, Walter Gordon was pressured to resign as federal Minister of Finance when it was discovered that he had employed certain non-civil servants, who had been sworn to an oath of secrecy, to assist him in the preparation of the budget.[11] In more recent times, a summary of a federal budget was given to a journalist who broadcast its contents on television; a journalist found portions of an Ontario budget in the trash of a printing firm; and a Nova Scotia newspaper printed advance reports of the provincial budget, which proved to be remarkably accurate.[12] In none of these cases did the minister resign.

One of the persistent proposals for reform of the revenue budget process is that the convention of secrecy should be relaxed somewhat. Evert Lindquist describes four problems that arise from this secrecy:

> First, many businesses and individual citizens find it difficult to plan their affairs because they perceive a high likelihood of having their plans dislocated by surprise budget announcements. Second, many initial budget proposals must be redrafted and rethought because they are prepared in the absence of information available only from those affected by the measures. The cost of consulting with those who have the information would be to reveal government thinking. Third, long delays frequently occur between the date on which a proposed measure has effect and the (later) date when its provisions are fully specified. As with many problems occasioned by public-sector processes, the underlying issue in all these problems is the generation of additional uncertainties. Outside observers have also identified a fourth problem: a concentration on process rather than policy deflects scarce analytical resources away from important substantive issues.[13]

There have been a number of specific proposals for reform.[14] They all recognize that secrecy is important for the announcement of certain kinds of tax changes, but most proposals suggest there should be a clear delineation of certain areas where secrecy is not important.

> The government believes that the fundamental rationale for budget secrecy now, as always, is to prevent the possibility of profit from advance knowledge about matters to be announced in a budget. Should this not be the sole context in which the government interprets and applies the concept of budget secrecy? If this were the accepted notion of budget secrecy, alleged budget "leaks" that do not relate in any way to the possibility of financial profit would not be considered the "stuff" of ministerial resignations. Indeed, such exaggerated reaction only serves to trivialize the concept of budget secrecy, perpetuate confusion and inhibit consultation.[15]

A usual suggestion for reform is that the minister should announce that changes are being considered in a particular field and then invite consultation with interested parties. The original announcement could be made either through a speech in the legislature or the use of the coloured paper process as discussed in Chapter 6.[16] Different proposals vary at this point, but the general idea is that members of the public could then make their views known to a legislative committee[17] and/or a permanent committee of experts established for this purpose.[18]

In spite of considerable pressure to open up the system in some ways, governments of all stripes in both federal and provincial spheres have moved very haltingly in this direction. For example, in 1985 the federal Minister of Finance tabled some specific suggestions for improvements in the budgetary process in a number of areas, but his suggestions in the area of secrecy were very vague.[19] In 1985, the government of Ontario arranged for a "pre-budget consultation," which involved in camera presentations to the provincial Treasurer by 114 organizations.[20] Of course, secrecy required that this be a form of one-way consultation in that the groups could express their views to the Treasurer, but he could not respond to them in a meaningful fashion.

There are some disadvantages to opening up the budgetary process. One obvious disadvantage is that increased consultation usually leads to increased delay in implementation. A more serious problem could stem from the fact that consultation is always uneven; some groups are able to participate better than others.

> If governments invite public debate of tentative tax changes, it is probable that relatively concentrated, well-organized, and well-financed interests with much at stake will be the most intense and best prepared participants. Their views and assumptions will dominate in the policy arena . . . Changes unfavorable to business or other well-organized interests will be strongly resisted, while passive citizens, each losing a little, will be " 'nickelled' and 'dimed' into economic oblivion."[21]

The continuing closed nature of the revenue budget process has had the effect of inhibiting comment about the process of budget preparation. However, a great deal of discussion has taken place about the preparation of the expenditure budget.

STYLES OF THE EXPENDITURE BUDGET

There are many different styles of budgeting in use in different jurisdictions. There is no general consensus about the ideal approach to the expenditure budget; each organization seems to adopt a slightly different style. Regardless of the approach employed, it is usually argued that the ideal budgeting system has three factors: control, management, and planning and policy choice.[22]

"*Control* refers to the process of binding operating officials to the policies and plans set by their superiors."[23] A satisfactory budgeting system must have some method of ensuring that managers do not overspend their budgets or spend money on programs that have not been properly authorized.

A sound system of good *management* goes beyond simply ensuring that subordinates are following orders; it also ensures that work is organized so as to achieve efficiency and effectiveness. When the problems of legal control were deemed to be solved, effective management was added to the purposes of budgeting. The budget was seen as a management tool to ensure the economical and efficient operation of departments and programs. The introduction of labour-saving equipment, the streamlining of paper processing, the careful determination of employment needs, and the introduction of performance measurement procedures to relate results achieved to resources used, are among the typical activities associated with management control.[24]

"*Planning* involves the determination of objectives, the evaluation of alternative courses of action and the authorization of select programs."[25] If planning is a part of the budgetary system, the system can be used to provide information about the future, which can be used in making trade-offs among policies. The perfect budgeting system will combine all three factors, but attaining that ideal has been somewhat elusive.

In searching for this ideal style, a number of innovations have been introduced over the years. It is sometimes difficult to find precise dividing lines between approaches, but it is possible to identify four major styles of budgeting that have been employed in recent years: line-item, performance, program, and zero-base. Some of the characteristics of these styles are illustrated in Table 26.1, and each style will be discussed in more detail below. However, it is important to understand that these different styles are not mutually exclusive. There are many examples of organizations creating hybrid systems by borrowing from different styles.

Line-item Budgeting

Line-item budgeting was the first style of budgeting employed in modern public administration, and is usually considered to be the most rudimentary.[26] Table 26.2 illustrates a page from a line-item budget. This page covers the entire budget of one department and shows how the requested funds will be spent by object of expenditure, e.g., salaries, rent, supplies. This illustrates the manner in which the line-item budget focusses on *inputs used* rather than *outputs achieved*.

The key person in the preparation of this type of budget is the accountant, because the process basically involves reviewing last year's budget and making revisions based on inflation and changes in the size of the population served. This process is usually carried out on an annual basis; there is ordinarily no attempt at long-range planning.

The key agency is the operating department because the budget is prepared on a "bottom-up" basis. This means that the process begins with the operating department preparing a request for funds that it then passes upward to decision-makers who, frankly, have a great deal of difficulty making any revisions in the original request because of the very detailed manner in which it is prepared. This leads to a decentralized style of decision-making because decisions are made in operating departments with little opportunity for meaningful review by politicians.

The use of line-item budgeting makes it somewhat awkward to evaluate a manager's performance. The main sign of a good manager in this system is that he or she does not overspend the assigned budget; clearly, this is a minimal requirement for good management, but there is simply too little information available to make any other kind of judgment.

All of this adds up to a style of decision-making on budgetary allocations that can only be incremental, i.e., this year's budgetary allocation is determined by making incremental changes in last year's allocation. This usually means uniform, across-the-board increases in the allocations to all departments. Everyone involved in the process recognizes that this is inferior to a thoughtful process that seriously considers the needs of each department separately and provides more funding to agencies with greater needs. However, because of the dearth of

Table 26.1
COMPARISON OF DIFFERENT STYLES OF BUDGETING

	Line-item	Performance	Program	ZBB
Building Block	Object of expenditure	Unit cost and units of service	Program	Decision package
Key Expert	Accountant	Cost accountant	Economist	Multi-disciplined program analyst
Time Horizon	Annual	Annual	Multi-year	Annual (some longer-term considerations)
Direction of construction	Bottom-up	Bottom-up	Top-down	Bottom-up and top-down
Key Agency	Operating department	Operating department	Central agencies	Central agencies
Method of Evaluation of Manager	Does not overspend	Minimizes unit cost	Maximizes program performance	Maximizes program performance
Type of Decision-Making	Decentralized	Decentralized	Centralized	Centralized
Dominant Philosophy of Decision-Making	Incremental	Incremental	Rational	Rational
Strong Points	Emphasizes control Discourages conflict	More information for decision-makers Emphasizes: -productivity improvement -cost minimization	Emphasizes rational process Emphasizes program and planning	Focus on priority-setting Facilitates cost-cutting Equal competition between established and new programs
Weak Points	Emphasizes status quo Little information for decision-makers	No cross-program comparisons	High cost Dubious techniques	High cost Dubious techniques Morale problems

meaningful information generated in a line-item budgeting system, there is no alternative to the incremental approach.

Line-item budgeting emphasizes the control aspect of the budget. It makes it very easy to prevent overspending or to determine who is responsible if it does

Table 26.2
EXAMPLE OF LINE-ITEM BUDGET

CITY OF ANYTOWN
FIRE DEPARTMENT
FISCAL YEAR ENDING DECEMBER 31, 1991

Object of Expenditure	1991 (Budget)	1990 (Actual)
Salaries—Regular	120,000	110,000
Salaries—Overtime	10,000	9,000
Casual Labour	9,000	8,000
Employee Benefits	12,000	11,000
Firefighting Equipment	11,000	10,000
Uniforms	6,000	5,000
Building Rent	24,000	22,000
Stationery	6,000	5,000
Cleaning Supplies	3,000	2,000
Travel	5,000	4,000
Vehicle Maintenance	4,000	3,000
Miscellaneous Expenses	3,000	3,000
TOTAL	213,000	192,000

occur. It also limits some of the conflict found in other styles of budgeting because it tends to compartmentalize spending rather than emphasize trade-offs. This characteristic is also a political defect in line-item budgeting. The limited information about output that it generates makes it very difficult for decision-makers (politicians or senior managers) to make trade-offs about the quality of programs. Therefore, line-item budgeting does not lend itself to the management and planning and policy choice orientations that were discussed earlier.

Line-item budgeting is useful in the case of relatively small, simple organizations where all decision-makers can grasp the roles of the different organizational units quickly and intuitively. The dearth of output information generated by it, and its lack of a management or planning and policy choice orientation, makes it considerably less useful in large, dynamic organizations. Nonetheless, it is still used in some organizations largely because of its simplicity of operation and because the accountants who frequently control the budgetary process feel comfortable with it.

The basic problem in line-item budgeting is its lack of an output orientation, i.e., the absence of any measuring technique to determine what is being accomplished by the expenditures. Therefore, it is not surprising that the next improvement in the budgetary process addressed this concern for output measurement.

Performance Budgeting

The basic difference between line-item and performance budgeting was the output orientation of performance budgeting.[27] Line-item budgeting measured only inputs used; **performance budgeting** established a relationship between inputs employed and outputs attained. The basic building block of performance budgeting was the unit cost of providing a service (inputs) and the number of units of service provided (outputs). Thus, a budgetary allocation was established by multiplying units of service (clients served, miles of road paved) by the unit cost of providing each service.

The key budgetary expert now became the cost accountant because he or she possessed the esoteric skills needed to collect and calculate information about unit costs. The unit cost information created an additional method of evaluating a good manager, besides not overspending his or her budget. Managers performing similar duties could be evaluated by comparing the unit costs of their operations.

In making budgetary allocations, it was possible to escape from incrementalism in a limited way. Reasonable estimates could usually be made about changes in the demand for the service, although, even here, incrementalism frequently had to be used as an aid in calculation. The unit cost could be influenced somewhat by experience in other jurisdictions, but, in the final analysis, incrementalism was a frequent guide here as well.

The strong point of performance budgeting was that it added a management improvement focus to the control focus of line-item budgeting. It provided decision-makers with enough information to consider management improvement and cost minimization techniques. However, performance budgeting did not provide any techniques for future planning; nor did it provide enough information to make trade-offs among programs. These techniques would come later.

Program Budgeting

In proceeding chronologically through the various budgetary styles, one can see a steady ascendancy in the basic building block from the object of expenditure, to the unit of service, to the entire program. But there were many changes that came with program budgeting that involved more than just the emphasis on program.

In general, program budgeting was an attempt to adapt the rational decision-making techniques discussed in Chapter 6 to the budgetary process. **Program budgeting** concepts were described in a 1969 federal government publication as:

(a) the setting of specific objectives;
(b) the systematic analysis to clarify objectives and to assess alternative ways of meeting them;

(c) the framing of budgetary proposals in terms of programs directed toward the achievement of the objectives;

(d) the projection of the costs of these programs a number of years in the future;

(e) the formulation of plans of achievement year by year for each program;

(f) an information system for each program to supply data for the monitoring of achievement of program goals and to supply data for the reassessment of the program objectives and the appropriateness of the program itself.[28]

Note the similarity between these steps and those mentioned earlier under the general heading of rational techniques such as determining objectives, examining alternative methods of attaining objectives, implementing the optimum method, and installing feedback mechanisms to measure attainment of objectives.

In practice, the implementation of program budgeting, or Planning-Programming-Budgeting (PPB) as it was called in the federal sphere, involved the division of the activities of each department into discrete units called programs and the preparation of *multi-year* budgetary forecasts for each program. The purpose of the multi-year estimates was to alert decision-makers to the full future costs of programs, particularly in cases in which programs started with a limited use of resources and expanded in future years.

Program budgeting is frequently described as a "top-down" system because it encourages a centralization of decision-making by allowing decision-makers to escape the excessive detail contained in line-item and performance budgets. Instead, the decision-makers could communicate messages such as "we need to hold the line on social services," or "this is the year to provide a bit more to defence," by simply allowing smaller increases in social programs and greater increases in defence ones. This sort of movement of macro-levers is possible only because of the emphasis on broad programs instead of details of expenditure.

Program budgeting brought with it a large set of rational economic tools such as cost-benefit analysis, cost-effectiveness analysis, and systems analysis. These tools could maximize government performance by providing a rational, economic comparison of different methods of attaining goals and even comparing the worth of trying to attain particular goals. The most extreme proponents of this kind of thinking argued that the ultimate purpose of government was to maximize human well-being—economic, physical, social, psychological, etc.— and that this well-being could be measured and rational techniques employed to determine which government programs would best attain this maximization of well-being. Others stopped somewhat short of these beliefs, but all practitioners of program budgeting argued that there were rational, economic tools that could be used to make trade-offs between programs.

Since the economist was the primary person who employed these kinds of techniques, program budgeting caused the mantle of key expert to pass from the accountant to the economist. The other structural change that occurred at the same time was the ascendancy of central agencies, in particular Treasury Board. If decision-making is more centralized and trade-offs between departments are more important, then there is an obvious need for a central agency to deal with these various elements.

The strength of program budgeting is that it includes all three of the factors that are important for an ideal budgeting style—control, management, and planning and policy choice. In evaluating the worth of a manager, program budgeting emphasizes not just avoiding overspending or minimizing cost, but rather maximizing program performance. The multi-year focus allows for future planning and the use of rational, economic techniques allows for effective, informed policy choice.

There have been a number of innovations in program budgeting and a number of other management techniques grafted onto it over the years.

In the federal government, Management by Objectives (described more fully in Chapter 4) was added to it in some departments.[29] It would seem that these two objectives-oriented approaches should meld together well, but the two innovations were developed separately by separate groups—PPB by financial officials and MBO by personnel officials—and were never really merged.[30] Whether it was for this or other reasons, MBO was adopted only in a small number of departments.

At roughly the same time as MBO was being imported, Treasury Board was developing its own system to supplement PPB and MBO. The key to the operation of both these systems is good measurement of the performance, or outputs, achieved by programs. The Operational Performance Measurement System (OPMS) was meant to be the performance measurement aspect of PPB and MBO.[31]

The concept of OPMS began with the idea that the ultimate goal of all government programs is to foster "individual and collective well-being," as evidenced by such things as national integrity, social justice, national wealth, and individual fulfillment. Of course, it is impossible to measure most of these things in a tangible way, and, even if it were possible to measure overall change, measuring the impact of a *particular* program on national integrity would be most contentious.

Therefore, OPMS suggested the use of a hierarchy of proxy measures. It is, for example, impossible to measure the effect of industrial incentives on social justice. However, if we posit a series of means/ends relationships in which the use of industrial incentives begins a chain reaction that ultimately has an impact on social justice, then it is possible to measure some of these intermediate steps.

As a result of implementation problems and bureaucratic resistance, OPMS was never widely adopted in the federal government. It now stands as an interesting possible approach to a recognized problem, but not an approach that has any support in the federal government.

However, a few other notable innovations in program budgeting have been more widely used. As a part of the PPB system, federal departments were required to prepare their budgets in three parts. The "A" budget represents the continuation of existing programs with adjustments made for inflation and changes in the population served. The "B" budget is the request for either the establishment of new programs or the enrichment and enhancement of existing programs. The "X" budget is a listing of the programs that a department would eliminate if it were forced to reduce its budget by a stated percentage. In other words, "X" budget items are the lowest priority programs ranked by the department.

The idea was that "A" budget items would not be evaluated in depth because these programs were approved previously, but that there would be a thorough review of the costs and benefits of new programs—the "B" budget items—before they were implemented. As will be discussed in more detail later, the "A" and "B" budgets continue to play an important part in the federal budgetary process. The concept of the "X" budget is still discussed, but, understandably, it has not been warmly welcomed by departments.

Another innovation in program budgeting has been most prevalent in municipal governments. For each program, the manager is required to estimate the effects on the program, in terms of levels of service, if it were to operate at three different levels of funding—the same budget as last year (adjusted by inflation and population served), and, for example, 80 percent and 120 percent of last year's funding. This provides decision-makers with a significant amount of knowledge that they can use in deciding on funding levels.

PPB was clearly the major budgeting innovation of the 1960s and the early 1970s. Virtually every government of any size in North America experimented with some form of program budgeting. The success of those experiments has been mixed. PPB was significant in that it forced people to think in terms of programs and outputs. It was probably unrealistic to think that it could ever live up to its promise to turn budget-making into a totally rational process.

There are many reasons for the problems experienced with PPB.[32] As noted above, it is an attempt to apply rational modes of decision-making to the budget process. Therefore, many of the general criticisms of rational decision-making techniques are also applicable to PPB. The high cost in both dollars and time of implementing the system and the sheer complexity of some attempts were clearly problems. In some cases, the amount of time spent "getting ready to get ready" seriously weakened the credibility of those seeking to implement PPB. Also the attempt to impose one system of evaluation on diverse programs led to some difficulties. Schick argues that the success of PPB in the United States Department of Defense stems, in part, from the fact that it was home-grown there; its failure in other departments stems from its status as a foreign intruder unable to adapt to the local customs.[33]

There is one outstanding reason for the problems of PPB that is too often overlooked. Changes in budgeting systems are not minor technical adjustments in procedures significant only to accountants. Certain changes in budgeting systems amount to vast shifts of power within organizations.[34] This was the case with PPB. PPB usually involved a shift from a decentralized form of budgeting such as line-item or performance budgeting to a highly centralized one. In the decentralized systems, individual departments present budget requests, but little information, to politicians. The politicians, in turn, do not have a group of qualified experts from whom they can seek advice. The head of the department, then, has fairly broad latitude to manage the department with minimum scope for intrusion from either any other department or politicians.

PPB introduces a new actor to the scene—the strong central budget agency. If detailed documentation is to be prepared, cost-benefit analysis performed, and trade-offs made between various programs, there must be an organization to do these things. If the system is to function properly, this organization must have the right to request significant amounts of information from departments and evaluate that information in order to make recommendations to politicians. This would allow the budget agency to have a clear "window" into the operation of departments and so provide the agency with the ability to exercise some degree of control over operating departments. Thus, operating departments tend to oppose the introduction of PPB because they fear the increased exposure that this window provides.

Additional difficulties with a rational system of budgeting surround the related problems of specifying goals, measuring benefits achieved, and predicting future conditions.[35] Government programs usually serve multiple goals and people will disagree on the relative priority of those goals. Is the purpose of a youth employment program to have certain work activities carried out? To assist young people in developing good work habits? To provide funds to young people to continue their schooling? To buy votes? The likely answer is all of these, but which one is seen as paramount will have an effect on how the program is designed and evaluated.

A related problem is the inability to measure in a rigorous, quantified fashion the benefits derived from government services. Everyone agrees that it is beneficial that the garbage is picked up, but how is this value determined objectively in dollars and cents so that costs and benefits can be compared? Arguably, *some* of the public health benefits could be measured, but what about the aesthetic, practical, and other benefits?

A final problem involves the difficulty of predicting the future. Many programs have a large initial cost, and a stream of benefits that flow far into the future. The value assigned to those benefits can depend on the number of people who will enjoy them. For example, the total benefit derived from the construction of a second airport in Toronto is highly sensitive to whether one assumes that the level of usage remains steady, increases slightly, or increases significantly.[36] Yet no one is able to predict with sufficient precision which situation will occur.

For these and other reasons, many have suggested that PPB has failed. It might well be that PPB has not failed, but rather that some people expected (and others promised) more than PPB could ever deliver. Some felt that PPB was a rational device that would enable us to remove politics from the budgetary process. Programs would be selected using various economic techniques. Politicians and interest groups would be so swayed by the clear and unequivocal answers provided by these techniques, and by the totally impartial rationality of the system, that they would immediately confirm the results. In retrospect, this sort of thinking was naive. "[O]ne might wonder how a paper tiger such as PPB could possibly wreck the entrenched values defended by the armies of interest groups which patrol the budget scene."[37]

Zero-Base Budgeting

In the 1970s, as the glamour of PPB waned, it began to be supplanted by the latest budgetary innovation—**zero-base budgeting**. Of course, PPB is still very widely used, but the new technique of the late 1970s and 1980s was ZBB. Charles Beard, writing in 1917, provided a rationale for this shift: "Budget reform bears the imprint of the age in which it originated."[38] PPB was one of the casualties of the economic downturn of the mid-1970s. PPB is a budgetary system for a dynamic, expanding government. It evaluates new programs and helps determine which to implement immediately and which must be put off until next year. It is more difficult to use in times of fiscal restraint. Enter zero-base budgeting.

Zero-base budgeting derives its name from the fact that conceptually managers are required to justify every dollar requested from zero up.[39] The implication is that if they cannot, their programs will be reduced or eliminated. The building block of ZBB is the decision package. The decision package is basically the program under program budgeting divided into several elements. One decision package could be 80 percent of last year's funding for the program. A second package would be the increment from 80 percent to 100 percent; and the third could be an increment from 100 percent to 120 percent of last year's funding. A manager would then prepare a document for each decision package, which provided a large amount of quantitative and other information about each package. Systems vary, but some of the usual components are:

- description of actions performed;
- achievements from actions (both a narrative and some quantitative measures might be required);
- consequences of not approving package;
- alternative methods of accomplishing the same objective; and
- calculation of a benefit-cost or similar ratio.

This provides decision-makers with information not just about the total program, but about the outputs of various elements or levels of service of the program.

After preparation of these documents for each decision package, the ranking begins. It starts at the lowest level at which a manager has several decision packages under his or her control. This manager will rank these decision packages in order of priority and pass this ranking up to the next level in the hierarchy. The manager at this level will receive decision packages from a number of subordinates, which he or she in turn ranks in order of priority. This process continues up the hierarchy. In some organizations, as the process approaches the top levels of the hierarchy, committees are used to do the ranking. This frequently culminates in a final ranking done by committees of politicians (and sometimes administrators).

At the conclusion of this process, there exists a ranking of all decision packages from the most to the least attractive. At the same time that the ranking process is taking place, a decision is made concerning the level of total expenditure for the year. The final step is simply to start at the top of the list, add up proposed expenditures and accumulate until one arrives at the desired expenditure level. All programs above the line are accepted; all those below are rejected.

Zero-base budgeting can be viewed as both a "bottom-up" and a "top-down" approach, because it allows lower-level managers to participate in the ranking process but saves final decisions for politicians and senior managers.

Zero-base budgeting has a number of features that aid in cost-cutting and thus make it suitable for its time. In the first place, it evaluates *all* programs, not just new initiatives. The existence of the "A" and "B" budget systems in the federal government has meant that "A" items are usually not seriously reviewed for reductions. Instead, there is an emphasis on holding the line on new initiatives. Thus, this system does not provide any way to cut back. ZBB subjects existing programs to the same evaluation as new ones and so at least raises the possibility that existing programs could be eliminated, and possibly replaced by new, better ones.

Another important factor in ZBB that facilitates holding the line on spending is that the revenue constraint can be set first and the level of expenditure cut to fit it. This helps treasurers and other guardians of the public purse to withstand the onslaughts of spenders. This is likely one reason why ZBB has been most popular among municipal governments, which are not allowed to operate at a deficit.

Many of the criticisms of PPB are also applicable to ZBB. Both systems attempt to achieve rationality in expenditure management. This is both their strength and their weakness. An additional flaw of ZBB is the effect that this annual review to determine whether some programs will continue to exist has on the morale of employees. Presumably, large organizational units could be eliminated with great loss of jobs on the occasion of one of these reviews. If that is not really the case, then ZBB is not doing what it set out to do. This realization could well motivate managers to maximize their short-term successes with possible poor consequences for the longer-term.

There have been some limited evaluations of ZBB systems in practice.[40] The usual conclusion is that the system has some real value, although sometimes not as much as had been hoped. ZBB is no longer widely used. Its complexity and the lack of clear benefits have dampened the initial enthusiasm with which it was met. Most governments now use some variation on program budgeting, usually with some consideration of output measures, but without the rather naive belief that the calculation of sophisticated ratios will turn the budgetary process into a purely rational exercise.

UNDERSTANDING STANDARD BUDGETARY STRATEGIES

Regardless of the style of budgeting used or the specific processes established, there seem to be certain enduring strategies and tactics that participants in any budget-making exercise employ. It is important to understand that the skill with which the various actors employ these tactics will likely have a much greater impact on the eventual shape of the budget than any rational economic techniques.

One of the most common frameworks employed in parliamentary systems to analyze these strategies is "spenders and guardians."[41] Ministers in operating departments with large constituencies score points when they operate attractive, well-funded programs. These ministers are "spenders" not just because they want to aggrandize their own positions (although that could be one motivation), but because they come to understand that their clientele has very real needs that can be met only by adequately funded programs. Ministers also understand that one of their most important jobs is to keep their client groups contented—and therefore quiet. One way to accomplish this is by ensuring that programs affecting these groups are adequately funded. A recent survey indicates that ministers believe that they receive more political credit for launching new programs than for administering on-going ones.[42] These factors together can turn the most conservative, responsible minister into an avowed spender.

The "guardians" are the Minister of Finance and the President of the Treasury Board, who score points for reducing deficits and holding the line on taxes. The overall size of the budget and its allocation among programs is an outcome of the "game" played by the "spenders" and "guardians."

This framework is directly related to the bureaucratic or governmental politics style of policy-making discussed in Chapter 6. The bureaucratic politics approach sees the expenditure budget as the outcome of a bargaining process involving various governmental and some non-governmental organizations. Governments are not monolithic entities; rather, they consist of, on the one hand, many departments and agencies that are in competition with one another for limited resources and, on the other hand, agencies that are responsible for deciding how to divide up these funds. The budget, as ultimately determined, is the product of the to-ing and fro-ing that takes place between and among these entities. In spite of its name, this approach is not limited to bureaucrats; politicians and even representatives of non-governmental organizations become involved.

Just like any game, each side has certain strategies and tactics that it employs to enhance its position. The spenders have the greatest array of potential tactics. They can begin with fairly obvious ones like padding their original requests. However, that alone seldom works because guardians also understand the tactics of the game. Experienced spenders will supplement this basic strategy by a number of other tactics:

- *Mobilize constituency interest groups.* A spending minister will encourage interest groups to make great demands on his or her department, significantly increasing the minister's bargaining power in Cabinet. Business groups have been very good at this.

- *The thin edge of the wedge.* Start a program with a very small commitment of funds; when people become dependent on the program, the guardians cannot eliminate it and in fact will probably be pressed to increase funding.
- *Kill the Friendly Giant.* When pressed to make budget cuts, always cut the program that is most popular with the public, not least popular. This will bring public pressure to bear on the guardians who demanded the cuts in the first place. A few years ago, when CBC television faced severe budget restraint, it eliminated the popular program "Friendly Giant," which sparked great concern over the cuts.
- *End run.* In the ordinary budget cycle, when many requests for funding are arrayed against one another, the competition for funds is very keen. A resourceful minister will propose a new program part-way through the year and attempt to obtain a snap commitment from Cabinet, thus making an end run around the vicissitudes of the ordinary budget process.
- *This program saves money.* It is surprisingly easy to argue that a program that costs a significant amount of money in the short-run will actually result in a long-run saving. More money on fitness will reduce future health care costs. Business development grants will generate future taxes. Of course, these relationships cannot be proven, but they sound good.
- *Fire truck first.* There is an apocryphal story about one of the most audacious strategies. A fire chief wanted a new fire truck and a new fire station in the same year. When the city council told him that this was excessive in one year and that he could have either, but not both, he chose to buy the new fire truck. However, when the truck was delivered, it turned out that (you've probably already guessed) the existing fire hall was too small to accommodate the new truck.

Guardians also have tactics of their own, although it is possible that the rapid spending increases of the 1960s and 1970s were a result of an imbalance of power between spenders and guardians. Some of the responses to the above tactics are fairly obvious. For example, most recent budgetary systems have procedures to prevent "end runs," and the claims of program managers that "this program saves money" are usually met with requests to provide hard evidence. The one continuing tactic that guardians have is simply to underestimate revenue and so underestimate the amount available for expenditure. This allows them to paint the picture as being more bleak than it really is, and so increases their bargaining power.

Some people object to this "game" theory because they feel that it trivializes an important part of the governing process.[43] However, the theory strikes a responsive note for anyone who has been involved in the process. Game theory should not be equated with deception or a lack of concern for the public interest, but, rather, it can be seen as a committed group of people being certain that all options are considered in arriving at an optimum decision.

Budgeting as an outcome of bureaucratic politics has been fully described in the United States, where it is easy to analyze because the budget-making process is very open.[44] The work in Canada has been somewhat fragmentary,[45] but Donald J. Savoie's recent book, *The Politics of Public Spending in Canada*,[46] provides an excellent insight into the existing system.

The picture that Savoie paints is fairly negative. He uses the analogy of a number of people meeting for lunch and sharing the cost equally, regardless of how much each actually eats. Clearly, the incentive is for each person to eat and drink as much as possible, knowing that the cost will be shared by others. Even people who, at first, show restraint will soon loosen up when they see others gorging themselves. After all, if I am paying for someone else's extravagance anyway, why should I show moderation?[47]

There are simply no incentives for spending ministers to restrain themselves. On the contrary, ministers are frequently judged by their clients on the basis of how much money and how many new programs they can deliver. Regionalism is so important in Canada that ministers must also be seen to be delivering the goods to their regions. Savoie illustrates this with a rather depressing quotation from a minister.

> No doubt, I went for the Cadillac model instead of the Volkswagen model in the case of the golf course, the marina, the highways, the bridges, and so on. Yes, I had some second thoughts about the cost of it all. But that second thought lasted for all of five seconds. All you have to do is sit at the cabinet table and watch ministers from Toronto, Ottawa, and Montreal grab everything that goes by. If I went for the Cadillac model, they went for the Rolls Royce model. . . . I saw that whenever support for the party in Toronto dropped two points it sent Toronto ministers running around everywhere for new projects. I made sure that my region would get its share of federal spending. . . . *If Toronto ministers couldn't show restraint surely you don't expect me to do so.*[48]

A person quoted by Savoie expressed his concern about the unfairness of the closing of the CN yards in Moncton in this manner: "In government, especially in the federal government, there is a great deal of waste and inefficiency. Moncton is not getting its share of the waste. In losing the CN shops, we are now getting even less of our share."[49]

It is clear that the overall process is stacked in favour of the spenders. Not only are they more numerous than the guardians, but there are more good political arguments for spending money than for guarding it. This imbalance has been identified as a major problem and changes have been made in the budgetary process in recent years to redress this imbalance.

THE CURRENT FEDERAL BUDGETARY SYSTEM

This section will review recent changes in the federal budgetary process to set the scene for a description of how the current process operates. The last twenty years have seen three different budgetary processes—PPB (late 1960s-1979), the

Policy and Expenditure Management System (1979-1988), and "Ops and Chops" (1988-present).

Regardless of the details of the process employed, the major product of the budgetary process is a multi-volume set of documents entitled the *Estimates*, sometimes called the "Blue Book."[50] These volumes contain the details of the expenditure budget and are tabled in the House of Commons by the President of the Treasury Board before the beginning of the fiscal year. Part II, which is called the *Main Estimates*, is debated in Parliament and when it is passed, it represents the formal legislation that provides authority for spending by the executive. After it is passed, it is referred to as the Appropriation Act for that year. The remainder of this chapter will describe the process involved in the preparation of the *Estimates*.

Planning-Programming-Budgeting: Late 1960s-1979

The federal government implemented a Planning-Programming-Budgeting System (PPBS) in the late 1960s. This style of budgeting was discussed extensively earlier in this chapter and the details of the federal system will not be recounted here. The major contribution of PPBS was to start budget-makers thinking in terms of the output side of the budget and to force departmental managers to think more about goals and objectives. It also introduced an accounting system based on programs rather than line-items of expenditure.

PPBS never achieved the complete rationality that its early proponents promised, but it worked quite well during its time. The 1960s and 1970s were a period of fairly buoyant government revenue and PPBS helped manage the growth in government that was experienced at the time. Budgetary analysis focussed on the "B" budget, i.e., new spending initiatives, and PPBS provided a way to determine which programs would be implemented this year and which would be put off to next.

However, in the absence of the ill-fated "X" budget, PPBS had no mechanism to reduce expenditure. Instead, it provided a framework for the spenders' and guardians' game, with the usual outcome—the guardians were hopelessly defeated. A major part of the problem was that policies were frequently considered on a piecemeal basis and a number of individual programs were begun without any understanding that their *cumulative* impact on the federal budget would be very serious. In essence, the problem was that *policy initiatives were being considered apart from their budgetary implications.*

The Policy and Expenditure Management System (PEMS): 1979-1988[51]

The Policy and Expenditure Management System was, as the name suggests, a marriage of the policy-making and expenditure management systems. It was an attempt to force politicians to consider the budgetary implications of their actions.

PEMS was also sometimes called the "envelope system" because it involved division of the total expenditure budget into "envelopes." The process started when the Department of Finance prepared a five-year fiscal framework, which it updated each year. This was communicated to the Cabinet Committee on Priorities and Planning, which used the information to decide on the total level of government spending for a particular year, and then divided that pie into broad categories such as social development, external affairs, and defence. The "envelopes" that contained these allocations were then passed to the relevant Cabinet policy committees to further subdivide between departments and programs.

Sometimes, an "envelope" contained a "policy reserve." This was a pool of funds that the policy committee could use at its own discretion to launch new initiatives. Policy committees could create or add to their policy reserves by reducing expenditure on existing programs. There was also the possibility of a negative policy reserve, which would force the committee to search for savings in its area.[52] One of the most significant innovations of this system was the power it gave to the policy sector Cabinet committees to make budgetary and policy decisions in their sectors, as long as they stayed within their set expenditure limit.

"Envelopes" reflected not only cash expenditures, but also included new tax expenditures. Departments could still use tax expenditures instead of outright grants if they wished, but tax expenditures were no longer "free" to departments as they had been under the previous system; they showed up in their envelope as an expense.

The major innovation of PEMS was breaking up the former game of spenders and guardians. Another innovative aspect of this system showed there was no bottomless pot to which departments could keep returning to request additional funding for new policy initiatives. If individual departments or ministers wanted to embark on new programs, they would have to find the needed funds in their "envelope." This might mean cancelling or rearranging existing programs or making them operate more efficiently so that new money could be made available. Instead of the game of spenders vs. guardians, departmental ministers were now forced to be both spenders *and* guardians.

The most basic problem that the Mulroney government identified with PEMS was, quite simply, that it had not been effective in limiting expenditure. In particular, ministers had never come to grips with "X" budgets, nor had they seriously considered statutory appropriations.[53] These appropriations are permanent appropriations, made under legislation other than the annual *Estimates*, for such items as family allowances, veterans' benefits, and interest on the public debt. Expenditure on these items has been approved under other legislation and so does not require annual approval. However, since statutory appropriations make up over 60 percent of the total budget, it is clear that any attempt to reduce spending must examine these programs carefully.

In sum, instead of ministers becoming both spenders and guardians as was hoped, ministers still continued as spenders, but forgot about being guardians altogether.

"Ops and Chops": 1988-present

One of the major concerns of the Mulroney government has been the reduction of the deficit. This concern increased significantly in the government's second term, beginning in 1988. This has had a major impact on both the substance and the process of the budget. After the 1988 election, Prime Minister Mulroney decided that the only way to control expenditure was to centralize decision-making on the expenditure budget. To accomplish this, he established two new Cabinet committees—Operations ("Ops") and Expenditure Review ("Chops").

The *Committee on Operations*

> is chaired by the deputy prime minister and has a small membership chosen from among senior P & P ministers [members of the Cabinet Committee on Priorities and Planning] who also chair other committees. It is responsible for overseeing the agendas of the policy committees and may itself handle any item of business if the appropriate policy committee is not soon to meet or if the "Ops" ministers so choose. Since it effectively sets the agenda of the Cabinet, and since he or she who sets the agenda gets to control priorities, "Ops" is a very powerful committee indeed.[54]

The *Expenditure Review Committee* is chaired by the Prime Minister. It "screens all policy proposals which have expenditure implications before they can be discussed by policy committees."[55]

"Ops and Chops," working together, are very effective gatekeepers in the policy-making system. A new proposal must get by "Ops" to get on the Cabinet agenda, and if the proposal requires additional spending it must also get through "Chops." These changes constitute a significant centralization of the system.

Describing a dynamic process like a budgeting system can be like describing a cloud—by the time the description is finished, it has changed its shape so much that it is barely recognizable. No two budget years are the same. With these caveats, this section will discuss the outline of the budgetary system as it seems to be developing during the Mulroney government's second term. Figure 26.1 provides a general outline of the budgetary process.

The Department of Finance consults with Treasury Board in recommending a fiscal plan. Treasury Board contributes information about "reference levels," i.e., the level of spending needed to continue existing programs at their current level. Finance then estimates the revenue likely to be generated in the coming year and provides some advice on the appropriate level of surplus or deficit needed to stimulate or slow down the economy. These recommendations constitute Finance's fiscal plan, which it then conveys to the Cabinet Committee on Priorities and Planning (P & P).

"Ops" and "Chops" also provide information on an on-going basis to P & P. All proposals for new spending must go through "ops and chops," and the Expenditure Review Committee also has a continuing role in examining existing programs to determine possibilities for cost savings.

Figure 26.1
FEDERAL GOVERNMENT BUDGETARY PROCESS, 1990

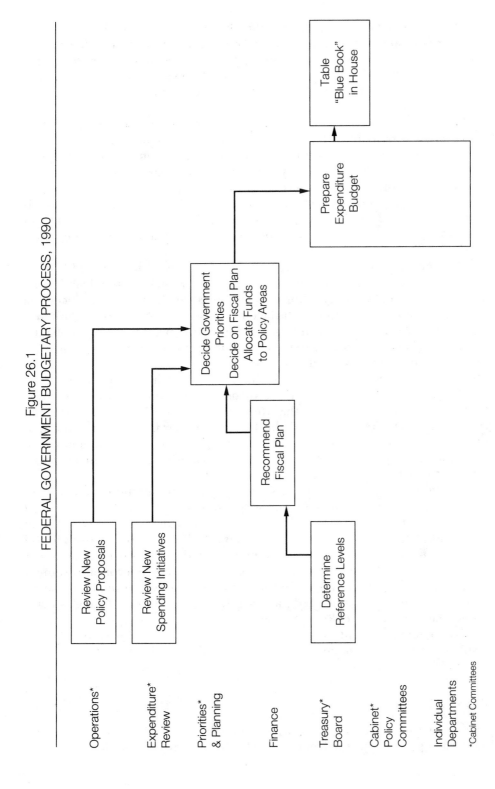

Operations*

Expenditure*
Review

Priorities*
& Planning

Finance

Treasury*
Board

Cabinet*
Policy
Committees

Individual
Departments

*Cabinet Committees

Review New
Policy Proposals

Review New
Spending Initiatives

Decide Government
Priorities
Decide on Fiscal Plan
Allocate Funds
to Policy Areas

Recommend
Fiscal Plan

Determine
Reference Levels

Prepare
Expenditure
Budget

Table
"Blue Book"
in House

The Cabinet Committee on Priorities and Planning has the key role in the system. This committee decides on overall government priorities for the coming year. The committee then converts these general guidelines into more specific ideas in the form of major policy initiatives, the desired fiscal plan (overall taxation and expenditure levels), and levels of expenditure allocated to general policy areas.

Within these constraints, the expenditure budget is then prepared as a result of discussions involving Treasury Board, individual ministers, and the Cabinet policy committees. Individual ministers decide on details of expenditure within their departments. They can make minor program changes as long as they stay within their reference levels. Treasury Board is responsible for preparing the *Main Estimates*. The preparation phase of the budgetary process ends when the President of Treasury Board tables the *Estimates* in the House of Commons in January or February, shortly before the beginning of the new fiscal year on April 1.

It is too early to make a definitive assessment of the new "Ops and Chops" process, but some tentative statements can be made. First, it is quite clear that the ascendancy of the "Ops and Chops" committees has significantly reduced the power of the policy committees. The fact that these committees no longer have a significant role in allocating funds could turn them into vacuous debating societies. If that happens, ministers will probably find better ways to spend their time than attending these committee meetings.

Second, Savoie has pointed out that "Ops and Chops" are seen as preempting the role of the traditional guardians, yet the committees are composed mostly of spenders. He doubts that these committees will really be firmer in controlling spenders than would the traditional guardians. In fact, the new situation could constrain the guardians because when a new program has been given the stamp of approval by these committees, it will be very difficult for the traditional guardians to fight it.[56]

In a more general vein, there is some question whether there is any kind of structural fix that can produce painless spending cuts. Savoie has argued that "no expenditure budget system, no approach to policy making, and no cabinet committee structure can substitute for political will."[57] Indeed, the successful budget-cutting exercises that Savoie identified were all "cuts from above." For example, in 1978 Prime Minister Trudeau returned from an economic summit in Germany and simply announced without warning or consultation that $2 billion would be cut from the federal budget.[58] He then worked with guardians to see that this was done. Recent experience in Australia and Britain seems to confirm that cuts can only be made when the Prime Minister becomes directly involved and has the political will to say "no," even in the face of strong demands.

CONCLUSION

This chapter has focussed on the preparation phase of the budget. This is a very important part of the total budget cycle, because it is so important in the determination of overall government priorities. However, budget preparation is still only one-third of the total budget cycle. Adoption and execution are also important; these will be covered in the next chapter.

APPENDIX: HOW TO READ GOVERNMENT FINANCIAL STATEMENTS

The various financial documents prepared by governments contain vast amounts of information that can be very useful for research, but many students, and even some more experienced researchers, shy away from using them because they imagine that they are much too difficult for the uninitiated to understand. It is very easy to be overwhelmed by the size, complexity, and esoteric terminology of some financial statements. In truth, there are some statements whose full import can only be comprehended by specialists, but even the uninitiated can learn quite a bit from some statements with just a rudimentary knowledge of terminology. This appendix will use everyday language to introduce the wonders of government financial statements.

In the first place, the neophyte should not allow himself or herself to be overwhelmed by the volume of information. There are two major government financial documents that are important to understand—*Estimates* and *Public Accounts*. These are the two main financial documents prepared by the federal and provincial governments. Municipal governments prepare similar types of documents, but they have different names. This appendix will focus on the federal documents, but it should assist you in reading provincial local government financial documents as well.

Estimates

The **Estimates** or **"Blue Book"** is actually a multi-volume series of documents prepared before the beginning of the fiscal year as an output of the budgetary process described in the chapter. These volumes contain the expenditure budget and represent the formal legislation that, when passed by the legislature, provides authority for spending by the executive. These documents focus entirely on the expenditure budget and so contain no information about revenue.

Since the late 1970s, the format of the *Estimates* has undergone a major revision so that more information is provided in a more easily understandable fashion. The *Estimates* is now presented in three parts—each geared to a different level of detail.

Part I of the *Estimates* consists of one volume called the *Government Expenditure Plan*. It contains a multi-year listing of expenditure by envelope, department, and major program within department. It also contains brief descriptions about the activities of each department and explanations of major increases or decreases in expenditures from previous years. This document is a good starting point to obtain a general understanding of how much of the total budget is consumed by a particular department or program and what the trend is.

However, it does not usually provide enough detail about these activities to be satisfactory for most researchers.

Part II also consists of one volume, referred to as the *Main Estimates*. It begins with a slightly more in-depth overview than was presented in Part I. Table 26A.1 illustrates a page from the *Main Estimates* for the fiscal year 1989-90. On the left side of the page is a listing of the departments and agencies that have requested funds; on the right are the amounts requested, under several headings.

The major headings distinguish between budgetary and non-budgetary transactions. **Non-budgetary transactions** are loans or advances made to organizations, or investments in some entity.[59] These involve an outlay of cash, but it is expected that the funds will ultimately be repaid; therefore, they do not increase the government deficit. In accounting parlance, these involve the creation of an asset rather than an expense. **Budgetary transactions** represent expenses, i.e., a one-time outlay of funds for which no reimbursement is expected. To compare the two: the purchase of a Crown corporation, or a loan to any organization, is a non-budgetary transaction; the payment of salaries of government employees is a budgetary transaction. Both types of transactions are included in the *Estimates* because both require an outlay of cash. The difference between them is that a budgetary transaction affects the government's surplus/deficit position, while a non-budgetary transaction does not.

It is important to distinguish between these two types of transactions, but the distinction is sometimes abused because non-budgetary transactions do not increase the government's deficit, thereby making the government presenting the budget look more financially responsible. Governments sometimes consider transactions that ought to be budgetary as non-budgetary instead. For example, there is a temptation for a government to "loan" money to a Crown corporation, even though it realizes that there is little likelihood of it ever being repaid; this reduces the government deficit in the year the "loan" is made, but it creates a problem because these "loans" begin to pile up on the government's books. When the Liberal government came to power in Ontario in 1985, it tackled this problem by making large one-time adjustments in the government's financial statements.[60]

The *Estimates* are further broken down between funds requested "Under authorities to be voted" and "Under previous authorities (statutory)." The latter category is usually referred to as statutory appropriations. **Statutory Appropriations** are allocations of funds made under continuing legislation (not a part of the *Estimates*) that provide for a payment whenever a particular condition is met. Some examples of statutory appropriations are family allowances, veteran benefits, or payments made to provincial governments as a result of intergovernmental agreements. Funds under this heading do not need to be approved each year because their expenditure is authorized under the original, enabling legislation. They are included in the *Estimates* for purposes of information and completeness. While some amount is stated for information purposes, this amount could be exceeded because funds are paid to all claimants who meet the specified criteria, regardless of the amount shown in the *Estimates*.

The appropriations "Under authorities to be voted" are the annual appropriations that require the approval of the legislature each year. The only amount available to be spent on these programs is the amount specified in the *Estimates*; these limitations cannot be exceeded. Any funds allocated under annual appropriations that are not spent at the end of the year lapse, i.e., they cannot be carried over and spent in the following year.

As illustrated in Table 26A.1, statutory appropriations are higher than annual appropriations in some departments, e.g., Finance. For 1989-90, statutory appropriations amounted to 67 percent of total funds requested. This raises some concern that the ability of the legislature to reduce expenditure is severely limited by the existence of these statutory expenditures. However, there is no restriction on the ability of the legislature to modify the underlying legislation, but this can be rather awkward politically in some cases.

Close to the right margin, Table 26A.1 lists the full amount of funds requested this year and the amount requested last year. This allows legislators to identify departments that are requesting significant increases in funding.

Table 26A.2 illustrates a different grouping of information also found in Part II of the *Estimates*. This provides a breakdown of departmental allocations by vote. A **Vote** is the appropriation approved by Parliament. Roughly speaking, there is one vote per program, although there could be more where a program involves a large capital expenditure or large amounts of grants and contributions (transfer payments to organizations or individuals).[61] Since Parliament has approved funds on the basis of votes, a department must obtain parliamentary approval to move funds between votes. This is the mechanism that Parliament uses to control the ways in which departments spend funds. The votes with numbers in the left margin are annual appropriations; those with "(S)" are statutory appropriations.

Also in Part II is some additional information about each program, as illustrated in Table 26A.3. This provides a short description of the objectives and activities of each program, as well as some additional budgetary information.

Part II of the *Estimates* is very useful for research purposes. It provides both financial and narrative background information on the activities of each department. It allows the researcher to locate the organizational unit responsible for a particular activity, and a review of previous years' *Estimates* allows some consideration of expenditure trends.

Part III of the *Estimates*, referred to as *Expenditure Plans*, contains one volume for each department and major government agency. These volumes present a wealth of information about the activities of the various programs. Each volume takes a somewhat different approach, but the information provided involves details of departmental organizational structure, highlights of program performance in the previous year, new initiatives planned and updates on previous initiatives, and data on program effectiveness. Obviously, this provides a wealth of information for the legislator as well as the researcher. The data provided facilitates the identification of trends and the relating of expenditure information to output data.

Table 26A.1

General Summary

Section Department or agency	1989–90 Main Estimates		
	Budgetary		
	Under authorities to be voted	Under previous authorities (statutory)	Total
(thousands of dollars)			
8 Environment	810,120	60,996	871,116
9 External Affairs			
Department	1,017,332	30,376	1,047,708
Canadian Commercial Corporation	20,089	....	20,089
Canadian Institute for International Peace and Security	....	5,000	5,000
Canadian International Development Agency	1,891,650	95,551	1,987,201
Export Development Corporation	....	125,000	125,000
International Centre for Ocean Development	10,100	....	10,100
International Development Research Centre	108,500	....	108,500
International Joint Commission	4,528	307	4,835
10 Finance			
Department	52,561	46,943,711	46,996,272
Auditor General	45,918	5,005	50,923
Canadian International Trade Tribunal	6,097	747	6,844
Office of the Superintendent of Financial Institutions	2,757	....	2,757
Privatization and Regulatory Affairs	9,266	658	9,924
Tariff Board	....	....	....
11 Fisheries and Oceans	679,205	40,855	720,060
12 Forestry	198,486	8,452	206,938
13 Governor General	8,234	1,091	9,325
14 Indian Affairs and Northern Development			
Department	3,304,703	34,684	3,339,387
Northern Canada Power Commission	....	....	....
15 Industry, Science and Technology			
Regional Industrial Expansion	1,149,698	46,978	1,196,676
Cape Breton Development Corporation	32,000	....	32,000
Federal Business Development Bank	27,628	6,400	34,028
Investment Canada	8,632	926	9,558
Ministry of State (Science and Technology)	43,921	1,381	45,302
National Research Council of Canada	468,679	23,934	492,613
Natural Sciences and Engineering Research Council	388,810	1,065	389,875
Science Council of Canada	2,698	270	2,968
Statistics Canada	205,299	25,855	231,154
Canada Post Corporation	184,500	....	184,500

Non-budgetary (loans, investments and advances)			Total	1988–89 Main Estimates
Under authorities to be voted	Under previous authorities (statutory)	Total		
....	....	....	871,116	**796,235**
28,000	**2,000**	**30,000**	1,077,708	**939,663**
....	....	....	20,089	**18,651**
....	....	....	5,000	**5,000**
....	**18,000**	**18,000**	2,005,201	**2,225,566**
....	**64,000**	**64,000**	189,000	**117,000**
....	....	....	10,100	**8,000**
....	....	....	108,500	**114,200**
....	....	....	4,835	**3,791**
25,550	**70,500**	**96,050**	47,092,322	**38,884,149**
....	....	....	50,923	**48,337**
....	....	....	6,844	**....**
....	....	....	2,757	**1,843**
....	....	....	9,924	**18,148**
....	....	....	....	**2,741**
....	....	....	720,060	**679,287**
....	....	....	206,938	**234,870**
....	....	....	9,325	**7,758**
16,870	**1,452**	**18,322**	3,357,709	**3,032,155**
....	....	....	....	**24,534**
800	....	**800**	1,197,476	**1,348,433**
....	....	....	32,000	**40,600**
....	....	....	34,028	**37,019**
....	....	....	9,558	**9,254**
....	....	....	45,302	**37,721**
....	....	....	492,613	**430,027**
....	....	....	389,875	**354,461**
....	....	....	2,968	**2,797**
....	....	....	231,154	**221,949**
....	....	....	184,500	**305,500**

Source: *Main Estimates 1989-90*, Part II, pp.1-18, 1-19.

Table 26A.2

National Health and Welfare

Ministry Summary

Vote	(thousands of dollars)	1989-90 Main Estimates	1988-89 Main Estimates
	National Health and Welfare		
	Department		
	Departmental Administration Program		
1	Program expenditures	63,727	**61,534**
(S)	Minister of National Health and Welfare–Salary and motor car allowance	48	**46**
(S)	Contributions to employee benefit plans	6,788	**6,895**
	Total Program	*70,563*	*68,475*
	Health Services and Promotion Program		
5	Operating expenditures	40,657	**35,473**
10	Grants and contributions	44,733	**36,723**
(S)	Payments for insured health services and extended health care services	6,871,000	**7,031,000**
(S)	Contributions to employee benefit plans	1,993	**1,959**
	Total Program	*6,958,383*	*7,105,155*
	Social Services Program		
15	Operating expenditures	18,358	**13,279**
20	Grants and contributions	183,596	**125,688**
(S)	Canada Assistance Plan Payments	4,779,200	**4,471,800**
(S)	Contributions to employee benefit plans	1,735	**1,495**
	Total Program	*4,982,889*	*4,612,262*
	Medical Services Program		
25	Operating expenditures	496,943	**440,875**
30	Capital expenditures	23,233	**28,365**
(S)	Contributions to employee benefit plans	14,184	**13,766**
	Total Program	*534,360*	*483,006*
	Health Protection Program		
35	Operating expenditures	146,889	**117,888**
40	Capital expenditures	27,897	**21,491**
45	Grants and contributions	20,070	**. . . . .**
(S)	Contributions to employee benefit plans	13,081	**11,664**
	Total Program	*207,937*	*151,043*
	Income Security Program		
50	Program expenditures	68,290	**61,975**
(S)	Family Allowance payments	2,612,000	**2,586,000**
(S)	Old Age Security payments	11,885,000	**11,118,000**
(S)	Guaranteed Income Supplement payments	3,961,000	**3,887,000**
(S)	Spouse's Allowance payments	549,000	**525,000**
(S)	Contributions to employee benefit plans	12,333	**12,177**
	Total Program	*19,087,623*	*18,190,152*

Vote	(thousands of dollars)	1989-90 Main Estimates	1988-89 Main Estimates
	Fitness and Amateur Sport Program		
55	Operating expenditures	9,848	7,476
60	Contributions	62,959	54,118
(S)	Contributions to employee benefit plans	665	672
	Total Program	73,472	62,266
	XV Olympic Winter Games Program		
	Appropriation not required		
–	Program expenditures	. . . . .	1,927
	Item not required		
–	Contributions to employee benefit plans	. . . . .	93
	Total Program	. . . . .	2,020
	Total Department	31,915,227	30,674,379
	Medical Research Council		
65	Operating expenditures	4,469	3,891
70	Grants	197,146	178,331
(S)	Contributions to employee benefit plans	370	356
	Total Agency	201,985	182,578

Source: *Main Estimates 1989-90*, Part II, pp. 19-2, 19-3.

All three parts of the *Estimates* are tabled in Parliament just before the beginning of the fiscal year. Part II, the *Main Estimates*, constitutes the initial request made by the government for funding. During the fiscal year, the government will usually present three or four sets of *Supplementary Estimates* to take account of changed conditions. *Supplementary Estimates* are presented in roughly the same form as the *Main Estimates*; they could constitute a request for additional funds, or they could involve a transfer of funds between votes not requiring any additional total funds. When the various sets of *Estimates* are passed they are called the Appropriation Acts and become a part of the legislation passed in a particular Parliament. They can then be located in the Statutes of Canada for that Parliament.

Public Accounts

The second major financial document is the **Public Accounts**. The *Public Accounts* is prepared after the government's year-end and contains the government's year-end financial statements. The federal *Public Accounts* is a three-volume document. The first volume contains most of the important information about government financial activities during the year. The second volume contains a large amount of detail about the transactions summarized in volume one. The third volume contains financial information about Crown corporations.

Table 26A.3

National Health and Welfare
Department
Health Services and Promotion Program

Objective

To develop, promote, and support measures designed to preserve and improve the health and well-being of Canadians.

Activity Description

Health Insurance

Provides payments to provinces and territories in respect of the cost of insured health services, and certain extended health care services as provided under the Federal-Provincial Fiscal Arrangements and Federal Post-Secondary Education and Health Contributions Act, 1977; monitors compliance of provincial and territorial health care insurance plans in accordance with the program criteria and conditions of payment of the Canada Health Act.

Health Services

Provides leadership and co-ordination and gives technical and financial support to the provinces and territories, professional associations, and international organizations in the development and maintenance of health services and facilities. Financial support and consulting services are also provided to national voluntary health organizations to assist their development and improve the efficiency and effectiveness of health services. Information collection and dissemination in addition to collaborative efforts with the provinces and territories play an important and integral role in this activity.

Extramural Research

Fosters and supports public health research and related scientific activities, through the National Health Research and Development Program, which complement departmental programs and hold the potential to advance national health goals. Encompasses research projects, studies and demonstrations, the training and career development of research manpower in relevant disciplines, and forums for the development of research strategies and approaches and for the communication of research outcomes.

Health Promotion

Develops and implements, in co-operation with provincial and territorial governments and non-governmental organizations, health promotion programs directed to all Canadian residents and to special target groups including those at high risk and those responsible for the planning or provision of health and social services.

Program Administration

Provides program direction, program planning and policy development. Support is also provided to the Minister of State for Seniors through the Senior Secretariat.

Program by Activities

(thousands of dollars)	1989–90 Main Estimates					1988–89
	Authorized	Budgetary			Total	Main Estimates
	person years	Operating	Capital	Transfer payments		
Health Insurance	21	1,261	....	6,871,000	6,872,261	7,032,210
Health Services	66	6,864	....	3,274	10,138	9,862
Extramural Research	23	1,805	....	29,019	30,824	25,616
Health Promotion	129	26,056	....	12,440	38,496	34,823
Program Administration	49	6,648	16	....	6,664	2,644
	288	**42,634**	**16**	**6,915,733**	**6,958,383**	**7,105,155**
1988–89 Authorized person-years	286					

National Health and Welfare
Department
Health Services and Promotion Program

Transfer Payments

(dollars)	1989–90 Main Estimates	1988–89 **Main Estimates**
Grants		
Health Services		
Grants to national voluntary health organizations to assist with the operating costs of national offices	2,899,000	**2,899,000**
Health Promotion		
Grants to persons and agencies to support health promotion projects in the areas of community health, resource development, training and skill development, and research	4,500,000	....
Grant to the World Health Organization in support of the Regional/Inter-regional Project on Health Promotion based in the WHO Regional Office in Europe	68,000	....
Total grants	**7,467,000**	**2,899,000**
Contributions		
Health Insurance		
* (S) Payments under the Federal-Provincial Fiscal Arrangements and Federal Post-Secondary Education and Health Contributions Act, 1977:		
Insured Health Services Program	5,524,000,000	**5,756,000,000**
Extended Health Care Services Program	1,347,000,000	**1,275,000,000**
Health Services		
Contributions to organizations, groups and individuals to address problems encountered by victims of violence	375,000	**375,000**
Extramural Research		
Contributions to persons and agencies to support activities of national importance for the improvement of health services and in support of research and demonstrations in the field of public health	29,019,000	**24,009,000**
Health Promotion		
Contributions to persons and agencies to support health promotion projects in the areas of community health, resource development, training and skill development, and research	7,072,000	**8,640,000**
Contributions to agencies for research, development and delivery of improved treatment and preventive education programs on alcohol and other drug abuse	800,000	**800,000**
Total contributions	**6,908,266,000**	**7,064,824,000**
Total	**6,915,733,000**	**7,067,723,000**

*The Main Estimates show the cash portion of the federal contribution authorized by the Federal-Provincial Fiscal Arrangements and Federal Post-Secondary Education and Health Contributions Act, 1977 and proposed amendments. The following table shows the total federal contribution in respect of Insured Health Services and Extended Health Care, including the tax transfer also authorized by the legislation:

	1989–90	1988–89
	$	$
Payments per Main Estimates	6,871,000,000	7,031,000,000
Tax Transfers	7.056,000,000	6,174,000,000
Total	13,927,000,000	13,205,000,000

Source: *Main Estimates, 1989-90,* Part II, pp. 19-6, 19-7.

The first volume of *Public Accounts*, titled *Summary Report and Financial Statements*, contains information about all transactions that affect the Consolidated Revenue Fund. The **Consolidated Revenue Fund** is "the aggregate of all public moneys that are on deposit at the credit of the Receiver General."[62] This money is actually maintained in a number of separate accounts at a variety of financial institutions, but it is viewed as one fund. All funds collected by the government become a part of the Consolidated Revenue Fund, and all payments are made from the Consolidated Revenue Fund. The emphasis on "consolidated" stems from the fact that some governments maintain a number of separate accounts that are earmarked for specific purposes, such as highway expenditure or social services. The federal government feels that better cash management is obtained from accounting for only one fund, even though it is physically located in a number of different places and will be used for a number of different purposes.

Tables 26A.4 to 26A.7 illustrate the statements contained in the *Public Accounts*, which provide an overview of the transactions for the year. Table 26A.4 provides details on revenue obtained in the current and several previous years. The information shown here can be used to identify major sources of government revenue and the trend of those sources.

Table 26A.5 illustrates budgetary expenditures by function. This is the year-end listing of actual amounts spent, which is comparable to the budgetary transactions listed in the *Estimates*. Like the revenue side of the equation, this information can be used to compare major expenditure programs and the trend in those programs.

The government's *administrative budget* consists of all budgetary revenue and budgetary expenditure transactions. The surplus or deficit based on the administrative budget is the difference between budgetary revenue and budgetary expenditure. Computations from Tables 26A.4 and 26A.5 indicate a deficit in terms of the administrative budget for the year ended March 31, 1989 of $28,734 million. (Revenue of $103,981 million and expenditure of $132,715 million.) This administrative budget is not the same as the government's cash requirement, which will be discussed below.

Table 26A.6 illustrates non-budgetary transactions. Again, this is a year-end reflection of the figures shown in the *Estimates*. They show the net inflow or outflow of funds for loans, advances, and investments, i.e., the difference between loans and investments paid out and returns received in the form of loan repayments and sale of investments. For example, this statement shows that during 1988-89, the federal government provided a loan (net of any possible repayments) to the Canada Mortgage and Housing Corporation of $273 million. The negative figures indicate net repayments of previous loans and investments, i.e., net inflows of funds. The positive figures reflect net pay-outs by the government.

The government's *cash budget* determines the total amount that the government will need to borrow in the upcoming fiscal year. The cash budget is determined by the budgetary and non-budgetary transactions already discussed. The result of these transactions is then adjusted by foreign exchange transac-

Table 26.A4

TABLE 1.6

**GOVERNMENT OF CANADA
PUBLIC ACCOUNTS PRESENTATION
DETAILED STATEMENT OF REVENUE TRANSACTIONS
(in millions of dollars)**

	Year ended March 31									
	1980	1981	1982	1983	1984	1985	1986	1987	1988	1989
I. Budgetary transactions										
A. REVENUE, Section 3										
Tax revenue—										
Income tax—										
Personal	16,808	19,837	24,046	26,330	26,967	29,254	33,008	37,878	45,125	46,026
Corporation	6,951	8,106	8,118	7,139	7,286	9,379	9,210	9,885	10,878	11,730
Unemployment insurance contributions ..	2,778	3,303	4,753	4,900	7,259	7,553	8,719	9,558	10,425	11,268
Non-resident	787	867	1,018	998	908	1,021	1,053	1,355	1,162	1,578
	27,324	*32,113*	*37,935*	*39,367*	*42,420*	*47,207*	*51,990*	*58,676*	*67,590*	*70,602*
Excise taxes and duties—										
Sales tax	4,651	5,355	6,148	5,842	6,561	7,592	9,345	11,972	12,927	15,645
Customs import duties	2,996	3,185	3,435	2,828	3,376	3,794	3,971	4,187	4,385	4,521
Excise duties	895	1,042	1,175	1,274	1,356	1,462	1,473	1,470	1,459	1,453
Other	502	570	564	685	754	850	1,354	1,455	1,567	1,506
	9,044	*10,152*	*11,322*	*10,629*	*12,047*	*13,698*	*16,143*	*19,084*	*20,338*	*23,125*
Energy taxes—										
Excise tax—Gasoline	421	453	436	408	386	404	729	1,279	2,286	2,174
Petroleum and gas revenue tax		27	864	1,960	2,106	2,563	2,037	473	−75	105
Excise tax—Aviation gas and diesel fuel .							41	213	385	369
Natural gas and gas liquids tax		187	998	1,264	524	−15	−15	1		−1
Oil export charges	750	842	964	626	347	677	327		1	
Special petroleum compensation charge .			473							
Canadian Ownership special charge ...			786	889	805	850	229	−1	6	−1
	1,171	*1,509*	*4,521*	*5,147*	*4,168*	*4,479*	*3,348*	*1,965*	*2,603*	*2,646*
	10,215	*11,661*	*15,843*	*15,776*	*16,215*	*18,177*	*19,491*	*21,049*	*22,941*	*25,771*
Other tax revenue	96	99	120	132	126	107	126	144	207	265
Total tax revenue	37,635	43,873	53,898	55,275	58,761	65,491	71,607	79,869	90,738	96,638
Non-tax revenue—										
Return on investments—										
Bank of Canada	1,084	1,459	1,853	1,879	1,744	1,852	1,880	1,936	1,844	1,938
Canada Mortgage and Housing Corporation .	782	839	873	892	941	913	892	866	853	845
Farm Credit Corporation	210	243	285	346	408	452	403	372	324	301
Exchange Fund Account	719	850	711	435	345	224	−505	366	752	1,658
Interest on bank deposits	244	318	701	433	395	243	278	219	279	255
Other return on investments	607	606	641	631	539	568	791	475	496	512
	3,646	*4,315*	*5,064*	*4,616*	*4,372*	*4,252*	*3,739*	*4,234*	*4,548*	*5,509*
Other non-tax revenue	640	587	1,039	814	1,083	1,155	1,487	1,681	2,166	1,834
Total non-tax revenue	4,286	4,902	6,103	5,430	5,455	5,407	5,226	5,915	6,714	7,343
Total net revenue	41,921	48,775	60,001	60,705	64,216	70,898	76,833	85,784	97,452	103,981

Source: *Public Accounts of Canada 1989*, Vol. I, p. 1-6.

tions, e.g., transactions that the government makes to adjust the value of the dollar on international markets. The net of these transactions determines the amount that the government needed to borrow in the past year.

Table 26A.7 illustrates the calculation of the federal government's cash requirement for the fiscal year ended March 31, 1989. Budgetary expenditures exceeded budgetary revenues by $28,734 million, but for non-budgetary transactions, inflows exceeded outflows by $6,762 million, reducing the net cash requirement at that point to $21,972 million. The increased investment in foreign currency increased the final requirement to $27,702 million. Govern-

Table 26A.5

COMPARATIVE STATEMENTS OF TRANSACTIONS

TABLE 1.7
GOVERNMENT OF CANADA
PUBLIC ACCOUNTS PRESENTATION
DETAILED STATEMENT OF EXPENDITURE TRANSACTIONS
(in millions of dollars)

	Year ended March 31									
	1980	1981	1982	1983	1984	1985	1986	1987	1988	1989
I. Budgetary transactions										
B. EXPENDITURE: Section 4										
Social development—										
Old age security benefits, guaranteed income supplements and spouses' allowances	6,320	7,418	8,585	9,643	10,406	11,418	12,525	13,445	14,349	15,202
Unemployment insurance benefits	3,922	4,524	5,446	9,823	9,782	10,052	10,036	10,444	10,487	10,972
Established programs financing—										
Insurance and medical care services	3,858	3,982	4,283	4,060	5,564	6,330	6,400	6,607	6,558	6,678
Education support	1,515	1,600	1,628	1,532	2,065	2,265	2,277	2,232	2,242	2,227
Canada Assistance Plan	1,653	1,941	2,298	2,832	3,288	3,745	3,916	4,051	4,246	4,556
Family allowances	1,725	1,851	2,020	2,231	2,326	2,418	2,501	2,534	2,564	2,606
Justice and legal	1,063	1,197	1,357	1,506	1,697	1,863	2,016	2,177	2,318	2,526
Social assistance—Indians and Inuit	870	1,015	1,202	1,664	1,786	1,985	1,951	2,238	2,330	2,509
Direct job creation and training	1,213	1,096	1,164	1,384	1,799	2,053	1,795	1,939	1,929	1,938
Veterans benefits	933	1,006	1,140	1,283	1,387	1,458	1,535	1,586	1,609	1,612
Housing	896	1,058	943	1,853	1,598	1,657	1,429	1,454	1,885	1,734
Television, film and radio	569	844	741	822	913	1,034	1,023	1,025	1,097	1,144
Other	1,707	2,420	2,985	3,691	4,025	4,261	4,415	4,838	5,022	5,387
	26,244	*29,952*	*33,792*	*42,324*	*46,636*	*50,539*	*51,819*	*54,570*	*56,636*	*59,091*
Economic and regional development	7,033	8,761	9,801	11,577	12,064	14,851	11,821	11,792	14,232	13,341
Defence	4,377	5,063	5,989	6,938	7,843	8,762	9,094	9,993	10,769	11,025
Fiscal arrangements	3,455	3,944	4,750	5,597	5,977	5,985	5,941	6,302	7,007	8,127
Services to Government	2,327	2,332	3,460	2,963	3,465	3,788	4,433	3,975	4,194	4,149
External affairs and aid	1,392	1,457	1,814	2,050	2,373	2,646	2,490	2,892	3,438	3,557
Parliament	100	130	153	169	180	196	198	207	231	242
Total program expenditure	44,928	51,639	59,759	71,618	78,538	86,767	85,796	89,731	96,507	99,532
Public debt	8,494	10,658	15,114	16,903	18,077	22,455	25,441	26,658	29,028	33,183
Total net expenditure	53,422	62,297	74,873	88,521	96,615	109,222	111,237	116,389	125,535	132,715

Source: *Public Accounts of Canada 1989*, Vol. I, p. 1-7.

ment borrowing increased during the year by $28,002 million so that its cash balance increased by $300 million.

The cash budget is important because it is a signal of the demands that the government will be making on the market in future and, therefore, has an effect on money markets. A high cash requirement can drive up interest rates by placing heavy demands on money markets. A low requirement might signal that there will be substantial amounts available for borrowing for business expansion.

There are other sections of the *Public Accounts* that break down each line of these three statements in considerably more detail by department and by specific non-budgetary transaction. Obviously, this information is very useful for research purposes.

The *Public Accounts* also contains the federal government's *Statement of Assets and Liabilities* (also called a balance sheet) as illustrated in Table 26A.8. Assets are defined as anything of value owned by the government. In the case of the federal government, the assets consist of loans and advances made by the government to Crown corporations and other organizations, foreign exchange held, and cash. The federal government values all of its fixed assets (land, public buildings, equipment, vehicles, etc.) at one dollar. Also, at the bottom of the left page is the

Table 26A.6

TABLE 1.9

GOVERNMENT OF CANADA
PUBLIC ACCOUNTS PRESENTATION
DETAILED STATEMENT OF OF NON–BUDGETARY TRANSACTIONS
(in millions of dollars)

	Year ended March 31									
	1980	1981	1982	1983	1984	1985	1986	1987	1988	1989
II. Non-budgetary transactions										
A. LOANS, INVESTMENTS AND ADVANCES,										
Section 6										
Crown corporations—										
Lending institutions—										
Canada Deposit Insurance Corporation			–200	60	140	–40	–895	–268	131	–361
Canada Mortgage and Housing Corporation ...	–366	–66	–199	–30	194	364	195	254	234	273
Export Development Corporation	–44	19	52	–40	–5	39	64	49	55	25
Farm Credit Corporation	–307	–270	–348	–394	–379	172	214	591	–179	230
Federal Business Development Bank	–245	101	125	145	172	157	119	93	51	
	–962	–216	–570	–259	122	692	–303	719	30	167
All other Crown corporations—										
Atomic Energy of Canada Limited	–216	697	8	3	37	38	67	19	20	21
Canada Development Investment										
Corporation				–308	5	18				
Canadian National Railway Company	–108	–8		–41	–62	2	9	352	29	12
Petro–Canada	–80	–440	–840	–1,354	–660					
Other	15	275	–354	124	159	–33	110	–291	1,371	–177
	–389	524	–1,186	–1,576	–521	25	186	80	1,420	–144
Allowance for valuation of assets			144	1,523	–60	100	–100	100	–400	1,000
	–1,351	308	–1612	–312	–459	817	–217	899	1,050	1,023
Other loans, investments and advances—										
Provincial and territorial governments	44	247	28	–41	35	67	110	89	37	28
National governments including developing										
countries	–185	–204	–276	–273	–167	–172	–142	124	81	132
International organizations (subscriptions										
less notes)	–134	–110	–166	–213	–335	–378	–220	46	15	–24
Veteran's Land Act Fund advances less										
allowance	43	37	29	28	31	32	31	26	24	20
Joint and mixed enterprises	–27	–52	8	–42	7	–93	–61	237	319	36
Miscellaneous	–29	–19	–17	–42	–145	–163	140	65	–117	66
	–288	–101	–394	–583	–574	–707	–142	587	359	258
Allowance for valuation of assets	553	–376	500	393	569	599	400	–100	100	–200
	265	–477	106	–190	–5	–108	258	487	459	58
Total loans, investments and advances after										
allowance for valuation of assets	–1086	–169	–1,506	–502	–464	709	41	1,386	1,509	1,081
B. SPECIFIED PURPOSE ACCOUNTS. Section 7										
Liability accounts—										
Canada Pension Plan Account	113	173	170	165	152	211	511	1,556	1,002	769
Superannuation accounts	1,966	2,307	3,014	3,483	3,862	4,302	4,680	4,995	5,423	5,825
Government Annuities Account	–14	–15	–21	–22	–26	–29	–35	–36	–37	–39
Deposit and trust accounts..................	78	32	909	–473	264	259	413	14	–45	–523
Provincial tax collection agreements account ...	118	728	–56	–384	277	309	–227	57	1,050	–731
Other...................................	28	29	47	48	62	72	96	110	89	130
Total specified purpose accounts	2,289	3,254	4,063	2,817	4,591	5,124	5,438	6,696	7,482	5,431
C. OTHER TRANSACTIONS. Sections 8 and 11										
Cash in transit	–130	–693	16	–736	689	–6	189	225	–854	387
Other liabilities..........................	296	1,236	3,053	2,435	2,382	2,689	–1,534	731	1,793	–137
Total other transactions	166	543	3,069	1,699	3,071	2,683	–1,345	956	939	250
Net non–budgetary transactions after allowance for										
valuation of assets	1,369	3,628	5,626	4,014	7,198	8,516	4,134	9,038	9,930	6,762
Summary—										
Net non–budgetary transactions before allowance										
for valuation of assets	816	4,004	4,982	2,098	6,689	7,817	3,834	9,038	10,230	5,962
Allowance for valuation of assets	553	–376	644	1,916	509	699	300		–300	800
Net non–budgetary transactions after										
allowance for valuation of assets	1,369	3,628	5,626	4,014	7,198	8,516	4,134	9,038	9,930	6,762

Source/requirement (–)

Table 26A.7

GOVERNMENT OF CANADA

Statement of Transactions
for the Year Ended March 31, 1989
(in millions of dollars)

	1989	1988
BUDGETARY TRANSACTIONS		
Revenue	103,981	97,452
Expenditure	−132,715	−125,535
Deficit	−28,734	−28,083
NON-BUDGETARY TRANSACTIONS		
Loans, investments and advances	1,081	1,509
Specified purpose accounts	5,431	7,482
Other transactions	250	939
Net source	6,762	9,930
Financial requirements (excluding foreign exchange transactions)	−21,972	−18,153
FOREIGN EXCHANGE TRANSACTIONS[1]	***−5,730***	***−7,149***
Total financial requirements	−27,702	−25,302
UNMATURED DEBT TRANSACTIONS[1]	***28,002***	***22,217***
Change in cash	300	−3,085
CASH BALANCE AT BEGINNING OF YEAR	***1,533***	***4,618***
CASH BALANCE AT END OF YEAR	***1,833***	***1,533***

The accompanying notes are an integral part of this statement.
Cash requirements (−.)
Details can be found in other sections of this volume.
   [1]Unmatured debt payable in foreign currencies, −$2,962 million in 1989 (−$715 million in 1988), has been included as part of foreign exchange transactions.

August, 15, 1989

Source: *Public Accounts of Canada 1989,* Vol. I, p. 2-6.

government deficit accumulated over the years, which amounted to $320,918 million as of March 31, 1989.

The right side of the statement lists all government liabilities, i.e., obligations on the part of the government to pay out funds in the future. These consist of accounts payable to suppliers, and Canada Savings Bonds and other long-term bonds.

Liabilities also include large amounts in "specified purpose accounts" or what might be generally called trust accounts. This is money paid to the government that is being held for some special purpose, sometimes on a long-term basis. For example, all funds contributed to the Canada Pension Plan are liabilities from the standpoint of the federal government because they must be repaid at some future time. Payments out of the account reduce the government's liability. The balance shown in the account of $37,603 million is the net amount held in trust to be paid out to contributors in the future. The $32,058 million figure represents the amount of CPP funds loaned to provincial governments. The difference of $5,545 million is the only portion of these funds that the federal government still has on hand.

It is interesting to note that one reason the accumulated government deficit seems so high is that all fixed assets owned by the government are valued at one dollar, yet the liabilities incurred to purchase those assets are shown at the amount needed to repay them. If the value of the fixed assets was changed to reflect their original purchase price or even current market value, the accumulated government deficit would automatically be reduced rather substantially.

Supplementary statements in the *Public Accounts* contain a large amount of detailed information about items listed in the *Statement of Assets and Liabilities*. This includes details of transactions in the trust accounts, e.g., Canada Pension Plan, detailed lists of loans, advances, and investments, and details of unmatured debt. Again, this is an important source of information for anyone doing research on these trust funds, the financial situation of Crown corporations or agencies, and government indebtedness.

The *Public Accounts* also contains the opinion of the Auditor General of Canada on the accuracy of the statements presented by the government. Anyone using the *Public Accounts* should look at this section to determine how the Auditor General views the accuracy of these statements. In the last several years, the Auditor General of Canada has stated that, in his opinion, certain procedures followed by the federal government have the effect of misstating certain transactions reported in these statements. This is a technical accounting disagreement rather than something that reflects on the credibility of the government, but it can have an effect on how one uses the figures reported.

Volume II of the *Public Accounts*, referred to as *Details of Expenditure and Revenue*, contains a vast amount of information, mostly about the expenditure items contained in Volume I. Most of this volume is devoted to a listing of the names of individuals and companies to whom government funds were paid during the year. For a particular kind of research, this information can be used to track down the nature of the relationship between a department and an individual or company. Volume II of the *Public Accounts* is not ordinarily an important research tool.

Volume III of the *Public Accounts*, titled *Financial Statements of Crown Corporations*, is frequently very useful, but the information is not always as complete or as helpful as that contained in the corporation's annual report. Also, the *Public Accounts* contains information about only some of the corporations in which the government has a financial interest.[63]

The *Public Accounts*, like the *Estimates*, contains a great deal of financial information. It is preferable to use financial information from the *Public Accounts* because it contains the audited figures prepared after the year-end, whereas the *Estimates* reflect amounts requested at the beginning of the year, which are subject to significant change during the year as a result of supplementary estimates or underspending. However, the advantage of the *Estimates* is that it tends to have more detail about the activities of departments. In practice, it is

Table 26A.8

GOVERNMENT OF CANADA

Statement of Assets and Liabilities
as at March 31, 1989
(in millions of dollars)

	1989	1988	Net increase or decrease (−)
FINANCIAL ASSETS			
LOANS, INVESTMENTS AND ADVANCES, Table 6.1, Section 6—			
Crown corporations (Notes 8 and 17)—			
Lending institutions—			
Canada Deposit Insurance Corporation	1,695	1,334	361
Canada Mortgage and Housing Corporation	8,904	9,177	−273
Export Development Corporation	697	722	−25
Farm Credit Corporation	3,472	3,702	−230
Federal Business Development Bank	294	294	
	15,062	*15,229*	*−167*
All other Crown corporations[1]—			
Atomic Energy of Canada Limited	669	690	−21
Canada Development Investment Corporation	396	396	
Canadian National Railway Company	2,452	2,464	−12
Petro-Canada	4,299	4,299	
Other	370	193	177
	8,186	*8,042*	*144*
Less: allowance for valuation	4,400	3,400	1,000
Total Crown corporations	18,848	19,871	−1,023
Other loans, investments and advances—			
Provincial and territorial governments	883	911	−28
National governments including developing countries (Note 9)	4,191	4,323	−132
International organizations (Note 9)	4,621	4,564	57
Less: notes payable	1,907	1,874	33
	2,714	*2,690*	*24*
Veterans' Land Act Fund advances less allowance for conditional benefits	91	111	−20
Joint and mixed enterprises[1]	629	665	−36
Miscellaneous	843	909	−66
	9,351	*9,609*	*−258*
Less: allowance for valuation	5,800	6,000	−200
Total other loans, investments and advances	3,551	3,609	−58
TOTAL LOANS, INVESTMENTS AND ADVANCES	**22,399**	**23,480**	**−1,081**
FOREIGN EXCHANGE ACCOUNTS, Table 9.1, Section 9—			
International reserves held in the Exchange Fund Account, Table 9.2, Section 9			
(Note 10)	17,422	14,779	2,643
International Monetary Fund—Subscriptions	4,534	5,038	−504
	21,956	*19,817*	*2,139*
Less: International Monetary Fund—Notes payable	3,985	4,480	−495
Special Drawing Rights allocations	1,201	1,335	−134
	5,186	*5,815*	*−629*
TOTAL FOREIGN EXCHANGE ACCOUNTS	**16,770**	**14,002**	**2,768**
CASH IN TRANSIT, Table 11.1, Section 11	*1,935*	*2,322*	*−387*
CASH, Table 11.2, Section 11	*1,833*	*1,533*	*300*
TOTAL FINANCIAL ASSETS (Note 15)	**42,937**	**41,337**	**1,600**
FIXED ASSETS (valued at one dollar), Section 11			
ACCUMULATED DEFICIT (Note 7)	**320,918**	**292,184**	**28,734**
TOTAL	**363,855**	**333,521**	**30,334**

	1989	1988	Net increase or decrease (−)
LIABILITIES			
SPECIFIED PURPOSE ACCOUNTS, *Table 7.1, Section 7—*			
Canada Pension Plan Account (Note 11)	37,603	36,021	1,582
Less: provincial and territorial government securities held by the Canada			
Pension Plan Investment Fund	32,058	31,245	813
	5,545	*4,776*	*769*
Superannuation accounts (Note 12)	57,913	52,088	5,825
Government Annuities Account	948	987	−39
Deposit and trust accounts	1,267	1,790	−523
Provincial tax collection agreements account	1,766	2,497	−731
Other	979	849	130
TOTAL SPECIFIED PURPOSE ACCOUNTS	**68,418**	**62,987**	**5,431**
OTHER LIABILITIES, *Table 8.1, Section 8—*			
Interest and matured debt	10,389	11,605	−1,216
Less: unamortized discount on Canada and Treasury bills	3,266	2,005	1,261
	7,123	*9,600*	*−2,477*
Accounts payable	9,674	6,777	2,897
Outstanding cheques and warrants	2,369	2,723	−354
Allowance for employee vacation and termination benefits	2,250	2,500	−250
Allowance for borrowings of agent Crown corporations expected to be repaid by the Government—			
Borrowings of agent Crown corporations, Table 6.10, Section 6 (Notes 8 and 13)	15,022	14,833	189
Less: borrowings expected to be repaid by these Crown corporations	14,572	14,383	189
	450	*450*	
Miscellaneous	214	167	47
TOTAL OTHER LIABILITIES	**22,080**	**22,217**	**−137**
UNMATURED DEBT, *Tables 10.1 and 10.10, Section 10 (Notes 3 and 14)—*			
Payable in Canadian currency—			
Marketable bonds	115,748	103,899	11,849
Canada savings bonds	47,756	53,323	−5,567
Special non-marketable bonds issued to the Canada Pension Plan Investment Fund	3,005	2,492	513
Treasury bills	102,700	81,050	21,650
	269,209	*240,764*	*28,445*
Less: Government's holdings of unmatured debt	4,172	3,729	443
	265,037	*237,035*	*28,002*
Payable in foreign currencies—			
Marketable bonds	5,373	6,323	−950
Notes and loans	1,911	3,926	−2,015
Canada bills	1,131	1,045	86
	8,415	*11,294*	*−2,879*
Less: Government's holdings of unmatured debt	95	12	83
	8,320	*11,282*	*−2,962*
TOTAL UNMATURED DEBT	**273,357**	**248,317**	**25,040**
TOTAL (Notes 16, 17 and 18)	**363,855**	**333,521**	**30,334**

The accompanying notes are an integral part of this statement.
Details can be found in other sections of this volume.
[1] The 1988 amounts for loans and investments in Air Canada have been reclassified under joint and mixed enterprises.

August 15, 1989

Source: *Public Accounts of Canada 1989*, Vol. I, p. 2-8.

usually necessary to use data from both reports, but the difference in the basis of the reports should not be forgotten.

All provincial governments prepare *Estimates* and *Public Accounts* documents, although in some cases the accounting assumptions and formats vary significantly from the federal government. However, the variance is usually not so great that it is impossible to understand the statements after reading this section. It is always necessary to read the notes accompanying the statements carefully and, in some provinces, there is a fair amount of supplementary information that is also helpful.

Municipalities also prepare budget requests at the beginning of the year and year-end statements, although these bear a myriad of different names. Because of certain technical aspects of municipal accounting, these statements can become very complicated. There are usually publications of the provincial Department of Municipal Affairs, which can be helpful in unravelling the mysteries of these statements.

NOTES

1. Allan M. Maslove, "Introduction: Budgeting in Provincial Governments," in Allan M. Maslove, ed., *Budgeting in the Provinces: Leadership and the Premiers* (Toronto: Institute of Public Administration of Canada, 1989), p. 1.
2. The illusions involved in tax expenditures are described in Kenneth Woodside, "The Political Economy of Policy Instruments: Tax Expenditures and Subsidies in Canada," in Michael M. Atkinson and Marsha A. Chandler, eds., *The Politics of Canadian Public Policy* (Toronto: University of Toronto Press, 1983), pp. 175-76 and passim.
3. G. Bruce Doern, Allan M. Maslove, and Michael J. Prince, *Public Budgeting in Canada* (Ottawa: Carleton University Press, 1988), pp. 55ff.
4. Douglas G. Hartle, *The Revenue Budget Process of the Government of Canada: Description, Appraisal, and Proposals* (Toronto: Canadian Tax Foundation, 1982), p. 6. (Footnotes omitted.)
5. Michael H. Wilson, *The Canadian Budgetary Process: Proposals for Improvement* (Department of Finance, 1985), p. 8. A similar argument is made in Allan J. MacEachen, *The Budget Process: A Paper on Budget Secrecy and Proposals for Broader Consultation* (Department of Finance, 1982), p. 7.
6. Hartle, *The Revenue Budget Process*, p. 31. (Footnotes omitted.)
7. There seem to be only two major discussions of the revenue budget process in addition to Hartle's: David A. Good, *The Politics of Anticipation: Making Canadian Federal Tax Policy* (Ottawa: Carleton University, School of Public Administration, n.d. 1980?), ch. 6; and Evert Lindquist, *Consultation and Budget Secrecy* (Ottawa: The Conference Board of Canada, 1985), ch. 2.
8. Hartle, *The Revenue Budget Process*, p. 8.
9. Ibid., pp. 28-29.
10. Robert J. Bertrand, Alice Desjardins, and René Hurtubise, *Legislation, Administration and Interpretation Process in Federal Taxation*, Study for the Royal Commission on Taxation, no. 22 (Ottawa: Queen's Printer and Controller of Stationery, 1967), pp. 44-45.
11. Walter L. Gordon, *A Political Man* (Toronto: McClelland and Stewart, 1977), ch. 8.

12. Robert Martin, "Kerr Won't Quit Over Budget Leak," *The Globe and Mail,* April 19, 1986, p. A4.

13. *Consultation and Budget Secrecy,* pp. 3-4.

14. The major proposals are recounted in Hartle, *The Revenue Budget Process,* ch. 4.

15. Wilson, *The Canadian Budgetary Process: Proposals for Improvement,* p. 27.

16. D. J. Sherbaniuk, "Budget Secrecy," *Canadian Tax Journal* 24 (May-June 1976): p. 227.

17. Ontario, Ministry of Treasury and Economics, *Reforming the Budget Process: A Discussion Paper* (Toronto: Queen's Printer for Ontario, 1985), pp. 5-8.

18. The most complete inventory of suggested reforms is contained in Lindquist, *Consultation and Budget Secrecy,* ch. 4.

19. Wilson, *The Canadian Budgetary Process: Proposals for Improvement,* pp. 25-27.

20. Ontario, Minister of Treasury and Economics, *Reforming the Budget Process: A Discussion Paper,* p. 1 and Appendix.

21. Robert A. Young, "Business and Budgeting: Recent Proposals for Reforming the Revenue Budgetary Process," *Canadian Public Policy* 9 (September 1983): 354. (Footnote omitted.)

22. Donald Gow, *The Process of Budgetary Reform in the Government of Canada* (Ottawa: Information Canada, 1973), p. 1.

23. Allen Schick, "The Road to PPB: The Stages of Budget Reform," *Public Administration Review* 26 (December 1966): 244. (Emphasis in original.)

24. Paul G. Thomas, "Public Administration and Expenditure Management," *Canadian Public Administration* 25 (Winter 1982): 678-79.

25. Schick, "The Road to PPB: The Stages of Budget Reform," p. 244. (Emphasis in original.)

26. A good general discussion of the chronological development of the different styles of budgeting is contained in James Cutt and Richard Ritter, *Public Non-Profit Budgeting: The Evolution and Application of Zero-Base Budgeting* (Toronto: The Institute of Public Administration of Canada, 1984), chs. 4-7. A specific description of how the evolution occurred in the Canadian federal government is given in Gow, *The Process of Budgetary Reform in the Government of Canada.*

27. A good description of the strengths and weaknesses of performance budgeting is contained in V. N. Macdonald and P. J. Lawton, *Improving Management Performance: The Contribution of Productivity and Performance Measurement* (Toronto: Ministry of Treasury, Economics and Intergovernmental Affairs, 1977), pp. 32-33.

28. Honourable C. M. Drury, *Planning-Programming-Budgeting Guide* (Ottawa: Queen's Printer, 1969), p. 8.

29. J. S. Hodgson, "Management by Objectives—The Experience of a Federal Government Department," *Canadian Public Administration* 16 (Fall 1973): 422-31.

30. H. L. Laframboise, "Administrative Reform in the Federal Public Service: Signs of a Saturation Psychosis," *Canadian Public Administration* 14 (Fall 1971): 312.

31. Treasury Board, *Operational Performance Measurement, Vol. I: A Managerial Overview* and *Vol. II: Technical Manual* (Ottawa: Information Canada, 1974); D. G. Hartle, "Operational Performance Measurement in the Federal Government," *Optimum* 3, no. 4 (1972): 5-18; and Henning Frederiksen, "Is Operational Performance in Government Measureable?" *Optimum* 6, no. 4 (1975): 23-41.

32. The strongest critic of the system in Canada is one of its veterans, D. G. Hartle, "Techniques and Processes of Administration," *Canadian Public Administration* 19 (Spring 1976): 24-29. One of the most prolific and perceptive critics of PPB in general

has been Aaron Wildavsky, "The Political Economy of Efficiency: Cost-Benefit Analysis, Systems Analysis, and Program Budgeting," *Public Administration Review* 26 (December 1966): 292-310, and "Rescuing Policy Analysis from PPB," *Public Administration Review* 29 (March-April 1969): 189-202.

33. Allen Schick, "A Death in the Bureaucracy: The Demise of Federal PPB," *Public Administration Review* 33 (March-April 1973): 147.

34. This shift in power is described very well in A. Clayton, "Brother Could You Spare A Dime?" *Optimum* 12, no. 1 (1981): 7-19.

35. Peter Self, *Econocrats and the Policy Process: The Politics and Philosophy of Cost-Benefit Analysis* (London: Macmillan, 1975).

36. Sandford F. Borins, *The Toronto Airport(s)*, Case Program in Canadian Public Administration (Toronto: Institute of Public Administration of Canada, 1977).

37. Schick, "A Death in the Bureaucracy," 149.

38. As quoted in Schick, "The Road to PPB," 247.

39. The definitive work about ZBB has been written by the man who developed it, Peter A. Pyhrr, *Zero-Base Budgeting* (Toronto: John Wiley & Sons, 1973).

40. Cutt and Ritter, *Public Non-Profit Budgeting*, chs. 8-11; Stephen L. Gould, Alan A. Oldall, and Fred Thompson, "Zero-Based Budgeting: Some Lessons From An Inconclusive Experiment," *Canadian Public Administration* 22 (Summer 1979): 251-60.

41. These terms were popularized by Hugh Heclo and Aaron Wildavsky, *The Private Government of Public Money*, 2nd ed. (London: The Macmillan Press Ltd., 1981), ch. 4.

42. Douglas G. Hartle, "Perceptions of the Expenditure Budget: Survey of Federal and Provincial Legislators and Public Servants," *Canadian Public Administration* 32, no. 3 (Fall 1989): 437.

43. Ibid., 434.

44. There are so many of these studies that it is impossible to mention even the main ones, but some of the classics are Aaron Wildavsky, *The Politics of the Budgetary Process* (Boston: Little Brown, 1964); Richard F. Fenno, Jr., *The Power of the Purse: Appropriation Politics in Congress* (Little, Brown, 1966); John P. Crecine, *Governmental Problem-Solving: A Computer Simulation Model of Municipal Budgeting* (Chicago: Rand McNally, 1969).

45. Douglas G. Hartle, *The Expenditure Budget Process in the Government of Canada* (Toronto: Canadian Tax Foundation, 1978); Richard French, *How Ottawa Decides* (Toronto: James Lorimer, 1980); Richard Van Loon, "The Policy and Expenditure Management System in the Federal Government: The First Three Years," *Canadian Public Administration* 26 (Summer 1983): 255-85.

46. (Toronto: University of Toronto Press, 1990).

47. Ibid., pp. 19-20.

48. Ibid., pp. 200-201. (Emphasis added.)

49. Ibid., p. 257.

50. The contents of the *Estimates* will be discussed in more detail in the appendix that follows this chapter.

51. This system is very well-described and analyzed in C. Lloyd Brown-John, André LeBlond, and D. Brian Marson, *Public Financial Management: A Canadian Text* (Scarborough, Ont.: Nelson Canada, 1988), ch. 8. Much of the material in this section comes from there.

52. Treasury Board of Canada, *Policy and Expenditure Management System Manual*, p. 2.2.

53. A more complete discussion of statutory appropriations is presented in the appendix to this chapter.

54. Richard J. Van Loon and Michael S. Whittington, "Kaleidoscope in Grey: The Policy Process in Ottawa," in Michael S. Whittington and Glen Williams, eds., *Canadian Politics in the 1990s* (Scarborough, Ont.: Nelson Canada, 1990), p. 453.
55. Ibid., p. 454.
56. *The Politics of Public Spending in Canada*, pp. 352-53.
57. Ibid., p. 352.
58. Ibid., ch. 7.
59. Greater elaboration is provided in Treasury Board of Canada, *Guide on Financial Administration for Departments and Agencies of the Government of Canada*, 2nd ed. (Hull: Supply and Services Canada, 1979), p. 2.2.2; and Ontario, Ministry of Treasury and Economics, *Province of Ontario: Financial Report 1985*, p. 16.
60. Robert F. Nixon, *1985 Ontario Budget* (Toronto: Ministry of Treasury and Economics, 1985), pp. 2-4, 39-44.
61. The general criteria to determine what constitutes a vote is set out in Treasury Board, *Policy and Expenditure Management System Manual*, ch. 8; and, Canada, Treasury Board, *Report on the Study of the Accounts of Canada* (Ottawa: Minister of Supply and Services Canada, 1976), p. 140.
62. R.S.C. 1970, c. F-10, s. 2.
63. See Chapter 9 for a discussion of how this circumstance came about.

BIBLIOGRAPHY

Aucoin, Peter. "Organizational Change in the Machinery of Canadian Government: From Rational Management to Brokerage Politics." *Canadian Journal of Political Science* 19 (March 1986): 3-27.

Bertrand, Robert J., Alice Desjardins, and René Hurtubise. *Legislation, Administration and Interpretation Process in Federal Taxation*. Study for the Royal Commission on Taxation, no. 22. Ottawa: Queen's Printer and Controller of Stationery, 1967.

Bird, Richard M. *The Growth of Government Spending in Canada*. Toronto: Canadian Tax Foundation, 1970.

Borins, Sandford F. "Ottawa's Expenditure Envelopes: Workable Rationality at Last?" In G. Bruce Doern, ed., *How Ottawa Spends Your Tax Dollars: National Policy and Economic Development–1982*. Toronto: James Lorimer, 1982 pp. 63–85.

———. *The Toronto Airport(s)*. Case Program in Canadian Public Administration. Toronto: Institute of Public Administration of Canada, 1977.

Brown-John, C. Lloyd, André LeBlond, and D. Brian Marson. *Public Financial Management: A Canadian Text*. Scarborough, Ont.: Nelson Canada, 1988.

Canada. Treasury Board. *Operational Performance Measurement, Vol. I: A Managerial Overview* and *Vol. II: Technical Manual*. Ottawa: Information Canada, 1974.

———. *Report on the Study of the Accounts of Canada*. Ottawa: Minister of Supply and Services Canada, 1976.

Clark, Ian D. "Recent Changes in the Cabinet Decision-Making System in Ottawa." *Canadian Public Administration* 28 (Summer 1985): 185-201.

Clayton, A. "Brother Could You Spare a Dime?" *Optimum* 12, no. 1 (1981): 7-19.

Crecine, John P. *Governmental Problem-Solving: A Computer Simulation Model of Municipal Budgeting*. Chicago: Rand McNally, 1969.

Cutt, James, and Richard Ritter. *Public Non-Profit Budgeting: The Evolution and Application of Zero-Base Budgeting*. Toronto: The Institute of Public Administration of Canada, 1984.

Danziger, James N. *Making Budgets: Public Resource Allocation*. Beverly Hills, Calif.: Sage

Publications, 1978.

Dobell, Rod. "Pressing the Envelopes," *Policy Options* (November/December 1981): 13-18.

Doern, G. Bruce, Allan M. Maslove, and Michael J. Prince. *Public Budgeting in Canada.* Ottawa: Carleton University Press, 1988.

Downs, Anthony. *An Economic Theory of Democracy.* New York: Harper & Row, 1957.

Drury, C. M. *Planning-Programming-Budgeting Guide.* Rev. ed. Ottawa: Queen's Printer, 1969.

Dye, Thomas. *Understanding Public Policy.* Englewood Cliffs, N.J.: Prentice-Hall, 1972.

Falcone, David J., and Michael S. Whittington. "Output Change in Canada: A Preliminary Attempt to Open the 'Black Box.' " Paper presented to the Annual Meeting of the Canadian Political Science Association, Montreal, Quebec, June 4, 1972.

Fenno, Richard F., Jr. *The Power of the Purse: Appropriation Politics in Congress.* Boston: Little, Brown, 1966.

Frederiksen, Henning. "Is Operational Performance in Government Measureable?" *Optimum* 6, no. 4 (1975): 23-41.

French, Richard. *How Ottawa Decides.* Toronto: James Lorimer, 1980.

Golembiewski, Robert T., and Jack Rabin, eds. *Public Budgeting and Finance: Behavioral, Theoretical, and Technical Perspectives.* New York: Marcel Dekker, 1983.

Good, David A. *The Politics of Anticipation: Making Canadian Federal Tax Policy.* Ottawa: Carleton University, School of Public Administration, n.d. 1980?

Gordon, Walter L. *A Political Man.* Toronto: McClelland and Stewart, 1977.

Gould, Stephen L., Alan A. Oldall, and Fred Thompson. "Zero-Base Budgeting: Some Lessons From an Inconclusive Experiment." *Canadian Public Administration* 22 (Summer 1979): 251-60.

Gow, Donald. *The Process of Budgetary Reform in the Government of Canada.* Ottawa: Information Canada, 1973.

Hartle, Douglas G. *The Expenditure Budget Process in the Government of Canada.* Toronto: Canadian Tax Foundation, 1978.

——. "Operational Performance Measurement in the Federal Government." *Optimum* 3, no. 4 (1972): 5-18.

——. "Perceptions of the Expenditure Budget: Survey of Federal and Provincial Legislators and Public Servants." *Canadian Public Administration* 32, no. 3 (Fall 1989): 427-48.

——. *The Revenue Budget Process of the Government of Canada: Description, Appraisal, and Proposals.* Toronto: Canadian Tax Foundation, 1982.

——. "Techniques and Processes of Administration." *Canadian Public Administration* 19 (Spring 1976): 21-33.

——. *A Theory of the Expenditure Budget Process.* Toronto: Ontario Economic Council, 1976.

Heclo, Hugh, and Aaron Wildavsky. *The Private Government of Public Money.* 2nd ed. London: Macmillan, 1981.

Hodgson, J. S. "Management by Objectives—The Experience of a Federal Government Department." *Canadian Public Administration* 16 (Fall 1973): 422-31.

Johnston, Donald J. *Guide to the Policy & Expenditure Management System.* Minister of Supply and Services Canada, 1980.

Laframboise, H. L. "Administrative Reform in the Federal Public Service: Signs of a Saturation Psychosis." *Canadian Public Administration* 14 (Fall 1971): 303-325.

Lindquist, Evert. *Consultation and Budget Secrecy.* Ottawa: The Conference Board of Canada, 1985.

MacDonald, V. N., and P. J. Lawton. *Improving Management Performance: The Contribution of*

Productivity and Performance Measurement. Toronto: Ministry of Treasury, Economics and Intergovernmental Affairs, 1977.

MacEachen, Allan J. *The Budget Process: A Paper on Budget Secrecy and Proposals for Broader Consultation.* Department of Finance, 1982.

Macnaughton, Bruce D. "Public Finance for Political Profit: The Politics of Social Security in Canada, 1941-1977." Ph.D. diss., Carleton University, 1980.

Macnaughton, Bruce D., and Conrad J. Winn. "Economic Policy and Electoral Self-Interest: The Allocations of the Department of Regional Economic Expansion." *Canadian Public Policy* 7 (Spring 1981): 318-27.

Maslove, Allan M., ed. *Budgeting in the Provinces: Leadership and the Premiers.* Toronto: Institute of Public Administration of Canada, 1989.

Niskanen, William A., Jr. *Bureaucracy and Representative Government.* Chicago: Aldine-Atherton, 1971.

Ontario. Ministry of Treasury and Economics. *Province of Ontario: Financial Report 1985.*

——. *Reforming the Budget Process: A Discussion Paper.* Toronto: Queen's Printer for Ontario, 1985.

Pryor, Frederick. *Public Expenditures in Communist and Capitalist Nations.* London: George Allen & Unwin, 1968.

Pyhrr, Peter A. *Zero-Base Budgeting.* Toronto: John Wiley, 1973.

Savoie, Donald J. *The Politics of Public Spending in Canada.* Toronto: University of Toronto Press, 1990.

Schick, Allen. "A Death in the Bureaucracy: The Demise of Federal PPB." *Public Administration Review* 33 (March-April 1973): 146-156.

——. "The Road to PPB: The Stages of Budget Reform." *Public Administration Review* 26 (December 1966): 243-58.

Self, Peter. *Econocrats and the Policy Process: The Politics and Philosophy of Cost-Benefit Analysis.* London: Macmillan, 1975.

Sherbaniuk, D. J. "Budget Secrecy." *Canadian Tax Journal* 24 (May-June 1976): 223-30.

Thomas, Paul G. "Public Administration and Expenditure Management." *Canadian Public Administration* 25 (Winter 1982): 674-95.

Treasury Board of Canada. *Guide on Financial Administration for Departments and Agencies of the Government of Canada.* 2nd ed. Hull: Supply and Services Canada, 1979.

——. *Operational Performance Measurement, Vol. I: A Managerial Overview* and *Vol. II: Technical Manual.* Ottawa: Information Canada, 1974.

——. *Policy and Expenditure Management System Manual.* n. d.

Van Loon, Richard. "Ottawa's Expenditure Process: Four Systems In Search of Co-ordination." In G. Bruce Doern, ed., *How Ottawa Spends: The Liberals, the Opposition & Federal Priorities–1983.* Toronto: James Lorimer, 1983, pp. 93-120.

——. "The Policy and Expenditure Management System in the Federal Government: The First Three Years." *Canadian Public Administration* 26 (Summer 1983): 255-85.

Van Loon, Richard J., and Michael S. Whittington. "Kaleidoscope in Grey: The Policy Process in Ottawa." In Michael S. Whittington and Glen Williams, eds., *Canadian Politics in the 1990s.* Scarborough, Ont.: Nelson Canada, 1990, pp. 448-67.

Wildavsky, Aaron. "The Political Economy of Efficiency: Cost-Benefit Analysis, Systems Analysis, and Program Budgeting." *Public Administration Review* 26 (December 1966): 292-310.

——. *The Politics of the Budgetary Process.* Boston: Little, Brown, 1964.

——. "Rescuing Policy Analysis from PPB." *Public Administration Review* 29 (March-April 1969): 189-202.

Wilson, Michael H. *The Canadian Budgetary Process: Proposals for Improvement.* Department of Finance, 1985.

Woodside, Kenneth. "The Political Economy of Policy Instruments: Tax Expenditures and Subsidies in Canada." In Michael M. Atkinson and Marsha A. Chandler, eds., *The Politics of Canadian Public Policy*. Toronto: University of Toronto Press, 1983, pp. 173-97.

Young, Robert A. "Business and Budgeting: Recent Proposals for Reforming the Revenue Budgetary Process." *Canadian Public Policy* 9 (September 1983): 347-61.

CASES

In *Case Program in Canadian Public Administration* (Toronto: Institute of Public Administration of Canada):

The Elusive IPB System. By Walter Baker

Spenders, Guardians, and Policy Analysts: A Game of Budgeting Under the Policy and Expenditure Management System. By Sandford F. Borins and David A. Good

The Fiscal Framework Problem: First Steps in the Formulation of a Provincial Budget. By Paul C. Leger

Resource Allocation in a Provincial Government: The Frustration of Respecting Global Expenditure Levels. By Paul C. Leger

The Allocation of a National Housing Budget. By Barbara Carroll

STOL: A Benefit-Cost Analysis. By Allan M. Maslove and Gene Swimmer

Resource Allocation Problems in Health Care Institutions. By Ellen Pekeles

Cases developed by the Canadian Centre for Management Development and distributed by the Case Program in Canadian Public Administration:

A Delicate But Unavoidable Evaluation. By Richard Marceau, Pierre Simard, and Michel Paquin

27

The Management of Financial Resources

The previous chapter discussed the budgetary process, i.e., the process of allocating funds to be spent on specific programs. This chapter will consider what happens to those funds after they have been appropriated. Of course, operating departments have the main role because they operate programs and therefore spend the bulk of the funds. However, there are a number of other agencies involved in the process of ensuring that funds are spent wisely and with appropriate controls. This chapter will examine in detail each of the agencies involved in the process.

THE FINANCIAL ADMINISTRATION ACT

The **Financial Administration Act**[1] establishes the responsibilities of the Treasury Board and the Department of Finance in the area of financial management. It establishes the general rules for the handling and safeguarding of public funds and other assets. It specifies rules for the management of the public debt and sets out procedures for maintaining the government accounting system. It also establishes the accountability regime for Crown corporations and other agencies. In sum, the Financial Administration Act provides the general framework of financial and administrative management within which the departments and agencies of the federal government must function.

PARLIAMENT

The best way to view the system is as an annual cycle as illustrated in Figure 27.1. The process begins when Parliament appropriates funds for a new fiscal year, which begins on April 1.

Most aspects of the appropriation process were covered in the previous chapter, but it is important to remember that it is a basic tenet of responsible, parliamentary government that Parliament must approve the expenditure of any funds *before* the expenditure occurs. This is the first step in the financial administration cycle.

As discussed in the previous chapter, quite a bit of work goes into the preparation of the budget before it is tabled in the House of Commons. In this

Figure 27.1
ANNUAL CYCLE OF FINANCIAL ACCOUNTABILITY

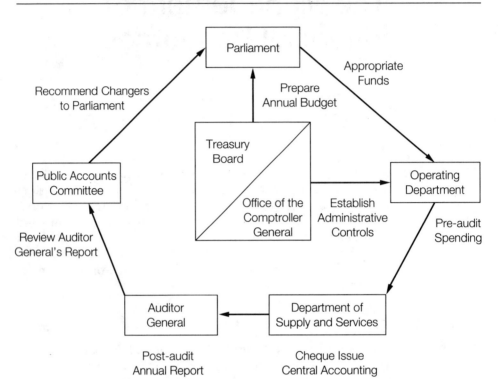

chapter, the role of Parliament in the approval of the expenditure budget will be considered.

The President of the Treasury Board begins the process, usually in January or February of each year, by tabling a series of documents collectively referred to as the *Estimates*. These documents list the budget allocations requested by each department, as well as some supporting detail about the operation of the programs for which funding is requested. In recent years, this supporting information has expanded so that the estimates of each department now constitute several volumes providing supplementary information about programs such as the number of clients served, the number of units of service provided, and the unit cost of providing a service.[2]

The *Estimates* and all other "money bills," as they are called, are always tabled and approved in the House of Commons before going to the Senate. This is a long tradition stemming from the fact that the House of Commons is the elected body of Parliament and is, therefore, the only body that is directly responsible to the electorate.

After the *Estimates* documents have been tabled in the House of Commons, they are then sent to the various committees of the House for further consideration. Each committee specializes in a department or a related group of departments so that the *Estimates* are divided up and sent to the appropriate committees for more in-depth consideration. Since this usually takes some time and since the *Estimates* are not tabled until a rather short time before the beginning of the fiscal year on April 1, it is unlikely that Parliament will approve the *Estimates* before the beginning of the fiscal year. Obviously, this creates a rather serious problem because departments cannot begin to spend money until Parliament has appropriated it. To circumvent this problem, Parliament provides Interim Supply before the beginning of the fiscal year.

Interim Supply is a piece of legislation that provides for the operation of the government for the period from April 1 to June 30 by appropriating approximately one-fourth of the total budget requested. This allows departments to continue operating even though the full budget has not yet been considered. It is customary that interim supply should include funds only for the continuation of existing programs. Funding for new programs must usually await the approval of the *Estimates*.

Shortly after the *Estimates* are tabled, the various parliamentary committees begin to hold hearings on the part of the *Estimates* that most closely concerns them. Usually, ministers and senior officials will appear before these committees to defend and explain their budget requests. The committees also like to hear from clientele groups and interested experts. The committees then recommend to Parliament what the appropriate budgetary allocation ought to be. Since these committees usually operate along highly partisan lines, it is unusual for the committee recommendation to deviate from the government's request, but that should not be taken as a sign of the committees' impotence. These budget hearings are an excellent place for Opposition members to learn about the activities of departments, and can also provide an important forum for holding ministers and public servants accountable.

After the committee reports have been received by the House of Commons, there is a vote on the full budget as contained in the *Estimates*. This vote is very important because the expenditure budget is always a matter of "confidence," meaning that if the budget were defeated it would be an indication that the government no longer had the "confidence" of the House and, therefore, as a matter of convention, ought to resign.

The rules of the House provide that if a budget has not been acted upon by the House before June 30 then it is voted upon on that date. This means that the Opposition is free to *defeat* a budget, but it cannot hamstring the government by merely *delaying* the passage of the budget. In fact, the *Estimates* are almost always passed in exactly the form proposed by the government. When the *Estimates* document becomes law, it is known as the **Appropriation Act** for that year.

The government always attempts to estimate its needs as accurately as possible when it prepares its *Estimates* at the beginning of the year, but it is not surprising that sometimes these beginning-of-the-year estimates do not prove completely accurate. Since all expenditures require parliamentary approval, the government cannot unilaterally shift funds from one program to another or spend more than was allotted by Parliament in the original Appropriation Act.

In order to meet unforeseen circumstances, the government presents **Supplementary Estimates** to the House at various times during the fiscal year. The *Supplementary Estimates* are pieces of legislation that request either additional funds beyond those originally approved or a shift in funds between programs. In recent years, governments typically have presented *Supplementary Estimates* from two to four times each year, usually beginning in November or December.

There is one other way of dealing with these unforeseen circumstances. **Governor General's Warrants** can be issued to meet an *unforeseen need* at a time when *Parliament is not in session*. In this case, the President of the Treasury Board notifies the Governor General that funds must be spent even though there has been no parliamentary appropriation. The Governor General then issues a warrant authorizing the expenditure of these funds.

To ensure that the use of these warrants is not abused the government is required to provide official notice whenever they are used. First, they are always announced in the *Canada Gazette*, which is the publication of the Government of Canada in which all official government announcements are publicized. Then, the issuance of these warrants must be approved by Parliament when it resumes sitting before it considers any new expenditure legislation.

While there is nothing that Parliament can do at this point to recapture the funds that have already been spent, it is an opportunity for the Opposition to question the government about the expenditure of these funds. The warrants are a limited violation of the principle that all expenditure requires prior parliamentary approval, but they are an important safety valve. For example, Governor General's Warrants were used extensively during the 1979-80 period when, because of transitions in government, Parliament was not sitting for an extended period. Without some mechanism such as these warrants, absolutely no money could have been spent in that rather lengthy period.

The role of Parliament in financial administration is crucial. Legally, it is Parliament—and only Parliament—that can start the process by appropriating funds. Still, there have been criticisms of Parliament's role. Some Members of Parliament have complained that they have very limited time to consider the lengthy and complex *Estimates* before they are passed. The Royal Commission on Financial Management and Accountability echoed this concern when it suggested that individual MPs were overworked in terms of their committee activities,[3] and when it further pointed out that there was no single committee that was charged with an overview of the budget and the economy.[4] However, at this time, while it seems that most people recognize the existence of the problem, no action has been taken to resolve it.

TREASURY BOARD

Treasury Board is a Cabinet committee consisting of six Cabinet ministers including the President of the Treasury Board and the Minister of Finance. The board has been called the Cabinet committee on the expenditure budget and the Cabinet committee on management.[5] In fulfilling its first role, it assembles the budget requests of departments and recommends the budget to Parliament.

This aspect of its work was covered in detail in the previous chapter. In this chapter, the main focus will be on the latter role.

There are two things that distinguish the Treasury Board from other Cabinet committees. First, there is a rather large group of civil servants working directly under the supervision of the President. In 1989, there were approximately eight hundred employees in the Treasury Board Secretariat, as the bureaucratic organization reporting to the President is properly called. The effect of this bureaucratic contingent is that the Treasury Board has a considerably higher profile as a committee touching on the day-to-day activities of public servants than other Cabinet committees.

Treasury Board is also distinguished from other Cabinet committees in that its existence has been established by an Act of Parliament (the Financial Administration Act), unlike the other Cabinet committees which are created by, and can be abolished by, a decision of the Prime Minister. The Financial Administration Act establishes the general framework for financial and administrative management in the federal government, and as a part of that framework it establishes the Treasury Board's status as a central control agency, meaning that the board has supervisory powers over certain activities of operating departments. Specifically, the board has the power to make regulations in most areas of general administrative and financial management. Some examples of the board's authority are set out below.

- establishing allotments, i.e., subdivisions of Parliamentary appropriations, that cannot be varied without Treasury Board approval;
- prescribing rules for the disbursement of public funds, i.e, procedures to be followed before a cheque can be issued;
- prescribing rules for the receipt and control of funds paid to the government;
- prescribing rules for the safeguarding of public property,
- ensuring coordination of administrative functions and services within departments and within government as a whole, i.e., ensuring effective interdepartmental coordination;
- prescribing the form and manner in which government accounting records will be maintained; and
- establishing regulations for entering into contracts and for purchasing.

Treasury Board also has a number of responsibilities in areas other than financial management, which are discussed in other chapters.

A perusal of these activities indicates that the main role of Treasury Board is to ensure prudence and probity in government, and to ensure uniformity in administration between operating departments. In a small organization, this kind of function would not be necessary, but this sort of role is frequently found in large organizations. It is necessary to have some organization to ensure that all the diverse and decentralized units of the organization are conducting their administrative activities in an appropriate and reasonably uniform manner.

In order to carry out this function, Treasury Board has prepared a number of manuals containing guidelines and regulations that are binding on all departments and agencies of the government. The regulations sometimes specify in great detail rules for everything from the steps that must be followed before a government cheque can be issued, to the size of offices for officials of various ranks. In some cases, a department can obtain an exemption from following certain regulations if it is able to make a satisfactory argument to Treasury Board that special circumstances require this exemption. The staff of the Auditor General's Office is familiar with the Treasury Board regulations and uses them in the performance of audits.

The status of Treasury Board as a central control agency gives it a key role in the system of financial administration. However, it is precisely this status that frequently leads it into conflict with operating departments and raises questions about accountability.

Operating departments usually feel a great deal of pressure to organize programs so that significant results are produced quickly. Officials in these departments sometimes see uniform, cross-departmental regulations as obstacles to smooth and efficient service delivery.

Treasury Board is not unsympathetic to this problem, but officials in the Treasury Board Secretariat are mindful that regulations are established to serve particular purposes and should not be circumvented lightly. The operating department might see that there are ways of saving time and money by cutting certain corners, for example, by shortcutting certain purchasing procedures or by skimping on some financial control mechanisms. This raises the classic staff-line conflict, but it is exacerbated in this case because Treasury Board, unlike the classic staff agency, has *control* over some aspects of the department's work.

This raises the question of accountability. Is it really appropriate to hold the line department accountable for results if it does not have full authority to take whatever action is necessary to obtain those results? This is an old question, which really cannot be answered in the abstract. Every situation is slightly different. The important point to be made is that some controls over the activities of line departments are important, but a certain sensitivity must be employed in exercising this control so as not to cripple unduly the activities of operating departments.

OFFICE OF THE COMPTROLLER GENERAL

The Office of the Comptroller General (OCG) is a relatively new organization.[6] It was established by an amendment to the Financial Administration Act in 1978, which was a response to continuing pressure from the Auditor General to create a "chief financial officer" for the Government of Canada. The higher profile given to financial administration by the creation of a separate office is important, but, in fact, most of the duties of the OCG were simply spun-off from the Treasury Board. This is reflected in the fact that most of the OCG's initial staff complement came from the Treasury Board Secretariat.

Throughout most of the 1970s, the Auditor General was James J. Macdonell—a somewhat larger-than-life figure who will be considered in greater ᵗail later in this chapter. When he became Auditor General in 1973, after a lengthy career in the private sector, he was surprised to find that while Treasury Board had general responsibility for financial management, along with many other things, there was no one *individual* who could be called the "chief financial officer" of the Government of Canada. This meant that there was no focal point for ensuring high quality financial management in the Government of Canada.

Under the terms of the Financial Administration Act, this was the responsibility of the Treasury Board. The problem was that because the board had so many other responsibilities, there was no guarantee that financial management would have the status within the board that the Auditor General felt it should. Therefore, beginning with his 1976 report, Macdonell began urging the creation of an Office of the Comptroller General.[7] This agitation was rewarded in 1978 when the office was created.

The relationship between the new Office of the Comptroller General and the Treasury Board has always been a convoluted one because the OCG has taken over certain responsibilities that were previously carried out by the board. The Comptroller General has the rank of deputy head—the same rank held by the Secretary of the Treasury Board—and reports to the President of the Treasury Board. Many publications bear the joint stamp of the Treasury Board and the Office of the Comptroller General. It is somewhat difficult to delineate exactly the role of the OCG, but the first Comptroller General, Harry Rogers, carved out certain areas that became his primary focus of interest.

The OCG is responsible for developing government-wide policies for financial and operational management. This involves publication of the *Guide on Financial Administration for Departments and Agencies of the Government of Canada*,[8] which sets out in great detail the procedures that must be followed with regard to receipt and payment of public funds, handling inventories and other assets, and so forth. The OCG also shares with the Department of Supply and Services the responsibility for developing government accounting policy and the system of accounts used in the preparation of the *Public Accounts*.

The other major role that the OCG has carved out for itself is in the evaluation of government programs—a process that has been of great concern in the federal government recently. *Evaluation*, which was discussed in detail in Chapter 7, involves the systematic, in-depth review of a program to determine its contribution to public policy.

The OCG does not actually evaluate the programs itself; that is better left to the operating departments which understand their programs better than would outsiders. However, the OCG has developed expertise in the evaluation area so that it can advise departments on undertaking evaluations and, to some extent, evaluate the evaluations. In general, it provides leadership in this area by using both moral suasion and producing publications such as *Principles for the Evaluation of Programs by Federal Departments and Agencies*.[9]

In the previous section, some of the tensions that exist between Treasury Board and line departments, and some of the problems of accountability caused by these tensions, were discussed. Many of the same comments could be repeated with regard to the role of the OCG. As a central control agency, it has a mandate to impose certain operating rules on departments—rules that the departments sometimes find onerous. This brings it into the same kind of conflict sometimes experienced by Treasury Board, and so the same problems of line-staff relationships and muddled accountability exist here as well.

OPERATING DEPARTMENTS

The line departments are involved in actually operating most large government programs, and so this is where the bulk of government expenditure takes place. These departments are clearly in the front line, in terms of making expenditure decisions, but the above discussions about the roles of the Treasury Board and the Office of Comptroller General should make it clear that the authority of a department to act unilaterally is somewhat limited.

Departments are required to establish appropriate *pre-audit procedures*—procedures to ensure that appropriate conditions have been met *before* payment is approved. These procedures must ensure that the expenditure has been authorized by Parliament, that adequate funds still remain in the appropriation, that appropriate goods or services have been received, and that these were in line with the contract.

If the payment is a grant or transfer payment, obviously the specific procedure is different, but the general idea is the same. The department must establish procedures to ensure that the person receiving the payment is entitled to it. These procedures are called a pre-audit because they are required, by Treasury Board-Comptroller General guidelines, to occur before any public funds are paid out. These same guidelines specify similar rules for the protection of revenue received and the safeguarding of non-cash assets such as inventories.

Departments are also responsible for establishing an internal audit group with free access to the deputy minister. The purpose of this is to provide the deputy with objective information about the adequacy and effectiveness of the management framework that each department has established for:

1. the achievement of its operational and program objectives;
2. the reliability and integrity of the information;
3. the economical and efficient use and safeguarding of resources; and
4. compliance with policies and regulations.

The Office of the Comptroller General is particularly interested in ensuring that all departments have an adequate internal audit function in place.

Departments receive a budgetary allocation and approve the payment of funds to be charged to that allocation, but they do not actually issue cheques. This is done by the Department of Supply and Services.

DEPARTMENT OF SUPPLY AND SERVICES

The Department of Supply and Services (DSS) is responsible for many common services provided to all departments and agencies, such as purchasing and ʾral accounting. It is this latter function that will be discussed in this chapter.

DSS is the central accounting agency of the Government of Canada. This means that the Receiver General for Canada, which is another title that the Minister of Supply and Services always holds, is responsible for the receipt and disbursement of all public funds and for accounting for those funds in the Consolidated Revenue Fund. The *Consolidated Revenue Fund* is the one large cash account that the government maintains for all federal funds that are not earmarked for some specific purpose. The title comes from the fact that at one time there was a large number of cash funds held by a variety of different agencies and used largely for their own purposes. This created some confusion and raised the possibility of inappropriate use of, or accounting for, government funds. For this reason, it was felt desirable to consolidate all government funds in one account under the control of one minister—the Receiver General—and his or her department—the Department of Supply and Services.

DSS receives cheque requisitions from operating departments and agencies and then issues cheques as requested. Before the cheque is issued, DSS ensures that the department will not be overspending its appropriation, but it undertakes no other reviews beyond that, because it assumes that the department has conducted a proper pre-audit.

DSS handles all receipts and deposits of public funds and acts as a central accounting agency; it shares with the Office of the Comptroller General responsibility for the establishment of the government accounting system.

DSS is also responsible for the preparation of the government's year-end financial statements referred to as the *Public Accounts.* These statements contain the government's balance sheet, which lists assets owned and liabilities owed, the *Statement of Revenue and Expenditure,* and certain other financial statements. The *Public Accounts* also contains a great deal of detailed information about sources of revenue and objects of expenditure by program and activity. This makes it a valuable source of information for researchers.[10]

DSS is responsible for *preparing* the government's financial statements, but these statements must bear the scrutiny of an audit by an independent agency.

AUDITOR GENERAL

The Office of the Auditor General (OAG) is one of the most visible and well-known actors in the financial management system. The **Auditor General** can be seen as having two roles—one narrow and one much broader. The narrow role is the least contentious and requires the Auditor General to act in the same manner as an auditor would act in the private sector. The Auditor General's more contentious, broader role requires him or her to be something of a watchdog of government spending.

In the Auditor General's narrow role, he or she performs an attest audit. An *attest audit* is an audit performed to ensure that the financial statements accurately reflect the financial position and activities of the government. The outcome of the attest audit is the auditor's opinion, which becomes a part of the *Public Accounts.* This opinion should be read by anyone working with the *Public*

Accounts to provide an insight into the level of accuracy of the statements presented.

In recent years, the Auditor General has issued an opinion indicating that the statements are not as accurate as they could be if certain better accounting principles were employed.[11] This is a rather strong statement, but it must be seen in perspective. The Auditor General is clearly not suggesting that any fraudulent or otherwise culpable activity has occurred. He has merely stated that improvements could be made in the presentation of the statement that would make them more reflective of the government's actual financial position.

In order to fulfill this attest function, the staff of the OAG must undertake a *post-audit* of a random selection of financial transactions that occurred during the year. This post-audit means that these selected transactions are traced through the accounting process to evaluate the adequacy of the pre-audit performed within departments, and to determine the accuracy of the accounting records. This is how the Auditor General forms an opinion as to whether the financial statements contained in the *Public Accounts*, and prepared by the Department of Supply and Services, accurately reflect the financial position of the government.

In addition to the attest audit, the Auditor General is also responsible for the performance of a compliance audit. A *compliance audit* is an audit performed to ensure that all legislative enactments and government regulations have been complied with in the operation of programs. It goes beyond the attest audit in ensuring not just that expenditures have been recorded correctly, but that there was appropriate statutory authority for all expenditure, and further, that the regulations specified by the Comptroller General and the Treasury Board have been followed. This role of the Auditor General has never been very contentious because it can usually be objectively established if rules have been violated.

However, the Auditor General's broader role has always been somewhat more contentious. The Auditor General is an officer of Parliament, rather than simply an ordinary public servant. This means that he or she has the right to report directly to Parliament and has protection from arbitrary dismissal from office by the government, which will be discussed in more detail later. In this role, the Auditor General is frequently seen as Parliament's watchdog on government spending. To carry out this role, the Auditor General is required to prepare an annual report for Parliament. Different Auditors General have used this report in different ways.

Under the terms of legislation in existence prior to 1977, the Auditor General was charged with reporting on any "non-productive expenditure." Previous Auditors General who have taken this responsibility to heart have produced annual reports that contained lists of "horror stories." These were 'ists of specific incidents that, in the opinion of the Auditor General, indicated ̄e sort of inappropriate expenditure by the government. This kind of report ̄ch loved by the media, because it provided a succession of juicy headlines. ̄e most widely heralded examples was the story of the refitting of the ̄er *Bonaventure*.[12] The Auditor General found numerous examples of ̄ınd excessive prices paid during the refit. Then, to add insult to injury, the ship was sold for a very low price almost immediately after the refit was complete.

These kinds of findings are important in reminding ministers and public servants that there is a check on their activities and that, therefore, they must carry out their responsibilities with due care. However, not all of the Auditor General's "horror stories" were as clear-cut as the *Bonaventure*.

In 1969, the government of the day became incensed over the Auditor General's criticism of its expenditure on a study of a causeway to Prince Edward Island.[13] The federal government had commissioned a feasibility study of the construction of the causeway. After considering the findings of the study, it was decided not to build the causeway at that time. At this point, the Auditor General suggested in his annual report that the cost of the study was a non-productive expenditure. The government of the day argued that this finding was unfair because it made more sense to study the feasibility of a major project first, rather than build it and then discover that it was unnecessary. This incident provides some insight into the problems that the Auditor General encounters when he or she goes beyond the narrow confines of the attest audit.

In 1977, provisions governing the Auditor General were removed from the Financial Administration Act, and the Auditor General's Office was for the first time governed by its own legislation. In this new legislation, the phrase "non-productive expenditure" was replaced by a requirement to report on any case in which "money has been expended without due regard to economy or efficiency."[14]

At about this time, the style of the Auditor General changed from an emphasis on individual "horror stories" to a more systematic approach to general problems in financial management. This change came about partly because of misunderstandings such as the causeway, and partly because the accounting profession was taking a more systematic approach to auditing. However, the change mostly came about as a result of the coming to office of James J. Macdonell—an individual who had spent his entire career in accounting and management consulting in the private sector. Macdonell moved away from the "horror stories" approach and toward the more systematic approaches of what was first called "value-for-money" auditing and then comprehensive auditing.

Comprehensive auditing is a broader approach to auditing than the narrow attest function, because its emphasis is on the three Es—economy, efficiency, and effectiveness.[15] *Economy* is defined as obtaining the appropriate goods and services needed at the best possible price. *Efficiency* is defined as arranging resources in such a manner as to obtain the maximum output from the resources employed. *Effectiveness* is defined as maximizing the attainment of a particular objective. These three Es are obviously complementary, and it is possible to maximize some of them, but not others. For example, one could maximize economy in obtaining resources, but then employ those resources in an inefficient manner. Probably the more usual situation is that economy and efficiency are present, but they are misdirected in some way so that effectiveness is not served, i.e., steps toward the desired objective are not maximized.

The introduction of comprehensive auditing caused a change in the style of auditing. In the former style, staff of the audit office reviewed the activities of each department and agency in as much depth as time allowed, performing mostly a post-audit, but always with an eye to uncovering horror stories.

In comprehensive auditing, there is still a concern for the ordinary attest function and post-audit. However, the random search for horror stories was replaced by a systematic and detailed review of a limited number of programs each year. An extensive, but shallow, approach was replaced by a selective, intensive approach.

The style and content of the annual report also changed. The listing of horror stories was replaced by two main types of chapters. One type reported on the comprehensive audits of specific programs, and the second type dealt with government-wide reviews of a general nature, such as the use of computers or photocopy equipment. In both cases, the Auditor General's comments were not confined to dealing only with financial activities. For example, in a 1989 report on the operation of the Canadian Parks Service, the Auditor General's report argued that it did not have an appropriate strategic plan, was not pursuing resource protection policies as strongly as it could, and did not have any way to evaluate visitors' satisfaction with programs at the parks.[16]

However, even this new approach did not deliver the Auditor General from controversy. In fact, in some ways the comprehensive audit approach increased the level of controversy. Governments ought to be concerned with all three Es, and proper accountability requires that ministers be held responsible for maximizing all three. The Auditor General can be one element in ensuring that accountability, but there is a rather difficult problem with this.

It is within the appropriate sphere of the Auditor General to comment on economy and efficiency, but a consideration of effectiveness frequently requires some comment on government objectives that clearly goes beyond the mandate of the Auditor General and may venture into political territory. The Auditor General must exercise care lest at some point he or she usurp the role of the Leader of the Opposition.

> The auditor general in the last ten years has moved light-years beyond the role of auditor, towards a broad assessment of government management and decision-making. Ironically, as there is less waste and fewer horror stories to report, the AG's annual report goes further and further towards a general second-guessing of government.[17]

Comprehensive auditing attempts to avoid this dilemma by limiting its role to commenting on economy and efficiency. These are not such contentious areas. In principle, there is no attempt to comment on effectiveness as such, but Macdonell took the position that all programs should have indicators to measure effectiveness, and that his office ought to have responsibility to comment existence (or non-existence) and adequacy of those indicators. This define the Auditor General's role more carefully has probably limited omewhat, but Mr. Macdonell has been accused of overstepping his e.[18]

One of the most significant conflicts occurred around the Cabinet decision to allow Petro-Canada to use $1.7 billion in public funds in the Canadian Ownership Account to purchase Petrofina.[19] The Auditor General felt that he needed supporting information to determine whether these funds were spent with appropriate regard to economy and efficiency. Initially, both Petro-Canada and the relevant government departments refused to allow him access to the information on the grounds that these documents were secret Cabinet documents. This principle of the secrecy of Cabinet documents is important for the maintenance of a neutral public service, which is discussed in Part IV of this book.

In the face of the government's continuing refusal to release the information, the Auditor General eventually took the matter to the Supreme Court of Canada. The court ruled that the Auditor General did not have right of access to confidential Cabinet documents. The ruling held that, where access is denied, the Auditor General can report that to Parliament, but it is then up to Parliament to decide what should be done.

The Auditor General must be careful about becoming involved in political controversies. The audit function derives its credibility from its penchant for objectivity. While it is very tempting to move into controversial areas, this constitutes a movement away from pure objectivity to greater subjectivity, which could weaken the credibility of the office.

Many people, especially the Opposition parties, would like to use the Auditor General for their own political ends. For example, one journalist has already suggested that the Auditor General was opposed to the Meech Lake Accord.[20] While this is a significant overinterpretation of what the Auditor General actually said, it is an indication of how people want to use the high status of the Auditor General to support their causes. In this environment, the Auditor General must move very carefully to avoid weakening the office by bringing it into political controversy.

In order to carry out the audit function appropriately, the Auditor General must have what private sector auditors refer to as "independence," i.e., the auditor must not be under the direct control of the organization being audited—in this case, the executive branch of government.

One aspect of this independence is ensured by the fact that the Auditor General is an officer of Parliament. In practice, this means that he can deliver all reports directly to Parliament without intervention by the government; he can appeal directly to Parliament if he feels that his office is not being funded appropriately; and he can be dismissed only for cause after an address of both Houses of Parliament. This last point means that an Auditor General can be dismissed only for some inappropriate behaviour, and even then only after a majority vote of the House of Commons and Senate, and the concurrence of the Governor General. This is the same procedure that is followed for the dismissal of a judge.

The method of appointment also helps ensure the independence of the Auditor General. The appointment is made by Parliament on the nomination of the Prime Minister. However, to help ensure the highest quality appointment, there is a tradition that, in making this nomination, the Prime Minister will rely on the advice of a committee of professional accountants. Once appointed, the Auditor General serves a fixed term of ten years or until he or she reaches sixty-five years of age, whichever comes first. The independence of the Auditor General is very important, and there is a general consensus that this independence is adequately served by the safeguards that are in place.

PUBLIC ACCOUNTS COMMITTEE

The Public Accounts Committee (PAC) is a committee of the House of Commons charged with the responsibility for reviewing the Auditor General's annual report. In most ways, it functions just as any other parliamentary committee with the exception that, by tradition, the chairperson of the committee is a member of the Opposition. It is quite possible that the committee will be composed of a majority of members from the government party, but this does not make the chairperson powerless. The chairperson establishes agendas and provides leadership to the committee. The presence of an Opposition member as chairperson ensures that important topics will be on the agenda and will be discussed in the presence of interested Members of Parliament and media. This high visibility does much to ensure accountability even if the contents of the committee's reports are dominated by government input.

The committee reviews the Auditor General's annual report on a section-by-section basis. Usually, it considers the comprehensive audits of each program separately. Relevant ministers and/or senior public servants are invited to appear before the committee to comment on the findings of the Auditor General, and possibly explain what steps have been taken to solve the problems. Throughout the process, the members of the PAC are advised by staff of the Auditor General's office.

> The auditor general and the public accounts committee must work hand in hand to ensure effective accountability. Without the auditor and his report the committee is unable to dig into government's finances, or to choose from among the millions of transactions and thousands of issues those which are important and deserve study. Without the committee the auditor general can only report and express an opinion; he has no backing or guidance by parliament, and his findings have less publicity and attention without the media interest in proceedings of the public accounts committee.[21]

During the course of the hearings, the committee sends a series of short reports to Parliament, providing its recommendations for what ought to be done as a result of each of the Auditor General's observations.

This series of reports closes the loop that was set out in Figure 27.1. 'iament will have the comments of the Public Accounts Committee before it 'eciding what to do about the continued funding of a particular program 't budget.

' very important in providing the proper feedback to Parliament. It ':ism of auditing, committee hearings, and similar activities that they constitute closing the barn door after the horse has escaped. This is not a valid criticism if the feedback loop is closed quickly enough. Actions can be taken to restructure or even terminate programs that are not performing as desired. In recent times, this entire cycle has taken approximately eighteen months to complete. The fiscal year ends on March 31. The Auditor General is required to produce a report by the end of December—a deadline that has always been met by recent Auditors General. Hearings by the Public Accounts Committee can begin shortly after that. The length of those hearings depends entirely upon the desires of the committee members, but in recent years the committee has usually concluded its deliberations on the Auditor General's report by the following summer. Eighteen months seems like a rather long feedback cycle, but considering the enormity of the task, it is probably the best that can be expected.

It is difficult to assess the significance of the role of Parliament in this process, since it does not typically alter the *Estimates* as presented by the government. However, it is likely that the government would want to move to correct problems identified by the Auditor General and the Public Accounts Committee before having to take strong criticism in the House and the media. In this sense, the benefits of these organizations are sometimes more real than apparent.

ASSESSMENT OF THE EXISTING SYSTEM

Since Maxwell Henderson's tenure as Auditor General, there has been a great deal of concern about financial accountability and the quality of financial management in the federal government. The government has responded to this concern in a number of ways: the Office of the Comptroller General was established and the staff of the Office of the Auditor General has been increased significantly; the Comptroller General has worked with the Treasury Board Secretariat to prepare comprehensive manuals dealing with financial and general administrative practices; program evaluation has been implemented across the government, and the internal audit function has been emphasized. These steps have made managers much more conscious of the need for good financial management.

However, some people are now questioning whether all of these changes have gone too far and become dysfunctional. Timothy W. Plumptre has written of "an overdose of "accountability" in Ottawa."[22] In particular, he takes issue with the specific forms of accountability employed, which he describes as "finan-centric"—a view of accountability "which places accounting and financial administration at its heart, subordinating all other dimensions of management."[23] He argues that this form of accountability focusses too much on whether managers are dotting their i's and crossing their t's, and not enough on whether overall goals are being attained. It is entirely possible that inappropriate forms of accountability can both prevent good managers from being innovative and provide a hiding place for incompetent managers, who can say "I followed all the rules."

Governments also need to be realistic about the impact of better financial management and accountability on controlling expenditure and public debt. Good management and proper accountability are important, but hopes that better financial management will significantly reduce public expenditure are misplaced. The reason that Canada is in its current financial state is because elected politicians have consciously chosen to implement major expenditure programs, but not increase taxes in order to fund them. Better financial management will have an impact at the margin, but major changes in Canada's financial situation can be effected only by tough political decisions that no one seems to want to make.

This is not a plea to lessen accountability. Clearly, proper accountability is important. Rather, this is a plea to choose carefully the mechanisms of accountability to ensure that they assist managers in accomplishing their goals.

NOTES

1. R. S. C. 1985, c. F-11.
2. The content of the *Estimates* is discussed in more detail in the appendix following Chapter 26.
3. *Final Report* (Hull: Supply and Services Canada, 1979), ch. 22.
4. Ibid., pp. 381-83.
5. A. W. Johnson, "The Treasury Board of Canada and the Machinery of Government of the 1970s," *The Canadian Journal of Political Science* 4 (September 1971): 346-66.
6. The role of this federal office should not be confused with an organization with a similar title that exists in most provinces. The role of the provincial comptrollers general is very different. See C. Lloyd Brown-John, André LeBlond, and D. Brian Marson, *Public Financial Management: A Canadian Text* (Scarborough, Ont.: Nelson Canada, 1988), pp. 417-18.
7. This story is told in Sonja Sinclair, *Cordial but not Cosy* (Toronto: McClelland and Stewart, 1979), ch. 8.
8. (Minister of Supply and Services Canada, 1979).
9. (Minister of Supply and Services Canada, 1981).
10. The *Public Accounts* document is described in more detail in the appendix to Chapter 26.
11. Receiver General for Canada, *Public Accounts of Canada—1985: Volume 1: Summary Report and Financial Statements* (Ottawa: Minister of Supply and Services Canada, 1985), pp. 2-18.
12. Sinclair, *Cordial but not Cosy*, p. 69.
13. *Report of the Auditor General to the House of Commons for the Fiscal Year Ended March 31, 1967* (Ottawa: Queen's Printer and Controller of Stationery, 1968), pp. 54-56.
14. R. S. C. 1985, ch. A-17, s. 7(2) (d).
15. The most complete reference on comprehensive auditing is Canadian Comprehensive Auditing Foundation, *Comprehensive Auditing in Canada: The Provincial Legislative Audit Perspective* (Ottawa: Canadian Comprehensive Auditing Foundation, 1985). also *Report of the Auditor General of Canada to the House of Commons—Fiscal Year 31 March 1983* (Ottawa: Minister of Supply and Services Canada, 1983), pp.

eral of Canada, *Report of the Auditor General of Canada to the House of*

Commons—Fiscal Year Ended 31 March 1989 (Minister of Supply and Services Canada, 1989), ch. 11.

17. John L. Manion, "New Challenges in Public Administration," *Canadian Public Administration* 31, no. 2 (Summer 1988): 240.

18. Sharon Sutherland, "On the Audit Trail of the Auditor General: Parliament's Servant, 1973-80," *Canadian Public Administration* 23 (Winter 1980): 616-44; and by the same author, "The Politics of Audit: The Federal Office of the Auditor General in Comparative Perspective," *Canadian Public Administration* 29 (Spring 1986): 118-48.

19. This story is told from the Auditor General's perspective, but quite accurately, in Auditor General of Canada, *Report of the Auditor General of Canada to the House of Commons, Fiscal Year Ended 31 March 1989*, pp. 23-27.

20. "Auditor General Signals Meech Danger," *The Gazette* (Montreal), December 14, 1988, p. B3.

21. C. E. S. Franks, *The Parliament of Canada* (Toronto: University of Toronto Press, 1987), p. 239.

22. *Beyond the Bottom Line: Management in Government* (Halifax: The Institute for Research on Public Policy, 1988), p. 185.

23. Ibid., p. 187.

BIBLIOGRAPHY

Auditor General of Canada. *Report of the Auditor General to the House of Commons.* (Various years.)

Brown-John, C. Lloyd, André LeBlond, and D. Brian Marson. *Public Financial Management: A Canadian Text.* Scarborough, Ont.: Nelson Canada, 1988.

Canada. Office of the Comptroller General. *Guide on Financial Administration for Departments and Agencies of the Government of Canada.* Ottawa: Minister of Supply and Services Canada, 1979.

Canada. Receiver General for Canada. *Public Accounts of Canada.* (Various years.)

Canada. Royal Commission on Financial Management and Accountability. *Final Report.* Hull: Supply and Services Canada, 1979.

Canadian Comprehensive Auditing Foundation. *Comprehensive Auditing in Canada: The Provincial Legislative Audit Perspective.* Ottawa: Canadian Comprehensive Auditing Foundation, 1985.

Johnson, A. W. "The Treasury Board of Canada and the Machinery of Government of the 1970s." *Canadian Journal of Political Science* 4 (September 1971): 346-66.

Manion, John L. "New Challenges in Public Administration." *Canadian Public Administration* 31, no. 2 (Summer 1988): 234-46.

Savoie, Donald J. *The Politics of Public Spending in Canada.* Toronto: University of Toronto Press, 1990.

Sinclair, Sonja. *Cordial but not Cosy.* Toronto: McClelland and Stewart, 1979.

Sutherland, Sharon. "On the Audit Trail of the Auditor General: Parliament's Servant, 1973-80." *Canadian Public Administration* 23 (Winter 1980): 616-44.

——. "The Politics of Audit: The Federal Office of the Auditor General in Comparative Perspective." *Canadian Public Administration* 29 (Spring 1986): 118-48.

CASES

Cases developed by the Canadian Centre for Management Development and distributed by the Case Program in Canadian Public Administration:
  Grants and Contributions. By John William Pullen

APPENDIX

How to Write A Research Paper in Public Administration

One of the assignments frequently required of students in public administration courses is the writing of a major essay. This kind of assignment not only increases and reinforces a student's knowledge in the field but also develops research and writing skills. However, it can be a very difficult task when a student is just becoming familiar with a new field of study. This appendix provides some guidance on choosing a good topic and on researching it.

The starting point of a good essay is selecting a good topic, if a specific topic or list of topics is not provided by your instructor. The topic should interest you and there should be an adequate amount of background material available. One obvious source of ideas is either this book or a similar overview text such as: Richard J. Van Loon and Michael S. Whittington, *The Canadian Political System: Environment, Structure and Process*, 3rd ed. (Toronto: McGraw-Hill Ryerson, 1981); Michael Whittington and Glen Williams, eds., *Canadian Politics in the 1990s*, 3rd ed. (Scarborough, Ont.: Nelson Canada, 1990); Robert F. Adie and Paul G. Thomas, *Canadian Public Administration*, 2nd ed. (Scarborough, Ont.: Prentice-Hall, 1987); G. Bruce Doern and Richard W. Phidd, *Canadian Public Policy* (Toronto: Methuen, 1983); or V. Seymour Wilson's *Canadian Public Policy and Administration* (Toronto: McGraw-Hill Ryerson, 1981).

Check the table of contents and decide which chapter interests you most. Read that chapter to see the areas covered. There will always be some ideas mentioned that could be extended or reviewed in a research paper. For example, Chapter 9 of this book discusses the accountability regime of federal Crown corporations. You could compare this regime to that of your province. Which is better? By what criteria? Chapter 12 discusses certain administrative values held by public servants. To what extent are these same values important in your province?

Another potential source of ideas for topics is articles contained in scholarly and professional journals. Spend some time in the library flipping through the main journals in the field (see below) to get an idea of which topics have been covered by others. Do you see an article with which you strongly disagree? Your paper could be a detailed critique of that article. Do you see an idea applied in one context that you would like to apply in another? If you see an article that tests a hypothesis about a particular department, you could test the same hypothesis in another department.

The articles can also serve as general models for your essay. Note how the authors present their arguments and make their major points. You should also note some more technical points such as the use of charts, tables, and footnotes.

Alternatively, your paper could take the form of a case study. This book, like most textbooks, focusses on how things *should* work. Is there some incident that occurred recently that allows you to test whether the real world operates in this manner or not? For example, Chapter 10 suggests that regulatory agencies *should* be kept at arm's length from the partisan political fray. Is there a recent example where this principle was violated? Were the consequences beneficial or detrimental? You could examine some published case studies (see below) to see what others have done.

When you have selected a topic or had one assigned to you, your next task is to do research to determine what has already been written about it. It is dangerous to form your own conclusions before you have reviewed what experts in the field have said.

A good place to start your research is the bibliographies at the end of the chapters of this book or one of the other overview books mentioned above, but these contain only the main sources. You will have to go considerably further than this. The *Canadian Public Administration Bibliography* published by the Institute of Public Administration of Canada is especially helpful in this regard. This bibliography was originally published in 1972; periodic supplements have been published since, the latest covering the period to 1985. It contains a complete listing of books and articles about public administration in Canada, but the 1985 version is the last supplement that has been published.

Therefore, you should check the subject and/or keyword index of your library's card or computer catalogue for recent books. You should also peruse recent editions of the periodicals in the field. The main Canadian journal is *Canadian Public Administration*, published by the Institute of Public Administration of Canada. It is published four times per year and contains an annual index (as do most other journals). *Canadian Public Policy* is another valuable source of information about public policy formulation. The federal government publishes two periodicals that contain very good information on the latest management innovations in the federal government. *Optimum* is published by the Bureau of Management Consulting of the federal Department of Supply and ˙vices, and *Manager's Magazine* is published by the Treasury Board Secretariat. ˙ are analogous publications in some provinces that you can locate in your ˙ library or in provincial government libraries. *Policy Options* is a maga-˙ed by the Institute for Research on Public Policy that contains short ˙e less weighty, in an academic sense, than those in the above ˙more current.

In addition, there are journals that specialize in areas other than public administration, but which contain some valuable articles. The *Canadian Tax Journal* is written primarily for tax lawyers and accountants, but it is also a valuable source of information about federal and provincial budgets, and it publishes the occasional article on the revenue or expenditure budget process. The journals of the learned societies such as the *Canadian Journal of Political Science*, the *Canadian Journal of Economics*, and the *Canadian Review of Sociology and Anthropology* are all very useful in their own particular areas.

There are also many excellent journals published in other countries that can be helpful, particularly for theoretical or comparative papers. The main international journal is the *International Review of Administrative Sciences*. The main journal in the field in Britain is *Public Administration*; in Australia, it is the *Australian Journal of Public Administration*. *Public Administration Review* is the most widely read public administration journal in the United States, but several others, such as the *American Journal of Public Administration, Administration and Society*, and the *Journal of Comparative Administration*, are also useful.

You can also communicate directly with government departments to obtain information on current policy. Most governments publish a directory that provides a brief description of the responsibilities of departments and agencies. This can direct you to the agency that is responsible for the field in which you are interested. These directories also provide some valuable addresses and telephone numbers. The federal government publishes the *Index to Federal Programs and Services* (Ottawa: Minister of Supply and Services Canada, annual publication); the Ontario government's equivalent publication is the KWIK *Index to Services of Your Ontario Government* (Toronto: Ministry of Government Services, annual publication).

You should not overlook popular magazines and newspapers as sources of topical information. Reports in these publications do not carry the same weight in an academic paper as articles from academic journals, but they are valuable sources of information on recent events. *Le Devoir* and *The Globe and Mail* both publish lengthy analysis articles on national issues. *The Citizen* (Ottawa) provides in-depth coverage of issues concerning the federal public service, and the newspapers in most provincial capitals contain similar coverage about provincial governments. Some of the most useful magazines are *Maclean's, L'Actualité*, and *Canadian Forum*.

There are a number of indexes that provide easy access to articles in these publications. Some of the most useful are ABC Pol Sci, ABI/INFORM, Business Periodicals Index, Management Contents, PAIS Bulletin, International Political Science Abstracts, Canadian Periodical Index, and Canadian Business and Current Affairs. Most of these indexes are issued in annual volumes with more frequent updates. Many are also available in CD-ROM (compact disk-read only memory) format on computers in your library. Computer searching is much easier and less tedious than searching through piles of books, updates, etc. Your librarian can assist you in choosing the appropriate index and beginning your search.

If you are interested in the case approach, you should be familiar with the many cases published in the Case Program in Canadian Public Administration, sponsored by the Institute of Public Administration of Canada. The cases cover almost all major areas of Canadian public administration. The Case Program is also the sales agent for cases developed by the Canadian Centre for Management Development. These cases deal with management issues in the federal government setting. Perusing the titles of these could give you some ideas for your own topic. Relevant cases are listed at the end of the chapters, and a free catalogue can be obtained by writing to the Institute, 897 Bay Street, Toronto, Ontario M5S 1Z7.

Now that you have selected a topic and begun to find information, it's time to sit down and actually do the research and write the paper. Some of the books that provide general information about preparing and organizing a paper are *How to Write a Research Paper Step by Step* by Phyllis Cash (New York: Monarch Press, 1977), *A Guide to Writing Essays and Research Papers* by Gordon Coggins (Toronto: Van Nostrand Reinhold Ltd., 1977), and *Making Sense: A Student's Guide to Writing and Style* by Margot Northey (Toronto: Oxford University Press, 1983). Some of the best books about writing style and grammar are *Canadian Style: A Guide to Writing and Editing* (Toronto: Dundurn Press and Department of the Secretary of State, *The Practical Stylist* by Sheridan Baker (New York: Harper & Row, 1981), and *The Elements of Style* by William Strunk and Elwyn B. White (New York: Macmillan, 1979). You might also need some advice about actual preparation of the paper—typing, charts, footnotes. The best source in this area is *A Manual for Writers of Term Papers, Theses, and Dissertations* by Kate L. Turabian (Chicago: University of Chicago Press, 1987).

Good luck!

GLOSSARY

Note: The numbers in brackets following each item refer to the page numbers where further elaboration on that item can be found.

Access to Information Act. A statute designed to provide a right of access to government information for the public. Provides for the exemption or exclusion of certain types of information from disclosure, and for a review by an Information Commissioner and/or a court of decisions by ministers and public servants not to disclose certain information. Also referred to as a freedom of information act. (469)

Accountability. *See* Administrative accountability.

Adjudication. In the context of employer-employee relations, the process by which an employee presents a grievance in relation to a collective agreement or arbitral award, or in relation to disciplinary action leading to discharge, suspension, or a financial penalty. (552)

Administrative accountability. The obligation of public servants to be answerable for fulfilling responsibilities that flow from the authority given them. Similar in meaning to the concept of objective responsibility. (282, 322-24)

Administrative discretion. The element of choice or judgment left to individual public servants in their interpretation and application of laws, rules, regulations, policies, and procedures. (299-300)

Administrative ethics. Principles and standards of right conduct in public organizations. Normally used interchangeably with the term "administrative morality." (324-25)

Administrative law. The branch of public law that is concerned with relations between the government and individual citizens. It deals with the legal limitations on the actions of governmental officials, and on the remedies that are available to anyone affected by a transgression of these limits. (401)

Administrative responsibility. The inclination and the capacity of public servants to respond to the needs and demands of both political institutions and the public. (283)

Advisory council. An organization composed of private citizens created by the government to provide an independent source of advice to a minister. It is established outside the normal departmental bureaucracy and does not ordinarily have responsibility for administering programs. (263-65)

Affirmative action. *See* Employment equity.

Appropriation Act. The law annually passed by Parliament that allows the government to spend public funds. (613)

Arbitral award. *See* Arbitration.

Arbitration. In the context of collective bargaining, the procedure by which an individual or a board hears arguments from both the employer and the union sides of an interest dispute and makes a decision called an arbitral award, which is binding on both parties. In the federal government, one of the two available routes of dispute settlement; the other is the conciliation-strike route.

Auditor General. The officer of Parliament who performs an annual audit of the *Public Accounts* and prepares an annual report to Parliament on the government's financial stewardship. (619-24)

Bargaining agent. An employee organization (a union) that has been certified, for example, by the federal Public Service Staff Relations Board, as the organization responsible for bargaining on behalf of a particular bargaining unit. Examples include the Public Service Alliance of Canada and the Professional Institute of the Public Service of Canada. To be certified as a bargaining agent, the union must prove that it has support of the majority of employees in the bargaining unit. (548)

Bargaining unit. A group of two or more employees that has been designated as constituting a unit of employees appropriate for collective bargaining. (548)

Blue Book. *See* Estimates.

Budgetary transaction. A revenue or expenditure transaction that affects the government's surplus or deficit position. (588) *See also* non-budgetary transaction.

Bureaucracy. A form of organization characterized by hierarchical structure, unity of command, hiring and promotion by merit, and specialization of labour.

Bureaucratic politics. An approach to the study of policy-making that focusses on interactions among individuals, in the form of conflict, bargaining, compromise, and persuasion, as determinants of the actions of a government. (122-23, 343)

Canada Gazette. An official publication of the government of Canada in which appear official announcements such as orders in council and regulations. (168)

~otive agency theory. A theory that holds that regulatory agencies eventually ~ne captive of, or controlled by, the interests they were established to ~ (240-41)

~cy. An agency that has a substantial amount of continuing legiti~ to intervene in and direct the activity of departments. (172-74)

~ystem of organization that involves minimal dispersal of ~sion-making units outside the centre of power.

Citizen participation. The direct involvement of individual citizens and citizens' groups in government decision-making. (461)

Classical federalism. A concept according to which the powers of government are divided "so that the general and regional governments are each, within a sphere, co-ordinate and independent." (418)

Classification standard. A definition of the category within which each occupational group falls, the groups within each occupational category, and the descriptions of benchmark positions to be used as guides for assessing jobs and rating them according to their level in the group. (514)

Collective agreement. An agreement in writing between the employer and the bargaining agent regarding terms and conditions of employment.

Collective bargaining. A method of determining wages, hours, and other conditions of employment through direct negotiations between the employer and the union.

Collective ministerial responsibility. The responsibility of ministers as a group (that is, as members of the Cabinet) for the policies and management of the government as a whole. (341) *See also* Individual ministerial responsibility.

Coloured paper. *See* Green paper or White paper.

Comprehensive audit. A review of a program that considers its economy, efficiency, and effectiveness. (621)

Comprehensive rationality. A style of policy-making based on a scientific assessment of alternative actions and conscious choice of the course of action that will yield the maximum benefit. (116)

Comptroller General (Office of the). A central agency reporting to Treasury Board that has particular responsibility for program evaluation and financial management and internal audit in departments. (178, 616-18)

Conciliation. A process by which an impartial person tries to resolve interest disputes in collective bargaining by seeking compromise or voluntary agreement between the two parties. Unlike arbitration, the recommendations of the conciliator (or mediator) are not binding on the parties. In the federal public service, conciliation must precede legal strike action.

Conditional grants. Payments by the federal government to a provincial government (or by a provincial government to a municipal government) in which the receiving government undertakes programs according to conditions specified by the granting government. Often referred to as shared-cost programs. (421)

Conflict of interest. A situation in which a public employee has a private or personal interest sufficient to influence or appear to influence the objective exercise of his or her official duties. (327)

Consolidated Revenue Fund. The fund in which is recorded all receipts and expenditures of public funds that are available for general governmental purposes. (596)

Contingency theory. A theory that suggests that there is no one ideal type of organizational structure. It argues that organizational structure should be contingent on such factors as predictability of the task performed, the technology employed, and the size of the organization. (72)

Control. That form of power in which A has authority to direct or command B to do something. Sometimes referred to as "authority of position" or "position power." (276)

Cooperative federalism. A term used to describe federal-provincial relations when the constitutional division of powers is preserved but federal and provincial ministers and public servants engage in consultation and coordination to reach joint decisions on matters of mutual concern. (419)

Coordination. The process by which two or more parties take one another into account for the purpose of bringing their decisions and/or activities into harmonious or reciprocal relation. (289)

Crown corporation. A corporation "in the ordinary sense of the term, whose mandate relates to industrial, commercial, or financial activities but which also belong to the state." (187) *See also* Mixed enterprise and Public enterprise.

Decentralization. A system of organization that involves placing actual decision-making power in the hands of units outside the centre of power, either geographically or organizationally. (50) *Contrast with* Deconcentration.

Deconcentration. The physical dispersal of operating units with only very limited delegation of decision-making authority. (50) *Contrast with* Decentralization.

Departmental minister. A minister who heads an operating department. (169)

Deputy minister. The administrative head of a government department. Appointed by the Prime Minister or Premier. Also referred to as the deputy head. (179-80, 365-66)

Deregulation. The elimination of government regulatory control over an industry so that it can operate through the dictates of the private enterprise system.

Double-image federalism. A term used to describe federal-provincial relations characterized by a combination of interaction between the central government the provinces and a special relationship between French- and English-ng Canadians. (419)

The acquisition of goods and services at the best possible price. (621) 'veness and Efficiency.

reasure of the extent to which an input of resources achieves To be distinguished from the related concept of efficiency.

Efficiency. A measure of performance that may be expressed as a ratio between input and output. The use of administrative methods and resources that will achieve the greatest results for a specific objective at the least cost. (282-83)

Emergency federalism. A term used to describe federal-provincial relations during the two World Wars and the Depression; these relations were characterized by a growth in federal power vis-à-vis the provinces. (418)

Emergent process view. An approach to management which suggests that organizations grow and develop as a part of a broader environment, and that managers have only a limited amount of control over how the organization develops. (73-74)

Employment equity. An approach or program designed to identify and systematically remove employment policies, practices, and procedures that exclude or place at a disadvantage certain groups that have been historically under-represented in the public service. (531) *See also* Representative bureaucracy.

Equalization. A program through which the federal government makes unconditional grants to provinces with a weak tax base. The program's purpose is to allow the so-called "have-not" provinces to provide adequate public services to their citizens without imposing excessively high taxes. (422)

Established Programs Financing (EPF). A transfer payment program begun in 1977 when the federal government terminated three very large conditional grants to the provinces and replaced them with a combination of cash payments and tax room. (422)

Estimates. The series of documents that contains the government's request for an annual appropriation and the necessary supporting documentation. When approved by Parliament, this becomes the Appropriation Act. (587-593)

Evaluation. An in-depth analysis of a program carried out to determine its worth and to locate any needed administrative or policy changes. (146)

Executive federalism. A term used to describe federal-provincial relations characterized by "the concentration and centralization of authority at the top of each participating government, the control and supervision of intergovernmental relations by politicians and officials with a wide range of functional interests, and the highly formalized and well-publicized proceedings of federal-provincial diplomacy." (419)

Expectancy theory. A theory which holds that people are motivated by their expectations about how their behaviour will help them satisfy their needs, desires, and goals. (95-98)

Federalism. A political system in which the powers of the state are formally divided between central and regional governments by a written constitution, but in which these governments are linked in a mutually interdependent political relationship. (417)

Federal-Provincial Relations Office (FPRO). A central agency that is responsible for advising the Cabinet and operating departments and agencies on the conduct of federal-provincial relations. (176)

Finance (Department of). The central agency most concerned with macro-economic policy and preparation of the revenue budget. (179)

Financial Administration Act. The statute that governs the regime of financial accountability for federal departments and agencies. (611)

Freedom of information. *See* Access to Information Act.

Governor General. The representative of the Queen in Canada; functions as the head of state when the Queen is not in Canada. (162)

Governor General in Council. Refers to the Governor General acting on the formal advice of the Cabinet. When the decisions of Cabinet have been approved by the Governor General, they can be formally described as acts of the Governor General in Council. (163)

Governor General's Warrants. An authorization for the government to spend in the absence of a parliamentary appropriation; used only for unforeseen expenditures when Parliament is not in session. (614)

Green paper. A statement prepared by government to stimulate discussion about the possibility of changing policy in a particular area. It is not a statement of government policy; rather it lists the options that the government is considering and the advantages and disadvantages of each. (129)

Hierarchy of needs. A concept developed by Abraham Maslow that suggests that workers can be motivated by the satisfaction of a number of different needs, ranging from basic shelter and food to self-actualization. As workers' lower-level needs are satisfied, they are motivated by desires to satisfy higher-level needs. (60)

Human relations school. An approach to management and motivation that emphasizes the dignity and needs of workers in the workplace. Usually associated with social psychologists such as Elton Mayo, Roethlisberger, and Dickson. (57)

Human resource planning. The process through which a government strives to ensure that it has the appropriate quantity and quality of employees to carry out its responsibilities. (516-17)

Incrementalism. A style of policy-making based on small, marginal changes from existing policies. (117)

Individual ministerial responsibility. The responsibility of the minister, as the political head of the department, to answer to the legislature and through the legislature to the public both for his or her personal acts and for the acts of departmental subordinates. (342, 379) *See also* Collective ministerial responsibility.

Influence. That form of power in which B conforms to A's desires, values, or goals on grounds of suggestion, persuasion, emulation, or anticipation. A more general and pervasive form of power than control. Sometimes referred to as "authority of leadership" or "personal power." (276)

Institute of Public Administration of Canada. An association of public servants from all spheres of government and academics. Devoted to improving the study and practice of public administration in Canada. Publishes the journal *Canadian Public Administration.* (6)

Interest groups. *See* Pressure groups.

Intergovernmental relations. The interactions between and among the federal, provincial, and municipal governments in the Canadian federal system. (418)

Interim Supply. A limited appropriation of funds provided by Parliament at the beginning of the fiscal year until the full *Estimates* have been approved. (613)

Interstate federalism. "The distribution of powers and financial resources between the federal and provincial governments as well as the relations between those two orders of government." (420)

Intrastate federalism. "Arrangements whereby the interests of regional units—the interests either of the government or of the residents of these units—are channelled through and protected by the structures and operations of the central government." (420)

Job classification. The process by which jobs are assigned to an occupational group within an occupational category and to a level within that group. (514)

Job evaluation. The analysis of a job in terms of its duties, its physical and mental demands, the knowledge and skills it requires, and the conditions under which it is performed; the writing of a job description that explains the duties, working conditions, and other aspects of the job; and the assessment of these job characteristics against the classification standard established for the relevant occupational group. (514)

Lieutenant Governor in Council. The representative of the Queen in a province; functions as the head of state. (163)

Line. The part of an organization that is directly involved in producing the organizations's output. (47) *Contrast with* Staff.

Line-item budgeting. A style of budgeting that emphasizes the object of expenditure (salaries, stationery) rather than the purpose of the expenditure. (569)

Lobbying. A legitimate means by which groups and individuals try to influence government decisions by means of direct contact with politicians or public servants. Usually associated with the activities of pressure groups or interest groups. (440)

Main Estimates. *See* Estimates.

Management by Objectives (MBO). A system of management that emphasizes supervisors and subordinates working together to agree on sets of objectives to be attained in the coming year. Commonly associated with Peter Drucker and George Odiorne. (63-65)

Management Category. An occupational category in the federal public service composed of about 4,600 senior public servants with responsibility for policy development; program formulation and delivery; the design and operation of management machinery; and the management of personnel, finances, and public affairs. (515)

Management information system (MIS). An organized method of collecting information about the internal operation and the external environment of an organization. It provides information for planning, control, and operation. (488-89)

Memorandum to Cabinet. The key mechanism by which policy proposals are brought forward by ministers for consideration and approval by their Cabinet colleagues. The formal means by which deputy ministers provide confidential policy advice to their ministers. (353-55)

Merit principle. A principle according to which 1) all citizens should have a reasonable opportunity to be considered for employment in the public service, and 2) selections must be based exclusively on qualification or fitness for the job. To be distinguished from the merit system. (302)

Merit system. The mechanism in use at any time by which the goals of the merit principle are achieved. An administrative device that can and should be adapted to changing circumstances. (302)

Minister of State for a Specified Purpose. A minister who heads a Ministry of State. (169)

Minister of State to Assist a Minister. A minister responsible for only a limited portion of a full department. (170)

Minister without Portfolio for Designated Purposes. A minister who does not have responsibility for a department, but is responsible for representing a particular interest in Cabinet, e.g., multiculturalism. (170)

Ministry of State. A small department responsible mainly for research and for coordinating the activities of other departments. (169)

Mixed enterprise. A corporation "in which the federal government has taken a direct equity position in common with other participants for the purposes of implementing a public policy or satisfying a public need." (187, 215) *See also* Crown corporation and Public enterprise.

New public administration. A movement of public administration scholars and practitioners in the United States in the late 1960s and early 1970s concerned with social equity, sensitivity to, and representation of, disadvantaged minority groups, increased citizen participation in government decision-making, and new forms of public organization. (297)

Non-budgetary transaction. An advance to, or investment in, some agency or corporation that is expected to be repaid; also the repayment of any of these items. These transactions do not affect the government's surplus or deficit position. (588) *See also* Budgetary transaction.

Objective responsibility. The responsibility of a person or an organization *to* someone else, outside of self, *for* some thing or some kind of performance. Similar in meaning to accountability or answerability. (322) *Contrast with* Subjective responsibility.

Occupational category. A broad range of occupations of the same type, distinguished by the nature of the duties performed and the education required. Examples in the federal public service are the Management and the Operational categories. (514)

Office of the Comptroller General. *See* Comptroller General.

Ombudsman. An official authorized by statute to investigate complaints from citizens about improper, unfair, or discriminatory treatment by public servants. Reports to the legislature and is independent of the political executive and the bureaucracy. (386-87)

Open systems approach. An approach to the study of organizations that emphasizes that organizations are a part of, and must interact with, their environment. (70-72) *Contrast with* a closed systems approach, which sees organizations as self-contained entities.

Operating department. "An administrative unit comprising one or more organizational components over which a minister has direct management and control." (163)

Order in council. An official proclamation made by the Governor General in Council; usually a government regulation. (168)

Organization development. A participative approach to management that emphasizes team development and allows members of the organization to work together to identify and correct problems. (65-67)

Organizational humanism. *See* Human relations school.

Organizational socialization. The process through which individuals learn the expectations attached to the position they occupy in the organization, and through which they selectively internalize as values some of the expectations of those with whom they interact. (286)

Participatory management. A style of management that emphasizes the desirability of workers actually being involved in decision-making. (63)

Partisan mutual adjustment. A process by which a very large measure of coordination in government takes place without any deliberate or conscious attempt to coordinate. (290)

Patronage. The appointment of persons to government service or their advancement within the service on the grounds of contributions, financial or otherwise, to the governing party rather than of merit. (302)

Pay equity. A system that permits comparisons to be made between different jobs performed for the same employer. A short-hand term for equal pay for work of equal value. To be distinguished from equal pay for equal work, which requires that men and women be paid the same for doing the same job. (539-40)

Performance budgeting. A style of budgeting that relates expenditure to specific activities to determine unit costs of providing services. (572)

Performance evaluation. The process whereby information about the performance of employees over time is systematically collected and analyzed. Also referred to as "employee appraisal." (521-22)

Political neutrality. A constitutional doctrine or convention according to which public servants should not engage in activities that are likely to impair—or appear to impair—their impartiality or the impartiality of the public service, for example, public statements about government policies or involvement in election campaigns. (294)

Political parties. Organizations that seek to get their members elected to political office and to gain and maintain control of the government. Their major functions include the aggregation and articulation of interests, the recruitment and training of political leaders, and the education and socialization of the public on political matters. (452)

Politics-administration dichotomy. The idea that a sharp distinction can be made between the responsibilities of elected executives, who make policy decisions, and the responsibilities of public servants, who execute these decisions. (295)

Power. "The capacity to secure the dominance of one's values or goals." There are two forms of power—control and influence. (276)

Pressure groups. Organizations composed of persons who have joined together to seek their mutual interest by influencing government decisions and actions. Often referred to as interest groups. (440)

Prime Minister's Office (PMO). The central agency that provides partisan policy advice to the Prime Minister. It is most concerned with relations between the Prime Minister and the media and the party. (174-75)

Privacy Act. A statute which gives individuals access to their personal information held by the government, and which protects the privacy of individuals by limiting those who may see this personal information. Also sets out principles of fair information practices. (475)

Privative clauses. Statutory provisions designed to prevent judicial review of the decisions of administrative tribunals. (409)

Privatization. Turning over Crown corporations to the private sector by sale or other means. (211-14)

Privy Council Office (PCO). The central agency that provides policy advice and administrative support to Cabinet and its committees. (175-76)

Program budgeting. A style of budgeting that allocates funds by program and attempts to measure the impact of expenditures on the goals and objectives of programs. (572-77)

Public Accounts. The series of documents that contains the government's year-end financial statements. (593, 596-604)

Public bureaucracy. The system of authority, people, offices, and methods that government uses to achieve its objectives. The means by which the practice of public administration is carried on. (5) *See also* Bureaucracy.

Public choice. The use of economic principles to analyze political activity. It suggests that people take political action to further their self-interest. (120-22)

Public enterprise. Crown corporations and mixed enterprise. (187)

Public interest group. A form of pressure group whose members try to influence government decisions in the name of the "public interest." Distinguished from special interest groups, which are primarily motivated by particular, selfish interests. (442)

Public participation. A broad range of direct and indirect forms of participation by members of the public in government decision-making. Includes such forms of participation as membership in political parties, pressure groups, and advisory bodies. A broader concept than "citizen participation." (461)

Public policy. "Whatever governments choose to do or not to do." (114-16)

Public Service Commission. An independent agency that serves Parliament as the guardian of the merit principle in human resource management. It is responsible for recruitment, staffing, and promotion in the public service. (388)

Quasi-federalism. A term used to describe the early decades of the Canadian federation during which the federal government dominated the provincial governments, in part by making frequent use of the federal constitutional powers to disallow and reserve provincial legislation. (418)

Recruitment. The process of identifying candidates for public service positions by such methods as inviting job applications from within and from outside the public service and using a human resource inventory system. (517)

Regulatory agency. A body that administers, fixes, establishes, controls, or regulates an economic, cultural, environmental, or social activity by regularized and established means in the public interest and in accordance with general policy guidelines specified by the government. (225-26)

Representative bureaucracy. The idea that the social composition of the bureaucracy should reflect that of the population as a whole. Also that larger numbers of persons from certain underrepresented groups (e.g., women, minority groups) should be brought into the public service. (526-28) *See* Employment equity.

Responsiveness. *See* Administrative responsibility.

Royal commission. A temporary organization constituted to investigate either specific incidents or general policy concerns and to report to government. It usually is disbanded after it delivers its report and so is not involved in the implementation of its recommendations. (255-57)

Scientific Management. A management style that emphasizes tailoring the physical nature of work to the physical abilities of workers. Characterized by time-motion studies and precise work standards. Usually associated with Frederick W. Taylor. (39-41)

Selection. The process through which candidates for public service positions are screened by such means as application forms, written examinations, and interviews. (517-18)

Shared-cost programs. *See* Conditional grants.

Socialization. The process by which individuals learn from their environment the social patterns and values of their culture. The socializing agencies involved in this process include family, peer groups, schools, prior employment, and adult organizations. (286)

Span of control. The number of subordinates reporting to a particular supervisor. (43)

Staff. The part of the organization that supports the line function, but is not directly involved in producing the organization's output (e.g., accounting or personnel). (47)

Statutory appropriation. A continuing appropriation of funds that does not require approval in the annual *Estimates* because there is already some legislative authorization. (588-89)

Statutory instruments. The rules, regulations, orders, etc., made by the executive under delegated legislative authority. (390)

Strategic planning. "A disciplined effort to produce fundamental decisions and actions that shape and guide what an organization (or other entity) is, what it does, and why it does it."

Subjective responsibility. The responsibility that a person *feels* toward others. Often described as *personal* or *psychological* responsibility. Similar in meaning to identification, loyalty, and conscience. (322) *Contrast with* Objective responsibility.

Sunset legislation. Legislation that establishes an agency or program for a finite period and requires an assessment of the value of the agency or program before it is continued. (246)

Supplementary Estimates. A request for funds in addition to the original *Estimates*. Usually requested toward the end of the fiscal year. (614)

Task force. *See* Royal commission.

Tax expenditure. A tax reduction available to a taxpayer who does (or refrains from doing) something desired by government. (564)

Theory X–Theory Y. Developed by Douglas McGregor to describe different managers' views of workers. Theory X holds that workers are basically lazy and need to be closely watched. Theory Y holds that workers are highly motivated and will voluntarily work hard. (60-61)

Transfer payments. *See* Conditional grants and Unconditional grants.

Treasury Board (TB). A Cabinet committee consisting of the President of the Treasury Board, the Minister of Finance, and four other Cabinet ministers. Responsible for preparation of the expenditure budget and for administrative management in departments. (176-77, 614-16)

Treasury Board Secretariat. The central agency that assists the Treasury Board in carrying out its responsibilities. (177-78)

Unconditional grants. Payments by the federal government to a provincial government (or by a provincial government to a municipal government), which can be used for any purpose the receiving government desires. (422)

Unity of command. The bureaucratic principle that holds that all employees must report to one, and only one, supervisor in order to minimize confusion and misdirection. (36)

Values. Enduring beliefs that influence the choices made by individuals, groups, or organizations from among available means or ends. Values are organized into value systems in which values are ranked in terms of their relative importance. (281)

Vote (as a part of the Estimates). The basis on which Parliament appropriates funds to departments and agencies; usually, there is one vote for each program. (589)

White paper. A statement of government policy. Usually provides a statement of policy in everyday, non-legislative language accompanied by an explanation and defence of the particular course of action chosen. (129)

Zero-base budgeting. A style of budgeting that emphasizes the ranking of programs in priority order and the allocation of funds on this basis. (577-78)

NAME INDEX

SUBJECT INDEX